CORE

ColdFusion 5.0

ISBN 0-13-066061-2

PRENTICE HALL PTR CORE SERIES

Core PHP Programming, 2/e, Atkinson

Core Python Programming, Chun

Core Java Media Framework, Decarmo

Core Jini, 2/e,* Edwards

Core Servlets and JavaServer Pages,* Hall

Core Web Programming, 2/e,* Hall/Brown

Core ColdFusion 5, Hewitt

Core Java 2, Vol I–Fundamentals,* Horstmann/Cornell

Core Java 2, Vol II–Advanced Features,* Horstmann/Cornell

Core JSP, Hougland & Tavistock

Core CSS, Schengili-Roberts

Core C++: A Software Engineering Approach, Shtern

Core Java Web Server, Taylor & Kimmet

Core JFC, 2/e, Topley

Core Swing: Advanced Programming, Topley

Core Web3D, Walsh & Bourges-Sévenier

**Sun Microsystems Press titles*

CORE ColdFusion 5.0

EBEN HEWITT

Prentice Hall PTR
Upper Saddle River, NJ 07458
www.phptr.com

A CIP catalog record for this book can be obtained from the Library of Congress.

Editorial/Production Supervision: Faye Gemmellaro
Acquisitions Editor: Mark Taub
Editorial Assistant: Sarah Hand
Marketing Manager: Bryan Gambrel
Buyer: Maura Zaldivar
Cover Design Director: Jerry Votta
Cover Designer: Nina Scuderi
Cover Illustration: Karen Strelecki
Art Director: Gail Cocker-Bogusz
Interior Series Design: Meg VanArsdale

Prentice-Hall, Inc.
Upper Saddle River, NJ 07458

Prentice Hall books are widely used by corporations and government agencies for training, marketing, and resale. The publisher offers discounts on this book when ordered in bulk quantities. For more information, contact:

Corporate Sales Department
Prentice Hall PTR
One Lake Street
Upper Saddle River, NJ 07458
Phone: 800-382-3419; FAX: 201-236-7141
E-mail (Internet): corpsales@prenhall.com

Printed in the United States of America

10 9 8 7 6 5 4 3 2 1

ISBN 0-13-066061-2

Pearson Education LTD.
Pearson Education Australia PTY, Limited
Pearson Education Singapore, Pte. Ltd.
Pearson Education North Asia Ltd.
Pearson Education Canada, Ltd.
Pearson Educación de Mexico, S.A. de C.V.
Pearson Education—Japan
Pearson Education Malaysia, Pte. Ltd.

For Alison, of course—the sine qua non

CONTENTS

Preface

"… and what is the use of a book," thought Alice, "without pictures or conversations?"

—Lewis Carroll, *Alice in Wonderland*

Core ColdFusion 5 is the book I wish I'd had when I began writing applications. One way of teaching programming is for the author to entice you, gentle reader, into the Technicolor landscape of the programming language at hand—the author is your friendly guide, pointing out the dazzling array of colors and scents, while you, the Maui-shirted, floppy-hatted tourist, peer dimly into your map as you stand gawking dead center at the intersection of 42nd and Broadway. You get your required caramel milkshake at Ellen's Stardust Diner and move on to stand in line for *Cats* tickets. Or something like that.

This is a different kind of book.

I learned ColdFusion on the fly—devouring websites and books devoted to the topic, nosing about in newsgroups and loitering on lists while I tried to get my first applications up and running. I learned by reading, by asking endless questions, by trying things over and over until something clicked. I learned from the generosity of hundreds of programmers it has been my pleasure to work with. I don't view it as an academic subject. This learning process was all very glamorous, but I think I wasted a lot of time that I didn't need to waste.

The approach is this: programmers are, above all, problem solvers. That's what they get paid to do. Therefore, the language is presented as a set of tools that are available to you to solve business problems. The code you will work with will consist of numerous non-trivial, practical examples that you can build on and incorporate into your own websites. My belief is that you can learn best how it all fits together by seeing it in action, working together. For instance, it's fun to learn about cookies, and it's great to know that by using the CFLOCATION tag in your templates you can quickly jump to another URL. This is the sort of thing one learns as a programming tourist. Only when discussing a real-world application *where all the parts have to fit together* do you discover that, because of HTTP headers, you can't effectively set a cookie in the same template that you use CFLOCATION to get out of. But that's exactly the sort of thing you need to know when you sit down to write ColdFusion.

You are a person in the world where people live. This indicates a certain relationship with space and time. This book was designed with these key factors in mind. There is only so much space in a book, so what you've got in your hands is the set of tools with which to continue on your own: There's the complete tag and function reference. There are lists of dozens of websites where you can get ColdFusion code, find more information on related topics, discover hundreds of places where you can host your ColdFusion website, and more. You get a list of the common ColdFusion errors you'll run into when debugging your applications, what they mean, and how to fix them. You put together a ColdFusion application for Web-enabled cell phones and a working e-commerce site, complete with rotating banner ads.

The idea is to save your walls from the repeated impact of your head. This book will give you everything you need to get up and running quickly, effectively, and with an understanding of the real-world implications of developing with ColdFusion.

The remainder of this preface briefly illuminates key things you will need to start using this book, and ColdFusion, quickly.

Who You Are

This book was written for anybody who wants practical knowledge of how to make Web applications on an easy, scalable, powerful platform.

You know HTML already. You do not need to know another application programming language. You do not need knowledge of Web servers or data servers.

Maybe you know ASP or JSP and want to learn another language. This book is perfect for you. Maybe you just took an IT job at Symantec or Doctor Solomon's or Bank of America or the University of Utah or the Recording Industry of America. Or maybe you were just elected Senator of your fine state, and, while browsing at http://www.Senate.gov noticed the little ".cfm" extension on your website and wondered what it was. All of the above organizations entrust their Web transactions to ColdFusion. And with good reason.

This book was also written for Web developers and for people who have done a static website or two and want to make their next one dynamic. The ability to create an online store, to interact with data warehouses via enterprise-level features such as stored procedures and data probing, lets you get really serious. The ability to personalize your website, catering its content to each individual visitor, will allow you to create truly compelling relationships with your users. The ability to search and share documents in just about any format will allow your organization to stay ahead of the information cycle.

Project managers and sales engineers will benefit from this book's discussions of planning an enterprise-level website and making all of the components come together.

Despite a seemingly universal predilection toward Mountain Dew, Web programmers are a diverse species. Whether you are a pleasantly dressed coed working in a college computer lab with well-modulated air, or if you're grinding out 18-hour days in a high-tech job shop and have recently started looking like the long-lost fourth member of ZZ Top, or whether you're all by yourself in your basement playing gladiator with IIS and scramming the cat from chewing your cables, this is the right book for you.

What You Need

You will need several things to work successfully through the exercises in this book. You will need a computer with a text editor. You will need access to ColdFusion Server 5 software, a Web server, and an Internet connection. A 30-day evaluation version of ColdFusion 5 comes on the CD-ROM with the book, Notepad or Pico comes with your OS, and Apache is free, so you're in pretty good shape.

What You Get

This is a practical book. Its purpose is to answer the questions you need answered by showing you how everything works together (HTTP 1.1 headers, the Web server, your applications, conditional logic, and so forth). Some of this may be old hat to you. I have therefore tried to flag you about beginner material that you may want to skip.

Here is what you get:

- A clear, detailed explanation of the ColdFusion language and how you can leverage it to build fantastic Web applications.
- Information, tips, and tricks about becoming a ColdFusion Certified Developer.
- Thousands of lines of complete, working code.
- On the CD-ROM, you get 30-day evaluation versions of Macromedia ColdFusion Enterprise Server 5.0 for Windows, HP-UX, Sun Solaris, and Linux; ColdFusion Studio 4.5.1 (the optional development environment for creating ColdFusion templates); HomeSite 4.5.1, Macromedia's award-winning HTML editor; The Harpoon Flash Toolkit; ColdFusion Express, the nonexpiring, limited-functionality product for serving ColdFusion pages; JRun 3.0.1, the award-winning server for Java Server Pages, Servlets, and Enterprise Java Beans; Macromedia Spectra 1.5 for Windows and Sun Solaris, the packaged application solution for content management, e-commerce, and personalization—written in ColdFusion!
- A website companion to the book filled with even more ColdFusion resources. The website is located at http://www.CoreColdFusion.com. Check out http://www.conditionallogic.com as well.

How This Book Is Organized

This book begins where HTML left off. We start with an overview of how the Internet works and an overview of what ColdFusion does. We then move into a discussion of SQL (the Structured Query Language), the language used to create and manipulate databases and their data. If you have a solid understanding of relational databases and SQL, you can probably skim Chapters 9 and 10.

Each chapter will have roughly the same structure. You will be introduced to the key concepts in a general way, and quickly move into details as they pertain to ColdFusion or application development. You'll come out of most chapters with a working example that you can take with you.

Because each chapter builds on the last, it is a good idea to read the book from beginning to end. If you're used to programming in another Web application language such as PHP, you might want to at least skim the introductory chapters on the World Wide Web and HTTP, as well as the SQL chapters, just so I don't make unfortunate assumptions.

As the book continues, and you've got the key concepts and a number of tags and functions under your belt, we'll start putting together bigger applications with a number of pieces that have to fit together. That is the only way you can learn how to work with ColdFusion in large-scale websites.

Many of the examples in this book were created with the ColdFusion Application Server running on a Windows 2000 with IIS 5. The database used in most cases is Microsoft SQL Server 2000. Oracle 8*i* is used in some examples. Access has generally been eschewed because, while it is inexpensive and therefore easier to get hold of, it is desktop software and unsuited to a production environment. You can make most of the examples in this book work with Access or Paradox with little or no modification. You can even use Excel spreadsheets and plain text files with some modification. That's a fabulous aspect of ColdFusion, and just one demonstration of its flexibility. However, I try to discourage the use of desktop database software with ColdFusion for applications that are likely to have more than a couple of concurrent connections or any frequency of use.

About the Website

If you point your browser to http://www.CoreColdFusion.com, you will discover the companion website to this book. It is meant to provide you with a resource for taking your applications to the next level and continuing your work.

Some features of the website include:

- Databases, files, and code from the book
- Code for creating the website
- Enhancements and expansions to discussions in the book
- Links to ColdFusion hosting providers
- Resource links for ColdFusion User Groups and the most useful ColdFusion sites on the Web
- Information about becoming a Macromedia ColdFusion Certified Developer
- A newsletter with product and informational updates on ColdFusion and Spectra

- A forum for reader feedback—tell me what you think!
- A schedule of ColdFusion and Spectra training seminars happening every month, all over the United States
- Fun things like the ColdFusion challenge—a compendium of tips and tricks
- Security bulletins

Conventions Used in This Book

Notes, which are boxed, illustrate a little tidbit that I couldn't force into the paragraph without an intolerable inelegance of style. They look like this:

<NOTE>

Hello, I am a note. I say something useful or I make a handy reminder.

You will also see such boxes populated with a <TIP> or even a <SOAPBOX>.

If I've done my job, this book will teach you what you need to know about ColdFusion in order to go do it in the real world. Hopefully it will also prove useful long after you know what you're doing—it has been organized to serve also as a reference. It's got the complete language in it, updated for ColdFusion 5. And it's got working examples that represent the most commonly needed tasks in Web programming today.

You can give me feedback at *writer@CoreColdFusion.com.* I welcome your comments and suggestions for future editions.

Thank you for picking this up. I really hope you like it.

Acknowledgments

Core ColdFusion 5 is the product of the time, energy, and knowledge of a great number of people, and I am grateful for their efforts.

Thank you to Marilou Landes, certified ColdFusion developer at University of Illinois Urbana-Champaign, and Susan Matteson, senior Web developer at CyberTrails, who served as the technical reviewers. Their comments, suggestions, and insight were invaluable in helping to make this book clear, concise, and technically accurate.

I appreciate the support of Ted Taylor and everyone at CyberTrails.com.

Thank you to the *Core* series editor Cay Horstmann; I am proud to have been included in this excellent series, and his comments and revision suggestions immeasurably improved the book.

Thanks to Tucker Walsh, Jason Knell, and Bill Sahlas at Macromedia for their support. The Beta team at Macromedia was responsive as the product evolved, and I appreciate the time they took with me to answer questions.

I am pleased to thank Ben Forta. In an exchange regarding conditional logic, Mr. Forta suggested that the topic might make a good book. *Core ColdFusion 5* is the result of that initial conception, and I am grateful for his correspondence and his enthusiasm for ColdFusion.

Thank you to my teachers, especially Bryan Short and Christine Ney, for having high expectations.

It is now clear to me why Prentice Hall is a publishing leader. The team that put this book together is comprised of exceptionally quick, dedicated, utterly professional people. I am lucky to work with Lisa Iarkowski and Faye Gemmellaro in Production and Bryan Gambrel, Executive Marketing Manager. I am very excited to be working with Senior Editor Karen McLean on making the CD-ROM training course version of this book.

The ColdFusion developer community has been fabulous. I am continually inspired by the efforts of all the coders who make it a point to help beginners learn, for no other apparent reason than that they like what they do and they want others to get the most out of their work. The websites devoted to ColdFusion, the teachers and trainers, and the makers of listservs are all a crucially important aspect of ColdFusion development. Thank you to Robert Diamond of Sys-Con Media for the ColdFusion Developers Journal and list. Thank you to everyone who writes in and makes it such an excellent resource.

I am very grateful to Mark Taub, Editor-in-Chief of Prentice Hall Professional Technical Reference. Mark has been open, flexible, thoughtful, and supportive throughout this project. I couldn't have asked for a smarter, more energetic editor. I'm lucky to know you, and I look forward to continuing our work. P.S. I found out what "autodidactic" means—it means others teach you.

Thank you to my sweetheart, Alison Leigh Brown. You're the best writer I know, and my happiest thing, absolutely. Thank you for helping me make this book. You fantasticate. Thank you also to Tom and Sheila Brown for their encouragement and support, and to our Zoë, a best thing, for her understanding. Now we can go on a scooter ride.

Programming, like all work, is political.

GETTING THE LAY OF THE LAND

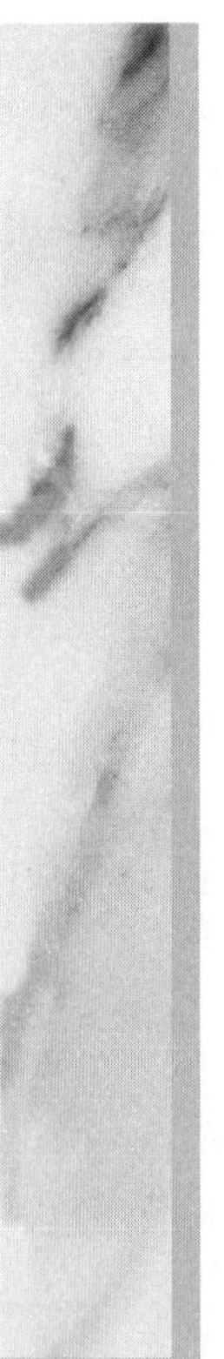

Topics in This Chapter

- What is ColdFusion?
- Why ColdFusion?
- What's new in ColdFusion 5?

Chapter 1

The world is full of problems, which is lucky for programmers. Then we get to have jobs. In a sense, ColdFusion is a set of tools that meet the challenges posed by business and communications. You can use ColdFusion to quickly and easily create data-driven websites. If you're familiar with HTML's tag-based structure, you can start making dynamic websites in short order with ColdFusion.

What Is ColdFusion?

ColdFusion is a couple of things: it's the ColdFusion Markup Language (CFML)—a tag-based language you can use to quickly and easily create dynamic, interactive, data-driven websites; it's also the ColdFusion Application Server (CFAS). CFAS is the software that translates the tags into commands that gather and manipulate data from the Web environment.

First, a bit of history. Two brothers, J. J. and Jeremy Allaire, founded Allaire Corporation in 1995 to bring ColdFusion, the world's first Web application server, to life. ColdFusion, the company's flagship product, was marketed entirely on the Web, fueled by a personal investment of $18,000 by J. J. Allaire. Jeremy Allaire, Macromedia's Chief Technology Officer, graduated from Macalaster College with Bachelor's Degrees in both Political Science and Philosophy. In 1999, the brothers began to expand their core product and made Spectra, the world's first packaged system for content management, e-commerce, and personalization. Six years later, in March 2001, Macromedia purchased the company for over $360 million.

You've heard of software and hardware. ColdFusion is *middleware.* Middleware is any software that performs some kind of translation or conversion. It serves an intermediary function by translating the code you write using ColdFusion tags into an HTML document so that it can be displayed in a Web browser.

It's a Web Programming Language

By now, we're immersed in dynamic websites—that is, websites whose content changes based on user interaction. E-commerce sites and news sites are prominent examples of dynamic sites; they pull their content from databases and deliver an experience to the user based on the user's interests. Intranets (private websites for an organization's internal use) and extranets (websites that provide a private tunnel between two or more organizations) are often dynamic.

To hardcode such sites in HTML would be an endlessly expensive and exhausting task. So, along with the "static" portions of our website (the parts that rarely change), we write web applications. A web application is a shopping cart on an e-commerce site, an online scheduler and contact book, webmail program, or password-protected area that allows office administrators to update the content of the site via a Web interface without touching a line of code. It's software that runs only on the Web.

ColdFusion is a terrific tool for Web applications because it's relatively easy to learn, it's tag based (so it seems familiar to people who know HTML), it's scalable (so it's easy to adapt as your needs adapt), it plays well with others (meaning it can communicate with the Java Programming Language (Java), COM, and CORBA objects), and it's flexible (you can even make your Web apps available for PDAs and Web-enabled cellular phones, which we'll learn how to do later in this book).

ColdFusion is a full-featured Web programming language. You write ColdFusion using conditional logic, tags (about 85 altogether), scripting, and functions. ColdFusion functions are similar in syntax and style to functions in other languages. Both regular expressions and complex data types are available to you, such as structures, arrays, and lists.

It's a Web Application Server

The function of the ColdFusion Application Server is to process all inbound requests that are passed to it by the Web server. CFAS processes all the ColdFusion tags and functions, turns them into HTML pages, and delivers that content to the client. To understand how to approach creating Web applications, it is important first to see that Web applications are ways of solving business problems and replicating business logic. But what do *those* things mean?

In a sense, many things we do each day involve challenge and response. We might have to figure out how to get three people in different cities on the same conference call at the same time, or how to make the city council meeting notes easily available to the public. Maybe we're charged with making Velma and Phyllis—who have hated each other for years—talk to each other now that they're in the same cubicle set. These things are *business problems.* They are challenges that organizations face which require a solution

Often, too, there is a certain way that certain things must be done—the pink paper goes in the blue folder on Tuesday, and yellow papers go in the red folder once they're signed, but they *all* go in the green folder on Friday. Perhaps you receive a statement from a supplier that needs to be resolved into a quote for a client, once you've marked it up. This is what we refer to as *business logic.* It is the process or series of events contingent on one another that allow everything to move forward.

You will code more efficiently, faster, and smarter, with a greater chance to reuse your code, if you consider your ColdFusion applications within a framework of business problems and the accompanying business logic. This book was written with this tenet at the forefront.

And now, with ColdFusion 5, you have access to even more powerful reporting tools via probes, advanced logging, and (on Windows Servers) a direct communication with the Performance Monitor—a sort of cardiogram of your system, applications, and resources.

With ColdFusion you get an interactive debugger, which we'll examine later, which gives you a great deal of information regarding your pages as they execute. This makes it easy to figure out what's going wrong in your code, how long your database queries are taking to execute, what the local and passed variables are, and more.

It's a Web-Based Administration System

ColdFusion 5 ships with what is referred to as the ColdFusion Administrator. It is a web-based application, itself written with ColdFusion tags and functions, that allows you to manage your datasources, manage your ColdFusion log files, create Verity collections, and more. Now with ColdFusion you can set up probes to retrieve information about the health of your applications and the ColdFusion server. Another new feature of the administrator is the ability to interact with advanced third-party management systems, or deploy entire applications as one ColdFusion Archive (CAR) file. The administrator is the interface from which you handle these things.

It's Secure

You can use ColdFusion templates over a Secure Sockets Layer, or disallow use of certain advanced ColdFusion tags such as CFREGISTRY (which allows you to view, edit, and delete keys in the server's registry). If you want to offer a shared hosting environment, the Advanced Security Feature lets you set up sandbox security on your server so that roles- and rules-based interaction can be permitted with granular control. It also allows you to easily "turn off" the use of certain advanced ColdFusion tags.

What Can It Do for You?

Using ColdFusion, you can do a lot more than write dynamic Web pages and shopping carts. You can do really fantastic things with standard tags that would take dozens of lines of code in other languages. You can send and retrieve email over the Web, and exchange data with COM, CORBA, and Java objects. You can use a subset of XML (Extensible Markup Language) called WDDX (Web Distributed Data eXchange) to serialize and expose packets of data as generic XML; with this power, you can communicate with Active Server Pages, retrieve news headlines from MoreOver.com, and much more. You can also perform file and directory manipulation, perform FTP post and retrievals, and use a tag called CFHTTP to retrieve entire Web pages and dynamically incorporate them into yours. It's powerful stuff.

Communicate with Relational Databases and Other Data Sources

With ColdFusion and ODBC, OLE-DB, or native database drivers, you can manipulate stored data on Microsoft SQL Server, MySQL, Postgre, Oracle,

Access, Paradox, IBM DB2, and Sybase databases. You can even manipulate the databases themselves. You can create and drop (delete) databases, create, alter, and drop tables, insert, update, view, and delete data—in fact, you have the full power of the SQL available to you.

You can even use other sources of data, including Microsoft Excel spreadsheets and plain text files.

Why ColdFusion?

There are a lot of languages for you to choose from when you develop Web applications—ASP, JSP, CGI, and JavaScript, to name a few. These are all widely accepted, and have books and popular websites devoted to them. ColdFusion can take the Pepsi Challenge with all of them (see Table 1.1).

Table 1.1 ColdFusion, ASP, and CGI Compared

	ColdFusion	*Microsoft ASP*	*CGI/Perl*
Rapid Deployment	Fast	Slower	Slower
Cost of Software	$1,200–$5,000*	Free with IIS	Free
Scalability	Good	Good	Good
Flexibility	Excellent	Okay	Okay
Reliability	Excellent	Okay	Excellent
Runs on Windows, Linux, Solaris, and HP-UX	Yes	No†	Yes

*Depending on whether Professional or Enterprise edition is purchased
†Adaptive software, such as from ChiliSoft, is available at extra charge

You can check out a much more comprehensive comparison chart online at http://www.infinitywebsystems.com/CF_vs_ASP.html.

Don't be daunted by the cost of the software. With programmers' costs spiraling above lawyers' hourly rates, the speed at which you can plan, write, debug, and deploy your applications has far more impact on Total Cost of Ownership than the price you pay for the software. Because of the readability of the language, minor changes and updates to ColdFusion applications can be worked on by interns or others in your office with only a beginning knowledge of ColdFusion. This frees up the heavy hitters to do what they do best—and saves the company money.

For instance, compare the two snippets of code below. First, in ASP (VBScript):

```
<%
Dim RandomFraction
Randomize
RandomFraction = Rnd
Response.Write(RandomFraction)
%>
```

We can write code in ColdFusion that accomplishes the exact same thing. It looks like this:

```
1. <cfset RandomFraction = Rand()>
2. <cfoutput>#RandomFraction#</cfoutput>
```

I'll let you judge which one is easier to read, faster to debug, and simpler for beginners to get their mitts around. *Hint:* One is twice as long as the other.

Just to whet your appetite, let's take a quick look at this code. First, we notice that the code is inside < and > signs, which, we remember from HTML, indicate the beginning and end of a tag. Then we notice that the text inside the tags begins with "CF," which stands for ColdFusion. In fact, every ColdFusion tag starts with "CF," which is how the CFAS knows to interpret the tags. So right off the bat we see that the above code has two different ColdFusion tags: <CFSET> and <CFOUTPUT>.

We use the CFSET tag to declare a variable—that is, to say, "I want to reserve this name for a moment because it's going to hold some value that I will refer to later." In this case, that variable name is "RandomFraction."

We then call the ColdFusion *function* Rand(), which tells ColdFusion to "generate a random decimal number between 0 and 1." So in the first line we've declared a variable and set it to a particular value. At this point (the end of line 1), ColdFusion has a value and has a way to refer to that value. But it hasn't done anything with it. For example, it hasn't displayed (output) it on the Web page. We need to use another ColdFusion tag, <CFOUTPUT>, to display the contents of a variable. Just as ColdFusion knows that it should specifically process tags that begin with <CF, it recognizes the hash mark (or pound sign) as surrounding variables, results, and functions. We'll discuss functions in depth later.

If we were to rewrite the above two lines of code in plain English, they would look like this:

Line 1: Reserve a little space in memory and give it the name "RandomFraction" to distinguish it from other places reserved in memory. Make it equal to a randomly generated decimal number between 0 and 1.

Line 2: Output to the web browser whatever the value of the "RandomFraction" variable is.

We might also write:

```
1. <cfset FirstName = "Eben">
2. <cfoutput>#FirstName#</cfoutput>
```

This time we don't use a function. We just set the value of the variable FirstName to the text string "Eben." Then we output the value of the variable just as before. If we saved our little file with a .cfm extension and uploaded it to a Web server running ColdFusion, we might see output like this:

```
0.86965744
```

If we then hit "Refresh" in the browser, we would see a new randomly generated decimal between 0 and 1.

This just gives you a small idea of how easy it is to start working with ColdFusion, and how straightforward the language can be. The fun part will be discovering how powerful it is. Let's look now at what's new in ColdFusion 5.0.

What's New in Macromedia ColdFusion 5?

If you've had a little experience with ColdFusion, the thing that's obviously new is the name (it used to be Allaire ColdFusion). It also gets a new Macromedia look. ColdFusion 5 represents a pretty significant upgrade from 4.5. Here are some of the major new features:

Enhanced Productivity

- **User-Defined Functions**—create reusable functions to accelerate development
- **Streamlined Security Configuration**—quickly and easily secure applications
- **Business Intelligence Capabilities**—provide enhanced decision support

- **Charting Engine**—create professional quality charts and graphs from data queries
- **Reporting Interface for Crystal Reports 8.0** (for Enterprise Edition only)—create professional quality tabular reports from data queries
- **Enhanced Verity K2 Full-Text Search**—index and search up to 250,000 documents using the embedded Verity K2 search engine with an easy upgrade path to index unlimited documents

Enhanced Performance

- **Query of Queries**—reduce database overhead by querying cached data sets or join queries from multiple data sources
- **Incremental Page Delivery**—improve response time by delivering page output to users as it is built
- **Wire Protocol Database Drivers**—provide high-performance, reliable database connectivity

Easy Management

- **Application Deployment Services**—reliably package, deploy, archive, or restore entire applications
- **Enhanced Application Monitoring**—monitor server performance and availability with customizable alerts and recovery
- **SNMP Support**—monitor ColdFusion applications from enterprise management systems
- **Server Log Analysis**—quickly detect and diagnose problems

Expanded Integration

- **Expanded Linux Support**—new support for SuSE and Cobalt Linux distributions
- **Enhanced Hardware Load Balancer Integration**—optimized, agent-based support for hardware load balancers including new support for the Cisco CSS 11000

- **Enhanced COM Support**—easier integration with COM components

What Difference Does the Macromedia Merger Make?

Along with these major upgrades come some interesting new capabilities for those of you familiar with the Macromedia product line. The larger company has greater resources behind it, and can now offer products that take advantage of the combination of server-side software, development tools, and dynamic content generation.

Harpoon

With Harpoon, a free download developed in Spring of 2001, you can easily create and customize Macromedia Flash interfaces for your ColdFusion forms. Programmers at www.figleaf.com have helped turn this into a really exciting new tool. Check out Figleaf Software's site for a number of helpful documents and answers to questions you might have about Harpoon and how it can enhance your forms. The basic idea is that your application can perform data checks without making a round trip to the server. And the interfaces have a great look and feel as well. A copy is included on this book's CD-ROM.

Generator

Macromedia Generator is the solution for dynamically updating the content of sites that implement Flash. ColdFusion interacts with Generator to create scheduled (offline) content updates, and rich graphical charts for data reports. Using the <CFGRAPH> tag, it's easy to represent your data relationships by creating Gantt charts, pie charts, and more.

Speed

If you're deciding whether or not to upgrade from a previous version of ColdFusion, you'll be happy to know that ColdFusion 5 processes more than 75% faster than 4.5.

Still Need a Reason (Got Java?)

Whether you're a developer, a server admin, a project manager, or a student just starting a career, you've got a lot to work with when you choose ColdFusion. If you write Java, you want to know that you're on a platform that can support you.

Not only does ColdFusion allow you to send and receive information from Java objects via the <CFSERVLET> and <CFOBJECT> tags, but there's an entire line of support for you as you continue to develop Java applications.

JRun

JRun software offers a complete IDE for writing, testing, and deploying server-side Java applications. It's a visual environment which respects your code as you create Servlets and Enterprise Java Beans. ColdFusion uses existing architecture within JRun to take advantage of increased performance and other new features.

Kawa

Macromedia's Kawa software offers a complete IDE for writing, testing, and deploying server-side Java applications. It's a visual environment which respects your code as you create Servlets and Enterprise Java Beans. It also integrates with JRun.

Neo

The next version of ColdFusion, 6.0, is currently code-named "Neo." It is scheduled to be released in 2002. The major difference between the current version and Neo is that Neo will be rewritten in Java, and will therefore be able to offer greater platform support, and leverage more significant interaction with your existing Java applications. You won't need to know any Java at all to work with Neo, any more than you need to know C right now to work with ColdFusion 5. Your applications will just run faster, and incorporate better Java support.

In ColdFusion 6, the tag language will be implemented as Java Server Page tags. That means that ColdFusion tags will compile to Java Servlets, and programmers will be able to freely mix ColdFusion and Java.

So let's get to work. We're going to have a lot of fun.

THE WORLD WIDE WEB AND HTTP

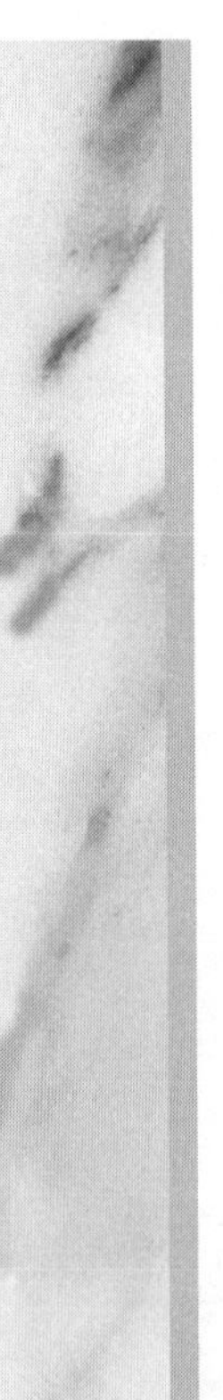

Topics in This Chapter

- What is the Internet?
- Networks
- IP
- DNS
- ColdFusion templates
- Request and response
- How the ColdFusion server operates

Chapter 2

"The first thing in a visit is to say 'How d'ye do?' and shake hands!"
—Lewis Carroll, *Through the Looking Glass*

This chapter is devoted to ensuring that you're confident about how general aspects of the Internet work within the context of ColdFusion. If you already have a pretty good grasp of the concepts of HTTP 1.1, how web servers work, and the Client-Server relationship, you can skip this section. Turn to the "ColdFusion Templates" section instead.

The main idea is that if you understand what the numbers mean and how they go together, you will be sensitive to issues of load later on when you're designing your applications. You'll also get a pretty good handle on HTTP requests and responses, which is important for understanding a number of development shortcuts available to you.

This chapter will not make anyone a network administrator. You can certainly develop ColdFusion applications without understanding even very much of this chapter. However, if you have a more complete knowledge, you can know what to expect on a practical level if you're looking to go out developing on your own. I briefly touch on topics concerning protocols, the web, and HTTP requests and responses.

What Is the Internet?

In general terms, the Internet is simply the world's largest network. It is made up of a series of connected smaller networks, which are themselves made up of a number of even smaller networks. A little information about how they work is important to aid in your understanding of how to craft reliable, fast-loading, user-friendly websites written in ColdFusion.

It would be fun right about now to generate a number of cute remarks about how there is no definition of a life form that is not also true of the Internet, and like that. But I'll resist the temptation. Several people in my family happen to be lawyers. So instead, I'll offer you the legal (that's right) definition of the Internet:

The Internet refers to the global information system that has three key components:

1. It is linked together by a globally unique address space based on the Internet Protocol (IP).
2. It is able to support communications based on the Transport Control Protocol/Internet Protocol (TCP/IP) standard, and/or other compatible protocols.
3. It provides, uses, or makes accessible, either publicly or privately, high-level services layered on the communications and related infrastructure of the above.

This definition gives us a couple of things to work with: infrastructure, and protocols. We'll look at them in some detail in a moment.

The Internet was created during the Cold War as a defense against possible military attacks. The idea was that if any part of the Internet went down, the communications infrastructure would still work. The reason it would still be able to work is called *packet switching.*

Data travels across networks in packets, which are small collections of related information. They also carry a "from" address and a "to" address. We'll refer to Internet addressing in a bit. When you send or retrieve data over the Internet, hardware devices called *routers* read the address on each packet and choose the best route to its destination. Think of the airlines, or regular postal mail. If there is a problem in Chicago, I can still go through St. Louis to get to New York.

Let's take a moment to look more closely at how these packets get sent and retrieved. We start with networks, which provide the physical transport mechanism for the Internet.

Networks

Cities and countries are connected by large cables and wireless data-transmission devices that carry very large amounts of data. These are called *backbones.* While these backbones carry large amounts of data, they're handling millions of different users at once. So your computer breaks up any one request for data into many different packets, each with your address on them, and an identifier, and sends them all out. When all of the packets arrive at their destination, they are reassembled. If any packet is missing, the destination sends back a message saying "Hey, we lost one; send it again," and the source of the request sends it again.

IP

IP is the Internet Protocol, which, like any other protocol, is a set of rules governing actions. We might say that one facet of our current social protocol in America is to begin and end our conversations with phrases like "hello" and "goodbye." When you hear the phone ring, you pick it up and say, "How d'ye do?" Then the voice at the other end of the line says, "Hello, this is your credit card company." After you have worked out the details of how you can retrieve your repossessed car, you both signal the end of the conversation with "ta ta" (or some equivalent).

Chunks of data sent over the Internet, referred to as *packets*, do the same thing. But how do they know where to go? The answer is a "globally unique address space," or IP address.

An IP address looks something like this: 203.165.42.18. It's a 32-bit number separated by four dots. The number before each dot is an *octet* and can be from 0–255. Every computer connected to the Internet has an IP Address. On a private network, your IP address can be randomly assigned. If your network is running DHCP (the Dynamic Host Control Protocol), your IP address can even change every time you connect to the Internet. Each octet in the address is a different identifier regarding the particular network and a particular host on that network.

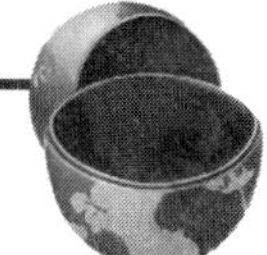

If you are interested in this subject, there are a number of good books. Charles Petzold, the well-known C++ author, has written a lovely book called Code *(Microsoft Press, 2000) which explains how computer languages work at a fundamental level. Another excellent book on the subject is* The Pattern In the Stone *(Perseus Books, 1999) by Daniel Hillis.*

Although IP can support millions and millions of addresses, we are gradually running out of numbers. In order to combat this, IP is very slowly being replaced by CIDR, or "Classless Internet Domain Routing," which allows for a trailing slash at the end of the address; each number after the slash can hold thousands of addresses more. It will be some time before we see this fully realized, however.

DNS

DNS is the Domain Name Service, which is actually its own network. Computers on the DNS network hold huge databases of information about domain names. These databases store mappings of IP addresses with their associated domain names. A domain name is the alphabetical name reserved by each website. For instance, http//www.CoreColdFusion.com is the domain name of the website that accompanies this book. Every domain name must be unique. And every Web server must have a Name Server to associate the IP addresses with the domain names of the sites it serves.

But the Internet doesn't really understand domain names. It has to use DNS to find out which domain goes with which IP address. One can quickly see that it is easier to remember and type http//www.CoreColdFusion.com than 162.42.161.27—but they both get you to the same place.

If this site were on a cluster, each of the computers in the cluster could resolve the same domain name to different IP addresses. Or rather, DNS would resolve the same name to any of a number of IPs. This capability is provided because some heavily trafficked sites would slow to a crawl if everyone were trying to retrieve files from them across the same poor little Network Interface Card. It is called *load balancing,* a feature which ColdFusion Enterprise supports nicely. This also allows you to support *failover;* that is, you can make a back-up server in case your primary Web server fails for some reason.

There are about thirteen total top-level domain name servers in the world. Ten of these are in the United States. When you type a URL (Uniform Resource Locator) into your browser and hit Enter, that name is sent first to your ISP. If your ISP has a copy of the page you're looking for, it will send that one back. This saves trouble for your ISP; your request doesn't have to go hunting the Internet.

Another advantage is that if you move your website to a different host, everyone can still find your website.

So this is why if you buy a domain name it often takes about 48 hours for it to propagate throughout the Internet—each DNS server needs to know that if it gets handed a certain name, there's a number that goes with it.

Proxy Servers

A *proxy* is something done for you by someone else on your behalf. A proxy server lends you an IP address for the time that you are connected to the Internet. It acts as a central location through which requests get routed. Since there are only about 4 billion IP addresses in the world, this is a good thing.

A proxy server can use a few IP addresses to service a great number of clients. This is the way that WebTV, AOL, and a lot of local networks access the Internet. This is why it isn't a great idea to try to track your users based on their IP addresses—they could be going incognito through a proxy.

One can quickly see how this benefits end users. If you're going through a proxy for your requests, your computer, and all the others on your local network, are hidden from the outside world. In this way, the proxy acts as a kind of firewall, or protection. It is important to understand just the fact of proxy servers at this point. They can impact your ColdFusion writing in terms of accessibility and user tracking.

Anatomy of a Web Address

What are you typing in your address bar when you visit a website? A typical Web address looks like this: http://www.macromedia.com. It has this structure:

```
[protocol://]Domain_Name.TopLevelDomain[/Path/File
.MIMEType]
```

So there are a number of parts to this address.

The first part indicates the *protocol* to use. On the Web, it's generally http (Hypertext Transfer Protocol). You may have visited an FTP site, in which case the address you're looking for begins with FTP (File Transfer Protocol). For instance, you could type ftp://ftp.redhat.com to download the latest version of RedHat Linux.

The protocol determines a number of things about your Internet connection:

- Data compression method
- Kind of error handling to be used
- How a signal will announce the beginning of a transmission
- How a signal will announce the end of a transmission

Other protocols on the Internet include NNTP and SMTP. NNTP (Net News Transfer Protocol) is a newsgroup protocol, and SMTP (Simple Mail Transfer Protocol) is used for sending email messages.

The second part of your Web address is the domain name, discussed above. You can purchase domains at http//www.networksolutions.com, http//www.register.com, and many other sites, or through your ISP.

The third part of the address is the top-level domain. See Table 2.1 for a list of common domains and what they are used for.

Table 2.1 Top-Level Domain Names

Top-Level Domain	*Use*
.com	Commercial
.edu	Education
.gov	Government
.mil	Military
.org	Nonprofit organizations
.net	Network providers

The International Consortium for the Assignment of Names and Numbers, which assigns top-level domains, has recently appointed several new top-level domains. The reason is that we are already running out. As of this writing, there are about 30 million domain names registered throughout the world. So they came up with .tv, .name, .biz, .info, and .cc in order to open up millions more.

Note that each country has its own top-level domain as well. For instance, http://www.tate.org.uk takes you to the Tate Gallery's website in the United Kingdom.

The *path* is a folder that holds more folders, and files. So for the address ColdFusion5.com/Book/Chp1/index.html, the path is /Book/Chp1/index.html. The particular file requested has two key parts: the file name, and the file type (or MIME type).

The server will default to trying to find a particular file if only a folder is specified. For instance, if you simply type http//www.CoreColdFusion.com into your browser, you're still getting a particular file. But since you haven't specified one, the Web server will look for a default. Usually the default page is called "index." It goes down a list of default files, defined by the server administrator, looking for one of these. It also checks the *extension* or file type (MIME type). A ColdFusion template has a .cfm extension. Pages written in Wireless Markup Language have a .wml extension. The MIME type will define what application should process the request. We'll learn a lot more about MIME types later as we discuss the <CFCONTENT> tag, in the Appendix on WAP Development.

The World Wide Web

You may remember from the preface that ColdFusion is middleware. You may also have been struck by the broad definition of middleware. In fact, the

Web itself is middleware. It uses a combination of protocols (such as HTTP and TCP/IP), languages (such as HTML and ColdFusion), and a presentation layer (the browser) to translate its programs.

So what's the real difference between a regular Web page and a ColdFusion page?

ColdFusion Templates

To begin with, the difference between a regular Web page and a ColdFusion page is that ColdFusion pages are referred to as *templates*. The distinction is not merely academic.

First of all, ColdFusion is a *preprocessor* (like PHP—the "PHP Hypertext Preprocessor"). This means that when the Web server sees a file with a ".cfm" extension, the page is sent to the ColdFusion Application Server (CFAS). It is processed by ColdFusion before the client request is honored. We therefore refer to the .cfm file as a template, since it is unfinished for presentation.

Once the CFAS receives the template, the ColdFusion code is interpreted, any necessary database calls are made, and the CFAS creates an HTML page to be returned to the browser. So the second reason we call a .cfm file a "template" is that it could have any number of possible outcomes as an HTML page, depending on the instructions in the template. In this way, the file is like a template in a Word document, or a kind of boilerplate: any number of different instantiations of a page can be created from the one overarching resource.

At this point one can see where a little knowledge of Object-Oriented thinking is helpful. While ColdFusion is not an Object-Oriented language, it is important to consider your code in terms of use-case scenarios. That is, you must create the conditional logic on your templates that best utilizes the possible user interactions with it, in order to maximize code reuse, efficiency, modularity, and readability. If you aren't familiar with use-case, conditional logic, or any of this, we will consider these in detail as we approach creating large ColdFusion applications.

HTTP

Tim Berners-Lee wrote the first specification for the Hyper Text Markup Language in late 1990 as a way to standardize the structure of documents so they could be shared easily. HTML, the language used to create Web pages, is an application of the SGML (Standard Generalized Markup Language). Soon thereafter, he wrote HTTP for transferring them.

Hypertext Transfer Protocol is the primary form of information delivery on the Web. It was developed by the Swiss particle physics laboratory CERN in 1991.

<NOTE>

Just for fun:

Here is the definition of HTTP 1.1 as stated by the W3C, the governing organization for the standardization of the Web: "The Hypertext Transfer Protocol (HTTP) is an application-level protocol for distributed, collaborative, hypermedia information systems. It is a generic, stateless, protocol which can be used for many tasks beyond its use for hypertext, such as name servers and distributed object management systems, through extension of its request methods, error codes and headers. A feature of HTTP is the typing and negotiation of data representation, allowing systems to be built independently of the data being transferred."

I urge you to read the full specification at http://www.w3c.org.

State

As stated above, HTTP is a stateless protocol. That is, each request and response set is a discrete transaction; the "state" of the previous page is not "carried" into any subsequent page requests. The server sends its response, and the transaction is complete. It is possible to associate a series of requests with each other by using cookies, session variables, or the like. This is known as *carrying state.* A familiar example is a shopping cart in an e-commerce site which continues to "know" what items are in your cart as you move from page to page.

Requests and Request Headers

HTTP requests are primarily comprised of *headers.* The header consists of three parts: the Request Method, the URL of the data requested, and the protocol version. Other information is also made available in the request. This includes information regarding the client (brand and version number of the requester's browser), and the character set and language in use on the client.

Since this information is available in the request sent to the server, it is de facto available to ColdFusion. For instance, it is very easy in ColdFusion to discern and record what browser your visitors are using and what their operating system is. This information could be useful for displaying different pages based on browser type, or for recording demographics.

When you make an HTTP request, you are sending a message to the Web server. Here is an example of a typical request:

```
GET / HTTP/1.1
Accept: image/gif, image/x-xbitmap, image/jpeg,
        image/pjpg, */*
Accept-Language: en-us
Accept-Encoding: gzip, deflate
User-Agent: Mozilla/4.0 (compatible;
        MSIE 5.5; Windows 5.0)
Host: cybertrails.com
Connection: Keep-Alive
```

Here is what this request header tells the server: "I (the browser) use HTTP version 1.1. I will accept a number of defined image documents (specified by MIME type), as well as undefined documents—the "*" is a wildcard, which in this instance means all extensions of all file types. I accept messages in American English, and I am using the gzip type of compression." The User-Agent line tells the server what brand of browser is being used, what version, and what operating system its running. The Host line tells the server what hostname it is looking for. The last line admonishes the server to keep the TCP connection open until explicitly told to close (disconnect) it.

<NOTE>

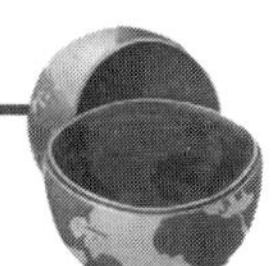

You can do advanced work with HTTP in ColdFusion via the <CFHEADER> tag, which is used to manipulate these variables and others. For instance, we will use it later to force the server to give us a noncached copy of a page.

Response Headers

If the server is able to honor this request, it returns a *response.* A response header looks similar to a request header. You can use these server variables to add functionality to your ColdFusion applications. It is also a good idea to know what is going on under the hood.

Below is a typical response header:

```
HTTP/1.1 200 OK
Date: Sun, 06 May 2001 22:43:26 GMT
Server: Apache/1.3.6 (Unix)
Last-Modified: Fri, 11 Aug 2000 13:55:01 GMT
```

```
ETag: "3d4ef-765-435f3ce7"
Accept-Ranges: bytes
Content-length: 144
Connection: Close
Content-type: text/html
<title>Hello</title>
<h1>Hello World</h1><br>
This is my web page content.
```

The first line responds to the client with the version of HTTP in use, and what is called a *status code*. "200 OK" is probably the most common status code returned in responses. It means, "I have the file you're looking for, everything looks in order, so I am returning it to you as requested." You probably know the "404 File Not Found" status code, since 404 is one of the few response status codes that returns a value visible to the client. "200 OK" is invisible to the user. Then we've got the time on the server, as well as the Web server software it's running. We get a timestamp of the date and time that the requested document was last modified. This timestamp is used, as you might guess, to determine caching obligations. The "ETag" is an *entity tag*, which is how the server uniquely identifies a particular client. This tag is also used for caching purposes. We are then told that the length of the document returned is 144 bytes. The "Connection" line tells the client that the TCP connection protocol will close following the fulfillment of the response, and therefore another request needs to be made for any subsequent interest. The "Content-type" specifies the MIME type of the document returned. In this case it is HTML, though it could be, for instance, a Microsoft Word document, in which case the Content-type is application/ms word. What follows is the fulfillment of the requested document itself.

<NOTE>

If you are interested in reading the specification, which is a great idea, you can do so at:

http://www.w3c.org/Protocols/rfc2616/rfc2616.html

Application Servers

As complex as Web server software tends to be, its job is rather straightforward: a client requests a page, and the server returns it. *Applications servers,* like ColdFusion, extend this power and make it possible to do a number of things you couldn't do otherwise. You can create dynamic pages, access databases, send and retrieve email, work with objects, and more.

How the ColdFusion Server Operates

When your Web server receives a request from a browser, it checks the file type. If the page requested is a ColdFusion application page (a file or "template" written in ColdFusion and saved with the .cfm extension), it will get handed off to the ColdFusion server to be processed at runtime. The ColdFusion *daemon* (pronounced *demon*) is a process that runs in the background of your server, listening for .cfm requests. On Windows, you might be used to hearing about Services or System Agents; same thing.

So when a .cfm file is requested, a number of things happen:

1. The Web server passes the files over to the ColdFusion server.
2. The ColdFusion server scans the page, processing all of the ColdFusion Markup tags and functions from top to bottom.
3. Any necessary calls to a database are made. Cached result gets stored in memory.
4. ColdFusion Server generates HTML code (including any JavaScript) that contains the result of interpreting the template.
5. The server sends back the resulting HTML code to the browser.

Now we are ready to prepare the environment to install ColdFusion, which is the subject of Chapter 3. Just glance at the hardware requirements and go on to Chapter 4, "Installing ColdFusion 5," if you're comfortable with Web servers and databases for large websites.

PREPARING YOUR COLDFUSION ENVIRONMENT

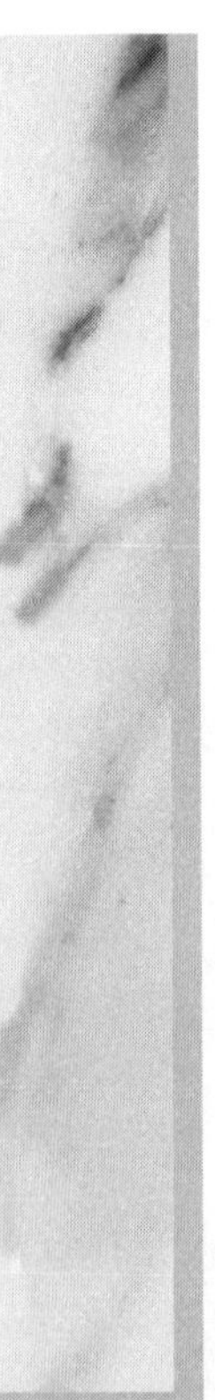

Topics in This Chapter

- Operating-system requirements
- Hardware requirements
- Choosing a Web server
- Choosing a data server
- Choosing a version of ColdFusion 5
- Where to get ColdFusion

Chapter 3

ColdFusion is available for a rich variety of platforms and can communicate with a number of different Relational Database Management Systems. The selection of Web server and data server environment to use with your ColdFusion applications is an important consideration that can have long-term effects on the scalability, power, and ease of deployment of your applications.

This chapter will cover pricing, licensing, and hardware and operating-system requirements for ColdFusion 5. Note that they are different than previous versions. For instance, although memory allocation is more efficient in version 5, more RAM is required. Version 4.5 of ColdFusion supported only RedHat on Linux. Now, Cobalt and SuSE are supported as well.

We will also examine different options for Web server and database software.

Operating-System Requirements

Before you begin to install ColdFusion, make sure that your system meets the minimum requirements. Table 3.1 lists the minimum requirements for running ColdFusion 5. Please make sure you have the right software for your system before you begin.

Table 3.1 ColdFusion Server 5 Requirements by Operating System and Version

OS	*CF Pro Windows*	*CF Ent Windows*	*CF Ent Solaris*	*CF Pro Linux*	*CF Ent Linux*	*CF Pro HP-UX*
Windows 95, 98, ME	X					
Windows NT (service pack 4+)	X	X				
Windows 2000 (Pro and Server)	X	X				
Solaris 2.6,7,8			X			
RedHat Linux 6.2				X	X	
SuSE Linux 6.4				X	X	
Cobalt RAQ3/4 and XTR				X	X	
HP-UX 11.0						X

When determining which OS to use, there are a number of considerations for ColdFusion and operating systems:

1. As of this writing, ColdFusion is lab-tested most frequently and thoroughly on Windows platforms.
2. Expect Linux releases of ColdFusion to trail Windows releases by a month or two.
3. ColdFusion for Linux does not currently support COM and has limited support for CORBA. A COM release for UNIX is being worked on.
4. Windows ME and Windows 98 will run ColdFusion with Personal Web Server. That's okay for development, but it's hard to determine how your applications will run for an end user in a production environment. But these also do support certain functions (such as GetMetricData) and certain server monitoring tools.

Hardware Requirements

Generally hardware selection is not a significant issue in running ColdFusion, as long as you meet the minimum hardware requirements. ColdFusion will run on Sun SPARC and Intel-based hardware. The hardware requirements for

Generator and JRun, which ColdFusion automatically installs in modified versions, are assumed in the requirements and need not be considered separately.

Table 3.2 shows the minimum hardware requirements for running ColdFusion 5.

Table 3.2 Minimum Hardware Requirements for ColdFusion 5

	Supported Operating Systems	*Processor*	*RAM*	*Hard Disk Space*	*Supported Web Servers*
ColdFusion Windows	Windows 98; Windows NT 4.0 SP6a; Windows 2000 SP1	Intel Pentium or later	256 MB Required; 512 MB Recommended	400 MB	Microsoft IIS 4.0 or later; Netscape/iPlanet 3.51 or later; Apache Web Server; O'Reilly WebSite Professional 2.0 or later; WebSite Server API (WSAPI)
ColdFusion Solaris	Solaris 2.6, 7, 8	Sparc	256 MB Required; 512 MB Recommended	350 MB	Netscape/iPlanet 3.51 or later; Apache Web Server
ColdFusion Linux	Red Hat 6.2 or later; SuSE Linux 7.0 or later; Cobalt; RAQ3/RAQ4	Intel Pentium or later	256 MB Required; 512 MB Recommended	350 MB	Netscape/iPlanet 4.1; Apache Web Server
ColdFusion HP-UX	HP-UX 11.0	PA_RISC 1.1 or 2.0	128 MB Required; 256 MB Recommended	120 MB	Netscape/iPlanet 2.01, 3.01, 3.6, 4.0; Apache Web Server*

*Your Apache Web server must be binary compatible with Apache 1.3.6 (up to and including 1.3.19).

<NOTE>

All Windows versions must be running MDAC 2.0 and MFC (MSVCP60.DLL). Go to http://www.microsoft.com/data to download the latest versions of these files.

In previous versions of ColdFusion, there was not a maximum allowable number of processors. As you select your hardware, remember that as of ColdFusion 5, regular ColdFusion licenses cover you for only one or two processors.

Choosing a Web Server

First, let's get this out of the way: if you are already running a Web server and are simply adding ColdFusion as a service, then this discussion is probably not for you. Just keep running your Web server as you have been and don't worry about it. It's a separate issue in many respects; I am treating it here for those who are not up and running yet. Just make sure that ColdFusion supports your Web server API (those on the list in Table 3.2 do): while you can use ColdFusion via CGI interface, this is discouraged.

Determining the appropriate Web server for your ColdFusion sites is a very important part of insuring the success of your Web application endeavors. There are a number of things to consider, many of which we will take a look at now.

ColdFusion will run on the Web servers mentioned in Table 3.2. But what do the different options really mean for your organization?

Once you have your site up and running, it can be somewhat difficult, time consuming, and expensive to migrate to another Web serving platform. You therefore need to address several issues before committing yourself to a Web server.

Total Cost of Ownership

Cost may be an issue for you or your organization. Just as with ColdFusion itself, be careful not to make the mistake of thinking that a product with a price tag is necessarily more expensive than a free product.

Is "Free" Really Free?

Apache is a free Web server, which can run on a free operating system like RedHat. Microsoft's IIS 5 comes free with Windows 2000 Server products. Netscape Enterprise Server is not a free product. But this is not the end of the story. For instance, Apache is far and away the most widely used Web server on the Web, with a market share of something like 65%. There is no charge for using the software, but it requires a good deal more experience to set up and maintain than the others. You can see that you need to take into account several factors that create the Total Cost of Ownership of your platform.

Application Purpose and Audience

This is something that we will often return to throughout the book. Rhetoricians consider it their first duty to determine two things when they create an argument: who is the audience and what is my purpose. I firmly believe that these very same two things are your first concern as an application designer. As it relates to choosing Web server software, you can save yourself a lot of trouble by asking these questions first.

Techie Time

Who is going to maintain your Web server? You should know what your role is in your organization, and how things work. You may be in a big and fancy operation where you've got the luxury of having one person for every specific job requirement. Or you may be in an office of three where you're also the accountant and the human resources department, as well as the host master. For either of these situations, how much is it going to cost you to have someone come in and handle Web server problems? Be realistic about how much you know, how much time you have, and how many different areas of your company have you listed as the Emergency Contact on their field day permission slips. In a surprising number of cases, it's cheaper to pay someone $100 an hour to come fix something or fine-tune it than it is to do it yourself.

Vendor Viability

It is important to consider the focus and viability of your vendor's business when choosing a platform. For instance, in March of 2001, O'Reilly announced that the company would drop its flagship software product, the O'Reilly website Web server. While another vendor is likely to assume its manufacture, the product may be quite different. If your software becomes unsupported, you may find it expensive to migrate to another platform later.

Authentication

What do you use for authentication in your company? Say you choose Netscape Enterprise Server. It runs on Sun Solaris and on Windows NT/2000. Since it maintains its own user list, security is not integrated with the operating system. At this point, people often turn to LDAP (Lightweight Directory Access Protocol). If you have a number of remote users, this may be costly to set up and maintain.

The Community

83% of ColdFusion licenses are for Windows. If you've got a hassle and you're running Windows, it may be easier to find help regarding that pesky p-code error.

What About Your Other Applications?

If you are migrating from one platform to another, you need to carefully consider what other applications you have running. If you have existing applications that you want to migrate, you need to make a thorough inventory of what programs and scripts they rely on and what databases they connect to (and the location of those). For instance, I have seen Apache Web servers that run off Linux for a year without ever being restarted. However, if I have a client whose Web applications require a data dump to a Word document, I'll probably need to use COM, so Linux isn't the best choice. Perhaps then I would want to consider running Apache off Windows.

Maybe you've got only a few pages of an existing site that use ASP, and you want to run a Linux/Apache combination. It's probably cheaper to rewrite those few ASP pages in ColdFusion than to go out and buy ChiliSoft's plug in for ASP.

The idea here has been to persuade you to take a wide variety of factors into account when planning your Web application environment. There are too many variables to discuss here in detail. ColdFusion has historically been engineered for Windows platforms, and ColdFusion 5 seems to integrate very efficiently and optimize memory usage exceptionally well on Windows 2000.

On the other hand, Netscape Enterprise Server is a powerful work horse that runs some of the largest sites out there—including Excite, Lycos, E*Trade, and Schwab.

Once you have considered the above questions, determined what your purpose is and who your audience will be, and taken an inventory of what software you've got to run and what resources you have available to help you maintain it, I expect the right answer for you will be clear.

Choosing a Data Server

The glory of ColdFusion is really apparent in its work with relational database systems. While there are things that you can do in ColdFusion without a database, it will surely not be long before you require the power and flexibility that comes with integrating a database with your Web application.

With ColdFusion, you create what are called "datasources." A *datasource* is a name and placeholder for the connection that ColdFusion will use to communicate with a particular database. We will go into these in more depth later, but for now, it is enough to know that ColdFusion supports a great variety of databases for you to use in your applications. The discussion here is meant to illuminate some key advantages and disadvantages to the different RDBMSs out there.

<TERM>

An RDBMS is a Relational Database Management System. This way of storing data keeps information in tables that relate to one another through unique identifiers. These are distinguished from flat file databases, such as Fox Pro. The main difference is that relationships between tables are enforced only by the programmer, not by constraints defined in the database. Some RDBMSs that you may be familiar with are Oracle, MS SQL Server, DB2, and MS Access. RDBMSs are what we will be concerned with throughout this book.

In ColdFusion we can retrieve information from databases for manipulation or display on the Web. We can also insert new data into a database, or update existing data. You can create tables, relationships, and constraints, and even create or delete entire databases via ColdFusion. In fact, anything you can do with an SQL statement, you can do through ColdFusion.

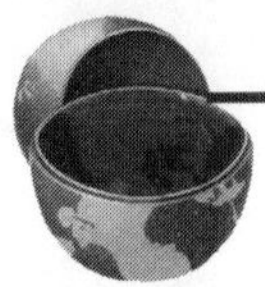

<CAUTION>

While it is possible, I do not recommend using ColdFusion to Alter, Create, or Drop tables or databases. These operations are quite delicate, and the username and password you provide for ColdFusion to connect to your database should be restricted from performing such operations. Otherwise, you may seriously compromise the security of your database.

We will discuss working with databases in later chapters. For now, we just need to select the right one for you.

There are different ways of connecting to databases. A common way is through ODBC, or Open DataBase Connectivity. ODBC was developed by Microsoft Corporation. Its goal is to enable accessing data from any application, regardless of the database handling the data. That's why you can connect to Excel files and even plain text (.txt) files via ODBC. This connectivity is possible because the ODBC driver, which is a small software program, inserts a middle translation layer between the database and the calling application. For this reason, both the database and the application must be ODBC compliant; that is, they both can understand ODBC, so the translation can take place.

Fittingly enough, the frequency of occurrence of the Microsoft name is apparent in Table 3.3, which lists the databases that ColdFusion supports.

Table 3.3 Databases Supported by ColdFusion

Database
Microsoft SQL Server 6.5, 7.0, 2000
Oracle 7.3, 8.0, and later
IBM DB2
Sybase 11 and later
Informix 7.3 and later
Microsoft Access database (.mdb)
Microsoft dBase driver (.dbf)
Microsoft Visual Fox Pro
Microsoft Excel spreadsheets (.xls)
Plain Text (.txt, .csv) files

If your database is not on this list, you may still be able to use it with ColdFusion. Check your documentation and poke around on the Macromedia website. If you have a Windows machine, you can see any ODBC connections you have running by going to the Control Panel and choosing ODBC Datasources. There you will notice, for instance, that you can also add a Paradox driver if you want to use ColdFusion with Corel's Paradox database.

Another set of drivers that ColdFusion communicates with is OLE-DB. *OLE*, which stands for Object Linking and Embedding, is another Microsoft invention to help applications take advantage of embedded objects. This means that you can communicate with SQL Server, Lotus Notes, and Microsoft Exchange 2000.

ColdFusion also offers native driver support for products such as Sybase11, Oracle 7.3, Oracle 8, Informix 7.3, and DB2.

New ColdFusion 5.0, Merant ODBC 3.7 drivers are available. You can connect with a clientless driver on Informix 9, and your Sybase driver no longer requires client libraries.

<NOTE>

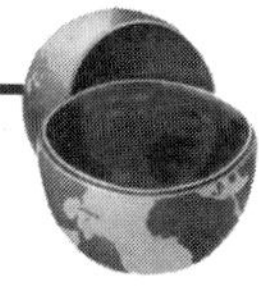

In late April of 2001, IBM announced plans to purchase the Informix database product line. If you use Informix, or are thinking of using Informix, watch for breaking news about this product line: it's likely to change.

You can also use open-source, free databases such as MySQL and Postgre. You can use the ODBC drivers that ship with ColdFusion, and it's just as easy as connecting to any other kind of database.

Questions to Ask Yourself When Choosing a Database

If you have a database administrator hanging around, then he or she will likely prescribe what you can work with. That's fine and dandy. But maybe you're just starting out. Or maybe you were minding your own business one day, casually sipping a Dr. Pepper while playing Quake, and the boss came in, pointed at you and said, "Hey, Fred, you're the new web app guy. Figure it all out and have something up by five, capiche?" At this point you need to ask yourself several questions.

- What is the purpose of my database?
- Who is the audience for my database? That is, who will receive this information? How many at once? For how long? Via what middleware other than ColdFusion?

- How flexible does my data need to be? Do I plan on using XML to expose my data for content syndication? Do I need to import data via XML?
- Will I have a number of internal users who will require their own usernames and passwords? What kind of security will I need to handle them?
- What are my current database needs? Do I have various database platforms I need to support? Would it be more cost effective to continue supporting those platforms, or to migrate them to one system?
- What are my business partnerships?
- What is my budget for a database? You can pick up Access for around $150. SQL Server with an Internet connection is around $7000, and Oracle, depending on which services you select, is often around $12,000. IBM's DB2 is around $20,000.
- Who will administer the database? How much does that person know? What are the other constraints on that person's time?
- If it breaks, who's going to fix it? How available are they?
- What support options do I need?

You get the idea. What I'm trying to suggest is that it is a crucial decision that will affect your business at a fundamental level. Few things will more greatly benefit the general health and performance of your ColdFusion applications than a solid database platform and design.

A Word about Desktop Databases

Desktop database systems are products such as Microsoft Access 2000 and Corel Paradox 9. They even share a number of the features of enterprise database systems such as Oracle and SQL Server. They are intended for people in an office to use in storing and sharing information. A Microsoft Access database will support only about 25 concurrent connections before performance seriously deteriorates. On the other hand, Microsoft SQL Server withstands 689,000 hits per minute and can successfully hold databases several gigabytes in size.

Desktop database systems are great learning tools and excellent products. You can learn a lot using Access or Paradox before you graduate to an enterprise server. Once you move into a production environment, however, do not be tempted to port these desktop applications. It's bad form, and you're risking the health of your site. Just don't do it.

For now, we focus on your having in place the appropriate environment for your needs. Hopefully you now have the tools to get the information you need in order to determine what is best for you *in the long run.* Knowing what databases are available to us, we need to choose the appropriate version of ColdFusion.

Choosing a Version of ColdFusion 5

Once you have selected the appropriate system requirements and gathered your hardware, you need to determine which version of ColdFusion is best for you.

Despite the differences in operating systems, there are really four different expressions of ColdFusion. They are Developer, Express, Professional, and Enterprise. Though we will generally be concerned with the Enterprise version in this book, we will look at them briefly here so you know your options.

Developer

The Developer version of ColdFusion 4.5 ships with ColdFusion Studio 4.5. It is free of charge and does not expire. The limitation is that it supports only one HTTP connection at a time. It is perfect for developers who are trying out ColdFusion or ColdFusion Studio, but don't have enough time to really get the full use of the evaluation product during the 30-day period. Beyond this restriction, the Developer version is more or less the Professional version of ColdFusion 4.5, so it does not merit further discussion in its own right.

Express

ColdFusion Express comes on the CD included with this book. It is available for free, and it does not expire. It is similar to the developer version in these regards, but has two major differences. The first is that it supports more than one connection. However, it is a scaled-down version and does not support the complete tag set. The full ColdFusion language contains about 85 tags;

Express understands only about 25 of them. Express supports only a limited number of desktop databases.

Professional or Enterprise?

The Professional and Enterprise versions of ColdFusion are the comprehensive commercial products. They both support the entire tag and function set of the ColdFusion Markup Language (CFML). There are a few differences that account for their respective price tags, and it is very important that you know these differences, understand the audience for your ColdFusion applications, and can anticipate what your needs will be several months from now. The main differences in the Enterprise version are the following:

- available on Sun Solaris and HP-UX
- allows for dynamic load balancing via Cluster CATS
- supports Automatic Server Failover
- allows for connectivity to Enterprise Java Beans and CORBA
- supports native drivers for Oracle and Sybase, as well as Merant drivers
- features server sandbox security

Questions to Ask Yourself When Choosing a Version

If it still seems unclear what version you want, then ask yourself a few questions:

- How mission-critical is my website? That is, if my site goes down, can I fail over to another box automatically?
- Will I be hosting multiple applications or websites developed by third parties who need only selective access to services?
- What databases do I need to support? Will I be using Oracle or SQL Server?
- Will ColdFusion need to run on a cluster now or in the next several months?

If the answer to any of the above questions is Yes, then you should strongly consider the Enterprise version of ColdFusion.

In brief, the Enterprise version of ColdFusion is meant for medium to large organizations who need to do everything they can to insure that their sites (or their clients' sites) are up the maximum possible time, and who need to support the fastest and most reliable databases and operating systems.

Getting ColdFusion 5

Once you have determined which version is right for you, you need to get your hands on a copy. You can get ColdFusion 5 from a variety of sources. Determining the appropriate license structure for your organization is an important step; you should carefully consider your options before purchasing a ColdFusion license.

How Much Does It Cost?

One of the benefits to ColdFusion is its low cost. While this may sound funny to members of the Linux community who are used to free, open-source solutions such as PHP, or Windows users who receive ASP for free with their server purchase, it actually makes sense. Think long term, and total cost of ownership. As you learn to develop ColdFusion applications, you can use ColdFusion Express, or the developer's version.

Once you are ready to purchase a ColdFusion license, you will already have realized how much more quickly you can work in ColdFusion's tag-based language than in other Web application languages. Programmers' time is a considerable expense for many job shops. They have to pass this cost on to their clients. Because you can work so fast with ColdFusion, the money you save on time-to-market will significantly decrease your development expense. Some estimates contend that with ColdFusion's ease of use, you recoup your investment in about one month.

<NOTE>

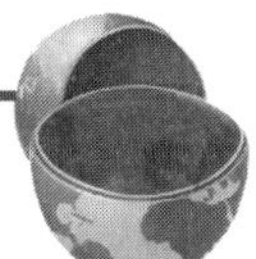

On April 26, 2001, Macromedia announced a new ColdFusion license—the Hosting License. This license was to be required for companies hosting multiple ColdFusion applications or sites owned by various third parties. When the developer community protested given license subscriptions, and the poor timing of the announcement, Macromedia promptly dropped the hosting license altogether. Since ColdFusion 5 is a product built entirely on

developer requests, this act of Macromedia's was just another example of how responsive the makers of ColdFusion are to their community.

You can purchase a subscription to ColdFusion as well, which gives you free product upgrades for two years from the date of purchase.

Where Can I Get It?

Generally, ColdFusion is expensive enough that it is not available at the regular software stores in your local mall.

On the Web

ColdFusion 5 is available for electronic download in many online stores. You can purchase it directly from Macromedia at http://www.Macromedia.com. You might find it competitively priced at http://www.Outpost.com, http://www.PriceWatch.com, or your favorite Web software vendor.

From a Partner

Check out the Partners section of the Macromedia website to find a vendor in your area. These Partners must undergo an application process with Macromedia and generally keep on staff a few dedicated ColdFusion developers as well as a few dedicated ColdFusion salespeople.

From a VAR

Value Added Resellers are cropping up with some frequency in today's market. You might find certain job shops that sell OEM versions of ColdFusion that they bundle along with their own products. For instance, since the e-commerce solution AbleCommerce requires ColdFusion, Able Solutions (the creator of Able Commerce) offers you the ColdFusion license if you don't already own it.

At the University

If you are a current university student or faculty or staff member, you can purchase ColdFusion through your university bookstore or software store, usually at a significant discount.

What's Next?

The next few chapters will focus on getting you familiar with the ColdFusion Server environment, understanding the basic precepts and functionality of CFML (the ColdFusion Markup Language), and getting a quick application or two up and running.

INSTALLING COLDFUSION 5

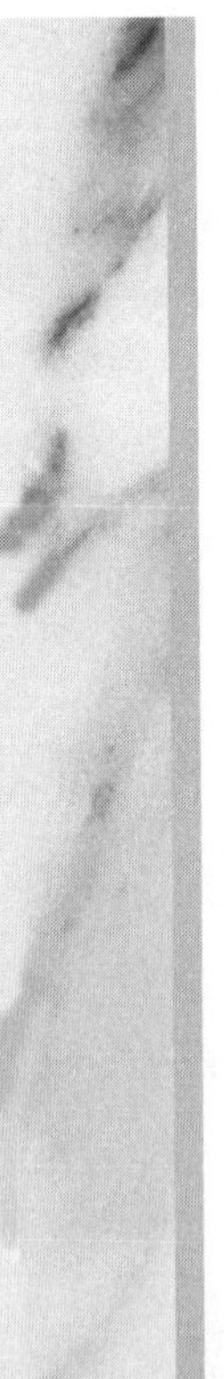

Topics in This Chapter

- Installing ColdFusion 5 on Windows
- What ColdFusion puts on your machine
- Troubleshooting your installation
- Installing ColdFusion 5 on Linux
- Uninstalling ColdFusion

Chapter 4

This chapter covers everything you need to know about installing ColdFusion 5.0. Each step is covered, so that if you run into any problems, you can return here and look it up. While installing ColdFusion 5 is not a very difficult process, or particularly time consuming, you'll be a smarter, more conscientious programmer if you know what files ColdFusion produces, where it puts them on your machine, and how all of this works. It is also somewhat different from previous versions of ColdFusion.

Once you have read the hardware and software requirements in Chapter 3, "Preparing Your ColdFusion Environment," you should be ready to begin. Note that you should already have installed your Web server before you attempt to install ColdFusion 5.

Installing ColdFusion will take about twenty minutes if nothing goes wrong. The process is very similar on different platforms. Here we will cover installing ColdFusion on Windows 2000.

Step 1: Checking Installation Requirements

Get a chug-size Mountain Dew. Put the CD-ROM in your CD-ROM drive. If you downloaded ColdFusion from the Web, then navigate to the folder in which you saved it. Make sure that you have your serial number handy.

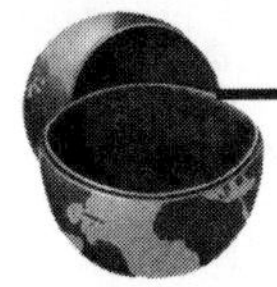

<NOTE>

If you are installing ColdFusion from the CD-ROM provided with this book, then you are installing an evaluation version, which will expire automatically in 30 days. ColdFusion does not "die" after this time period, however; you still can enter a valid serial number later if you purchase a license. This means you don't have to reinstall. It also means that you can choose whichever version, Professional or Enterprise, you have purchased and enter your license key. The evaluation version will "become" that version.

If you downloaded ColdFusion, click on the "CFServer5.exe" icon. The installation program will start.

Choose a Default Document Location

ColdFusion will prompt you to select your default document location, as shown in Figure 4.1.

Figure 4.1 Choosing the default installation location will save you headaches later.

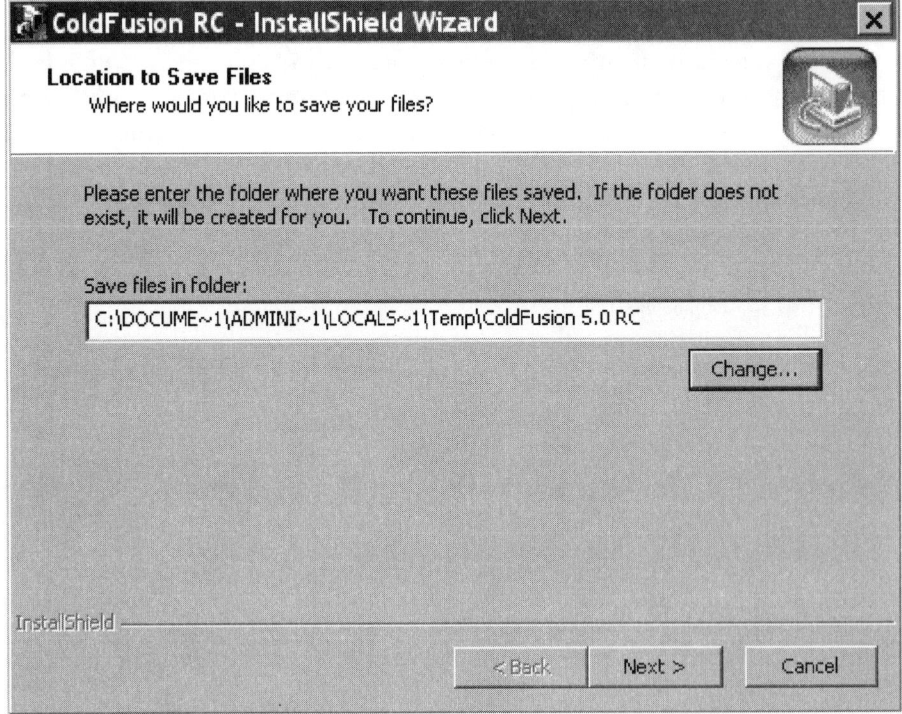

You can choose the default location and click "Next." Unless you have a very good reason for changing it, let ColdFusion go to the default directory. The Install Shield wizard will begin extracting files. These include .exe's, a few .cab and .cfm files, and a Microsoft Access Database used for logs during the setup.

ColdFusion will then begin the process of checking your system for installed components and verifying that there are no problems with any of them that might affect your installation. This is shown in Figure 4.2.

ColdFusion determines a number of things at this point:

- First, it checks to make sure that the user logged in has administrative privileges on this machine. You must be the Admin or have installation privileges in order to continue.
- ColdFusion checks that you have a Web client installed. Note that a Web browser is necessary to use the ColdFusion administrator.
- It finds your Web server and records the version.

Figure 4.2 Checking installation requirements.

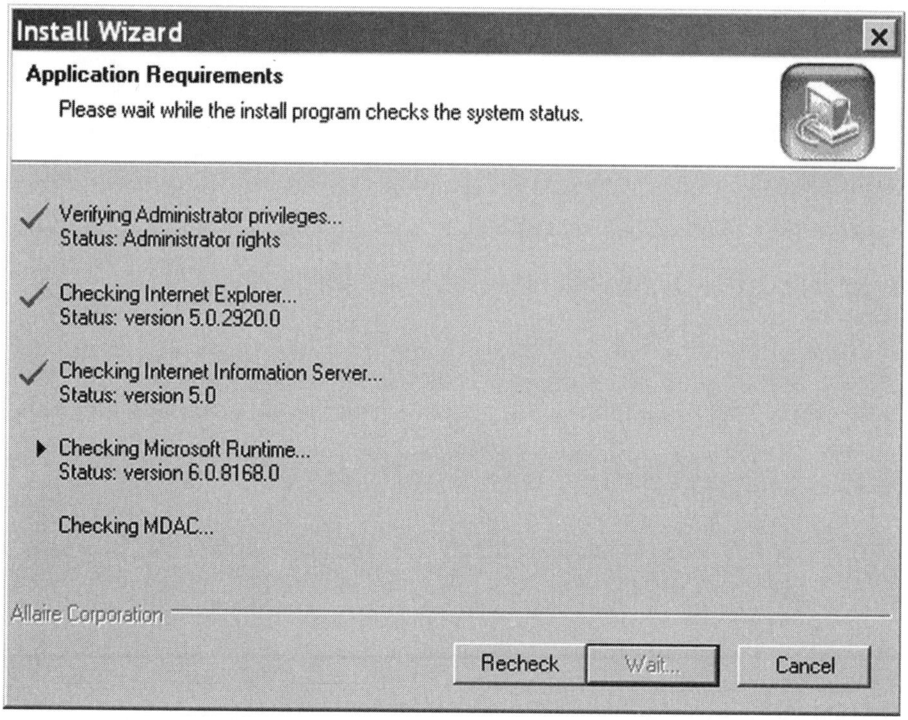

- It checks your system's Microsoft Runtime libraries to insure that current .dlls are installed. These include user and system files and OLE-related files.
- Finally, it checks to see that you have current Microsoft Data Access Component files installed. If you are running Windows 2000 Service Pack 1, you should have version 2.5 installed already, and this works fine.

Click "Next."

Step 2: License Agreement

You should now see the End User License Agreement for using this software (Figure 4.3). You must accept the agreement to continue the installation.

An interesting thing about this license agreement is that it prevents you from reporting benchmark findings. There has been a lot of discussion about this fact; we'll see if it comes up in the future. Once you have read and accepted the license agreement, click "Yes" to continue.

Figure 4.3 Accept the license agreement to continue.

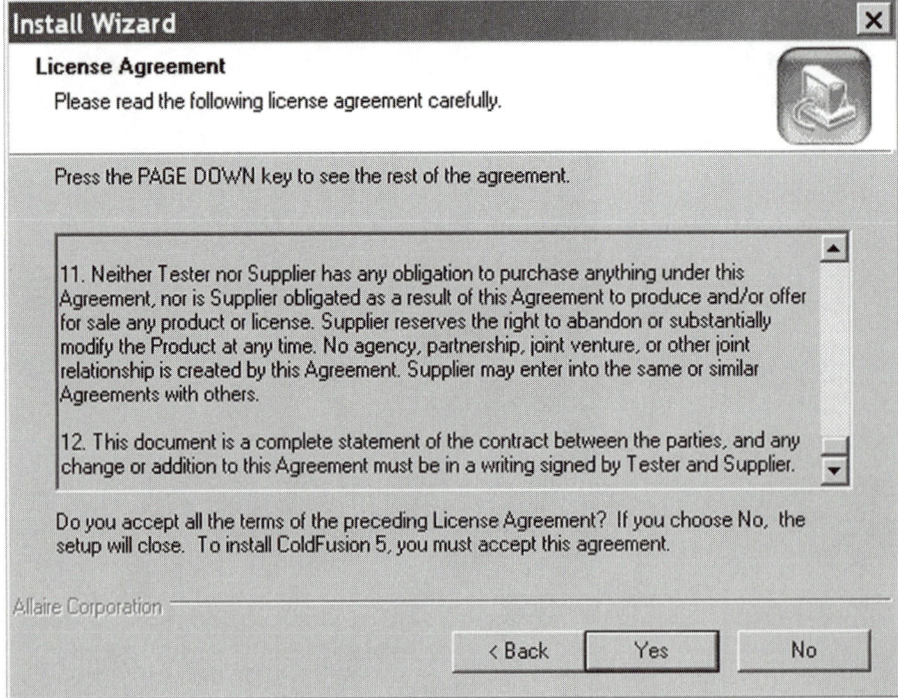

Step 3: Customer Information

Once you have entered your name and company information, type the serial number. If you are using an evaluation copy, you can leave the serial number field blank. In this case, ColdFusion will revert to a single-IP development copy after 30 days. If you are upgrading from a previous version, you must have your old serial number handy as well. ColdFusion 5 has a completely reengineered registration and encryption process that is far more secure than its predecessors. When you have typed in a valid license number, the "Next" button will appear so you can continue.

Step 4: Web Server

ColdFusion should automatically detect your Web server. For Windows users running IIS, Peer Web Server, or Personal Web Server, you can leave the default button selected. If you have multiple Web servers installed, you can choose which one you want to use with ColdFusion.

This screen is shown in Figure 4.4.

Figure 4.4 Choosing a Web server.

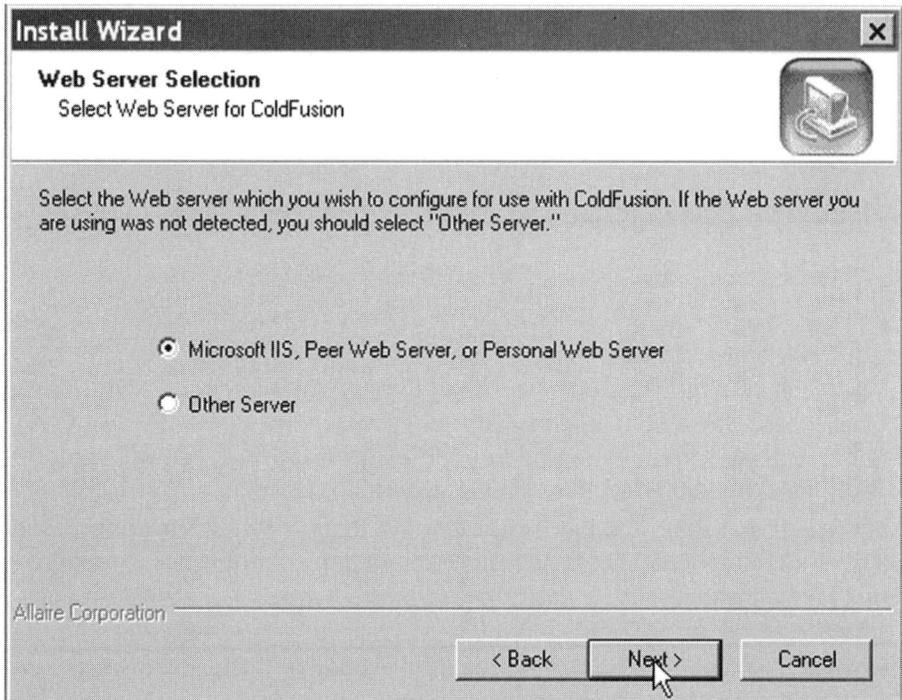

ColdFusion needs to be able to communicate directly with your Web server. If it does not automatically detect your Web server, cancel the installation. Check to make sure that your Web server is running, and check your error logs. Attempt the installation again.

Step 5: Choose Destination Path

You now need to choose the appropriate destination for the ColdFusion application files and the root of your Web server. Again, I recommend leaving the default for the ColdFusion application files.

The default C:\CFusion is displayed. ColdFusion will create several subfolders in this location, including the documentation files, the example application files, and the necessary Java applets. Click "Next."

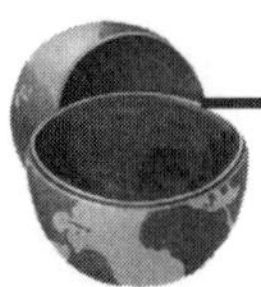

<NOTE>

ColdFusion comes with a few different example applications to help you quickly learn the power of ColdFusion. These require setting up a datasource. These files come unencrypted so that you can read the code and see how the best developers make their applications. If you're in a development environment, I encourage you to check the example applications out.

Step 6: Choose Components to Install

Now you are prompted to choose which components of ColdFusion 5 you want to install (see Figure 4.5).

There are far more choices here than in previous versions of ColdFusion. You should make your selections carefully at this point. While you can come back and install certain components later, I have found that you will get more reliability by knowing exactly what you want ahead of time.

If you're in a development environment, you probably will want to install all of the components, including the example applications and documentation. This will offer you the most help as you're learning.

Let's quickly go over each item in the list so we know what is being installed.

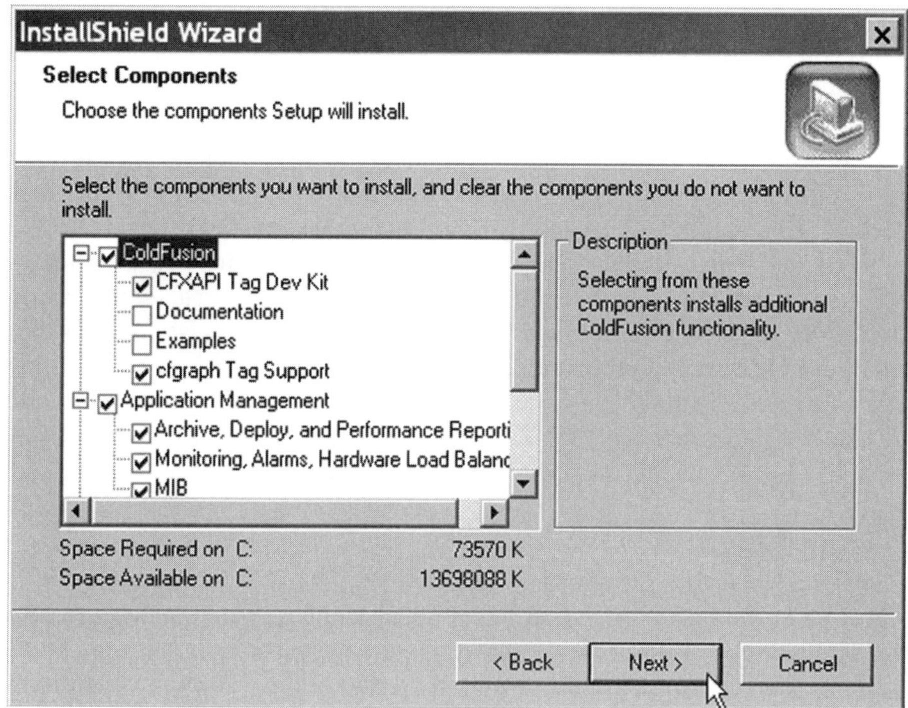

Figure 4.5 Choosing the components to install.

ColdFusion

You probably want to mark this checkbox, as you won't get much farther without it. This installs the files ColdFusion requires to run.

CFXAPI Tag Dev Kit

The CFXAPI Tag Dev Kit allows you to write your own ColdFusion custom tags in Java and C++. This will install by default to ease the process of creating custom tags. If you don't write in Java or C++, you can still create custom tags in ColdFusion itself. If you want to save disk space, skip this one—you'll save about 18 MB.

Documentation

You can choose to install the documentation, which is Web based. The documentation is about 9 MB, and includes a full tag and function reference for

CFML. I find it's handy, and the docs have sample code for each tag that helps you see how it is used.

However, if you are installing ColdFusion on a production server, I would advise against installing the documentation. Open your favorite search engine and do a search for any ColdFusion tag; just type something like "cfoutput." As you browse down the list of query results, you will start to see URLs that contain cfdocs/CFML_Language_ Reference/. This is a bad thing.

What that means is that search engine spiders have indexed production servers that have the documentation installed. In this way, I can get information about the structure and location of a ColdFusion installation. Knowing that the ColdFusion administrator is always in the same place, it is seconds before anyone can get to a login prompt for the ColdFusion Administrator. It just gets worse from there. The complete tag and function reference has been included at the back of this book for your convenience.

Examples

These include an e-commerce site, a webmail client, a small human resources application, and like that. These are a great way to learn ColdFusion from experts, and they are all open source. So if you're on a development box, I encourage you to snoop around them.

<CAUTION>

The example applications also pose somewhat of a security risk, as a hacker who knows a touch about ColdFusion can easily find them and potentially exploit their code to find information about your server or use them to run code against you.

Don't give them the chance. If you do install these on a production server, I strongly recommend that access be restricted by removing Anonymous access to those directories.

<CFGRAPH> Tag Support

This tag is new with ColdFusion 5. It works in conjunction with Macromedia Generator to create visual charts and graphs on the fly from real-time data. You can specify a pie graph or a bar graph for instance, specify a set of data that you want to represent, and ColdFusion will hand off to Generator to create a spiffy chart in milliseconds. The result is a Flash chart built from your database query which you can zoom in on and drag around. It's a great new tag, and one of the exciting features of ColdFusion 5.

Application Management Components

The Application Management Components are also new with ColdFusion 5 in a number of ways. These are sophisticated tools that help insure the integrity of your applications. They include probes, logging tools, and the new CAR file ability (ColdFusion Archive file) that cut your deployment time even more.

Archive, Deploy, and Performance Reporting

Choosing this option allows you to back up your sites conveniently, store them as archives, and then deploy entire applications as one file. This is a very exciting new tool that should help insure the integrity of your work in all of its stages.

Improved Performance reporting options means that you can easily view statistics regarding your ColdFusion server and the applications running on it. You also can view summaries of server state. This means you can really drill down to analyze what is happening in your applications. This is one you definitely want to install.

Monitoring, Alarms, Hardware Load Balancing

This component will help you cut down on down time by keeping you informed of your server's state when critical events happen. If you have hardware like Cisco Director that lets you load balance, you'll need to install this to make sure ColdFusion is able to take advantage of it.

MIB

The Management Information Base allows you to access all of ColdFusion's management data. This feature is used with third-party products such as Computer Associates' Unicenter, IBM Tivoli, or BMC Patrol. A major benefit is support for SNMP (Simple Network Management Protocol).

Cluster CATS

Installing the Cluster CATS components is necessary only if you are on a cluster running more than one ColdFusion machine. A *cluster* is a group of independent servers that use network intercommunication to form a kind of multiprocessor system. The advantage of clusters in a Web serving environment is that you can spread your application (website) out over multiple servers and thus provide faster, more reliable service for very high-volume websites.

Load Balancing

Allows HTTP requests to be redirected in this software-based load balancer. *Load Balancing* uses hardware and/or software to distribute HTTP requests evenly across servers in a cluster in order to improve website performance. Each component that is a subset of the Cluster CATS install option should be installed only if you install the initial package.

Web Server Failover

This allows Cluster CATS to assume the IP address of a server that has gone down and to accept the HTTP requests it receives in the failed server's place.

Advanced Security

Advanced Security allows you to designate "sand boxes"—or directories where individuals are allowed to work. You can also implement roles-based security on your server. You'll need it if you ever want to run Spectra, or if you're in a hosting environment where you allow multiple outside developers to configure their applications. Installs server sandbox security. Includes support for a number of ColdFusion tags and functions. It is a good idea to install this option. It is not selected by default.

Once you have selected all of the components you need for this installation, click "Next."

Step 7: Assign Passwords

Next you will be asked to choose two passwords, as shown in Figure 4.6.

The first password box asks you to choose a password for ColdFusion administrator. This will be the password that you use to access the Web-based administration features via this link: http://yourserver.com/cfide/administrator/index.cfm. This password is required.

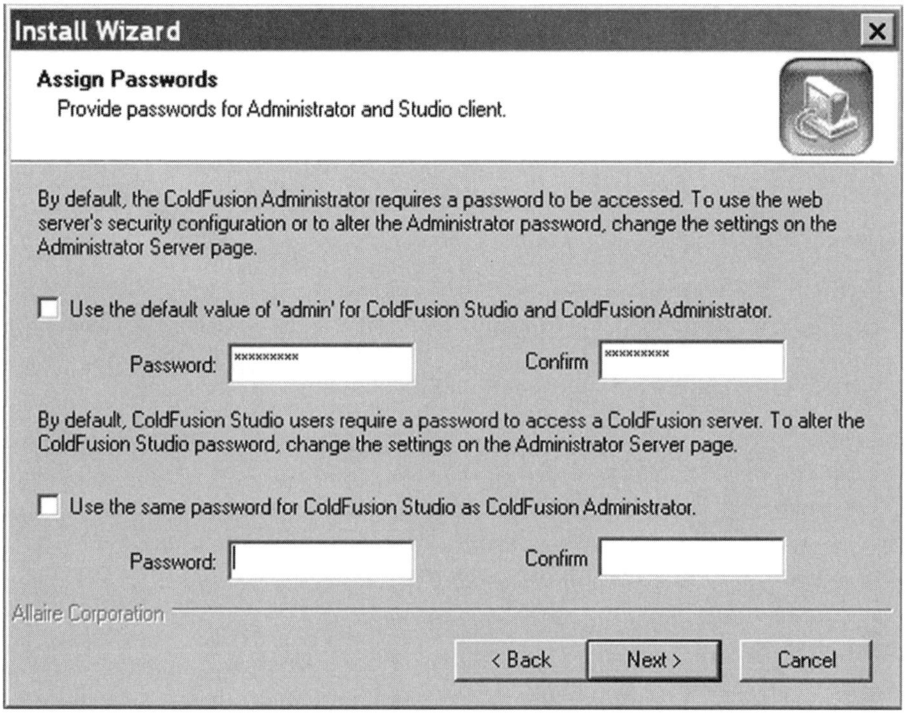

Install Wizard

Assign Passwords
Provide passwords for Administrator and Studio client.

By default, the ColdFusion Administrator requires a password to be accessed. To use the web server's security configuration or to alter the Administrator password, change the settings on the Administrator Server page.

☐ Use the default value of 'admin' for ColdFusion Studio and ColdFusion Administrator.

Password: xxxxxxxxx Confirm xxxxxxxxx

By default, ColdFusion Studio users require a password to access a ColdFusion server. To alter the ColdFusion Studio password, change the settings on the Administrator Server page.

☐ Use the same password for ColdFusion Studio as ColdFusion Administrator.

Password: Confirm

Allaire Corporation

< Back | Next > | Cancel

Figure 4.6 Assigning passwords for ColdFusion Administrator and Studio.

The second field is for ColdFusion studio access. Studio is the code-centric IDE for developing and deploying ColdFusion applications. You can remotely connect to your ColdFusion server via studio's Remote Development Services. So if you are using studio, you certainly want to create a password here.

You can update both of these from within the administrator at any time. Once you type in the passwords you want and click "next," you are asked to Confirm the selections you have made.

Step 8: Confirm Selections

You are presented a list of all of the information you have specified thus far. You can print this list if you desire.

Once you click "next," Set Up will begin installing the files you selected.

Step 9: Install Files

A common installation without documentation, example applications, or Cluster CATS support will be approximately 74 MB.

This process will take a few minutes, depending on which items you choose to install. In our typical installation, you will see Set Up speeding through the following:

- Installs a version of the JRun Java Server engine.
- Verity 2K, for creating searchable collections of over 250,000 documents.
- Database drivers.
- .cfm files. The ColdFusion Administrator is just a big ColdFusion application itself that serves as a Web-based front end for working with files, directories, databases, and even the registry.
- Help files.
- .cab files for, among other things, displaying the Java-based forms such as <CFSLIDER>, <CFTREE>, and <CFGRID>. These have been completely rewritten for version 5.
- Installs Advanced Security features, so you may see a .mdb and a .sql file or two.
- Configures ColdFusion as a service for NT.
- Installs <CFGRAPH> support, which means that it installs a version of Macromedia Generator for ColdFusion's use, and a number of .swt files.
- Under the JRun directory, ColdFusion installs the CFAM (ColdFusion Application Manager) and Management Repository Server.

Assuming everything goes smoothly, you should see a screen similar to Figure 4.7.

I strongly suggest that you restart your computer immediately. The setup process is *not* totally finished yet, as ColdFusion needs to make sure it can connect to the Web server when it restarts. Since there are a number of keys entered into the server's registry when ColdFusion installs, you want to restart right away before something else in the system changes.

Figure 4.7 You must restart your computer, since ColdFusion makes a great number of updates to the Windows registry.

<NOTE>

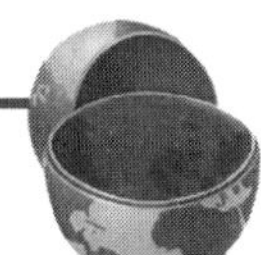

The Registry is a database within a Windows platform computer that stores information about the system. This includes information regarding files, users, performance, software and hardware, and printers and display. You can view or edit items in the registry from the command line by typing regedit, *or by using the ColdFusion* <CFREGISTRY> *tag. Do not attempt to edit the registry unless you are an expert, as your system could become irretrievably unstable.*

Once your server has rebooted, login, and your Web browser should automatically open to the following page:

```
http://127.0.0.1/CFIDE/administrator/docs/index.htm.
```

This page contains a helpful list of contact information, links to product documentation, and more (Figure 4.8).

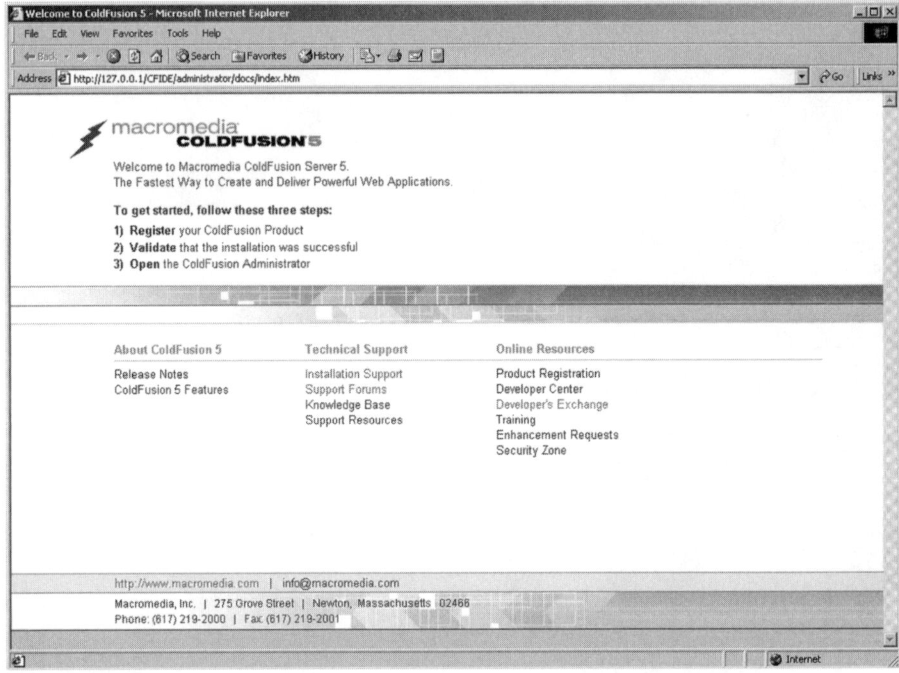

Figure 4.8 Upon restarting your computer, ColdFusion automatically opens a page allowing you to register, validate your installation, or go directly to the ColdFusion Administrator.

Choosing the first option, "Register your ColdFusion product," launches a new browser window and opens to the Macromedia website. Here you can enter your serial number to register.

At this point we haven't necessarily verified that the ColdFusion service is running. Let's do that now by clicking the second option, "validate that the installation was successful" (Figure 4.9).

Clicking "Test Installation" should return a result set from the ColdFusion Administrator's own log file, as shown in Figure 4.10.

Since choosing this option opens a new browser window, you can just close the Verify Installation window and return to the welcome screen.

To get the administrator, you can also type in this address:

```
http://127.0.0.1/cfide/administrator/index.cfm.
```

<NOTE>

127.0.0.1 always refers to the address of the local machine. That is, even if your machine has an IP address assigned, 127.0.0.1 will always identify you as well. This address is also known as LocalHost.

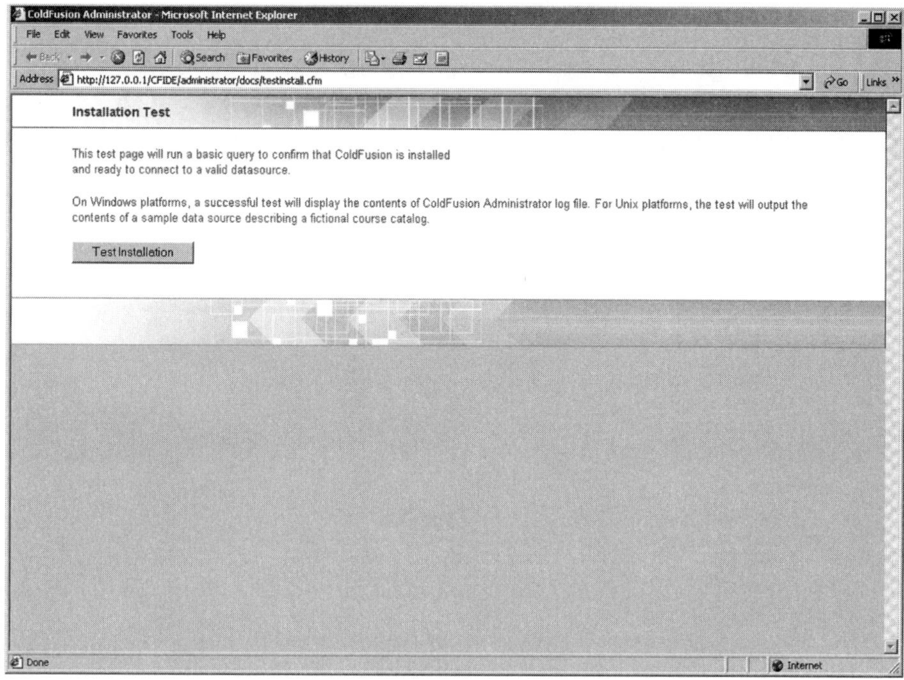

Figure 4.9 Verifying the installation by running a sample database query.

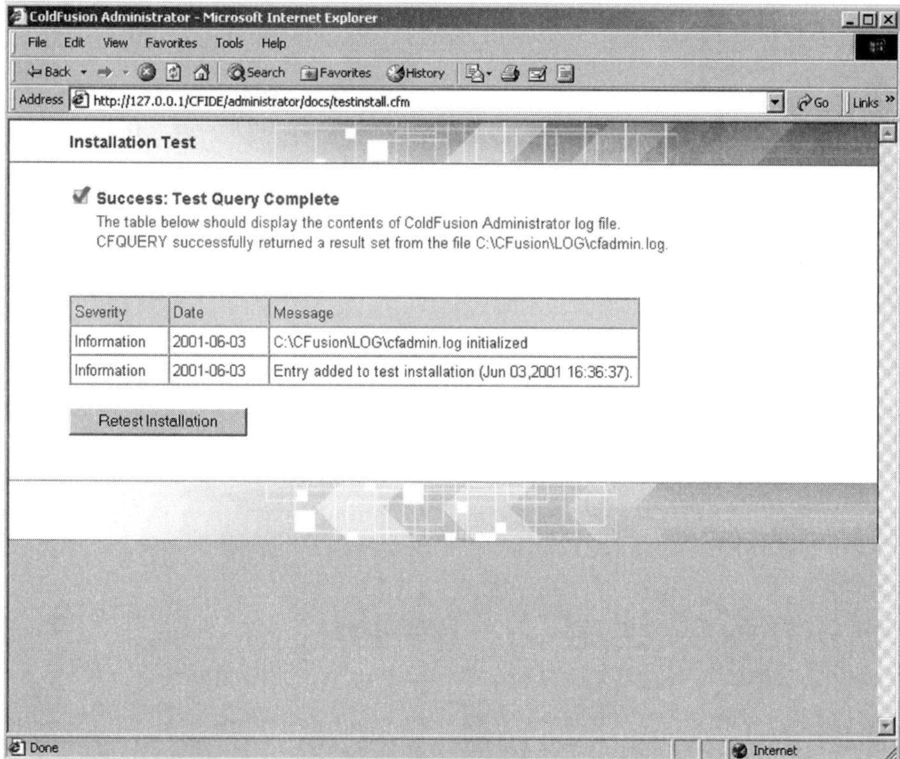

Figure 4.10 This live query of the ColdFusion Administrator log verifies that your installation was a success.

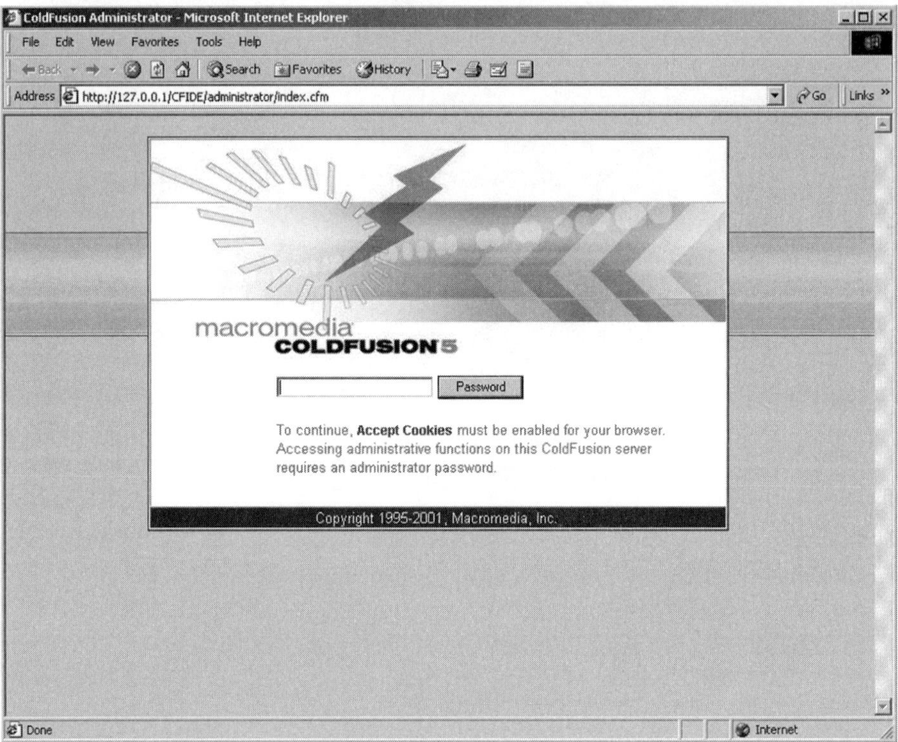

Figure 4.11 The new ColdFusion 5 login screen.

> *You can verify that your TCP/IP connection is working properly by calling up the command line and typing this:* ping 127.0.0.1. *You should see three "replies" and then it will stop. This tells you that you're online. Alternatively, you can also use* ping localhost.

Alternatively, you can click the "Open the ColdFusion Administrator" link to launch the ColdFusion Administrator. Figure 4.11 shows the new login screen. Once you login, you will see the Administrator screen (Figure 4.12). Before we familiarize ourselves with the configuration interface, let's poke around a bit and examine what ColdFusion has installed.

What ColdFusion Installs on Your Machine

It is by no means necessary to read the following section to learn ColdFusion. However, you now have 80 MB of stuff on your machine that you didn't have

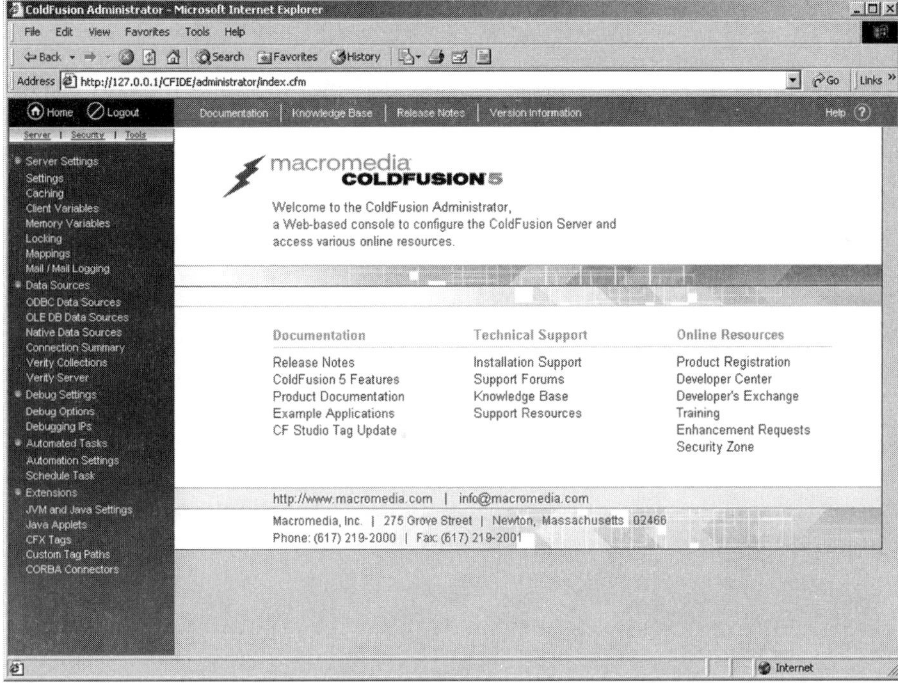

Figure 4.12 The interface for ColdFusion 5 Administrator has changed a lot since ColdFusion 4.5.

a few minutes ago. This section will introduce you to what is under the hood, so to speak, and give you a sneak preview at some of the power of ColdFusion.

Seeing what has been installed will benefit you in a number of ways. It will help familiarize you with options when you want to extend ColdFusion using custom tags. It will give you the power to quickly fix things (or at least know where to look) if something goes wrong later. It will introduce you to the power that you now have available to you: it will show you some of what you can do with ColdFusion tags, and it will touch on how they interact with the program.

<NOTE>

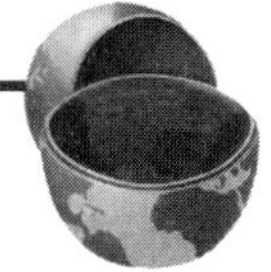

There is no specific call to read (and certainly not to modify) the files specified below. I include this section so that advanced users or administrators can have the familiarity with the system that high-powered development and troubleshooting may require.

If you are new to ColdFusion, you can skip this section, or read it for academic interest.

C:\CFUSION

This directory gets created upon installation, and 13 directories are added within it. We won't go over what's in all of these, but there are a few to be aware of so that you can manually change your settings.

Cfdist.ini

This file contains information regarding start up. If you want to modify this file, you can do so by using Notepad to open it; it's plain text (like all .ini files). For instance, ColdFusion by default will encrypt the data sent between the Web server and the ColdFusion server using an ASCII string. You can choose to turn off this setting, or specify a new string to use as the encryption key. You may increase security by setting the "Key" variable to another value. You can also choose to have ColdFusion listen for incoming .cfm requests on a different port if your configuration requires it.

Cfremote.ini

This file is used to specify the address and document root locations of a remote machine you are using to run ColdFusion. Remoting is set to off by default.

C:\Cfusion\BIN

This folder contains all of the crucial files for running ColdFusion. It includes the cfserver.exe file and a number of .dlls that translate the CFML commands, interface with LDAP, and so forth. Help files, the Uninstaller, and other files are in here, too.

There are a few items of interest here that you might be happy to know about.

Parser_data.xml

This is a very interesting file. You can open it by double clicking, and you should be able to view its contents in Internet Explorer. You can see an XML document that uses regular expressions to define aspects of the CFML. For instance, near the bottom, you can see explicitly what characters are allowed in a ColdFusion tag name.

Import.cfm and Export.cfm

By opening this file you can discover the location in the registry where ColdFusion stores the password for the Security Admin login. This is useful if you forget your ColdFusion Administrator login password. You can read it off the registry key using the encryption string specified in these files.

I mention this file also because you must be careful not to modify it, or you might not be able to get into the Administrator. I also mean to stress the grave security issue if you allow a number of people access to your directories and files.

Cfencode.exe

Right-click on this application file and click Open. You'll get a menu highlighting the uses of the CFEncode Template Encryption Utility. This is a command-line utility that allows you to encrypt your ColdFusion templates after you have written them. In effect, your code is turned into gibberish, and only ColdFusion can read it.

This is a handy tool that has been offered for a number of versions. If you download a custom tag from the Developer's Exchange, and it's all mucked up when you try to open it, the writer has used this utility. A number of products written in ColdFusion use this utility to distribute regular versions and Open Source versions of their products to great effect.

Beware that the encryption process cannot be undone. That said, you should also know that while encrypting your templates in this way is enough to ward off the casual browser, it will not keep serious hackers from reading your code (that is, of course it can be undone). We'll see how to use it in the chapter on custom tags.

C:\Cfusion\BIN\CFTags

If you open the CFTags folder, you'll see that ColdFusion tags are written in ColdFusion itself. Try to open one of the files by double-clicking on it. You'll see the encryption tool mentioned above in action.

<WARNING>

Do not attempt to modify the files or directories being referred to in any section of this chapter. This discussion is to familiarize you with the changes to your computer, and to see under the hood a little bit. Modifying any of

these files in the slightest way could result in abnormal, interrupted, or irretrievably impeded ColdFusion service.

C:\Cfusion\CFAM\Support

In this folder you will find a number of log files. You can read these manually to get information about the state of your system.

C:\Cfusion\Cfx\Examples\DirectoryList\ReadMe.txt

This file offers advanced users information about the tools available to them in writing Java and C++ extensions to the ColdFusion language. The other folders in your Cfx directory contain similar instructions on using the C++ and make files with the wizard.

C:\Cfusion\LOG

This directory contains four plain text files: application.log, server.log, cfadmin.log, and webserver.log. Open one of these up. You see a quoted list at the top, and matching columnar values on each line thereafter. By creating a text file in this manner, you can actually treat it as a database. Actually, it *is* a database. These files are where ColdFusion writes information regarding errors or operations. I suggest you read these periodically to make sure that there's no monkey business going on.

C:\Cfusion\Mail

Similar to the LOG folder, this folder contains information about the email that ColdFusion receives, delivers, and tries to deliver. Once you get into using the <CFMAIL> tag, which allows you to easily send and receive email via ColdFusion, you will appreciate being able to monitor your mail logs here. The "UnDelivr" folder tracks mail that ColdFusion was unable to send. For future reference, you can move any unsent mail into the "Spool" folder, and ColdFusion will automatically attempt to resend it.

C:\Cfusion\Scripts\CFForm.js

ColdFusion allows you create forms with the <CFFORM> tag. By using this tag instead of a regular HTML form tag, you can create forms that use client-side validation to insure that users have entered the required information in the appropriate format. To do this, ColdFusion automatically generates 50–100 lines of JavaScript that are sent back to the browser. If you have used ColdFusion before, you're likely aware of this feature. Ever wonder where that JavaScript comes from? It ain't magic—this is the file.

C:\Cfusion\Verity\Collections

ColdFusion offers you the power of the Verity 2K engine to create searchable document indexes of up to 250,000 documents. In minutes you can create a Verity collection, which can contain .pdf, .doc, .ppt, .htm, .txt, .cfm, .xls, .wpd, and many more file types. A couple of minutes more, and you've got a Web interface for it. This is the default location for Verity collections.

C:\Cfusion\Database

This folder contains, among other things, nine MS Access 2000 databases. They are used in conjunction with the example applications, and will therefore be present only if you installed them. These are not crucial to your ColdFusion install, and can be deleted if you so desire.

Troubleshooting Your Installation

Few things go wrong with ColdFusion installations. I have noticed the problem below however, and highlighting it here may save you some trouble.

ntJavaConsole Using 100% of CPU Cycles

You may not use special characters in your Administrator password, or the ColdFusion Application manager will spawn a process that eats up all of your available processes.

Can't Find the Server Specified

ColdFusion should install itself to point automatically to the local host address. If, after you have installed ColdFusion, your browser complains that it cannot find the specified page (404 error), then you may have to make a modification or two.

It seems that sometimes this happens when a network is configured with a firewall or an irregular gateway. Often reinstalling will not affect this behavior for those reasons. What you need to do is configure ColdFusion to point to the true IP address of the machine.

Try getting to the Administrator like so: http://205.225.205.225/cfide/administrator/index.cfm, where 205.225.205.225 is the IP address of your machine. If the administrator comes up, it means the following things:

- ColdFusion will serve .cfm pages perfectly normally
- You will need to access the administrator with its true IP
- You will likely also have issues with Advanced Security features

Figure 4.13 Sometimes ColdFusion can't see the localhost IP immediately after installation.

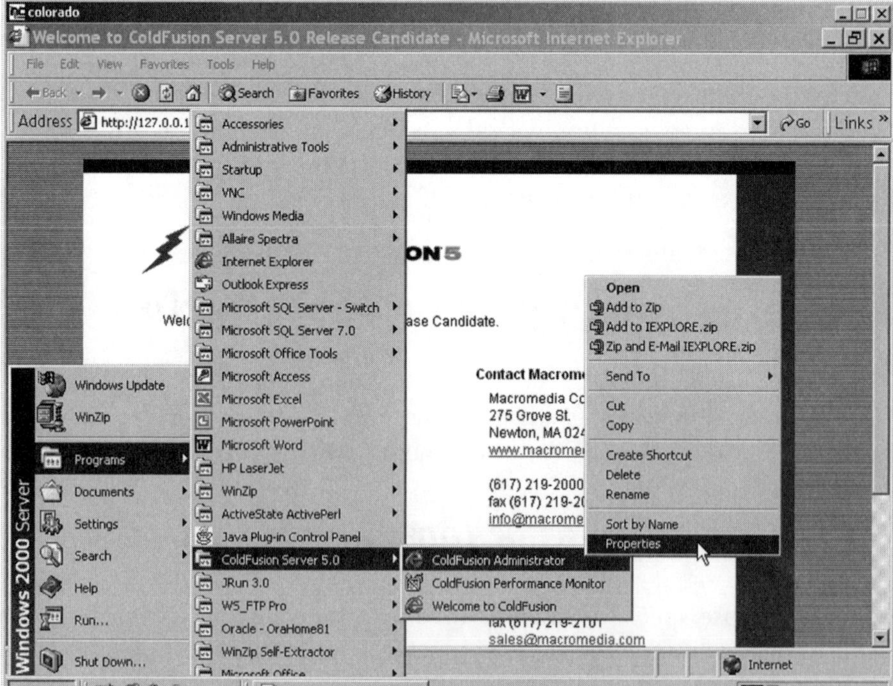

So you will probably want to change your shortcuts to refer to the new IP address if necessary. You can do this like so:

When you right-click on the ColdFusion Administrator shortcut, you will see the menu in Figure 4.13. Choose Properties. In the ShortCut dialogue box that comes up, just replace the local host address with the IP address of your machine in the Target field.

This has been an occasional problem with CF 4.5. We'll see if the problem continues with release 5, though it seems to have been alleviated. Anyway, now you know how to fix it, so hopefully it doesn't matter!

Installing ColdFusion on Linux

Installing ColdFusion 5 on Linux is a relatively simple process and is not radically different from installing on Windows. You can run ColdFusion for Linux on RedHat 6.2 or later, SuSE Linux 7.0, or Cobalt RAQ3/RAQ4 on an Intel Pentium. 256 MB of RAM is recommended; 512 MB is better.

This section will cover installing ColdFusion on a Red Hat Linux 7.0. Note that you need to be logged in as root to install ColdFusion.

<NOTE>

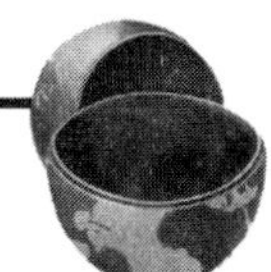

As of this writing, ColdFusion 5 for Linux was still a release candidate. Your installation process may vary slightly.

If you downloaded ColdFusion or are installing from the CD-ROM included with this book, untar (uncompress) the install file by issuing the following command:

```
: tar xvfz cf5serverlinux.tar.gz
```

Depending on whether or not you are installing an evaluation version or a Professional or Enterprise version, this file name might differ slightly.

Once you've done this, Linux will list the directory contents:

```
[root@spiderman cfusion]# tar xvfz cf5serverlinux.tar.gz
coldfusion-50-rc-linux/
coldfusion-50rc-linux/README
coldfusion-50rc-linux/releasenotes.htm
coldfusion-50rc-linux/new.htm
coldfusion-50rc-linux/cfremove
coldfusion-50rc-linux/data.tar
coldfusion-50rc-linux/cfinstall
```

```
coldfusion-50rc-linux/cfam_tar
coldfusion-50rc-linux/cfam_install
```

It is a good idea to read the README, release notes, and new files. You can open a text editor to read the README file by issuing this command:

```
[root@spiderman cfusion]#pico README
```

Doing so lets you view system requirements, late-breaking news, and known installation issues. You can quickly view the .htm files in the Lynx text browser by typing this:

```
[root@spiderman cfusion]#lynx new.htm
```

When you're ready to install ColdFusion, change to the directory containing the cfinstall file and data.tar file. For instance, if you're installing the Enterprise version, you might type this:

```
[root@spiderman cfusion]# cd coldfusion-50ent-linux
```

Then as root, run cfinstall:

```
[root@spiderman cfusion]# ./cfinstall
```

You should see the welcome screen as shown below. The rest is a piece of cake; just answer the prompts.

```
****************************************
**    Welcome to ColdFusion 5.0       **
**                                    **
**                                    **
**                                    **
** Thank you for choosing ColdFusion! **
**                                    **
****************************************
```

The command line will keep you informed of the current status of the installation as it goes along. First, ColdFusion detects your operating system:

```
It appears you are running on RedHat Linux.

Please enter the absolute path of the directory where you'd
like ColdFusion installed. ColdFusion will be installed into
a subdirectory, named 'coldfusion', of the directory you
specify here. You do not need to create the 'coldfusion' sub-
directory (this install will create it for you), but the par-
ent directory you specify here must already exist..

Enter the installation directory for ColdFusion [/opt]:
```

Choose the directory to install ColdFusion into. Default options are given to you in brackets. If you accept the default location, you can just hit Enter. Otherwise, type the path to the folder you want to install it into. The following text appears:

```
In order for ColdFusion to be able to receive requests your
web server must be configured to recognize CFML files.

For Apache, a ColdFusion dynamically loaded module must be
configured. For a Netscape server, the installation can in-
stall a NSAPI plugin to do this. If you are running another
web server, you must configure a CGI program.

What type of web server are you running (apache netscape
other) [apache]:
```

At this step, ColdFusion needs to do a couple of things. First, it needs to configure your MIME types to recognize the .cfm extension, and then insure that the Web server can communicate with the ColdFusion server.

```
Automatically configure your Apache server [y]:
```

It is best to allow ColdFusion to automatically configure itself to work with your Web server. Then you are asked to enter the location of the httpd.conf file, which dictates a number of things regarding your Web server, including permissions and other configuration issues.

```
Please enter your httpd.conf file
[/etc/httpd/conf/httpd.conf]
```

Press Enter to accept the default, or type in the location of your http.conf file.

```
In order to install the ColdFusion Administrator and the
ColdFusion documentation, files must be copied into the
document directory (usually called the document root) of
your web server.

Enter your web server's document root directory
[/var/www/html/]
```

Press Enter to accept the default, or type in the location of your Web root and press Enter. You are prompted to decide whether or not to install documentation:

```
Do you want the ColdFusion documentation (HTML files)
installed? [y]
```

Press Enter to install the documentation, or type “n” and press Enter to not install the documentation. There are potential security concerns for installing the documentation, which are mentioned above in the Windows installation section. If you have the documentation installed on a production server, spiders pick up these pages, and it becomes very easy for anyone with access to Yahoo to get to a login prompt for your ColdFusion server. It is similar for the example applications that ColdFusion ships with. These contain databases and a good deal of functionality to teach you how to write good ColdFusion applications. They are potentially exploitable.

```
It is not recommended that the ColdFusion example applications
be installed on a production server due to potential
security concerns.

Do you want the ColdFusion example applications installed?
[n]
```

Press Enter to accept the default of No. If you wish to install the applications, type "Y" and press Enter.

```
Please enter the user name of the account under which you
would like ColdFusion to run. This must be a valid, existing
user account. Is [sic] is a good idea to create an account
specifically for ColdFusion.

It is not recommended that the ColdFusion server run as root.

Enter an existing login name [nobody]:
```

You can accept the default of "nobody" or select another account for ColdFusion to run under. Press Enter. Next you choose the auxiliary services you would like ColdFusion to install. Refer to the section for installing under Windows above if you need to decide which of these components to install.

ColdFusion Management Services are optional features including service monitoring and alarms; system reporting; ColdFusion site archiving and deployment; load balancing support with Cluster CATS or LocalDirector integration; and ColdFusion SNMP MIB reporting.

```
Do you want to install any of these features? [y]
```

Press Enter to install one or more of these features. Type "N" to choose not to install any of them and go to the next step.

```
Do you want to install the Reporting and Archive/Deploy
features? [y]
```

If you want to install Reporting and CAR support, press Enter. Otherwise, type "N" and press Enter.

```
Do you want to install Monitors, Alarms, and Load-Balancer
Integration? [y]
```

You can install the Monitors and other probes, as well as load balancing support; press Enter.

```
To support the ColdFusion SNMP MIB, your server must have
UCD-SNMP 4.2 installed. If not, respond No at the prompt.

Do you want to install the ColdFusion SNMP MIB? [n]
```

Make your choice and press Enter. Once you're ready, press Enter again, and ColdFusion will begin installing all of your chosen components.

```
Ready to begin the installation. Press ENTER to continue..
```

ColdFusion will start installing files. Your response output may vary, depending on whether or not you are upgrading from a previous version of ColdFusion.

```
Preserving user-modified files from the existing
installation. . .
Copying files. . . . . . . .
```

The dots appear incrementally, like the blue bar in Windows. This will take several minutes. You will be updated a bit more specifically as the installation continues, and your responses will vary based on what components you have chosen to install:

```
Migrating existing Verity Collections. . .
Setting up uninstall links
Initializing ColdFusion settings
ColdFusion registry initialized
Customizing ColdFusion startup scripts. . .
  Restoring saved start script
  Restoring saved odbc.ini
Configuring ODBC.ini with sample datasources
Running the installation script for your selected
Enterprise extensions. . .
Configuring the ColdFusion Apache Module
Restarting Apache. . .
Shutting down http: . . .          [OK]
Starting ColdFusion servers. . .   [OK]

ColdFusion installation completed successfully.
The ColdFusion Application Server is now running!
```

You do not need to restart as you do with Windows. Type in the following address to get to the login prompt:

```
http://spiderman/CFIDE/Administrator/index.cfm
```

where "spiderman" is the name of your box. Of course, http://localhost/CFIDE/Administrator and http://127.0.0.1/CFIDE/Administrator work as well. If the login screen appears, ColdFusion is running. Note that if you are upgrading from a previous version of ColdFusion, you will not be asked for a password for ColdFusion administrator—it will be the same as before.

Uninstalling ColdFusion

To uninstall ColdFusion from your Linux machine, issue the following command as root:

```
[root@spiderman cfusion]# /opt/coldfusion/uninstall/cfremove
```

where opt is the path to your `coldfusion` directory.

Now that you've got ColdFusion Server installed, let's examine the ColdFusion Markup Language. In the next chapter, we'll learn how to set and output variables, and create our first ColdFusion application.

COLDFUSION MARKUP LANGUAGE AND VARIABLES

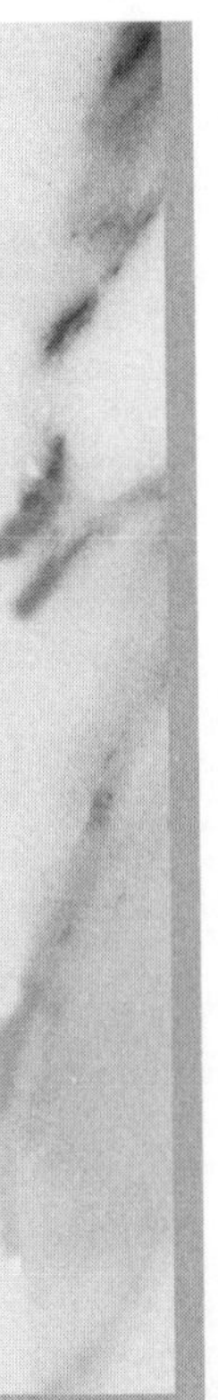

Topics in This Chapter

- Introduction to CFML
- How to begin
- Your first ColdFusion template
- Setting variables
- Commenting your code
- Outputting variables
- Setting and outputting rules

Chapter 5

It is time to start writing some code. We will create a short application that you can use in your websites to easily create a bit of personalization. The purpose of this chapter is to introduce you to the ColdFusion Markup Language (both tags and functions) and to help you write your first ColdFusion application.

By the end of this chapter, you will see just how easy and fast it is to build a solid Web application in ColdFusion. It's just not very far from "Hello World!" to real personalization for the visitors of your ColdFusion website. You will learn how to set variables, read their values, use functions, and incorporate conditional processing.

Introduction to the ColdFusion Markup Language

The ColdFusion Markup Language consists of about 80 tags and nearly 200 functions. The tags can be generally classified into one or sometimes two of the categories below:

- Database Manipulation
- Data Output

- Exception (Error) Handling
- Variable Manipulation
- Flow Control
- Internet Protocol
- Java Servlets and Java Objects
- File Management
- Web Application Framework
- Advanced ColdFusion Forms
- Extensibility
- Miscellaneous tags

ColdFusion tags all begin with <CF so that the ColdFusion engine knows that it's supposed to interpret them. Just like HTML, there are tags that do not require an end tag (such as <CFSET>), and tags that do (such as </CFOUTPUT>).

When a Web page that is a ColdFusion template (saved with the .cfm extension) is called, ColdFusion interprets the CFML on the page, performs whatever operations are required by the markup, and generates an HTML page from this, which it returns to the client browser.

Concise Code

One big advantage of writing in ColdFusion is that it is fast. A lot of functionality is encapsulated in the tags that make up the language. For instance, consider querying a database to retrieve information from it. You must first make a connection to the database, send it an SQL Statement saying what information you're interested in and what you want to do with that information, and then get it back in a workable form. Here's how you might connect to an Oracle database to retrieve a record in Java Server Pages:

```
<%@ page import="java.sql.*" %>
<% Connection conn;
PreparedStatement stmt;
 %>
<%! public void jspInit() {
    try{
          String url =

    "jdbc:oracle:thin:@www.corecoldfusion.com:8080:book";
          String user = "eben";
          String password = "wxyz";
```

```
          String sql =
          "SELECT firstname, lastname " 1
                "FROM users" 1
                "WHERE firstname = 'eben'";
          Class.forName("oracle.jdbc.driver.OracleDriver");
          conn = DriverManager.getConnection(url, username,
password);
          stmt = conn.prepareStatement(sql);}
      catch(SQLException e){}
      catch(ClassNotFoundException e){}
           };
            %>
<% public void jspDestroy()
    {try stmt.close();
           conn.close(); }catch(SQLException e){}
      }
%>
```

And that's the *short* version.

Or, we could just do the same thing in ColdFusion like this:

```
<cfquery name="getName" datasource="MyDB">
    SELECT firstname, lastname
    FROM Users WHERE firstname = 'Eben'
</cfquery>
```

Both do more or less the same thing (retrieve a record from a database). But which one is easier to write, and faster to debug?

Don't worry about what all of this means right now. The point is that you can really work fast in ColdFusion, since the tags encapsulate a lot of the code you'll commonly need.

Custom Tags

What if there isn't a tag for what you want to do? Then you create it yourself.

ColdFusion supports Custom Tags, which is a powerful feature (one that you may be familiar with if you're used to JSP). With Custom Tags, you can write a template in ColdFusion, use it over and over again across multiple applications, and it will work more or less just like the other tags in the language. Once you've written one you really like, you can even upload it to the Macromedia Developer's Exchange, where others can download it for free or for a charge.

The Developer's Exchange is filled with thousands of useful extensions to the CFML. Many of these are utility tags that perform some useful function that the language might be missing. Others are small applications in themselves.

For instance, I've written a custom tag that you can download for free called <CF_Classifieds>. With this tag, you've got an entire interface for allowing users to post a classified ad of their own in one of many categories. It then sends an HTML-formatted email to the site administrator with the contents of the ad. Click on the "Approve" link, and the ad automatically displays on the site and will expire by itself in three weeks. Click "Delete," and the ad is deleted. With ColdFusion, all of this is accomplished in fewer than 300 lines of code!

We will explore custom tags extensively later in this book.

Functions

If you have written in a language other than HTML, then you are likely to be familiar with functions. *Functions* are named operations that take this form: functionName(variable). In ColdFusion, not only can you write your own tags, but you can create user-defined functions as well (this feature is new with ColdFusion 5).

Functions should be creatures familiar from algebra. They perform an operation on a variable. For instance, let's say that we wanted to convert a text string, "HELLO, How Are YOU?," into lowercase letters. A ColdFusion function called "LCase" will do this for us. It's a string manipulation function that we call like this: Lcase("HELLO, How Are YOU?"). This would convert our string to this: hello, how are you? We will examine functions in Chapter 8.

How to Begin

Here are the tools you will need to complete this chapter successfully:

- A text editor such as Notepad or ColdFusion Studio
- A Web browser and Internet connection
- Access to the Web server on which ColdFusion is installed
- An FTP client or local network connection

Your Text Editor

ColdFusion is written as nothing but plain text, just like HTML. Therefore, you won't ever need a fancy editor to write ColdFusion. You can just open Notepad on Windows, or Pico on Linux, and get going. However, like most fancy things, there are many real benefits to having an editor that specifically supports ColdFusion. I highly recommend Macromedia ColdFusion Studio 4.5 (Studio was not released in 5.0 version with the server). An evaluation copy of Studio 4.5 is included on the CD-ROM with this book. Many others are available to you, but I recommend Studio for ColdFusion developers. It won't rewrite your code, and you can take advantage of these features:

- Remote Development Services, which allows you to edit remote files.
- Query Builder, which allows you to quickly write complex queries.
- Tag and Function support. Studio knows the attributes of the tags you write, and lets you select your attributes with just a click.
- Tag Insight and Tag Completion. These cut down on typing drastically, and help insure that your documents are well formed.
- Interactive Debugger and multiple views mean you can always drill down to specific places in your templates and focus on just what you need.

Figure 5.1 shows what it looks like.

Figure 5.1 ColdFusion Studio is a complete IDE for ColdFusion, but it's not required.

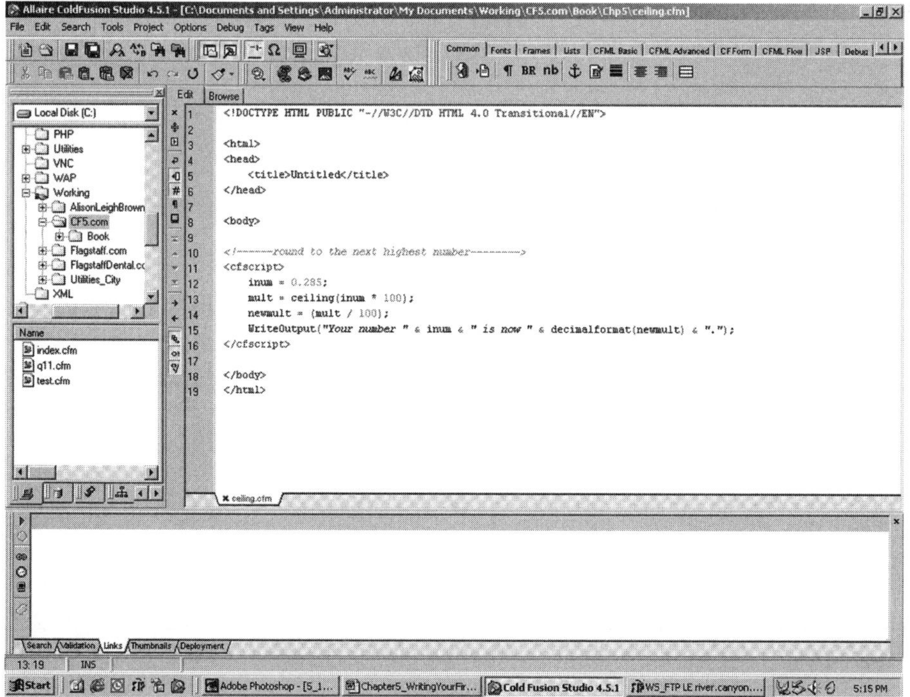

I really recommend Studio. Macromedia bundles it with UltraDev so that you can integrate your work with the graphic designers on your team. The point is that it's not necessary, but it will speed your development and your understanding of ColdFusion.

<NOTE>

You don't need ColdFusion Studio to use this book (or in any situation where you're writing ColdFusion). But I think it's a great help as a text editor in writing ColdFusion, and it's just what I use, so I'm going to refer to it throughout the book. You can install a 30-day evaluation copy from the CD-ROM included with this book.

The HTML that you write should be compatible with all of the browsers you need to support. Check out this book's appendix on writing ColdFusion applications for WAP (Wireless Application Protocol), which tells you how to get browsers that display web documents written for cell phones and PDAs.

FTP Client or Network Connection

If you installed ColdFusion on your local machine, you won't need this to complete the exercises. If you've installed ColdFusion on a test server somewhere, you just need a way to get your ColdFusion files over to it.

Now that we've got all of our tools together, we can begin writing.

Your First ColdFusion Template

HTML can create only static pages. *Static* pages never change unless you rewrite the code. When you use only HTML, large sites that need to change frequently become extraordinarily expensive and time consuming to maintain. Also, you are likely to have a number of errors on your site—the more times people touch something, the greater the chances are that it will break.

ColdFusion lets you write *dynamic* pages. That means that we separate the business logic (the code that does the dynamic work) from the presentation layer (the HTML tables and images used to create what people see in their browsers). With dynamic pages you can set variables, use loops, perform function operations on data, and manipulate data in databases for display on the Web. While not a full-fledged programming language like Java or C++, you can harness some of the power of these languages from within ColdFusion.

In the following section, we will create a ColdFusion template and introduce you to two tags: <CFSET> and <CFOUTPUT>.

Let's create a simple template, load it, and see how this works.

<NOTE>

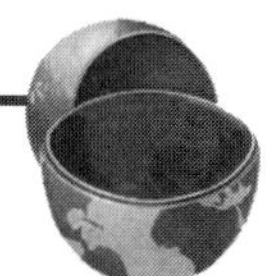

I recommend that you create a folder called CF5 on your hard drive (and wherever your ColdFusion installation is, if it is on a different machine). Throughout the book, you can just save your files there—this will make it easier to follow along so that you can concentrate on the code.

I have created a folder called MyDocuments\Working\CF5.com\Book\Chp5. This is where I will store the documents we create in this chapter. I will continue to follow this scheme throughout the book, so that you can easily stay organized with me.

In Studio, select File > New so we've got a clean slate to work with. Type the following code:

Listing 5.1 goodbye.cfm

```
<!DOCTYPE HTML PUBLIC "-//W3C//DTD HTML 4.0
    Transitional//EN">

<html>
<head>
    <title></title>
</head>

<body>
<!---
    Template: goodbye.cfm
    Author: Eben Hewitt
    Purpose: output "Goodbye Cruel World" to the browser
    Use: this is an independent template
    Date Created: 10/10/01
    Last Modified:
--->
<!---Create three variables with cfset--->

<cfset farewellPhrase = "Goodbye">
<cfset locationType = "Cruel">
<cfset location = "World">

<!---Output the values of the variables to the browser
    using cfoutput--->
```

```
<cfoutput>#farewellPhrase# # locationType# #location#
</cfoutput>

</body>
</html>
```

I'm going to save this file as MyDocuments\CF5\Book\Chp5\goodbye.cfm. If you've installed ColdFusion locally, then you can reference your virtual directory to call the file. If you installed ColdFusion locally, your address is something like http://127.0.0.1/corebook/goodbye.cfm.

Your page should look like mine (Figure 5.2). Congratulations! You've written your first dynamic ColdFusion page.

If Something Went Wrong

What if your page did not print "Goodbye Cruel World" when you loaded it in your browser? There are a couple of things that might have gone wrong, and you should check for them now, and try again:

Figure 5.2 Your first ColdFusion template.

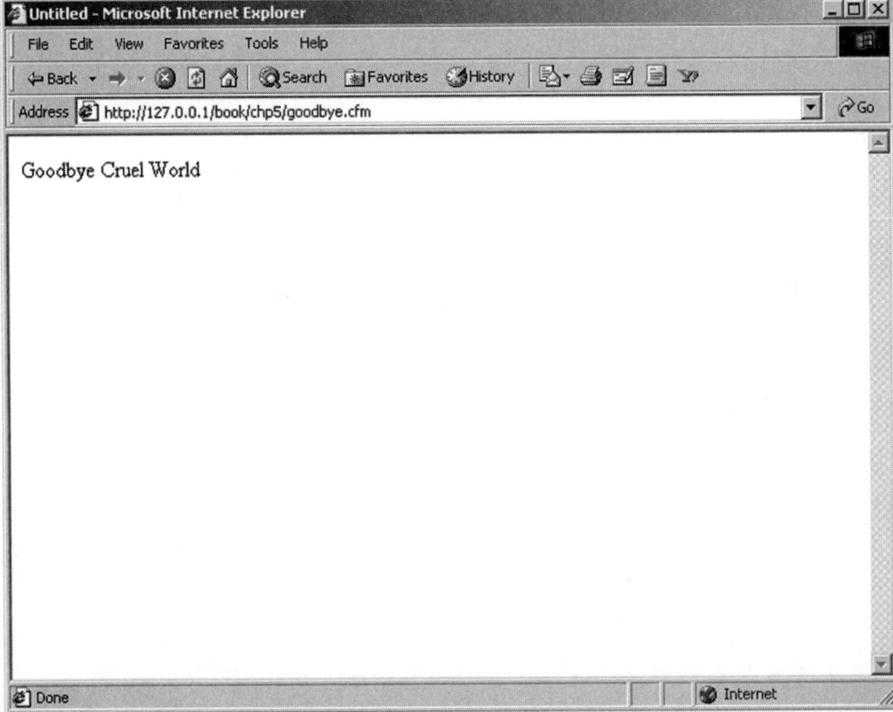

- If you got a 404 Error (File Not Found), then you should make sure that you typed the correct path to the file.
- If you got a 500 Internal Server Error, make sure that you installed ColdFusion correctly, and that the service is running.
- If you got a 403 Error, make sure that ColdFusion has execute permission for the directory you're storing your work in.

Perhaps you got a terrible-looking error message like the one in Figure 5.3.

In a simple template like this, an error message is almost always a typing error. These ColdFusion error messages are very useful in helping you locate problems with your templates. We will discuss them in depth later on, but for now, you should go back to your file and make sure that you typed everything exactly as it is written above.

In order to generate the error in Figure 5.3, I set the variables "farewellPhrase" and "locationType," but not the "location" variable. ColdFusion processed the page as far as it could.

Figure 5.3 A ColdFusion error page.

Untitled - Microsoft Internet Explorer

File Edit View Favorites Tools Help

Address http://127.0.0.1/chp10/err.cfm

Goodbye Cruel

Error Occurred While Processing Request

Error Diagnostic Information

An error occurred while evaluating the expression:

#location#

Error near line 15, column 45.

Error resolving parameter **LOCATION**

ColdFusion was unable to determine the value of the parameter. This problem is very likely due to the fact that either:

1. You have misspelled the parameter name, or
2. You have not specified a QUERY attribute for a CFOUTPUT, CFMAIL, or CFTABLE tag.

The error occurred while processing an element with a general identifier of (#location#), occupying document position (15:44) to (15:53).

Date/Time: 06/04/01 10:14:12
Browser: Mozilla/4.0 (compatible; MSIE 5.01; Windows NT 5.0)
Remote Address: 127.0.0.1

Done Internet

If you're still having problems, check the "Common Errors" chapter in the appendices for possible solutions.

Working with Variables

In this section we'll discuss what you wrote, and in the process we'll come to understand more about variables.

Naming Variables

There are certain guidelines that you must follow when naming your variables:

- Variable names must begin with letters
- Variable names may contain only letters, numbers, or the underscore character (_). Do not use spaces in your variable names.

The following are valid variable names:

- GetNumberofEmployees
- July30th
- Nom_de_Plume

The following are **not** valid variable names:

- @myPad
- 30thofJuly
- _MyParty
- Yeah,Baby!

Naming your variables is an important part of programming. That is, naming your variables in a clear, consistent, verbose manner is important. For instance, you could probably tell what sort of information to expect as you read the variable named "location." You would not have such luck had I been selfish enough to name the variable "loc" or "z29."

Additionally, you should always be consistent when naming your variables. For instance, I could have been lazy and done this:

```
<CFSET locationType = "Cruel">
<CFSET place = "World">
```

In English, the words "place" and "location" mean roughly the same thing. And ColdFusion doesn't care—the output would have been the same. But it simply makes your code more difficult to anticipate and debug. And it's easier to be consistent. Just get in a routine and follow it.

One thing I usually do is start a long variable name with lowercase letters, and then use capitals for other words in the name. For instance, I might call my variable classifiedAdTitle instead of ClsAdTtl. Doing this will make things easier for you.

Avoid giving your variables names like "ID" and "Type" and "User." Generic words like this often are reserved words in other languages you may be working with. You will get into trouble later. You can refer to the appendices in the back of this book for a list of words reserved by SQL, for instance.

<CFSET>

Let's examine what you wrote. A *variable* is a named place in memory. When you declare a variable, what you're doing is saying to the server, "Set aside a little space for me to hold some information." Then you give that space a name, so that you can refer to it consistently.

You might remember variables from algebra: $x + y = z$. Or maybe you're familiar with Java variables, like these:

```
boolean Flag
int TimesDisplayed
```

The Java variables above declare first their type, and then the name of the variable. ColdFusion is a *typeless* language. That means that we don't need to specify a variable's type.

In our example above, we set three variables, "farewellphrase," "locationType," and "location." The way we set variables in ColdFusion is by using the <CFSET> statement, like this:

```
<CFSET myVariableName = "MyValue">
```

The <CFSET> tag is used to define a local or global variable. If the variable exists already, ColdFusion will reset the variable to the new value. <CFSET> takes no attributes.

<NOTE>

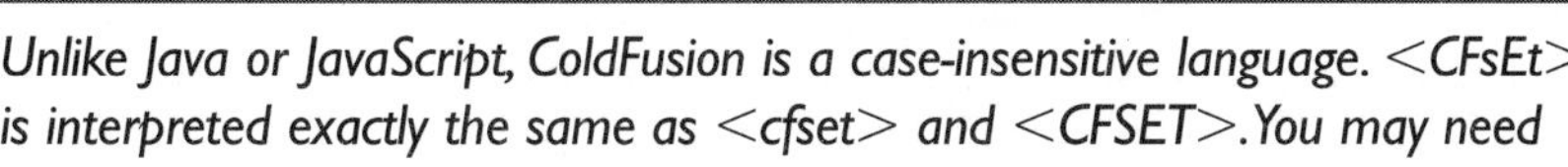

Unlike Java or JavaScript, ColdFusion is a case-insensitive language. <CFsEt> is interpreted exactly the same as <cfset> and <CFSET>. You may need

the flexibility of being able to run your same code on Linux, however. For this reason, I suggest that you be at least consistent throughout your code.

Comments

In this bit of code, I have used comments to give you information about what the code is doing, who the author is, and more. You're probably used to comments in various forms:

```
<!--I am an HTML comment-->

; I am a comment in an .ini file

// I am a JavaScript comment

/* I am a comment in SQL */
```

ColdFusion comments are like HTML comments, except that they require three dashes, not two:

```
<!---I am a ColdFusion comment. I do not display--->
```

There are two other ways to write comments in ColdFusion, but they can be used only inside a <CFSCRIPT> block. CFScript is a scripting language introduced in version 4 of ColdFusion that allows you to write ColdFusion in JavaScript-like syntax rather than using tags. A CFSCRIPT block looks like this:

```
<CFSCRIPT>
    // I am a single line comment. No one can see me.
    /* I am a comment that
         spans multiple lines. The following code will
         set the value of the variable "mult" to 28.5. It
         works just like the CFSET tag. Neat */
    inum = 0.285;
    mult = inum * 100;
</CFSCRIPT>
```

We will have a lot of fun writing CFSCRIPT later on.

Unlike HTML comments, which can be read if your user does a View Source in the browser, ColdFusion comments will not appear here. The user will just see blank space in its place, so you can safely write information about your code.

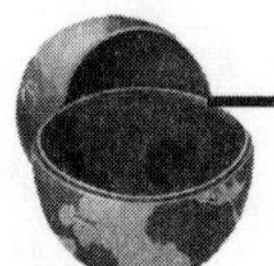

<SOAPBOX>

Please comment your code. *It is not uncommon for a rather complex ColdFusion website to result in 100,000 lines of code. Imagine inheriting 600*

ColdFusion templates after the programmer relocates to parts unknown, and sitting there in front of the screen with no pointers whatsoever as to what the code is doing—or what else will break if you change something.

If you need to go in and change things later, you will be disappointed if there are no comments. What seems perfectly normal and explicit to you today could look like the work of a lunatic in six months. Do yourself a favor. Comment everything constructively. This means you include the following items at the top of every template you write:

Author's name and email
Date Created
Date Last Modified
Purpose of the file
How the file relates to others that it impacts (or that impact it)

Noted ColdFusion developer Marilou Landes says: "I also include in the comments at the head of each template any templates that are included, any custom tags that are called, and any modules that are used." Smart.

<CFOUTPUT>

Now that we have a variable ("farewellPhrase") with an assigned value ("Goodbye"), we can output the value of the variable using the tag <CFOUTPUT>. Such an operation is short work in ColdFusion: you simply surround what you want to output with hash marks (also known as pound signs) like this: #MyVariable#. Then you surround that with a starting and closing <CFOUTPUT> tag, like this:

```
<CFOUTPUT>#MyVariable#</CFOUTPUT>
```

You can include more variables within a <CFOUTPUT>. You can write regular text and HTML code inside it, like this:

```
<CFSET firstName = "Eben">
<CFOUTPUT>My first name is <b>#firstName#</b>.</CFOUTPUT>
```

With these changes, this would be our output to the browser:

```
My first name is Eben.
```

As you can see, it is easy to combine HTML and text inside a CFOUTPUT block.

<NOTE>

The ColdFusion Application Server (CFAS) will start looking for CF markup to interpret the moment it knows it's inside a CFOUTPUT block. Therefore, try to keep your CFOUTPUT tags very close to the code that you want ColdFusion to resolve into a value. If you don't, your page will load more slowly.

<CFOUTPUT> is used to print the value of ColdFusion variables. <CFOUTPUT> takes five attributes: Query, Startrow, Maxrows, Group, and GroupCaseSensitive. These five attributes generally apply only when you are working with results from a database query or nested <CFOUTPUT>s. We will therefore revisit the CFOUTPUT tag when we discuss databases.

Setting and Outputting Rules

Certain rules surrounding the use of the <CFSET> tag, the <CFOUTPUT> tag, and pound signs (#), if learned at the outset, alleviate common problems and bloated code for the developer. Later on, you can use this section as a reference.

<CFSET> Usage

There are a number of things to keep in mind when using the CFSET tag. This section puts them into a neat little package:

- You may use only letter characters (a–z), numbers (0–9), or the underscore (_).
- Variable names must start with a number or a letter only.
- Use a period in a variable name only to separate a variable from its scope.
- Always close your quote marks and your tags! For instance, this is correct: <CFSET FirstName = "Eben">. This is incorrect: <CFSET FirstName = "Eben>.
- ColdFusion does *not* use more resources to reference a long variable name than a short one.
- Do not use quote marks around the name of the variable unless your variable is dynamic. This is incorrect: <CFSET

"FirstName" = "Eben">. This is correct: <CFSET "#FirstName#" = "Eben">.

- When setting a string that contains both text and variables, separate the string from the dynamic variable, using an ampersand (&) to concatenate them, like this: <CFSET FullName = "Eben"&FORM.LastName>.
- You do not need the pound signs (#) around a variable referenced in the CFSET tag. For instance, this is correct: <CFSET FirstName = FORM.FirstName>.
- If you are going to set three or more variables at once, it is more efficient to do so within a <CFSCRIPT> block. We will discuss how to do this in the <CFSCRIPT> chapter.

<CFOUTPUT> and Pound-Sign Usage

This section outlines basic rules regarding what situations call for use of pound signs. It also shows you some commonly misunderstood aspects of using the <CFOUTPUT> tag. This section is meant to start you off with good practices. It's also meant to serve as a reference later on as you develop.

- Within a <CFOUTPUT> block , use pound signs to reference *variables*. The variables in this code block will be interpreted by ColdFusion: <CFOUTPUT>My name is #FirstName# #LastName#.</CFOUTPUT>. If they don't exist, an error will be thrown.
- Within a <CFOUTPUT> block, use pound signs when using *functions*. For instance: <CFOUTPUT>The cosine of 0 is #Cos(0)#</CFOUTPUT>.
- Use pound signs around variables in a <CFQUERY> statement.
- Do not overuse pound signs in <CFSET> statements. For instance, <CFSET FirstName = FORM.FirstName> works just fine.
- Pound signs are necessary only when you need to distinguish expressions or variables from text—for instance: <CFSET Greeting = "Hello, #FirstName">.
- Be careful when using pound signs inside a <CFOUTPUT> block. You must *escape* these references by using two pound signs in a row, as with the hexadecimal value inside a font tag:

<CFOUTPUT><font color=##c0c0c0>#Greeting#</font> </CFOUTPUT>.

- You must use pound signs for the value of the test expression in a <CFSWITCH> tag, like this: <CFSWITCH expression = "#value#">.
- Pound signs must be used around parameter arguments in <CFOUTPUT> <CFQUERY>, and <CFMAIL> tags.

Now that we understand a bit about variables, it is important to understand just where those variables reside, how they are visible, and when to use them. Also, the variables discussed in this chapter are visible only to the current template, they do not persist, and they cannot be referenced from another request. We can pass variables between templates using HTML forms and in URL parameters. You will learn how to do this in ColdFusion in the next chapter.

PASSING DATA BETWEEN TEMPLATES

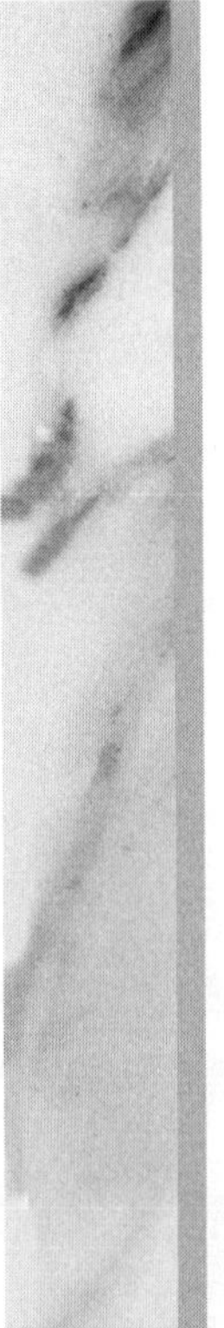

Topics in This Chapter

- What is scope?
- Using forms to display input data
- Using the URL scope to pass parameters
- URLEncode and URLDecode functions
- The CGI scope

Chapter 6

Now that you know how to set simple variables and output their values, this chapter will cover how to pass data between templates. First we'll define scope, then quickly move on to detailed coverage of working with variables in the FORM, URL, and CGI scopes.

At the end of the chapter we'll outline what variables are available in the REQUEST, QUERY, FILE, COOKIE, and CLIENT scopes.

What Is Scope?

In the last chapter we output the value of the `firstName` variable. If you are familiar with other programming languages, such as Visual Basic, you may be wondering what happened to the scope of that variable. For those who aren't familiar with the term, *scope* defines the visibility of a variable. That is, you can access variables in different parts of your program based on which scope they reside in.

ColdFusion defaults to the VARIABLES scope. This means that the `firstName` variable above is really in the VARIABLES scope, even though we did not declare it as such. So we could reference FirstName differently and still get the value returned to us, like this:

```
<CFSET firstName = Eben>

My first name is
<CFOUTPUT>#VARIABLES.firstName#</CFOUTPUT>.
```

The only change is that we are explicitly stating that we are looking for the value of the FirstName variable in the VARIABLES scope. However, this simple variable is available only to the current request, and cannot be referenced for any other request.

It is a central feature of dynamic applications that one can pass data between templates. ColdFusion has a number of scopes that you can use to such advantage. Two common ones are the FORM scope, which holds values that have been passed from HTML forms, and the URL scope, which holds parameters passed in the URL.

Figure 6.1 Incorrectly referenced variable scope.

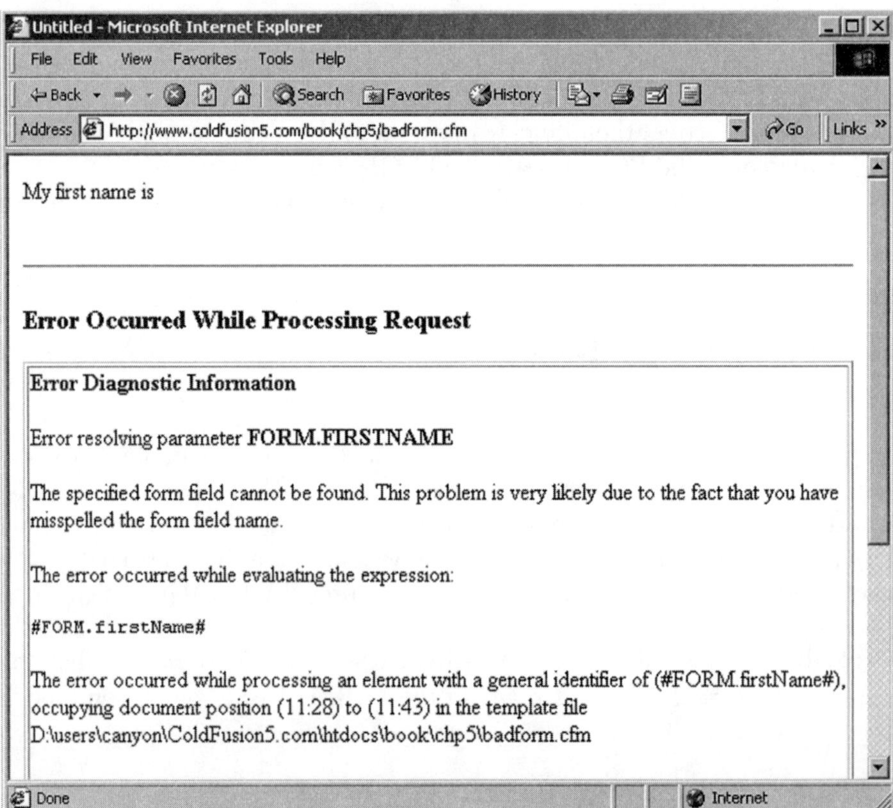

Untitled - Microsoft Internet Explorer
File Edit View Favorites Tools Help
Back Search Favorites History
Address http://www.coldfusion5.com/book/chp5/badform.cfm
Go Links
My first name is
Error Occurred While Processing Request
Error Diagnostic Information
Error resolving parameter FORM.FIRSTNAME
The specified form field cannot be found. This problem is very likely due to the fact that you have misspelled the form field name.
The error occurred while evaluating the expression:
#FORM.firstName#
The error occurred while processing an element with a general identifier of (#FORM.firstName#), occupying document position (11:28) to (11:43) in the template file D:\users\canyon\ColdFusion5.com\htdocs\book\chp5\badform.cfm
Done
Internet

To demonstrate a common error that occurs when one references variables in the wrong scope, type the code below into Studio and load it in your browser:

```
<CFSET firstName = "Eben">
My first name is <CFOUTPUT>#FORM.firstName#</CFOUTPUT>.
```

You should see a screen similar to Figure 6.1. This error message is telling us that it does not know the value of the #FORM.FirstName# variable. That's because this variable is not present in the FORM scope, it is present in the VARIABLES scope (which is the default, since we didn't explicitly set it).

Scopes Available to ColdFusion

Table 6.1 presents the different scopes available to ColdFusion, and what they can be used for.

Table 6.1 Scopes Available to ColdFusion

Scope	*Purpose*
QUERY RESULT	Prefixed with the name of a query that has run (as in, getUsers.FirstName), these variables refer to results returned from a database.
VARIABLES	These are page-level or local variables. You can refer to them only within the current template; then they are lost.
CGI	These are created every time a template request is fulfilled. There are more than 20 CGI variables, and they are always read-only. They return information about the user, such as IP address, the name of the current template, the user's browser type, and more.
FILE	File variables give you information regarding file-manipulation operations. For instance, when you upload a file to the server using the CFFILE tag, you can access the FILE.ServerFile variable to see what it is now named on the server.
URL	These are variables passed from one template to another via a URL parameter in a query string.
FORM	FORM variables are passed from one template to another via HTML forms. The names of all form variables are in a

Table 6.1 Continued

Scope	*Purpose*
	comma-separated list in the variable FORM.FIELD-NAMES. The value of each field name is referenced by its FORM-scoped field name.
COOKIE	Reference variables in a cookie set on the client machine.
CLIENT	Stores information about a particular client. Automatically creates seven variables such as CLIENT.LastVisit (which returns a date and time value) and CLIENT.HitCount (which returns an integer representing the number of times a user has accessed a site).

If you do not prefix your variables with the name of their scope (also known as "scoping your variables"), then ColdFusion has to figure out what scope they are in for itself. So beyond helping keep yourself organized, scoping your variables will make sure your pages process faster.

You also get more control over how your page processes when you scope your variables. ColdFusion will look for a referenced variable in all of the scopes listed in Table 6.1 *in that order.* So if it finds a variable called "UserName" in the URL scope, it won't bother checking the FORM or COOKIE or CLIENT scopes.

<NOTE>

There is a special scope called the Request scope. The Request scope extends the reach of a variable into the entire HTTP request. This makes it easy to expose a variable to nested tags and custom tags. You refer to the Request scope like any other scope: Request.myVariable. If you use a lot of custom tags in your applications, the Request scope is a terrific way to make sure your variables can always be seen.

Using Forms to Display Input Data

One of the goals of our form application is to allow the user to input her name, and then display the name back to her in the greeting. So we will set up a regular HTML form and pass it to a second page called an *action* page. The purpose of an action page is to process the instructions given on a previous page. In this example, we have a form page which will accept user input, and an action page that will process and output that data.

Type the following into a blank file in Studio:

Listing 6.1 An HTML Form Template

```
<html>
<head>
        <title>Greeting</title>
</head>

<body>

Please type your first name:<br>

<form action="actGreeting.cfm" method="post"
name="frmFirstName">
         <input type="text" name="FirstName" size="20"><br>
         <input type="submit" name="Submit">
</form>

</body>
</html>
```

Save this file as greeting.htm and load it in your browser. Notice that we save this file as plain HTML, since there is no ColdFusion code on the page to be interpreted. We could have saved this same file with a .cfm extension, and it would have worked exactly the same way. However, we also would have forced the page to be unnecessarily processed by the CFAS.

Notice that the action attribute of the form tag specifies the name of a .cfm file that we will use to process the input. Let's create that file now.

Create a new file in Studio and type the following code:

Listing 6.2 An Action Page

```
<html>
<head>
        <title>Welcome!</title>
</head>
<body>

Welcome, <cfoutput>#FORM.FirstName#</cfoutput>!

</body>
</html>
```

Go back to your browser, type your name into the form input control and click the "Submit Query" button. When I do this, I see the following displayed on the action page:

```
Welcome, Eben!
```

It's a dynamically generated page that you will use as a building block for many ColdFusion applications.

There are actually a number of variables that your HTML form has passed. Any time you make a FORM, you automatically get the FORM.FieldNames variable passed to the action page. This contains a comma-separated list of all of the names of form controls passed. So for our page, FORM.FieldNames has the following value list: FIRSTNAME, SUBMIT (remember that the "submit" button itself is a form control). You can leverage these variables to perform conditional processing—for example, to test if a form has been submitted or not.

Passing Data with Hidden Form Fields

HTML allows a hidden input control, which can be used to pass data to a template, just as we have already seen. There is one difference, however: the data is not displayed on the page. You can create a hidden form field like this:

```
<input type = "hidden" value="someValue">
```

Hidden form fields are useful if you need to pass nonsecure data that you don't mind the user seeing. The form values are hidden from displaying on the page, but are right there in the code if the user views the page source. Therefore you must not use hidden form fields to pass data that can be modified by the user.

<NOTE>

An old hacker trick that exploits hidden fields can compromise the security of your application. The hidden field data can be saved, modified locally, and then passed back to an absolute URL. For this reason, don't even include product price information in hidden fields. It's mostly useful for passing info that doesn't need to be hidden, but won't hurt your application if it is modified.

Let's add a hidden field to our greeting form so that the user can't see it (without viewing the page source), but the value is still available to the action page. Modify your Studio file greeting.htm so that it looks like this:

Listing 6.3 Including a Hidden Form Field

```
Please type your first name:<br>

<form action="actGreeting.cfm" method="post"
```

```
name="frmFirstName">

        <input type="hidden" name="UserID" value="007">

        <input type="text" name="FirstName" size="20"><br>

        <input type="submit" name="Submit">
</form>
```

Hidden form fields are referenced just like any other form field. Modify the actGreeting.cfm page to display the hidden variable by including the following line:

```
Your user ID is <b>#FORM.UserID#</b></cfoutput>
```

Then load the file in your browser and enter a name into the input control. Click the "Submit Query" button. You will see that the UserID variable set in the form was passed just like the FirstName variable. Of course, the variable will still be available to the action page, regardless of whether or not it is displayed to the browser.

Using the URL Scope to Pass Parameters

Forms are an excellent way to pass parameters from one template to another when you require user input. Often you need to pass nonsecure variables from one page to another *without* requiring user input. In this case, you can pass parameters within the URL scope.

Just as it sounds, the URL scope is the set of variables available from the URL of a given template. URL variables, or *parameters,* are similar to form variables in one respect—they are not available to the page on which they are set: they are available only to the page that they get passed to.

Setting a URL Variable

URL parameters are passed in the query string of a given URL. You create a query string by appending a question mark (?) to your link. They take the form *parameter=value.* Let's say you have a page called "SomePage.cfm." You want to pass a value to "SomeActionPage.cfm." You structure your link as follows:

SomeActionPage.cfm?Parameter=Value

In the above example, "SomeActionPage.cfm" will receive the parameter value when the link on SomePage.cfm is clicked. Your URL variable will be available for further processing or display on SomeActionPage.cfm, but *not* on SomePage.cfm.

An example should quickly elucidate. Let's create these two pages and populate them with real values. In Studio, type the following code, and save your file as "SetURLParam.cfm":

Listing 6.4 Setting Parameters in the URL

```
<!DOCTYPE HTML PUBLIC "-//W3C//DTD HTML 4.0
         Transitional//EN">

<html>
<head>
        <title>Untitled</title>
</head>

<body>

        Choose your favorite color:
<br>
        <a href="URLAction.cfm?favecolor=Green">Green</a>
<br>
        <a href="URLAction.cfm?favecolor=Red">Red</a>
<br>
        <a href="URLAction.cfm?favecolor=Blue">Blue</a>
<br>

</body>
</html>
```

When you call up this page in your browser, it should look like Figure 6.2.

You now have three links that all point to the same action page but pass different parameters. Let's make an action page, "URLAction.cfm," that accepts your passed URL parameter and displays it. Type the following into Studio:

Listing 6.5 Outputting the Value of a Parameter Passed in the URL

```
<!DOCTYPE HTML PUBLIC "-//W3C//DTD HTML 4.0
        Transitional//EN">

<html>
<head>
<title>You chose <cfoutput>#URL.favecolor#</cfoutput></title>
</head>

<body>

 Your favorite color is
```

```
<b><cfoutput>#URL.favecolor#</cfoutput></b>.

</body>
</html>
```

When you click on a link in "SetURLParam.cfm," the "favecolor" parameter is passed in the query string of the link to "URL.Action.cfm." The value of that parameter is then available to the action page as "URLfavecolor." When you reference that parameter, its value is displayed (or available for further processing). Just as we did with form variables, we put the scoped variable inside a block of <cfoutput> tags. ColdFusion interprets the variable and assigns it the value passed. So your output should look like Figure 6.3.

Notice that you can reference URL parameters in the title of your document as well. Your browser will display dynamic output from ColdFusion here just as well as any other place.

<NOTE>

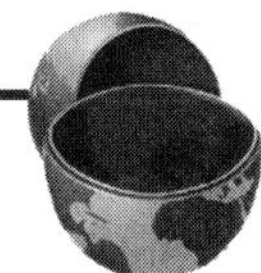

Just as a reminder, it is possible to reference your variables without their scope. We could also write <cfoutput>#favecolor#</cfoutput> in the above

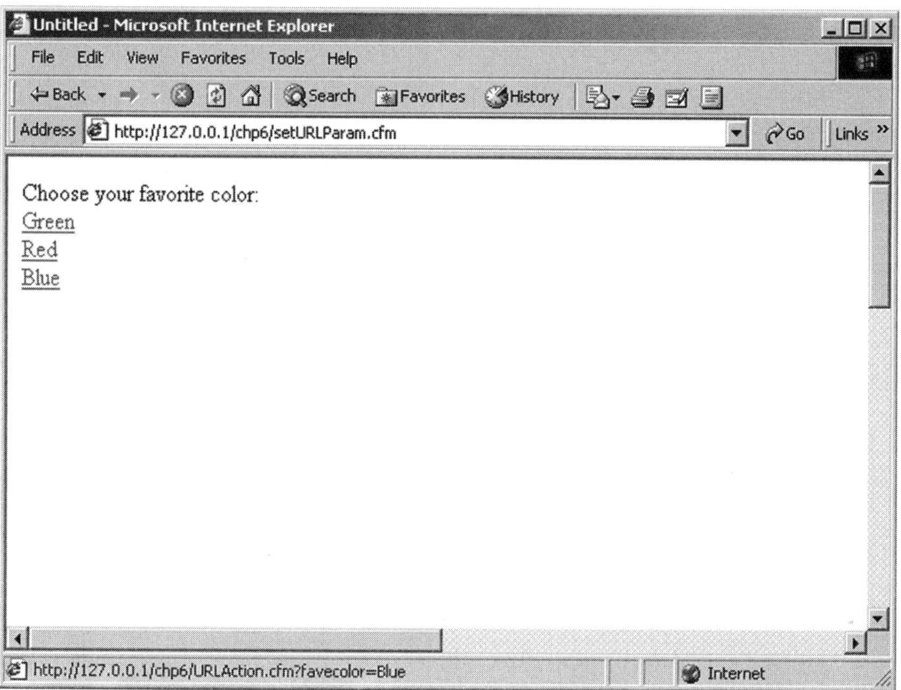

Figure 6.2 You can pass different values to the same page, depending on the parameters you append to the URL in the query string.

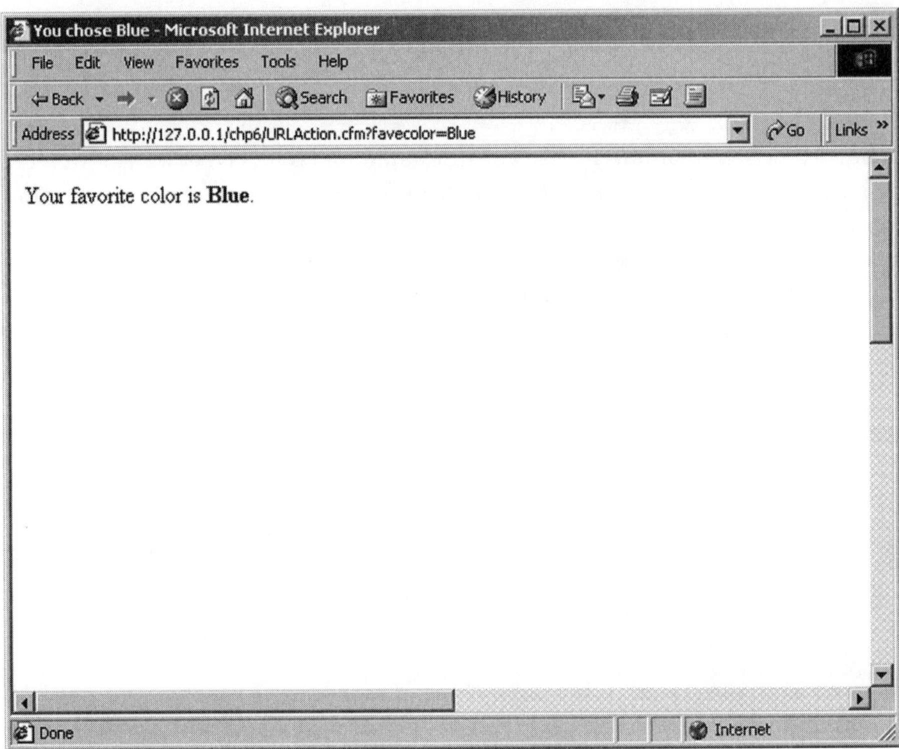

Figure 6.3 Outputting the value of the passed URL parameter.

code, and it would work. However, because ColdFusion will look for a parameter within each scope in a predetermined order until it finds one, forgetting the scope may lead to unpredictable results. Your code will process a bit faster, too, since ColdFusion doesn't have to go looking for a variable's scope.

URL Encoded Format

URLs may not contain spaces or any nonalphanumeric characters. If you are going to pass variables through a URL, you must define your parameter string to be acceptable for use in a URL. ColdFusion provides an easy way to do this: the URLEncodedFormat function.

The URLEncodedFormat function encodes the special characters and spaces within a string into a percent sign, followed by hexadecimal (16-bit) code. Nonalphanumeric characters are replaced with equivalent hexadecimal escape sequences. Spaces are replaced with plus signs.

URL variables are browser independent, which means that they will work on any platform. However, they sometimes work slightly differently, depending on how forgiving your browser is. For instance, Microsoft Internet Explorer will account for incorrectly formed URL query strings if it can and will insert the proper base-16 codes.

Netscape, on the other hand, is far stricter in its interpretation of URL parameters. I recommend you consider using Netscape as your development browser for just this reason. If it works in Netscape, you can usually be confident that it will work in Internet Explorer. Of course, it is prudent to test your code in a wide variety of browsers. I've found that this practice keeps me careful about working with URL parameters.

The URLEncodedFormat function takes one argument—the string to be encoded. You can therefore use it this way:

```
URLEncodedFormat(someString)
```

Let's say that we want to pass a parameter whose value contained spaces or special characters. We'll write some code very similar to the favorite color code we wrote before. However, this time we are going to choose our favorite cook. Since all of the choices of favorite cooks are first and last names, they need to contain spaces in the URL parameters in order to display correctly (with one space between the first and last names) on the action page. So let's quickly modify our favorite color code from above as written below, and save it as favecook.cfm. *Note:* This code will not perform reliably; we need to view it to make the point.

Listing 6.6 Setting URL Parameters with Spaces in the String

```
<!DOCTYPE HTML PUBLIC "-//W3C//DTD HTML 4.0 Transitional//EN">

<html>
<head>
	<title>Favorite Cooks</title>
</head>

<body>

Choose your favorite cook:<br>
<a href="Action2.cfm?cook=Julia Child">Julia Child</a>
<br>
<a href="Action2.cfm?cook=Martha Stewart">Martha Stewart</a>
<br>
<a href="Action2.cfm?cook=My Dad">My Dad</a>
<br>

</body>
</html>
```

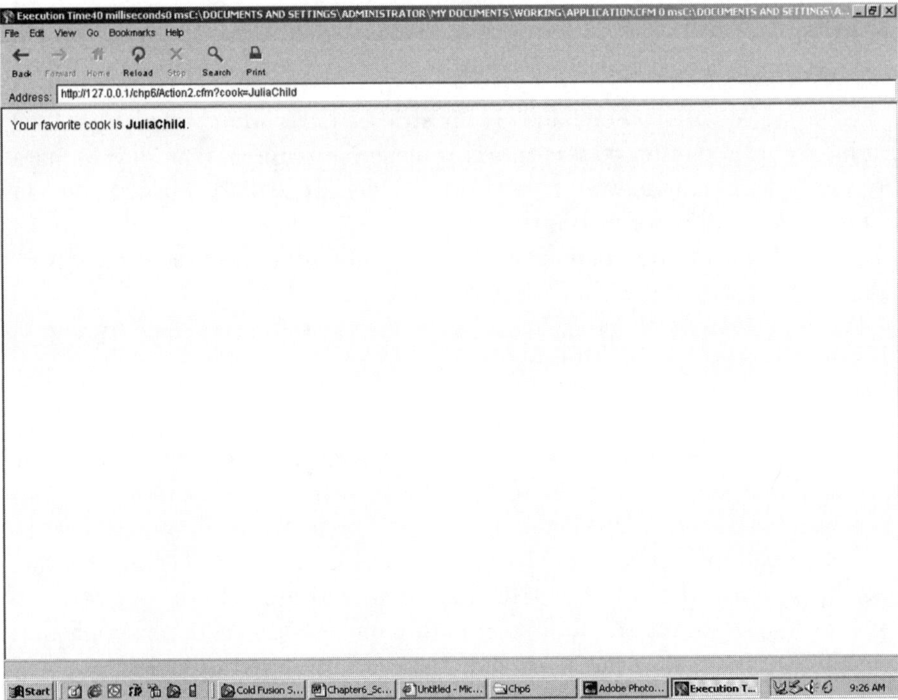

Figure 6.4 The action page viewed in Sun's HotJava 3 Browser.

We now need to create "Action2.cfm" to accept the "cook" parameter. You can easily modify "URLAction" to output the value of the #URL.cook# parameter like this:

Listing 6.7 You Can Sometimes Output the Value of Nonencoded Parameters Depending on Your Browser

```
<!DOCTYPE HTML PUBLIC "-//W3C//DTD HTML 4.0 Transitional//EN">

<html>
<head>
<title>Fave Cooks</title>
</head>

<body>
Your favorite cook is <b><cfoutput>#URL.cook#</cfoutput></b>.

</body>
</html>
```

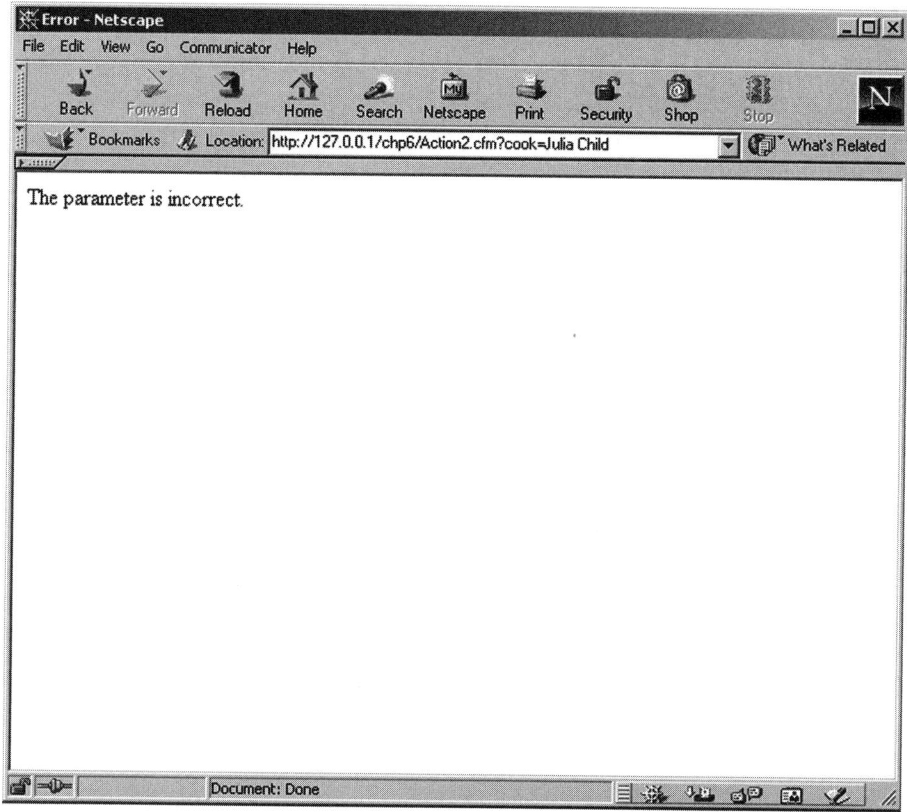

Figure 6.5 The same page viewed in Netscape 4.7.

I'm going to view this code just as it is in Sun's Hot Java 3.0 browser. Figure 6.4 shows the result of clicking on Julia Child.

As you can see, the HotJava browser tries to display something, even though it was passed an incorrectly formed URL parameter. But it mushed the two names together. Figure 6.5 shows the result of running the same code in Netscape 4.7.

As you can see, Netscape is not as forgiving as the HotJava browser. It returns an error stating that "the parameter is incorrect." Let's make it really tough. We'll change our code to include not only spaces but also two special characters: ' and &.

Create a file "FaveCookBook.cfm" with the following code:

Listing 6.8 Using the URLEncoded Format Function Handles the Problem

```
Choose your favorite cook book:<br>

<cfset cookbook1 = "Julia Child & Friends">
```

```
<cfset cookbook2 = "Martha Stewart's">

<cfoutput>
<a
href="Action2.cfm?book=#URLEncodedFormat(cookbook1)#">Julia
Child & Friends</a>
<br>
<a
href="Action2.cfm?book=#URLEncodedFormat(cookbook2)#">Martha
Stewart's</a>
</cfoutput>
<br>
```

Then, create a simple action page to accept these values:

```
<body>
Your favorite cook book is
<b><cfoutput>#URL.book#</cfoutput></b>.

</body>
```

Now, using the URLEncodedFormat function, we will pass these difficult parameters with ease to our action page. Assuming you choose Julia Child's book, your output should now look like Figure 6.6.

Figure 6.6 The encoded parameter displays correctly.

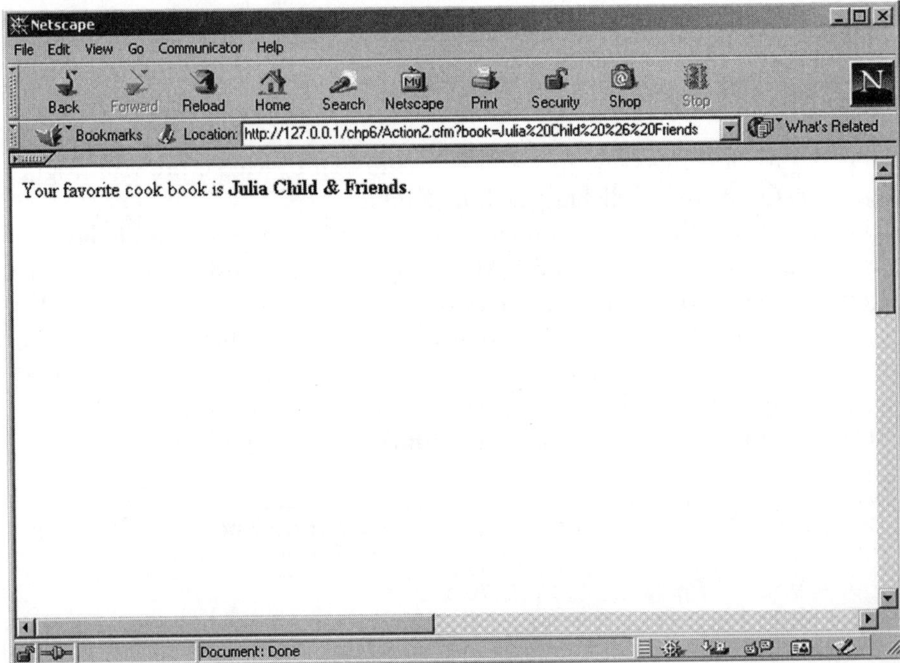

If you look in the address bar of your browser, you notice that the spaces have been replaced with %20, and the ampersand (&) has been replaced with %26. These are hexadecimal representations, which your browser can read.

Passing Multiple Parameters in One Query String

It is nice to be able to pass a parameter in a URL query string. However, you are not limited to one parameter per URL; you can *concatenate* (annex) parameters using an ampersand (&). Concatenated URL parameters in a query string look like this:

```
SomeActionPage.cfm?param1=value1&param2=value2&param3=value3
```

You are not limited as to the number of parameters you can pass in a URL. Browsers may limit the total size of a URL, but this limit is generally quite large (I have never heard of its being reached).

If we add one last bit to our cookbook code, we can see this in action. Let's add the date that each book was published by annexing the parameter "date" to our URL, like this:

Listing 6.9 Passing Multiple Parameters in the URL

```
<html>
<head>
        <title>Favorite Cook Books</title>
</head>

<body>

Choose your favorite cook book:<br>
<cfset book1 = "Julia Child & Friends">
<cfset book2 = "Martha Stewart's">
<cfoutput>
<a
href="Action2.cfm?book=#URLEncodedFormat(book1)#&year=1975">
Julia Child & Friends</a>
<br>
<a
href="Action2.cfm?book=#URLEncodedFormat(book2)#&year=2001">
Martha Stewart's</a>
</cfoutput>
<br>
</body>
</html>
```

Now we modify our action page to display this value:

Listing 6.10 Outputting multiple URL values

```
<!DOCTYPE HTML PUBLIC "-//W3C//DTD HTML 4.0 Transitional//EN">
<html>
<head>
	<title>Action2.cfm</title>
</head>

<body>
Your favorite cook book is
<b><cfoutput>#URL.book#</cfoutput></b>,
<br>published in <b><cfoutput>#URL.year#</cfoutput></b>.

</body>
</html>
```

Your browser output should look something like this:

> Your favorite cook book is **Martha Stewart's,**
> published in **2001.**

Just as a reminder, your users can see any parameters you pass in the browser. It is therefore not a good idea to pass passwords or other private information as URL parameters. They are very useful for the following:

- Passing nonsecure information
- Passing content or display preferences
- Cutting down on repetitive code

URLDecode

A matching function, introduced in ColdFusion 4.5, allows you to decode strings that are URL encoded. It takes one argument—the string to be decoded. We can see which high ASCII characters our special string characters will be converted into by writing using this function.

Type the following code into your browser and load it.

```
<cfset s = "%20">
%20 in ascii is a <cfoutput>#urldecode(s)#</cfoutput>.
<br>
<cfset s = "%26">
%26 in ascii is a <cfoutput>#urldecode(s)#</cfoutput>.
<br>
<cfset s = "%27">
%27 in ascii is a <cfoutput>#urldecode(s)#</cfoutput>.
<br>
```

Here we are simply setting and overwriting the variable "s" with a new ASCII value and then using the URLDecode function to output its value. Note that if you view this code in the browser, the first line will not appear to have a character. That's because the URL Encoded Format for %20 is a space.

One Last Note on URL Parameters

URL parameters are visible to ColdFusion as structures. Structures are a complex data type made up of key-value pairs, which we examine in a later chapter. ColdFusion creates URL variables as standard structures. They can therefore be manipulated and referenced just like any other ColdFusion structure.

The CGI Scope

Servers and clients create information that they pass back and forth to each other in the request headers and response headers, as we saw earlier. They also create a number of variables that are available for your use in ColdFusion. Here, we will examine what these variables are, and then we'll write a brief bit of code that displays a CGI variable value.

Using the CGI Scope to Display User and Server Data

CGI variables are created every time a template request is fulfilled. With the release of ColdFusion 5, there are now 45 CGI read-only variables available. Many of these have been added with the ColdFusion 5 release. They return information about the user, such as IP address, the name of the current template, the user's browser type, and more.

The names of CGI variables are fixed. You cannot create your own, and you cannot write to them. Listed below are the CGI variables available in ColdFusion 5 and their descriptions.

CGI Variables for Network Authentication

A few CGI variables are related to network authentication. These are set to empty strings if none is employed.

AUTH_PASSWORD The user's network password, if one was required.

AUTH_TYPE The type of server authentication employed (for instance, challenge/response), if any.

AUTH_USER The user's network username, if one was required.

CGI Variables for Secure Certificates and HTTPS

There are a number of CGI variables related to an SSL certificate, if any is present.

CERT_COOKIE The identifier of the cookie used in an SSL certificate, if present.

CERT_FLAGS An empty string unless a certificate is in use; otherwise, contains flags.

CERT_ISSUER The issuing company of a certificate, if one is in use. For instance, VeriSign.

CERT_KEYSIZE Size in bytes of the public key used in a certificate, if any.

CERT_SECRETKEYSIZE Size in bytes of the private key used in a certificate, if any.

CERT_SERIALNUMBER Serial number of the certificate, if any.

HTTPS Set to "on" or "off," depending on whether or not the HTTPS protocol is currently in use.

Other security-related variables are:

CERT_SERVER_ISSUER
CERT_SERVER_SUBJECT
CERT_SUBJECT
HTTPS_KEYSIZE
HTTPS_SECRETKEYSIZE
HTTPS_SERVER_ISSUER
HTTPS_SERVER_SUBJECT

CGI Variables for the Current Template

There are several CGI variables set about the current template. Some of these, such as HTTP_USER_AGENT, are created by the browser, not the server.

CF_TEMPLATE_PATH Returns physical path of the called template—for instance: `C:\CF5Book\Chp5\actGreeting.cfm`.

CONTENT_LENGTH Character length of client content.

CONTENT_TYPE MIME type of data attached to the current page. For instance, a page that accepts POSTed form data will look like this: `application/x-www-form-urlencoded.`

PATH_INFO Directory and template of requested page—for instance: `/bookchp5/actGreeting.cfm.`

PATH_TRANSLATED Requested template's path, converted from virtual to physical path—for instance:
`C:\Documents and Settings\Administrator\My Docments\Working\CF5.com\Book\Chp5\actGreeting.cfm.`

QUERY_STRING String of URL parameters passed to the current template after the ?, just as they appear in the URL.

SCRIPT_NAME The virtual path of the requested template. Returns the same value as `PATH_INFO.`

CGI Variables for the Connection

HTTP_ACCEPT MIME Types accepted by the client browser.

HTTP_ACCEPT_ENCODING Compression method sent in the client request, might be `gzip, deflate.`

HTTP_ACCEPT_LANGUAGE Default client language, also read from the request header.

HTTP_CONNECTION Read from the request header; possible values are `close` and `keep-alive.`

HTTP_CONTENT_LENGTH Read from the header; this value corresponds to the `CONTENT_LENGTH` value.

HTTP_CONTENT_TYPE Returns the same value as the `CONTENT_TYPE` variable.

HTTP_COOKIE `CFID=1; CFTOKEN=1235810.`

HTTP_HOST The host IP address.

HTTP_REFERER The URL of the document that contained the link or form submission that resulted in the current template's display.

HTTP_USER_AGENT The browser type of the requesting client. For instance, IE 5.0 returns this: `Mozilla/4.0 (compatible; MSIE 5.01; Windows NT 5.0).` Sun's Hot Java browser might return this: `Mozilla/3.0 (x86 en] Windows NT 5.0; Sun.`

CGI Variables about the Client

REMOTE_ADDR The IP address of the client.

REMOTE_HOST The host name of the client, if available.

REMOTE_USER Mimics AUTH_USER; this variable returns the username of the user requesting a protected template.

REQUEST_METHOD The method used to request the current template. This is generally GET or POST.

CGI Variables about the Server

GATEWAY_INTERFACE The CGI version in use on the server. It might look like this: `CGI/1.1`.

SERVER_NAME Name or IP address of the server.

SERVER_PORT Receiving TCP/IP port. For web servers, the default is 80.

SERVER_PORT_SECURE Receiving TCP/IP port for requests of pages in secured areas.

SERVER_PROTOCOL Protocol and version used to request the template—for instance, `HTTP/1.1`.

SERVER_SOFTWARE The name and version of the web server software on which ColdFusion is running. For example, this might be `Apache/1.3.12 (Unix) (RedHat/Linux)`. If you're running IIS 5.0, this would appear as `Microsoft-IIS/5.0`.

WEB_SERVER_API The API running on the server. For Windows, this value is generally ISAPI; on Netscape servers, it might be NSAPI.

Many of these values could be empty, depending on what your environment is. For instance, if I don't have an SSL certificate in use, the CERT_ISSUER variable will be empty. Also, not all servers or all browsers support every CGI variable; these will be set to an empty string as well.

How to Use CGI Variables in Your Templates

As explained previously, scoped variables take the form *SCOPE.VariableName*. Therefore, it should come as no surprise that you reference the CGI variable HTTP_USER_AGENT like this: CGI.HTTP_USER_AGENT.

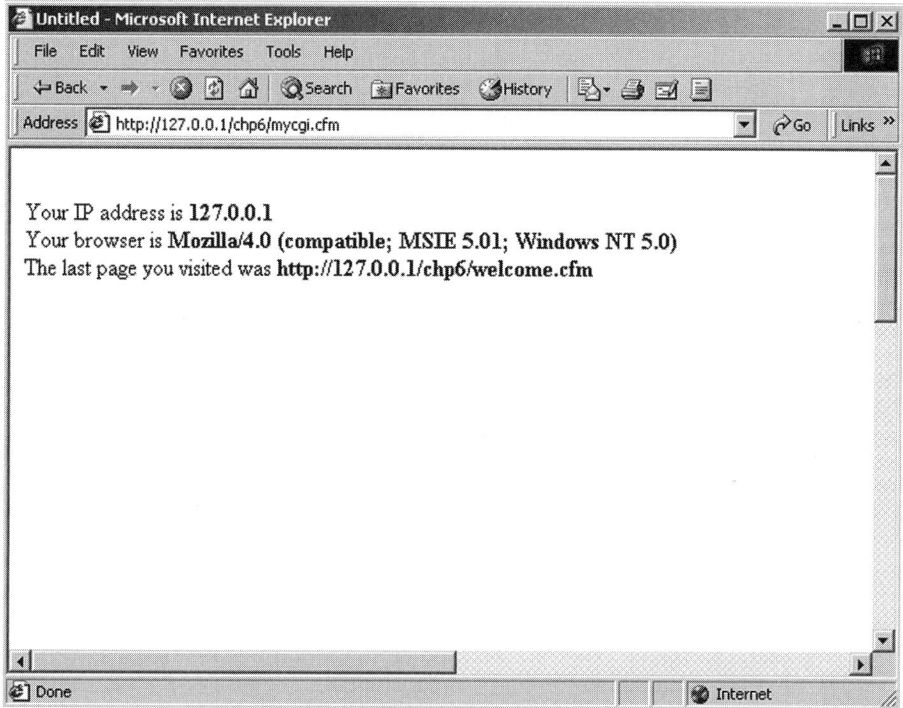

Figure 6.7 Outputting the value of CGI variables.

You might experiment with this scope to track information about users visiting your site. You could also run different code based on the information returned. For instance, you might be used to using the "pragma" parameter in HTTP 1.0 to force a page refresh. This meta value is deprecated in HTTP 1.1, so you might do this differently, based on what value the SERVER_PROTOCOL variable returns.

Let's use a variable or two from the CGI scope to freak out our visitor a little. Let's write a page called Welcome.cfm which contains a link to another page. Welcome.cfm looks like this:

```
I am Welcome.cfm<br>
Click <a href="mycgi.cfm">here</a> to go to a new page.
```

Then we quickly write a page that contains some CGI variables, like this:

```
<br>
<cfoutput>
Your IP address is <b>#CGI.REMOTE_ADDR#</b><br>
Your browser is <b>#CGI.HTTP_USER_AGENT#</b><br>
The last page you visited was <b>#CGI.HTTP_REFERER#</b><br>
</cfoutput>
```

Save the code above as "mycgi.cfm." Load "Welcome.cfm" in your browser. When you click on the link, you request the mycgi.cfm page, which will process and output the variables. Your screen should look something like Figure 6.7, depending on what browser and operating system you use.

Conclusion

There are a number of other scopes available to use when working with ColdFusion. These include the REQUEST, QUERY, CFFILE, COOKIE, ThisTag, and CLIENT scopes. Just as FORM variables are available only when working with HTML forms, and URL variables are available only when using links, each of the above scopes is available for specific contexts. For instance, you may only reference the QUERY scope when querying a database. So it makes more sense to talk about each of these as we come to them.

In this chapter you have learned about passing values in FORMs and URLs. You have also learned about auxiliary aspects of doing so, such as using hidden form fields and encoding and decoding URL parameter strings. You have learned about CGI variables, which your browser and the server create automatically with each request, and you have learned how to reference each of these to create dynamic and personalized pages for your website.

In the next chapter, we will take a close look at using functions to help you get the most out of your variables and perform complex data operations.

EXPRESSIONS, CONDITIONAL LOGIC, AND FLOW CONTROL

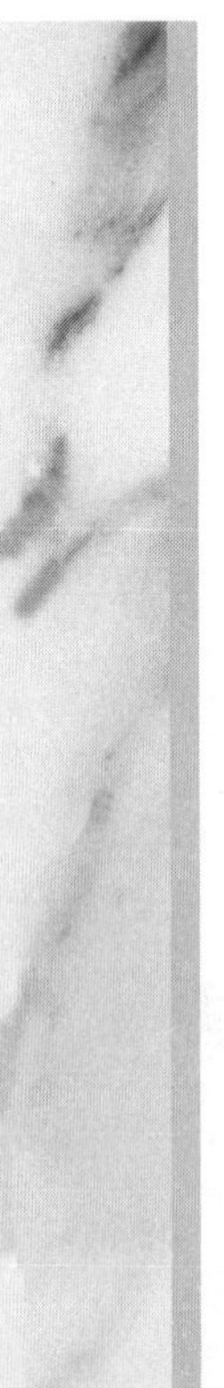

Topics in This Chapter

- Expressions and operators
- Conditional logic
- CFIF, CFELSE, CFELSEIF, CFPARAM
- CFSWITCH, CFCASE, CFDEFAULTCASE
- Flow control using CFINCLUDE, CFLOCATION and CFABORT
- A complete site flow control application

Chapter 7

"Contrariwise," continued Tweedledee, "if it was so, it might be; and if it were so, it would be; but as it isn't, it ain't. That's logic."
—Lewis Carroll, *Through the Looking Glass*

In this chapter you will learn how to create templates using ColdFusion expressions and conditional processing. You've got a bit of background now about ColdFusion, and you should feel comfortable setting and outputting variables locally and through forms and URLs. We will begin by working with expressions and the operators used with them. That will give us the foundation we need to work with conditional logic. This in turn will give us the tools to begin working with flow control.

Flow control is the art of implementing conditional logic in your templates for optimal processing. At the end of the chapter you complete a fully operational website using a flow control framework. Along the way, you will pick up no fewer than ten ColdFusion tags that you will use every day: <CFIF>, <CFELSE>, <CFELSEIF>, <CFPARAM>, <CFSWITCH>, <CFCASE>, and <CFDEFAULTCASE>. We will also learn to use <CFINCLUDE>, <CFLOCATION>, and <CFABORT>. Now things really start to get fun.

What Are Expressions?

An *expression,* in the most general sense, is any legal combination of symbols that represents a value. The same definition applies for regular spoken language, too, I suppose. More specifically, expressions are combinations of at least one *operand* and one or more *operators.*

Operands and Operators

An operand is a value, and an operator is a symbol that represents a performable action. Consider the example:

```
5 - Y
```

"5" and "Y" are operands and the "−" is the operator. By writing this expression, we make it available for evaluation. That is, we can possibly determine a result of the expression. Any given expression within ColdFusion will return a single value.

String Operators

We can also write expressions that contain *strings.* A *string* is a series of characters that are manipulated as a group. Strings make no reference to any other entity—that is, they don't stand for anything. Here are examples of strings:

```
100 N. Humphreys
8d8f(9dfd&6^lj@~kfff
Hello, world.
```

In our 5−Y example above, the operation performed is subtraction. If we knew the value of Y, we could output the result. Strings allow only one type of operator—concatenation. This operator is signified by the ampersand (&) and is used to fuse two strings together—like this:

```
<cfset FirstName = "Eben">
<cfset LastName = "Hewitt">
<cfset FullName = "#FirstName#" & " " & "#LastName#">
<cfoutput>#FullName#</cfoutput>
```

The code above will output "Eben Hewitt" to the browser. Two ampersands are necessary because there are actually three strings concatenated: the first name, a space, and the last name.

Arithmetic Operators

In ColdFusion, numerous mathematical operators are available to you. The first four are addition, subtraction, division, and multiplication. They work just as you would expect. Below is an example of a set of nested mathematical operations:

```
<cfset temp = ((3 * (4+2))/2)-8>
<cfoutput>#temp#</cfoutput>
```

When temp is output, its value is 1.

There are three binary operators: MOD, \, and ^.

Modulus, MOD, returns the remainder of a division (also known as the modulus). For example, 10 MOD 3 returns 1, since 10 divided by 3 is 3 with a remainder of 1. Here is an example of the syntax:

```
<cfset temp = 10 mod 3>
<cfoutput>#temp#</cfoutput>
```

The trailing or backward slash, \, returns the result of integer division. Therefore, 10\3 is 3. We can combine the two operators to demonstrate how they used to teach math in America:

```
<cfset temp = 10 \ 3>
<cfset rem = 10 mod 3>

<cfoutput>Result: #temp# R #rem#</cfoutput>
```

The caret, ^, raises the first number to the power of the second number. Therefore, 10^2 = 100.

The final two operators are known as unary operators. They set the sign of a number as either positive or negative; for instance, −23, or +75.

To discuss the remaining two categories of operators, Boolean and comparison, let us begin with a discussion of conditional logic.

What Is Conditional Logic?

For a programmer, *conditional logic* roughly means that you can execute certain code depending on whether or not a certain condition has been satisfied. This is a powerful aspect of every programming language.

To ask what "conditional logic" is, we would be prudent to begin by asking, "What is a condition?" A *condition* is precisely a particular state or mode. A "conditional" is therefore the expression of something's current state. Conditional logic allows us to base our actions on the current condition of our template, or the variables available to it.

We use conditional logic every day in our own lives to determine our actions, as in this example:

I am tired. Therefore, I will go to bed.

We might say about the above statements that the speaker's current state, or condition, is "tired." Because of that condition, the speaker will perform certain actions. In this case, the action will be "go to bed." We might extend this example by including other conditions or other actions:

If I am very tired, I will go to bed.

If I am just a little tired, I will keep working.

In order for conditional logic to make sense, there must be a reliable way to test the truth value of a statement. For instance, what measure does one use to determine the degree of tiredness?

Executing Code Based on Conditions

In order to determine the truth value of a variable's condition, we use comparison operators, as mentioned previously. We compare two variables and reduce the expression to TRUE or FALSE based on the comparison. For instance, any two given numbers can be equal to one another, or one can be less than the other. Those are the only two meaningful comparisons we can make regarding given numeric values. A common use of conditional logic is to determine whether or not a given variable exists at all, and to execute different code depending on the answer.

This is where things get sort of interesting. You may be thinking, "Wait a moment—you didn't mention numeric values that are *more than* other values." This is a reasonable objection. My omission is a matter of both efficiency and necessity: if x is less than y, y is *necessarily* more than x. So it is certainly true that a given number can be greater than another given number. We could just as easily have stated that. However, it would not have added to our knowledge regarding the comparative relation between two numbers.

While the point may seem pedantic, my illustration has another purpose. It is a good habit to get into, as you write conditional logic, to determine exactly what you know and do not know about the current state of your template at any given moment in its processing. Base your conditional logic on only the skeletal information you have about defined entities and their values at any given point in your application. This will help to combat the writing of bloated, unnecessary code.

Comparison Operators

ColdFusion offers a number of comparison operators that return Boolean values (which is to say, they evaluate to TRUE or FALSE). These are outlined in Table 7.1.

Table 7.1 Comparison Operators

Operator	*Description*
IS, EQUAL, EQ	Returns TRUE if values are equivalent, FALSE if they are not.
IS NOT, NEQ, NOT EQUAL	Returns TRUE if the left value and right value are not identical.
LT, LESS THAN	Returns TRUE if the left value is Less Than the right value.
GT, GREATER THAN	Returns TRUE if the left value is Greater Than the right value.
GTE, GREATER THAN OR EQUAL TO	Returns TRUE if the left value is Greater Than or Equal To the right value.
LTE, LESS THAN OR EQUAL TO	Returns TRUE if the left value is Less Than or Equal To the right value.
CONTAINS	Returns TRUE if the left value Contains the right value.
DOES NOT CONTAIN	Returns TRUE if the left value does not Contain the right value.

Note that in the case of string values, equivalency tests are case insensitive. Also, Table 7.1 separates alternative syntaxes with a comma where applicable. In case there is any confusion, by "left value" and "right value" in Table 7.1, I refer to sides of the operator. For instance:

```
"Bob" DOES NOT CONTAIN "Jim"
```

or

```
7 neq 8
```

Bob and 7 are left of the operators.

In order to create conditions in ColdFusion, we use the <CFIF> tag. In order to test for a condition, we use the comparison operators in Table 7.1. The comparison operator in our plain-language example above is "is": *If currentState* is *"tired," then go to bed.* Let's see how to use the CFIF tag.

<CFIF> and <CFELSE>

<CFIF> allows you to create simple or compound conditional statements. It accepts any expression as its value. It takes no attributes, but you do need a closing </CFIF> tag. It takes this form:

```
<CFIF expression>
       Any code here will be executed or output if the
       expression in the CFIF tag evaluates to TRUE.
</CFIF>
```

You use the <CFELSE> tag to specify code to run in the event that the expression in your <CFIF> clause evaluates to false. Note that the <CFELSE> tag must come before your closing </CFIF> tag.

Let's write a template that uses both of these tags in conditional processing. First we will set a variable and then output one of two statements to the browser, depending on the outcome of an expression:

Listing 7.1 Using CFIF and CFELSE

```
<!----Set a variable to test against--->

<CFSET CurrentState = "Energetic">

<!----Output a different statement depending on value of the
CurrentState variable--->

<CFIF CurrentState is "Tired">
       You should go to bed.
<CFELSE>
       Keep working.
</CFIF>
```

If you save this and load it in your browser, you will see the phrase "Keep working" printed, since we set the value to something other than "Tired." <CFELSE> works great if you may encounter a value that is not specifically accounted for.

<CFELESEIF>

It is often the case that you need to specify more than one condition. Using the <CFELSEIF> clause allows you to do this. Like <CFELSE>, <CFELSEIF> takes no attributes, and it must appear inside a <CFIF></CFIF> block. Listing 7.2 is an example of how the three tags work together. This time, we'll extend the example above to set a different

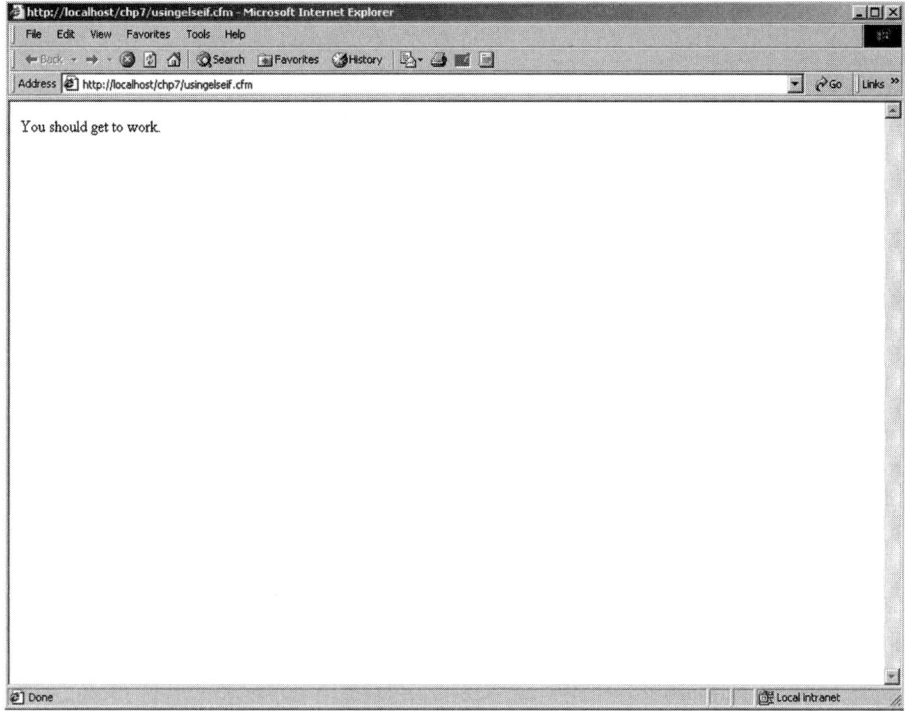

Figure 7.1 The result of executing different code based on a condition.

variable depending on the value of the CurrentState variable. Figure 7.1 shows the result of using the <CFELESEIF> clause.

Listing 7.2 Using CFELSEIF

```
<!---Set a variable so we have something to test against.--->

<CFSET CurrentState = "Busy">

<CFIF CurrentState IS "Lazy">

<!---The "do" variable will only be set to "watch a movie" if
the value of CurrentState is exactly "Lazy". Otherwise, this
block will be skipped entirely.--->

        <CFSET do = "watch a movie">

<CFELSEIF CurrentState IS "Busy">
<!---The "do" variable will only be set to "get to work" if the
value of CurrentState is exactly "Busy". Otherwise, this block
will be skipped entirely.--->
```

```
        <CFSET do = "get to work">

<CFELSE>
        <!---The code below will execute in the event that the
value of "CurrentState" is neither "Lazy" nor "Busy".--->

        <CFSET do = "take a sip of a refreshing beverage">

<!---Close the IF statement--->
</CFIF>

<!---Write the statement including the new "do" variable to
        the browser---->

<CFOUTPUT>You should #VARIABLES.do#.</CFOUTPUT>
```

Notice in Listing 7.1 that you may not use the = sign to test against string values. You use the IS or IS NOT comparison operators for strings. We'll see how to deal with ordinals in the next example.

For practice, try changing the value of the CurrentState variable in order to get each statement to execute.

Creating Personalization with Conditional Logic

We will now see how the CFIF-CFELSEIF-CFELSE construct you used previously can be expanded. In the next example we will use the same conditional logic building blocks, but you will learn how to use dynamic variables and functions to create a dynamic, personalized greeting for your site's visitors.

Write Listing 7.3 into Studio and save it as daytime.cfm.

Listing 7.3 Personalizing Your User's Experience with Conditional Logic

```
<html>
<head>
        <title>Greeting</title>
</head>

<body>

<!----Using the Now() and Hour() functions along with numeric
comparison operators, determine what time of day it is.--->

<cfif Hour(Now()) LT 12>

<!---Set the value of Variables.PartofDay depending on what
time of day it is.--->
```

```
        <cfset Variables.PartofDay = "Morning">

<cfelseif Hour(Now()) GT 18>
        <cfset Variables.PartofDay = "Evening">

<cfelse>
        <cfset Variables.PartofDay = "Afternoon">

</cfif>

<!---Set the greeting value based on time of day.
Include HTML in the variable to ensure there's always a break
------->

<cfset Variables.Greeting =
"<cfoutput>Good #Variables.Partof-Day#. You are not logged in.
<br></cfoutput>">

<!---output the greeting------->
<cfoutput>#Variables.Greeting#</cfoutput>

</body>
</html>
```

There are a number of new items in Listing 7.3. First, two new functions are introduced—the Now() function and the Hour() function. The Now() function returns the current system time in this format:

```
{ts '2001-06-10 11:30:34'}
```

The Hour( ) function returns the ordinal value of the hour, from 0 (for midnight) to 23 (for 11 pm). Functions will be discussed at greater length in Chapter 8.

You can see from the code that we can use two functions together. In our first <CFIF> expression, the Now() function, which takes no arguments, is run. The Hour() function takes one argument—the time that you want to determine the ordinal hour value for. So in this case, the Hour() function has a dynamic value—it is set to whatever the result of the Now() function is.

Since the Hour() function returns an ordinal, I decided that morning should be any time between 0 and 12 (that is, midnight and 11:59), and afternoon should be any time between 12 and 18 (that is, noon and 6 pm), and that any other time must be evening. In pseudocode, which often helps one think about how to write, we could say this:

```
morning is anytime from midnight up to but not including 12 pm;
evening is anytime from 7 pm up to but not including midnight;
afternoon is anything else (12 pm up to but not including 7 pm)
```

We can use the comparison operators GT (greater than) and LT (less than) and conditional logic to set the greeting variable based on the value of the hour ordinal. The conditional logic used in this example is also a bit more sophisticated than that used in the previous example. Let's take a closer look at it.

Know What You Know

It is important to note that conditional logic is used in a sophisticated way in Listing 7.3. When working with conditional logic, you have a number of choices. We could also have written the code in Listing 7.4, which illustrates bloated conditional logic.

Listing 7.4 Bloated Conditional Logic

```
<!---Is it earlier than noon?--->
<cfif Hour(Now()) LT 12>
      <cfset Variables.PartofDay = "Morning">
</cfif>

<!---Test to see if the current hour is greater than or
      equal to 12 AND IS ALSO less than 18--->

<cfif Hour(Now()) GTE 12 AND Hour(Now()) LT 18>
      <cfset Variables.PartofDay = "Afternoon">
</cfif>

<!---If the current hour is greater than or equal to 18,
then it is 6 pm or after, so it's evening--->
<cfif Hour(Now()) GTE 18>
      <cfset Variables.PartofDay = "Evening">
</cfif>
```

Listing 7.4 works perfectly well, but it is an example of what *not* to do. This may seem obvious to you, but I have seen application after application use conditional logic in this manner. What exactly is the problem with Listing 7.4? To begin with, it's slower to process and it's more code to read and manage. Also, because the programmer has not thought logically about the relationship between known values, there is unnecessary testing against values that don't matter. This is what I refer to as *bloated code*—it will work, but it is bigger and slower than it needs to be because of poorly thought-out conditions. It is completely unnecessary to find out if it is afternoon or not. Because there are only three possible times of day in the above example, anything that is not morning or evening is *necessarily* afternoon—which is how we test for the time of day in Listing 7.3, the correct example.

Every time the page with this code is accessed, it will output a different greeting depending on what time it is. This is a useful bit of personalization that you can incorporate into your websites.

Boolean Operators

To round out the discussion of conditional logic, we should discuss the final kind of operator: Boolean operators. Named for autodidact and English mathematician George Boole, these operators can only be used with Boolean values, and they return only Boolean values.

- **AND** returns TRUE when both conditions are true, FALSE otherwise.
- **OR** returns TRUE when at least one condition is true, FALSE otherwise.
- **NOT** negates (reverses) a value (turns TRUE to FALSE and vice versa)
- **EQV** returns TRUE when both values are true or both values are false.
- **IMP**—short for "implication"—returns TRUE when the statement "If A then B" is true. A imp B returns FALSE only when A is true and B is false.
- **XOR**—the Exclusive OR—returns TRUE ("Yes") when either one or the other value is TRUE, but not when both of them are.

Here is an example of the rarely used IMP in action:

```
<cfset A = 0>
<cfset B = 1>
<cfset temp = A imp B>

<cfoutput>#temp#</cfoutput>
```

This outputs YES to the browser. The code below demonstrates Exclusive OR; it will evaluate to TRUE:

```
<cfset A = 5 lte 10>
<cfset B = 4 eq 5>
<cfset temp = A XOR B>

<cfoutput>#temp#</cfoutput>
```

We will use AND, NOT, and OR extensively throughout the book.

In the preceding chapter we created a simple example of how to display information on an action page that was passed as a URL parameter from another page. We can expand on the concepts you've learned so far to create compact code when working with multiple templates.

Checking for Existence Using IsDefined( )

With conditional processing, we can create a *self-posting page.* A self-posting page uses functionality that normally would require two pages (a template including a form and an action page)—but it uses conditional logic to collapse this functionality into one page. This is a great way to cut down on the number of pages in an application and to be able to view all of the code you need at once.

You might recall our cookbook example from the last chapter. We used parameters set in the hyperlink of the first page to pass to the action page for output. Using conditional logic, we can test to see if the URL parameter is present (has been defined). If it is not present, we can be assured that no link has been clicked, and determine that we should show the cookbook choices. If the link has been clicked, we should perform the processing code to handle the user's choice as passed in the URL parameter.

Write this code into Studio, save it "Defined.cfm," and view it in your browser:

Listing 7.5 Defined.cfm

```
<html>
<head>
        <title>Favorite Cook Books</title>
</head>

<body>

<!---Use the isDefined function to determine if the URL.book
parameter exists---->

<cfif isDefined("URL.book")>
        Your favorite cook book is <b><cfoutput>#URL.book#</
cfoutput></b>,
        <br>published in <b><cfoutput>#URL.year#</cfoutput></
b>.
```

```
</cfif>

<br>
<br>
Choose your favorite cook book:<br>

<cfset cookbook1 = "Julia Child & Friends">
<cfset cookbook2 = "Martha Stewart's">

<cfoutput>
<a href="Defined.cfm?book=#URLEncodedFormat
(cookbook1)#&year=1975">#cookbook1#</a>
<br>
<a href="Defined.cfm?book=#URLEncodedFormat
(cookbook2)#&year=2001">#cookbook2#</a>
</cfoutput>
<br>

</body>
</html>
```

A number of things are introduced here. First, note that the isDefined() function takes one argument—the value whose existence is being tested for. IsDefined() returns TRUE if the value exists, and FALSE if the value does not exist.

<NOTE>

There is another function, ParameterExists(), that checks to see if a variable exists or not. This function has been deprecated since version 4.5 and should not be used. I mention it here because you are likely to come across it in older applications.

The first time this page is accessed, no link could have been clicked, so the URL.Book variable won't exist. Therefore the isDefined() function evaluates to FALSE, and the code inside that <CFIF> block is completely ignored. The rest of the template continues processing normally. Figure 7.2 shows our result.

Once we click on one of the choices, the URL.Book parameter is passed back to this page and is therefore defined, so the code inside the <CFIF> block does process. But the rest of the template processes, too—it is not

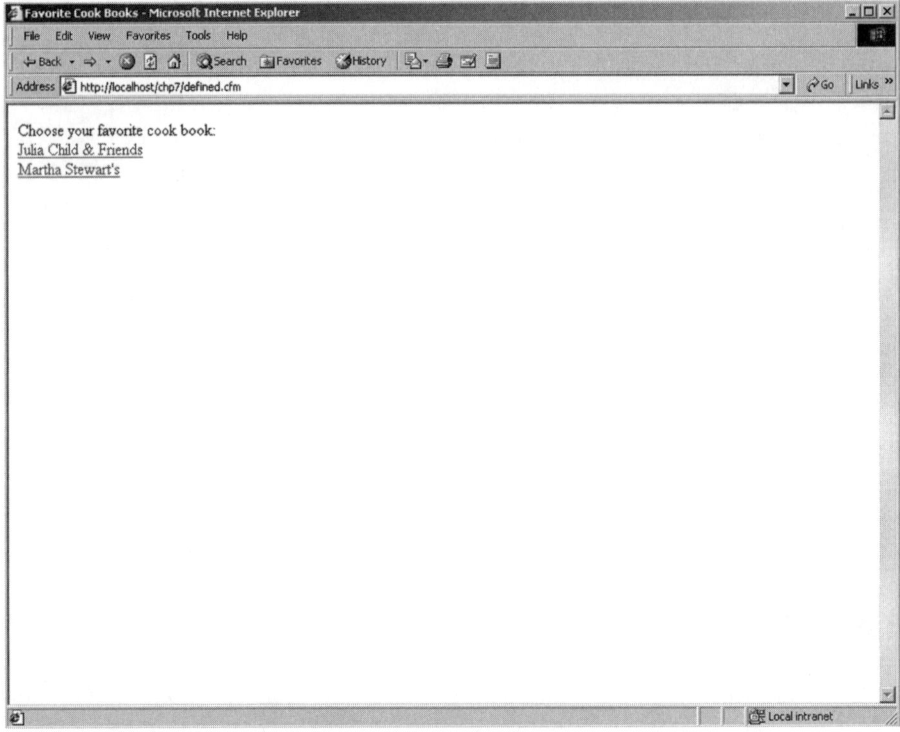

Figure 7.2 Using conditional logic to create a self-posting form.

inside the <CFIF> block and therefore has no constraints on it. The menu of cookbook choices will always be displayed. This is shown in Figure 7.3.

The way it's written now, this template allows you to go on choosing a different cookbook all day long, since the page posts to itself, and the menu is always displayed beneath the output. Let's say you want to show the menu only if the user has not clicked a link. In that case, the menu itself must be placed inside a conditional logic block. Here's how it looks:

Listing 7.6 Defined.cfm Updated

```
<html>
<head>
        <title>Favorite Cook Books</title>
</head>

<body>

<!---If they clicked a book title,
```

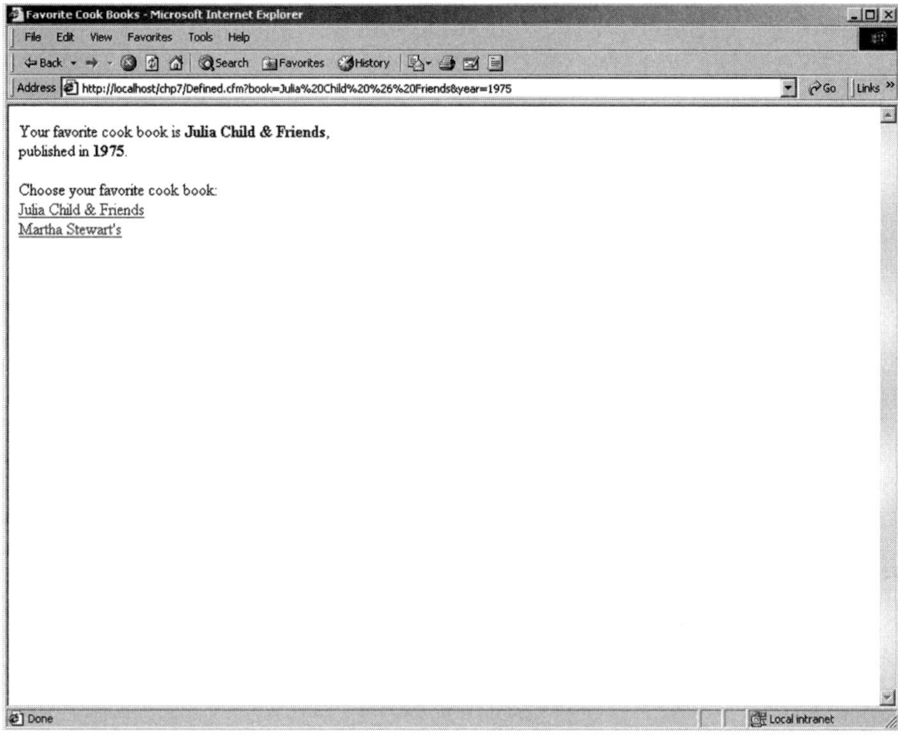

Figure 7.3 Passing the URL.Book parameter in the URL triggers the conditional logic statement.

```
process the code that outputs their choice---->

<cfif isDefined("URL.book")>
        Your favorite cook book is <b><cfoutput>#URL.book#</
cfoutput></b>,
        <br>published in <b><cfoutput>#URL.year#</cfoutput></
b>
<br>
<br>

<cfelse>
<!---Otherwise, the URL param is not defined, so they must
        not have clicked a link. Therefore, show them the
        menu.---->

Choose your favorite cook book:<br>

<cfset cookbook1 = "Julia Child & Friends">
<cfset cookbook2 = "Martha Stewart's">
```

```
<cfoutput>
<a href="Defined.cfm?book=#URLEncodedFormat(cookbook1)
#&year=1975">Julia Child & Friends</a>
<br>
<a href="Defined.cfm?book=#URLEncodedFormat(cookbook2)
#&year=2001">Martha Stewart's</a>
</cfoutput>
<br>

</cfif>

</body>
</html>
```

Notice that we leave the HTML <body> and <html> tags outside the <cfif> block so that they always process. Figure 7.4 shows the result in a browser.

Figure 7.4 Now that the entire page is inside a conditional block, the menu will display only the first time the page is accessed.

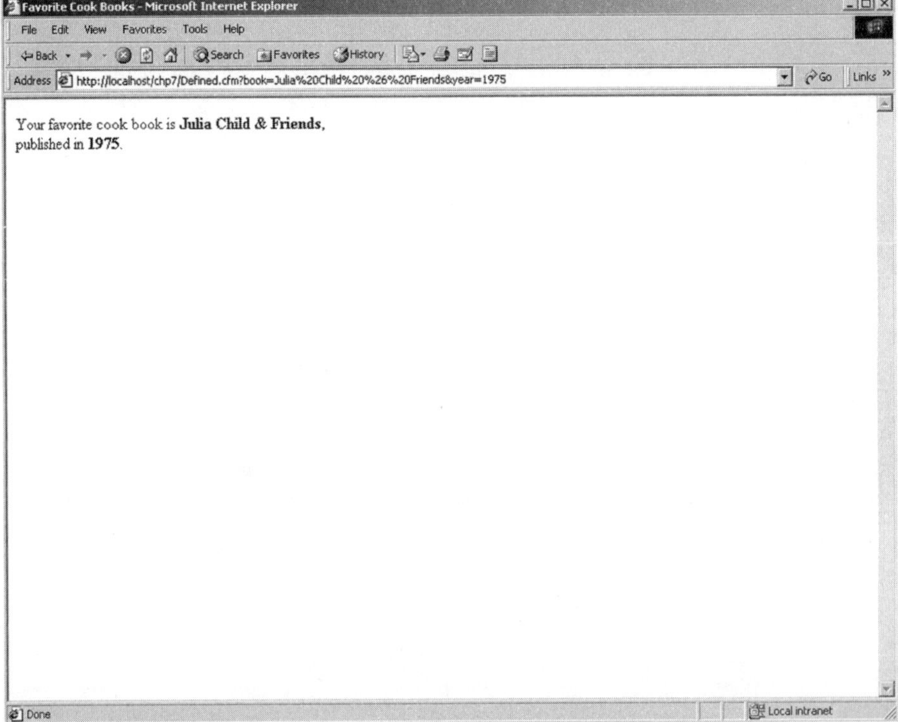

Nesting Conditional Logic

We can make our example a little more sophisticated by using nested <cfif> blocks. There is no theoretical limit to the number of layers deep you can nest your conditional logic, but application design generally dictates that more than three layers will give you a slight performance penalty. You do not need to do anything special to nest <cfif> blocks. You just write them as you otherwise would. Listing 7.7 is an example of how you would not just output the information passed in a URL, but do something extra and display different text depending on which choice the user made.

Listing 7.7 Nesting Conditional Logic

```
<html>
<head>
        <title>Favorite Cook Books</title>
</head>

<body>

<!---If they clicked a book title,
process the code that outputs their choice---->

<cfif isDefined("URL.book")>
        Your favorite cook book is <b><cfoutput>#URL.book#</
cfoutput></b>,
        <br>published in <b><cfoutput>#URL.year#</cfoutput></
b>.

        <cfif URL.Year less than or equal to "1983">

<!----The year the book was published is either 1983 or earlier.--->

Cook books published before 1983 or so use a lot of butter in
their recipes, <br>
and specify comparatively short cooking times for steaks.<br>

        <cfelse>
<!---The year is later than 1983, so make this statement.--->

Cook books from this period tend to focus on lighter recipes
that accommodate a fast-paced lifestyle.<br>

<!---End check for publication year--->
        </cfif>
```

```
<cfelse>
<!---The URL param is not defined, so they must not have
clicked a link. Therefore, show them the menu.------->

Choose your favorite cook book:<br>

<cfset cookbook1 = "Julia Child & Friends">
<cfset cookbook2 = "Martha Stewart's">

<cfoutput>
<a href="Defined.cfm?book=#URLEncodedFor-
mat(cookbook1)#&year=1975">Julia Child & Friends</a>
<br>
<a href="Defined.cfm?book=#URLEncodedFor-
mat(cookbook2)#&year=2001">Martha Stewart's</a>
</cfoutput>
<br>

</cfif>
</body>
</html>
</html>
```

Here we test to see what year the book they chose was published in. We can then make some vaguely witty remarks based on this information. Note that we could also have performed some conditional processing based on a test of the book title chosen—for instance, like this:

```
<cfif URL.Book is "Julia Child & Friends">
      Some code.

<cfelse>
     Some other code.

</cfif>
```

We have used indenting and comments in the above code to assist in readability. It is much easier to know which <cfif> statement you are ending if you make note of it and indent the block (see Figure 7.5).

<CFPARAM>

In the previous examples in this chapter, we have used the IsDefined( ) function to test for the existence of a URL parameter. The <CFPARAM>

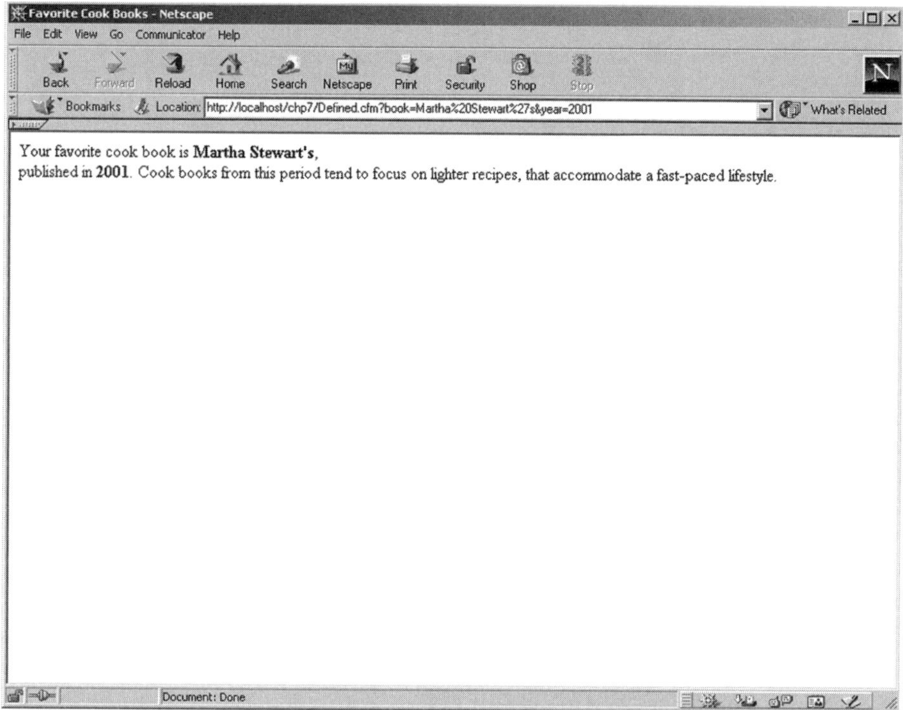

Figure 7.5 The result of running the page and clicking Martha Stewart's book.

tag allows you to test for the existence of a variable and to assign the variable a default value if it does not exist. The <CFPARAM> tag has the following structure:

```
<CFPARAM name="variable name"
         type="variable data type"
         default="default variable value">
```

The name attribute holds the name of your variable—for instance, "URL.Book." The optional type attribute holds the data type of the variable. If the type attribute is omitted, type is set to "any." Table 7.2 shows the possible values for this attribute.

Table 7.2 Possible Data Types for the <CFPARAM> Tag

Data Type	*Data Type*
Any	Query
Array	String

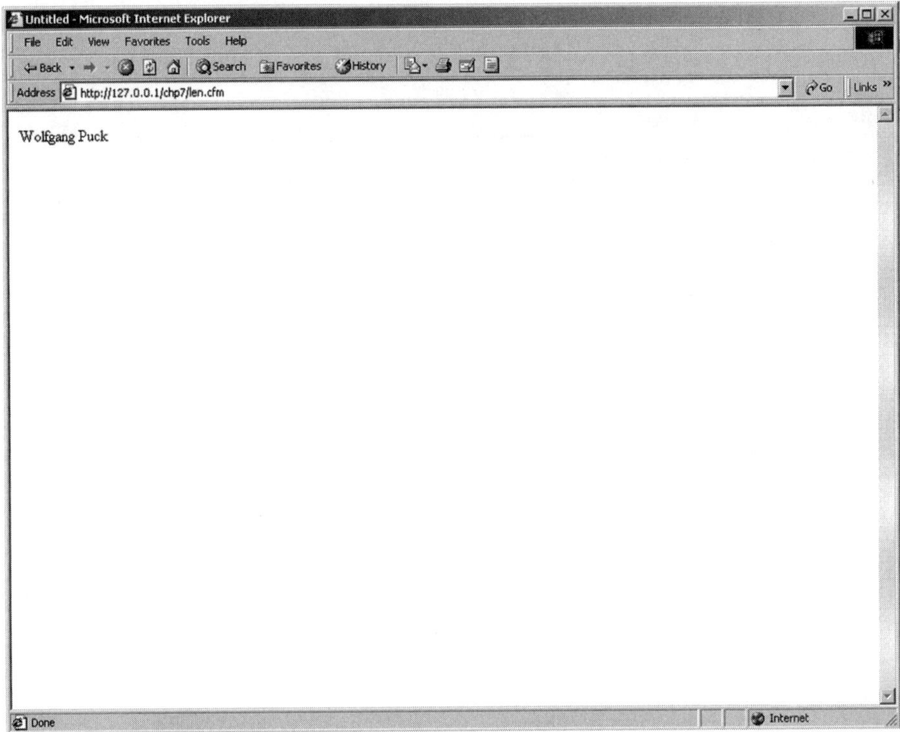

Figure 7.6 Outputting the value of a URL variable even though no URL parameter is appended to the URL.

Table 7.2 Continued	
Binary	Struct (a ColdFusion structure)
Boolean	UUID (a 31-character Universally Unique Identifier)
Date	Variable Name (a variable name)
Numeric	

The "default" attribute of the <CFPARAM> tag allows you to assign a default value to the variable specified in the name attribute if it does not exist. If it does exist, the current value will be used and the default value will be ignored.

<CFPARAM> can keep templates from crashing in the event that users attempt to access them without going though the proper channels.

For instance, we can use <CFPARAM> to assign a value to a URL variable in case none exists—like this (see Figure 7.6):

```
<CFPARAM name="URL.Book" default="Wolfgang Puck">
<cfoutput>#URL.book#</cfoutput>
```

That way the <CFOUTPUT> statement won't break the template if no URL.Book parameter exists, in the event that someone accesses the template without making a choice.

This tag can also cut down on coding time. It is just as good to write this:

```
<CFPARAM name="URL.Book" default="Wolfgang Puck">
```

as it is to write this:

```
<cfif NOT isDefined("URL.Book")>
        <CFSET URL.Book = "Wolfgang Puck">
</cfif>
```

This tag is also a key factor in writing your own ColdFusion custom tags, which we will explore in Chapter 14.

<CFSWITCH>, <CFCASE>, <CFDEFAULTCASE>

The <CFSWITCH>, <CFCASE>, and <CFDEFAULTCASE> tags work together to allow you to run code depending on the value of an expression. A Switch/Case set is similar to a series of if-elseif-else blocks, because it evaluates an expression passed to it. However, it evaluates more efficiently and is easier to read. If you have programmed in C or other languages, then you are familiar with this construction; ColdFusion uses it much the same way.

The <CFSWITCH> / <CFCASE> block has the following structure:

```
<CFSWITCH Expression="#Expression#">

       <CFCASE Value="SomeValue">
               Code to execute if the Expression variable is
equal to "SomeValue".
       </CFCASE>

       <CFCASE Value="SomeOtherValue" Delimiter="|">
Code to execute if the Expression variable is equal to any
item in pipe-delimited list called "SomeOtherValue".
       </CFCASE>
```

```
        <CFDEFAULTCASE>
              If the expression does not match a value
              in any of the CFCASEs above, then this
              default block will execute.
        </CFDEFAULTCASE>

</CFSWITCH>
```

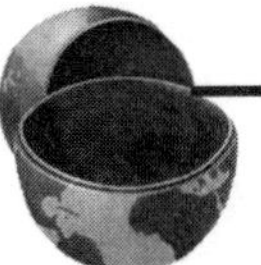

<NOTE>

These three tags must always be used together. ColdFusion returns an error if you attempt to use <CFCASE> without <CFSWITCH>.

If you have more than three conditional blocks (two or more <CFELSEIF> statements), consider using <CFSWITCH>. Your code will be cleaner and easier to manage. Also, it will perform faster, because you do not have to test against all possible conditions—ColdFusion will process the code within the first match it finds inside the <CFCASE> "value" attribute.

A nice feature of the <CFCASE> tag is that it allows you to enter multiple variables within the "value" attribute. Just separate them with commas, or specify a different delimiter using the "Delimiter" attribute. This is shown above, and demonstrated in Listing 7.6.

If we extend our cookbook example above, one can quickly see that we could proliferate different code blocks to execute based on publication year rather quickly. Right now, our example is manageable because we have only two options: before 1983 and after 1983. Let's say we wanted to make a different comment about a number of different years. This code would become very long, and it would be a drag because we would have to keep rewriting the expression. It would also perform comparatively slowly to using <CFSWITCH> and <CFCASE>. So let's modify our code to nest the Switch / Case block inside the IsDefined block.

Listing 7.8 Using Switch / Case

```
<html>
<head>
       <title>Favorite Cook Books</title>
</head>

<body>

<!---If they clicked a book title,
process the code that outputs their choice---->
```

```
<cfif isDefined("URL.book")>
        Your favorite cook book is <b><cfoutput>#URL.book#
</cfoutput></b>,
        <br>published in <b><cfoutput>#URL.year#</cfoutput></
b>.

<!---Evaluate URL.Year and output a different
        comment based on the value------->

<cfswitch expression="#URL.Year#">

        <cfcase value="1975">
                 Cooks books from 1975 are very comprehensive.
        </cfcase>
<!----The comment is the same for the years 1980 through 1982,
so put these values in a list in one CFCASE--->

        <cfcase value="1980, 1981, 1982">
             Cooks books from this year were often oversized.
        </cfcase>

        <cfcase value="1983">
                For some reason, most of the cook books from
                1983 are a shade of blue.
        </cfcase>

        <cfcase value="1984">

                I don't know why but not one of the cook books
                published in 1984 has any pictures whatsoever.
        </cfcase>

        <cfdefaultcase>
                I don't have a comment about that
                publication year.
        </cfdefaultcase>
<!--exit switch against URL.Year------->
</cfswitch>

<cfelse>
<!--The URL param is not defined, so they must not have
clicked a link.
Therefore, show them the menu.------->
Choose your favorite cook book:<br>

<cfset cookbook1 = "Julia Child & Friends">
<cfset cookbook2 = "Martha Stewart's">
```

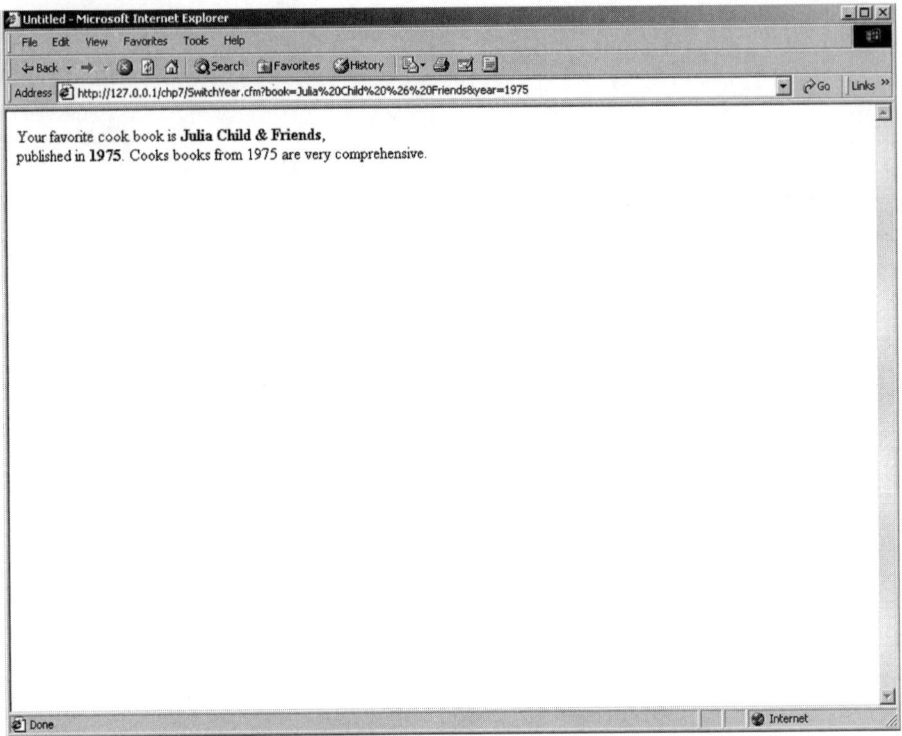

Figure 7.7 Only the code inside the CFCASE for 1975 executes, since URL.Year is 1975.

```
<cfoutput>
<a href="SwitchYear.cfm?book=#URLEncodedFor-
mat(cookbook1)#&year=1975">Julia Child & Friends</a>
<br>
<a href="SwitchYear.cfm?book=#URLEncodedFor-
mat(cookbook2)#&year=2001">Martha Stewart's</a>
</cfoutput>
<br>

</cfif>
</body>
</html>
```

The code above is the same as our previous listing, except that we don't nest the CFIF statements—we put a Switch / Case block in there instead. It's cleaner, it handles more values easily, and it executes faster (if you are testing against more than three values). See Figure 7.7.

We will use the concepts developed so far in this chapter as the building blocks of many applications we'll make. Let's explore how we can achieve flow control in our templates and applications by using conditional logic and Switch / Case blocks.

Flow Control

Flow control is the art of properly routing the execution of code. It refers to collections of statements (usually loops or conditional logic blocks) that control the order in which certain code is executed. Without flow control, your ColdFusion templates would execute top to bottom, all the way through. There would be so many different pages to account for that you might as well be writing in HTML.

<NOTE>

We will discuss loops in Chapter 12.

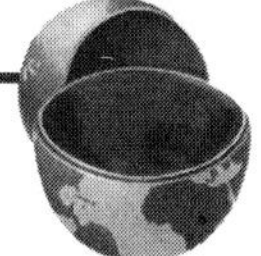

You can control the flow of our templates using not only statements, but any HTML or ColdFusion code inside your CFCASE blocks. Three main tags help us do this:

- <CFINCLUDE>
- <CFABORT>
- <CFLOCATION>

These tags are rather simple, so let's quickly examine each of them. We will then be able to create a flow control switch box for a website that allows us to separate the flow logic from any display code.

<CFINCLUDE>

The purpose of the <CFINCLUDE> tag is to include code from an outside template in the current template. Any text or code inside the included template will act as if it had been cut and pasted in its entirety into the exact location that you call the <CFINCLUDE> tag. <CFINCLUDE> takes one attribute: the template to be included. You may include files to any depth you wish. That is, you can include a file within an included file within another included file, and so on.

Let's say we have two templates: index.cfm and Footer.cfm. Index.cfm is our main page, and Footer.cfm has just the code that we need to make the footer, which is the plain text links that will appear on every page. We want to keep the footer separate in its own file so that, if a link changes, we don't have to go back through every single template in our site and change the code. We only have to change it in one place. We also don't have to look at it all the time when we are working on a different aspect of the application; the footer code won't be cluttering up our workspace. Another benefit of including files is that it helps you keep the graphic designers' work separate from your work. While you can use it for whatever you like, it can also be used in a manner similar to importing classes or including a library.

Here are the listings for each template.

Listing 7.9 Index.cfm

```
<html>
<head>
        <title>Flow Control</title>
</head>

<body>

I am the index page.
<br> I have a lot of content
<br>
<!---Include the footer--->
<cfinclude template = "Footer.cfm">

</body>
</html>
```

Listing 7.10 Footer.cfm

```
<br>

<hr width="150">

<br>
<center>
I am the footer template.
My job is to hold the navigation bar.
<br>

<!---navigation bar--->
```

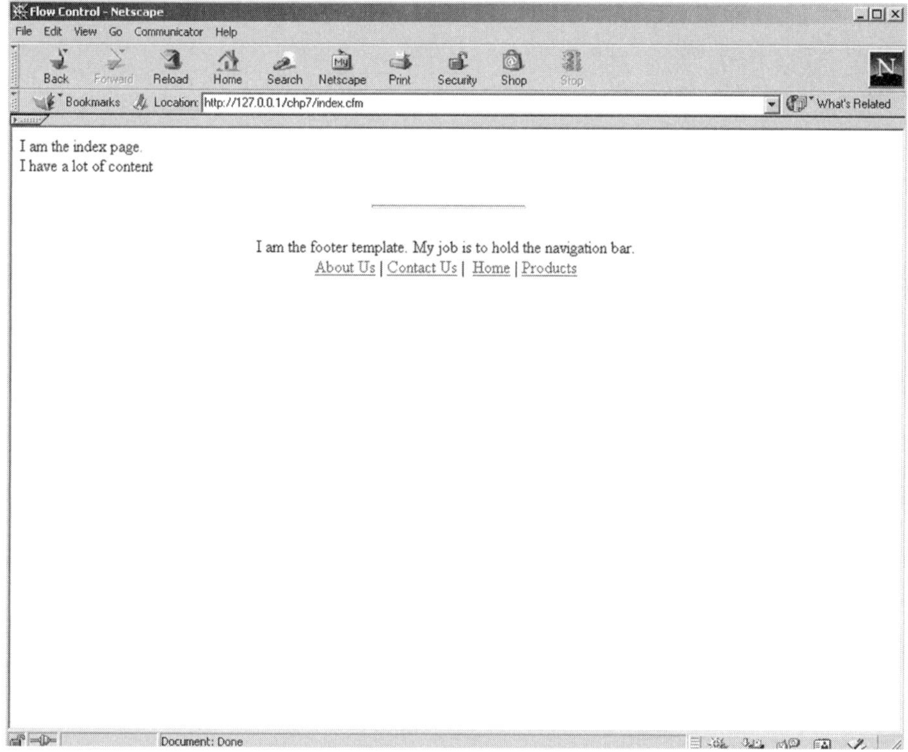

Figure 7.8 You can easily reuse code by putting it in a separate file and calling it with the <CFINCLUDE> tag.

```
<a href="about.cfm">About Us</a> | <a href="con-
tact.cfm">Contact Us</a> | 
<a href="index.cfm">Home</a> | <a href="prod-
ucts.cfm">Products</a>
</center>
```

As you can see, Listing 7.10 has no <body> or <html> tags. That's because those tags are already in index.cfm, and since the footer is included using the <CFINCLUDE> tag, all of the navigation bar code is just plunked right in at the point where we call the tag.

Load Index.cfm in a browser and give it a try. Figure 7.8 shows the results.

If you view the source of this file in your browser, you can see that the included footer file acts as if it were on the index.cfm page all along. We could do the same thing with the header. In fact, depending on how your page is laid out graphically, you could even include much of the main content of the page. We'll see how to do this in a moment.

<CFABORT>

The second flow control tag we will examine is <CFABORT>. This tag is used to stop template processing immediately at the location of the tag. ColdFusion will return everything on the template up to the point where the <CFABORT> tag is.

CFABORT takes one optional attribute: "showerror." This attribute is used to display an error message at the point that processing stops.

Returning to our index and footer page example above, we can demonstrate the CFABORT tag by placing it in the index.cfm page, immediately above the footer.cfm include.

Listing 7.11 Using CFABORT to Stop Page Processing

```
<html>
<head>
        <title>Flow Control</title>
</head>

<body>

I am the index page.<br>
I have a lot of content.
<br>

<!---Stop processing before we get to the footer--->

<cfabort showerror="This is my <b>customized</b>
        error message.<br>As you can see, I can put HTML in
here.">
<cfinclude template = "Footer.cfm">

</body>
</html>
```

Figure 7.9 shows the results of calling this page in the browser.

As you can see in Figure 7.9, using the CFABORT tag immediately halts page processing, so that the CFINCLUDE tag which includes the footer

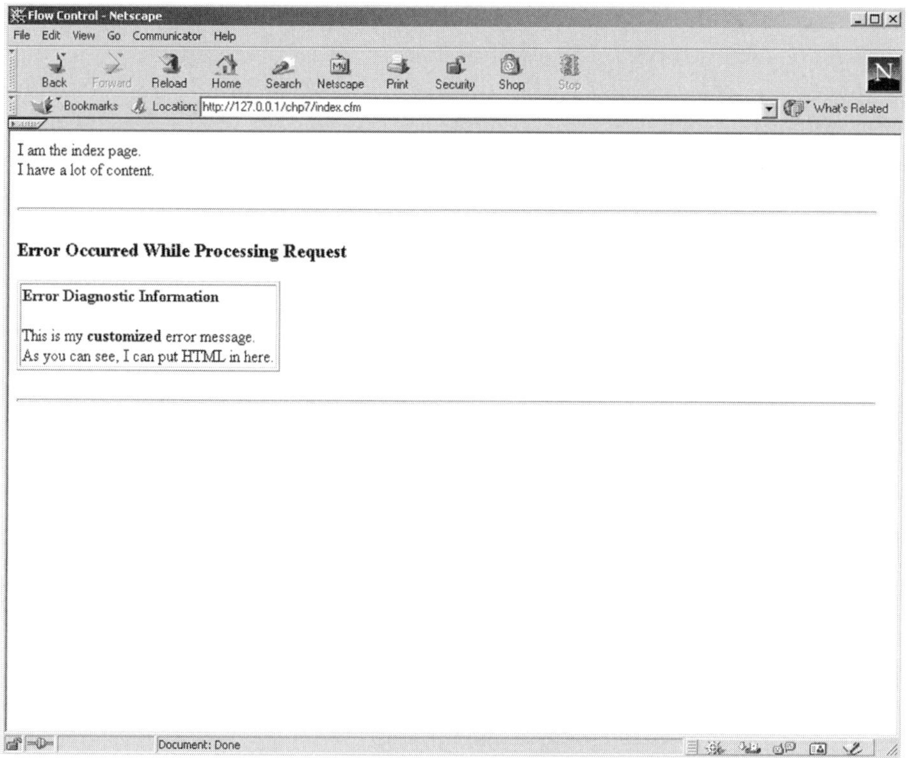

Figure 7.9 You can customize the error message returned by ColdFusion when halting page processing.

never gets called. In Chapter 25 we will learn a little more about using this tag in conjunction with CFERROR to produce elegant error-handling techniques.

<CFLOCATION>

The last flow control tag we will look at now is <CFLOCATION>. This tag is used somewhat like "location.href" in JavaScript. The main difference is that <CFLOCATION> does not return any information to the client. It simply immediately redirects to the page specified in the "URL" attribute.

CFLOCATION has the following two attributes: URL and AddToken. The value of the URL attribute can be any web resource. AddToken takes the value “Yes” or “No” and is used to maintain continuity between client requests. The AddToken attribute is necessary only when Client Management is enabled for the application and you want to append the client identifier strings to the URL. The Default is “No.” We will learn more about Client Management in Chapter 18.

Let’s replace the CFABORT tag we just wrote into the index.cfm page with a CFLOCATION tag. By setting the URL attribute to “http://www.macromedia.com,” we will be instantly whisked away to the Macromedia page without ever seeing the index.cfm page.

Listing 7.12 Using CFLOCATION to Go to Another Web Resource

```
<html>
<head>
       <title>Flow Control</title>
</head>

<body>

I am the index page.<br>
I have a lot of content.
<br>

<!---Since we cflocate right here, not only will the footer
not display, nothing on this page will display. It will be as
if we typed the Macromedia URL directly into the address bar
---->

<cflocation url="http://www.macromedia.com">

<cfinclude template = "Footer.cfm">
</body>
</html>
```

<NOTE>

You must not use <cflocation> on the same template that you need to set a cookie. The data will not be sent to the client, and your cookie will not be set. ColdFusion will not throw an error.

You can specify a local resource as well. Just reference it with the appropriate directory information. For instance, to do a CFLOCATION to a file one directory above the current directory, you would write this:

```
<cflocation url="../SomeFile.cfm">
```

A Complete Site Flow Control Framework

Using the tags we have learned in this chapter, you can implement a complete flow control framework for your applications. A flow control framework keeps the presentation of your pages (graphics and HTML layouts) entirely separate from your ColdFusion code. What's nice about this is that it offers a way around the smushing together of layers that plagues a tremendous number of websites. It also offers me an opportunity to demonstrate just about everything we covered in this chapter all in one neat package.

A Word about Fusebox

You may have heard of Fusebox. This is a methodology for writing ColdFusion sites created by Steve Nelson and cultivated a great deal by Hal Helms and many other developers. The idea is that every component of your application is one "fuse" of the application, like the fuses within the fuse box of a house. If one fuse goes out, the others remain on because your code is modular.

You can read more about it at Fusebox.org. This site, itself written with the Fusebox methodology, allows you to download the open-source code that makes up the site so you can see how it works. There is also a book available at www.SecretAgents.com if you want to learn how to work this way. Fusebox has a number of advantages and avid followers; it also has some disadvantages and the attendant detractors. While it makes debugging and adding or removing components very easy, it takes a good deal more up-front development time and can be confusing to a beginner.

It is worth checking out, especially because you are likely to come across it as you work, and it will be helpful to at least understand the basics.

I mention this methodology here because this framework, while not Fusebox, owes its logic to Fusebox. Also, it is an increasingly popular way to write

ColdFusion applications, so you're likely to hear about it. I appreciate the efforts of Mr. Nelson and more than 200 other developers in shaping this methodology.

Description of the Framework

We will create a main page, index.cfm, which will hold the "fuse box." The fuse box is just a <CFSWITCH>, which holds a <CFCASE> for the major components of our site. Each <CFCASE> is one "fuse," or one file component of the site. By using URL parameters in our hyperlinks to specify which page we want to view, we can separate the presentation from the logic entirely.

Here is a list of all of the components we need:

- An index page that holds a <cfswitch>. Each <cfcase> within the switch can route to the contents of one specific ColdFusion template.
- A header for the main graphic.
- A footer for the navigation bar.
- The "About Us" page.
- The "Contact Us" page.
- The default content for the index page.

You can put all of the listings below into a folder called "SwitchBox" and create a virtual site for the folder. Note that this is largely for demonstration of the concepts covered in this chapter. You may want to do things rather differently in a real-world application (though something similar has often been implemented in the real world). Otherwise, this will offer you a complete application framework, and you can easily add and substitute your own pages.

Listing 7.13 Index.cfm

```
<cfswitch expression="#URL.thisPage#">

<!---Include a different content page depending on
what was passed in the "thisPage" parameter.------->

<!---Notice that the AboutUs page is an HTML file.
  Just to make the point that it's okay to include
  other file types besides CFM.------->
  <cfcase value="About">
```

```
        <cfinclude template = "AboutUs.html">
  </cfcase>

  <cfcase value="Contact">
        <cfinclude template = "ContactUs.cfm">
  </cfcase>

  <cfcase value="Products">
        <cfinclude template = "Products.cfm">
  </cfcase>

<!---Since they haven't clicked on a link the first
time the page is accessed, the URL.thisPage variable
is an empty string. Therefore this code will run.------->
  <cfdefaultcase>
        <cfinclude template="Main.cfm">
  </cfdefaultcase>

<!---End switch against URL.thisPage.------->
</cfswitch>

<cfinclude template = "Footer.cfm">
```

Listing 7.14 Header.cfm

```
<!DOCTYPE HTML PUBLIC "-//W3C//DTD HTML 4.0 Transitional//EN">

<html>
<head>
      <title>Switch box</title>
</head>

<body>

<!---This header will be included at the top of every page,
since the index page is really the only page we're ever
actually "on"------->

<h3>Header</h2>
<br>
<h2>Core ColdFusion 5</h2>

<table bgcolor="#008000" width="80%" align="center">
<tr>
```

```
<td><font color="white" face="Verdana" size="+2">I am the
header.cfm page.</font></td>
</tr>

<tr bgcolor="#0000ff">
<td><font color="white" face="Verdana" size="+1">Put a nav bar
here.</font></td>
</tr>

</table>
<br>
```

Listing 7.15 Footer.cfm

```
<h3>Footer</h3>
<br>
<hr width="150">
<br>
<center>

<br>
My job is to hold the navigation bar.
<br>

<!---navigation bar. Notice that all the links point right
back to Index.cfm, they just pass a different "thisPage"
parameter. ------->

<a href="index.cfm?thisPage=about">About Us</a> | 
<a href="index.cfm?thisPage=contact">ContactUs</
a> | 
<a href="index.cfm">Home</a> | 
<a href="index.cfm?thisPage=products">Products</a>
</center>

</body>
</html>
```

Listing 7.16 AboutUs.html

```
<!---Include plain text and formatting for this information-
al page.------->
```

```
<h3>About Us</h3>
<br>

I have a lot of content
about how subversive our company is.
<br>
```

Listing 7.17 ContactUs.cfm

```
<h3>Contact Us</h3>
<br>

<cfif NOT isDefined("URL.method")>

You can <i>email</i> me.<br>
You can also <i>call me</i> on the phone.
<br>
<br>
Which method do you prefer?
<br>

<a href="index.cfm?thisPage=contact&method=email">Email</a>

<br>

<a href="index.cfm?thisPage=contact&method=call">Call</a>

<cfelse>

      <cfif URL.Method is "Email">
            <!---No email available, so show error.---->
            <cfabort showerror="Sorry, I don't have an
                                    email address.">

      <br>
      <cfelse>
            <!---Redirect them to the yellow pages
                                          website ----->
            <cflocation url="http://www.yellowpages.com">
      <!---End email/phone check--->
      </cfif>

<!---End Method exists check--->
</cfif>
```

Listing 7.18 Products.cfm

```
<!---This page is just informational content,
and so it includes text and formatting.------->

<h3>Products</h3>
I am the Products page.<br>
I have information on all the things we sell.
<br>
Here are some items:
<ul>
      <li> Skateboard
      <li> Switchblade
      <li> Cream Rinse
</ul>
```

Listing 7.19 Main.cfm

```
<!---This is the default content page.------->
<h3>I am Main</h3>
<br>
Here is the menu:<br>
<ul>
        <li><a href="index.cfm?thisPage=About">About Us</a>
        <li><a href="index.cfm?thisPage=Contact">Contact Us</
a>
        <li><a href="index.cfm?thisPage=Products">Products</a>
</ul>
<br>
```

If you browse to the INDEX.CFM page you've saved, you will see the content for the MAIN.CFM page. MAIN.CFM is included because no link has been clicked, so the value of the URL parameter, URL.thisPage, is an empty string, and the only case of the <CFSWITCH> statement that can be used is <CFDEFAULTCASE>. None of the other <CFCASE> statements are true. Once you click any other page, the "thisPage" parameter is passed, and the <CFCASE> that contains that parameter as its value will evaluate to true. ColdFusion will therefore follow the instructions inside that <CFCASE> clause. Those instructions are to <CFINCLUDE> a file, so that file will be the content you see between the header and footer (see Figure 7.10).

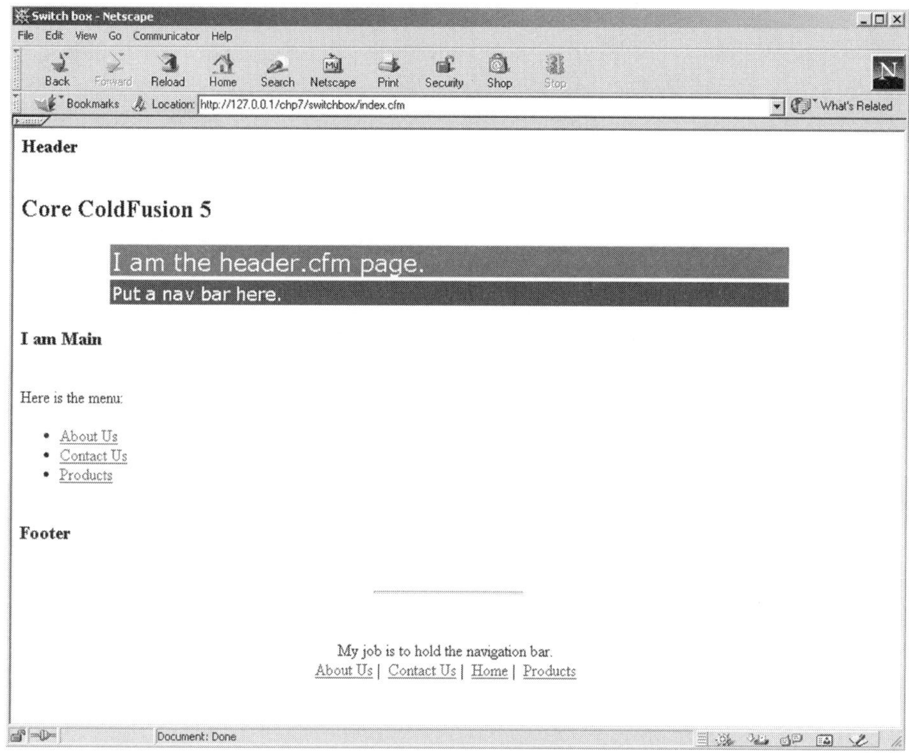

Figure 7.10 The default page displayed when you bring up the index.cfm page.

You've got an entire site framework that you can use. This kind of application scales rather well. I have written very large applications (more than 600 templates) using a similar technique, and I've found they perform quickly and are easy to maintain.

As you can see in the address bar (Figure 7.11), we have not left the index page, since anything the user sees is included.

<NOTE>

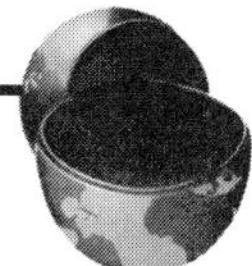

You don't want to use CFABORT in the way shown in Figure 7.12. It causes the "Error occurred while processing request" statement to show, and this isn't really an error. I include it in this way merely to illustrate again that the footer.cfm template does not execute, since the page was aborted. Otherwise, this is a pretty good framework to use.

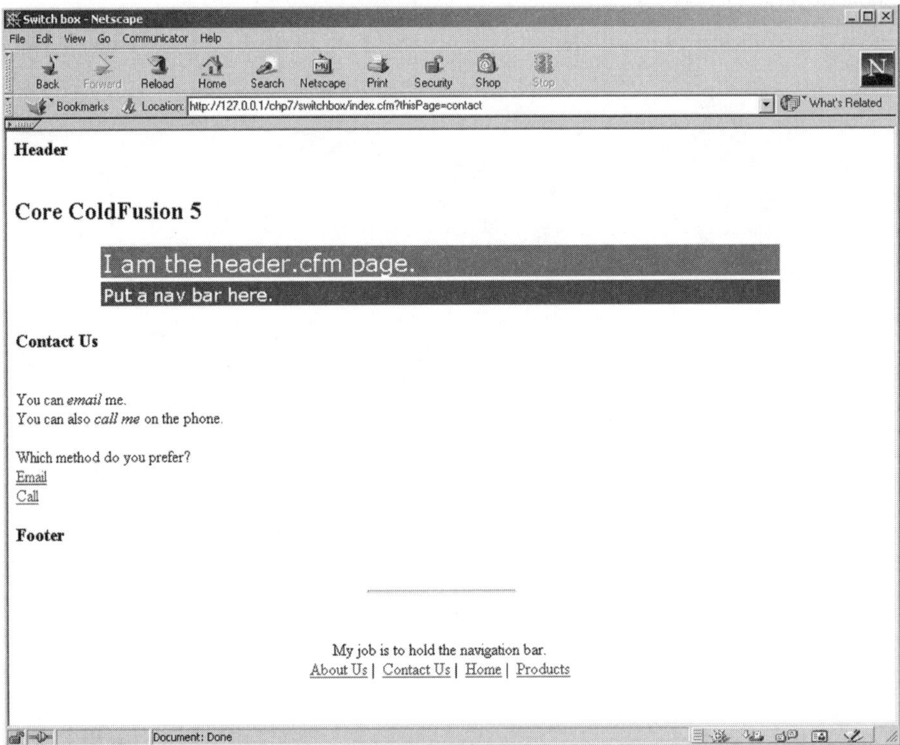

Figure 7.11 Clicking on the Contact Us link keeps the same header and footer and simply includes a separate middle content page.

This methodology is not strict Fusebox in any sense. This is an introduction to the concepts. If you find it a useful way to code your applications, that's terrific. If not, that's fine too. Either way, we'll revisit this method of coding many times throughout the rest of this book, and it has given me a good chance to put a number of the things we've learned into action all at once.

And now, on to working with lists, complex data types, and functions.

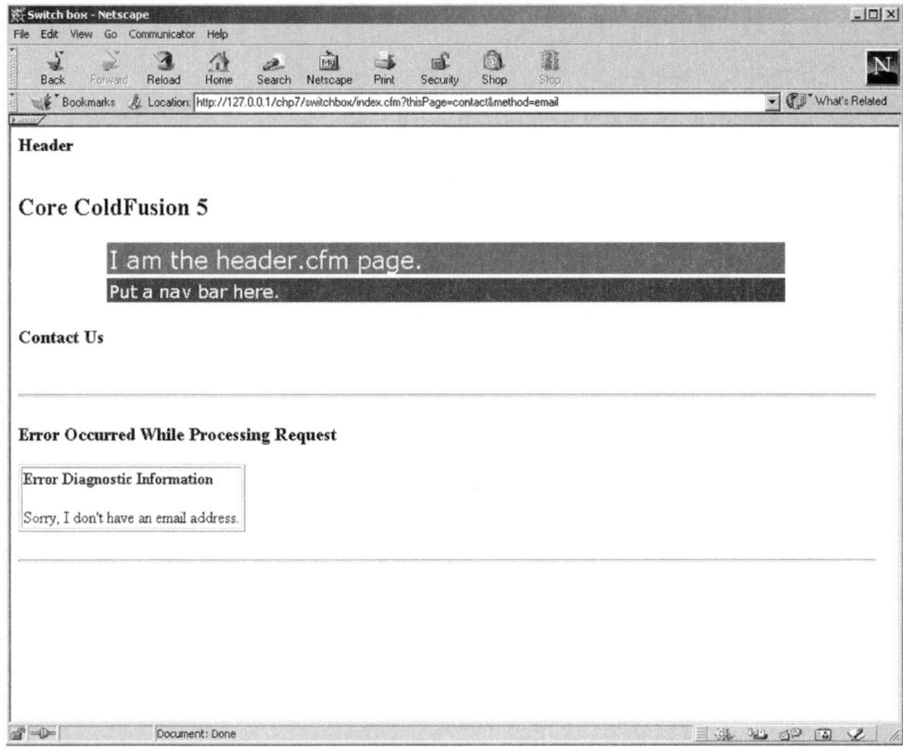

Figure 7.12 Clicking on the "Email" option causes our abort statement to run.

FUNCTIONS AND COMPLEX DATA TYPES

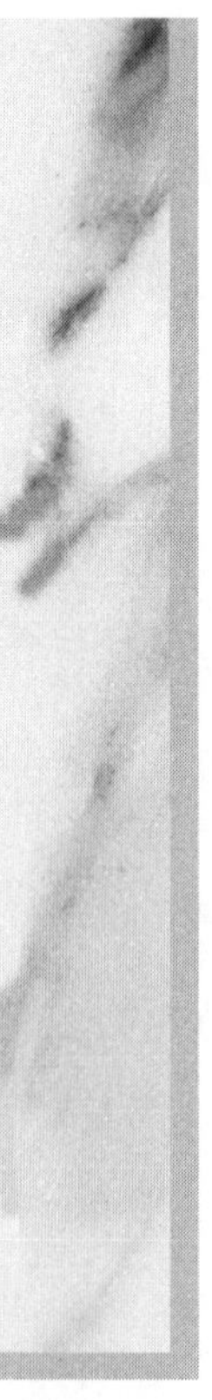

Topics in This Chapter

- What are functions?
- Different kinds of ColdFusion functions and how to use them
- Introduction to CFSCRIPT
- Creating user-defined functions
- <CFDUMP>
- Working with lists
- Working with arrays
- Working with structures
- <CFHTMLHEAD>
- Creating a complete HTML meta tag application

Chapter 8

By this point, we have already used a number of ColdFusion functions, including URLEncodedFormat, IsDefined(), Now(), and Hour(). ColdFusion has nearly 200 functions available for you to use, and new with ColdFusion 5, you can create your own user-defined functions to encapsulate typical operations. For this chapter I have put functions and complex data types together, because many functions exist specifically in order to perform some operation on complex data types. After a general discussion of functions, we will focus specifically on those used in dealing with lists, arrays, and structures. Along the way, we'll pick up a tag new with ColdFusion 5, <CFDUMP>.

What Are Functions?

Functions manipulate values for return, which is to say that in general they do not modify the data itself; they modify how the data is output, or what part is output. ColdFusion functions take the following structure:

FunctionName(argument)

Functions are the other half of the ColdFusion Markup Language, and they can be invaluable to your development. There are actually 16 different kinds of functions available to you in ColdFusion, if you include user-defined functions. In this chapter we will take a look at many different functions. Once you are familiar with their syntax, they are easy to use, and I encourage you to return frequently to Appendix B, "ColdFusion Function Reference," to see if a function you need hasn't already been written.

Here are the different kinds of functions and what they do. Note that some functions may overlap into different categories:

- **Array functions** create, convert, manipulate, and destroy one-, two-, and three-dimensional arrays.
- **Bit and Set manipulation functions** perform operations on bit-level data.
- **Client variable functions** let you manipulate variables in the CLIENT scope.
- **Data Formatting functions** manipulate the format of data.
- **Date and Time functions** create, convert, manipulate, and parse date and time variables.
- **Expression Evaluation functions** let you create and manipulate expressions.
- **International functions** support date and time values and other data for different locales around the world.
- **List functions** manipulate lists.
- **Mathematical functions** do calculations on numbers, create random numbers, and perform conversions.
- **Miscellaneous functions** let you check for existence of and format certain parameters.
- **Query functions** perform operations on queries and queried data.
- **Security functions** help you access security context information returned by the <CFAUTHENTICATE> tag.
- **String manipulation functions** are used to compare and convert text strings.
- **Structure functions** create, convert, manipulate, and destroy structures.
- **System functions** allow you to access and manipulate directory, temporary file, and path information.

- **User-defined functions** are functions that you write in order to encapsulate some functionality, give a name to it, and reference it as you would any other function.

Nested Functions and Mask Functions

You have already put nested functions to work in Chapter 7, when you used Now() and Hour() together to return only the ordinal value for the hour of the current time. You might define a *nested function* as just a function that takes another function as its argument. There is not a theoretical limit to how deep one can nest functions.

Here is a common example, also using date-time functions:

```
<cfset temp = DateFormat(Now())>
<cfoutput>#temp#</cfoutput>
```

Since the Now() function returns the current system time accurate to milliseconds, it is not always useful for display on its own. By using the formatting function DateFormat, we can manipulate the appearance of the value that the Now() function returns. Without specifying a *mask*—that is, a specific appearance for a value—the DateFormat() function will return a date in its default format, like this:

27-Dec-02

When working with Date and Time functions, you have a number of options when specifying the mask to use. In order to use a mask, which most of the formatting functions have available, you write a comma after the value and then use quote marks around the mask. For instance, to specify the date in this format:

6/10

for June 10, you write this in ColdFusion:

```
<cfset temp = DateFormat(Now(), "m/dd")>
```

<NOTE>

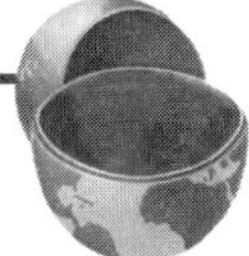

Check the function reference, Appendix B of this book, for complete information regarding data functions and formatting masks. There are far too many to consider in detail here, but we will use functions freely throughout the remainder of the book. If you have any questions about functions, Appendix B should answer them.

To create a more complex date value, we could add to the current date, and then format and output it. For instance, here is a way to add three months to whatever the current month is:

```
<cfset temp = DateFormat(DateAdd("m", 3, Now()), "m/dd")>
```

This example uses functions nested three deep to (1) get the current date-time, (2) add 3 to the month part of the value returned by Now(), and (3) format the output of that value with one place for the month (so no zero appears in front of it if it is a single-digit month), and always two digits for the day.

To spice things up, we can create a quick little form that allows a user to select a variable for ColdFusion to use in the DateAdd function. Check out Listing 8.1 to see how it works.

Listing 8.1 DateFor.cfm

```
<html>
<head>
	<title>Date Adder</title>
</head>

<body>

<h2>
Choose a number and I will tell you what the date will be
that many months from now.<br><br>
</h2>

<!----Check if the form has been submitted ----->

<cfif isDefined("FORM.MyDate")>

<!----Use a switch case to output a different suffix for the
number of month it is. For instance, "th" works well for
months 4-12, but outputting "the 2th month" would be incor-
rect.---->

Since today is the <cfoutput>
<CFSWITCH EXPRESSION="#Month(Now())#">
	<CFCASE VALUE="1">1st</CFCASE>
	<CFCASE VALUE="2">2nd</CFCASE>
	<CFCASE VALUE="3">3rd</CFCASE>
```

```
        <CFDEFAULTCASE>#Month(Now())#th</CFDEFAULTCASE>
</CFSWITCH>
</cfoutput> month, <br>

<!---Do the number crunching and format it---->
<cfset theDate = DateFormat(DateAdd("m", form.MyDate,
Now()), "mmmm dd")>

<!---Output the value--->
<cfoutput>#form.MyDate# months from now
                        will be #theDate#</cfoutput>

<!---End check for FORM.MyDate---->
</cfif>

<!---form that lets user choose from 1 to 6
                            months from now.------->

<form action="datefor.cfm" method="post">

<select name="MyDate">
     <option value="1">1
     <option value="2">2
     <option value="3">3
     <option value="4">4
     <option value="5">5
     <option value="6">6
</select>
       <input type="submit" name="Submit">
</form>

</body>
</html>
```

The output in Sun's HotJava Browser looks like Figure 8.1.

We can combine date functions with other kinds of functions as well. For our next example we'll introduce a number of new things. First, we will see how to use the IsDate function, which returns a Boolean true or false depending on whether or not the argument is a valid date. For debugging, we can employ the <CFDUMP> tag, new with ColdFusion 5, to output the variable being tested against.

First, let's use a valid date, such as Now() or "07-Jun-92," to see how this works (see Figure 8.2).

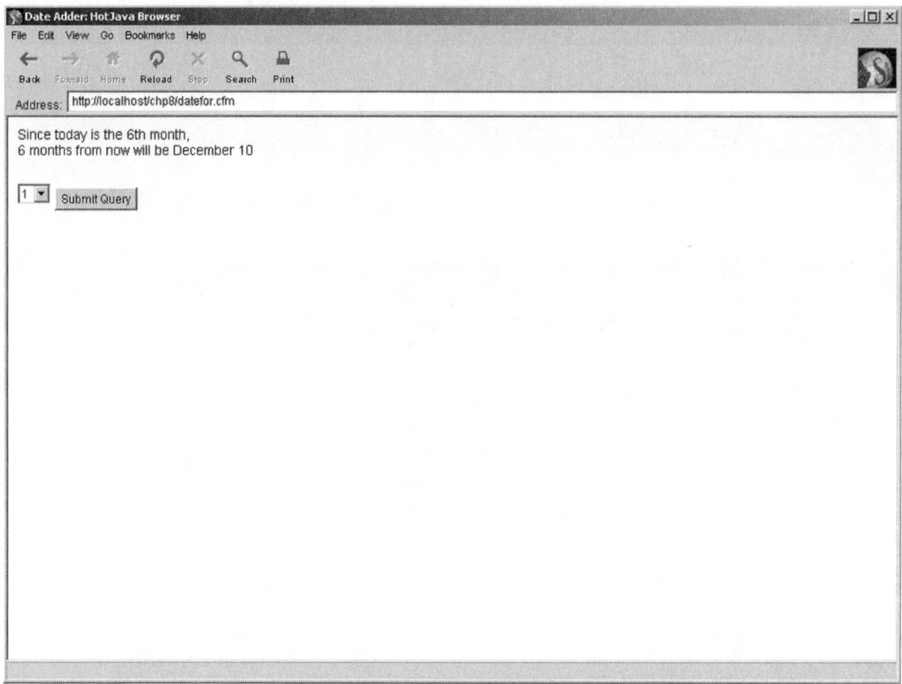

Figure 8.1 Functions nested three-deep output to the HotJava browser.

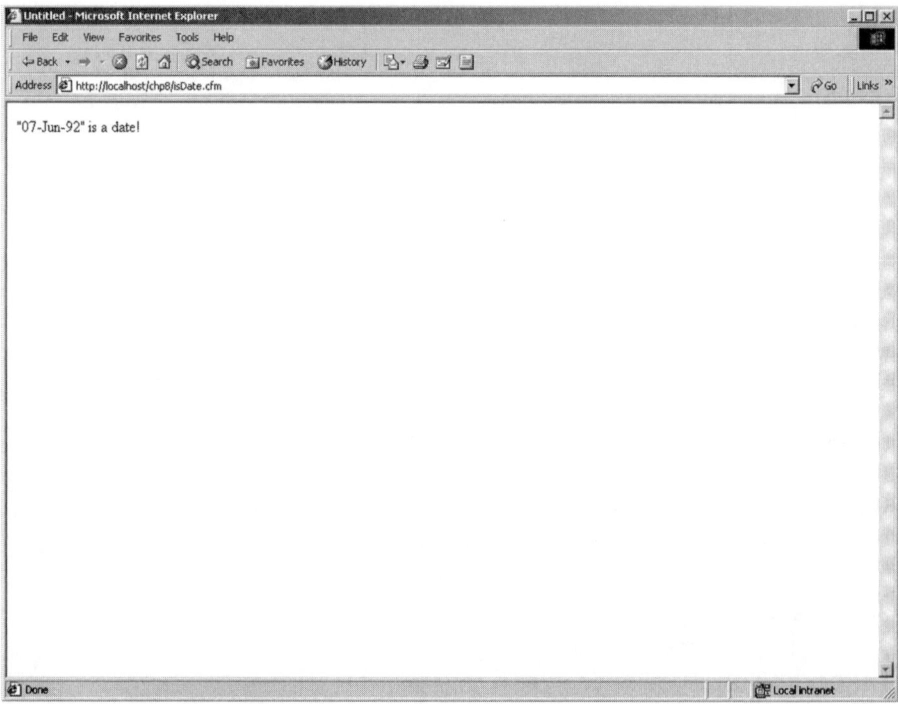

Figure 8.2 Checking for dates.

Listing 8.2 IsDate.cfm

```
<html>
<head>
       <title>IsDate</title>
</head>

<body>
<!---Date tester------->

<!---Set a string with a date value------->
<cfset Variables.myString = "07-Jun-92">

<!---Using the isDate function, determine whether
the MyString variable is a valid date.------->

<cfif isDate(Variables.MyString)>

<!---Use the DE (Delay Evaluation) function to
output the variable that was passed so we can
see what is being tested.------->

<cfoutput>#Variables.MyString#</cfoutput> is a date!

<cfelse>

<!---Use the new cfdump tag to output the variable--->

<cfdump var=#Variables.MyString#> isn't a date :(

<!----End check for isDate---->
</cfif>

</body>
</html>
```

Next, we can force a failure by using a regular text string, so we can see how <CFDUMP> works. It has one attribute, the variable to evaluate. Set the MyString value to "Bob." Here is your output:

```
Bob isn't a date :(
```

<CFDUMP>

The <CFDUMP> tag is useful for debugging. Ported over from Spectra, where it originated as <cfa_dump>, this tag displays simple variables, queries, arrays, structures, and WDDX packets. Previously, in order to output the key value pairs in a complex data type such as a structure, one had to perform a loop. For instance, to see all of the key-value pairs in the SESSION structure, you would have to write this:

```
<cfset strKeyArr = StructKeyArray(SESSION)>

      <cfloop from="1" to="#ArrayLen(strKeyArr)#"
             index="idx">
<cfoutput>Key #idx# is #strKeyArr[idx]#<br></cfoutput>
      </cfloop>
```

Now you've got that functionality encapsulated in the <cfdump> tag. In order to view the keys present in the session structure, and their values, you can just do this:

```
<cfdump var=#SESSION#>
```

The <cfdump> tag loops over all of the variables present in the specified variable or scope and outputs in a table. In Figure 8.3 we use <cfdump> to display all of the variables in the SESSION scope.

We'll use it occasionally in this chapter to check values in the arrays and structures we create. We will look at how this tag can be used in debugging in Appendix C, "Common Errors and What to Do About Them."

Now that you've got a sense of how to use functions with dates, you can refer to Appendix B, "ColdFusion Function Reference," for more information about specific functions.

String Functions

A string is a set of zero or more characters. We can manipulate string values with a number of functions. These include functions that help you format dates, complete Regular Expressions, encrypt and decrypt strings, and trim strings.

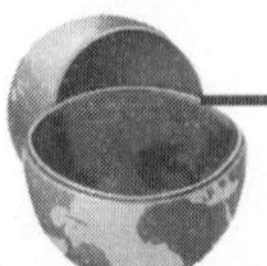

<NOTE>

The only limit on the length of a string in ColdFusion is the amount of memory available to the ColdFusion Server.

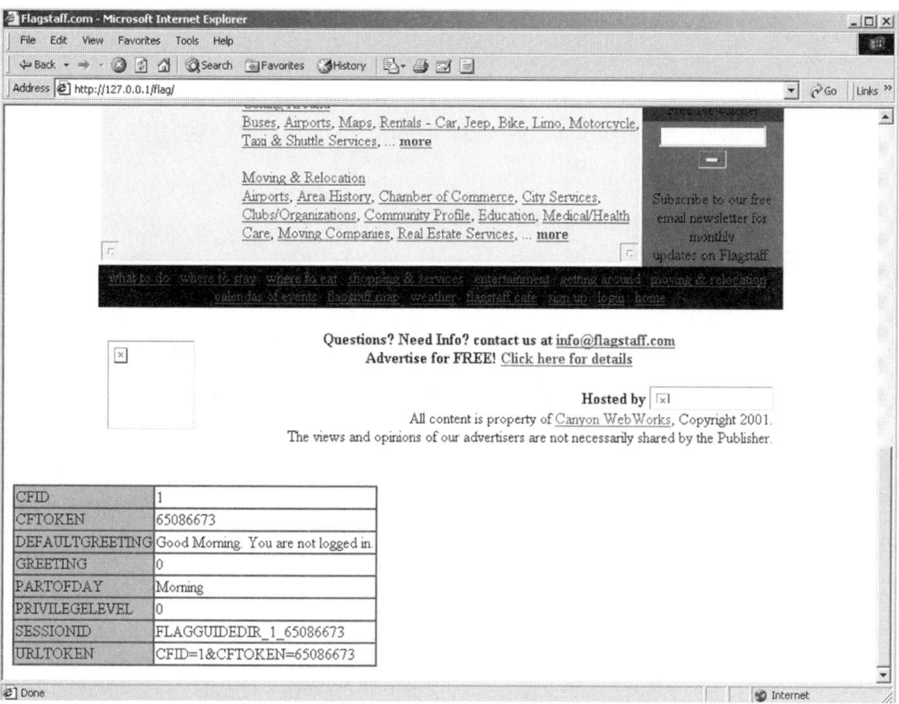

Figure 8.3 You can easily check the value of even complex data types such as structures using the new <cfdump> tag.

You will learn several string manipulation functions as we discuss how to create user-defined functions, the topic of the next section.

User-Defined Functions

User-defined functions are old hat to users of other languages, but they are new with ColdFusion 5. For instance, you can declare your own function in PHP like this:

```
Function myfunction ($argument1, $argument2...) {
        Echo "Some function.\n";
        Return $retval
}
```

The idea here is very similar, so if that syntax is familiar to you, you're in luck.

In ColdFusion, you declare your own functions using CFSCRIPT. We will discuss CFSCRIPT in depth in Chapter 13; for now, you will learn just enough to understand how to start writing your own custom functions. We will go in depth on these subjects in Chapter 13.

<CFSCRIPT>

ColdFusion Script is an alternate lexicon for writing ColdFusion. It is similar to JavaScript in my regards, and was created so that ColdFusion programmers who were used to working in other languages would have a way to feel comfortable right away in ColdFusion.

In order to write in CFSCRIPT, you just need to mark off a block that will contain only ColdFusion Script. You do this with the <CFSCRIPT> tag, which takes no parameters.

```
<CFSCRIPT>

// I am a comment in CFSCRIPT

script code here...

</CFSCRIPT>
```

There isn't much you can do in CFSCRIPT that you can't do using ColdFusion tags (the notable exception being creating user-defined functions). There are some distinct advantages to working with CFSCRIPT, however. To begin with, it processes generally faster than its counterpart tags. It is also more concise, and easier for programmers with backgrounds in, for instance, C, to work with.

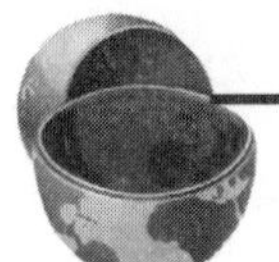

<NOTE>

The exception to the speed rule is a switch/case block, which performs slightly slower in CFSCRIPT than the tag version does. Remember, though, that in this context "slower" means a few milliseconds. Unless you've got a large application that is constantly hit, no one is likely to notice.

There are disadvantages to working with CFSCRIPT as well. The major drawback is that *you cannot use any ColdFusion tags* inside a CFSCRIPT block. That means that you cannot interact with FTP, LDAP, HTTP, or use the CFMAIL tag to send and receive email. There really are four reasons to use CFSCRIPT: to perform loops, to assign variables, to create conditional statements, and to invoke objects.

Writing User-Defined Functions

I think that we can kill a number of birds with one stone here. We will create our own user-defined function that you can use to delight your friends. Along the way, we will learn several existing string functions, such as Find, FindNoCase, Reverse, LCase, and a couple of Regular Expression functions.

User-defined functions have the following syntax in ColdFusion:

Listing 8.3 User-Defined Function Syntax

```
<cfscript>


function functionName( [paramName1[, paramname2...]] )
{
        CFScript Statements
}

</cfscript>
```

We will write a self-posting form that allows a user to enter a text string. We will then write a user-defined function called "isPalindrome()." A palindrome is a word that reads the same backward or forward. Therefore this function will read the passed string, reverse it, and check to see if the reversed string is equivalent to the original string. If it is, the string is a palindrome. We then call our custom function just as we would any other, which will tell the user if their string is a palindrome or not.

First, let's write the function. In order to create this function, we can make good use of the existing functions Reverse, which reverses a string, and Find, which finds a substring in a given string.

So that you can see how these are working, let's quickly look at them in their own right.

Reverse()

The Reverse() function returns the passed string with its characters in reverse order. Therefore, the result of this code:

```
<cfoutput>#Reverse("Alison Brown")#</cfoutput>
```

is this:

```
nworB nosilA
```

Find()

The Find() function returns the position of the first occurrence of *substring* in *string*. Therefore, the following code:

```
<cfoutput>#Find("o", "Alison Brown")#</cfoutput>
```

outputs this:

5

The reason is that the first occurrence of the substring "o" is in the fifth position of the string "Alison." Note that the Find() function is case sensitive.

Those two functions will be enough to get us started. Here are some quick rules about using CFSCRIPT:

- You use two forward slashes for single-line comments:

```
// I am a single-line CFSCRIPT comment
```

- Semicolons define the end of a statement, as in Java or JavaScript:

```
Some statement here;
```

- You can perform conditional logic, as you otherwise would using <CFIF> and <CFELSE>. It takes the following structure in CFSCRIPT:

```
if(expression) statement [else statement];
```

Here is an example:

```
<cfscript>

if ( 1 is 1) WriteOutput("Equal");
else WriteOutput("Not equal");

</cfscript>
```

The above code says, 'If 1 is equal to 1, output "Equal" to the browser, otherwise, they are not equal, so output "Not Equal" to the browser.' Note that line breaks and spaces are ignored.

- You perform variable assignment, as you otherwise would using <CFSET>, like this:

```
MyVariable = SomeValue;
```

That's enough CFSCRIPT to get us started writing user-defined functions.

First, declare a <CFSCRIPT> block. Next, tell ColdFusion that you are creating a user-defined function by writing "function" followed by a space, and then the name for your new function. Immediately following the function name, put any arguments you want your function to accept inside parentheses. Let's go slowly through the isPalindrome example; it looks long here, but it's mostly comments.

Listing 8.4 Creating the isPalindrome Function

```
<cfscript>
        // declare UDF and name it "isPalindrome".
        // It will accept one argument.

 function isPalindrome(MyString){

        // create a new variable called RevString, which
        // will reverse the order of the characters in the
        // passed string "myString"

RevString = Reverse(MyString); {

        // set up an if-else block. If the reversed
        // string matches the original string,
        // it is a palindrome

if (Find(RevString, MyString) is 1)

        // set the "theResult" variable. If the string is a
        // palindrome, set the value to "Your string
        // is a palindrome!"

         theResult = "Your string is a palindrome!";

        // the strings don't match, so set the
        // "theResult" variable accordingly.
else
        theResult = "Your string is not a palindrome :(";

        }

        // expose the "theResult" variable
         return theResult;

  }
</cfscript>
```

That's it. The comments within the code should explain what's going on line by line. Now that you have defined your function, you can call it like any other function within <CFOUTPUT> (as long as you have defined or included this function before the point on your template when you call it)—like this:

```
<cfoutput>#isPalindrome("pop")#</cfoutput>
```

Let's put the new UDF into a self-posting form so we can test it. Save the file as Palindrome.cfm and load it.

Listing 8.5 Putting the isPalindrome() Function to Work

```
<html>
<head>
	<title>UDF</title>
</head>

<body>

<cfscript>
 function isPalindrome(string){

 RevString = Reverse(MyString);
 {

if (Find(RevString, MyString) is 1)
 theResult = "Your string is a palindrome!";
 else
 theResult = "Your string is not a palindrome :(";
 }
 return theResult;

 }

</cfscript>

<cfif isDefined("FORM.MyString")>

<!---we can now call our custom function just like any other
function---->

<cfoutput>#isPalindrome(FORM.MyString)#</cfoutput>

</cfif>
<br>
```

```
<br>
Please type a string, and I will tell you if it is a
      palindrome or not:
<br>
<form action="palindrome.cfm" method="post" name="MyString">
       <input type="text" name="MyString" size="20"><br>
       <input type="submit" name="Submit">
</form>

</body>
```

Load palindrome.cfm in your browser and test it out. It's fun! There are obvious palindromes, such as "Mom," "Anna," and "Hannah." However, once you really put it to the test with longer palindromes, you come up against the limitation: isPalindrome() does not allow for any punctuation or spaces between words.

If you reverse the characters of "Race Car," the function will return false because of the space between the words, even though the letters reversed form a palindrome. The French palindrome, "Engage le jeu que je le gagne" ("Begin the game so that I can win") fails too, since it has not only spaces, but a capital letter. Any string with punctuation fails too.

So let's fix it up. First, we can easily tackle the capital letter problem by inserting the LCase function into the string manipulator. LCase is a standard ColdFusion function that forces all characters in a string to lower case. It accepts one argument—the string to force into lower case.

We could modify the reverse string by nesting the LCase function inside the reverse function, like this:

```
RevString = Reverse(LCase(mystring));
```

There is a better solution, however: using FindNoCase().

FindNoCase()

We must also update the expression inside the "if" block. In order to make sure that "Anna" and "anna" are both recognized as equivalent, we must use the FindNoCase() function. The Find() function is case sensitive and will therefore reject "Anna" as a palindrome. Using the FindNoCase() function in just the same way as its case-sensitive counterpart gives us the result we want.

Next, let's strip out any spaces that might be present in the string. To do this, we need to use the ColdFusion Regular Expression function REReplace.

REReplace

There are four ColdFusion Regular Expression functions, and they perform very complex string manipulation. They all begin with "RE." REReplace performs a case-sensitive search of a given string, finds a regular expression within *string*, and replaces it with *substring* in the given scope. Here is the structure:

```
REReplace(string, reg_expression, substring [, scope ])
```

We want to take the string passed as FORM.MyString, find all of the spaces in that string, and replace each space with an empty string. We want to do this for every instance of a space in the string, not just the first one we find. So we write:

```
mystring = REReplace(form.MyString," ","","ALL");
```

We set the variable mystring to the result of performing the `REReplace`. If we used <cfoutput> or <cfdump> at this point to view the contents of the variable MyString, all spaces would have been removed.

Now we can plug this into our script, send it a value with spaces, and see if it works. The bold code shows where we have made updates.

Listing 8.6 Updated Palindrome.cfm

```
<html>
<head>
        <title>Updated Palindrome</title>
</head>

<body>

<cfscript>
function isPalindrome(string){

        mystring = REReplace(form.MyString," ","","ALL");

        RevString = Reverse(mystring);

 {
if (FindNoCase(RevString, MyString) is 1)

        theResult = "<b>#form.MyString#</b>
                              is a palindrome!";
else
```

```
        theResult = "<b>#form.MyString#</b>
                              is not a palindrome :(";
        }
        return theResult;

}

</cfscript>

<cfif isDefined("FORM.MyString")>

<cfoutput>#isPalindrome(FORM.MyString)#</cfoutput>

</cfif>
<br>
<br>
Please type a string, and I will tell you if it is a
       palindrome or not:
<br>
<form action="UDFnocase.cfm" method="post" name="MyString">
        <input type="text" name="MyString" size="20"><br>
        <input type="submit" name="Submit">
</form>

</body>
</html>
```

There are a number of changes, but our application is much improved. Here's what we did:

- Used the regular expression function REReplace to strip out any spaces between words.
- Read the string case insensitive.
- Instead of the generic "your string," we displayed the string we checked.

Now we get better results, as shown in Figure 8.4.

<NOTE>

Variables created in a user-defined function are not visible outside the function, unless they are explicitly returned.

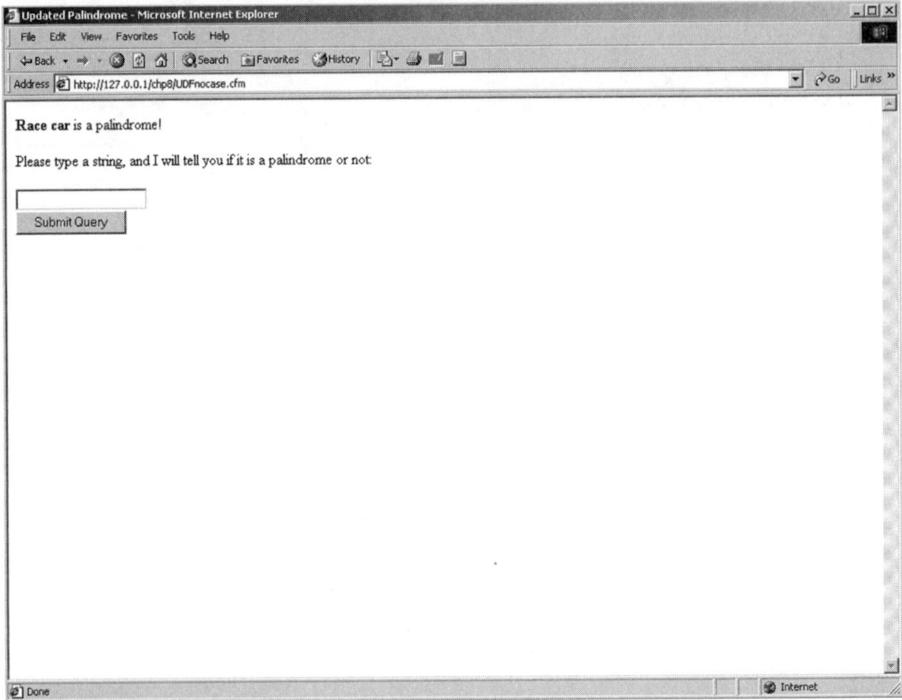

Figure 8.4 Improved isPalindrome function in action.

There is still an important flaw with our isPalindrome() function. If the function were passed this string:

Go hang a salami. I'm a lasagna hog?

it would return false, even though the string is a palindrome. That's because of the period, the apostrophe, and the question mark. In order to ignore these special characters, you can learn another string function: ReplaceList().

ReplaceList()

The purpose of the ReplaceList() function is to return *string* with all occurrences of specified characters in one comma-separated list of characters replaced with characters from another comma-separated list. It has the following structure:

```
ReplaceList(string, list1, list2)
```

<NOTE>

Unlike other replacement functions, ReplaceList() will replace all occurrences of a listed character; you do not have the option to specify a narrower scope.

Let's write our replace list to account for characters typically used in sentences, since that's what we are most likely to have to deal with. Our second list should be an empty string. Here's the function:

```
MyString=ReplaceList(form.MyString, "?,',"",:,.,!, ", "");
```

There are three items here. The first is form.MyString, which is the variable we want to replace special characters for. The second item is a comma-separated list in double quotes, which begins with a ? and ends with a space. This is the list of characters to look for in the variable form.MyString. Notice that one item is `""`. We have to *escape* the double quote marks; otherwise, ColdFusion thinks that you are ending the list. The third item is a list that simply contains an empty string: `""`.

I think we have a winner (see Figure 8.5).

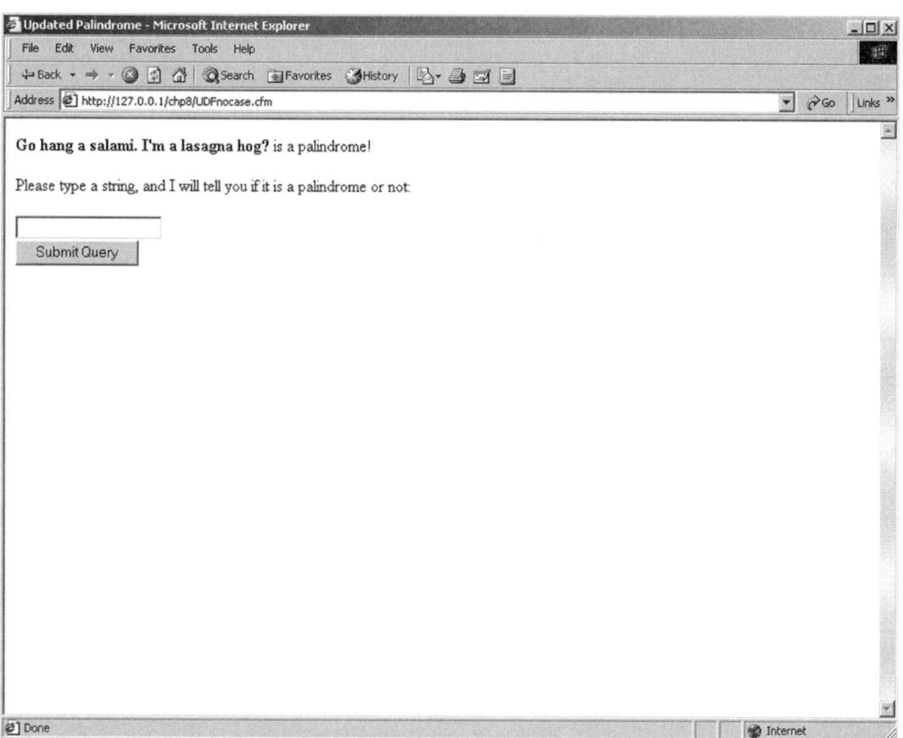

Figure 8.5 The complete isPalindrome() user-defined function; the ReplaceList function takes care of the period, single quote mark, and exclamation mark.

Some Considerations for User-Defined Functions

There are a number of things to remember when writing user-defined functions. Like most things, there are advantages and disadvantages. To begin with, UDFs process quickly, as do most things inside <CFSCRIPT>. UDFs will perform faster than ColdFusion custom tags, and they are sometimes easier to work with, since all variables and scopes are automatically visible from within a user-defined function. Also, a nice feature is that UDFs can call not just regular ColdFusion functions, but also other UDFs.

The disadvantages are nothing you don't already know:

- You must use <CFSCRIPT> to define your custom functions.
- You may not use tags inside a UDF.
- To call a UDF, you must have included the function definition itself directly in the template before you call it. Or you must use <CFINCLUDE> to bring it in. It's probably a good idea to have a definition library and include the custom functions you need.

<NOTE>

There is a project underway to create libraries of custom functions. We can read about this effort and download mathematical and string libraries at http://www.cflib.org.

In the remaining sections of this chapter we will discuss lists, arrays, and structures.

Working with Lists

A list is a set of data with zero or more elements, each of which is delimited in a common manner. For instance, the following is a list:

1, 2, 3, 4, 5

This is a list with five elements, separated by commas. But this is a list, too:

Alison Brown

It is a list with two elements, "Alison" and "Brown," delimited by a space. However, notice that it is also an *"o"-delimited list* of three elements: "Alis," "n Br," and "wn." My point is that any variable in ColdFusion is actually a list. You don't have to treat them all as such, but you can. It should be easy for us to discuss lists at this point, because lists are not truly a data type in ColdFusion—they are treated by ColdFusion as strings.

<NOTE>

Your list delimiter can be more than one character long. A comma is the default list delimiter.

A number of List functions are available to us. All of them begin with "List" and they all take a list as their first attribute. But there is not a function for creating a list. You can do it with <cfset>, like this:

```
<cfset GroceryList = "fettucine, red peppers, vodka, cream">
```

Because regular variables are lists, you can also use <CFSCRIPT>, as you saw earlier. The code below does the same thing:

```
<cfscript>
       GroceryList = "fettucine, red peppers, vodka, cream";
</cfscript>
```

You gain access to the elements in a list using any of the 21 list functions. These allow you to find whether or not a certain value is in a list, change the delimiters set for a list, delete an element at a specific location in a list, append and prepend values to a list, and more.

HTML forms pass their fields and values in a comma-delimited list. They are therefore a natural place to start when beginning to work with lists.

Let's create a short form that allows users to specify what kind of an ad they would like to place on your website. We won't make the full application, but we will learn how to manipulate lists and use them in decision making.

FORM.FieldNames

A variable that is always available to you on the action page for a form is one called FORM.FormFields. It is a comma-delimited list of all of the fields submitted in an HTML form. Let's set up our form and start putting these list functions to work.

Listing 8.7 A Simple Form

```
<html>
<head>
        <title>Lists</title>
</head>

<body>
<h2>Advertise with Us!</h2>
<cfif isDefined("FORM.FieldNames")>

<cfdump var=#Form.FieldNames#>

</cfif>
<br>
<br>
Please choose what kind of advertisement interests you:
<br>
<form action="list1.cfm" method="post" name="MyString">
        <input type="Checkbox" name="Banner"> Banner Ad<br>
        <input type="Checkbox" name="Feature"> Feature Ad<br>
        <input type="Checkbox" name="Listing"> Listing<br>
        <input type="submit" name="submit">
</form>

</body>
</html>
```

We start with a self-posting form that contains three checkboxes, each for a different kind of advertisement. When we first build a form, we want to make sure that we know what values we are passing and that things work. This will keep us from creating too many unknowns at once, running into an error, and not knowing where to start debugging.

So for now, we create the form, and on the action "page" we just dump the variable FORM.FieldNames. FORM.FieldNames contains a comma-separated list with three elements: BANNER, FEATURE, and SUBMIT. SUBMIT will always be present, no matter what its "name" attribute specifies, or what value you give the button.

Now that we know we're getting what we need, let's get to work. Here's what we're going to do:

- Find the length of the list (the number of elements in it).
- Delete the last element.
- Append a new element.

In order to determine the number of elements in the list, we use the ListLen() function.

ListLen()

ListLen() takes two arguments—the list and (optionally) the list delimiters. Therefore, if we choose two ads, running the ListLen() function against the FORM.FieldNames variables should return 3 (the two ads chosen and the submit button).

ListFindNoCase()

We can perform some decision logic based on the values in the list. We determine what values have been passed using the ListFindNoCase() function. This function is the case-insensitive version of the ListFind() function. It takes three arguments: the list to be searched, the value sought, and the (optional) delimiters. The default delimiter, as with all lists, is a comma.

<NOTE>

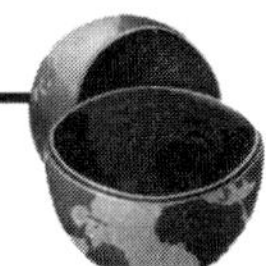

The <cfdump> tag is meant for debugging and should never be used in production code. It is not useful for data operations, since it outputs to the browser.

If the value you search for in the list is present, ColdFusion returns not a Boolean, as you might expect, but the value's position in the list. If the value is not found, ColdFusion returns 0. Therefore, this code:

```
Was the "Feature" box checked?
<cfoutput>
      #ListContainsNoCase(FORM.FieldNames, "FEATURE")#
</cfoutput><br>
```

returns 2 when the Banner and Feature boxes are checked.

ListFirst() and ListLast()

ListFirst() is a function that returns the first element in a list. The function takes two arguments: the list to find the first element of, and (optionally) delimiters. The ListLast() function returns the last element in a list. Even if you make no choices in our form, the submit button is present.

<NOTE>

ColdFusion ignores empty list elements. Therefore 1, 2, 3, , 4 is a four-element list. However, 1, 2, 3, , 4 is a FIVE-element list, since a space does not constitute an empty element. It is rather an element whose content is a space.

List Append() and ListPrepend()

You must be cautious using ListAppend(). This function will annex a value onto the end of your list, and ColdFusion will automatically insert the appropriate delimiter. However, here is a tricky thing to remember about ListAppend(). It is tempting to write something like this:

```
<cfset temp = ListAppend(FORM.FieldNames, "Step 2")>
```

The above statement will not throw an error, and it will appear that "Step 2" has been appended to the list. It should therefore be the last element, and the list should be one element longer. However, that is not exactly the case. The element is in fact added to the end of the FORM.FieldNames list, but the result of the function is assigned to a NEW variable called "temp." In order to change the FORM.FieldNames list, you must name FORM.FieldNames as the variable that receives the result of the function. The following code will append the value "Step 2" to the end of the FORM.FieldNames list, even though it was not submitted with the form:

```
<cfset FORM.FieldNames=ListAppend(FORM.FieldNames, "Step 2")>
```

The same holds true for ListPrepend(), which inserts a value into the first position in the list.

<NOTE>

List elements start at position 1, not 0 as in many other languages.

```
<cfset FORM.FieldNames=ListAppend(FORM.FieldNames, "First!")>
```

Let's catch up with our form page and see how this code affects our list. As you can see in Figure 8.6, the list functions can freely select and update information from the list. Listing 8.8 shows the code we've discussed altogether.

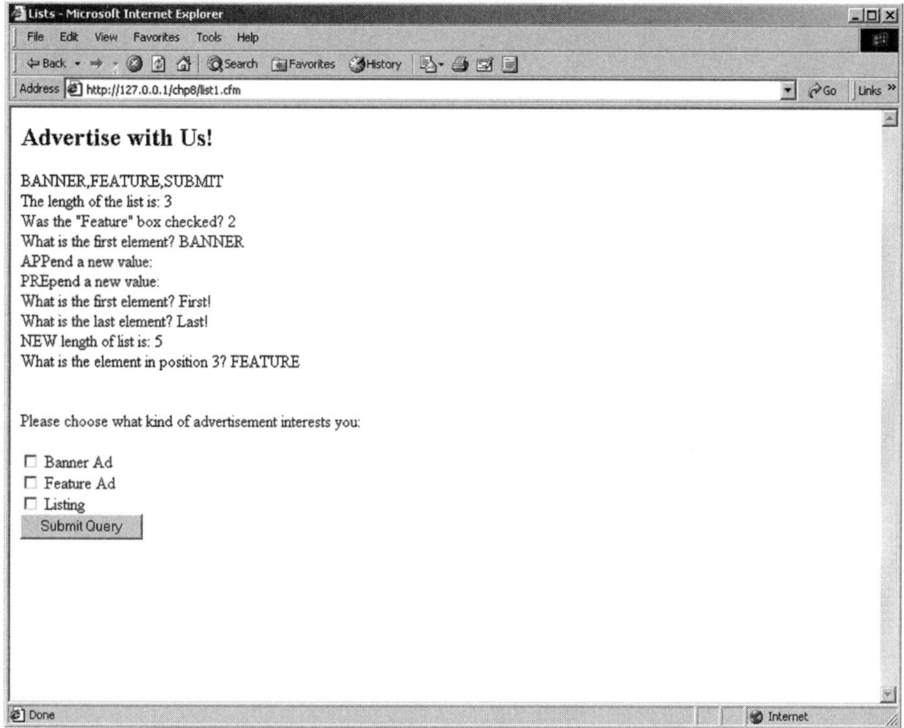

Figure 8.6 The results of performing list manipulation on form.fieldnames.

<NOTE>

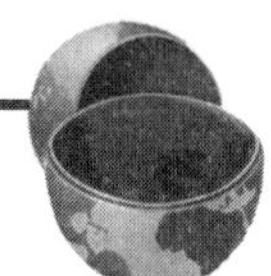

Lists are one of the least efficient ways you can assess data in ColdFusion. It therefore is not generally a good idea to keep frequently referenced or changing items in lists.

Listing 8.8 The Form Updated with List Functions

```
<html>
<head>
        <title>Lists</title>
</head>

<body>
<h2>Advertise with Us!</h2>

<cfif isDefined("FORM.FieldNames")>
```

```
<cfdump var=#form.fieldnames#>
<br>

<!---specify comma as the delimiter for illustration
purposes------->

The length of the list is:
<cfoutput>#ListLen(FORM.FieldNames, ",")#</cfoutput>
<br>

Was the "Feature" box checked?
<cfoutput>
#ListContainsNoCase(FORM.FieldNames, "FEATURE")#
</cfoutput>
<br>

What is the first element?
<cfoutput>#ListFirst(FORM.FieldNames)#</cfoutput>
<br>

APPend a new value:
<cfset FORM.FieldNames=ListAppend(FORM.FieldNames, "Last!")>
<br>

PREpend a new value:
<cfset FORM.FieldNames=ListPrepend(FORM.FieldNames, "First!")>
<br>

What is the first element?
<cfoutput>#ListFirst(FORM.FieldNames)#</cfoutput>
<br>

What is the last element?
<cfoutput>#ListLast(FORM.FieldNames)#</cfoutput>
<br>

NEW length of list is:
<cfoutput>#ListLen(FORM.FieldNames, ",")#</cfoutput>
<br>

What is the element in position 3?
<cfoutput>#ListGetAt(FORM.FieldNames, 3)#</cfoutput>
<br>

<!---End check for form submission---->
```

```
</cfif>
<br>
<br>
Please choose what kind of advertisement interests you:
<br>
<form action="list1.cfm" method="post" name="MyString">
<input type="Checkbox" name="Banner" value="Banner"> Banner
Ad<br>
<input type="Checkbox" name="Feature" value="Feature"> Feature
Ad<br>
<input type="Checkbox" name="Listing" value="Listing">
Listing<br>
<input type="submit" name="submit">
</form>

</body>
</html>
```

Since the other list functions work in very similar ways, let us now move on to arrays.

Arrays

An *array* is a data set that can store one or more values in a single variable. Many people think of arrays as tabular, like a spreadsheet. They can hold data in multiple dimensions. Arrays are stored in ColdFusion in a *Complex Data* format, which allows them to hold not only strings or integers, but lists, structures, or results from database queries.

ColdFusion arrays come in one, two, and three dimensions. You might think of a one-dimensional array as being very much like a list. It is an ordered series of elements. Like a list, an array has a numeric position that you can use to reference and manipulate its data. This position is called an *index.*

One might use a one-dimensional array to set values that could also be stored in a single row of multiple cells in a spreadsheet. Two-dimensional arrays can be thought of as containing not only rows, but columns, which means that you can reference an array by its coordinates. A two-dimensional array is really a one-dimensional array that contains a series of one-dimensional arrays. Each column acts independently of other columns.

Arrays are typically used to store information temporarily and when the order of data is important. If you are familiar with conventional arrays, there are a couple of important differences in ColdFusion arrays. Arrays in ColdFusion start at 1, instead of 0. That is, the first element in an array is referenced at position 1, not position 0. Also, if you are familiar with associative arrays, these are not arrays in ColdFusion, but are rather a kind of structure (we will discuss structures in the next section). Lastly, arrays in ColdFusion are *dynamic*, which means that they are resized on the fly, given the number of elements added to or removed from the array. In Java, you must declare the size of the array beforehand and stick to it.

Let's take a quick look at how one initializes and populates an array.

Initializing an Array

You create an array by using the ArrayNew() function and assigning a variable name to it, like this:

```
<cfset arrCustomer = ArrayNew(1)>
```

The <cfset> statement names the array, in this case "arrCustomer." You use standard variable naming conventions when naming an array; I usually prefix "arr" to the rest of the variable name so that I can easily remember that that variable is an array. Then you use the ArrayNew() function, which takes one argument—the number of dimensions for the array. An array may have 1, 2, or 3 dimensions. In our example above, arrCustomer is a one-dimensional array.

Now that you have created an array, you can populate it with data, which is referenced using square brackets that indicate the index. For example, let's create an array called arrCustomer, and then populate it with typical customer information:

Listing 8.9 Creating and Populating an Array

```
<!---Create the array---->
<cfset arrCustomer = ArrayNew(1)>

<!----Populate it with data---->
<cfset arrCustomer[1] = "Janet">
<cfset arrCustomer[2] = "Jackson">
<cfset arrCustomer[3] = "555 E. Route 66">
<cfset arrCustomer[4] = "Flagstaff">
<cfset arrCustomer[5] = "AZ">
<cfset arrCustomer[6] = "86001">
```

```
<!---Use cfdump to display the contents--->
<cfdump var = #arrCustomer#>
```

My result is shown in Figure 8.7.

The above set of statements insert one value each into the “cells” of the arrCustomer array. In order to reference that data, you use the same square-bracket syntax.

```
<!---Output the value in the second cell--->
   <cfoutput>#arrCustomer[2]#</cfoutput>
```

Using <CFOUTPUT> to reference the cell position in this manner gives us the value in the cell: “Jackson.” Try it with other values in the array to get the hang of it.

<NOTE>

One uses the term index *to refer to the position of an element in an array.*

Figure 8.7 The one-dimensional arrCustomer array populated with data.

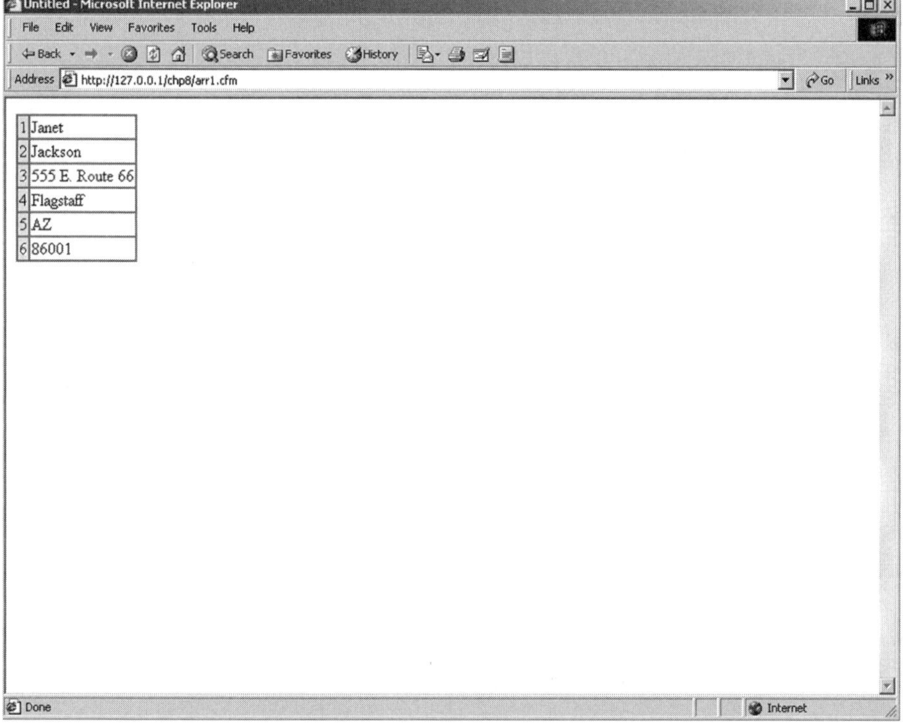

Referencing Array Data

Using block notation, you can reference or display the value of an array cell. You do so by naming the array and immediately referencing the cell number inside square brackets, as follows:

```
<cfoutput>#arrCustomer[3]#</cfoutput>
```

This example outputs the customer address information, since that's what is in cell 3:

```
555 E. Route 66
```

Updating Array Data

To update the data in a cell, you can just overwrite it. That's why you must be careful to keep track of the order of information in your cells. In our arrCustomer example, the street address is kept in cell 3. In order to update the data in that cell (change the address), we just set it again:

```
<cfset arrCustomer[3] = "222 Some New Street, Apt. 3">

<!---Output new value---->

<cfoutput>#arrCustomer[3]#</cfoutput>
```

Here is the output:

```
222 Some New Street, Apt. 3
```

Deleting Array Data

Once you are comfortable with the notation, it is easy to reference array-cell data to output its value and to update or delete the value. When you remove information from an array, the array automatically resizes. You can delete data using the ArrayDeleteAt() function, which takes two arguments—the name of the array, and the position to delete at:

```
<cfset ArrayDeleteAt(arrCustomer, 2)>
```

The above code will delete the value at position 2 and resize the array accordingly. Since this function returns only a Boolean (true or false) upon completion, you can put it inside a <cfoutput> block to check the value:

```
<cfoutput>#arrayDeleteAt(arrCustomer, 3)#</cfoutput>
```

Putting It to Work

Let's create the arrCustomer array, add data to it, update some data, remove data, and then clear the array altogether. We can do this on one page, and we'll use <cfdump> and <cfoutput> to display the array contents as it changes. I urge you to type in Listing 8.10 yourself and play around with substituting, adding, and deleting values.

Listing 8.10 Arrays.cfm

```
<html>
<head>
	<title>Array functions</title>
</head>

<body>

<!---Create arrCustomer------->

<cfset arrCustomer = ArrayNew(1)>

<!---Add data to it------->

<cfset arrCustomer[1] = "Janet">
<cfset arrCustomer[2] = "Jackson">
<cfset arrCustomer[3] = "555 E. Route 66">
<cfset arrCustomer[4] = "Flagstaff">
<cfset arrCustomer[5] = "AZ">
<cfset arrCustomer[6] = "86001">

<!---Display current contents------->

<cfdump var = #arrCustomer#>

<!---Make a new cell at position 2 to hold middle initial.
Notice that as of version 4.5, we do NOT have to use
a dummy variable such as "temp" to perform an insertion
function like this------->
<cfset ArrayInsertAt(arrCustomer, 2, "J.")>
<br>

<!---Output the value in the first, second, and
third cells--->
```

```
New name:
<cfoutput>
#arrCustomer[1]# #arrCustomer[2]# #arrCustomer[3]#
</cfoutput>

<!---Add the courtesy title by prepending------->

<cfset ArrayPrepend(arrCustomer, "Ms.")>
<br>

<!---Output the full name with title.
After the prepend, everything has shifted a cell.
So, for instance, the middle initial is now in cell [3]--->

New name:
<cfoutput>
#arrCustomer[1]# #arrCustomer[2]# #arrCustomer[3]#
#arrCustomer[4]#
</cfoutput>
<br>

<!---What is new length of the array? Set a variable to
this value and output the variable------->

<cfset temp = ArrayLen(arrCustomer)>
New Length: <cfoutput>#temp#</cfoutput>
<br>

<!---This time we will swap the values in cells 2, 3, and 4.

That way we can change the order of appearance of the full
name, like this: Ms. Jackson, Janet J.------->

<!---First, swap 2 and 4 (first name and last name------->
<cfset temp= arraySwap(arrCustomer, 2, 4)>

<!---Then swap 3 and 4 (middle initial and first name,
and output the new name.------->

<cfset temp= arraySwap(arrCustomer, 3, 4)>

<!----Note hard-coded comma after cell [2]------->

Name after cell swap:
<cfoutput>
#arrCustomer[1]# #arrCustomer[2]#, #arrCustomer[3]#
#arrCustomer[4]#
```

```
</cfoutput>

<br>
<!---Now delete the middle initial. This function, like
ArraySwap, returns a Boolean TRUE when completed success-
fully.------->

Was Middle initial deleted?
<cfoutput>#arrayDeleteAt(arrCustomer, 4)#</cfoutput>

<br>
<!---Send the entire contents to a list using the array to
list function. It takes two arguments: the array to use, and
the delimiter for the list------->

<cfset lsArray = ArrayToList(arrCustomer, ",")>

<!---Now it is in a list as well as the array------->

Show list: <cfoutput>#lsArray#</cfoutput>

<br>
<!---Now let's clear the array.
This function returns a Boolean------->

Array cleared? <cfoutput>#ArrayClear(arrCustomer)#</cfoutput>
<br>

<!---CF says it is cleared. Make sure------->

Is it really empty?
<cfoutput>#arrayIsEmpty(arrCustomer)#</cfoutput>
<br>

Does arrCustomer still exist?
<cfoutput>#isArray(arrCustomer)#</cfoutput>

<br>
How many cells does it have?
<cfoutput>#ArrayLen(arrCustomer)#</cfoutput>

</body>
</html>
```

My result is shown in Figure 8.8.

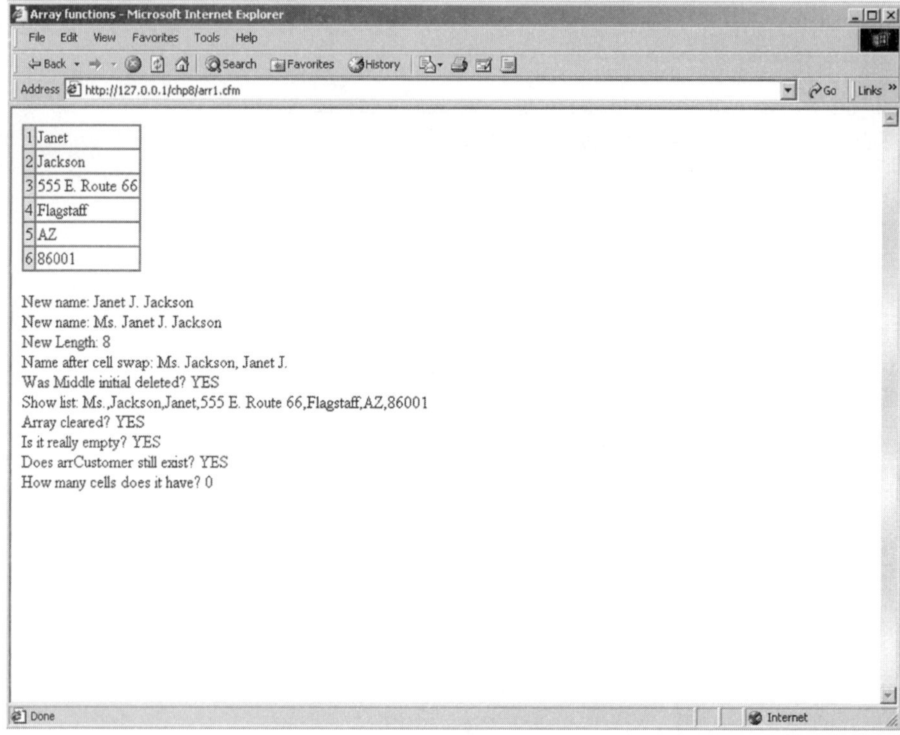

Figure 8.8 Result of running Listing 8.10 in a browser.

<NOTE>

If you are studying for the ColdFusion developer's exam, I highly recommend you follow Listing 8.10. This is a terrific way to understand how all of the pieces come together when working with arrays. Writing each function out like this and viewing your results is great practice before the exam, or before putting arrays to work in complex applications. I would do the same for lists and structures.

That should give you a pretty good sense of how all the pieces of a one-dimensional array fit together.

Two-Dimensional Arrays

Let's expand the example for a two-dimensional array. This time, we'll call the array arrCustomers (plural), as it will hold more than one customer. You create a 2-D array just like a 1-D array, except that your argument for the

ArrayNew() function is "2." You then reference cells with two square brackets, as shown in Listing 8.11.

Listing 8.11 A Two-Dimensional Array

```
<html>
<head>
       <title>2-D Array</title>
</head>

<body>
<!-----Make the array---->
<cfset arrCustomers = ArrayNew(2)>

<!----Set a value for the
first cell in the first row---->

<cfset arrCustomers[1][1] = "Janet">

<!---set the second cell in the first row------->
<cfset arrCustomers[1][2] = "Jackson">

<!---Set the first cell in the second row------->
<cfset arrCustomers[2][1] = "Latoya">

<!---Set the second cell in the second row------->
<cfset arrCustomers[2][2] = "Jackson">

<cfdump var=#arrCustomers#>

</body>
</html>
```

As you can see in Figure 8.9, there are two columns with two cells each, and they have corresponding values:

```
column 1 = customer 1
cell 1 = first name 1
cell 2 = last name 1

column 2 = customer 2
cell 1 = first name 2
cell 2 = last name 2
```

<cfdump> makes it easy to envision how arrays organize their data. What this example does not illustrate is that your columns do not need to have the

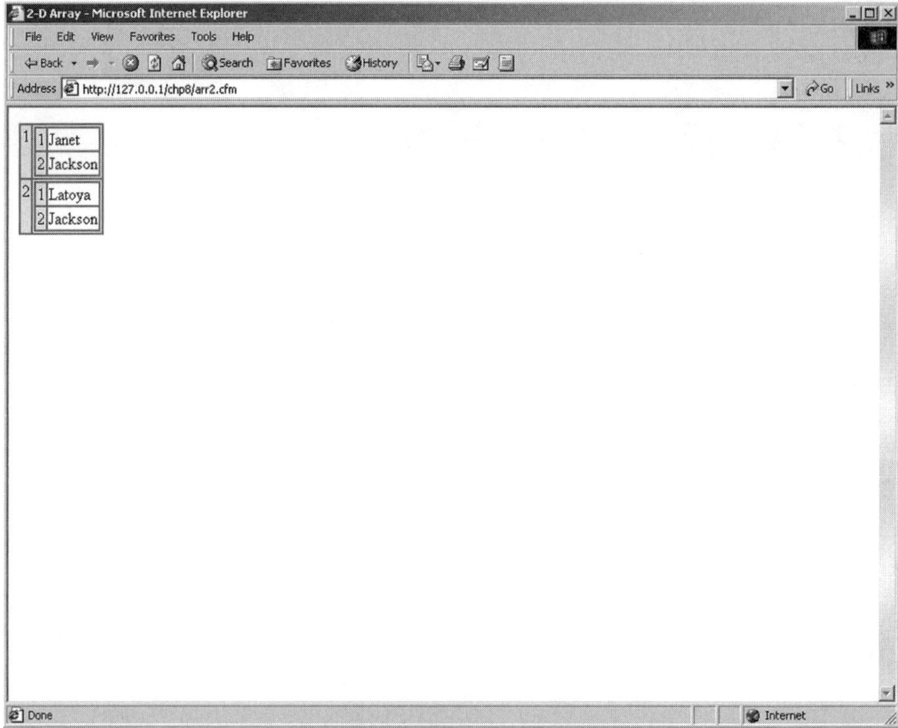

Figure 8.9 A two-dimensional array holds multiple cell values in a single column.

same number of cells. For instance, in Listing 8.12, we can make a third column that holds four values. (See also Figure 8.10.)

Listing 8.12 Two-Dimensional Array with Three Columns

```
<html>
<head>
        <title>2-D Array</title>
</head>

<body>
<!---Make the 2-D array---->
<cfset arrCustomers = ArrayNew(2)>

<!----Set a value for the
first cell in the first row---->

<cfset arrCustomers[1][1] = "Janet">
```

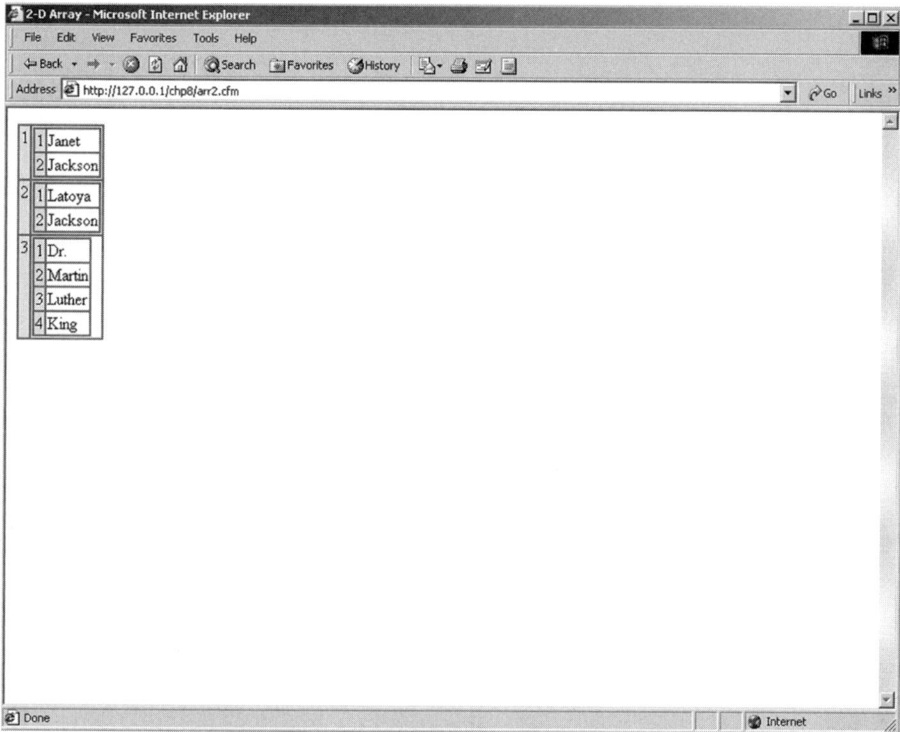

Figure 8.10 A two-dimensional array with three columns holding a different number of cells.

```
<!---Set the second cell in the first row------->
<cfset arrCustomers[1][2] = "Jackson">

<!---Set the first cell in the second row------->
<cfset arrCustomers[2][1] = "Latoya">

<!---Set the second cell in the second row------->
<cfset arrCustomers[2][2] = "Jackson">

<!-----Make a third column that holds four cells------>
<cfset arrCustomers[3][1] = "Dr.">

<cfset arrCustomers[3][2] = "Martin">

<cfset arrCustomers[3][3] = "Luther">

<cfset arrCustomers[3][4] = "King">
```

```
<cfdump var=#arrCustomers#>

</body>
</html>
```

Arrays are very useful for creating shopping carts in e-commerce sites. You can store all of the items in a customer's cart in an array, and delete items, update quantities, and add to them. There are also three-dimensional arrays, which you create and reference in the same manner as one- and two-dimensional arrays. We'll investigate this further in the chapter on CFSCRIPT.

One drawback to using arrays (and structures) is that, because they are not simple data types, they cannot be passed in a URL like lists can. However, a benefit of using arrays is that they can be stored in the APPLICATION, SESSION, or REQUEST scopes to hold complex data.

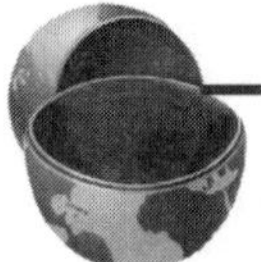

<NOTE>

The application scope is reserved space in memory that allows variables to be referenced throughout an entire application. Application variables are therefore available over multiple requests.

The session scope holds variables in the server memory that are specific to each user's interactions with your application. Session variables are therefore not available throughout an application.

The request scope was first available with ColdFusion 4.0.1, requested by the team who developed Spectra. It is all but undocumented, though it is a very useful tool. Request variables exist only for the duration of a single page request like local variables, but they are exposed to the entire request (nested custom tags, etc.). This makes them perhaps the most flexible data type to work with.

Storing Arrays in Arrays

Finally, let's take a quick look at how to store arrays in other arrays. We will create three arrays—the first will hold names of blues musicians, the second will hold names of crooners, and the third array will hold both of those arrays—one array in each column (Figure 8.11).

To spice things up a little bit, we'll use <CFSCRIPT> syntax to make and populate the second array, just so you can see how that looks. It is not very different, you just need to remember that you don't use <cfset> to set a variable, you just write variable = value, and end each statement with a semicolon.

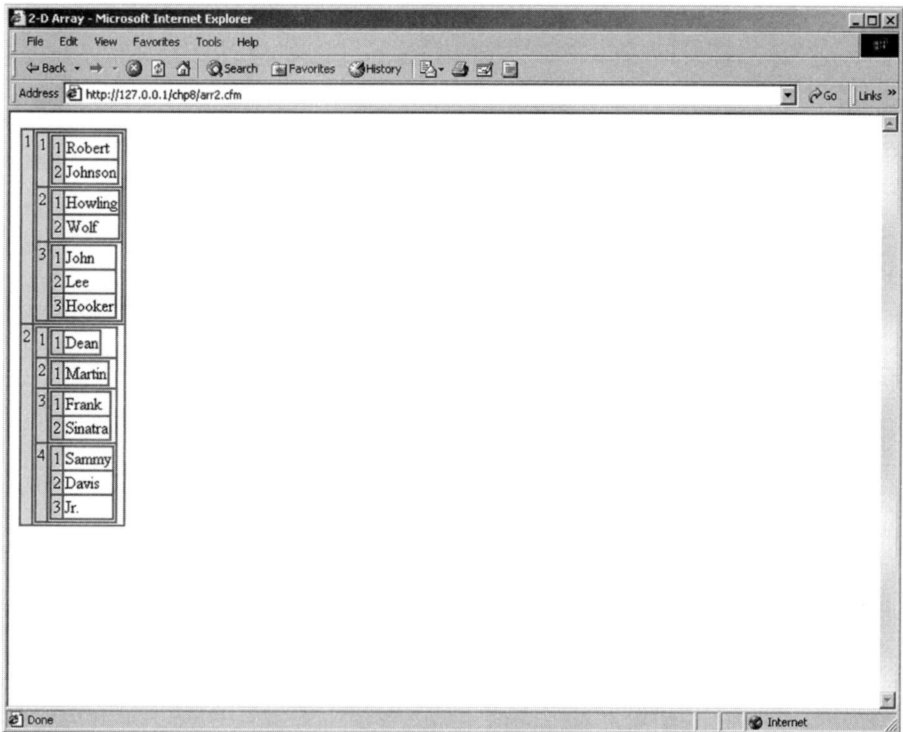

Figure 8.11 You can hold arrays within arrays.

Here is the code:

Listing 8.13 Storing Arrays in Another Array

```
<html>
<head>
        <title>2-D Array</title>
</head>

<body>
<!-----Make the Blues Musicians array---->
<cfset arrBlues = ArrayNew(2)>

<!----hold first blues musician---->

<cfset arrBlues[1][1] = "Robert">

<cfset arrBlues[1][2] = "Johnson">

<!-----hold second blues musician----->
```

```
<cfset arrBlues[2][1] = "Howling">

<cfset arrBlues[2][2] = "Wolf">

<!-----hold info for third blues musician------>
<cfset arrBlues[3][1] = "John">

<cfset arrBlues[3][2] = "Lee">

<cfset arrBlues[3][3] = "Hooker">

<!---For fun (and performance), use cfscript to create the
second array---->

<cfscript>

// make array for crooners
arrCrooners = ArrayNew(2);

// first crooner
arrCrooners[1][1] = "Dean";
arrCrooners[1][2] = "Martin";

// second crooner
arrCrooners[2][1] = "Frank";
arrCrooners[2][2] = "Sinatra";

// third crooner
arrCrooners[3][1] = "Sammy";
arrCrooners[3][2] = "Davis";
arrCrooners[3][3] = "Jr.";

</cfscript>

<!---Create an array called arrMusicians to hold all
musicians (Blues and Crooners)------->

<cfset arrMusicians = ArrayNew(1)>

<!---set the value of the first cell to hold the entire
arrBlues array---->
<cfset arrMusicians[1] = arrBlues>

<!---set the value of the second cell to hold the entire
arrCrooners array---->

<cfset arrMusicians[2] = arrCrooners>
```

```
<!---show the result------->

<cfdump var=#arrMusicians#>

</body>
</html>
```

While we have not studied loops in ColdFusion yet, we will do so shortly, and it would be a disservice to you to leave arrays at that. Half the battle of dealing with arrays is how to output them, and <cfdump> is only meant for debugging as you develop. Therefore, I will quickly demonstrate how you might use a nested loop to loop over the array of arrays to output its value in a flexible (usable) manner.

You may not simply output an array, since ColdFusion cannot convert this complex data type to a string. You must therefore loop over each array, and output each array column and cell value one at a time.

Append the code in Listing 8.14 to the code in Listing 8.13, before the closing </body> </html> tags.

Listing 8.14 Using Nested Loops to Output Array Values

```
<!----loop over blues array from 1
       to the length of the array.
       It will perform one iteration
       for each length of the array.
       In this case, it will loop three times.
 ------->

<cfloop index="BluesColCounter"
       from="1" to="#ArrayLen(arrBlues)#">

<!-----NESTED LOOP! Now we loop one
       time for each cell within each
       column. This will be two times,
       and then three times (for John, Lee, Hooker)
----->

       <cfloop index="BluesCellCounter"
              from="1"
              to="#ArrayLen(arrBlues[BluesColCounter])#">

              <!-----the BluesColCounter holds the
                     value for the outside loop,
                     which is looping once for each
```

```
                    column in arrBlues------->
        <cfoutput>
               #arrBlues[BluesColCounter][BluesCellCounter]#
        </cfoutput>
        <!---end Blues Cell loop------->
        </cfloop>

        <!----put the break AFTER the
               inside loop has finished,
               so each entire column is
               output on one line------->
        <br>

<!---end Blues Column loop------->
</cfloop>

<br>

<!---do the second array, Crooners. This is exactly like the
first set of loops------->

<!---column counter------->
<cfloop
index="CroonersColCounter"
from="1"
to="#ArrayLen(arrCrooners)#">

        <!-----nested cell counter----->

        <cfloop
        index="CroonersCellCounter"
        from="1"
        to="#ArrayLen(arrCrooners[CroonersColCounter])#">

        <!-----the CroonersColCounter holds the value for
               the outside loop, which is looping once
               for each column in arrCrooner--->

               <cfoutput>
#arrCrooners[CroonersColCounter][CroonersCellCounter]#
               </cfoutput>

        <!---end Crooners Cell loop------->
        </cfloop>

        <!----put the break AFTER the inside loop
```

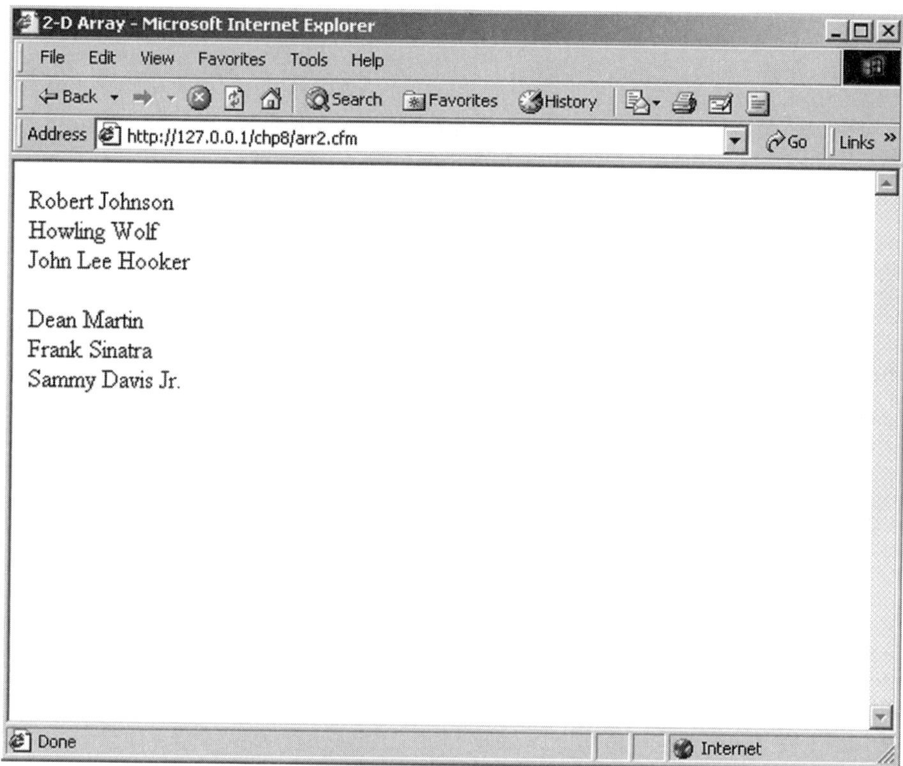

Figure 8.12 You can loop over multidimensional arrays to output their values.

```
                has finished so each column is output
                on one line------->
        <br>

<!---end CroonersColumn loop------->
</cfloop>
```

Figure 8.12 shows the output as desired.

Note that you can use loops to quickly populate arrays, or to quickly delete certain values in them. We will study loops in Chapter 12, and see more ways to employ arrays in your applications throughout the book. Now let us examine structures.

Structures

Structures are different sorts of things from arrays and lists. They are like arrays inasmuch as they are a complex data type, which matters only in terms of how they are stored in memory and how you can reference them. *Structures* are collections of key-value pairs. They hold related variables as a single unit. Unlike arrays, structures are not ordered.

You can use structures to pass related information in one neat package. Using structures, you can send complex data to different scopes. For instance, ColdFusion custom tags can accept a structure as an attribute collection.

Structures are powerful partly because they can hold other complex data types. Within a structure you can store database query result sets, other structures, or arrays.

It's a good idea to get comfortable using structures. Beyond the fact that they are a central and generally useful part of the ColdFusion Markup Language, they perform very, very fast—for a number of reasons. First, they store their data unordered. Second, keys are not really formatted—all structure keys are uppercase. Third, many of ColdFusion's internal data are actually structures. All variables with the following prefixes are stored as structures and can be manipulated as such:

- APPLICATION
- ATTRIBUTES
- CFCATCH
- CFERROR
- CGI
- COOKIE
- FORM
- REQUEST
- SESSION
- THISTAG
- URL

Creating a Structure

Create a structure using the function StructNew(), which takes no arguments. ColdFusion offers eleven structure functions, all of which begin with "Struct" (except for IsStruct()). You can create structures using <cfset>:

```
<cfset strMetaTags = StructNew()>
```

Or you can do it like this, with <cfscript>:

```
<cfscript>
strMetaTags = StructNew();
</cfscript>
```

<NOTE>

Many developers name structures beginning with "st" or "str" so that it is easy to determine that a variable is a structure. Spectra, which is written entirely in ColdFusion, uses hundreds of structures, and it follows this naming convention.

Once you have created it, you can populate it. In this example, we'll work with a structure that holds meta tags. Since meta tags are familiar, and they consist of string keys and paired values, this should make understanding structures easier. Let's say we're going to use the following meta tags in making a website:

```
<meta name="robots" content="all">
<meta name="resource-type" content="document">
<meta name="revisit-after" content="31 days">
<meta name="distribution" content="global">
<meta name="copyright" content="Copyright Cybertrails 2001">
<meta name="author" content="Cybertrails">
<meta name="rating" content="general">
```

We could write these into a structure using the "name" value as our key and the "content" value as our value.

Populating and Referencing a Structure

You can populate a structure using <cfset> like this:

```
<cfset StructureName.Key = Value>
```

You can also use <cfscript>, like this:

```
<cfscript>
        StructureName.Key = "Value";
</cfscript>
```

As you can see, the only difference between setting a structure key and a regular variable is that there are two terms, the structure and the key. This syntax is known as *dot notation*, referring to the fact that the structure and key are separated with dots. So in order to create a new key called "resource-type" and give it a value of "document," we write this:

```
<!----make the structure---->
<cfset strMetaTags = StructNew()>

<!---set the robots key to the value "all"---->
<cfset strMetaTags.robots = "all">

<!----output the value of the key---->
<cfoutput>#strMetaTags.robots#</cfoutput>
```

If you run the code above, your output will be "all."

Array Syntax

You can also reference a structure using *array syntax*, which uses square brackets in much the same way as an array uses them. There is no real performance difference in using one over the other, but there are situations when using array syntax is preferable. You want to use array syntax when your key contains special characters. For instance, the following code will throw an error:

```
<cfset strMetaTags.resource-type = "document">
```

That's because of the dash in "resource-type." Using array syntax gives us what we need:

```
<cfset strMetaTags["resource-type"] = "document">

<cfoutput>#strMetaTags["resource-type"]#</cfoutput>
```

Another way to insert data into a structure is by using the StructInsert() function. It has the following structure:

```
<cfset StructInsert(structure, key, value, allowoverwrite)>
```

You must give the name of the structure you wish to insert your key/value pair into, then the name of the key, whether it exists yet or not, and then the value. Finally, you specify whether or not to allow the function to overwrite any current key/value that may exist with the same name. The "AllowOverwrite" attribute is optional and has two possible values: TRUE and FALSE. Default is FALSE. Here it is in action:

```
<cfset StructInsert(strMetaTags, "rating", "general", true)>

<cfoutput>#strMetaTags["rating"]#</cfoutput>
```

There is also another way to reference a value in a structure. You can use the StructFind() function. StructFind() takes two arguments—the structure name and a key name. It returns the value of the specified key. You use it like this:

```
<cfoutput>#StructFind(strMetaTags, rating)#</cfoutput>
```

<NOTE>

Structures are like lists, arrays, and simple variables in that they do not persist across multiple requests. They are available only to the current template unless you pass them to another page or hold them in a persistent scope such as a cookie, a client variable, or a session variable. We'll learn how to do this in the chapter on application frameworks.

Changing Structure Data

To change the value of a structure key, use the function StructUpdate().

Listing 8.15 Using the StructUpdate Function

```
<!------Create the "revisit-after" key.
       Set its value to "31 days"------>
<cfset StructInsert(strMetaTags, "revisit-after", "31 days")>
<!---output the "revisit-after" key------->
<cfoutput>#strMetaTags["revisit-after"]#</cfoutput>

<br>
<!----change the value of the key------->
<cfset StructUpdate(strMetaTags, "revisit-after", "7 days")>

<!---output the new value, which is now "7 days"------->
<cfoutput>#strMetaTags["revisit-after"]#</cfoutput>
```

<NOTE>

When it makes sense to use a structure, do it. Structures offer the fastest way for ColdFusion to access values. They perform far faster than lists, and faster than arrays.

Removing Data from a Structure

To remove a key/value pair from a structure, use the StructDelete() function. It has this syntax:

```
<cfset StructDelete(structure, key, indicatenotexisting)>
```

After you specify the structure to delete the key/value from, and the key you wish to delete, you use the indicatenotexisting argument to specify whether or not you want ColdFusion to notify you if you attempt to delete a key that does not exist. Possible values are TRUE and FALSE. Default is false, and if you leave it this way, ColdFusion will return TRUE regardless of whether the key existed or not. To delete only the "robots" key and its value from our example, you'd write this:

```
<cfset StructDelete(strMetaTags, "robots")>
```

You can delete data from a structure using the StructClear() function, which empties all key and value pairs but leaves the structure. It is very simple, accepting the name of the structure to clear as its argument:

```
<cfset StructClear(strMetaTags)>
```

Putting It to Work

You learned earlier how to use a loop to output the values in an array. This time we will use a loop to insert key/value pairs into structure. Using a form, you can create a meta tags definition application that will build your HTML meta tags for you. The only purpose of this application is to demonstrate how many of the concepts we've discussed in this chapter can work together. There are obviously easier ways to do this. I think this is a helpful example because it offers some insight into how all the pieces fit together. It is rich in structure, array, and list functions and combines them all in complex ways.

<NOTE>

I know we haven't dealt with loops yet, but since this is the way you are likely to interact with arrays and structures once you're more comfortable, I include these loop examples.

In order to complete the meta tags application, you need to take a quick look at a ColdFusion tag called <CFHTMLHEAD>.

<CFHTMLHEAD>

Meta tags, as you know, belong in the HTML head of a Web document. The ColdFusion tag <cfhtmlhead> makes it possible to send information to the HTML head of a Web document, no matter where your code is. Without <cfhtmlhead>, our meta tags would end up in the body of the document, where they don't belong.

The <cfhtmlhead> tag has one attribute: "Text," which is the text you wish to send to the HTML head. Here is an example:

```
<cfhtmlhead text="<title>My Document Title</title>">
```

We will use this tag to send the meta tags generated from form inputs into the HTML head.

Creating a Meta Tag Maker

In order to demonstrate the concepts in this chapter, we will create an HTML meta tag maker application. First we'll build a form that allows a user to input content values for meta names. Then we'll pass those form values into a structure. Now, we could name out every key, and set the value of the key to a form variable with a matching name. Or we could use a loop and make both the meta name (structure key) *and* the value dynamic. Let's do that, since it is shorter and gives us more flexibility. This is the real power of ColdFusion, and Listing 8.16 shows how to do it.

<NOTE>

We have not discussed each of the functions used in the meta tag maker application. However, they should seem familiar, given everything you've learned so far, and you can refer to the ColdFusion function reference in Appendix B of this book for more information.

Listing 8.16 Meta Tag Maker

```
<html>
<head>
        <title>Meta tag maker</title>
</head>

<body>
```

```
<cfif isDefined("FORM.Fieldnames")>
<!----they have submitted the form, so process it------->

<!---we get form.fieldnames as a list.
The final value in this submitted form
is "submit", so let's get rid of it. To do that, we use
the ListDeleteAt function, and nest the ListLast function as
the value for the "position" argument. That ensures that
we will delete whatever the last value is.

Hold the list in the "newlist" variable.------->

<cfset newlist = ListDeleteAt(form.fieldnames,
(ListLen(form.fieldnames)))>

<!---set the list without the Submit field into an array
       using the ListToArray function.---->

<cfset arrList = ListToArray(newlist)>

<!---remember that structures output in alphabetical order.
So re-sort the array accordingly. Using the "text" argument
will order the array alphabetically.------->

<cfset ArraySort(arrList, "text")>

<!----recast the sorted array as a
       list again so that the key/value
       pairs match up in the structure.
       Specify a comma as the delimiter.------->

<cfset "fields" = ArrayToList(arrList, ",")>

<!---make a structure to hold the meta tags------->
<cfset strMetaTags = StructNew()>

<!---loop over the array and populate the keys
       with the arrList values.------->

<cfloop from = "1" to="#ArrayLen(arrList)#" index="idx">

<!-----give the new keys values from the
       "fields" list. Use the evaluate function
       to force ColdFusion to interpret the
       value of the field.
------>
```

```
        <cfset strMetaTags[#arrList[idx]#] =
                "#Evaluate(ListGetAt(fields, idx))#">
</cfloop>

<!-----use the StructKeyArray function to
        create an array containing all of the keys
        in the structure------>

<cfset strKeyArr = StructKeyArray(strMetaTags)>

        <cfloop from="1" to="#ArrayLen(strKeyArr)#"
                index="idx">

        <!---output metatags------->
                <cfoutput>
                <!---put the meta names into
                        lower case for fun------->
        <!---escape double quote marks--->
        <cfset tags =
"<meta name=""#Lcase(strKeyArr[idx])#""
        content=""#structFind(strMetaTags, ArrList[idx])#"">

<!---if we do not use the cfHTMLHead tag,
        our meta tags will end up in the body of the page,
        which we don't want.------->

                <cfhtmlhead text=#tags#>
</cfoutput>
        </cfloop>

The meta tags have been created.

<cfelse>

<!---the form is not defined, so display it.------->

<form action="MetaStruct.cfm" method="post"name="MyMetatags">

<!---the names of the form fields will be used as the
        "name" value in the meta tags---->

<h2>Meta Tag maker</h2>
<table border = 0>
<tr>
<td align="right">Please enter the values</td>
<td> </td>
```

```
</tr>
<tr>
<td align="right">Title:</td>
<td><input type="text" name="Title" size="50"></td>
</tr>
<tr>
<td align="right">Keywords:</td>
<td><input type="text" name="Keywords" size="50"></td>
</tr>
<tr>
<td align="right">Description:</td>
<td><input type="text" name="Description" size="50"></td>
</tr>
<tr>
<td align="right">Resource-Type:</td>
<td><input type="text" name="ResourceType" size="50"></td>
</tr>
<tr>
<td align="right">Copyright:</td>
<td><input type="text" name="Copyright" size="50"></td>
</tr>
<tr>
<td align="right">Author:</td>
<td><input type="text" name="Author" size="50"></td>
</tr>
<tr>
<td align="right">Revisit-After:</td>
<td><input type="text" name="RevisitAfter" size="50"></td>
</tr>
<tr>
<td align="right">Distribution:</td>
<td><input type="text" name="Distribution" size="50"></td>
</tr>
<tr>
<td> </td><td><input type="submit" name="Submit"
value="Make Meta Tags"></td>
</tr>

</form>

</table>

<!----End check for form.fieldnames definition----->
</cfif>

</body>
</html>
```

Figure 8.13 shows the values entered into the form.

Once the form is submitted, the meta tags have been generated and sent to the document header.

You can see the results in Figure 8.14. I have added line breaks so that you can see the entire output, but that is of no consequence to your browser.

You can save this information to a file that you can have ColdFusion read into documents later, or expand the application to allow a site administrator to associate these meta tags with certain objects in your website. You can also save this information to a database, or call it from a custom tag to include it in all of your ColdFusion sites. But its main purpose is just to demonstrate how to use lists, arrays, and structures, and their associated functions.

In the next chapter we will learn how to design and create databases for use with ColdFusion.

Figure 8.13 The values have been entered into the form.

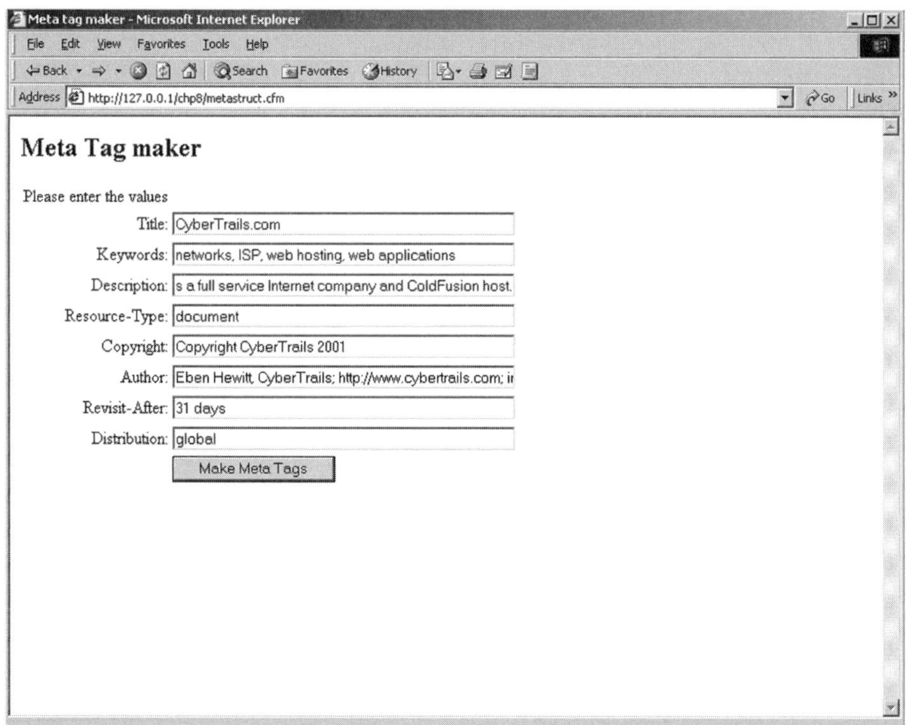

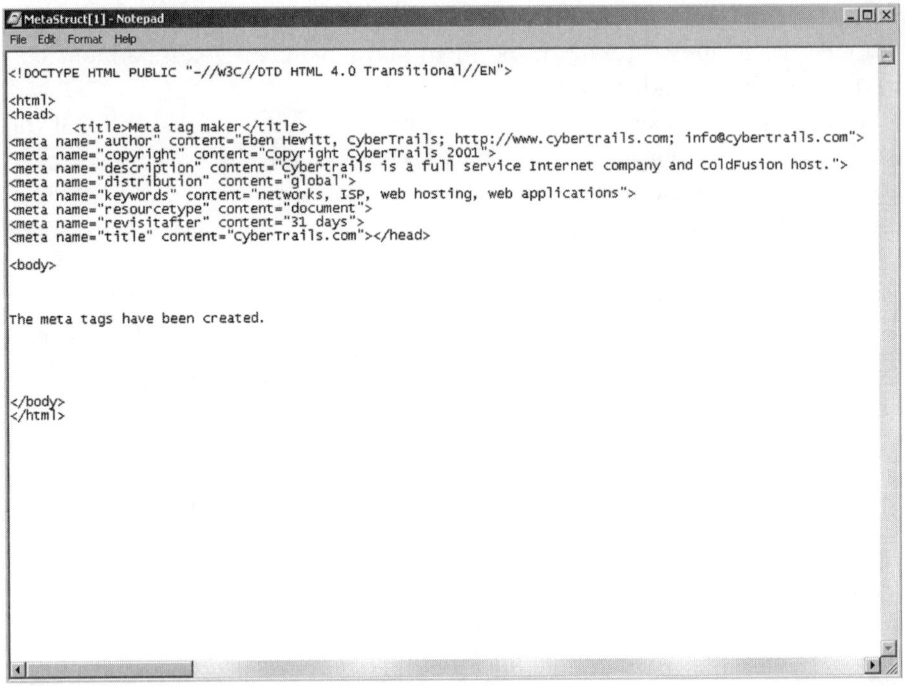

MetaStruct[1] - Notepad

File Edit Format Help

```
<!DOCTYPE HTML PUBLIC "-//W3C//DTD HTML 4.0 Transitional//EN">

<html>
<head>
	<title>Meta tag maker</title>
<meta name="author" content="Eben Hewitt, CyberTrails; http://www.cybertrails.com; info@cybertrails.com">
<meta name="copyright" content="Copyright CyberTrails 2001">
<meta name="description" content="Cybertrails is a full service Internet company and ColdFusion host.">
<meta name="distribution" content="global">
<meta name="keywords" content="networks, ISP, web hosting, web applications">
<meta name="resourcetype" content="document">
<meta name="revisitafter" content="31 days">
<meta name="title" content="CyberTrails.com"></head>

<body>


The meta tags have been created.




</body>
</html>
```

Figure 8.14 Once the meta tag maker is submitted, you can view the document source to check your results.

DESIGNING A RELATIONAL DATABASE

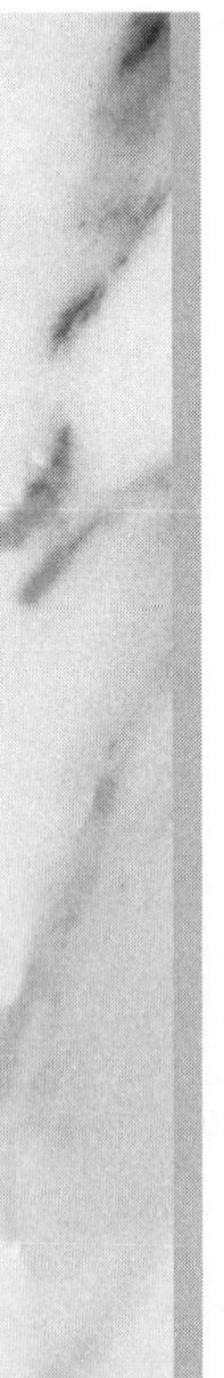

Topics in This Chapter

- Three-tier architecture
- What is a database?
- The relational model and normalization
- Database entities and relationships
- Example database creation script
- Database design tips

Chapter 9

"You see this? This is this. This ain't something else. This is this."

—*Robert DeNiro,* The Deer Hunter

In working with ColdFusion, interacting with databases will be a fundamental aspect of your applications. This chapter is a tutorial on how to design a sensible database that you can use in creating ColdFusion applications. If you are not responsible for creating databases within your organization, you may still find this chapter a useful introduction to the ideas behind database design that will help you develop ColdFusion more conscientiously.

We begin by discussing the relational model, then quickly cover some relational database design theory. We move next into a discussion of the entities that make up a relational database, and how they relate to one another. We will conclude with an example database creation script and some tips on how to write databases for Web applications.

There won't be much ColdFusion in this chapter, so if you are already familiar with database design, you can skip to Chapter 10, "Working with Relational Databases," though you may find my approach to describing database design somewhat unique.

Three-Tier Architecture

Many of today's dynamic websites are referred to as three-tiered Web applications. This architecture is implemented on three separate processes, each running on a separate platform. The three tiers refer to:

- *The Client Tier.* This generally means the user interface, which is not to be confused with a browser. It means the objects the user directly interacts with, such as menus, links, graphics, layouts, and forms. The browser is simply the mode of displaying the user interface. You will often hear this referred to as the "presentation layer."
- *The Application Server Modules.* The middle tier consists of the functionality that actually processes data, such as ColdFusion templates and the ColdFusion Application Server.
- *The Database Management System.* This tier is comprised of database software and the database itself. It runs on a second server called the data server.

The client is the requester of services, and the server provides the services. While this seems obvious now, it was somewhat revolutionary in the 1980s because of the file-sharing networks common at that time. This three-tier architecture provides data retrieval and manipulation mechanisms, as well as business logic and computational capabilities. Therefore less software is required to run on the client (a Web browser is all that's needed). That makes this architecture very powerful, because it makes rich data stores easily accessible. This book is generally devoted to the construction of the middle tier. We don't discuss the client tier, because HTML and a little graphic design knowledge solve that. But the middle tier doesn't do very much without the database behind it—which leads us to the main topic of this chapter.

What Is a Database?

A *database* is a structured collection of information. In this sense, a grocery list is a database. It is a collection of information—the items you want to buy—and it is structured inasmuch as it is discrete (the items on it are enumerable; that is, it has a verifiable beginning and end). Moreover, the information on the list is structured, inasmuch as it consists entirely of items you want to purchase from the grocery. We must make a distinction between a database as defined above, and a *relational database management system,* which is a product designed to let you work with relational databases. Such products include Microsoft SQL Server, Microsoft Access, Oracle, IBM's DB2, Informix, Sybase, and others.

It will serve us well to step back and examine the concepts surrounding relational databases in somewhat abstract terms. Let us eschew the approach that says that a database is what comes out of the box when you unwrap Access, put the CD in your computer, and click Next. It is tempting to jump directly into a discussion of how your company database can be filled with employees who have names and phone numbers, products that have sku's, and so forth. But this would be a disservice to you. Database design theory is not insignificant, and while it may be easy to drag and drop in Access, designing relational databases, especially for sites of any complexity such as you will be expected to build, is sophisticated work. Your database is often the cornerstone of your ColdFusion Web application. Your database design will affect how you can interact with the database from within your application, and it will greatly impact the overall speed, durability, scalability, and flexibility of your ColdFusion site. We will therefore proceed somewhat cautiously.

Relational Databases and the Relational Model

The *relational model* is a way of describing some defined aspect of the world. Dr. E.F. Codd was working as a research scientist at IBM in 1969 when he conceived of the relational model. When Dr. Codd described it, lack of order or hierarchy was in sharp contrast to other models of the time.

The relational model has a strong foundation in *set theory* as described by Georg Cantor, Bertrand Russell, Gottlob Frege, and others. Set theory is capable of describing and proving theories within complex mathematics and geometry, and in this sense serves as a foundation for mathematics.

A *set* is a collection. We talk about a set of encyclopedias or a deck of cards, which are also a set.

There are two ways to specify a set. The first is as a list, as in 1, 3, 5, 7, 9. In set theory, one specifies sets as property extensions, as in "$x \mid x$ is an odd natural number less than 10." One might say this as, "the set of all *x such that x* is an odd natural number less than 10." The most fundamental type of relation in set theory is that of *membership.* For instance, "7 is a member of the set of odd natural numbers less than 10." Of course, 7 is *also* a member of the set of *all* odd natural numbers, as well as a member of the integers set, and many other sets as one can quickly see.

Membership in a set is *determinate.* That is, it can be confidently determined—there is absolutely no ambiguity. "Laundry detergent" is either written on your grocery list or is not. Whether or not you actually buy laundry detergent once you get to the store is of no consequence. Because that is a different set—the set of things you bought at the grocery. This latter set, the set of things you bought at the grocery, is a *subset* of the total items in the grocery.

The *union* of sets A and B is the set of all members of A as well as all members of B. The union of the set of creatures with wings and creatures without wings is the set of all creatures. The *intersection* of sets A and B is the set of members common to both sets.

I urge you to think of things in terms of sets as you write relational databases. As you investigate relational databases you will come across these terms, and other set-theory terms such as "Cartesian products," with some frequency. In fact, you will first come across them in Chapter 10, "Working with Relational Databases."

The identity of a set is determined entirely by its members. The order of information within a set is indifferent, just as the order of the items on your grocery list is indifferent. Referring to the "order" of relations within a database is not meaningful.

<FOR FUN>

Just for fun, consider Bertrand Russell's famous paradox, which rests on this formulation: for any Property P, there is a set {x | x has P}. The paradox says, "Describe the set of all sets that are not members of themselves." What is the problem with that? If a set is a member of that set, it is NOT a member of that set, in which case it is a member of that set, in which case it is not. In the same way, one can never delineate the set of all sets, since it constitutes an infinite regress of inclusivity/exclusivity.

Relational Databases and the Real World

In this sense, a relational database is a discrete set of sets. It describes what some theorists refer to as a *problem space,* or what this specific database is concerned with addressing. The problem space is a well-defined aspect of the real world. In writing a database, you are deciding what real-world objects will and will not be necessary in describing that space sufficiently. Of course, "sufficiently" is relative. And thinking of the world in relational terms is not necessarily intuitive.

<NOTE>

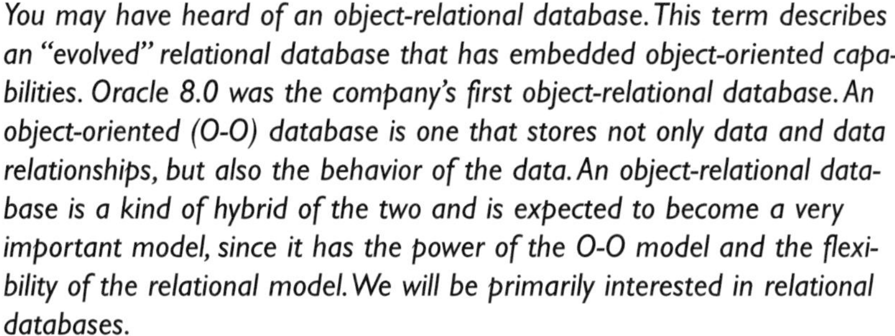

You may have heard of an object-relational database. This term describes an "evolved" relational database that has embedded object-oriented capabilities. Oracle 8.0 was the company's first object-relational database. An object-oriented (O-O) database is one that stores not only data and data relationships, but also the behavior of the data. An object-relational database is a kind of hybrid of the two and is expected to become a very important model, since it has the power of the O-O model and the flexibility of the relational model. We will be primarily interested in relational databases.

Consider that your challenge is to write an e-commerce site for your company. You could create a database to store product, customer, and order information, and then write a ColdFusion application to serve as the Web interface between the customers and the database. Your problem space is the determination of how to represent orders, customers, products, and anything else that is relevant. What are the sets that make a customer? Is it one set that contains all of the customer's contact information? What exactly does "contact information" mean? Where do you record the credit card number and expiration date—with the order, with the customer, or somewhere else? As in art and literature, deciding how to represent the world is a crucial aspect of database design.

The Relational Database

A *relational database* is a physical instance of the relational data model. It is an implementation of the abstract schema, as well as the data which the implementation structures. It has three main objectives:

- describe the way that data is represented
- define data integrity possibilities (how data can be protected)
- define how data can be manipulated

The term "relational database" comes not from the relationships between the sets of information in a database, but rather from the sets themselves, which Codd called *relations*, after the term in set theory that refers to the set of ordered pairs. We often refer to these sets as *tables*. A table is comprised of precisely rows (or *tuples*) and columns (or *attributes*). If you are familiar with spreadsheets, the visual representation is quite similar. A *record* is an intersection of one row and one or more columns.

<TIP>

You can read Codd's original specification first published in 1970 as "A Relational Model of Data for Large Shared Data Banks," Communications of the ACM, *Vol. 13, No. 6 (June 1970).*

For instance, I have created a little Access database for illustration purposes. I do not recommend using Access for Web applications, as it is meant for a very few concurrent users and has nothing like the power of more sophisticated relational database management systems, such as SQL Server or Oracle.

If you examine Figure 9.1, you can see a table called "Customers," which has five rows and eight columns. The columns are named CustomerID, FirstName, LastName, Phone, Address, City, State, ZipCode. Each column refers to a subset of the Users set. That is, since each user will have a first

Customers : Table

CustomerID	FirstName	LastName	Phone	Address	City	State	ZipCode
1	Eben	Hewitt	(520) 834-4454	606 Birch St.	Scottsdale	AZ	80622
2	Alison	Brown	(520) 834-7565	606 Birch St.	Scottsdale	AZ	80622
3	Zoe	Brown-Harvey	(520) 557-4454	11 E. Main St.	Champaign	IL	80622
4	Susan	Matteson	(777) 765-9888	22 Train Ave.	Miami	FL	87654
5	Trevor	Elliott	(212) 007-0123	212 E. 23rd St. Apt 14	New York	NY	11111
(AutoNumber)							0

Figure 9.1 A table consists of columns and rows.

name, we can refer to the set of first names in the database. And the set "name" doesn't mean anything without its superset "Customers." Each row is *one particular instance* of the table set. Each of the five users in the table is known by aggregates of the column values.

For example, the value for the "FirstName" column for the first row is "Eben." The value for the FirstName column in the second row is "Alison." Each row represents one particular user—one instance of the set.

Relations, or Tables

A relation, or table (we'll use the terms interchangeably), refers to an entity that has two structural properties: it is comprised solely of scalar values, and it is arranged as rows and columns (as in a spreadsheet).

Scalar in this context refers to the dictate that any particular row and column intersection must contain only a single value. What exactly constitutes a scalar value is not always hard and fast. For instance, what is a "name"? Should a name be stored in one column, or two columns, "FirstName" and "LastName" (as in our example above), or three columns "GivenName," "SurName," "MiddleInitial"? The answer depends on the requirements of your application and is also a bit subjective. In general, however, anything one might consider a list is not a scalar value.

Our users table example above might work okay if the users represented in the table were members of our website whom we didn't really need to contact. We might be storing their contact information just for reference purposes. What if this users table was meant to represent salespeople in the field? This would not be a very good design, because there is a serious limitation constituted by the "Phone" field. How many salespeople do you know with only one phone? Phones are a central concern to salespeople, and at least in my experience they have two or three. If you see that your application is imposing an artificial programmatic constraint that does not exist in the real-world problem space, then you should reexamine your schema.

In order to decide what tables to create in a database, you must examine the problem space. Each table should represent one thing. This is where most relational databases get into trouble. The designer chooses the wrong thing in the world to represent. When thinking about designing your database, it's a pretty good rule to think of nouns as things to be represented, but not verbs. For instance, when thinking about what will happen at your site, you can make a number of statements: "a customer browses the catalog," "a customer buys a product," "the order is received," etc. It seems clear that a "customer" is a thing that can be considered with some degree of discretion. A product, too, is a thing. "Browses" is a verb and therefore an action; that makes it hard to represent in a database. Furthermore, what is to be gained by even trying to represent "browses"? So it seems we have our candidates for tables.

But what about the "catalog"? It may seem at first that we want to have a catalog table. What would go into that table, though—that is, specifically what information would be represented? As we start to think about it, it seems that a catalog may not be an entity itself. Remember that a set is identified entirely by its members. The members of a catalog are just products, which we've already got. So we probably don't need a catalog table. But products do fit into categories. Should we make a categories table, and then put each product in that category into the table?

<NOTE>

The relational model only specifies that data be represented conceptually as a relation. Which means that a relation need not exist physically, since it can be determined from values extant in other relations.

The answer is somewhat complex, and we will need to examine how a database deals with uniqueness among records, and the relationships between tables in order to do it justice.

Uniqueness, Keys, and Relationships

Because, as noted above, the order of information within tables is indifferent, we need to have a way to refer to each item, or row, within a table. The model dictates that each row in a table be unique. In order to ensure this, you create what are called *primary keys.* A primary key is usually one column (in which case it is called a "simple key"), but it can be combinations of columns (in which case it is a "composite key"). In the customers access table in Figure 9.1 the primary key column is "CustomerID." The number in that column does not refer to anything.

Stability is the central concern here. You want to make sure that your primary key value rarely or never changes. For that reason, many relational database management systems (RDBMSs) create a special data type that will automatically increment each time you insert a new record into the database. In Microsoft Access, this is called Auto-Number. In other systems it is often referred to as an incremental column.

As you can see in Figure 9.2, a tiny key symbol is printed to the left of the CustomerID column, which signifies that this column is the primary key for the table. It is generally a good idea to stick with numeric, automatically

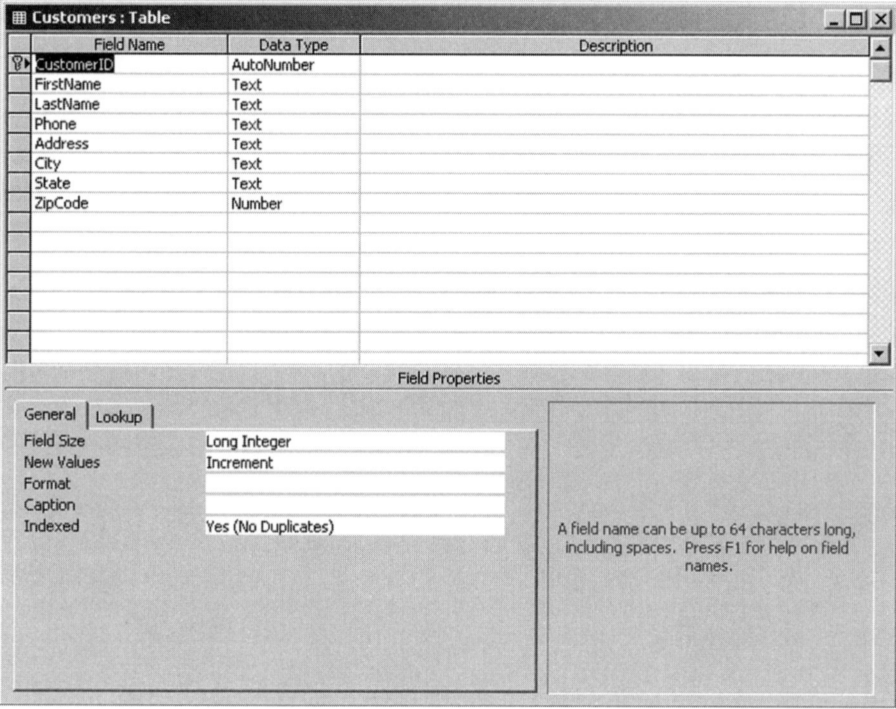

Figure 9.2 Using "design view" in Microsoft Access allows you to specify the data types of each column.

incrementing values for your primary key column, since it won't ever change, and because it is numeric it will be very fast for your database to retrieve.

You will see how to go about creating tables in a moment. For now, we still need to answer our product/category question. You could make a table that holds both the name of the product and the name of the category it is in. However, your data quickly becomes unmanageable. What if our product was a book? In a physical sense, a book is a discrete object. But in a very important sense in the real world, a book is in no way a discrete object; it is the product of, at least, an author and a publisher. The publisher is related to the book just as much as the author is. What if the book takes two or three or twenty people to write? We're back to our salesperson–phone dilemma. It may have a year of publication. What if it goes into multiple editions, each of which needs to be recorded? Perhaps you've got an e-commerce site that sells books, or a library site. How do you handle something like Joyce's *Ulysses*? It has multiple publishers. Shakespeare's plays are in the public domain, and anybody with paper and ink can publish them if they want to.

Asking Questions

My intention here is to impress upon you the need to really consider certain things before you write a database. Poor database design is often behind slow-performing sites that are difficult to scale. So the things to consider are this:

- What will my database represent in the real world? (Remember that the real world means interactions and events just as much as it means objects.)
- How can I make this purposive representation in its simplest form? Do I need to break it into smaller subsets? If so, what are the composite parts of the sets I wish to represent?
- What requests are going to be made of this database? What questions does it exist to answer?

That last item is important. When thinking of sets and representations it is easy to think of databases as passive things. That is a mistake. It is certainly true that they are repositories of information. However, that information must be structured not just to sit there, but to answer questions. It is a good idea to start with the result you desire, and then determine what you need in order to get there. You do that by considering all of the questions that will be (reasonably) asked of your system.

Redundant Data

For the questions that your database will get asked to be answered properly, your system must have its sets represented as rather specific subsets. If your database contains redundant data, you'll end up tying yourself in knots, and the question posed to your database will be difficult to answer. That's why you need the primary keys—they are unique identifiers, so they can be used to create a unique relationship between tables. Another consideration when determining how to store your data is consistency. When you have redundant data, it becomes very difficult to maintain the consistency of that data.

So you break up your entity into smaller, more flexible subsets. The process of creating these subsets is known as *normalization*.

Normalization

Normalization is what you do to optimally simplify the structure of your database. There are five *normal forms,* which are the rules of normalization theory specifying efficiency of structure. Each higher normal form dictates a more efficient design.

In this chapter we will discuss normal forms one, two, and three. Normal forms four and five are generally regarded as more theoretical than practicable and are rarely achieved. For our purposes, normalizing through third normal form will do just fine.

First Normal Form

We are now prepared to make a finer distinction than we did earlier. A "relation" and a "table" are not precisely equivalent. I have been using them interchangeably, because I want to encourage you to think of them in the same way. A *relation* has these specific characteristics:

- It describes only one entity.
- Its columns are unordered.
- Its rows are unordered.
- It contains no duplicate rows. There is therefore always a primary key available.

Make sure that your tables always conform to the definition of a relation. Remember that your relational database management system will not necessarily enforce these rules. They are part of the relational model. It is your job to make sure that your database complies.

A *relation is said to be in first normal form if every intersection of rows and columns is scalar, and it does not have repeating groups.* That means that you must store only indivisible values. Consider a library database that holds information about who has checked out what books. The example in Figure 9.3 violates first normal form.

By storing lists or arrays you quickly run into trouble. The table in Figure 9.3 is no easier for your RDBMS to understand than it is for you to understand. What exactly have people checked out here? In the second row, has user with UserID 3 checked out one book called *Prozac Nation, Credit Card Nation* or two books whose titles are separated by a comma? The third row is even worse. How could you determine what exactly has been checked out? You couldn't.

You might try to solve the problem above by making several columns in the "CheckedOut" table, each holding one book checked out by a library customer. Your table would then look like Figure 9.4.

This seems like an improvement, and for reporting purposes you are a little better off. However, first normal form also dictates that your tables must

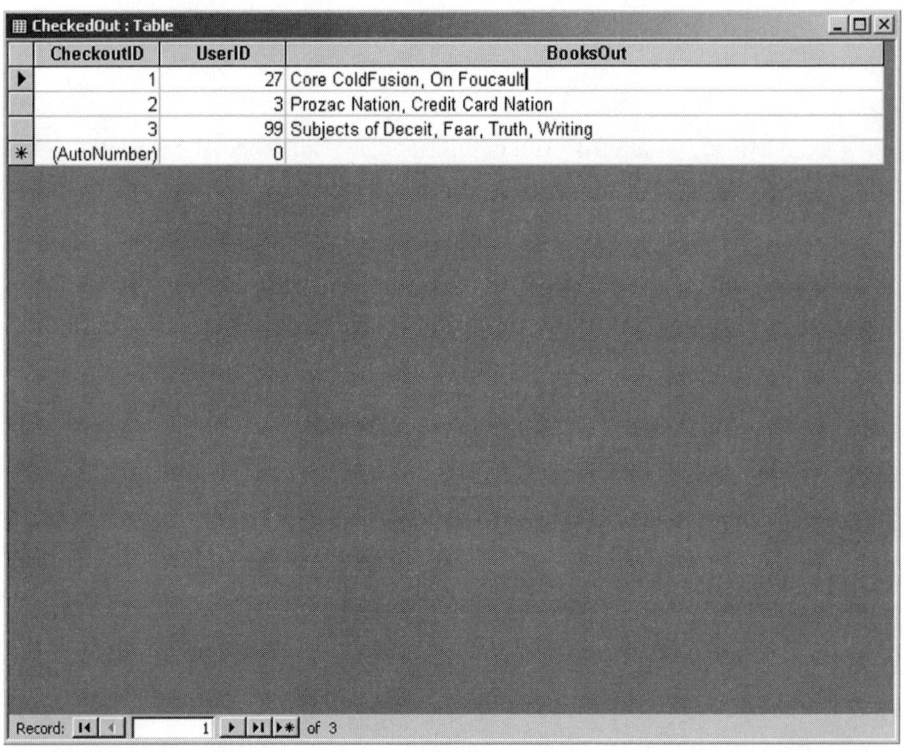

CheckedOut : Table

CheckoutID	UserID	BooksOut
1	27	Core ColdFusion, On Foucault
2	3	Prozac Nation, Credit Card Nation
3	99	Subjects of Deceit, Fear, Truth, Writing
(AutoNumber)	0	

Record: 1 of 3

Figure 9.3 This table violates first normal form, since it stores lists of values rather than individual values.

CheckOut2 : Table

CheckOutID	UserID	Book1	Book2	Book3	Book4	Book5
1	27	Core ColdFusion	On Foucault			
2	3	Prozac Nation	Credit Card Nation			
3	99	Subjects of Deceit	Fear, Truth, Writing			
(AutoNumber)	0					

Record: 2 of 3

Figure 9.4 This table also violates first normal form, since it has repeating groups.

not have repeating groups. What happens when I bring six books to the counter to check out? We have introduced an artificial system constraint by just deciding that users don't need to check out more than five books at once. Remember that the database reflects sets in the world; don't try to shape the world according to your database—the world will surely win.

So how do we get our table into first normal form, if we can't have repeating groups and we can store only scalar values? The key, as it were, is in the key.

Foreign Keys

There is a saying in database design: "The key, the whole key, and nothing but the key." The idea behind the saying is that you can relate tables to each other using their primary keys. Because the primary key implies uniqueness, you can reference unique rows from another table. Such a reference is called a foreign key. A *foreign key* is simply a column whose value is the primary key of another table, creating a *relationship* between the tables.

Relationships

In databases, as in the world, a relationship is simply an association between two entities. In the world, relationships are complex; there are few examples of entities that have a relationship with only one other entity. If you think about it in relational terms (or in binary terms for that matter), that's all you need. Anything in the world can be represented after a fashion in binary, if you have enough digits. Remember that database theory is rooted in set theory. In set theory, relationships are generally binary—because that's all you need.

There are three kinds of relationships in databases: one-to-one, one-to-many, and many-to-many. We will examine each of these before returning directly to the discussion of normalization.

One-to-One Relationships

In a one-to-one relationship each row in a table has one corresponding row in a second table. This type of relationship is rare in the real world and is therefore rare in database design. To illustrate the point, consider the following example. A taxicab company requires its drivers to have their own cabs. Each driver has only one cab, and each cab has only one driver. Because they are separate entities, they are represented in separate tables. We can create

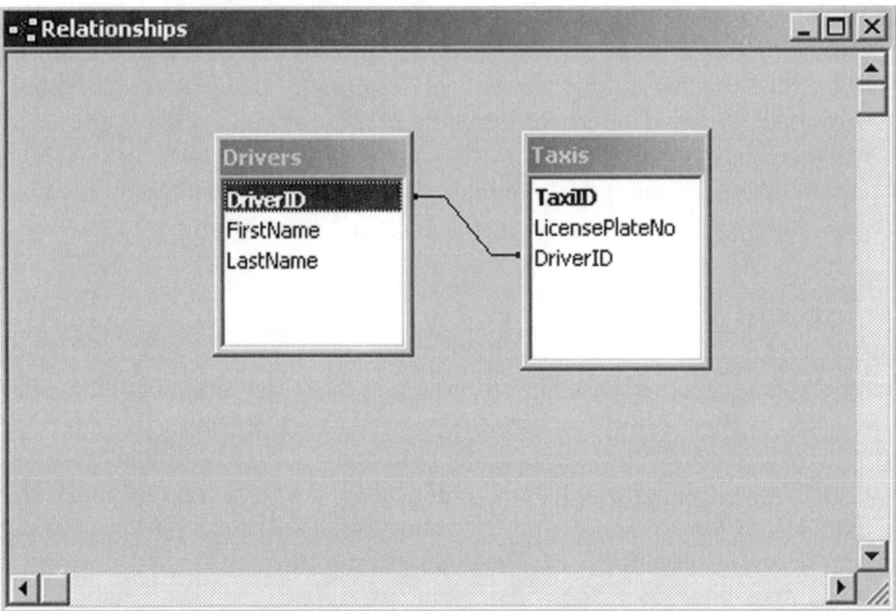

Figure 9.5 A one-to-one relationship.

these tables in Access and demonstrate the relationship between them with a line, as shown in Figure 9.5.

The taxi table is in a one-to-one relationship with the driver table, since each taxi has one and only one driver, and each driver has one and only one taxi. The limitation of this design is clear when you consider that things change over time. What if the cab company wanted to keep track of which drivers have had a certain taxi over time? If Travis leaves the company and Arthur is hired and assumes Travis's taxi, that record is gone. It is important to consider how things might change over time when you design your database.

One-to-Many Relationships

A one-to-many relationship is one in which each row in Table A can have zero, one, or more corresponding rows in Table B, and for every row in Table B there is exactly one row in Table A. This is a very common type of relationship. The normalization process often results in tables in one-to-many relationships. These are therefore the most common type of relationship.

For example, consider a website that has advertisers. Any given advertiser can have many different ads, but any given ad belongs to only one advertiser. The advertiser–ad relationship is one-to-many.

You create this kind of relationship using the primary key from the *one* table and copying that key into the *many* table. The many table now is referred to as the foreign relation, as it contains a foreign key to the one table.

It is useful to specify the relationships between entities in plain English to help make sure that you are thinking about the relationship in the right way. For instance, let's extend our advertiser–ad example. I ran into trouble once making a rather large database because I didn't consider the relationships carefully enough (this is generally what's behind problematic databases). I understood that an advertiser could have many ads, and that a particular ad could have only one advertiser associated with it. However, I stored more information in the advertisers table than I should have—I included that person's company name. I didn't think that would be a problem, since an ad only belongs to one company, right?

A company is a different sort of thing in the real world than a person is (which we know from tax laws). Even though an ad may be related to only one company, one person can work at or own several different companies. My database was fine for a long time until someone wanted to place an ad for a second company he owned. Since his first company was written into the advertisers table, it got really messy really quick. That's the kind of drag you want to anticipate and never face. Again, as in the taxi company example, change over time is a very important factor in considering your relationships.

Many-to-Many Relationships

A many-to-many relationship occurs when each record in Table A can correspond to multiple records in Table B, and each record in Table B can have multiple records in Table A. Let's return to the library example to illustrate. A given book may have only one title. The title will not change over time, if we consider that "edition" is a separate item from "title." One title can have multiple authors, however. And one author can write multiple books. So we have a dilemma, because one cannot represent many-to-many relationships in a relational database. The way we get around this is by using an intermediary table to create the relationship.

If we had a table called Titles and a table called Authors, these tables would be in a many-to-many relationship, with each title in the Titles table corresponding to one or more records in the Authors table, and each row in the Authors table corresponding to one or more records in the Titles table.

<NOTE>

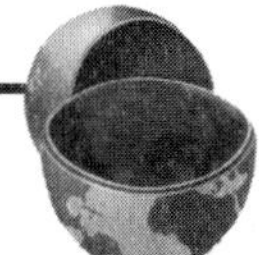

It occasionally will occur that, for instance, a title has no author. In this case, the Authors record that corresponds to that title would contain an empty set {Ø}. In databases, the empty set is referred to as NULL. Null is

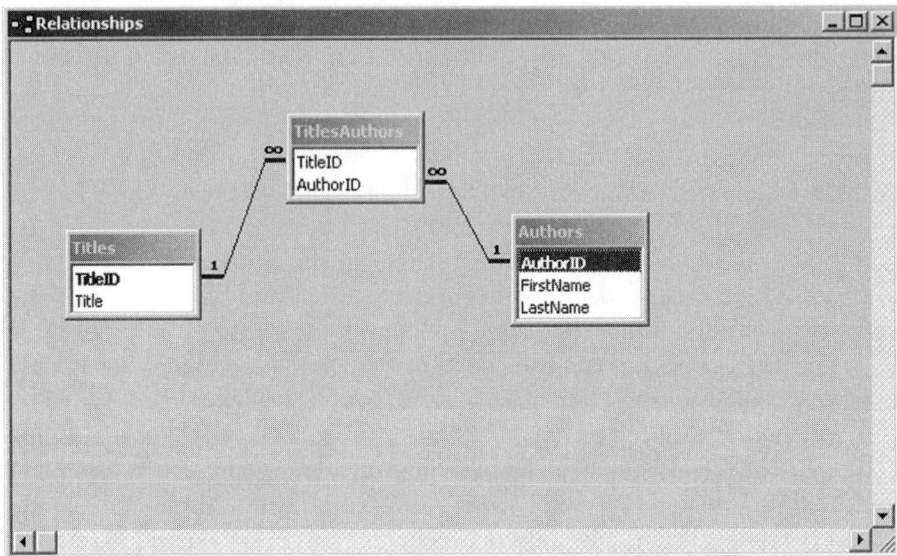

Figure 9.6 Many-to-many relationships are resolved with an intermediary table that holds only foreign keys.

not 0! Zero is a value! Null is simply "unknown"; it is a record that no record exists. The most fun definition of null I have heard is "that for which nothing can be said that is true." This definition is obviously problematic (being paradoxical in the same way as Russell's set of all sets that are not members of themselves), but it drives home an important point about null values: nulls are nonvalues and therefore cannot be less than, equivalent to, or more than any other value.

Let's create the Authors table with three columns: AuthorID (primary key), FirstName, and LastName. Then we make a Titles table that has two columns: TitleID and Title. We create a third table, usually called a *join* or *lookup* table, in order to resolve the many-to-many relationship. The join table, which we'll call TitlesAuthors, has two columns: TitleID and AuthorID. The values in both of these columns are the primary keys of their respective tables (so they are foreign keys). For instance, the TitleID column holds only the primary keys (TitleID) of the Titles column, and the Authors table holds only the primary keys value (AuthorID) from the authors table. This makes each column in TitleAuthors a foreign key column. When we *query* the database, or request information of it, which we will learn how to do in the next chapter, we can put together titles with authors via the join table. This is represented in Figure 9.6.

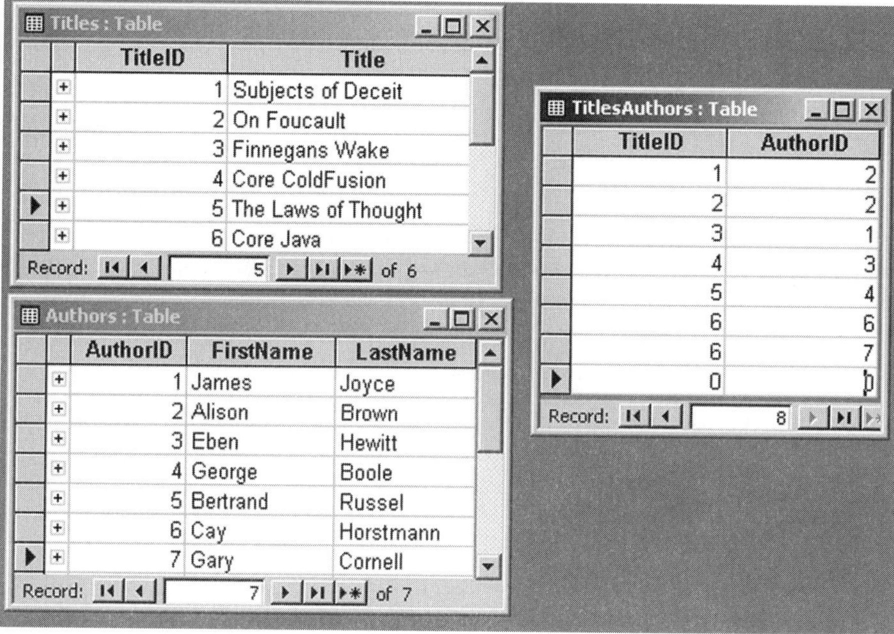

Titles : Table

TitleID	Title
1	Subjects of Deceit
2	On Foucault
3	Finnegans Wake
4	Core ColdFusion
5	The Laws of Thought
6	Core Java

Record: 5 of 6

Authors : Table

AuthorID	FirstName	LastName
1	James	Joyce
2	Alison	Brown
3	Eben	Hewitt
4	George	Boole
5	Bertrand	Russel
6	Cay	Horstmann
7	Gary	Cornell

Record: 7 of 7

TitlesAuthors : Table

TitleID	AuthorID
1	2
2	2
3	1
4	3
5	4
6	6
6	7
0	0

Record: 8

Figure 9.7 The three tables populated with data; you can tell who authored which books by using the foreign keys in the TitleAuthors table.

Notice in Figure 9.6 that the line connecting the Titles table and the TitleAuthors table has a small number 1 next to the TitleID and an infinity sign next to it. This is how Access represents a one-to-many relationship. The same is true for the Authors table and the TitleAuthors table. Authors and titles can be related indirectly via the join table. Figure 9.7 shows the titles table.

Another example may help you envision this. A common set of many-to-many relationships are those among students, teachers, and classes. Each class has many students, and each student has many classes. Each teacher teaches many classes, and each class can have more than one (many) teachers. So the relationship between students and classes is many to many, as is the relationship between teachers and classes.

At the RDBMS level you can specify constraints which ensure the integrity of your data across tables. You can also create "ad hoc" relationships on the fly between different tables by using Structured Query Language. SQL is the language used to interact with databases, and we will discuss it at length in the next chapter. For now, let us return to normal forms.

Second Normal Form

A table is in second normal form if it is in first normal form and it describes only one entity, and that entity is described by its primary key. We might say instead that every column is dependent on the primary key. I violated second normal form in the example above by not separating the company from the person; I tried to represent two distinct entities in the same table. Again, time becomes an issue. It worked fine for a while to have one company per advertiser, but over time that changed. As you create each entity, you really must ask yourself, "Will this be true for all time?"

When you break up one table into two tables this way, the process is known as *decomposition*.

Third Normal Form

A relation is said to be in third normal form if it is in second normal form and all non-key columns are mutually independent. By non-key columns is meant columns that are not part of the primary key (a primary key can be composed of multiple columns). Dependency between columns means that one column is not meaningful without another. An example is when you use calculated columns. Let's say you've got a table that stores the library's ordering information, and it has columns for TitleID, TitleCost, QuantityOrdered, and TotalCost. By multiplying the TitleCost by the QuantityOrdered, you arrive at a value for the TotalCost column. That column therefore holds a *calculated value.* That calculation is perhaps better handled at the programmatic level (i.e., have ColdFusion figure it for you, or have SQL figure it for you). The TotalCost column is dependent on the values in the TitleCost and QuantityOrdered tables, which is a violation of Third Normal Form.

There are two more normal forms in Codd's original model, but we will not consider these here. You really want to aim to make your database in third normal form.

The focus of this chapter has primarily been understanding the concepts behind database design. That is not a common approach to the topic in Web application books. It is not difficult to create a database using Microsoft Access or even SQL Server or Oracle. Access even has an "Upsizing Wizard" that allows you to create a database in Access and import it into SQL Server using a simple wizard.

Remember that the aim here is to work with ColdFusion in an intelligent manner, and in my view that requires a good understanding of relational databases and data sets. So we will write a database creation script that you can use later on to manage an "application framework" for your Web site, allowing you to authenticate users based on rules. Take a look at the syntax of the script, which you can basically cut and paste into Microsoft SQL Server 7 or 2000's Query Analyzer.

In the next chapter we will take an in-depth look at the Structured Query Language, which is used to interact with relational databases. That's what you really need to know when working in ColdFusion.

A Database Creation Script for Microsoft SQL Server

Below is a script that you can use to create a database and a few tables for it. While you can use graphical tools to do this in most RDBMSs, it is a very good idea to become familiar with the syntax. We don't have space to go into great detail here, but I have tried to comment the script so that it is clear what is happening.

If you have Microsoft Access 97, 2000, or XP, you can easily create a similar database. You shouldn't use this script, though. I encourage you to look through the script, determine what tables, fields (columns), and datatypes you need, and create the database in Access accordingly. Access and SQL Server both come with several sample databases, which help you see how good databases are structured.

This script will work with Oracle and Sybase with minor modification (for instance, drop the "Use Master" reference).

The tables created use an intermediary table with foreign keys to resolve the many-to-many relationship. We will refer to this database later on when we create an application framework to impose security for a website. There is another example of a database script in the e-commerce chapter, which is a bit larger and more complex.

After taking a look at the script, there are a number of ways you can get creative and extend the capabilities here. What are some ways you could handle phone-number information? How would you need to modify this script to handle international users? What tables and relationships would you need if your "users" were employees who worked in certain departments? Often a security framework will store security policies, which are groups of rules that can apply to different users, instead of referencing each rule at once. How would you extend this database to include Policies?

```
/*Eben Hewitt, eben@corecoldfusion.com */

/* Create a series of tables to hold
user login information and "rules information."
We could use a rule in a Web application to
give a user permissions at the object level.
A rule dictates what objects one is allowed to view.
For instance, instead of giving everyone access
to everything, once they successfully login,
we can have ColdFusion check the database
for the rules (or allowances) when a protected
object is encountered (menu items, links, or what
have you), and display it only if that
userID is associated with that ruleID.

We therefore need a Users table, a Rules table,
and a join table called UserRules. */

/* You must have Create Database permissions
on the server */

/* Create the database at 3 MB size, with a 5 MB log.
Both DB and log will grow in increments of 1 MB */

USE master

/* Go statement batches */

GO
CREATE DATABASE CoreCFDB
ON

/* specify to physically create the database file
on the d: drive, and call the data file "CoreCFDBdat.mdf" */

( NAME = CoreCFDB_dat,
  FILENAME = 'd:\mssql7\data\CoreCFDBdat.mdf',
  SIZE = 3,
  FILEGROWTH = 1 )

 /* create a log file for the database */

LOG ON
( NAME = 'CoreCFDB_log',
```

```
  FILENAME = 'd:\mssql7\data\CoreCFDBlog.ldf',
  SIZE = 5MB,
  FILEGROWTH = 1MB )
GO

/* now that the DB is created, create the tables*/

USE CoreCFDB
GO


/* ********* Create Users table************** */
/* test for existence of table; drop it if exists */
if exists
      (select * from sysobjects
            where id = object_id(N'[Users]')
            and OBJECTPROPERTY(id, N'IsUserTable') = 1)

drop table [Users]

GO
/* Make 10 columns in Users table: UserID which will
automatically increment by 1,
starting at 1, and will be the primary key;
make Username and Password
as varchar (variable-length character fields)
and allow them only 25 characters; make
Firstname and LastName to hold up to 50 characters.
Make columns to hold address info */

CREATE TABLE Users
(
          UserID                int IDENTITY(1,1)
                          NOT NULL PRIMARY KEY CLUSTERED,

          UserName        varchar(25)          NOT NULL,

          Password        varchar(25)          NOT NULL,

          FirstName       varchar(50)          NOT NULL,

          LastName        varchar(50)          NOT NULL,

/* don't force them to type an address (allow null) */

Address1 varchar(75) NULL,
```

```
Address2 varchar(50) NULL,

City           varchar(25) NOT NULL,

State          varchar(25) NOT NULL,

/* ZipCode must be 5 numeric characters.

We do this by specifying the data type as INTEGER (int) that
can be 5 digits.

Using the CONSTRAINT command  enforces this rule: the Zip-
Code column must have a digit between 0 and 9 for each of its
five digits. That means that one cannot enter fewer than five
digits*/

ZipCode    varchar(5) NOT NULL

CONSTRAINT CK_ZipCode CHECK
          (ZipCode LIKE '[0-9][0-9][0-9][0-9][0-9]')

)
GO


/* ********* Create Rules table************** */
/* test for existence of table; drop it if exists */

if exists

    (select * from sysobjects
          where id = object_id(N'[Rules]')
          and OBJECTPROPERTY(id, N'IsUserTable') = 1)

drop table [Rules]
GO


/* Make 2 columns in the Rules table:

RuleID, which is the primary key, and
RuleDesc, which is a large text field to hold
a description of the rule. */

CREATE TABLE Rules
(
```

```
    RuleID          int IDENTITY(1,1)
                NOT NULL PRIMARY KEY CLUSTERED,

    RuleDesc    text
                NOT NULL

)
GO


/* ********* Create UserRules table*************

This table depends on Users, and Rules

*/

/* test for existence of table; drop it if exists */
if exists

    (select * from sysobjects
         where id = object_id(N'[UserRules]')
         and OBJECTPROPERTY(id, N'IsUserTable') = 1)

drop table [UserRules]
GO


/* Make UserRules table as a join/lookup table.

Its job is to resolve the many-to-many relationship
between users and rules.

Therefore, make 2 columns in the UserRules table:

RuleID, which is a foreign key to the Rules
table and is therefore data type "int" (integer)

UserID, which is a foreign key to the Users table */

CREATE TABLE UserRules
(

/* RuleID is a foreign key to the Rules table,
RuleID column
*/
```

```
RuleID    int NOT NULL

FOREIGN KEY (RuleID)
REFERENCES Rules(RuleID),

/* UserID is a foreign key to the Users table,
UserID column
*/

UserID    int NOT NULL

FOREIGN KEY (UserID)
REFERENCES Users(UserID),


)
GO

/* batch completed */
```

Tips for Writing a Database and Planning Your Web-Based Application

The design of your database is a crucial factor in the success of your ColdFusion applications. There are a number of things you can do to make life easier as you plan your applications and design your databases. It's relatively inexpensive to pick up a copy of Visio, a drawing tool that has numerous built-in components for creating site navigation and conceptual charts, as well as database design tools. Figure 9.8 shows a site architecture plan in Visio.

First, I always start with a question that often seems left out: What is the aim of the client? Not the website's aim, the *client's* aim. What does this organization want to do in the world? Pretend the Web doesn't exist for a moment. What are they trying to do? I have seen site after site fail and get redone over and over because this question was never asked. Often your clients will show up at your office and say, I want an e-commerce site. Generally a less-than-witty dialogue ensues. Why? I want to sell stuff. To whom? Customers. Why? To make money. At which point it is easy enough to write them up a little store, put some pictures on it, and send them on their way.

In order to avoid the tedium of such a conversation, and to make your client's site a real success, dig a little deeper. Define the audience of the site

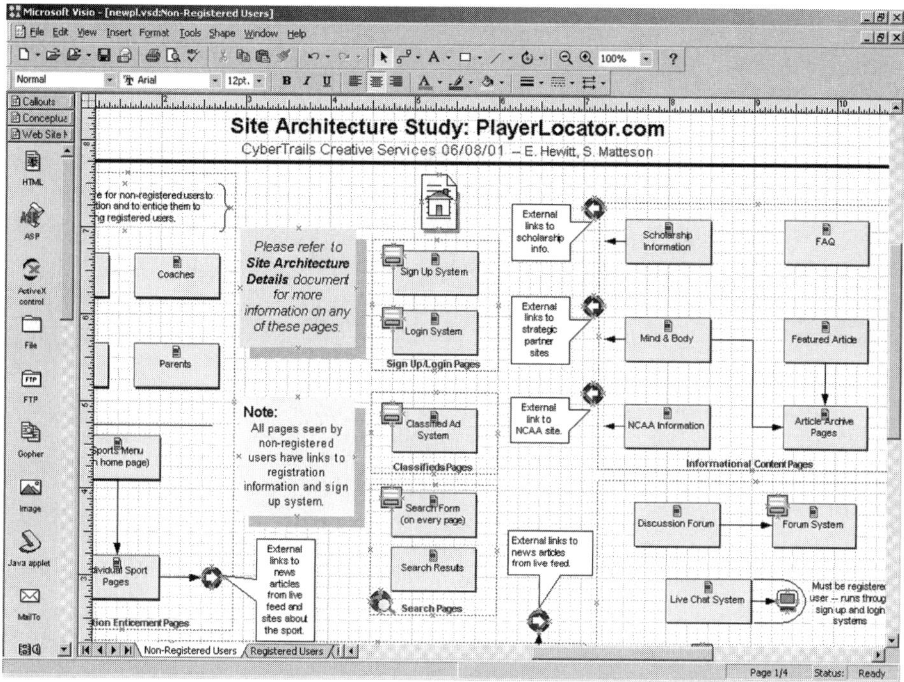

Figure 9.8 Creating a site plan is a good idea; you can do this on paper, on a whiteboard, or with a software program like Visio.

demographically. Who will be using the site—specifically? I once did research on a proposed website for high school athletes and recruiters. That turned out to be time very well spent, since I discovered something I never would have thought of. I assumed that the primary audience for the site would be teenage boys and girls, and that the design and content categories should reflect this. Upon doing my homework I discovered that a key audience for such websites is women in their late thirties and forties. Why would that be? Of course the answer is that they are the mothers of high school athletes, and have a great deal of concern for their athletic children's overall health, nutrition, scholarship information, and so on. We therefore quickly went back to the drawing board and modified the design somewhat to appeal to this demographic, and offered content categories that would be of interest to the parents of these kids. It was fabulous.

Once you have determined who your audience is and what the goal for the organization is, you can determine the goal for the website. Consider what will make a good return on investment for your customers. If they succeed, you succeed. Period. That means that you must consider each case individually.

For instance, Coca-Cola is a world dominator in its industry. While you could sell cans of Coke over the Web, is that what you would suggest they do if they came to you to build a website? Again, a little homework reveals that nearly 85% of their revenue does not come from people like you and me paying 75 cents a can in a machine. It comes from their business partners, such as their bottlers, and affiliates in the media. At this point I say, listen, let's sell Coke-related products over the Web, such as t-shirts, but let's focus the website on supplier/vendor/distributor channels in the form of an extranet, and make that automation the core Web business.

Now things start to get specific. Consider all of the interactions a user will have with your site. Will users need to login? Download something? Buy something? Break these down into steps until you can get basic nouns and verbs out of them. Once you get to thoughts like "A user places an order," the entities and relationships you need for your database almost start defining themselves.

Determine what the architecture in your site will be. Once you know what users need to do, you can figure out how they are going to do it. For instance, you know that they need to buy things. What will the shopping experience be? What is the product? When you go to the website for a car manufacturer, they don't make recommendations for your next car. They just focus on showcasing the few products they have. That's for a number of reasons, not the least of which is that people don't buy cars very often. Moreover, the cars they are selling don't change very frequently. So their sites don't need to be quite as dynamic, but they are more graphically oriented. Amazon.com, on the other hand, has thousands of products, they are cheap, you are likely to buy them with some frequency, and the product list changes frequently. It is therefore in their interest to cross-market products and make recommendations based on past purchases. The site is fast loading because it needs to be totally data driven, so it doesn't rely on many graphics. Write your application accordingly, and create your navigation with these factors in mind.

So, once you know the architecture, you can determine the objects and the rules that will apply to those objects. Perhaps you have an administrative navigation bar that only logged-in business users see. Maybe your site has members, and you want to show them a discounted price for products when they visit your site. You can do this with rules, using a database schema something like the script in the previous section.

Create the forms that users will use very early on. It's true that they will interact with menus and links more often, but the behavior of those objects is also much more predictable.

When you think you've finished with your database design *on paper* (or in a software program), then ask it all of the questions you will need to ask it.

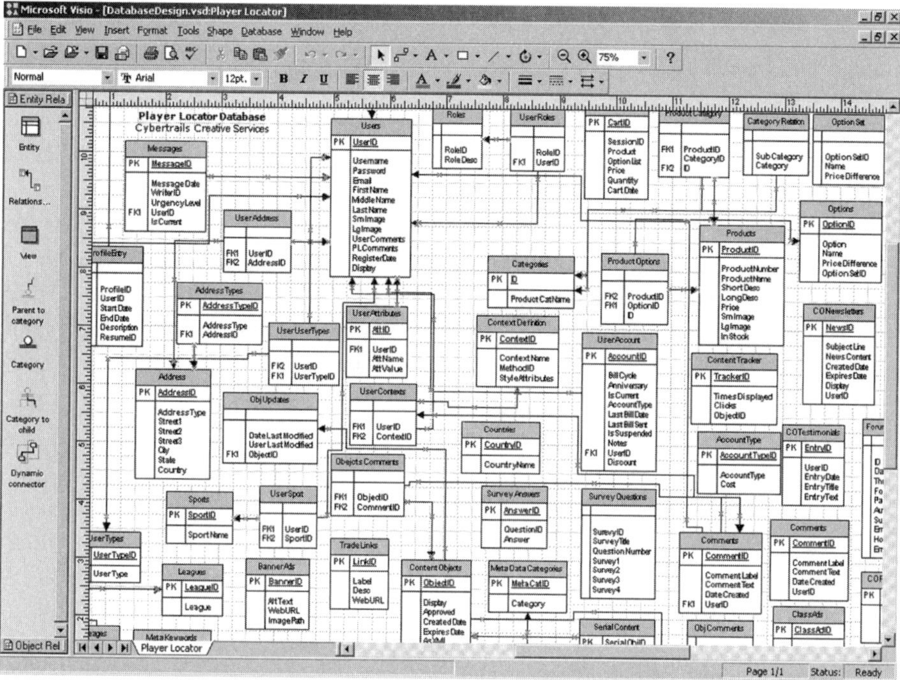

Figure 9.9 A database design layout in Visio.

Can your design give you that information? Look at your design. What in there will change over time? Look again. Have you accounted for those changes? (See Figure 9.9.)

Once you can ask your database all the questions you need to, and you get a reliable answer back, you can be pretty confident about your database. And that's an important step toward being confident about your Web application. In the next chapter you will see how to phrase those questions, once you've created your database.

Conclusion

The glamour of the Internet is over. When was the last time you picked up your telephone and were *delighted* to hear a dial tone? When was the last time you got in your car and thought, "That is so cool—when I turn the key, it starts, and then I push the pedal and it goes!" Web shops and Web hosts are now just a utility like the phone company. We who make websites aren't really that cool any more, either. People know now that it isn't magic. It is therefore important, more than ever before, to make sure that your focus remains steadfast on human interaction and the logic of business rules. Consider the world in sets, and represent it in your work. There is a good sample database in the e-commerce chapter that illustrates these "sets." The Web is just one tool, like a phone, to help people get things done. It's not a thing in itself that matters.

Databases get very complicated; a well-normalized database, even one for just a smallish website, can have dozens of tables. To make it right takes practice and a lot of paper. But if you remember the basic tenet that at the end of the day it's *people* that matter, not the Web, your database and your application will reflect that, and your site will be flexible, scalable, durable, and reliable. And that's the aim.

WORKING WITH RELATIONAL DATABASES

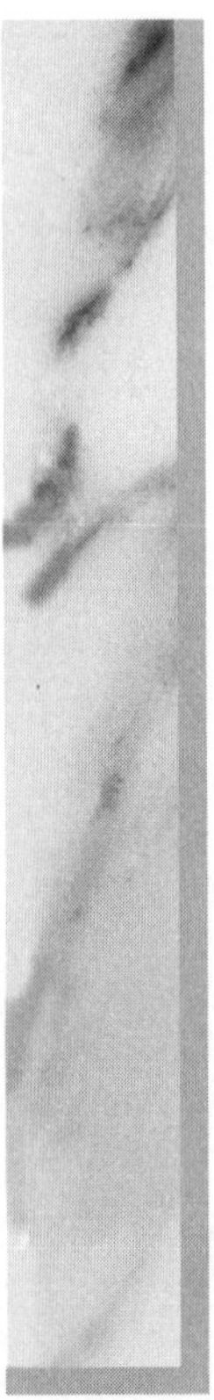

Topics in This Chapter

- Data manipulation language
- Connecting to a database
- The SELECT statement in detail
- Creating a datasource in the ColdFusion Administrator
- Retrieving data from a database with <CFQUERY>
- Inserting records
- Updating records
- Deleting records
- Query of queries
- Performing joins
- Creating a complete site searching application

Chapter 10

The aim of this chapter is to give you a solid foundation in using SQL (the Structured Query Language), which is the language used to retrieve and manipulate data in relational database systems. You will also learn how to connect to a database via ColdFusion so you perform any SQL task from within your ColdFusion templates. We will cover the basics of data retrieval and manipulation in a bit of detail. You will then learn how to set up a datasource in the ColdFusion Administrator to connect to a variety of databases, including a Microsoft SQL Server, Microsoft Access XP, and Oracle 8i.

In this chapter you will also learn how to use the <CFQUERY> tag, which encapsulates much of the complexity of working with databases through the web.

This chapter is not a complete coverage of SQL. There are numerous entire books devoted to the topic. The idea here is to give you a brief explanation, and then a practical example, of the kinds of data retrieval that ColdFusion developers generally need to do when creating web applications. So this chapter does not assume any knowledge of SQL. My hope here is to spare you the purchase of a whole new book on SQL, and to create a kind of reference for later on, such that once you really know what you're doing, you can easily refer back here and find the exact syntax of whatever statement you're working with.

Data Manipulation Language

In the last chapter you saw how to create a database using Data Definition Language statements. These allowed you to create, alter, and drop (delete) database objects and to grant or revoke permissions on those objects. The other kind of SQL statements are Data Manipulation statements. They allow you to SELECT, INSERT, UPDATE, and DELETE data in a database. This chapter will examine how to write these statements.

The statements we will write should work with little or no modification on most platforms, including Oracle, Access, Sybase, and so on. I will assume for convenience that you are running a version of Microsoft SQL Server 2000.

The thing about SQL is that one must be quite precise indeed when retrieving and manipulating data from a database. If you are not careful in specifying exactly what data you want, and exactly how you want to see it, the results of a query can be fiendishly and subtly very, very wrong. We will try to keep this in mind as we work through the chapter.

Connecting to a Database

We need to get a good grasp of SQL before we start running things through ColdFusion. Since database information will be a crucial facet of your work in ColdFusion, it would be unwise to jump immediately into this vast database sea and pick things up as we go along. A more comprehensive approach is to begin working natively in your database environment. It will then be easy to slip into using databases in our ColdFusion applications. Not surprisingly, in working with large ColdFusion data applications every day, I find that I often view and work on my databases from within the RDBMS itself every day, too. It is therefore prudent that we get at least a little comfortable in the native RDBMS.

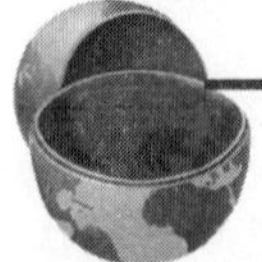

<NOTE>

Many of our examples in the early parts of this chapter will demonstrate database concepts directly within an RDBMS, such as Microsoft SQL

Server. You will very likely have to manipulate and retrieve data from within your database system itself, and it is therefore useful to become familiar with the environment.

The Query Analyzer in Microsoft SQL Server 7 and 2000 is a command-line tool, much like SQL *Plus for Oracle, which allows you to perform any interaction with your SQL database in plain text. While graphical tools are included for such business, such as the Designer, these don't help you learn the language, and, most importantly, they won't be useful in working from ColdFusion. So we'll stick to the command line.

To follow along with this chapter, you will need to have installed Microsoft SQL Server 6.5 or better, Access 97 or better, or Oracle.

<NOTE>

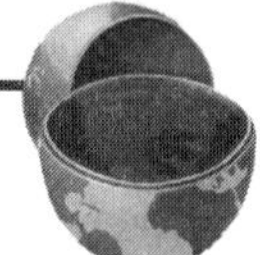

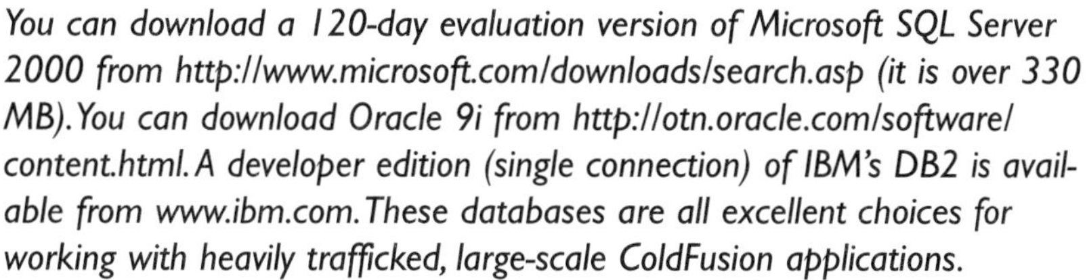

You can download a 120-day evaluation version of Microsoft SQL Server 2000 from http://www.microsoft.com/downloads/search.asp (it is over 330 MB). You can download Oracle 9i from http://otn.oracle.com/software/content.html. A developer edition (single connection) of IBM's DB2 is available from www.ibm.com. These databases are all excellent choices for working with heavily trafficked, large-scale ColdFusion applications.

Access 2000 and XP give you easy, graphical ways to build queries in a database. In order to be able to write your SQL statements from scratch, which you need to know how to do in order to query from ColdFusion, you need to follow these steps:

- Open Access 2000, and open the database you wish to work with.
- Click Queries in the side bar.
- Click Open.
- The Query Designer window will appear. From here you can drag and drop objects in your table to have Access build your query for you. Since we want to know what we're doing, *right-click* in the top pane.
- When the context menu appears, choose "SQL View." You can type your statements here, and click the red bang (!) to execute them.

The SELECT Statement

In Structured Query Language, you retrieve data from a database using the SELECT statement. We are using Microsoft SQL Server 2000 for our examples, but generally your statements will translate with little or no modification into other "dialects" of Structured Query Language. Where there is a major difference between the syntax that we discuss and other popular RDBMSs, I will take note of it.

The SELECT statement is the building block of data-driven applications. It is the statement that allows you to view the data in your database. The SELECT statement is ostensibly simple; however, as you will learn, you can perform very complex operations and data-retrieval methods with this statement. The basic structure looks like this:

```
SELECT columns
FROM tables
[WHERE condition]
```

The brackets above indicate that WHERE is an optional clause. The SELECT clause indicates the columns you want returned, and the FROM clause specifies the table they are in.

<NOTE>

Depending on your installation and your operating system, your SQL statements may need to be case sensitive. Generally, they are case insensitive. If you're not sure, be consistent, and the system will soon let you know.

The asterisk character (*) is a *wildcard* in SQL. It is used in place of "all." Our "ClassAds" table holds information about Classified Ads. It has a primary key column called ClassAdsID, then a column that holds the title of the ad, another that holds the text of the ad, and so on. To retrieve all rows and all columns from the "ClassAds" table, which holds information for classified ads, we could write this:

```
SELECT *
FROM ClassAds
```

<SOAPBOX>

*I advise against you using the wildcard in your SQL statements. It will give you a slight performance penalty, since you're forcing SQL Server to find out what list of columns the * stands for in the context of the specified*

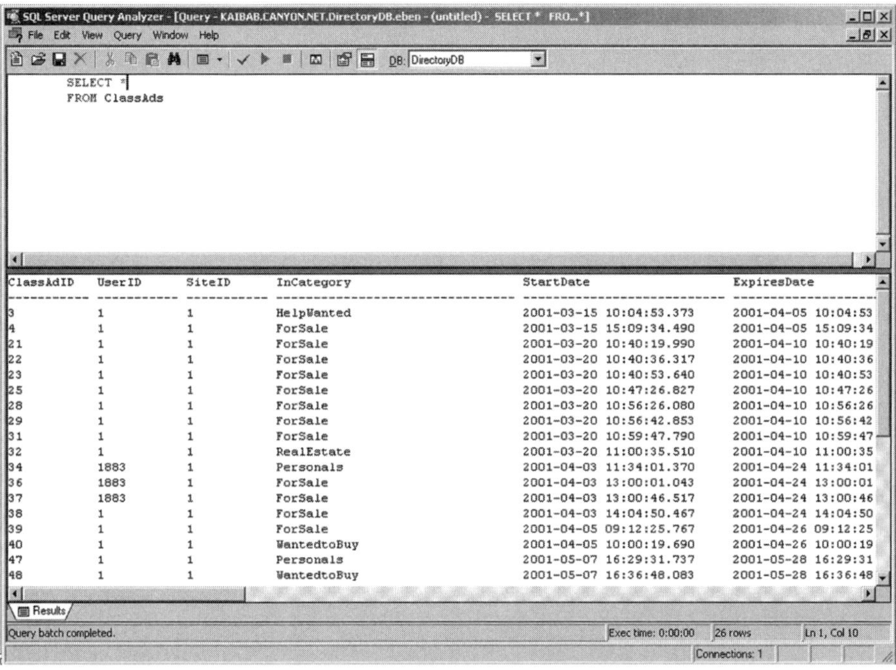

Figure 10.1 The results of selecting all columns using the SQL wildcard.

table. It is cleaner and more conscientious to list each column. Moreover, you often do not need every column returned to you; it is bad form to retrieve data you are not using. I mention it above because you will no doubt come across it.

If we run this statement in the Query Analyzer, our results look like Figure 10.1. You see every record in the table. In this case there are 26 records.

Selecting Only Certain Columns

Most of the time you will need to select only certain columns from the database. You do this, as mentioned in the note above, by specifying each column you want to retrieve (Figure 10.2). Replace the * used in the statement above with a comma-separated list of columns:

```
SELECT ClassAdID, ClassAdTitle
FROM ClassAds
```

Click the "Execute Query" button in the Query Analyzer to see the results.

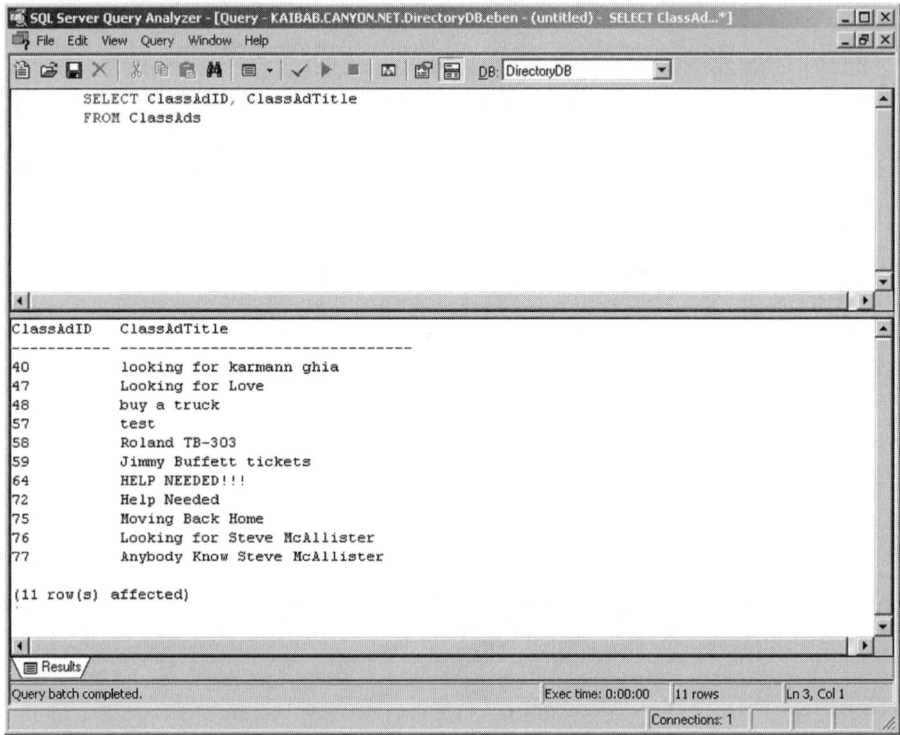

Figure 10.2 Selecting certain columns in the SQL Server Query Analyzer.

<NOTE>

Graphical tools that come with many Relational Database Management Systems make building queries simpler. ColdFusion Studio comes with a graphical tool similar to that provided with Microsoft Access 2000 and XP to create SQL Statements without having to remember all the syntax.

If we were to reference these columns in ColdFusion, we could do so easily, and it would not require too much typing. However, sometimes it is useful to be able to change how you reference a column. We do this with Aliases.

Using an Alias

When we reference a column returned by a query, we can use an *alias* as a subsequent reference for that column. An alias is useful if your column name is very long, or you want to easily distinguish it from other similarly named items.

We write an alias like this:

```
SELECT ClassAdID AS ID, ClassAdTitle AS ThisAd
FROM ClassAds
```

where "ID" is an alias for "ClassAdID," and "ThisAd" is an alias for the column "ClassAd." We can now reference "ID" and "ThisAd" when manipulating or outputting results.

String Manipulation

In Chapter 7 we learned about using expressions in ColdFusion. Expressions are also available to you in SQL. There are a few common SQL functions that help you manipulate your string data.

String Concatenation

Sometimes you need to see string data from two separate columns fused together as if the data were from one column. In this case, you can concatenate the strings. Commonly, you will see this when making a "FullName" from "FirstName" and "LastName" columns. You can concatenate strings in a query like this:

```
SELECT FirstName + ' ' + LastName AS FullName
```

Figure 10.3 shows the result of running this query in SQL Server 2000.

As you can see, the column is output as FullName, with data from both columns. The single quotes are included to indicate a space between the first and last names. If you wanted to format your data a bit, you can easily do so following the same principles. For instance, often you will want to display a name in this format: "LastName, FirstName." Then we write this:

```
SELECT LastName + ', ' + FirstName AS FullName
FROM Users
```

Figure 10.4 shows your results.

Notice that the SQL statement above has within the single quotes not only a comma, but also a space, which is necessary to separate the comma from the first name.

A Note about Oracle

In Oracle 8i, you need to use a slightly different syntax in order to accomplish the same thing. The Oracle equivalent of the Microsoft SQL Server Query

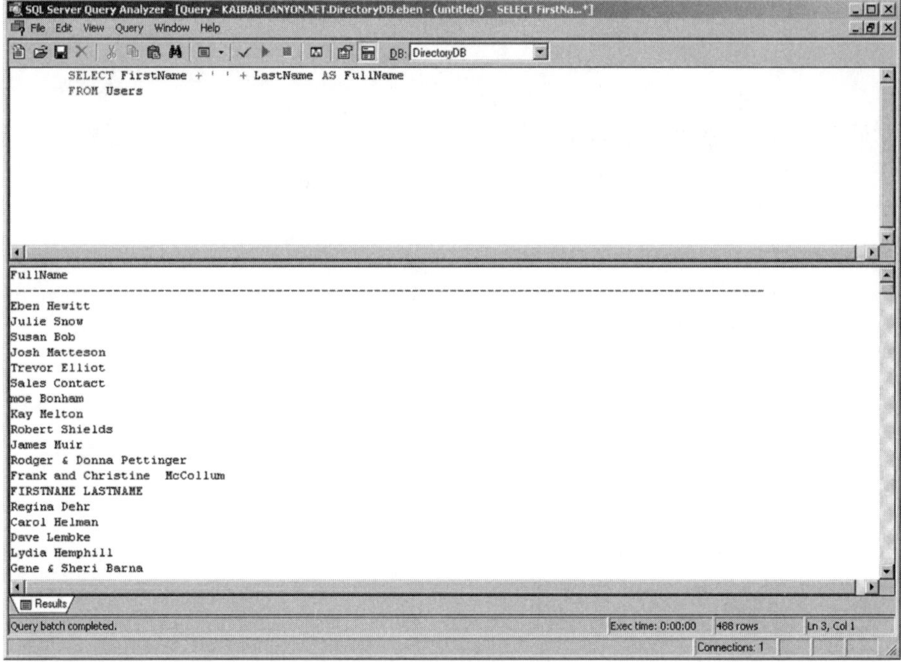

Figure 10.3 Concatenating strings allows you to merge multiple column values into one.

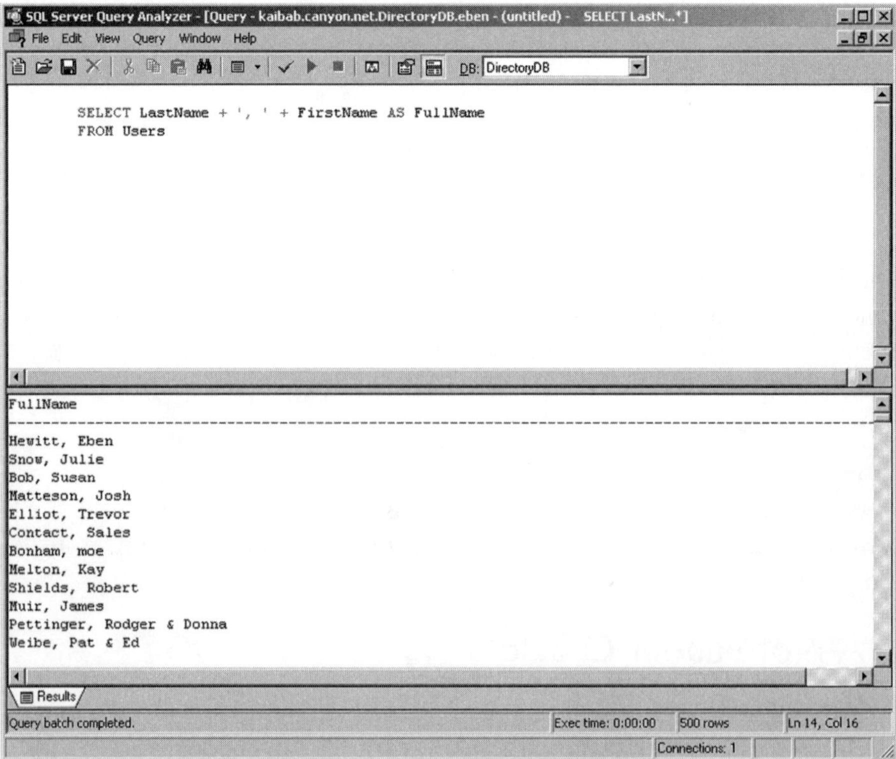

Figure 10.4 The results from multiple columns can concatenate into a single string.

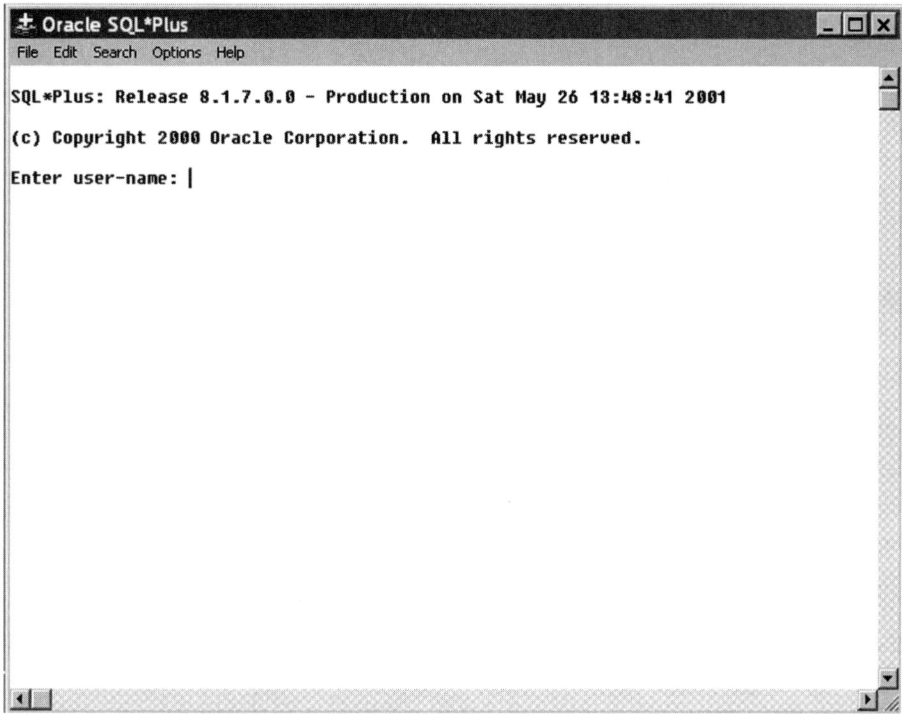

Figure 10.5 Oracle's SQL Plus offers a powerful text-based environment for running PL/SQL data retrieval and manipulation code.

Analyzer is PL/SQL. Both companies offer different flavors of the Structured Query Language that include extensions of the language. You are likely familiar with the differences in interpretation and extension between browsers; it's the same idea here. Instead of Transact-SQL, which is the Microsoft extension of standard SQL, Oracle uses PL/SQL. Many basic statements are the same. For some of the more complex examples, you will likely need to modify the code given in this chapter (see Figure 10.5).

To run the above concatenation code in Oracle for Windows, choose Start > Programs > Oracle – Orahome8i > Application Development > SQL Plus. Enter the username and password given to you by the administrator:

```
SELECT lastname || ', ' || firstname AS fullname
FROM users;
```

As you can see, in Oracle 8i, two pipes (||) are used for concatenation, instead of the + sign used in T-SQL.

Complex Concatenations and Trims

Just as functions are available to you in ColdFusion, they are also available in SQL (and many of them are the same). It is sometimes useful to be able to perform complex string manipulations from within your database before it is returned to ColdFusion. Opinions vary regarding where to perform operations that are possible in your RDBMS and ColdFusion. Many developers recommend that you let your database do what it was built to do, and perform as many operations as possible from within your database. With that in mind, let's look at how to write more complex manipulations of strings from within the RDBMS.

Often you will find that your database has been populated with imperfect data. For instance, it is common to see data with whitespace around it. You do not want to return trailing whitespace to ColdFusion because it is unnecessary, and it may mar your display of the data. In order to insure that your data is returned without trailing whitespace, you can use the "rtrim" (right trim) function of SQL to trim it off. Similarly, you can use the "ltrim" (left trim) functions to shave leading whitespace from the left of your string. Whitespace is most commonly found to the right of a string. If you are pulling data that will become part or all of a URL, it is imperative that you use these functions. Many browsers will crash when passed a URL containing whitespace.

The rtrim and ltrim functions have the same structure, so I will just demonstrate rtrim. The rtrim function has the following structure:

```
rtrim(string)
```

To make sure that the "FirstName" string we return to ColdFusion does not contain any trailing whitespace, we write this in SQL:

```
SELECT rtrim(FirstName)
FROM Users
```

Our output need not be noticeably affected, since you cannot see whitespace itself, but only its offset.

Suppose we need to return not the Full name of a user, but only the initial of the first name and the entire last name. We do so by employing the SUBSTRING function, which has the following structure:

```
SUBSTRING(string, position, length)
```

The SUBSTRING function extracts from the given string `length` characters, starting at the indicated position. Therefore, to select the first initial of the first name and the entire last name, we write this:

```
SELECT LastName, SUBSTRING(FirstName, 1, 1)
FROM Users
```

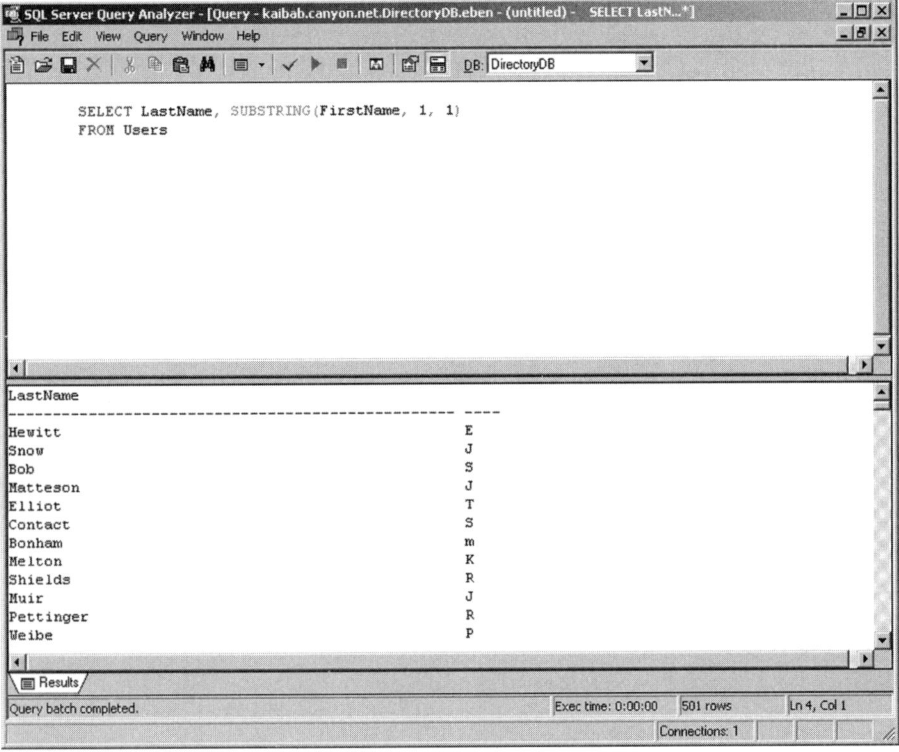

Figure 10.6 Manipulating data output with the SQL SUBSTRING function.

The SUBSTRING function extracts one character from the first position in the string. Figure 10.6 shows the result.

So we just add an alias, and everything's fine:

```
SELECT LastName, SUBSTRING(FirstName, 1, 1) AS FirstName
FROM Users
```

What you notice in Figure 10.6 is that, because we did not give the substring an alias, the result set does not appoint a column name for it. Therefore, the result set isn't really useful from within ColdFusion. If we were to run a this statement from within a ColdFusion page (as we'll learn how to do shortly), we would get an error like the one shown in Figure 10.7, notifying us that ColdFusion cannot determine the value of FirstName.

In the next section we will see how to connect to a database and output query results. For now you need to know that, if you use the SUBSTRING function, you must alias your column name.

When you use SUBSTRING in this way, the FirstName and LastName columns are still separate entities. You can create a more complex substring,

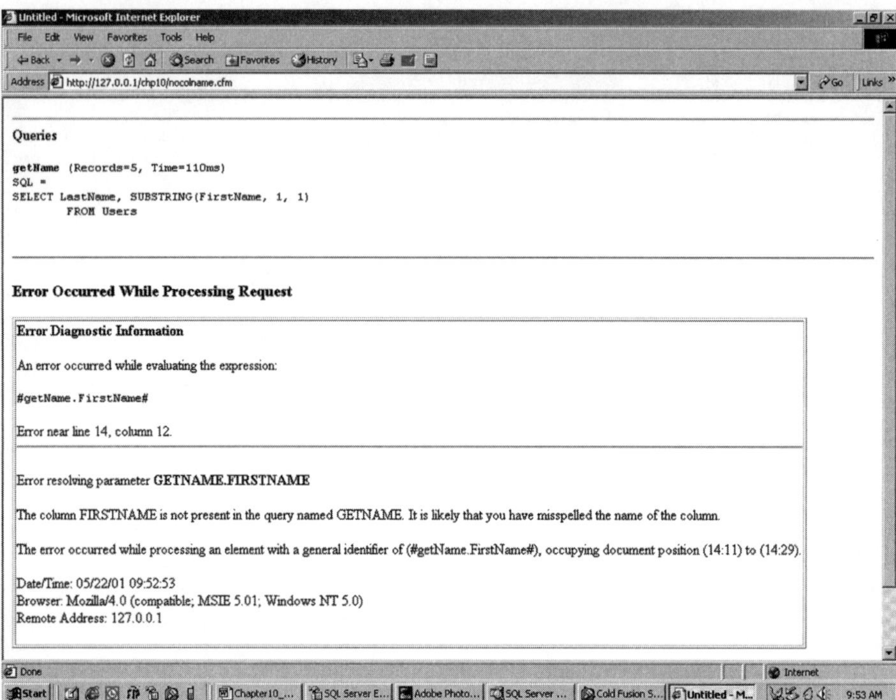

Figure 10.7 A nonaliased substring returns an error when you try to output its value in ColdFusion.

however, in order to use the result as one data object. The following example shows you how to combine functions to create a useful data string object:

```
SELECT rtrim(LastName) + ', ' + substring(FirstName, 1, 1) +
'.' AS theName
FROM Users
```

Your results would look something like those shown in Figure 10.8.

Then the complete string is available to ColdFusion as the alias name ("theName"). Notice that the query above also returns 3220 rows. You will often need to limit your result set to specific rows. We will now learn how to do so.

Selecting Particular Rows: TOP

You can retrieve only the top number of rows using, not surprisingly, the TOP command. You write a statement using the TOP command like this:

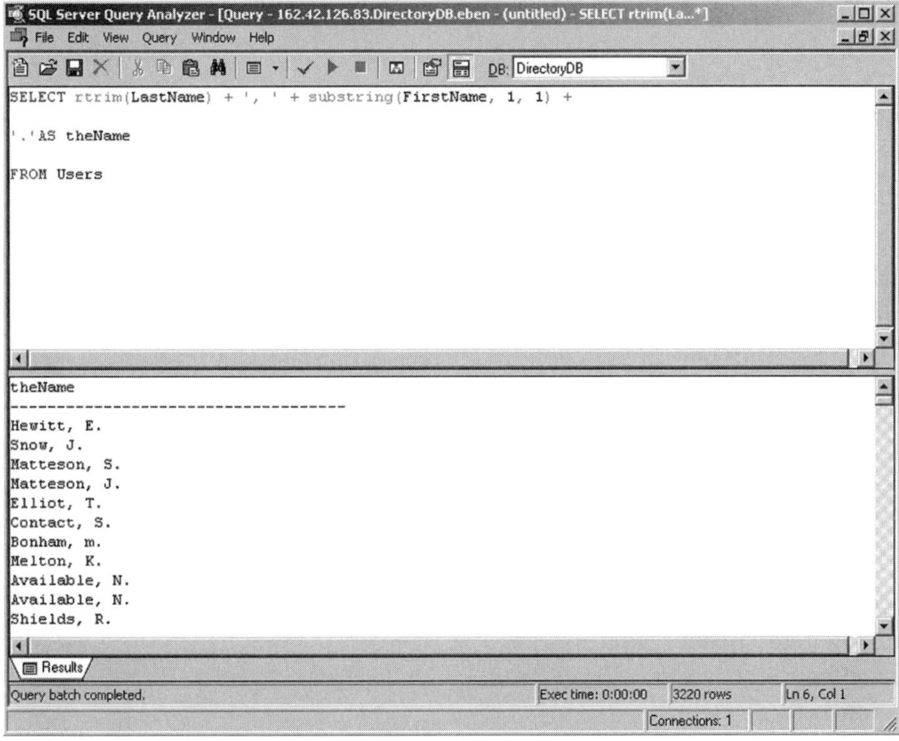

Figure 10.8 You can create and reference more complex substrings.

```
SELECT TOP 5 FirstName
FROM Users
```

<NOTE>

Remember that SQL is case sensitive, depending on your installation. I write it this way just to be consistent, but "select top 5 fiRSTnaMe" would work just as well in my environment.

One could also retrieve only the top *x* percent rows from a table, like this:

```
SELECT TOP 10 PERCENT LastName
FROM Users
```

This statement retrieves all rows inclusive in the first 10 percent of the total row count for the table. If your Users table has 1700 rows, the above statement returns the first 170 records.

Selecting Particular Rows: WHERE

A method often used for choosing only certain rows to be returned is WHERE. It takes this form:

```
SELECT columnlist
FROM tablelist
WHERE expression
```

which is to say, "Show me all of the rows in the table WHERE this thing is the case." For instance, in order to return the last names of all records in the Users table where the first name is "John," we write this:

```
SELECT LastName
FROM Users
WHERE FirstName = 'John'
```

As you can see, the structure of the WHERE clause is this:

WHERE *columnname* *operator* *value*

The operators available for use within a WHERE clause are the general SQL Server comparison operators, listed in Table 10.1. These operators allow you to compare two values, much like the ColdFusion comparison operators you learned in Chapter 7.

Table 10.1 Comparison Operators

Operator	*Description*
=	Equal to
!=	Not equal to
<>	Not equal to
>	Greater than
<	Less than
>=	Greater than or equal to
<=	Less than or equal to

<NOTE>

In Oracle, you can also use ^= to indicate inequality (it's the same as != and <>).

The value that you specify in a WHERE clause can be a constant (such as "Alison" or 237) or an expression that returns a value, such as AVG (DISTINCT Price). You may also manipulate the column value with T-SQL functions. We will do this together later in this chapter using DATEPART.

AND

We can narrow our result set even further by employing the AND operator. AND allows you to specify multiple conditions for your WHERE clause. To return every column for users who have the first name "John" and who have the last name "Strand," write:

```
SELECT *
FROM Users
WHERE FirstName = 'John'
       AND LastName = 'Strand'
```

You can use more than one AND clause in your SQL statement if you need to. Simply append the next AND statement, as shown below. Note that you do not need to separate the clauses in any way:

```
SELECT *
FROM Users
WHERE FirstName = 'John'
        AND LastName = 'Strand'
        AND State = 'AZ'
```

Nonequivalency Operators

When you need to retrieve a row, often you don't have enough information to perform an equivalency check. For instance, in a search function on your site, you need to return rows that are not only equal to the string the user entered, but similar to the strings the user entered. Or you may have only part of a string. In such cases, you might use the LIKE, BETWEEN, or OR operators, rather than the = operator.

LIKE

The LIKE operator in SQL determines whether or not a given character string matches a given pattern. That pattern can include both wildcards and regular characters. Recall that a wildcard is a character that can stand for any appropriate set.

There are four wildcard characters in T-SQL. These are shown in Table 10.2.

Table 10.2 T-SQL Wildcard Characters

Wildcard Character	*Description*	*Example*
%	Any string of zero or more characters.	`WHERE ProductName LIKE '%ColdFusion%'` finds all products that have the string "ColdFusion" anywhere in the ProductName
_(Underscore)	Any single character.	`WHERE Word LIKE '_ood'` finds all records in the Word table that have exactly one letter, followed by the string "ood." For instance, "good" and "wood," but not "brood" or "moody."
[ ]	Any single character within the specified range ([a-d]) or set ([abcd])	`WHERE ProductName LIKE [a-d] oldFusion` might find BoldFusion and ColdFusion, but not GoldFusion.
[^]	Any single character NOT within the specified range ([^a-d]) or set ([^abcd])	`SELECT LastNameFROM users` `WHERE LastName like '[^a-d]s%'` returns Hsu, Osborne, and Eskridge, but NOT Ashinhurst

Note that in Table 10.2 I've spiced things up a bit by demonstrating the use of two different wildcard characters at once in the last cell.

To continue our example from the last section, perhaps you know the person's first name, and you have only the first initial of their last name. In this case, you need to use the LIKE operator. So we would include the single quote marks, because we are using a text string, the letter that we do know (in this case, an "s") and the % character. Our statement looks like this:

```
SELECT LastName
FROM Users
WHERE FirstName = 'John'
      AND LastName LIKE 's%'
```

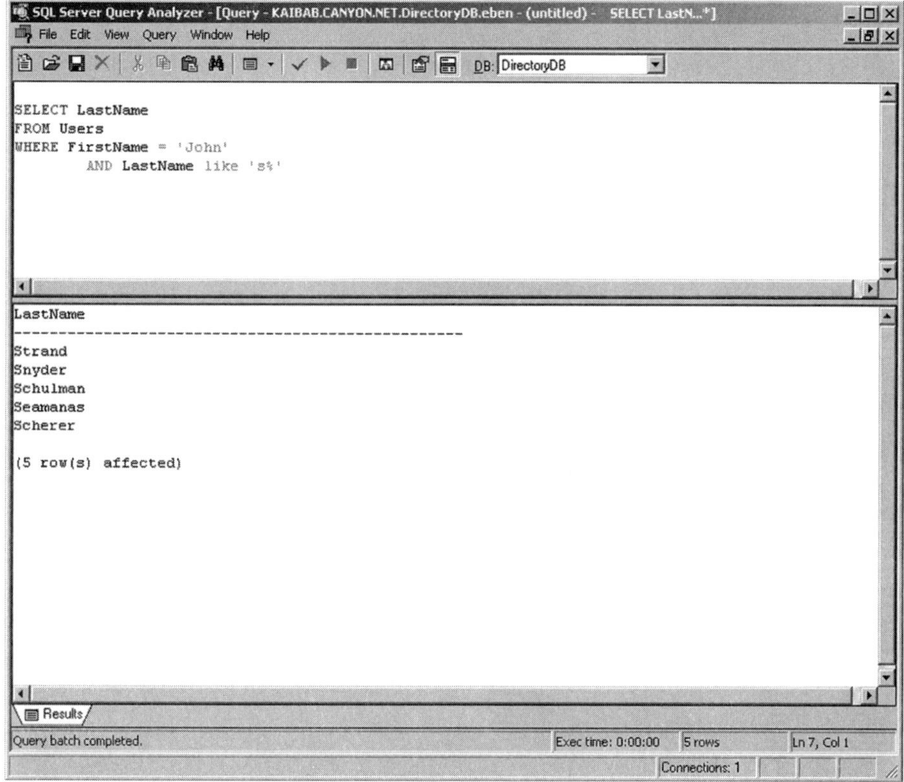

Figure 10.9 Results of using the LIKE operator.

<NOTE>

Remember that SQL doesn't care about spacing or carriage returns any more than an HTML browser does. Use indenting to make your statements more readable.

Running the above statement in SQL Server Query Analyzer produces the results shown in Figure 10.9.

In plain English, you are saying to SQL Server: show me the last names of people in the Users table who have the first name "John" and whose last name begins with the letter "S." The % wildcard character stands for one or more characters, so this will find last names of any length. Of course, you can also move the wildcard characters around to produce different results. For

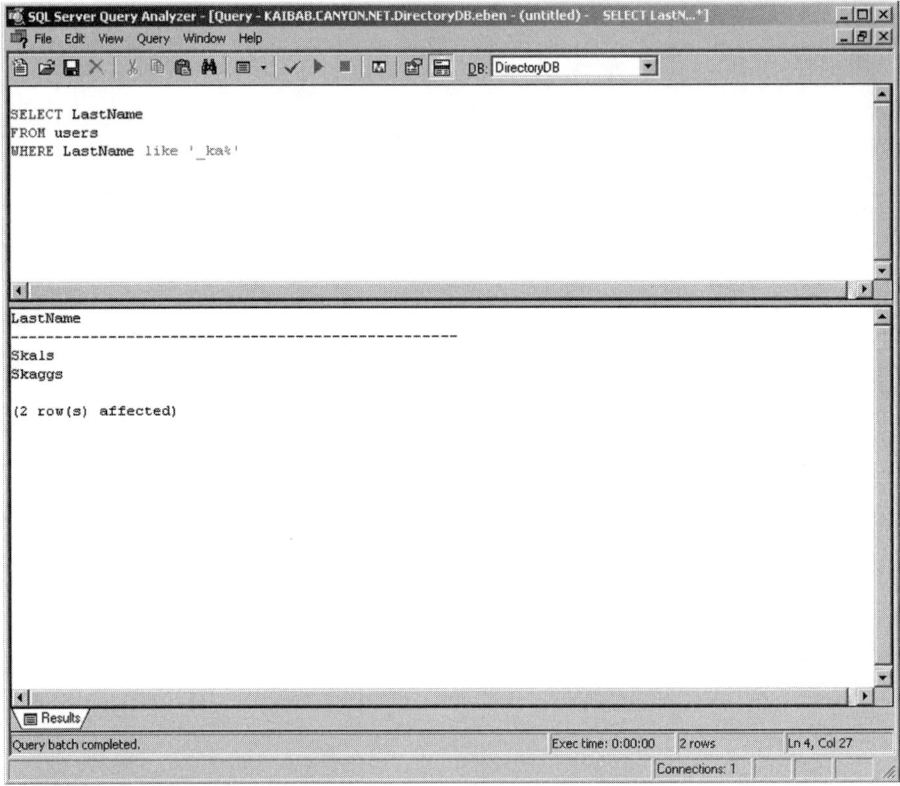

Figure 10.10 You can combine wildcards to create powerful search functionality.

instance, to find anyone named "John" whose last name *ends* in "s," move the wildcard to the front of the search parameter:

```
SELECT LastName
FROM Users
WHERE FirstName = 'John'
        AND LastName like '%s'
```

In this particular table we get two results:

```
Collins
Seamanas
```

Now let's combine two different wildcard operators (Figure 10.10). In order to retrieve the users' lastnames that have exactly one letter followed by "ka" followed by zero or more characters, we write this:

```
SELECT LastName
FROM users
WHERE LastName like '_ka%'
```

OR

You can use the OR logical operator much as we saw in Chapter 7, "Expressions and Conditional Logic." The OR operator will return true if any one of its conditions is true. And, like its counterpart in ColdFusion expressions, the SQL OR clause is evaluated before an AND clause, unless parentheses are used.

Shown below is a way we could specify that we want to find the last names of users where the last name does not have a, b, c, or d for its first letter, *does* have "s" for its second letter, and then has zero or more letters following, *or* the last name is "Johnson."

```
SELECT LastName
FROM Users
WHERE LastName like '[^a-d]s%'
        OR LastName = 'Johnson'
```

And here are our results:

```
LastName
-------------------------
Johnson
Johnson
Hsu
Osborne
Eskridge

(5 row(s) affected)
```

<NOTE>

As you may have noticed, I think it is often a good idea, as you're starting out, to write in plain language what you want your SQL statement to do. Often developers write bloated, overblown SQL statements because they have not thought out their query in plain language beforehand. You should always be able to quickly translate in this fashion. I have also found this technique useful for debugging very long, complex queries.

As mentioned, you can use parentheses to separate your clauses (just like in algebra!) so that the OR statement completes before the AND statement is run when you use the two together:

```
SELECT LastName, CompanyType
FROM Users
WHERE (CompanyType LIKE 'S%' OR CompanyType = 'Internet')
       AND LastName = 'Elliot'
```

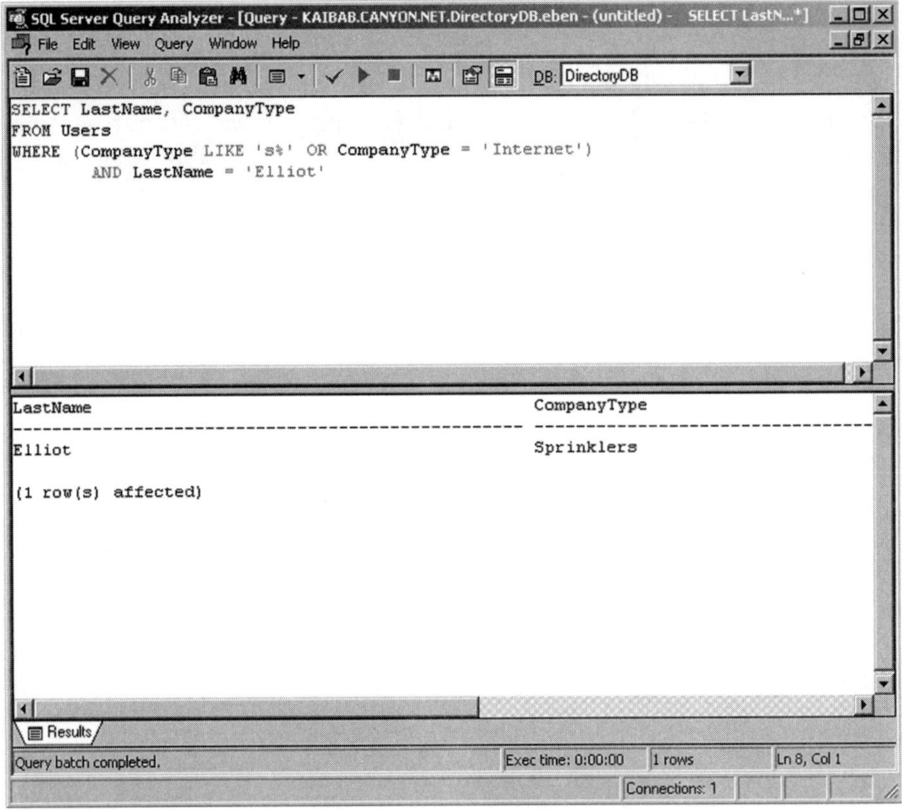

Figure 10.11 You can combine wildcards to create powerful search functionality.

Running this statement in the Query Analyzer returns the results shown in Figure 10.11.

As you can see, since CompanyType in this case is "Sprinklers," the first clause within the parentheses found a record ("Sprinklers" begins with an "S"), and there are many CompanyTypes of "Internet" in this table. Therefore, we know that after the entire parenthetical clause is evaluated, only then is the AND clause run.

NOT

NOT, the most powerful operator in logic, negates an expression that results in any Boolean input.

There are a number of ways to express NOT in SQL. In order to select all first names that are not "John," one could write the following:

```
SELECT FirstName
FROM Users
WHERE FirstName != 'John'
```

Using the bang (!) before the equals sign negates the equality comparison operator. One could also write it like this to produce the same results:

```
SELECT FirstName
FROM Users
WHERE FirstName <> 'John'
```

We can also combine the NOT keyword with more complex operations. You can negate an entire clause by writing NOT in front of it. Let us modify our earlier statement a bit:

```
SELECT LastName, CompanyType
FROM Users
WHERE LastName = 'Hewitt'
AND NOT (CompanyType LIKE 'S%' OR CompanyType = 'Internet')
```

This tells SQL Server to find the last name and company type in the Users table where the last name is "Hewitt" and the CompanyType does not begin with the letter "S," nor can the CompanyType be "Internet." We get one record that satisfies this set of conditions:

```
LastName          CompanyType

----------------- ---------------------------
Hewitt            Web Applications
(1 row(s) affected)
```

BETWEEN

BETWEEN returns rows that are found between specified markers. For instance, we want to find the last names of everyone in the table who has the first name John, and whose user ID is between 1500 and 1599. We write it like this:

```
SELECT LastName
FROM Users
WHERE FirstName = 'John'
       AND UserID BETWEEN 1500 AND 1599
```

Escaping and Dealing with Dates

It is sometimes frustrating to work with dates in ColdFusion or RDBMSs. It is delicate business that can produce very unpredictable results if one is not careful. So let's take a moment to examine how we can look for an order placed between two specific dates.

First, we must determine just how the date is stored in the database. Sometimes developers will modify the date of, say, a transaction, and store it as a string. Sometimes they will use the default time stamp in a date/time datatype column. There are various reasons to make either of these choices. In an application where the date is ornamental—for instance, in a guest book application—you might choose to store the date as a formatted string. This would be a very poor choice, however, for an e-commerce application, where the date, and often the second, of a transaction is very important to be able to locate precisely.

Since we don't have any dates in the Users table, let's shift to an "Orders" table that holds a transaction date for when an order was placed. The BETWEEN operator is perhaps the intuitive choice for such an operation, but it's not very easy to use in this context. Here we will learn a couple of things: escaping a column name, and working with dates in a practical manner.

In SQL Server, "Date" is a reserved word, since it is part of the SQL language. If you choose to name your table or column a word that is reserved, you must escape it. You might recall escaping the # character for ColdFusion within <CFOUTPUT> blocks. The way to escape a column name in T-SQL is to surround it with brackets ([ ]).

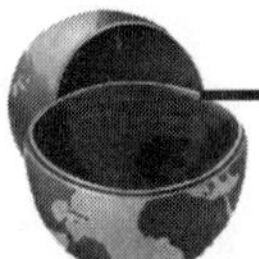

<NOTE>

Check out Appendix I, "Common SQL Functions," for a list of numerous datetime functions and their usage. They might make your life a bit easier.

Let's say that we have a column unfortunately named "Date" in our Orders table. The problem is this: the application uses a timestamp to record the date and time of the transaction when the order is placed. The timestamp recorded in the database looks like this:

```
2000-12-21 12:47:37.410
```

It has the following structure:

YEAR-MONTH-DAY HOUR:MINUTE:SECOND.MILLISECOND

Therefore, we need to do a bit of rearranging before we can work with this date. It will be difficult to determine an equality (or any other comparative relationship) unless we can extract the parts we need. Luckily, we've got the DATEPART function.

We need to retrieve all of the orders placed in the month of December. Here's how we do it. First, escape the "Date" column name by surrounding it with brackets, for reasons explained above. Next, specify the "Orders" table. Here comes the tricky part. Using DATEPART, we can specify part of the date we need to retrieve. DATEPART takes two arguments: the part of the date we want (month, year, day, etc), and the column where SQL can find the date. It is structured like this:

```
DATEPART(datepart, column_name)
```

Therefore, we can achieve the result we want by writing the following statement:

```
SELECT [Date]
FROM Orders
WHERE DATEPART(m, [Date]) = 12
```

Here we have written, "Get all the order dates where the month part of the date is equal to 12, which is December." We get the following results:

```
Date
---------------------------
2000-12-20 17:18:25.610
2000-12-21 12:47:37.410
2000-12-21 15:04:02.470

(3 row(s) affected)
```

Table 10.3 shows all of the DATEPART arguments available for use in Transact-SQL for Microsoft SQL Server 7 and 2000.

Table 10.3 T-SQL DatePart Abbreviations for Arguments

Date Part	*Abbreviations for Argument*
year	yy, yyyy
month	mm, m
quarter	qq, q
dayofyear	dy, y
day	dd, d
week	wk, ww
weekday	dw
hour	hh
minute	mi, n
second	ss, s
millisecond	ms

<NOTE>

If you think you will ever need to compare two dates, or if you are storing dates that you will need to work with for any reason other than recovery, do NOT use timestamp in your column. Timestamp generates a databasewide unique value which changes when the row is updated.

Between Dates and the CONVERT Command

What if you need to find, not a specific date, but the values in a range of dates? This section will show you how to do that using the CONVERT command with BETWEEN.

DATETIME columns in Microsoft SQL Server can store dates from January 1, 1753, through December 31, 9999 (therefore those of you who made it safely through Y2K can look forward to readdressing this issue in about 8000 years). As the name implies, DateTime fields store the time, which is often irrelevant in, for instance, a reporting application. In fact, you may not get the results you need unless you convert your date/time field to a string when referring to it. This is a little sophisticated for where we are right now, but I want you to be able to refer back to this section and find what you're looking for, since I bet this will come up in your work. Don't concern yourself too much with the example if it is confusing at this point. Just remember that it's possible, and check back again later after you've had time to let things soak in.

The job of the CONVERT function is to convert a column value from one datatype into another. We will use the CONVERT command to change our datetime column into a varchar (character string) column so we can find the orders between December 19, 2000, and December 21, 2000. Quickly, here's how we do it:

- Choose the date column, escape it, and alias it "OrderDate."
- Remember that because we are working with nested columns, SQL Server will work from the inside out, just as in algebra. So the second thing we do is CONVERT the values in the date column to varchar datatype, with a style specification of 120. 120 is the appropriate style for converting datetime into string.
- Then, again, moving outward, we use the LEFT function to chop off and keep only the first ten characters of the string. Notice that, the way the year-month- day segment is formatted, this is exactly ten characters.

- Compare that result with the expression following the BETWEEN operator, namely, where the result is between "2000-12-19" and "2000-12-21."

```
SELECT [date] AS OrderDate FROM orders
WHERE LEFT( CONVERT(varchar, [ Date], 120), 10)
        BETWEEN '2000-12-19' and '2000-12-21'
```

Running the above query returns the following results:

```
OrderDate
---------------------------
2000-12-20 17:18:25.610
2000-12-21 12:47:37.410
2000-12-21 15:04:02.470
(3 row(s) affected)
```

NOT BETWEEN

As you might imagine, NOT BETWEEN isn't really a function in itself; it is a concatenation of the NOT operator and the BETWEEN operator. Therefore, we can modify our statement above to find all of the orders placed at any time that is NOT BETWEEN December 19 and December 21, 2000.

<NOTE>

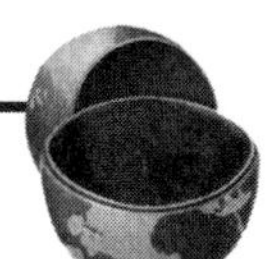

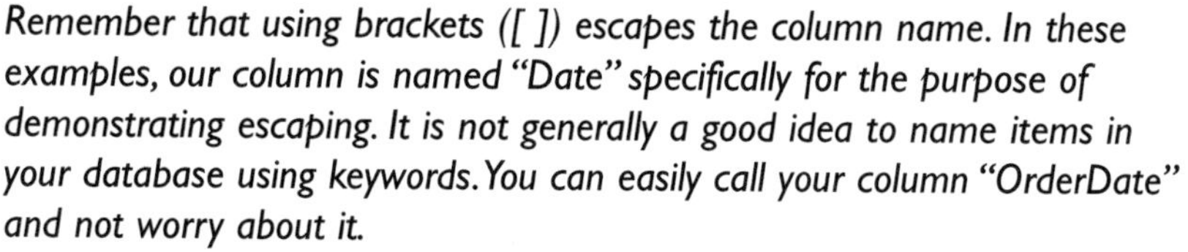

Remember that using brackets ([ ]) escapes the column name. In these examples, our column is named "Date" specifically for the purpose of demonstrating escaping. It is not generally a good idea to name items in your database using keywords. You can easily call your column "OrderDate" and not worry about it.

Let change this a bit to find the orders placed at any time except between March 15, 2000, and March 15, 2001. Notice that you must specify a double-digit month date, or your results will be off. SQL Server won't throw an error, so you must be careful to remember this aspect of working with dates in this fashion.

Here is the modified query:

```
SELECT [date] AS OrderDate FROM orders
WHERE LEFT( CONVERT(varchar, [Date], 120), 10)
        NOT BETWEEN '2000-03-15' and '2001-03-15'
```

And here is the result:

```
OrderDate
---------------------------
2001-03-16 14:23:44.700
(1 row(s) affected)
```

Sorting Data: ORDER BY

For simplicity's sake, let's return to our FirstName and LastName columns to demonstrate ORDER BY. The ORDER BY clause tells SQL Server (or Oracle, or Access, etc.) how to sort the output. A sort column can be a name or column alias, an expression, or a nonnegative integer representing the position of the name, alias, or expression in the select list. It is sometimes easier to specify the number location of the column in the select list when working with joins, which we will do later in this chapter. I include it in the definition here for completeness.

When we select all of the FirstNames and LastNames in the Users table, the results are ordered by record number, ascending—that is, from lowest to highest—in the order in which they were entered into the database. We can sort this data in a number of different ways by specifying a column for ORDER BY. Note that the sort is performed first, and then the results are output.

Let's do a plain old select for only the first eight firstnames in the table, and add the ORDER BY clause with the keyword ASC, which means ASCENDING.

```
SELECT FirstName, LastName
FROM Users
        ORDER BY firstname ASC
```

Here is our result, truncated for brevity:

```
FirstName                LastName
------------------------ -----------------------
Abdul                    Khan
Adam                     Cordon
Alan                     Hube
Albert                   Zalfini
Alice                    Fennell
Alison                   Brown
Allen                    Madle
Amy                      Keach
Amy                      Nadio
Andy                     Kuo
Angel                    Gloria
Ann                      Pollock
Anna                     Swift
Annette                  Pranckey
```

We can also choose to ORDER BY first name, descending, which means from the bottom up:

```
SELECT FirstName, LastName
FROM Users
order by firstname DESC
```

That gives us the following (truncated) results:

```
FirstName           LastName
------------------- ------------------------------
Yolanda             Pelayo
Yancy               Gatheright
Winnie              Hanseth
William             Hargrave
William             Mosley
William             Neu
William             Ortiz
William             Perry
William             Robinson
William             Rowland
Wally               Blanchard
Vincent             Bifano
Victor              Cortes
```

As you can see, the default sort order is ASCending. So when there are ties, the remaining columns are sorted in ASCending order—unless it is explicitly stated to be DESCending. In this result set, "William" appears seven times in the FirstName column; every accompanying last name is ordered alphabetically.

Let us modify the current query and choose only the TOP 8 first names; we get the first eight records entered into the table.

```
SELECT TOP 8 FirstName
FROM Users

FirstName
--------------------------------------
Eben
Julie
Susan
Josh
Trevor
Sales
Moe
Kay

(8 row(s) affected)
```

To generate the first eight rows in alphabetical order, we simply include the ORDER BY command, right?

```
SELECT TOP 8 FirstName
FROM Users
ORDER BY FirstName
```

But here is our output. Is it what you expected?

```
FirstName
-------------------------------------------
Abdul
Adam
Alan
Albert
Alice
Alison
Allen
Amy

(8 row(s) affected)
```

Remember that ORDER BY is a clause that is not modified by the TOP *n* modifier; rather, TOP is a limit that's placed on the result set *after* the WHERE and ORDER BY clauses are applied. Always double check and make sure that the data you are getting returned to you is in fact what you intended.

DISTINCT and COUNT

Often records have at least one column with the same value. For instance, you might have a number of FirstName = John records. In order to show just the first record when SQL encounters a resolution, you can use the DISTINCT keyword.

For a string, such as a name, the DISTINCT keyword looks like this:

```
SELECT DISTINCT FirstName
FROM Users
WHERE Firstname = 'John'
```

This statement will retrieve only one record for each instance of a value if there are duplicate first-name values. If there are 72 records in the table where the first name is John, and 37 records with the first name "Mary," then the above statement will return exactly one record: John.

You can use the COUNT keyword to have your database return to you the number of times a record occurs. If you wanted to know the number of Users who have the first name John, you could write this statement:

```
SELECT COUNT (FirstName)
FROM Users
WHERE FirstName = 'John'
```

And here is the result:

```
-----------
18

(1 row(s) affected)
```

This tells you that there are 18 records in the Users table with the first name John. Here is how you could view the number of users with any first name:

```
SELECT FirstName, COUNT(FirstName) AS FNCount
FROM Users
GROUP BY FirstName
ORDER BY FirstName
```

The result is:

```
FirstName                FNCount
------------------       ---------
John                     72
Mary                     37

(2 row(s) affected)
```

<NOTE>

We'll examine the GROUP BY clause shortly.

Related Functions

What if we wanted to find the average price of products? Or the most expensive item in a catalog? Or perform more complex calculations? You can use SQL functions such as SUM, MAX, and MIN. You can also use the DISTINCT keyword combined with these functions to aggregate values. Let's say we've got 5 items, with the prices listed below:

```
ItemID        Price
----------    -----------
1             2
2             3
3             4
4             4
5             4
```

If we perform a simple average, our result is 3.4:

```
SELECT AVG(Price)
From Item
```

```
 ---------------------
 3.4
```

However, choosing the distinct prices, and then averaging them returns a different answer:

```
SELECT AVG(DISTINCT Price)
FROM Item

---------------------
3

(1 row(s) affected)
```

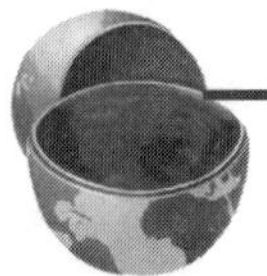

Please see the SQL Function reference for more information on SQL functions.

ColdFusion Datasources

Now that you have a solid understanding of what sort of data retrieval and manipulation you can do with SQL, it will be quite easy to introduce the <CFQUERY> tag. This tag's entire purpose is to encapsulate all the work of connecting your ColdFusion application pages to a database. Its syntax is very straightforward, and anything that you can do with SQL and your database, you can do from within the <CFQUERY> tag.

If you have ever worked with JDBC (Java Database Connectivity), you will be delighted at the ease of querying databases from within ColdFusion. There are only two steps. The first is registering your database with the ColdFusion Administrator. This is called *creating a datasource.* A *datasource* is a name for your database that ColdFusion can use for reference. When you create a datasource, you also verify that ColdFusion can establish a working connection with your database. Let's walk through the steps right now.

Creating a Datasource in ColdFusion Administrator

This section will demonstrate how to create a datasource in ColdFusion Administrator. First, open ColdFusion Administrator in your web browser.

This address will be http://yourservername/CFIDE/Administrator/index.cfm, where "yourservername" is the IP address or domain name of your server. If you installed ColdFusion on your local web server, you should be able to access it via either of the following equivalent addresses:

```
http://localhost/CFIDE/Administrator/index.cfm
```

or

```
http://127.0.0.1/CFIDE/Administrator/index.cfm
```

Once the login screen appears, type in your password. This is the password that you choose during the installation process. You will be admitted to the ColdFusion Administrator, where we can set up a datasource (see Figure 10.12).

<NOTE>

We will look at the features of the ColdFusion Administrator in Chapter 11, "A Note About the ColdFusion Administrator."

Figure 10.12 Choosing ODBC DataSources from within the ColdFusion Administrator main server screen.

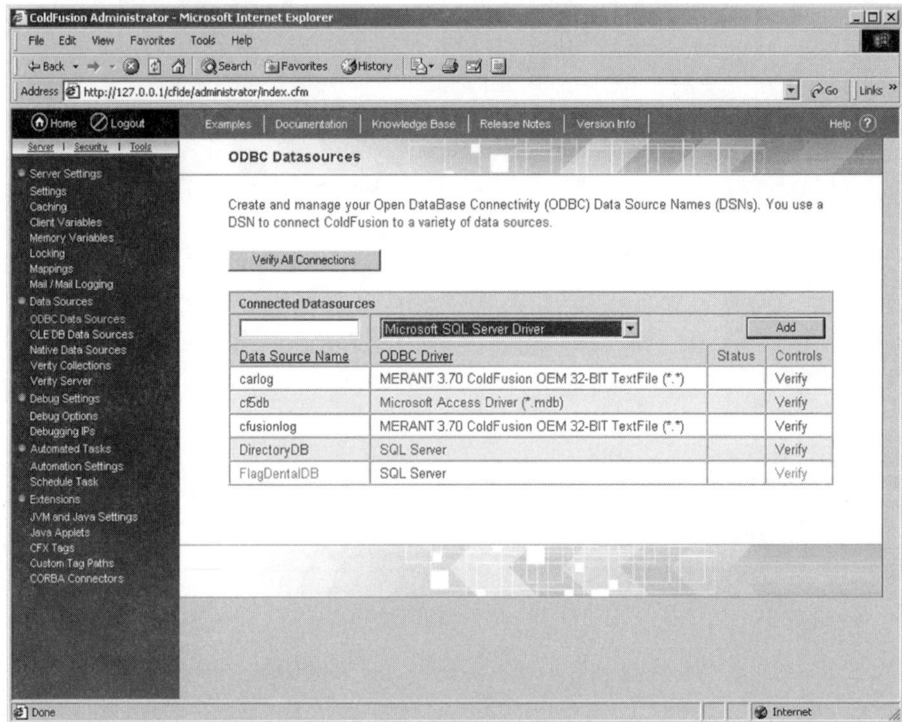

Figure 10.13 Create and manage your ColdFusion datasources here.

On the left-hand side of the screen is the menu. The administrator should open by default to the "Server" section, where you will see the heading "Data Sources." Underneath this, the first menu item is a link "ODBC Datasources," which we will click to set up our data source.

You will see the ODBC Datasources screen, as shown in Figure 10.13.

The rest of this section will take you through the slightly different steps for setting up a ColdFusion datasource with different kinds of databases.

Creating a Datasource for Microsoft SQL Server

Right underneath where it says "Connected Datasources," you will see a text input control. Type a name for your new datasource here. Note that ColdFusion reserves the names "Registry" and "Cookie" for its own use, so you should never use either of these names. Then, from the drop-down menu next to this input control, choose "Microsoft SQL Server Driver" as shown

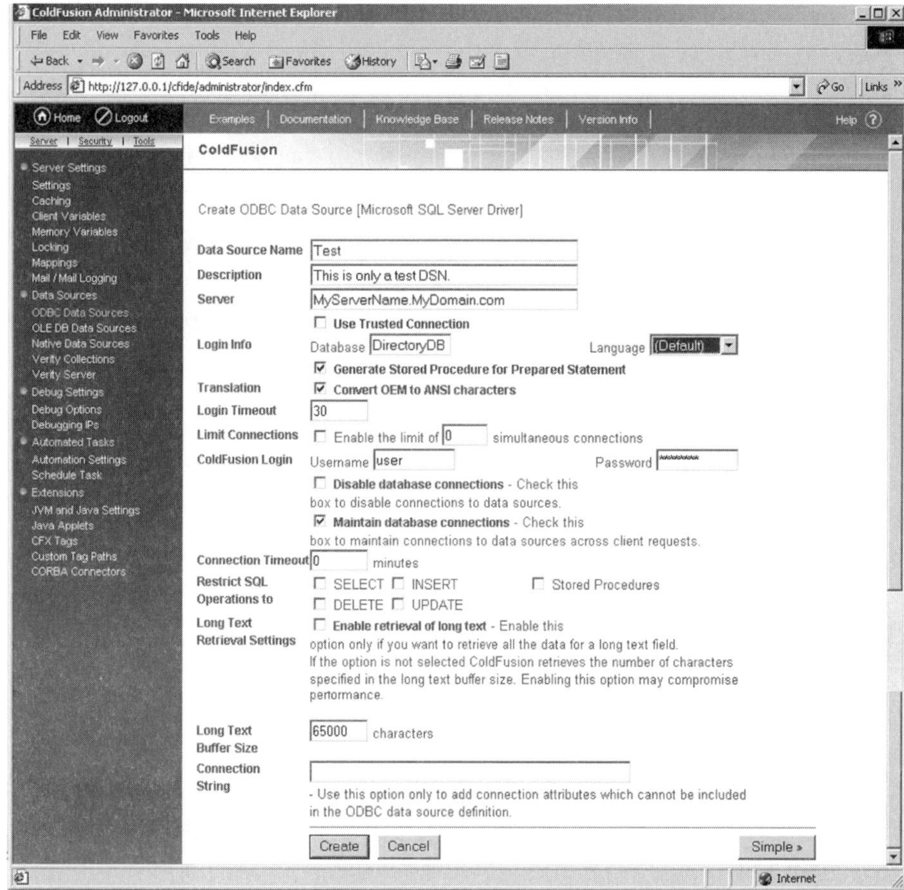

Figure 10.14 Clicking CF Settings gives you more detailed control over your datasource.

above, and click "Add." You will be able to cancel this process at any time and start over by clicking "Cancel."

Click "CF Settings" on the resulting screen. This will display a more detailed option menu, like the one shown in Figure 10.14.

Next we will see how to choose the appropriate settings for your database.

Choosing Datasource Settings

The name you choose automatically populates the name input control. Below this you can type a description for your datasource to remind you what application this datasource is for, or make other quick notes.

In the Server input field, type the IP address or domain name of your data server. If the data server housing the database you want to connect to is named data.CyberTrails.com, that's what you write in this box.

Next, find the paired fields called Username and Password next to "ColdFusion login." This is the SQL Server login that has at least "data reader" permission for the database you want to connect to. I do not recommend using the dbo role to connect ColdFusion. If a hacker became interested in your application, he could potentially hijack your application and cause serious damage to your database by passing destructive SQL statements through URLs. It is a good idea to create a login specifically for ColdFusion in your applications, and give the ColdFusion login only the exact permissions it will need in your database. This way, you are at least offering a bit of defense against hackers wishing to alter the structure of your database (by dropping tables, for instance).

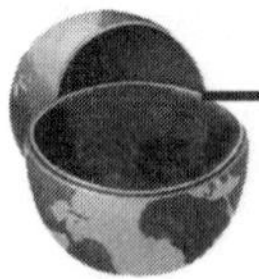

<NOTE>

If you have an experienced database administrator on site, you might consider implementing the following security framework. It will slow down your development time, but your databases will be very safe:

Create the ColdFusion login as "connect only"—don't even give it datareader privileges.

Set up a number of different usernames and passwords in four categories: read, write, update, delete. Make the usernames and passwords in each of these categories match only the particular tables upon which you need to perform any of these operations.

Use the Username and Password attributes of the <CFQUERY> tag in each SQL statement to implement a different username and password combination, depending on which statement you need to run. That means you leave blank the Username and Password section of this form in the ColdFusion Administrator.

Have a different set of usernames and passwords for development than you do for production.

This way, your DBA has total granular control over what's happening in the database, and very precise logs. That is probably extreme for many situations, but it's very secure.

For now, leave the rest of the settings at their default values.

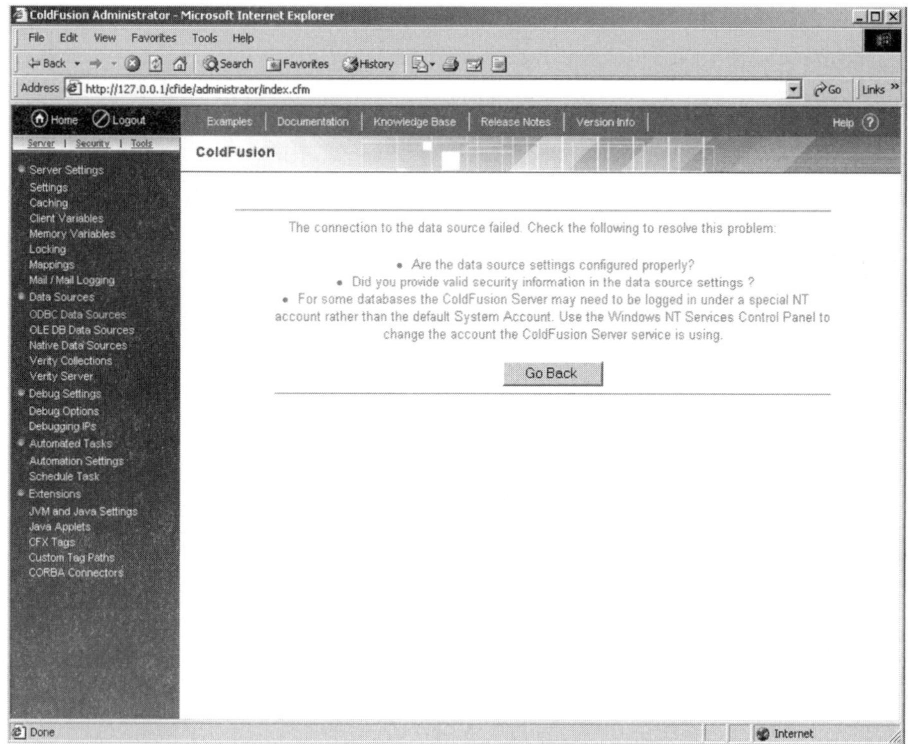

Figure 10.15 You see this screen when ColdFusion cannot verify a connection to your datasource.

<NOTE>

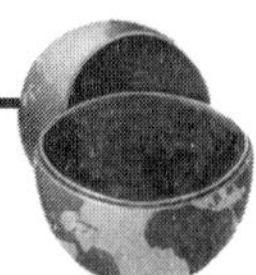

For now, we will limit our discussion to what is required for setting up a datasource on a couple of different databases."

Once you have typed in a username and password with permission on this database, click "Create" to create the datasource. ColdFusion will automatically register the datasource name (DSN) and attempt to verify the connection to the database. You will be redirected to the datasource page, and ColdFusion will tell you whether the connection failed or could be verified. If your connection was successful, you are ready to begin using this database with ColdFusion.

If your connection failed, it may have timed out, or there might have been a wacky glitch in the connection for that moment. Try it again by clicking the "Verify" link. If it still doesn't work, you will see the screen shown in Figure 10.15, and you will know that you must revise your settings.

Here are some common situations when a datasource connection cannot be verified:

- Are you certain you spelled everything correctly? Try retyping your username and password, and double-check that you have correctly entered the name of the server where your database resides.
- Are you sure that you typed the name of the database exactly as it is is Registered in SQL Server?
- Does the username and password you used have proper permission in that database? Is it a registered login for that specific database, or the Database Owner?

You can go back and revise your settings if necessary by clicking on the name of the datasource.

Once ColdFusion can establish a connection to your SQL Server database, you are ready to retrieve and manipulate data in the database with ColdFusion!

Creating a Datasource for Oracle 8i on Linux Red Hat

The process for setting up a datasource for an Oracle or Microsoft SQL Server database is roughly the same, so we will only touch on the differences here. This section assumes that you have Oracle installed already on Red Hat Linux. There are just a couple of extra steps you may need to take to prepare Oracle to work with ColdFusion:

- At the console, login to Oracle's SQL *Plus, the command-line tool for working with Oracle databases:

```
sqlplus user@database.domain
```

- Make sure that ColdFusion is ready to talk to Oracle. To do this, you need to edit the /opt/coldfusion/bin/start script with a text editor, such as vi or pico:

```
pico /opt/coldfusion/bin/start
```

- Uncomment the ORACLE_HOME line. Depending on where you have installed Oracle, your line might look like this:

```
ORACLE_HOME=/home/oracle/u01/app/oracle/product/8.1.6
```

- Change the LD_LIBRARY_PATH so that it looks like this:

```
LD_LIBRARY_PATH=$CFHOME/lib;$ORACLE_HOME/lib
```

At this point, you should be ready to set up a DSN for your Oracle database just as described above in the Microsoft SQL Server section: choose the MERANT Oracle 8 Driver, type the database name, data server name, username and password. Click "Create," and you're ready to access your database from ColdFusion using the <CFQUERY> tag.

Creating a Microsoft Access Datasource

You can easily create a DSN for a Microsoft Access database via ColdFusion Administrator. While this is a practical learning tool, please do not use Access databases for live production websites. Access is a desktop database that handles few concurrent connections and does not give you the speed, scalability, or power of a more full-featured database system.

For learning ColdFusion, Access will work just fine. Once you are ready to make a production site, you can "upsize" your Access database into an SQL Server database through a wizard. Note that, while I'm using Transact-SQL for many of the examples in this book, much of the SQL statement code will work with little or no modification in Access.

In this example, we will connect to an Access database which happens to be running on my local machine (though it could be on another machine on your network). You must have already created the Access database to continue.

It is a good idea to choose the same name for your DSN as for your database. It makes it easier to remember later. If your application is expected to be rather large, you might use a number of different datasources for the same application. In this case, name the databases appropriately, given their function within the larger application.

First, in ColdFusion Administrator, choose ODBC Data Sources. Type a name for your datasource. This is the name that you will write in your ColdFusion templates so that ColdFusion can connect to the database.

In the drop-down select box, choose Microsoft Access Driver (*.mdb) and click Add. In the description box, type a brief description of this database. Next, click "Browse Server" to locate the file on your machine or network.

If this is the first time you have been to this screen, you will be prompted to download a plug-in that ColdFusion will use to display the Java applet that will let you browse for your .mdb file (Figure 10.16).

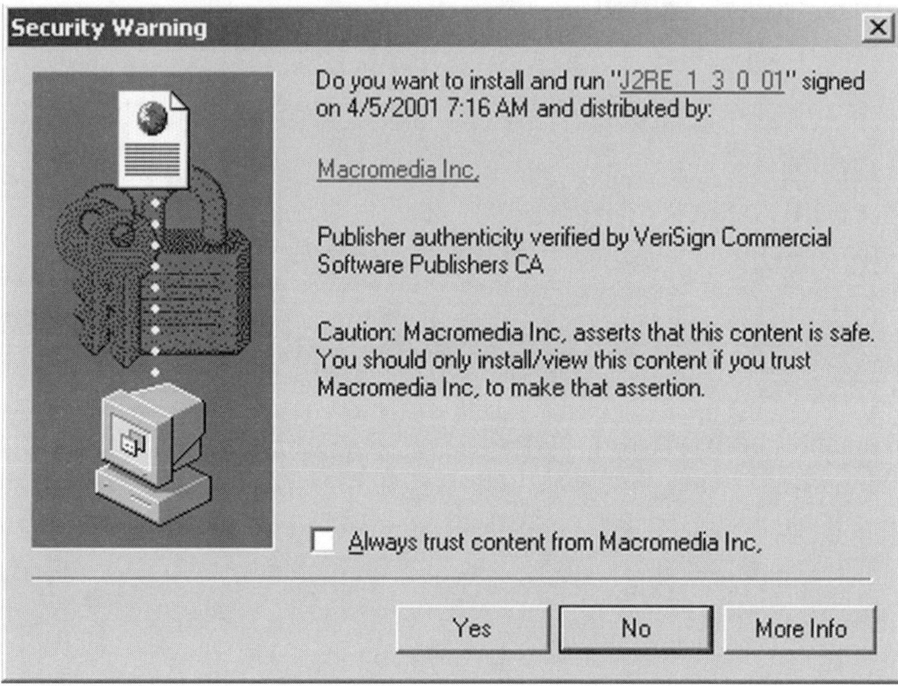

Figure 10.16 ColdFusion Administrator prompts you to install the necessary components for using the enhanced Java form when browsing for a database file for the first time.

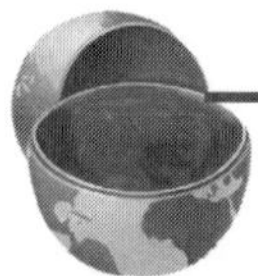

<NEAT THING>

ColdFusion Administrator, as you might recall, is really just a ColdFusion application itself, and it uses the <CFTREE> tag, which is one of the enhanced form tags that is a standard part of the language, to create this file-browsing interface. When you download the Macromedia cabinet file once, you won't have to do so again when you start working with the ColdFusion Java forms. If you are familiar with earlier versions of ColdFusion, you will be happy to know that these forms have been completely rewritten. They now perform faster and more reliably.

Now you are ready to browse for your Access database. Click the small, boxed plus signs (+) to expand and contract drives on your machine, and continue until you find the Access database you want. This form will display only folders and .mdb files, so you shouldn't have a hard time navigating to it. Once you find it, click on it; ColdFusion Administrator will

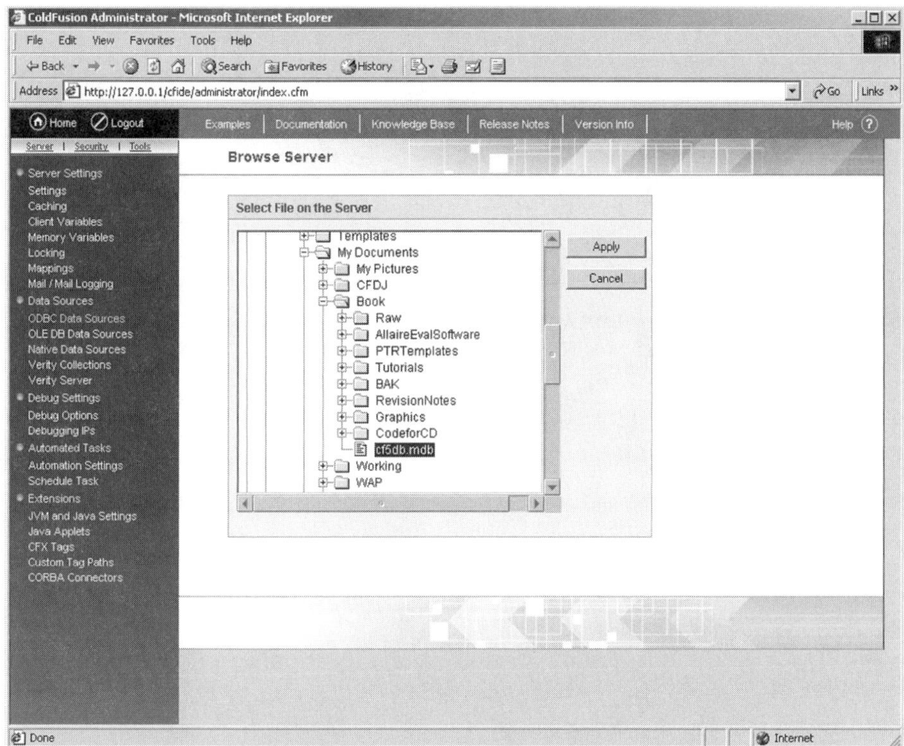

Figure 10.17 This particular database is located in the Book folder, within the My Documents folder.

highlight your selection. Click the "Apply" button to choose this database (see Figure 10.17).

At this point, you can create a security context for this database by locating a system database. This file is usually winnt/system32/system.mdw, but we'll ignore this setting for now. Unless you have set up login permissions within Access for this database that require you to enter a username and password, you can click "Create." ColdFusion will attempt to connect to this database. If it can, you will see "OK" in the Status column next to your new datasource. You are now ready to start using the <CFQUERY> tag to connect to your datasource.

<CFQUERY>

Once you have created a datasource in the ColdFusion Administrator, you are ready to begin running all of the SQL statements we have studied throughout this chapter from ColdFusion.

Here's the basic structure:

```
<CFQUERY datasource="DatasourceName" name="NameForThisQuery">
        Put your SQL statements here. . .
</CFQUERY>
```

That's it! You've opened and closed the connection and retrieved your data, which is now available for further processing, manipulation, or display from ColdFusion.

From now on, we will move from using the Microsoft SQL Server Query Analyzer to writing our statements, and outputting our results, in ColdFusion. We will learn how to do more sophisticated things, like work with stored procedures, in a later chapter. For now, you have a rather solid foundation for retrieving and manipulating data in your database, and it doesn't work any different via ColdFusion than it does from within your RDBMS. The <CFQUERY> tag is just a mask for the complexity of creating the connection.

If you set up your datasource properly, there isn't much that can go wrong on a Windows system when you use the <CFQUERY> tag. Despite this, <CFQUERY> probably generates more errors than any other tag in ColdFusion. That is generally because the programmer has used incorrect syntax when writing the SQL statements the tag passes to the data server.

Querying a Database

Before we examine the complete attributes of the <CFQUERY> tag, let's see how it works in its most basic form. Note that using the <CFQUERY> alone will get your database results, but it won't display them. You therefore always need to use <CFOUTPUT> in conjunction with a query.

Open a new document in ColdFusion Studio and write the following:

```
<!DOCTYPE HTML PUBLIC "-//W3C//DTD HTML 4.0
       Transitional//EN">

<html>
<head>
       <title>My First Query</title>
</head>

<body>

<!----The value of the Datasource attribute is the name of a
verified datasource that you have set up in ColdFusion
Administrator------->
```

```
<!--Select all user's first and last names--->

<cfquery datasource="CF5DB" name="getUsers">
        SELECT FirstName, LastName
        FROM Users
</cfquery>

<!----Display query results------->

<h2>Here are the users in the users table:</h2>
<br>

<cfoutput query="getUsers">
#getUsers.LastName#, #getUsers.FirstName#<br>
</cfoutput>

</body>
</html>
```

The results of running this code appear in Figure 10.18. Your results will vary, depending on what names you have in the database.

First we query the database using SQL statements just as we would write them in their native environments (such as Oracle, Access, SQL Server, MySQL, etc). Then you wrap a <CFQUERY> tag around your SQL statement, specifying the datasource name, and a name for the query. You need the query name to refer to the query result set when you output it. Then you use the <CFOUTPUT> tag to display the result set. Note that above we have chosen to combine a bit of punctuation—we displayed the last name, followed by a comma, and then the first name. Column names are scoped using the value of the NAME attribute used in the CFQUERY tag.

The <CFOUTPUT> tag will output a result set just as you tell it to, iterating over each row in the result set like a loop. Had we not included the HTML <br> tag, our results would have output immediately next to each other, all on one line.

If You Get an Oracle Driver Error

If you are running Oracle for Linux, and you got the following error the first time you loaded your <CFQUERY> template, ColdFusion had a problem locating the driver:

```
ODBC Error Code = IM003 (Specified driver could not be
loaded)
```

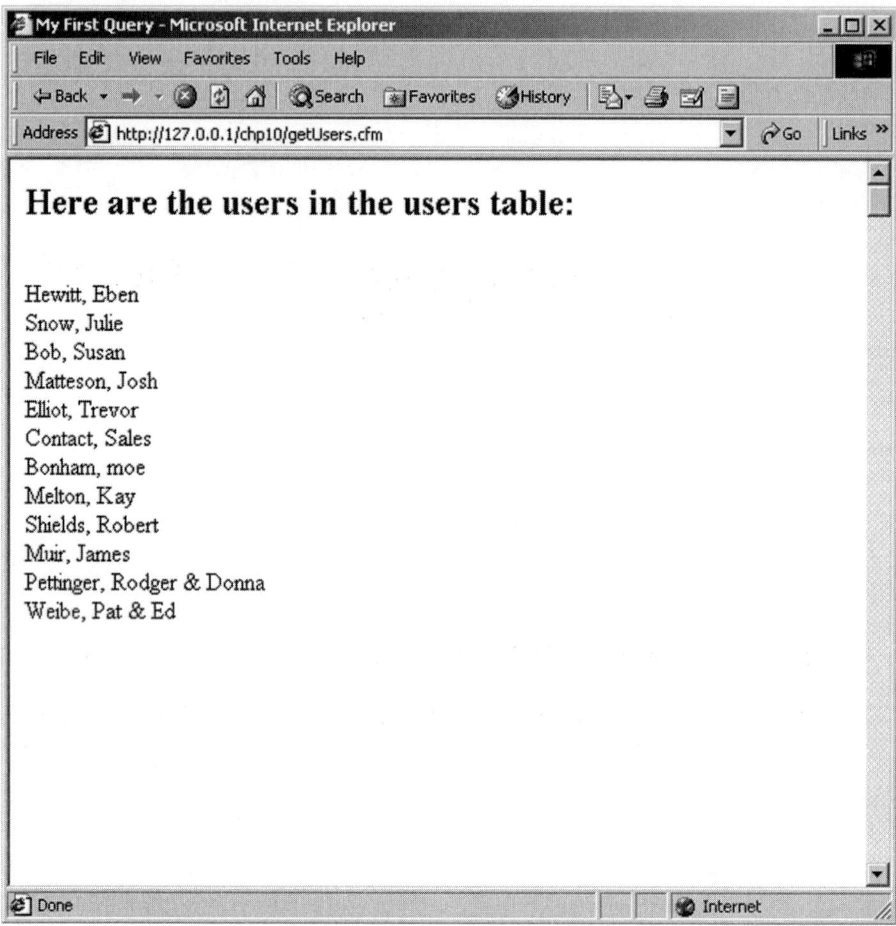

Figure 10.18 Querying a database allows you to make dynamic pages on the fly.

You have a couple of possible remedies for this. Try changing permissions on the Oracle home directory to 755 if they aren't already. Restart the ColdFusion server, and try it again. If it still gives you trouble, set the LD_LIBRARY_PATH and execute the ldd command against the driver:

```
ldd /opt/coldfusion/lib/CFor815.so
```

You should be able to determine the libclntsh.so it's looking for. By default, the ColdFusion user is nobody. If you changed the ColdFusion user at any point (or even if you didn't), make sure that the ColdFusion user has correct permission on the Oracle directories.

A Quick Word about Batches

If you are used to writing long SQL statements within SQL Server, you may not use the batch command "go" from within ColdFusion. For instance, the following statement is fine in SQL Server directly, but will *fail* when used from <CFQUERY>:

```
<cfquery name="go" datasource="cf5db">
set quoted_identifier on
go
select Numbers
from Col1
INNER JOIN Col2 ON Numbers = MoreNumbers
</cfquery>
```

CFQUERY Attributes in Depth

Before we continue, let us first cover the many attributes of the <CFQUERY> tag. Note that you can pass any SQL statements through the <CFQUERY> tag, including those that create tables or drop databases.

```
<CFQUERY NAME="query_name"
    DATASOURCE="datasource_name"
    DBTYPE="type"
    CONENCTSTRING="string"
    DBSERVER="dbms"
    DBNAME="database name"
    USERNAME="username"
    PASSWORD="password"
    MAXROWS="number"
    BLOCKFACTOR="blocksize"
    TIMEOUT="milliseconds"
    CACHEDAFTER="date"
    CACHEDWITHIN="timespan"
    PROVIDER="COMProvider"
    PROVIDERDSN="datasource"
    DEBUG>
Put your SQL statements here. . .

</CFQUERY>
```

The following list details the attributes of the <CFQUERY> tag,

NAME

(Required.) The name you assign to the query. Query names must begin with a letter and may consist of letters, numbers, and the underscore character (spaces are not allowed). The query name is used later in the page to reference the query's record set.

DATASOURCE

The name of the data source to run this query against. The datasource attribute is REQUIRED if the DBTYPE is not QUERY.

DBTYPE

(Optional.) The database driver type:

Query—New in ColdFusion 5, specifying dbtype as Query means you want to query a subset of a previously run query.

ODBC (default)—ODBC driver.

Oracle73—Oracle 7.3 native database driver. Using this option, the ColdFusion Server computer must have Oracle 7.3.4.0.0 (or greater) client software installed.

Oracle80—Oracle 8.0 native database driver. Using this option, the ColdFusion Server computer must have Oracle 8.0 (or greater) client software installed.

Sybase11—Sybase System 11 native database driver. Using this option, the ColdFusion Server computer must have Sybase 11.1.1 (or greater) client software installed. Sybase patch ebf 7729 is recommended.

OLEDB—OLE DB provider. If specified, this database provider overrides the driver type specified in the ColdFusion Administrator.

DB2—DB2 5.2 native database driver.

Informix73—Informix73 native database driver.

CONNECTSTRING: Set of parameters to pass to the RDBMS when making the connection.

DBSERVER

(Optional.) For native database drivers and the SQLOLEDB provider, specifies the name of the database server machine. If specified, DBSERVER overrides the server specified in the data source.

DBNAME

(Optional.) The database name (Sybase System 11 driver and SQLOLEDB provider only). If specified, DBNAME overrides the default database specified in the data source.

USERNAME

(Optional.) If specified, USERNAME overrides the username value specified in the data source setup.

PASSWORD

(Optional.) If specified, PASSWORD overrides the password value specified in the data source setup.

MAXROWS

(Optional.) Specifies the maximum number of rows you want returned in the record set.

BLOCKFACTOR

(Optional.) Specifies the maximum number of rows to fetch at a time from the server. The range is 1 (default) to 100. This parameter applies to ORACLE native database drivers and to ODBC drivers. Certain ODBC drivers may dynamically reduce the block factor at runtime.

TIMEOUT

(Optional.) Lets you specify a maximum number of milliseconds for the query to execute before returning an error indicating that the query has timed out. This attribute is not supported by most ODBC drivers. TIMEOUT is supported by the SQL Server 6.x or above driver. The minimum and maximum allowable values vary, depending on the driver.

CACHEDAFTER

(Optional.) Specify a date value (for example, 3/27/01, March 27, 2001, 3-27-01). ColdFusion uses cached query data if the date of the original query is after the date specified. You can effectively use the CACHEDAFTER attribute only if query caching has been enabled in the ColdFusion Administrator. To use cached data, the current query must fulfill these requirements: use the same SQL statement, data source, query name, user name, password, and DBTYPE as the cached query. For Sybase native drivers, it must have the same DBSERVER and DBNAME.

Years from 0 to 29 are interpreted as 21st century values. Years 30 to 99 are interpreted as 20th century values.

When specifying a date value as a string, make sure it is enclosed in quotes.

CACHEDWITHIN

(Optional.) Enter a timespan using the ColdFusion CreateTimeSpan function. Cached query data will be used if the original query date falls within the time span you define. The CreateTimeSpan function is used to define a period of time from the present backward. Effective only if query caching has been enabled in the ColdFusion Administrator. To use cached data, the current query must use the same SQL statement, data source, query name, user name, password, and DBTYPE. Additionally, for native drivers it must have the same DBSERVER and DBNAME (Sybase only).

PROVIDER

(Optional.) Name of the COM provider. Used only for OLE-DB.

PROVIDERDSN

(Optional.) Data source name for the COM provider (OLE-DB only).

DEBUG

(Optional.) Used for debugging queries. Specifying this attribute causes the SQL statement actually submitted to the data source and the number of records returned from the query to be output. This takes no parameters. Just append it inside your <CFQUERY> tag.

The <CFQUERY> tag returns not only the result of the query, but also metadata about the query. You can reference CFQUERY.ExecutionTime, which returns the time it took the query to execute in milliseconds.

<CFQUERY> automatically creates a query object, which always gives you access to three variables every time a query is run.

Table 10.4 CFQUERY Object Variables

Variable Name	*Description*
QueryName.RecordCount	Total number of records the query returned.
QueryName.ColumnList	A comma-delimited list of all columns referenced in a query.
QueryName.CurrentRow	The current row of the query.

Table 10.4 shows the variables returned with every query you run. You can reference these within a <CFOUTPUT> block to display them on the page as you debug. A common use for the RecordCount variable is for displaying to the user the number of records retrieved for a particular search string. We will see how to construct a site data search at the end of this chapter. And that will be really fun.

Dynamic Queries

Another terrific thing about the <CFQUERY> tag is that you can create totally dynamic queries. You can use conditional logic and ColdFusion variables inside your SQL statements. That's because the statement you write inside the <CFQUERY> tag, along with any ColdFusion code, gets prepared by ColdFusion and *then* sent off to the database. That means that you don't have to worry about database connection time when using complex conditional queries—though it will increase your ColdFusion processing time.

Below you will learn the remainder of the important SQL commands—INSERT, UPDATE, and DELETE. They are far less complex than the SQL SELECT statement, so it shouldn't take long to pick them up. Also, now that you know your SQL pretty well, it will be a piece of cake to start using it inside the <CFQUERY> tag. Below I will use examples of dynamic queries in demonstrating each of the remaining statements, so you can get a sense of how that works before we make our little search application.

Inserting Records

How do you get all of this data we've been selecting into the database in the first place? The answer is the INSERT statement. Its syntax differs from that of the SELECT statement:

```
INSERT INTO Table
       (Column1, Column2)
VALUES
       (Column1Value, Column2Value)
```

The INTO part is optional, but I always use it to make the code more readable. The real difficulty with using the INSERT statement is that the columns and corresponding values are separated out. If you have a long list of values, you must be careful to put everything in the correct order.

The following INSERT statement takes an email address typed in from a form and inserts it into the database along with a preset value of 1, which will populate the Active column for the same record:

```
<cfquery name="InsertNewsSubscriber" datasource="cf5DB">
        INSERT into NewsletterSubscribers
                (EmailAddress, Active)
        VALUES ('#FORM.EmailAddress#', 1);
</cfquery>
```

Updating Records

The UPDATE statement allows you to change the value of an existing record. It has this structure:

```
UPDATE Table
SET Column = Value
WHERE Condition
```

This syntax is a little different from the others, but it is intuitive enough to remember easily. While it is not necessary to use the WHERE clause, you need it to indicate exactly which row(s) you want to update. If you don't, your *entire table* will be updated. Therefore, the following is generally a very *bad* idea:

```
UPDATE Users
SET FirstName = 'Eben'
```

Every record in the database instantly has the first name "Eben" and there isn't a way to undo it. I mention this right away so that you have it uppermost in your mind. You can SELECT away all day long, willy-nilly. You do not have the same luxury with UPDATE and DELETE statements. Just be careful when updating.

They are changing the area code where I live. Instead of 520 it will be 928. Let's say that you want to update your database of ColdFusion programmers living in Arizona to reflect this very thing. You need to tell SQL Server, "Find all the programmers who have a 520 area code. Then make that area code 928." Here's how you would do it:

```
UPDATE Programmers
SET AreaCode = 928
WHERE AreaCode = 520
```

Easy enough.

If you want to update multiple columns, you can do that, too. You simply need to separate your value assignments with commas. Let's say that you wanted to change the contact info for only one of these programmers. We'll assume that the programmer in question has filled out a form, and the UserID is passed in the URL of the form action:

```
<cfquery name="UpdateContactInfo" datasource="cf5DB">

UPDATE Programmers
SET
Address1 = '#FORM.Address1#',
Address2 = '#FORM.Address2#',
AreaCode = 928,
Phone = '#FORM.Phone#'

WHERE ProgrammerID = #URL.ProgrammerID#;

</cfquery>
```

As you can see, the difference when updating multiple columns at once is that you separate the column/value pairs with a comma. The optional semicolon included at the end of the entire statement is just good practice—it tells the SQL Server that that's the end of this statement. Remember, too, that single quotes are necessary for character strings, and no single quotes are used for numeric values.

Dynamic SQL Statements with Conditional Logic

We can also write the statement above using a bit of conditional logic. Remember that ColdFusion builds the appropriate SQL statement as a result of interpreting all of the ColdFusion on the page—even when it's inside the <CFQUERY> tag. Suppose it is not necessary for programmers to type a value in the "Phone" control—they only have to tell you their phone number if they feel like it. Then we can use conditional logic inside the <CFQUERY> tag to check if the "Phone" field has anything typed in it, and if it does, then include it as part of the UPDATE statement. Like this:

```
<cfquery name="UpdateContactInfo" datasource="cf5DB">

UPDATE Programmers
SET
Address1 = '#FORM.Address1#',
Address2 = '#FORM.Address2#',
AreaCode = 928

<cfif Len(FORM.Phone) GT 0>

, Phone 5 '#FORM.Phone#'

</cfif>

WHERE ProgrammerID = #URL.ProgrammerID#;

</cfquery>
```

Here we use the ColdFusion Len function, which returns the character length of a given string, to determine if the Phone field was filled out. If the length is greater than 0, then the SQL inside the <cfif> block is included. On the other hand, if we were to submit this form without having typed anything in the "Phone" field, ColdFusion might pass off to the database a statement like this:

```
UPDATE Programmers
SET
Address1 = '22 Some St.',
Address2 = 'rm.3G63',
AreaCode = 928
WHERE ProgrammerID = 3;
```

An SQL UPDATE statement cannot end with a comma—a comma is used to separate column-value pairs. Therefore, the comma was included inside the conditional (the <cfif> part), so that it would be present only if the Phone column was included in the statement. And the Phone column is only included in the statement if its length is greater than 0.

Deleting Records

The DELETE statement permanently removes one or more records from the database. The syntax is much like that for the SELECT statement:

DELETE FROM *table* WHERE *condition*

Note that the WHERE clause is not necessary. Without it, however, you will delete *every row* in your table.

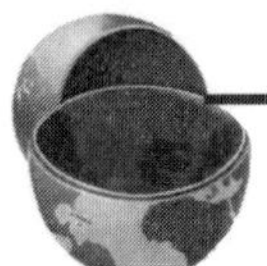

<TRICK>

*Here's a neat trick you can use to make sure that your delete statement deletes only the exact rows you want it to: write the delete statement as a SELECT statement first, and execute it. When you see the result set, you'll know the exact rows the statement affects. Then just change the SELECT * to a DELETE when you've determined that your statement is right. I figured this trick out one pleasant afternoon after erasing a few hours of someone else's data entry work.*

With the DELETE statement, unlike SELECT, you may not use the wildcard (*). It's not necessary. You must use great caution when working with the DELETE statement. It is permanent. Your only remedy for deleting data you didn't mean to is to have your admin restore the database from a current backup. One is quick to see the inherent difficulties here; if you have been working directly with the database and delete a load of rows you didn't mean to, it is a tedious process to discover exactly what rows have changed since the last backup.

Here is a dynamic SQL delete statement. This statement deletes all the rows in the Users table that have the matching UserID as passed in the URL (there will be only one, since UserID is a primary key):

```
DELETE FROM Users WHERE UserID = #URL.UserID#
```

Note that we do *not* use single quotes around the UserID variable, since it is an integer data type.

Sending Two Statements at Once

It is a common need in websites to display a banner or advertisement of some sort. You advertisers will generally appreciate that you record the number of times their banner was displayed, and you would likely need the same number for billing purposes. This requires two actions then—one SQL SELECT statement to retrieve the banner ad, and another SQL UPDATE statement to add one more hit to the TimesDisplayed integer column for that advertisement. Luckily, that's quite easy with <CFQUERY>. You don't even have to write two separate <CFQUERY> tags—just separate the two statements and hand them off to the database at once. Here is an example:

```
<!—Get the banner ad with passed ID and update
      TimesDisplayed—->

<cfquery name="getOneBannerAd"
       datasource="#Request.App.datasource#" maxrows5"1">

SELECT AdID AS AffiliateID, ImageName, AltText, WebsiteURL
        FROM Ads
        WHERE AdID = #VARIABLES.thisBannerID#;
UPDATE Ads
        SET TimesDisplayed 5 TimesDisplayed + 1
        WHERE AdID = #VARIABLES.thisBannerID#;

</cfquery>
```

Recall that spacing was applied above only for readability.

<NOTE>

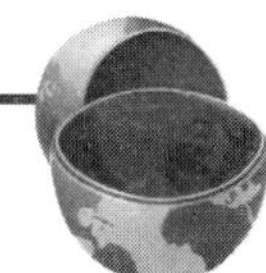

Ending your SQL statements with a semicolon is usually a good idea. It tells SQL Server that it's the end of the statement (kind of like putting a period at the end of a sentence). When using two statements in one <CFQUERY> tag, it is required.

Union

A union combines the results of two different SELECT statements into a single set. Both of your SELECT statements must have the same number of fields, they must be listed in the same order in both queries, and they must have the same data type. Also, you may not use fields with data types of memo (Access), text (SQL), image, or any other kind of Binary Large Object. Below is an example of a UNION with our two tables that hold the numbers 1 though 9 and 6 through 14:

```
SELECT Numbers
FROM Col1

UNION
```

```
SELECT MoreNumbers
FROM Col2
```

Fourteen rows are output, with the four duplicate entries (6, 7, 8, 9) forgotten.

While not very commonly used itself, union can be an important aspect of the new Query of Queries feature of ColdFusion, which we will examine next.

Query of Queries

The ability to query a previously run query result set is new in ColdFusion 5. This powerful new feature allows you pull memory-resident data without having to hit the database again to select a subset of the initial query. The primary benefit here is performance; it is obviously faster to pull a result set out of memory than to go back to the database. The thing I really like about it is that you can join results from disparate datasources to create a new result set.

The Query of Queries feature supports a subset of the SQL 92 standard that we have addressed in this chapter. The supported subset is shown in Table 10.5.

Table 10.5 Query of Queries SQL Support

SQL Item	

Aggregate Functions:
`Count([DISTINCT][*] expr)`
`Sum([DISTINCT] expr)`
`Avg([DISTINCT] expr)`
`Max(expr)`
`Min(expr)`
No nesting of aggregate functions is allowed.
	Boolean predicates: NOT, LIKE, IN, BETWEEN, AND, OR, NOT IN, NOT BETWEEN

Computed Columns	*GROUP BY*
SQL Item	
AS (Aliasing)	DISTINCT
DML	HAVING
Multiple Queries	OUTER JOINS

How do you query a query? A new DBTYPE is now available for the <CFQUERY> tag="query"; using this attribute value will load a driver that will interpret the SQL within the tag. So all you have to do is set that attribute and then specify the name of an available query to use as the table.

Combining Queries from Different Datasources

Let's put this new feature to work. Consider a university that has many different departments. Each department runs a different database server with different operating systems, so that they can not only hold their data, but give the students and faculty access to different kinds of systems. But they are also likely to hold at least some of the same kind of information.

With a Query of a Query, it is easy to retrieve, for instance, a single list of the employee names and their positions in their different departments—even if some overlap. The listing below shows how to perform a Query of a Query using the SQL UNION operator to combine the results of two query sets from two different data sources—one of them Oracle, and the other SQL Server. Then it outputs the result simply.

```
<html>
<head>
	<title>Untitled</title>
</head>

<body>

<!----First, retrieve the list of names and positions from
the Human Resources department, which runs an Oracle 8i data
server---->

<cfquery name="Names1" datasource="HRDB"
	dbtype=" Oracle80">

SELECT FirstName
FROM Users;

</cfquery>

<!-----Next, we query the second data server, which is a
Microsoft SQL Server box. Our datasource is set up with the
OLEDB driver instead of the ODBC driver---->

<cfquery name="Names2" datasource="AccountingDB"
	dbtype="OLEDB">
```

```
SELECT TOP 10 FirstName
FROM Users;

</cfquery>

<!----We then use the SQL UNION command to join the two que-
ries together. Notice the DBTYPE now is "Query", and we do
not need to specify a datasource, since no connection info is
used---->

<cfquery name="QofQUnion" dbtype="Query">

SELECT FirstName
FROM Names1
UNION
SELECT FirstName
FROM Names2
ORDER BY FirstName ASC

</cfquery>

<!---Output the results---->

<h2>First Names in Both Human Resources and Accounting</h2>

<cfoutput query="QofQUnion">

#QofQUnion.FirstName—<br>

</cfoutput>

</body>
</html>
```

Figure 10.19 shows what it looks like with debugging output turned on.

Simple enough. Also with Query of Queries, you are freed of the UNION constraints regarding HAVING and GROUP BY clauses; ColdFusion supports their full functionality. We will take a look at HAVING and GROUP BY shortly.

The ability to join two datasources in the manner described above is very powerful indeed. This feature will save you a lot of hassle when working with enterprise applications. You can achieve smarter reporting over larger data landscapes to support business decisions. You can leave existing data applications in their native environments to create large web projects without the expense of migrating data. It's pretty terrific.

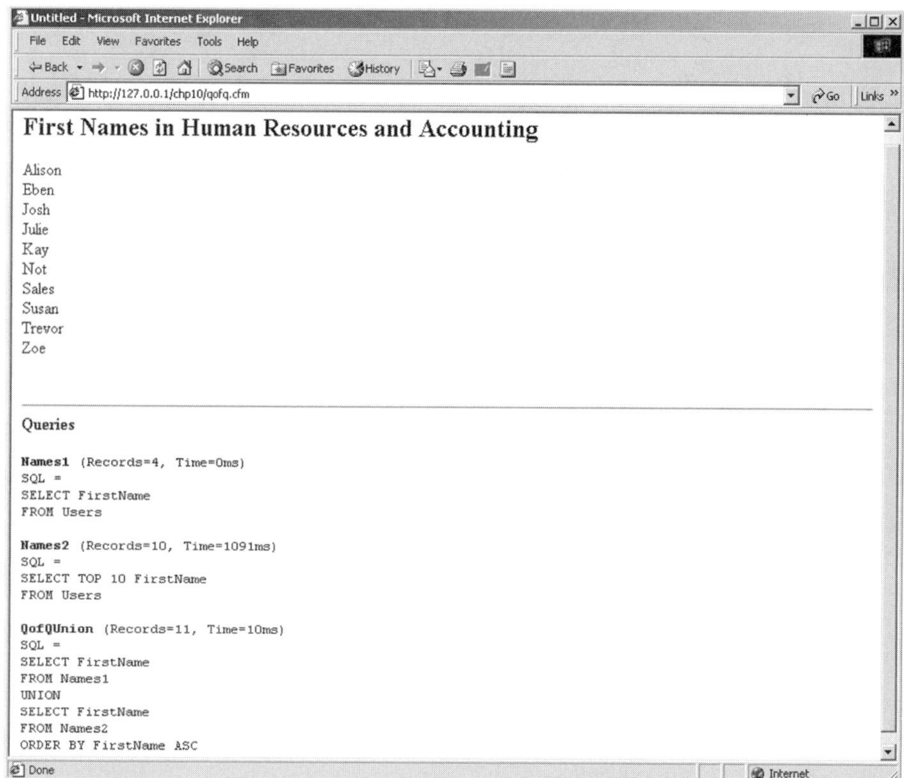

Figure 10.19 The new Query of Queries feature of ColdFusion can combine result sets from disparate datasources.

ConnectString

The ConnectString attribute of the <CFQUERY> tag is new with ColdFusion 5. It allows you to dynamically override the ODBC connection information that you provided in the ColdFusion Administrator. You can also specify connection attributes that are not set in the Administrator. To do so, use the connectstring attribute in any CFML tag that connects to a database: cfquery, cfinsert, cfupdate, cfgridupdate, and cfstoredproc.

Let's create a connection to our SQLServer data source using a connect string to specify the Application and Work Station ID.

```
<cfupdate datasource = "mssql"
  connectstring = "APP=ColdFusion;WSID=howard"
  tablename = "department">
```

Dynamic Datasources

New in ColdFusion 5, you can specify a datasource dynamically. That is, you don't have to create it as a datasource in the ColdFusion Administrator first. It requires two steps: first, specify the "DBTYPE" of the <CFQUERY> tag as "dynamic." Then, using the ConnectString attribute, you can specify all of the information ColdFusion needs to connect to the database and run your query.

Listing 10.1 Connecting to an Undefined Datasource Dynamically

```
<html>
<head>
        <title>Dynamic Datasource</title>
</head>
<body>
<!----Specify the DBYTYPE and ConnectString attributes---->

<cfquery name="getUsers"
  dbtype = "dynamic"
  ConnectString=
  "DRIVER=Microsoft Access Driver (*.mdb);
  DBQ=C:\Documents and Settings\Administrator\My Docu-
ments\CoreBook\cf5db.mdb;
MaxBufferSize=1024;FIL=MS Access">

  SELECT Firstname, LastName From Users WHERE FirstName =
'Eben';

</cfquery>

<!---Output the result------->
The first name is:<br>

<cfoutput query="getUsers">#firstname# #lastname#</cfoutput>
</body>
</html>
```

If you are used to writing in ASP, you are likely familiar with this syntax and approach. The *connectstring* attributes for the database will be somewhat different, depending on which database you're connecting to. Here is the same example, modified to demonstrate the connect string you can use for a SQL Server database:

Listing 10.2 Using the ConnectString and DBTYPE Attributes to Connect to an SQL Server Database without a Datasource Previously Defined in the Administrator

```
<html>
<head>
        <title>SQL Server Connection String</title>
</head>

<body>

<html>
<head>
        <title>SQL Dynamic Datasource</title>
</head>

<body>
<!----Specify the DBYTYPE and ConnectString attributes---->
<cfquery name = "getItems"
  dbtype = "dynamic"
  connectstring = "Driver={SQL SERVER};
Server=data.ct.net;
Database=CoreCFDB;
UID=MyUsername;
pwd=MyPassword;">

  SELECT FirstName, LastName
FROM Users
WHERE FirstName = 'Eben'

</cfquery>

<!---Output the result like normal------->
My SQL Server result:<br>

<cfoutput query="getItems">#FirstName# #LastName#</cfoutput>
</body>
</html>

</body>
</html>
```

Not Just for Databases

You are not limited to joining different datasources, however. You're not even limited to using the <CFQUERY> tag to generate the initial query. ColdFusion allows your initial query to be any ColdFusion tag or function that generates a query result set, including cfldap, cfhttp, cfstoredproc, cfpop, cfindex, cfdirectory, and the Query functions.

Joins

Often in a properly normalized database design, the data you want to view is in more than one table. Joins are the means for recognizing shared values in different tables, and returning rows that meet the join condition. Using a unique identifier, such as primary and foreign keys, you can perform table joins with some ease.

Here is a sort of abstract example. Say you have two separate tables, Table1 and Table2. Each holds a list of numbers. You could perform a join on the tables to see which numbers they shared. Writing SELECT * FROM Table1, which has the Numbers column, returns the following rows:

```
Numbers
-----------
1
2
3
4
5
6
7
8
9

(9 row(s) affected)
```

Writing SELECT * FROM Table2, which holds the MoreNumbers column, displays its entire list of numbers:

```
MoreNumbers
-----------
6
7
```

```
8
9
10
11
12
13
14

(9 row(s) affected)
```

So each has nine numbers, but only some of them are the same. In order to return all of the rows that are shared between the tables, we perform a join, which has this structure:

```
SELECT Column_List
FROM Table
JOIN TYPE Table2 ON JoinCondition
WHERE Conditions
```

This syntax I find less intuitive than the more basic SQL syntax, but it is perfectly sensible. It says, in effect, "Choose all the rows where whatever I specify in the join condition is true for both rows, *and* the conditions in the WHERE clause are satisfied."

It is good to remember that the column names do not have to be the same for each table, nor do the data types have to be the same. However, if they aren't the same, SQL Server will attempt a conversion, and it may not always work. So it is generally good practice to join on columns of the same datatype.

Inner Joins

Inner Joins return only the rows for which the join condition is true. These are far and away the most common type of join. Recall from the previous example that we have two tables, each with one column: "Numbers" and "MoreNumbers." So to join our Numbers column with the MoreNumbers column to find out which numbers are the same for both columns, we would write this:

```
SELECT Numbers
FROM Table1
INNER JOIN Table2 ON Numbers = MoreNumbers
```

And here are the results:

```
Numbers
----------
6
7
```

```
8
9

(4 row(s) affected)
```

Looking back at our number lists in both tables, these are indeed the only matches.

<NOTE>

Remember that tables are often referred to as relations. This can be a bit confusing, but relation is really the proper term.

Often you will use a foreign key and primary key in creating the join relationships. In Oracle and SQL Server, you can give tables Aliases when you perform joins. This helps keep the columns you refer to unambiguous when they have the same names in different tables.

For instance, here is a query that retrieves the User's privilege level from the UserPrivilege table. In this example, I have made the datasource name a variable:

```
<cfquery name="GetUserPrivilegeLevel"
        datasource="#VARIABLES.Datasource#" maxrows="1">

SELECT U.Username, U.FirstName, U.LastName, UP.UserID,
UP.PrivilegeID
        FROM Users U
        INNER JOIN UserPrivilege UP
               ON U.UserID = UP.UserID
        WHERE U.Username = '#FORM.Username#'
                AND Password = '#FORM.Password#'
</cfquery>
```

This query gets the user's first name and last name from the Users table, it gets the match for this user's UserID that should be in the UserPrivilege table. It knows which UserID to use, because there can be only one (or no) match for the particular username and password combination supplied by the form.

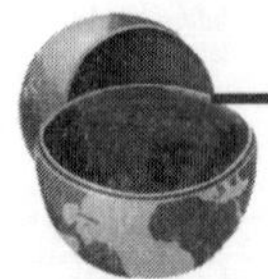

<NOTE>

Remember that character strings take single quote marks around them and numeric values do not.

Outer Joins

On occasion it is useful to return all of the rows from one or more tables, even if they don't have matches in another joined table. In this case, you perform an *outer join*. There are three different kinds of outer joins: left, right, and full.

Left Outer Joins

A *left outer join* returns all of the rows from the left table in the result set, even if they don't meet the join condition; it also returns rows in the right column that do meet the join condition. Columns in the right table that don't meet the join condition return as NULL.

Modifying the Username and Privilege example from above, you could find all of the users who indeed have an assigned privilege in the UserPrivilege table, as well as those who do not (those records will return NULL for UP.PrivilegeID):

```
SELECT U.Username, U.FirstName, U.LastName, UP.UserID,
UP.PrivilegeID
        FROM Users U
        LEFT OUTER JOIN UserPrivilege UP
               ON U.UserID = UP.UserID
        WHERE U.UserID < 10
```

To illustrate the point more consistently, let us use a Left Outer Join to find all of the numbers in the Numbers column, and only the matching numbers in the right-hand table:

Listing 10.3 Left Outer Join with Dynamic Datasource

```
<html>
<head>
        <title>Left Outer Join</title>
</head>
<body>
<html>
<head>
        <title>Dynamic Datasource</title>
</head>

<body>
<!—Specify the DBYTYPE and ConnectString attributes—>
<cfquery name = "getItems"
```

```
   dbtype = "dynamic"
   blockfactor = 10
   connectstring = "Driver={SQL SERVER};
Server=data.ct.net;Database=CF=DB;UID=test;pwd=MyPassword;">
   SELECT Numbers, MoreNumbers
   FROM Col1
   LEFT OUTER JOIN Col2
   ON Numbers = MoreNumbers;
</cfquery>

<!--Output the result------->
Numbers</b><br>
<cfoutput query="getItems">#Numbers#</cfoutput><br>
<br>

<b.More Numbers</b><br>
<cfoutput query="getItems">#MoreNumbers#</cfoutput><br>
</body>
</html>
```

Figure 10.20 shows the result set of the Numbers/More Numbers tables joined with a Left Outer Join.

Right Outer Joins

A *Right Outer Join,* as you might imagine, returns every row from the right table of the JOIN clause, even if they don't meet the join condition. It is almost exactly like the Left Outer Join in this way—exact same structure. It's just the other table that has only the matching values return.

You can combine different types of joins in the same statement. You can also join more than two tables using different kinds of joins, as shown below:

```
SELECT Cols
FROM table1
       LEFT OUTER JOIN table1.c3 = table2.c3
       RIGHT OUTER JOIN table3
       LEFT OUTER JOIN table4         ON table3.c1
       ON table2.c3 = table4.c3
```

Full Outer Join

The rarely used Full Outer Join returns all rows from both tables. It returns the same results as the UNION command. If a row from either the left or the right table does not match the selection criteria, a Full Outer Join specifies

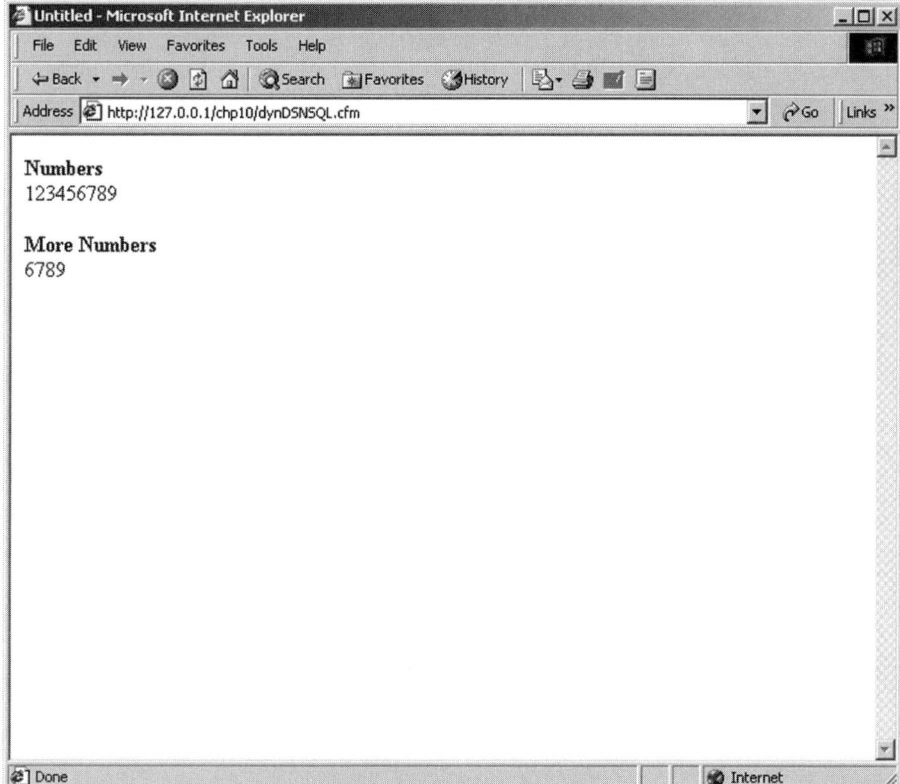

Figure 10.20 A Left Outer Join shows you all the rows from the left table, and only the matches from the join condition of the right table. This query also uses a dynamic datasource.

that the row be included in the result set, and that outputs columns that correspond to the other table set to NULL.

The syntax is similar to that of other types of joins. We can use a Full Outer Join to return all the numbers in the two tables, including matching rows.

```
SELECT Numbers, MoreNumbers
from Table1
full outer join Table2 on Numbers = MoreNumbers
ORDER BY Numbers ASC, MoreNumbers ASC
```

Here is the result set. Because the combined columns include only the numbers 1 though 14, exactly 14 rows are returned.

```
Numbers     MoreNumbers
----------- -----------
NULL        10
NULL        11
```

```
NULL        12
NULL        13
NULL        14
1           NULL
2           NULL
3           NULL
4           NULL
5           NULL
6           6
7           7
8           8
9           9

(14 row(s) affected)
```

Cross Join

The Cross Join kind of join returns a Cartesian product of both tables. That is, a Cross Join returns all possible row combinations from both tables specified in the join. For example:

```
SELECT Numbers, MoreNumbers
from Table1
CROSS JOIN Table2
ORDER BY Numbers ASC, MoreNumbers ASC
```

Each table in this statement has exactly nine rows. Can you guess how many records will be in our result set? Cross Joins are useful for looking at your data as sets. They aren't used much in application development, but I thought it would be good to include a brief reference in case someone asks you about them at a cocktail party.

The answer to the above question is 81.

GROUP BY

GROUP BY combines rows with the same values in the column(s) specified into a single row. The GROUP BY command lets you work with aggregate functions in SQL with some ease. Remember that aggregate functions allow you to perform filtering and mathematical operations on the data retrieved in your SELECT statement and return a single value. You cannot use the wildcard character (*) when using the GROUP BY command.

<NOTE>

See Appendix I, "Common SQL Function Reference," for a list, explanations, and examples of common SQL functions.

```
SELECT  count(A.AdType) as adtypes
       FROM Ads A
GROUP BY A.AdType
```

Here are the results of executing the above query. They tell us how many of each ad type exist in the ads table, assuming four different types of ads.

```
adtypes
-----------
43
1583
4
2

(4 row(s) affected)
```

Let's quickly look at another example. The basic structure is standard, so a generic GROUP BY structure will look like this:

```
SELECT Column1, Column2, SUM(Column3)
FROM table
WHERE Column1 > Column 2
       AND Column1 < 10
GROUP BY Column1, Column2
ORDER BY Column1
```

It will also work great in Oracle. The main thing to understand here is that the GROUP BY clause handles summarizing of the data as they are retrieved, and the ORDER BY list determines the sorting arrangement for the retrieved rows.

HAVING

The primary difference between HAVING and WHERE is that the HAVING keyword is meant to filter data *before* they are grouped. The HAVING clause restricts the rows returned by GROUP BY, much as the WHERE clause restricts data returned by a SELECT statement. To this end, the syntax for the HAVING clause is very much like that for the WHERE clause. The difference is that the HAVING clause can incorporate aggregate functions from the SELECT column list. You must reiterate any aggregate functions stated in the SELECT list. Here is an example:

```
SELECT A.AdID, Count(S.SiteID) as thisSite
        FROM Ads A
        INNER JOIN Sites S ON A.SiteID = S.SiteID
GROUP BY A.AdID
        HAVING count(S.SiteID) = 1
```

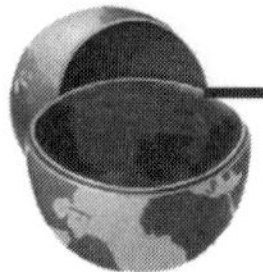

<NOTE>

You may not use the column alias in the HAVING clause.

A Complete Search Engine Application

Now we can combine our knowledge of SQL operators, FORM variables, conditional logic, <CFOUTPUT>, and the <CFQUERY> tag to create a complete search engine for a website. This will show you how to put together a number of the components you have learned so far. It will also be terrifically fun because it will show you the real evolution of writing a ColdFusion application. It would be a disservice to you, in my view, to plunk down a load of code and say, "Here's your search app, tiger," because it wouldn't show you the process that you will have to go through yourself when you write your own applications. After all, that's the idea here.

Since this search engine will retrieve only data stored in a database, it will not retrieve information stored in documents, such as Word documents, .pdf files, or the like. You can do that in ColdFusion, however, using Verity 2k collections.

First, let's determine the general scope of this application. We will make a search function that allows users to search for products in the CF5DB database. This Microsoft SQL Server database contains product descriptions, names, and prices. The Item table looks like Table 10.5.

Table 10.5 Description of the Item Table

Column Name	*Data Type*
ID	Int, with Identity set On (in Access, use AutoNumber)
ProductNumber	Int (in Access, use Number)

Column Name	*Data Type*
Name	VarChar (in Access, use Text)
Description	Text (in Access, use Memo)
Price	Money (in Access, use "Currency")

Create this table in your database using a query or graphical tool. Populate the database with some dummy information that you can use to complete this chapter. For this example, I am using ski accessory items, such as hats and gloves.

Next, we need to determine exactly what things are going to happen in this little application. These are known as *use-case scenarios* (though formalists might object, it's good enough for our purposes at this time):

- A user can type a string to search into an input control.
- If the user's search yields fewer than 2 results, let him know, and display a hint on how to get more results.
- If the user's search yields 2 or more results, display an abbreviated version of the result.
- Make the product name a hyperlink on the abbreviated result page, so that the user can click on a product name to see a complete listing for a particular item.
- Minimize the amount of code and number of pages involved in creating this application: make the search results and item detail display in the same template, using conditional logic.

According to our requirements above, we can write this entire application using only one ColdFusion template. It may seem at first that you need three pages: one for the form to display to the user, a second for the search results, and a third for detailed product information.

Using conditional logic, you can create a self-posting form. This is a good idea for a search application, since you will likely want to have the search form always display to the user. Why make them go Back to type in another search string?

Let's make the HTML form component first, working from the inside out, just as in algebra. This is often the way that I write; I find it helps me zero in very quickly on errors, and I can write with confidence as my application gets more complex, because I know that each individual component works correctly before I begin the next.

First, create the simple search form:

```
<!DOCTYPE HTML PUBLIC "-//W3C//DTD HTML 4.0 Transi-
tional//EN">
```

```
<html>
<head>
      <title>Site Search</title>
</head>

<body>

<cfset thisPage = cgi.script_name>

<h3.Search for products:</h3>

<cfoutput>

<form name="siteSearch" action="#thisPage#" method="post">
        <input name="SearchString" type="text" maxlength="25".
        <input type="Submit" name="Submit" value="Search">
</form>

</cfoutput>

</body>
</html>
```

Here we have written a simple form. Of note, here are the small additions that will cut down on the number of CF templates we have to keep track of. First, we set a variable, "thisPage," to the name of the current template. The read-only variable "CGI.SCRIPT_NAME" is always available to us, as we learned in Chapter 6. We use it here as the value of the action attribute in the form tag. That means that when the user types in a search string and clicks the "Search" button, the search string form variables will post to the same page they came from. This practice, making a "self-posting" form, is an excellent way to streamline your work. Also it makes it easier to see all the parts of your form and action "page" at once. This is a common practice in Macromedia Spectra applications as well.

In order to create a self-posting form, we need to test for the existence of the form variables. If they don't exist, then the user has not filled out the form and pressed "Submit" yet. In that case, we should just show the user the form. If the variables do exist, the user has filled out the form and hit the "Search" button, so we need to process the information submitted.

Use your browser's "View Source" function to make sure that your "thisPage" variable is pointing to the page you want it to. It will be a relative path.

Before we go any further, let's test that this self-posting form works. We will add the necessary conditional logic, like the code shown in bold below:

```
<html>
<head>
	<title>Site Search</title>
</head>

<body>

<cfset thisPage = cgi.script_name>

<h3>Search for products:</h3>

<cfoutput>

<form name="siteSearch" action="#thisPage#" method="post">
	<input name="SearchString" type="text" maxlength="25">
	<input type="Submit" name="Submit" value="Search">
</form>

</cfoutput>

<cfif isDefined("FORM.SearchString")>
	You want to search for something.
</cfif>

</body>
</html>
```

Since we want to display the search form every time, we need only test whether the form was submitted; we can leave the form controls outside the conditional logic. Using the function IsDefined, we can control the flow of our processing.

<REMINDER>

We discussed conditional logic, flow control, and the IsDefined function in Chapter 6. If you need to brush up on these things, refer to that chapter.

Once you have typed the code above, load the page, which I have called "SearchSite.cfm," into your browser. You should *not* see the "You want to search for something" string. Type anything into the input field and press "Search." You now see the search control, ready to accept a new string, and you see the message, "You want to search for something."

Now that we have verified that our form works, and our conditional logic is correct, we need to make sure that we are passing and accepting the search string correctly. Let's modify the above code slightly. We will output to the

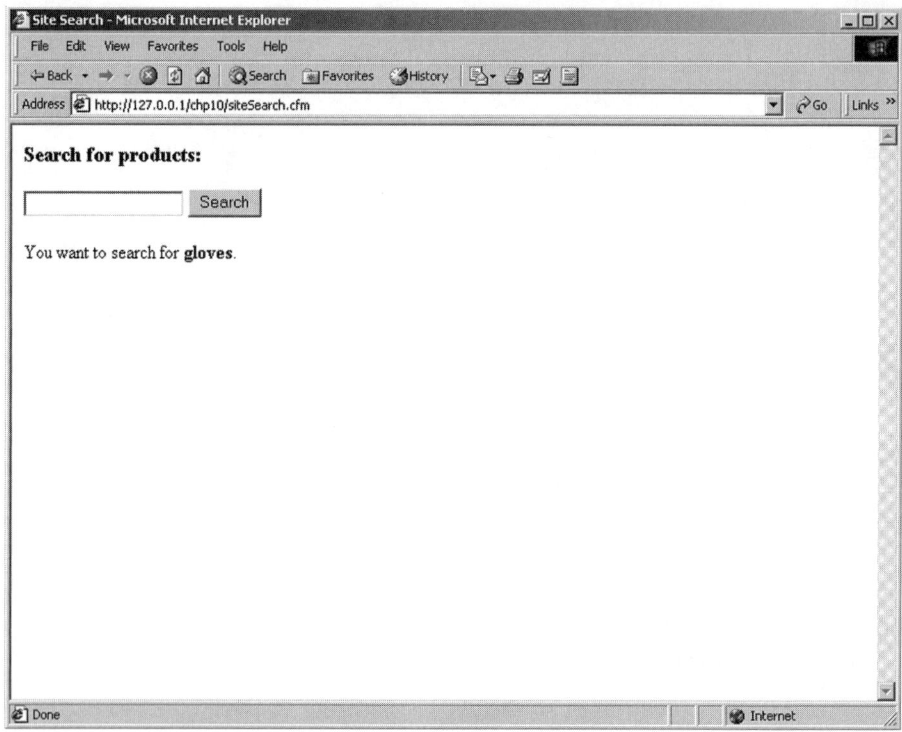

Figure 10.21 Using conditional logic, you can create a compact, self-posting form.

browser the search string submitted by the user. This step insures that we will pass the correct information to the <CFQUERY> tag.

```
<cfif isDefined("FORM.SearchString")>
You want to search for
<cfoutput>
        <b>#FORM.SearchString#</b>
</cfoutput>.
</cfif>
```

If you type a name into the field and click "Search," your string should be output to the browser, as shown in Figure 10.21.

Now that we have confirmed that we are passing the search string successfully, we can send it on to the <CFQUERY> tag to retrieve matches in the database. Then we will make our form a little more sophisticated.

Update your code to include the <CFQUERY> tag inside the <cfif> clause. We don't want to run the query if no search string was provided. But as it is now, a user could submit this form without entering a search string. So, every bit of code used in processing the form variables must be included inside the <cfif> clause—it acts like a separate action page altogether, and it's not a bad idea to think of it that way for now.

<NOTE>

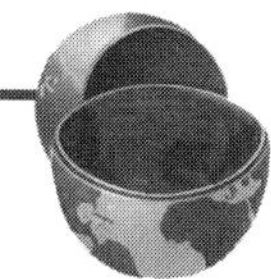

There are a few ways to check if a particular form field has any kind of value, once it has been submitted. A popular and fast-performing way is by checking that the length of the string is more than 0. Like this:

```
<cfif Len(FORM.SearchString) GT 0>
        They typed at least one character.
</cfif>
```

Since you can test for multiple expressions, you could also write this in the Search Site application:

```
<cfif isDefined("FORM.SearchString") AND Len(FORM.SearchString) GT 0>

        The form has been submitted and the field has a value.
<cfelse>
        <!—Passed an empty string—>
        You must enter some text to search for!
</cfif>
```

Here is the updated template that queries the database and outputs matching product names:

```
<cfset thisPage = cgi.script_name>
<h3>Search for products:</h3>
<cfoutput>
<form name="siteSearch" action="#thisPage#" method="post">
       <input name="SearchString" type="text" maxlength="25">
       <input type="Submit" name="Submit" value="Search">
</form>
</cfoutput>

<cfif isDefined("FORM.SearchString")>

<!--Add the ID to the query, since we'll need a unique
       identifier--->
<cfquery name="searchItems" datasource="cf5DB">
        SELECT ID, Name
        FROM Item
        WHERE Name LIKE '%#FORM.SearchString#%'
```

```
</cfquery>

Your search for
<b><cfoutput>#FORM.SearchString#</cfoutput></b> results:
<br>
<cfoutput query="searchItems">
#searchItems.Name#<br>
</cfoutput>

</cfif>
```

We changed things just a bit. We changed our text slightly to make some grammatical sense when results are returned. More importantly, we used the <CFQUERY> tag to choose all of the product names in the Item table that are *like* what the user typed into the form.

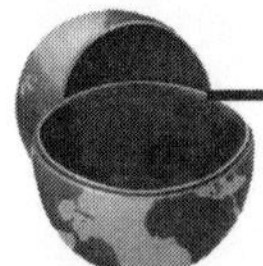

<NOTE>

For usage and syntax of the SQL LIKE keyword, refer to the discussion earlier in this chapter.

When outputting the results of a query, it is important to use the "query" attribute of the <CFOUTPUT> tag. The value of the query attribute should be the same as the value of the name attribute for the <CFQUERY> tag. So in this case it's "searchItems." This tells ColdFusion that this block is intended to output directly from a query, and to include all results. If you leave out the query attribute, ColdFusion will output only the first record. While you need not prefix your variables with the query name, it is a very good idea. It helps to keep your query variables distinct from other variables, and saves ColdFusion from having to check different scopes until it finds your variable's value.

At this point, our basic database search functionality works. But it is not particularly useful or user friendly. It doesn't tell us how many records were found, and it doesn't let us see detailed information in a drill-down fashion.

Making Drill-Down Data Retrieval Functionality

First, let's modify the output to generate a link for each specific record. By clicking on the link, the user gets more detailed information about a product. This is commonly referred to as *drill-down* functionality. In order to do this, we need to wrap our matched output in an anchor tag and set a dynamic URL

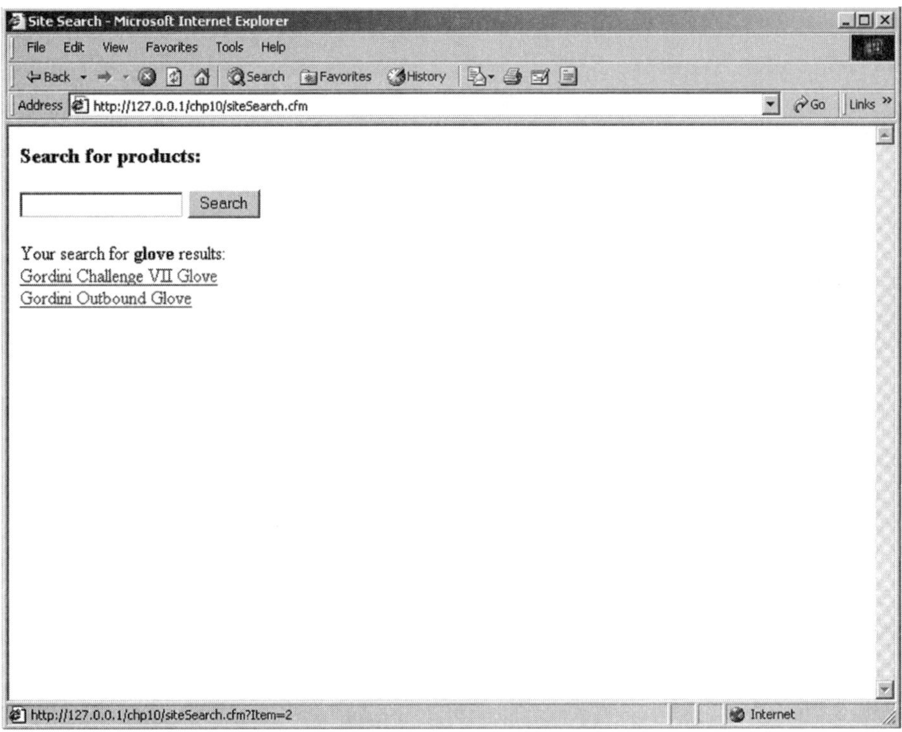

Figure 10.22 Notice the URL parameter dynamically assigned to each link; this will let us view detailed information about each result individually.

parameter. This parameter should be a unique identifier, such as the item ID, so we can refer to only one record in our drill-drown.

Modify the output section of your template to look like this:

```
<cfoutput query="searchItems">
<a href="#thisPage#?Item=#searchItems.id#">#searchItems.Name#
</a>
<br>
</cfoutput>
```

This code will now make each search item a link, and assign each URL parameter the value of the "id" column retrieved from the query. Figure 10.22 shows the result of loading your new page in a browser.

Notice how when we mouse over Gordini Challenge VII Glove, the status bar at the bottom left of the browser displays the URL of the link. In the case of this item, it's /chp10/siteSearch.cfm?Item=2.

In order to achieve the drill-down, let's work in some conditional logic, similar to that which we used to check for the existence of FORM variables in this template. We'll then pass the URL.Item parameter, which holds the value of the "id" first query, on to a second query to get the detailed information.

Go back to your file and modify your code so that it looks like this:

```
<html>
<head>
	<title>Site Search</title>
</head>

<body>

<!--Set the page name so we can reference it easily when
self posting—>
<cfset thisPage = cgi.script_name>

<h3>Search for products:</h3>

<!--Use cfoutput tags around the form so we can use the
"thisPage" variable-->

<cfoutput>
<form name="siteSearch" action="#thisPage#" method="post">
	<input name="SearchString" type="text" maxlength="25">
	<input type="Submit" name="Submit" value="Search">
</form>
</cfoutput>

<!—If the user has clicked the submit button, run the
query to retrieve product items—>

<cfif isDefined("FORM.SearchString")>
	<cfquery name="searchItems" datasource="cf5DB">
		SELECT id, ProductNumber, Name, Description
		FROM Item
		WHERE Name LIKE '%#FORM.SearchString#%'
	</cfquery>

	Your search for
<b><cfoutput>#FORM.SearchString#</cfoutput></b> results:
	<br>
<!—Display the results of the query—>
	<cfoutput query="searchItems">

	<a href="#thisPage#?Item=#searchItems.id#>
	#searchItems.Name#</a>
<br>
	</cfoutput>
```

```
</cfif>

<!—if the user clicked on an item link, pass the URL item
parameter into the query, and retrieve the description for
only that item.—>

<cfif isDefined("URL.Item")>
        <cfquery name="ItemInfo" datasource="cf5DB">
                SELECT id, ProductNumber, Name, Description
                FROM Item
                WHERE id = #URL.item#
        </cfquery>

         <h4>Here is your detailed info:</h4>
         <cfoutput query="ItemInfo">
         <b>#ItemInfo.Name#</b><br>
         Product #ItemInfo.ProductNumber#<br>
         ItemInfo.Description#
         </cfoutput>
</cfif>


</body>
</html>
```

Remember that <CFOUTPUT> will loop over the query results, and therefore all code within the output block will execute once for every iteration of the loop. That means that had you written this:

```
<cfoutput query="searchItems">
Your search for <b>FORM.SearchString#</b> results:
<br>

<a href="#thisPage#?Item=#searchItems.id#">
#searchItems.Name#</a><br>

</cfoutput>
```

your search results would have looked like this:

```
Your search for glove results:
Gordini Challenge VII Glove
Your search for glove results:
Gordini Outbound Glove
```

Correctly placing your <CFOUPTUT> tags (especially when working with HTML tables) is therefore a crucial aspect of outputting dynamic data. Figure 10.23 shows the results of incorporating the new code and clicking on an item.

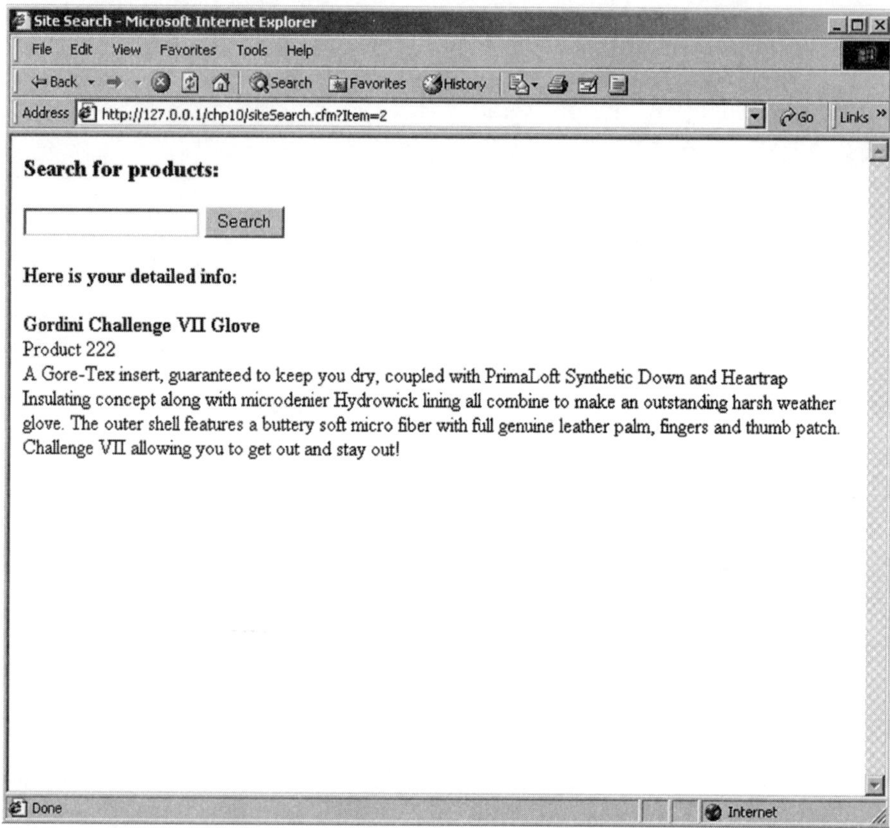

Figure 10.23 Drill-down item detail results.

Now we can easily display the number of records found using the variable Queryname.RecordCount. Remember that this <CFQUERY> variable is automatically created every time a query is run.

Making a More User-Friendly Search

We need to expand our application a bit. We've got things working correctly, but we should probably upgrade things at this point. First of all, the only field searched in the database that is of interest to the user is "name." We need to search other columns, too. This should be easy enough to add, using the OR keyword in our SQL statement.

Next, we'll add a little more conditional logic to account for the number of items a user might find. Right now our application just goes blank if no matches are found. Let's display a little message instead. We will use the automatically created RecordCount variable to do this.

Neither of these should require too much effort, given what you already know. Update your code to read like the listing below. New sections are in bold typeface:

```
<html>
<head>
      <title>Site Search</title>
</head>

<body>

<!---Set the page name so we can reference it easily when
self posting---->
<cfset thisPage = cgi.script_name>

<h3>Search for products:</h3>

<!---Use cfoutput tags around the form so we can use the
"thisPage" variable----->

<cfoutput>
<form name="siteSearch" action="#thisPage#" method="post">
      <input name="SearchString" type="text" maxlength="25">
      <input type="Submit" name="Submit" value="Search">
</form>
</cfoutput>

<!----If the user has clicked the submit button, run the
query to retrieve product items. Include not just ID and
"name" column, but also "description"---->

<cfif isDefined("FORM.SearchString")>
      <cfquery name="searchItems" datasource="cf5DB">
              SELECT id, ProductNumber, Name, Description
              FROM Item
              WHERE Name LIKE '%#FORM.SearchString#%'
              OR Description LIKE '%#FORM.SearchString#%'
      </cfquery>

<!---Show user number of records returned.--->


Your search for <b><cfoutput>#FORM.SearchString#</b> returned
      <b>#searchItems.RecordCount#</cfoutput></b> results:
      <br>
```

```
<!--If the search produced fewer than 3 results, show a
hint-->

<cfif searchItems.RecordCount LT 3>
      Hint: Modify your search by typing in word roots, for
      instance, "hat" instead of "hats".<br>
</cfif>

<!—Display the results of the query—>

      <cfoutput query="searchItems">

<a href="#thisPage#?Item=#searchItems.id#">
#searchItems.Name#</a>
<br>

      </cfoutput>
</cfif>

<!—if the user clicked on an item link, pass the URL item
parameter into the query,
and retrieve the description for only that item.—>

<cfif isDefined("URL.Item")>
      <cfquery name="ItemInfo" datasource="CF5DB">
            SELECT id, ProductNumber, Name, Price,
                    Description
            FROM Item
            WHERE id = #URL.item#
      </cfquery>

      <h4>Here is your detailed info:</h4>
      <cfoutput query="ItemInfo">
      <b>#ItemInfo.Name#</b><br>
      Product #ItemInfo.ProductNumber#<br>
      Price: #DollarFormat(ItemInfo.Price)#<br>
      #ItemInfo.Description#
      </cfoutput>
</cfif>


</body>
</html>
```

Just for a final touch, we've added the price column to the query, and we've output it along with the rest of the product information. Use the dollar for-

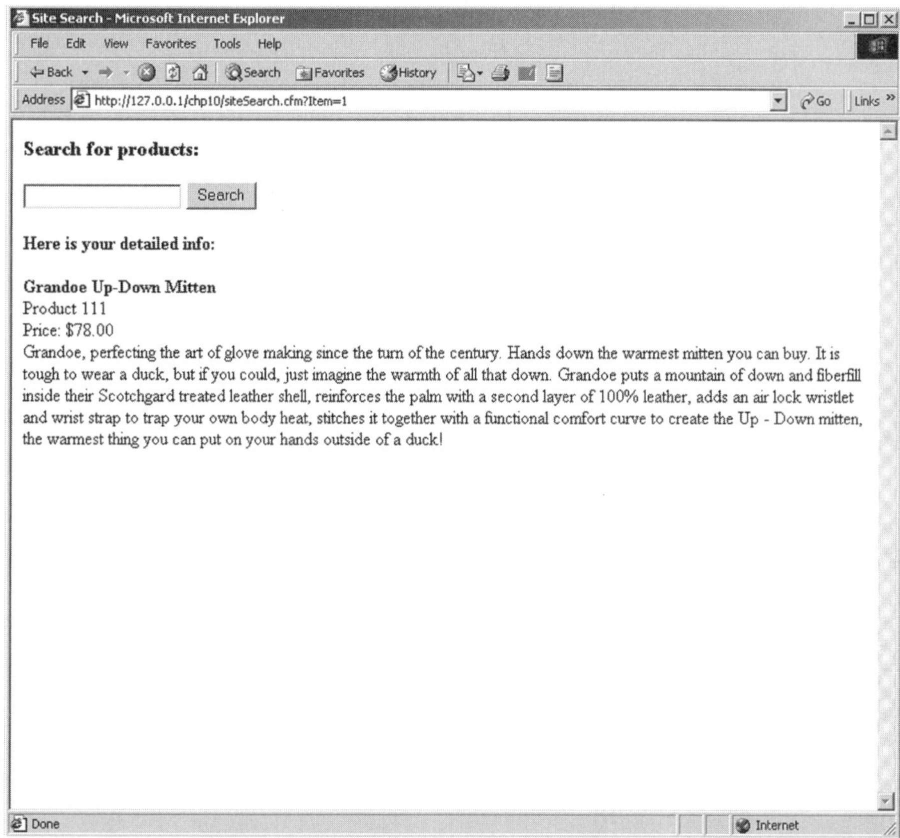

Figure 10.24 The drill-down search application with the dollar formatting function incorporated.

mat function around the Price output. This will format your data by putting a dollar sign ($) where it belongs, and putting two decimal places after the integer. Your final result should look like Figure 10.24.

Project Suggestions

This application gives you a good running start for creating sophisticated search functionality for your website. While it is ready to use in your existing website, if you want to take this application to the next level, here are a few suggestions:

- Make the search string more sophisticated. Use conditional logic inside your SQL statement.

- Allow users to choose a second auxiliary search string, combined with the first by Boolean logic. Users can choose the Boolean logical operator, or choose no auxiliary search string. This will require a select box for the Boolean operator, and another input box for the second text string.
- For an advanced project, create two columns in the Item table for images. Store the relative path to a small image and a relative path to a large image in the table. When you drill down to an item, display the picture under the title. *Hint:* Use the HTML <img> tag with a dynamic "src" attribute.

You should be able to create this functionality, given everything that you have already learned about ColdFusion and a little imagination.

Conclusion

Congratulations! You have created a fairly complex, efficient, and practical ColdFusion application. You have learned a tremendous amount of SQL in this chapter. The Structured Query Language is very large and complex, and it is always evolving. The SQL that you've learned in this chapter should cover much of what you need to use on a regular basis in writing ColdFusion, but it is really just a start.

Relational Database Management Systems and relational database theory are very complex subjects which demand careful attention in their own right. There are many good books on the subject of database design. I recommend *Designing Relational Database Systems* by Rebecca M. Riordan, and *The Database Relational Model* by C. J. Date, which offers insight into the original relational model as conceived by D. F. Codd.

You also learned to use the <CFQUERY> tag with some panache. The new Query-of-Queries functionality was addressed, as was how to set up a datasource in the ColdFusion Administrator. You then applied what you learned in a complete, working search application that you can use with little modification on your own web site.

In the next chapter we will take a quick look at the ColdFusion Administrator, a web-based interface that allows you to configure the ColdFusion Server and implement serverwide settings for your applications.

A NOTE ABOUT THE COLDFUSION ADMINISTRATOR

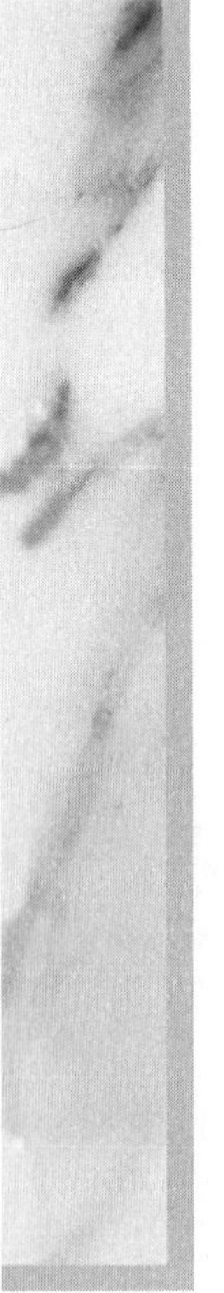

Topics in This Chapter

- An overview of the features in the ColdFusion Administrator

Chapter 11

The aim of this book is to give you the tools you need to write in ColdFusion. This means demonstrating the functionality that you will need in order to create applications. Therefore a lot of code is provided throughout the book that shows you how to make complete applications. We aren't left with much room to examine the rich features of the ColdFusion Administrator. We will therefore take just a quick overview of what the Administrator is and how you can do the tasks entailed in writing applications.

The ColdFusion Administrator is a Web-based interface that lets you configure settings and manage your ColdFusion server. It has changed a lot in the current release. Apart from other documentation about the language, ColdFusion now ships with 500 printed pages on how to configure ColdFusion Server and perform advanced administrative tasks. The release of ColdFusion 5 marks a new era for ColdFusion in a number of ways. It used to be the case that ColdFusion programmers and administrators were the same people, because the Administrator interface was not particularly complex. You could enable variables and change some settings, and that's all you needed to do. It's a different deal now. The Administrator has a number of advanced and complex features including probes, monitoring, alarms, and advanced logging. You now have the ability to create CAR files (ColdFusion Archives) that allow you to archive and deploy website configuration information, files, and entire applications. It is increasingly apparent that organizations have administrators to handle these features, and developers to write the applications. We're focusing here on the writing. The online documentation within the Administrator is far more extensive than it used to be, and it's context sensitive. So we will just do a quick overview of the things available to you in the Administrator, and what you need to make your applications. Each time we come to a new concept that requires some action in the Administrator, we will address it in that chapter.

The ColdFusion Administrator is installed automatically when you install ColdFusion. It is a Web-based application, itself written in ColdFusion. It is located at http://127.0.0.1/CFIDE/Administrator. Its menu is divided into three main sections: Server, Security, and Tools. We will glance at what's in each one and point out items that will affect your day-to-day development.

Server

The Server menu appears by default when you first log in. It contains several submenus that relate to the settings and behavior of your server. Let's look at these briefly.

Server Settings

Here you can specify information about how many queries to keep in the server cache, and the size of the cache. You can set up client, session, and application variables here, which allow you to persist variables across multiple requests. We will learn how to do that in Chapter 14. You can also set how ColdFusion handles locking of variables in a shared memory pool. You can have ColdFusion perform single-threading for you automatically, or you can lock these variables programmatically. You will learn how to do this in Chapter 14. Mapping allows you to create logical names for physical locations on your hard drive.

If you click on the Mail / Mail Logging link, you can specify an SMTP mail server that will allow you to send email from ColdFusion. You can also have ColdFusion log information about mail messages here. We will learn how to write complete email applications in Chapter 16.

Data Sources

Data sources are collections of names and connection information pertaining to a database for use with ColdFusion. We looked at configuring a new datasource in Chapter 10. You can quickly verify connections to datasources, which can be not only Enterprise RDBMSs, but also spreadsheets and plain text files. This section also allows you to create Verity 2K Collections. Verity Collections allow you to index collections of documents that you can search through ColdFusion. These documents can be HTML files, plain text, PDFs, Word or Excel files, and more.

Debug Settings

The Debug Settings links are very important to you in the development stage. In the Administrator you can specify what debug info you want output to the browser with every ColdFusion request. It is very helpful to have information regarding passed FORM and URL variables and SQL statements. Clicking Debug Options allows you to choose which variables you want to see in your debug output. Clicking Debugging IPs allows you to select only certain IP addresses to receive the debug output.

Automated Tasks

This section of the Administrator allows you to schedule tasks such as the creation of daily sales reports or statistical information pages. The task scheduler lets you enter the URL of the ColdFusion template you want to run and other parameters. Some developers use this to delete old data from a database or to make a new HTTP request or file read.

Extensions

Under the Extensions section of the Server menu you will find links that help you configure ColdFusion to work with Java and CORBA. You can also connect to CFX tags. These are extensions of the ColdFusion language written in C++ and saved as .dlls that you can connect to. Now you can also specify multiple paths for ColdFusion custom tags. Custom tags are ColdFusion tags that you write yourself, in ColdFusion. This is a really fun aspect of application development that we will learn how to do in Chapter 18. In previous versions of ColdFusion, you could specify multiple custom tag paths only by directly editing the registry.

Security

The Security menu has two submenus: Basic and Advanced. The Basic security area lets you change the password you use to login to the Administrator

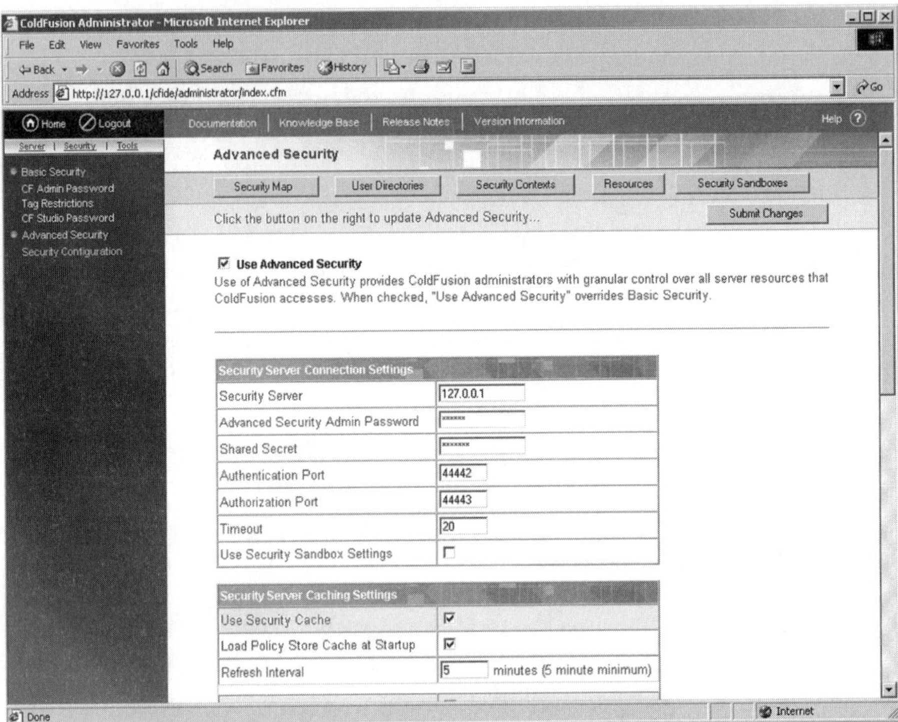

Figure 11.1 The Advanced Security screen of the Security menu in the ColdFusion Administrator.

and the password that lets ColdFusion Studio connect to your ColdFusion server. The Advanced Security section lets you specify user directories in a database or an LDAP directory. You can create rules and security policies (which are collections of rules) that govern who has access to what resources on your ColdFusion server. This is useful especially for Web hosting companies who need to give many different users access to their ColdFusion server, but restrict their interactions with it. Note that Advanced Security ships only with ColdFusion Enterprise (see Figure 11.1).

Tools

The Tools menu has several different facilities for logging and monitoring your ColdFusion environment. You can generate statistical reports, deploy system probes, and create and deploy archive files.

Logs and Statistics

A number of the items on the Tools menu are new. Logging ColdFusion has been greatly enhanced. Not only can you use the new <CFLOG> tag to log site actions, you can integrate with UNIX and NT internal logging facilities. In the Administrator you can view not only the log files that come built in with ColdFusion that log application, server, and cfadmin activity, but also the log files you create yourself with <CFLOG>. The log viewer allows you to download, store, and search log files.

The Server Reports link is a great new feature that lets you view very detailed information about the processes on your system. You can sort and filter data such as average ColdFusion memory usage, thread count, performance counters, throughput per hour, and more. You can summarize this data, and view the "Change Log," which records and displays every change made to the ColdFusion Administrator, shown by hour.

These are terrific new tools to make sure your server is running optimally.

System Monitoring

This menu includes tools for monitoring and updating load-balancing hardware such as Cisco Local Director. You can configure your connection to the Cisco Local Director by clicking the Hardware Integration link. The Web Servers link lets us view the status and control interactions of load-balancing devices The Alarms link lets you set a different email address to send messages when events occur that threaten the health of the server.

Server Probes are new with ColdFusion 5. A probe is a test that is used to verify the availability and integrity of a resource on your system. For example, you create probes to run against a known ColdFusion template and search for a particular string and return a success value. The Probes link lets you create, edit, and delete probes, as well as view their status.

Archive and Deploy

The Archive and Deploy menu is entirely new to the Administrator. It contains the links you need to set up application archiving and deployment. With application archiving you can back up complete applications and all attendant resources, including files and directories, datasources, applets, and directory mappings. With Archive Security, you can encrypt and digitally sign your archives for secure electronic transmission. You must have a certificate (SSL) to digitally sign CAR files.

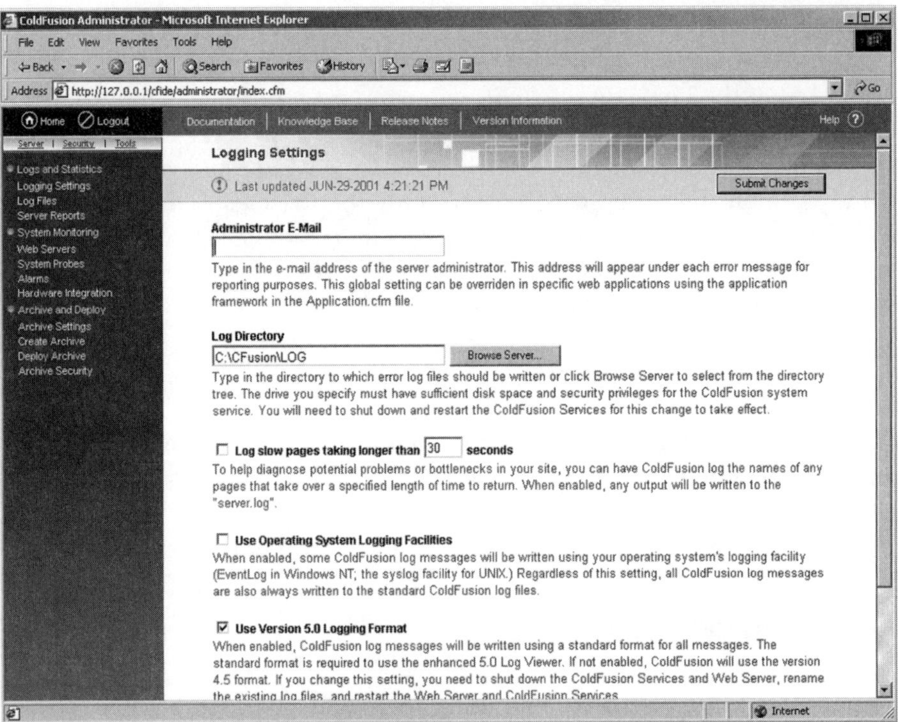

Figure 11.2 The Tools menu in the ColdFusion Administrator.

Once you have archived an application, you can deploy it, which means you can restore your CAR (ColdFusion Archive file) to your machine or network location for live use. You can retrieve a CAR file via FTP or HTTP if it is posted to a website. Note that these tools are available only with ColdFusion Enterprise edition (see Figure 11.2).

When we need to configure certain settings as we write, we will address that specific aspect of the Administrator as we go. The new help system in the Administrator is extensive. You can find a good deal of information, links to knowledge-base articles, and more to cover all of these topics. Also, the help link in the upper right-hand corner is context sensitive, so you can get information on any aspect of the administrator very quickly. So I will leave it to you to explore it as you need to—let's start writing applications.

LOOPS

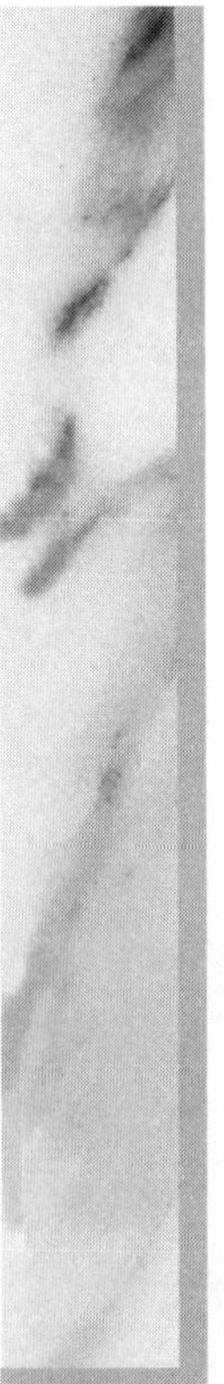

Topics in This Chapter

- What is a loop?
- Conditional loops
- Index loops
- List loops
- Collection loops
- Nested loops
- <CFFLUSH>>

Chapter 12

ColdFusion has several different kinds of loops that you can use to perform complex operations in your templates. You have already had a preview in Chapter 8 of how they work. In this chapter we will discuss in greater depth the different types of loops, which we will use throughout the rest of the book. You will also learn a tag new with ColdFusion 5 called <CFFLUSH>.

What Is a Loop?

A loop is a program element that causes a block of code to execute repeatedly. You can use ColdFusion loops to execute a code block a certain number of times. For instance, you could use a loop to repeat once for each number of days in the week. But because you can use all of ColdFusion's dynamic properties in working with loops, you don't need to know in advance the number of times you want to loop. It is more common to use a loop to execute some code one time for each element in a list of *x* length, or once for each record returned from a database query.

<TERM>

Each pass through a loop is called an iteration, which comes from the Greek word meaning "to say or perform again; to repeat."

You can also use a loop to allow instructions to repeat until a certain condition is met or to execute as long as a certain condition is true. For instance, you could use a loop to repeat a block of code as long as the number of the current iteration was less than or equal to a certain number.

Pretty much anything you can do in ColdFusion you can do inside a loop. You can use loops to insert a bulk set of records into a database, output HTML, delete elements from an array one at a time, and so forth.

We use the <CFLOOP> tag to perform each type of loop, simply specifying a different set of attributes for the tag depending on what type of loop you want to perform.

A Quick Word About Infinite Loops

Infinite loops are loops that are formed paradoxically. Infinite loops are constructed such that it is impossible for any condition to ever be satisfied. Since no condition can be satisfied or no end can ever be reached, the loop will continue processing until you stop the services altogether.

Note that a poorly written <CFLOOP> block is not the only way to cause an infinite regress of instructions. Using flow control and conditional logic in your ColdFusion templates can be tricky business when your site starts getting large. I bring up infinite loops at this point because they are what really taught me the power and use of loops.

I must admit that I found loops hard to get my mind around for a long time. Their purpose became very clear to me only when I got myself into trouble. Did you ever see the movie *Fantasia*? You may remember the Sorcerer's Apprentice scene where Mickey Mouse casts a spell that doesn't have an ending clause built in. The broomsticks he appoints to bring buckets of water to fill the vat do exactly as they were instructed. They keep bringing buckets of water, dumping one and then returning with another. Since he did not think to give them an end condition, they just keep repeating their instructions until the entire place is flooded.

I once caused a similar flood. When working on a website comprised of hundreds of ColdFusion templates, I got myself into an infinite loop, much like Mickey's. I had written several <cfinclude> tags, nested inside one another, which worked fine. The last of the included templates had a simple job: sending me an email notification whenever the template was called. Everything was fine until I wrote that the email notification template should include its calling template immediately after sending the notification. It looked like this in pseudocode:

```
<!---I am a template called "Parent.cfm"---->

<cfinclude template = "Notify.cfm">


<!----I am Notify.cfm---->

...Code that sends email to administrator goes here...

<cfinclude template = "Parent.cfm"---->
```

As I proudly put on my coat to go to lunch, I thought I'd check my email before stepping out. Sure enough, I received an email notification from my website, and, ever the proud papa, I called my colleagues over to give me a pat on the back for a job well done. Strangely, I received another notification. Then a moment later, another. I peered closer at the screen, as if doing so would somehow reveal the reason for this odd behavior. Then came that special moment of terror. The mail kept coming. Forever. My inbox was flooded. I was finally able to shut off the service and restart before anything really terrible happened, but not before I had received more than 1,100 email messages from myself.

So, as you write loops, it is important to know with certainty that your code is capable of reaching a conclusion. In general, a runaway loop will stop only when you stop the ColdFusion service on your server, or when it eats up enough cycles that it crashes your server itself. ColdFusion works. It will do exactly what you tell it to do. Make sure that you're telling it exactly what you mean.

Classified in ColdFusion as a flow control tag, <CFLOOP> allows you to create five types of loops: conditional, index, collection, query, and list loops. We now examine each of these individually.

The Query Loop

Since we learned queries in the last chapter, and since they are probably the simplest kind of loop in ColdFusion, let us begin with the query loop.

One uses a query loop to iterate a set of statements one time for each record returned in a query. When you use the QUERY attribute of the <CFLOOP> tag, you can use only two other attributes: STARTROW and ENDROW, both of which are optional (Table 12.1).

Table 12.1 Attributes of the CFLOOP Tag When Used for a Query

Attribute	*Description*
QUERY	The name of the executed query to loop over.
STARTROW	(Optional) Specifies the first row of the query to be included in the loop.
ENDROW	(Optional) Specifies the last row of the query to be included in the loop.

You can output records retrieved from a database query using <CFOUTPUT> inside a <CFLOOP>:

Listing 12.1 Outputting Query Results with a CFLOOP

```
<html>
<head>
       <title></title>
</head>

<body>

<cfquery name="MyQuery" datasource="CoreCFDB">
       SELECT LastName from Users
</cfquery>

<cfloop query="MyQuery" startrow="1" endrow="8">
       <cfoutput>#MyQuery.LastName#<br></cfoutput>
</cfloop>

</body>
</html>
```

The loop in Listing 12.1 demonstrates the use of the STARTROW and ENDROW tags, which you can use for using "Next *n*" type interfaces. This query retrieves 1742 records, which takes 200 milliseconds. Retrieving only the eight records used executes in 30 milliseconds (see Figure 12.1).

It will often arise that you want to output the results of a query using <CFOUTPUT query="MyQuery">. This works great, as we have seen. However, if you want to nest <CFOUTPUT> tags within one another, things can become difficult, because you need to specify a GROUP. Try something like the code in Listing 12.2 and you'll get an error:

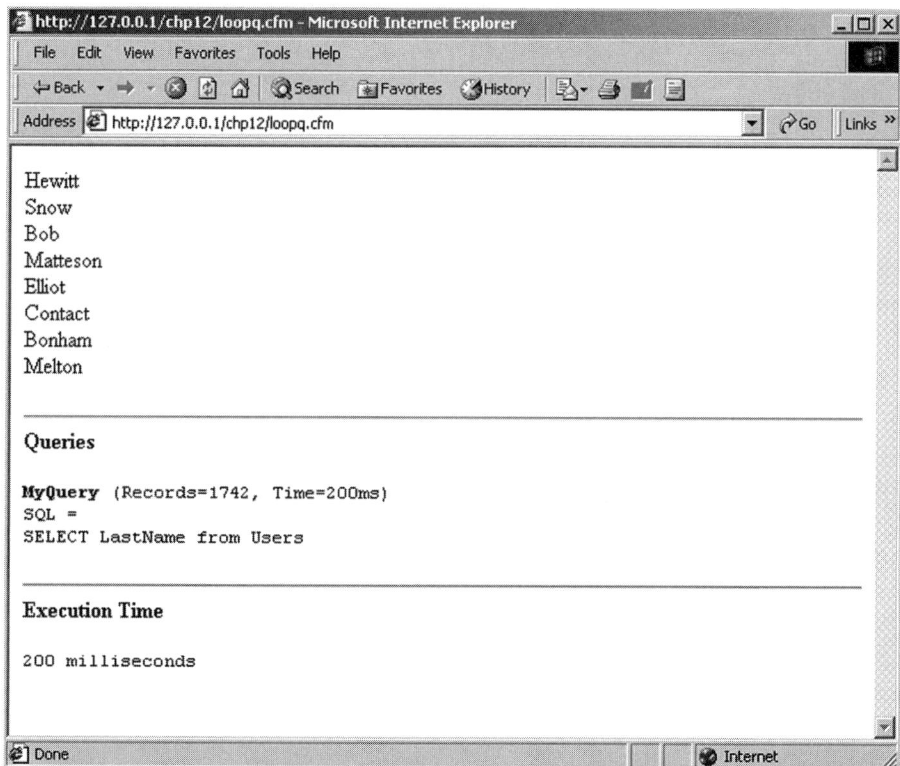

Figure 12.1 The results of retrieving 1742 records, and outputting only eight with debugging output turned on in ColdFusion Administrator.

Listing 12.2 Nesting CFOUTPUTs

```
<body>
<cfquery datasource="CoreCFDB" name="MyQuery">
select top 8(LastName) from Users

</cfquery>

<cfset thisPage = "Using a Query Loop">

<cfset message = "All Done.">

#thisPage#

<!---top level cfoutput---->
<cfoutput>
```

```
<!----nested cfoutput to dump the query results---->
<cfoutput query = "MyQuery">

#LastName#<br>

</cfoutput>

<br>
#message#

</cfoutput>

</body>
```

Were you to run this code, you'd get an error message telling you that you've tried to nest <CFOUTPUT>s without specifying a GROUP. You can get around this problem by using looping over the query and outputting it that way. This fixes it.

```
<html>
<head>
       <title>Query Loop</title>
</head>

<body>

<!---get some records---->

<cfquery name="MyQuery" datasource="CoreCFDB">

       SELECT top 8 (LastName) from Users

</cfquery>

<!---set variables to output---->
<cfset thisPage = "Using a Query Loop">

<cfset Message = "All done.">

<cfoutput>
<!---output variable------->
<h2>#thisPage#</h2>
<br>
Here are your records:<br>
```

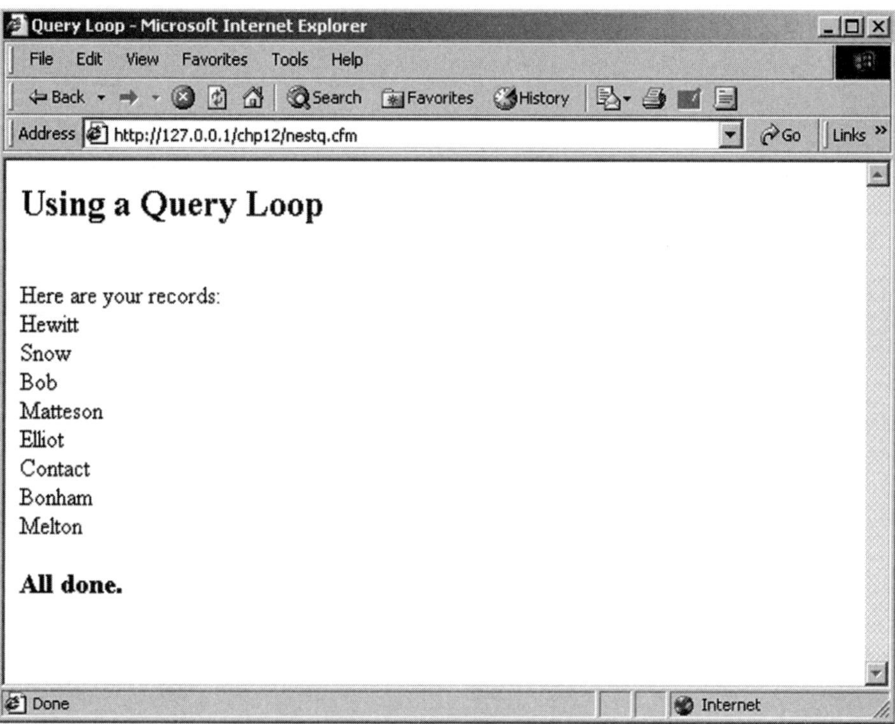

Figure 12.2 Using <CFLOOP> to output a query result set.

```
<!---output query result. Break after each record, or they
will be output continuously on one line------->

<cfloop query = "MyQuery">
     #MyQuery.LastName#<br>
</cfloop>


<h3>#VARIABLES.message#</h3>
</cfoutput>

</body>
</html>
```

The loop works fine inside a <CFOUTPUT>. The results are shown in Figure 12.2.

The query loop functions much as <CFOUTPUT> with a query attribute. If you are doing any processing with the output, ColdFusion will perform better with a query loop than with <CFOUTPUT>.

The Conditional Loop

Generally known as a while loop, a conditional loop executes as long as a particular condition is true. The specified condition is evaluated the instant ColdFusion enters the loop; if it returns false, the loop is never run.

A conditional loop takes only one attribute: condition = "expression."

Listing 12.3 A Conditional Loop

```
<!---get 8 records------->
<cfquery name="MyQuery" datasource="CoreCFDB">
      SELECT top 8 (ID) from Orders
</cfquery>

<cfset idx = 0>
<!---while MyNum is less than or equal to the number of
records retrieved from a query, output each increment--->
<cfloop condition="idx lte MyQuery.RecordCount">
      <cfset idx = idx + 1>
      <cfoutput>#idx#<br></cfoutput>
</cfloop>
```

The output of the above loop is always the numbers 1 through 9—not through 8, even though that is the number of records retrieved. That's because on the final iteration of the loop (when the value of idx is equal to the value of MyQuery.RecordCount), the "idx" variable is set to one greater than itself (9), and output.

<NOTE>

QueryName.RecordCount is a variable automatically created every time a query is run. Its value is the number of rows returned by the query.

List Loops

A list loop iterates over a ColdFusion list. It takes the three attributes listed in Table 12.2.

Table 12.2 Attributes of the CFLOOP Tag When Used with Lists

Attribute	*Description*
INDEX	Name of the variable to hold the value of the list element for each iteration.
LIST	Name of the list to loop over.
DELIMITERS	(Optional) List element delimiter. Default is a comma.

Listing 12.4 A List Loop

```
<!----create a list------->
<cfset Children="Becky, John, Alison, Tommy, Elizabeth,
       Michael">

<!---loop over list, output not just each child's name, but
their ordinal place in the list------->

<cfloop list="#Children#" index="idx" delimiters=",">

<cfoutput>
Child #ListFind(Children, idx)# is #idx#.<br>
</cfoutput>

</cfloop>
```

Here is the output:

```
Child 1 is Becky.
Child 2 is John.
Child 3 is Alison.
Child 4 is Tommy.
Child 5 is Elizabeth.
Child 6 is Michael.
```

As with any other list, you can use functions to manipulate the data inside of a list loop.

Looping over Structures

In order to loop over a structure, you specify two attributes of the <CFLOOP> tag: Collection and Item. The collection attribute holds the name of the structure you want to loop over, and the Item attribute functions much like the "Index" attribute of a list loop: it holds the value of the structure key for each iteration.

Listing 12.5 A Collection Loop

```
<!---create a struct to hold employee info------->
<cfset StrEmps = StructNew()>

<cfset StrEmps.FirstName = "Phineas">
<cfset StrEmps.LastName = "Fogg">
<cfset StrEmps.Phone = "(212) 999-7777">

<cfloop collection="#strEmps#" item="thisKey">
<cfoutput>The value of #thisKey# is #strEmps[thiskey]#<br></
cfoutput>
</cfloop>
```

Here is the output:

```
The value of FIRSTNAME is Phineas
The value of LASTNAME is Fogg
The value of PHONE is (212) 999-7777
```

Things get more complicated when we have an array as the value of the structure key. Were we to simply attempt to perform a collection loop over a structure which had arrays for its values, an error would ensue, telling us that the value cannot be converted to a string. When looping over an array, one uses an index loop. Therefore, we can nest them to get the result we desire.

Listing 12.6 Looping over an Array Nested inside a Structure

```
<!---create a struct to hold employees------->
<cfset StrEmps = StructNew()>

<!----create array to hold first employee------->
<cfset arrEmp1 = ArrayNew(1)>
<cfset arrEmp1[1] = "Phineas">
<cfset arrEmp1[2] = "Fogg">
<cfset arrEmp1[3] = "(212) 999-7777">

<!----put first employee array into structure----->
<cfset StrEmps.Emp1 = arrEmp1>

<!-----loop over the collection------->
<cfloop collection="#strEmps#" item="thisKey">
```

```
<!---within the collection loop, loop over the array--->

<cfloop index="thisEmp" from="1"
              to="#ArrayLen(StrEmps.Emp1)#">

        <!----output the key value------->
<cfoutput>The value of #thisKey# is #arrEmp1[thisEmp]#
<br>
</cfoutput>
       </cfloop>
</cfloop>
```

Let's use the previous code listing as a starting point for creating an array that holds a structure that holds a list. The contents of this array will be products, as from an online catalogue. We will use a complex set of loops to find each item and output it to the browser. Listing 12.7 shows you one way to do this.

Listing 12.7 Working with Lists, Arrays, and Structures to Assign Values as in a Shopping Cart

```
<!---create a cart------->
<cfset arrCart = ArrayNew(1)>

<!---create a struct to hold each product------->
<cfset strCart = StructNew()>

<!----try populating the lists dynamically,
for instance, by submitting a form------->

<cfset lstItems = "Blue Jeans, Shirt, Perfume">
<cfset lstItemCats = "Clothing, Clothing, Cosmetics">
<cfset lstPrice = "69.99, 39.99, 140.00">
<cfset lstQty = "1, 2, 1">

<cfloop index="idx" from="1" to="#ListLen(lstItems)#">

<cfset strCart.Item = "#ListGetAt(lstItems, idx)#">
<cfset strCart.ItemCategory ="#ListGetAt(lstItemCats, idx)#">
<cfset strCart.Price = "#ListGetAt(lstPrice, idx)#">
<cfset strCart.Qty = "#ListGetAt(lstQty, idx)#">
<cfset #arrCart[idx]# = "#strCart#">


<cfloop collection="#strCart#" item="thisKey">

        <cfloop index="thisItem" from="1" to="1">
```

```
        <!---output the key value------->
        <cfset thing = StrCart[thisKey]>
        <cfoutput>
               The value of #thisKey# is #thing#<br>
        </cfoutput>
        </cfloop>
</cfloop>

</cfloop>
</html>
```

Here is the output:

```
The value of ITEM is Blue Jeans
The value of ITEMCATEGORY is Clothing
The value of PRICE is 69.99
The value of QTY is 1
The value of ITEM is Shirt
The value of ITEMCATEGORY is Clothing
The value of PRICE is 39.99
The value of QTY is 2
The value of ITEM is Perfume
The value of ITEMCATEGORY is Cosmetics
The value of PRICE is 140.00
The value of QTY is 1
```

This code base can be used as the building blocks for creating a shopping cart. Instead of outputting these items to the browser, try creating the list from form fields and inserting them into a database. Later we will see how we could persist the value of the cart using session or client variables.

<CFFLUSH>

<CFFLUSH> is new with ColdFusion 5. It's job is to flush the data currently available to the client. This is very useful if you've got a complex page that takes a long time to load. In general, any template you send to the ColdFusion Application Server should return parsed faster than 250 milliseconds. However, complex or nested loops, queries with a number of joins or many calculative operations, or any of the protocol tags (such as <CFHTTP>, <CFLDAP>, or <CFFTP>), or any Spectra application, can take a thousands of milliseconds to run. You can use the <CFFLUSH> tag to deliver information incrementally to the clients so they don't get frustrated or concerned that the site is slow or not working. It's polite.

You can also use this tag to create some interesting textual effects to delight your users. We will use <CFLOOP> to do some time-consuming counting, and output the lines of Edgar Allan Poe's poem "The Bells" with phrasing that imitates the rhythm of speaking it aloud. We can use the loop index to increase the font size. Here's the code to do it:

Listing 12.8 Using <CFFLUSH> to Deliver Pages Incrementally

```
<!---flush the page  with
      every five bytes sent------->

<cfflush interval=5>

<!--- create a loop from 1 to 7, since we want to output
"bells" 7 times.------->

<h2>The Bells</h2>
by Edgar Allan Poe
<br>
<center>
Hear the sledges with the bells- <br>
Silver bells! <br>
What a world of merriment their melody foretells! <br>
How they tinkle, tinkle, tinkle, <br>
In the icy air of night! <br>
While the stars that oversprinkle <br>
All the heavens, seem to twinkle <br>
With a crystalline delight; <br>
Keeping time, time, time, >br>
In a sort of Runic rhyme, <br>
To the tintinnabulation that so musically wells <br>

<!----iterate once for each "bell"------->

From the
<cfloop index="outidx" from="1" to="7" step="1">

<!-------cause 20,000 iterations of a second loop, and perform
a ceiling calculation for extra work------>
  <cfloop index="idx" from="1" to="20000" step="1">
    <cfset num = ceiling(idx + "0.131313")>
  </cfloop>
  <cfoutput>
    <font size="#outidx#">bells</font>
  </cfoutput>
</cfloop>
```

```
<!----end the stanza---->
<br>
-From the jingling and the tinkling of the bells.
</center>
</body>
</html>
```

COLDFUSION SCRIPTING

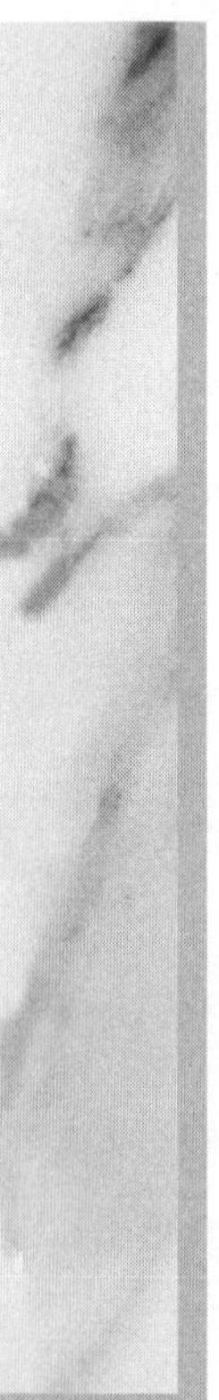

Topics in This Chapter

- Introduction to CFScript
- Setting variables and expressions
- Conditional logic
- Loops
- Another user-defined function

Chapter 13

In addition to writing ColdFusion using tags, you can perform many typical processing tasks using CFScript—a script version subset of the ColdFusion language. Using a syntax similar to JavaScript, CFScript allows you to read and set variables, perform conditional processing, and loop. However, as a subset, it has limitations. To begin with, there is nothing that you can do inside CFScript that you can't do with tags. Until ColdFusion 5, CFScript didn't really extend the functionality of ColdFusion. Now, it is an important facet of the language, since you must use CFScript to write user-defined functions. Furthermore, it makes the language more accessible for programmers used to other scripting languages, and it speeds up your performance in certain situations.

It's a good idea to go over scripting at this point, since often it is a smart alternative as you write, and we will be using it with some frequency in the remainder of the book. Examining scripting is also helpful as a refresher for some of the functionality that we have discussed up to this point.

How Does CFScript Work?

In order to write ColdFusion script, you must surround your script code with a ColdFusion tag, <cfscript>. This tag takes no attributes, and the closing tag is required. The chief limitation of CFScript is that you may not use any ColdFusion tags inside a script block. Variables you set inside a script block are visible just like any other variables in ColdFusion. You can manipulate data inside the script block, and it is visible to the rest of your request.

Setting Variables and Commenting

You set a variable by simply writing the name of the variable you wish to set, an equal sign, and the value. If the variable does not exist, ColdFusion creates it. Let's set a simple variable to see how this works.

Listing 13.1 Setting a Variable

```
<!-----first declare that you're about to write
script by using the <cfscript> tag.------>

<!---then create a variable called "drink". Set its value to
"coffee"----->

<cfscript>

      Drink = "coffee";

</cfscript>

<!---output the variable value------->

<cfoutput>#drink#</cfoutput>
```

The variable set inside the block is just the same as if you had created it using <cfset>. The output to the browser is "coffee." One thing you probably noticed is the presence of a semicolon at the end of the line. Commands must end in a semicolon within CFScript.

There are two ways to create comments inside a script block. To write a one-line comment, you use two slashes:

```
<cfscript>
// set the drink variable. I am a comment.

      Drink = "coffee";

</cfscript>
```

In order to create a multiline comment, you use a /* combination, as you would in SQL or C. Like this:

```
<cfscript>

/* I am a
      multiline comment */

      Drink = "coffee";

</cfscript>
```

You will not see a performance benefit in using CFScript to set only one or two variables in this manner. However, once you have to set three or more at once, you will see a performance increase. The reason is that ColdFusion does not have to read and interpret each successive <cfset> tag one by one. Instead, the entire <cfscript> block gets passed to the ColdFusion server and interpreted at once. You *will* see a performance increase when setting more than three variables at once.

Conditional Processing

You can use conditional processing inside script blocks. You can make both if/else and switch/case statements. Then syntax is a bit different, so first let's see how a simple "if" statement looks.

Listing 13.2 An "if" Statement in CFScript

```
<cfset "MyNumber" = 9>

<cfscript>
      // check if the number is less than 10

      if (MyNumber lt 10)  {

//if it is, output a message to the browser

      WriteOutput("Your number is less than 10");
      }
</cfscript>
```

To use conditional processing, you type “if,” followed by the condition you wish to test for. Then you use curly brackets to surround the code you want to run if the condition is true. In this case, we use the “WriteOutput” function to output a message to the browser. This function is similar to “Write” in JavaScript. Then we end the statement with a semicolon as always, end the brackets, and close the </cfscript> block.

<NOTE>

Curly brackets are not required, but they help keep your statements organized. It's generally considered good practice to use them.

Since you cannot use tags, such as <CFOUTPUT>, inside ColdFusion script blocks, you use the WriteOutput function to accomplish this task. It works much as <CFOUTPUT> does, so if you load the above script in your browser, you'll see the message:

```
Your number is less than 10
```

Note that when using WriteOutput, you must enclose what you want to output in parentheses and double quotes. If the string inside your WriteOutput function contains quotes, you must escape them, like this:

```
<cfset "MyNumber" = 9>

<cfscript>
        // test for the variable's existence
        if (MyNumber lt 10)  {

WriteOutput("She said, ""Your number is less than 10"".");
        }
</cfscript>
```

You can create additional conditional clauses using “else” and “elseif,” as follows:

Listing 13.3 Using if-elseif-else Inside <cfscript>

```
<cfset "MyNumber" = 256>

<cfscript>
        // test for the variable's existence
        if (MyNumber lt 10)  {
        WriteOutput("She said, ""Your number is less than
10"".");
```

```
        }
        else if (MyNumber lt 20) {
        WriteOutput("Your number is between 10 and 19");
        }
        /*  note that we can use HTML tags and variables set
outside the script block in our WriteOutput */

        else {

        WriteOutput("Your number, <b>#MyNumber#</b>, is
greater than 20");
        }
</cfscript>
```

Here's the output to the browser:

```
Your number, 256, is greater than 20
```

As you notice, the rules regarding use of expressions and operators are the same as in ColdFusion Markup.

Switch Case in CFScript

The use of switch case tags in CFML differs from the performance of the same operation in CFScript. You must use a BREAK statement inside each CASE. The BREAK statement tells ColdFusion to exit the switch case once a condition has been satisfied. If you don't include it, ColdFusion will not throw an error: it will run the DEFAULT case *in addition* to the CASE that evaluated true. Here is the syntax:

Listing 13.4 Switch Case

```
<cfscript>
        // set a variable to test against
        MyNumber = 18;

        /* unlike in regular CFML,
                the switch expression needn't be
                surrounded with pound signs */

        switch (MyNumber) {

                case 1: {
                // if the number is 14, this code will run
```

```
                    /* note how the case value is referenced.
                           we don't use the "value" keyword,
                           but use colons */

                    WriteOutput("Your number is ONE.");
                    /* use break to exit the case. since it is a
                       statement, too, end it with a semicolon */
                    break;
                           }

                    case 2: {

                    // we can use multiple values for one case
                    WriteOutput("Your number is TWO");
                    break;
                           }

                    default: {
                    // note that we don't use "defaultcase", but
//simply "default"
                    WriteOutput("Your number is neither one nor
two.");
                    }
        }
</cfscript>
```

And here is the resulting output to the browser:

```
Your number is neither one nor two.
```

Note that we are testing for numeric values here. If your CASE statement were testing against a string, you would need to use quote marks around the value.

In general, it is preferable to use switch case in its tag form, since it processes faster, and you are not as limited by the script syntax, which does not allow you to specify multiple values for a case.

Looping

You can create several different types of loops within a script block. Just as you specify different attributes of the <CFLOOP> tag within CFML's tag-based syntax, loop statements take different elements when used inside <cfscript>.

For Loop

A "for" loop will iterate as long as a condition returns true. The code has the following structure: specify "for," and then put three loop elements inside parentheses. The loop elements are separated with semicolons. The first specifies an initiator, which will run before the loop iterates. The second specifies the condition to test against, and the third specifies the loop step.

To illustrate, let us output the numbers 1 to 10 to the browser.

Listing 13.5 A FOR Loop

```
<cfscript>

// output the loop index in each iteration

for (idx = 1; idx lte 10; idx = idx +1) {

      WriteOutput("#idx#<br>");
}
</cfscript>
```

We start with a variable declaration (idx = 1), which initializes the counter. Then we specify the condition to test for (loop as long as the idx value is less than or equal to 10). Then we add one to the counter variable each time the loop iterates. Finally, we output the current value of "idx" and an HTML <br> so that each loop outputs on its own line. The following is output to the browser:

```
1
2
3
4
5
6
7
8
9
10
```

You may have thought that it would output the numbers 1 to 11. However, the third element in the loop runs only after the condition has evaluated to true. The loop will terminate the instant the condition is false, and therefore won't execute the code remaining inside the loop.

While Loops

The while loop is similar to using the <CFLOOP condition = "expression"> tag. It loops as long as the expression is true. The statement will therefore not execute at all if the expression specified is false to begin with. It looks like this:

Listing 13.6 While Loop

```
<cfscript>
	idx = 1;

	while (idx lte 10) {

	WriteOutput("#idx#<br>");

	idx = idx + 1;
}

</cfscript>
```

The output to the browser is this:

```
1
2
3
4
5
6
7
8
9
10
```

Set the variable to 1, then loop once while the variable is less than or equal to 10. Immediately after we output to the browser, we add one to the current "idx." When the loop goes to iterate again, "idx" has the new value, which is retested. The loop stops when the condition is false.

Do-While Loop

A do-while loop is the same as a while loop except that it tests the condition *after* each iteration of the loop—not before.

Listing 13.7 Do-While Loop

```
<cfscript>

idx = 1;

do {
      WriteOutput("#idx#<br>");

      idx = idx +1;
      }
while (idx lte 10);

</cfscript>
```

Here is the output:

```
1
2
3
4
5
6
7
8
9
10
```

For-In Loops

A For-In Loop is the final item to examine in <cfscript>. For-In loops execute one time for each element in a ColdFusion structure variable. This is the script version of writing <CFLOOP collection = "#StructName#">. This can be a very useful loop in CFScript, as ColdFusion stores much of its internal data as structures (for instance, COOKIE variables, APPLICATION, and SESSION variables are stored as structures). Let's create a new structure and loop over it with For-In. Figure 13.1 shows the results.

Listing 13.8 For-In Loop

```
<cfscript>
// create the structure

strProducts = StructNew();
```

```
// populate the structure

strProducts.Name = "Core ColdFusion 5";
strProducts.Price = "44.95";
strProducts.sku = "0119299377";

// loop over it and output the key-value pair

for (idx in strProducts) {


        WriteOutput("#idx# is #strProducts[idx]#<br>");
}
</cfscript>
```

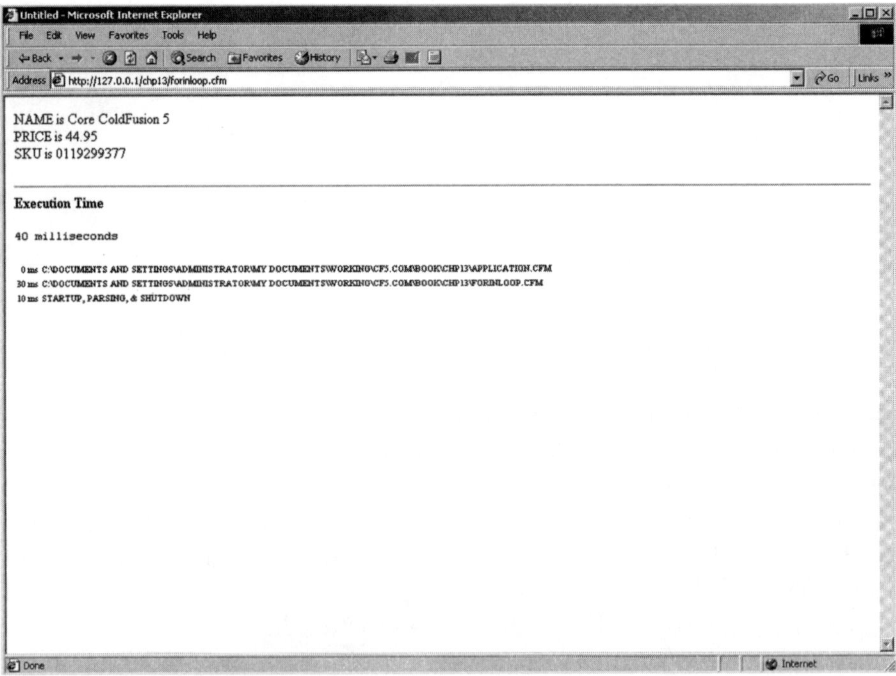

Figure 13.1 The results of the For-In loop over a structure are like those of using the <CFLOOP> tag with the "collection" attribute.

Another User-Defined Function

ColdFusion script is also important to learn early on, because you use it exclusively to write user-defined functions. For instance, I have a User-Defined Function that performs a similar task to a very popular and well-known custom tag written by Ben Forta. Because this function is written in script, the code is concise, and it executes quickly. Mr. Forta's tag is called <CF_EmbedFields>, and its job is to take any values in the comma-separated FORM.FieldNames list passed to a page and create them as hidden fields on the calling template. This can be accomplished with CFScript as well. We might write it like this:

Listing 13.9 User-Defined Function to Create Hidden Form Fields

```
<!--- PassHiddenFields------->

<cfscript>

// this UDF sets passed form fields as hidden
function PassHiddenFields(){

idx = 0;

// loop over length of form.fieldnames

if (isDefined("FORM.fieldnames")){
while (idx LT ListLen(FORM.fieldnames)){
idx = idx + 1;


// output the hidden fields
WriteOutput
("<input type=""hidden""
name=""#ListGetAt(FORM.fieldnames, idx)#""
value=""#Evaluate("#ListGetAt(FORM.fieldnames, idx)#")#"">");
}}
}
</cfscript>
```

Now we could include the template on which this script is written, and then simply write

```
<cfset PassHiddenFields()>
```

to invoke the function.

Let us suppose that we wanted to loop over the fields, but keep a certain field from getting written to a hidden form field. We might desire this because the form field contains sensitive information we want to keep from the browser, or because we want to set that variable manually ourselves. We would do this using the "continue" statement. "Continue" prevents that iteration of the loop from running; ColdFusion simply goes to the next iteration.

Here is an example of how we might use the Continue statement. Let's say that we knew that FORM.thisPage was going to get passed to the template on which we call PassHiddenFields(). We need to set the "thisPage" variable manually on the calling page and therefore do not want to create a conflict between the new variable and the passed variable. We can keep the "thisPage" variable from being set into a hidden form field using "continue." Listing 13.10 shows the modified code, with the new part set in bold.

Listing 13.10 Using the Continue Command

```
<!--- PassHiddenFields------->

<cfscript>

// this UDF sets passed form fields as hidden
function PassHiddenFields(){

idx = 0;

// loop over length of form.fieldnames

if (isDefined("FORM.fieldnames")){
while (idx LT ListLen(FORM.fieldnames)){
idx = idx + 1;

// set thisPage variable manually
// so it doesn't get overwritten

if((ListGetAt(FORM.fieldnames, idx)) eq "thisPage") continue;
```

```
// output the hidden fields
WriteOutput
("<input type=""hidden""
name=""#ListGetAt(FORM.fieldnames, idx)#""
value=""#Evaluate("#ListGetAt(FORM.fieldnames, idx)#")#"">");
}}
}
</cfscript>
```

The above user-defined function will set all passed form variables into hidden fields, except for any form variable called "thisPage."

Conclusion

This chapter has provided a solid introduction to CFScript, covering everything that this subset of the ColdFusion Markup Language does. Since CFScript performs faster and is more concise and readable than tags in many cases, we will use it often throughout the remainder of this book.

THE COLDFUSION APPLICATION FRAMEWORK

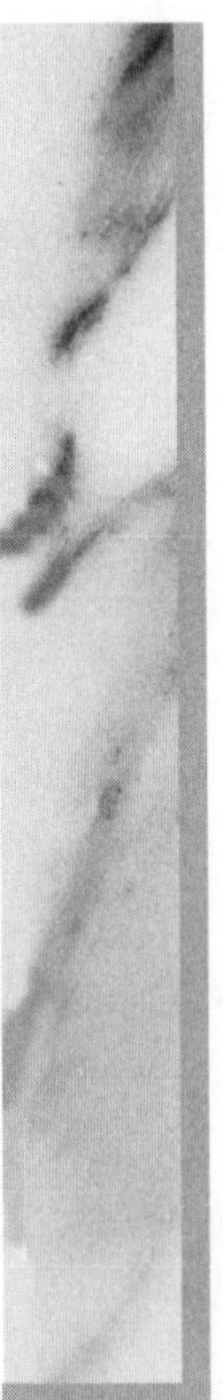

Topics in This Chapter

- Defining the application framework
- Application.cfm, <CFAPPLICATION>, and OnRequestEnd.cfm
- Application variables and <CFLOCK>
- Session variables
- Client variables
- Server variables
- Error handling with <CFERROR>
- Logging site information with <CFLOG>
- A site personalization application

Chapter 14

In this chapter you will learn how to implement the ColdFusion Application Framework to create applications that "carry state" across requests, set global variables, and more. You will learn how to use client variables and session variables to maintain user information. We will also take a brief look at the error-handling capabilities that the application framework provides. At the end of the chapter we will put much of this all together by creating a complete personalization application component.

Defining the Application Framework

So far we have written independent templates that honor individual requests. These templates have not been related to each other in any way. Perhaps they've been in the same directory, or we've passed parameters between them using form and URL variables, but they haven't formed a coherent unit. In addition, we haven't had a way to track what a user is doing across multiple requests. We've seen a number of errors as we've written ColdFusion templates thus far. While the typical black-and-white ColdFusion error message is informative, it can surprise users with its starkness, and may provide information about your application that you don't necessarily want anonymous users to have. The ColdFusion application framework addresses these issues, so let's look at them in turn.

The root of your application is the uppermost directory in a branch of your Web server document root. Everything underneath the document root can be considered as one coherent application. For instance, in the final chapter of this book we create a complete e-commerce application. The application root is called "Store," and it contains several folders within it, such as "Images," "Shop," and "Checkout." We can specify that ColdFusion consider the documents in these folders to be a unique, unified application. We do this with two primary tools: a special template called "Application.cfm" and a tag, <CFAPPLICATION>.

Application.cfm

Every time a request is made for a .cfm file, ColdFusion automatically checks for the existence of a file called "Application.cfm" within the current directory. If the file is found, it is executed prior to the execution of the requested template. If it is not found, ColdFusion checks the parent directory for Application.cfm; if it is not found, the parent directory of *that* directory is checked.

ColdFusion will check for an Application.cfm file *all the way up to the root of the hard drive.* Many developers mistakenly believe that ColdFusion stops when it gets to the Web server root. This is not the case. What that means is that you might want to create an Application.cfm file that's blank if you don't plan on using it. You will save your ColdFusion server the effort of looking in every directory all the way up the hard drive for it.

Once found, the Application.cfm file is included in the requested template, just as if you had used <CFINCLUDE>. That means that you can use it to define global variables. For instance, you might want to define the name of your data source here, a default color or font, or an image path. Then you can reference these variables like any other variables in your template code.

You will occasionally inherit code that includes presentation-layer code in the Application.cfm file. This is a very unfortunate practice. You must avoid the temptation to include graphics or any HTML in this file. The Application.cfm file is a powerful aspect of the logic layer of your site; don't conflate it with the presentation layer.

You can also use the Application.cfm file to implement the application framework. This is similar to the Globals.asa file in ASP. To create the file, just create a new template called "Application.cfm." If you're on a UNIX platform, you must use a capital A in naming this file; it can't be lowercase.

Let's type some simple code into the new file to see how this works. However, you never call the Application.cfm file directly. ColdFusion will throw an error if you try to do so. Therefore we also need to create another template that will be the page a user actually requests. We'll call this page "index.cfm." Its purpose will be to have a page to request, and to demonstrate how the variables set in Application.cfm can be referenced. Create a new directory folder on your web server to put them in.

Listing 14.1 Index.cfm

```
<html>
<head>
        <title>Index</title>
</head>

<body>

<cfoutput>
I am the <font size="#defaultSize#" face="#defaultFace#">
index page</font>.
</cfoutput>

<br>

</body>
</html>
```

Now we create the Application.cfm file in the same directory to set these default variables.

Listing 14.2 Application.cfm

```
<!---set an applicationwide font definition------->

<cfset defaultFace = "Verdana, Arial, Helvetica">

<cfset defaultSize = "+3">
```

Any ColdFusion template in this directory or any subdirectory will automatically execute Application.cfm, and these variables will be available just as if the code were copied and pasted into the called template.

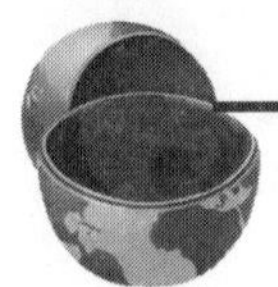

<NOTE>

You can have multiple Application.cfm files within one application. ColdFusion will simply execute the first one it finds, and no others. However, you can use <CFINCLUDE> to execute the Application.cfm file in the parent directory if you desire. You might do this, for example, if you wanted to define different global variables for each department in an intranet.

Implementing the Framework

As mentioned previously, the most powerful aspect of Application.cfm is that you can use it to define an application. You do this using the <CFAPPLICATION> tag. The attributes of this tag appear in Table 14.1. Only the "Name" attribute is required.

Table 14.1 <CFAPPLICATION> Tag Attributes

Attribute	*Description*	*Value*
NAME	A name for your application.	Any name, unique to the server.
APPLICATIONTIMEOUT	A time limit for keeping application variables.	#CreateTimeSpan (days, hours, minutes, seconds)#
CLIENTMANAGEMENT	Enables client variables.	YES/NO
CLIENTSTORAGE	Specifies where ColdFusion should store client variables.	Registry/Cookie/ Datasource
SETCLIENTCOOKIES	Specifies whether ColdFusion should set cookies with client and session variables.	YES/NO
SETDOMAINCOOKIES	Specifies whether ColdFusion should set CFID and CFTOKEN cookies at the domain level for a cluster environment.	YES/NO

Attribute	*Description*	*Value*
SSIONMANAGEMENT	Enables session variables.	YES/NO
SESSIONTIMEOUT	A time limit for keeping session variables.	#CreateTimeSpan (days, hours, minutes, seconds)#

When you specify a name for your application in the NAME attribute of the <CFAPPLICATION> tag, the application scope is initialized. This gives you access to application variables, which are stored in server memory and are available to all pages within an application. You can create client and session variables using the attributes of this tag. We'll see how to do this in a moment.

The <CFAPPLICATION> tag in its simplest form allows you to specify a name for this application, and then set and use application variables. The values of application variables are kept for the duration specified in the "applicationTimeout" attribute. If this value is not set in the <CFAPPLICATION> tag, ColdFusion will use the default application timeout as specified in the ColdFusion Administrator. Let's login right now and see how to modify these values.

Application Variables in ColdFusion Administrator

Log into the ColdFusion Administrator and click "Memory Variables." You'll see the page for setting Application and Session variables. These are both enabled by default, and there isn't any terrific reason to turn them off. If you're trying to save your server's RAM by disabling these variables, I'd say it's time to by more RAM. But you can disable them by unchecking the box and submitting your changes.

On the Memory Variables screen, you can change the values for when you want your application and session variables to timeout. Because the application timeout specified in the ColdFusion Administrator applies to all applications on your site, the value you specify in the <CFAPPLICATION> tag will override the administrator setting. However, you may not specify a value higher than the maximum set in the administrator (see Figure 14.1).

Listing 14.3 Initializing an Application

```
<!---initialize the app------->
<cfapplication name="CoreCF">
```

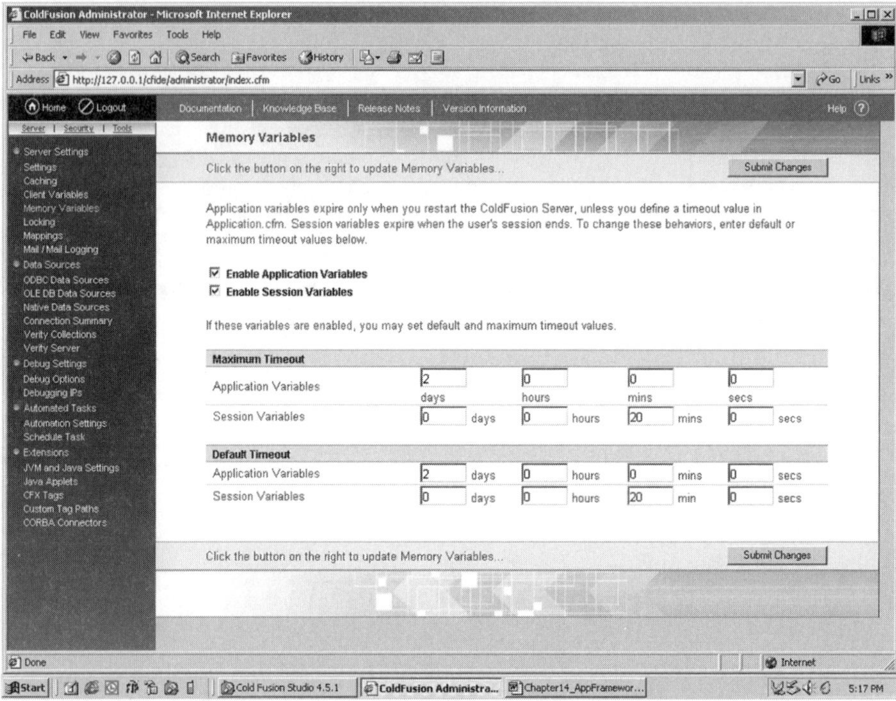

Figure 14.1 Default and maximum settings for application and session variables in the ColdFusion Administrator.

```
<!---set a datasource in the application scope------->
<cfset application.datasource = "MyDatabaseName">

<!----used in the HTML title tag--->
<cfparam name="application.title" default="Core CF">
```

You don't need to reference the name of the application again. It is for ColdFusion to know which templates belong together. You can now set variables in the application scope by prefixing the variable name with "application." These variables are now available to any page that is controlled by this application.cfm. For instance, we could have ColdFusion use this default title in the HTML title tag, like this:

```
<head>
        <title>
                <cfoutput>#application.title#</cfoutput>
        </title>
</head>
```

You can store arrays and query result sets in application and session variables.

For instance, to dump a query result of a previously run query called "qName" into the application scope, you simply write this:

```
<!----note that one doesn't use quote marks here----->
<cfset application.getNames = getNames>

<!---output the query column "FirstName", now in the
      application scope---->

<cfoutput>#APPLICATION.getNames.FirstName#</cfoutput>
```

Note the dot syntax used. Application variables, like much of ColdFusion's internal data, are stored in structures and can therefore be manipulated as such. In the last chapter, when we write the e-commerce site, we'll manipulate session variables with query result sets using structure functions.

In general, application scope variables are well suited for data that you read often and write infrequently. Remember that all instances of application variables are available to the entire application.

Locking

While the foregoing is the proper way to set application-scoped variables, it is not really the proper way to reference them. ColdFusion server handles multiple requests simultaneously, and it is possible for the server to attempt to read data in one request that is being updated by another simultaneous request. This can cause a corruption of memory that can lead to instability in your server. Application, session, and server variables are stored in server memory, so you must place a lock around any reference to variables in these scopes. Not doing so can cause a memory leak or other problems, including Unknown Exception errors, crashing of the cfserver processes, or an unstable operating system. In order to make sure that your data and your server are not compromised, you lock any reference to application, server, or session variables with the <CFLOCK> tag. If you have used previous versions of ColdFusion, you will find its usage has changed a bit since version 4.0.

Read-Only Locks

Read-Only locks allow multiple requests to concurrently access the locked data or CFML. For that reason, you specify Read-Only when you want to read, and not write to or modify the shared data. If another request has an

Exclusive lock on the data, the Read-Only lock will have to wait until the Exclusive lock is released.

Exclusive Locks

Exclusive locks create single-threaded access to the data and CFML inside the lock. Single-threading means that up to one request may process the code inside the lock at any given time. If any subsequent request attempts to access the shared constructs inside the lock, it will have to wait for the request holding the initial lock to finish processing. Locks are issued on a first-come-first-serve basis.

In order to lock your code, you use the <CFLOCK> tag. In invoking this tag, you generally use three attributes: SCOPE, TIMEOUT, and TYPE. The SCOPE attribute allows you to specify the scope—"Session," "Server," or "Application"—that this lock will apply to. The TIMEOUT attribute specifies the maximum time in milliseconds that you want to allow ColdFusion to wait to obtain the lock. This is often a number between 10 and 30.

To modify our template above, we should lock the application variables we set in the Application.cfm. This is straightforward.

Listing 14.4 Locking Application Variables

```
<!---initialize the app------->
<cfapplication name="CoreCF" sessionmanagement="yes">

<cflock scope="APPLICATION" timeout="20" type="EXCLUSIVE">

<!---set a datasource in the application scope------->
<cfset application.datasource = "MyDatabaseName">
<!----used in the HTML title tag--->
<cfparam name="application.title" default="Core CF">

</cflock>

<!---set an applicationwide font definition------->
<cfset defaultFace = "Verdana, Arial, Helvetica">

<cfset defaultSize = "+3">
```

You can specify locking settings in the ColdFusion Administrator. Click "Locking" in the Server menu to specify how much lock checking you want ColdFusion Server to do for you. This is useful chiefly for maintaining old code that has been poorly locked. The more lock checking you have ColdFusion

Server do, the more stable your applications are, but the slower they are, too. Please see the online help in the Administrator to learn more about these options.

The rule to remember is this: if you see the words APPLICATION, SESSION, or SERVER in your code, you had better see a lock as well.

OnRequestEnd.cfm

Before we turn to a discussion of session variables, we must note the other file that is part of the application framework, OnRequestEnd.cfm. This file is the counterpart to Application.cfm; it executes *after* each page request. ColdFusion will look in the same directory as the Application.cfm file of the current page. If found there, it will execute. Otherwise, it will not. ColdFusion does not perform the same searching for OnRequestEnd.cfm as it does for Application.cfm. Just as with Application.cfm, you should not write HTML or any presentation layer code inside this template.

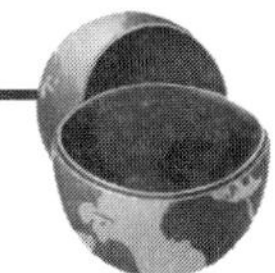

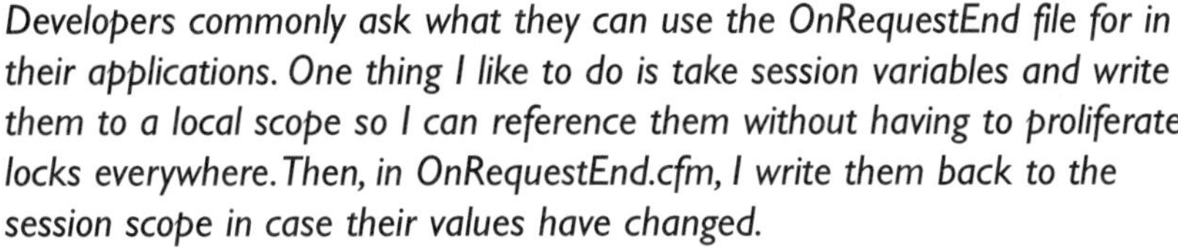

<TIP>

Developers commonly ask what they can use the OnRequestEnd file for in their applications. One thing I like to do is take session variables and write them to a local scope so I can reference them without having to proliferate locks everywhere. Then, in OnRequestEnd.cfm, I write them back to the session scope in case their values have changed.

Note that on case-sensitive UNIX systems, you must name your file precisely this: OnRequestEnd.cfm.

ColdFusion provides you with two ways of tracking users across multiple requests in your applications: session variables and client variables. First we will discuss session variables.

Session Variables

It is best to use session variables for tracking users across multiple requests in a single sitting. They are available for only a single application, and any data is lost when the session timeout ends. So a shopping cart in an e-commerce site is a good candidate for session variables. Another common use of session variables is to have a form that allows users to specify preferences for an application, and then retrieve that information from a database and store it in session variables upon their next visit. It is very common to see session variables used in administration areas of websites where users must log in. They are stored in memory and therefore are quickly accessed and needn't be retrieved in a later session. As with application-scope variables, you must lock all session variables.

Before you can use session variables, you must enable them in the <CFAPPLICATION> tag. To do so, you set the sessionmanagement attribute to "Yes." You may optionally specify a specific timeout for your session using the CreateTimeSpan function. Here is an example:

```
<!---initialize the app and set session vars to
            timeout in 30 minutes------->

<cfapplication name="CoreCF"
            sessionmanagement="yes"
            sessiontimeout = "#CreateTimeSpan(0,0,30,0)#">
```

Session variables are stored in ColdFusion as structures. You can therefore use structure functions to manipulate variables in this scope. For instance, in the e-commerce site we create in the last chapter, we want to make sure that a user's shopping basket is deleted instantly, once the order is placed. That way, they can't refresh the page or use the browser's Back button and mistakenly place the order twice. Here is how we delete the items in their basket, which is stored in the session scope:

```
<!---order has been placed, clear the basket---->
<cfset StructClear(session)>
```

Standard Session Variables

Four read-only variables are automatically created with a session-enabled application, as shown in Table 14.2.

Table 14.2 Read-Only Session Variables

Variable	*Description*
Session.CFID	The client ID, stored as a cookie on the client.
Session.CFToken	The client security token, stored on the client as a cookie.
Session.URLToken	A combination of CFID and CFToken, stored as two URL parameters. If the client does not support cookies, you can use this variable to pass client session info with each page request.Ω
Session.SessionID	A unique session identifier.

We use session variables extensively in Chapter 22 to create a complete online store.

Client Variables

In order to enable client variables you use the <CFAPPLICATION> tag. Client variables maintain state as session variables do, but they also accomplish different tasks. To begin with, the data in client variables is accessed more slowly than in session variables. That is because they are not stored in memory. For the same reason, many developers argue that client variables are more stable. You can specify where to store client variables: in the system registry (default), a cookie, or a datasource. It seems to me that you should base your choice of what kind of variables to use on what job you need done. Session variables are more suited for sustaining user information across a single request, whereas client variables are well suited for maintaining user information across many different requests. For instance, if you want to allow a user to specify his or her own fonts and colors for your site, this information is best stored in client variables. An advantage of client variables over session variables is that you do not have to lock client variables.

State without Cookies

It is possible to maintain state in ColdFusion without the use of cookies. However, doing so requires that you pass the CFID and CFToken variables in the URL or in hidden form fields of every request. To do so, set the <setClientCookies> attribute of your <CFAPPLICATION> tag to "No," and then refer to the Client.URLToken variable to maintain state.

Enabling Client Variables

In order to enable Client variables for tracking long-term information about a particular client, you need to set the clientManagement attribute of the <CFAPPLICATION> tag to "Yes." Next, you must specify where you want to store the client variables. By default they are stored in the system registry. However, this is not a terrific idea, since inappropriate modification of your registry can cause the system to become unstable. Moreover, the registry was not necessarily intended to store potentially infinite amounts of data. You have two other options here: cookies or an SQL database. Either way, you must choose the appropriate method for your application, as they are mutually exclusive.

You can override the default setting by specifying a storage location in the <CFAPPLICATION> tag's clientstorage attribute. If you wish to store client data in cookies, you specify "cookie" as the value for this attribute; in order to store client information in a database, you simply provide the name of a datasource which has already been configured in the ColdFusion Administrator. Using a datasource is generally the faster-performing method.

Below is a sample Application.cfm file which illustrates how to enable client variables and specify a datasource to use for storing those variables.

```
<!---initialize the app. store client variables in the
CoreCFDB database, which has been set up as a DSN in
       the Administrator------->

<cfapplication name="CoreCF"
             clientmanagement="Yes"
             clientstorage="CoreCFDB">
```

The read-only client variables shown in Table 14.3 are created automatically when client management is enabled.

Table 14.3 Read-Only Session Variables

Variable	*Description*
Client.CFID	The client ID, generally stored as a cookie on the client.
Client.CFToken	The client security token, generally stored on the client as a cookie.
Client.HitCount	The number of page requests made by this client.
Client.LastVisit	The time the client last visited this application.
Client.TimeCreated	The time the CFID and CFToken client variables were first created for this client.
Client.URLToken	A combination of CFID and CFToken in the form of CFID=*ID*&CFToken=*Token*. If the client does not support cookies, you can use this variable to pass client session info with each page request.

You can reference client variables like this:

```
<cfset MyName = "#Client.MyName#">
```

```
Welcome back, <cfoutput>#MyName#. You have visited this site
#Client.HitCount# times.</cfoutput>
```

A major difference between client variables and session variables is that you needn't lock client variables, since they are not stored in memory.

Storing Client Variables

Once you have enabled client variables in the <CFAPPLICATION> tag, you must specify a storage location. By default, they are stored in the system registry. You have two other options for client variable storage: a datasource and a cookie.

It is most efficient to store client variables in a datasource. The registry is not necessarily made to store large amounts of data for fast retrieval on your website. Cookies are generally limited to 4 K of data, and ColdFusion will throw an error if you attempt more. Additionally, browsers generally limit the number of cookies allowed to 20 per host. Because ColdFusion automatically sets three of them right off the bat—CFID, CFToken, and CFGLOBALS (which contains data about the client)—you are limited to 17 unique applications per host. That's not really viable over the long term. Therefore, let's set up a datasource that we can use to store client variables for our application.

Configuring a Datasource for Client Variables

You can manage the storage of your client variables in the ColdFusion Administrator. Log in to the Administrator and click "Client Variables" on the "Server Settings" menu. If you have your applications hosted with a ColdFusion host, you will likely need to have them do this for you.

Once you have opened this page in the Administrator, you'll notice that the drop-down menu near the top displays all of the datasources already available to ColdFusion. You can also change the default setting for client variable storage if none is specified in the <CFAPPLICATION> tag (see Figure 14.2).

Choose which datasource you want to hold client variables for this application, and click "Add to Client Variable Store." Once you select a datasource, ColdFusion Administrator will ask you a few questions about how you want it configured.

At the top of the page is a checkbox for selecting whether or not you want to have ColdFusion automatically purge data that has not been retrieved in some time. It is a good idea to have ColdFusion delete client variables that have just been sitting around for a long time, unless you need to persist them

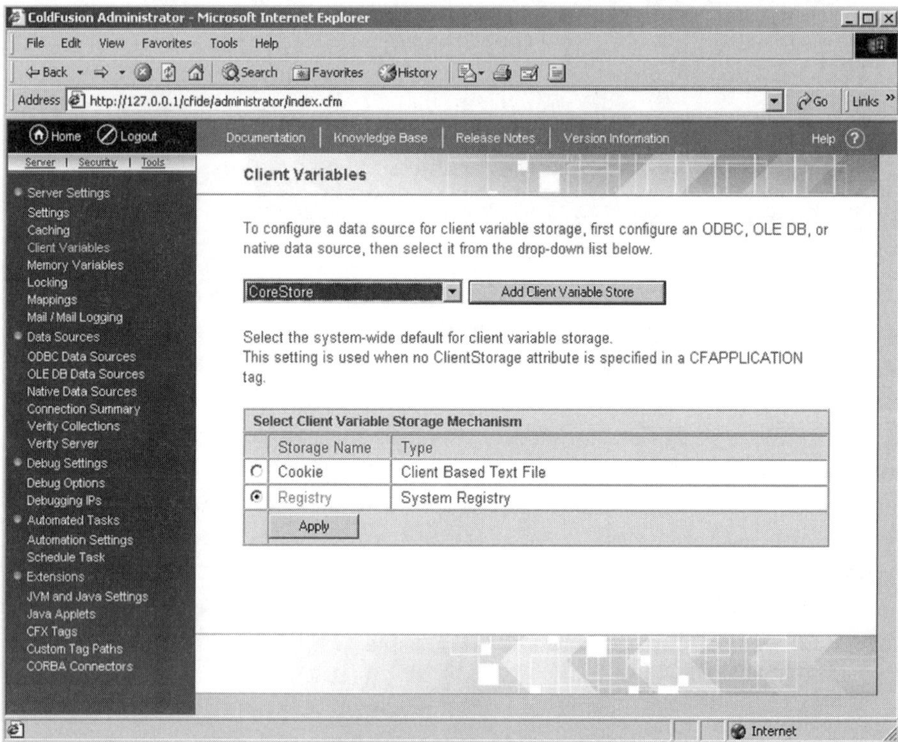

Figure 14.2 To store client variables in a datasource, you must first configure the datasource in the ColdFusion Administrator.

for programmatic or reporting purposes. You can change the number of days here; the default is 90.

Next, you can disable updates to the system-generated client variables such as to LAST VISIT and HIT COUNT to save system resources and improve the performance of your pages. If you disable this option, ColdFusion will only update global client variables.

The last item allows you to specify whether or not to Create Client Tables. You must have this box checked the first time you configure the datasource, and unchecked every subsequent time you modify client variable settings for this datasource. If the datasource has already been configured to store client variables, SQL will throw an error, because you will be trying to create tables that already exist. Since this is the first time we're configuring this datasource to hold client variables, leave the box checked, and hit Submit.

<NOTE>

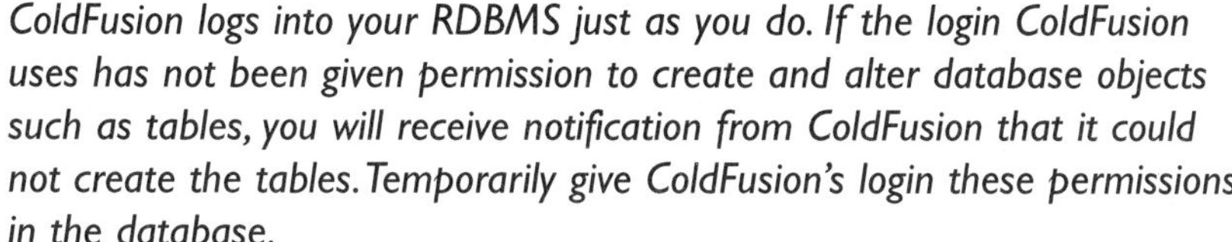

ColdFusion logs into your RDBMS just as you do. If the login ColdFusion uses has not been given permission to create and alter database objects such as tables, you will receive notification from ColdFusion that it could not create the tables. Temporarily give ColdFusion's login these permissions in the database.

ColdFusion will create two tables in your database: CDATA and CGLOBAL. The CDATA table has the following fields: CFID, APP, and DATA. The CGLOBAL table holds these fields: CFID, DATA, and LVISIT. Some of the information stored here is generated by ColdFusion automatically, such as LVISIT. The DATA field in the CDATA table will hold variables and values that you write to the client scope in your applications. The CGLOBAL DATA field will hold the system-generated values, in this format:

```
HITCOUNT=3#LASTVISIT={ts '2001-06-27 11:45:52'}
#TIMECREATED={ts '2001-06-27 11:26:44'}#
```

Retrieving the Client Variable List

You can view all of the client variables stored on a particular client using the standard GetClientVariablesList() function, which takes no arguments. This function returns a comma-separated list of all client variable names for the current application. It does *not* return the standard system client variables.

Deleting a Client Variable

You can delete client variables that you create using the function DeleteClientVariable("ClientVariableName"). This function will destroy only client variables associated with the current application, and will *not* destroy system-created variables such as Client.CFID, and Client.HitCount.

Server Variables

Server variables exist for the whole server and are therefore available to every application. There are several built-in variables in the server scope that you can reference in your templates.

Server.ColdFusion.ProductName
Server.ColdFusion.ProductVersion
Server.ColdFusion.ProductLevel
Server.ColdFusion.SerialNumber
Server.ColdFusion.SupportedLocales
Server.OS.Name
Server.OS.Version
Server.OS.BuildNumber

You can write to the server scope as well if you want to share data across all applications on your server. Server variables are stored as structures and can be referenced and manipulated accordingly. As with application variables, you will loose any information you write to the server scope when the server is restarted.

It is uncommon to see Server variables in use in production environments. ColdFusion Administrator uses them internally, however.

Error Handling

Debugging your ColdFusion applications is easy with the new `<CFDUMP>` tag. And the appendix "Common ColdFusion Errors and What to Do About Them" will help you to determine why you're getting certain error messages so you can fix them. But what about your users?

Using the <CFERROR> tag in your Application.cfm file, you can display custom HTML pages when errors occur. That means you can keep your users from the stark standard ColdFusion error message, and you can notify a site administrator by email when an exception occurs. Table 14.4 shows the attributes of the <CFERROR> tag.

Table 14.4 <CFERROR> Tag Attributes

Attribute	*Description*
Type	Required. The type of error that the custom error page handles (validation or request).
Template	Required. The relative path to the custom error page.

Attribute	*Description*
MailTo	The email address of the administrator to be notified of the error. The value is also available in your custom error page in the MailTo property of the error object, as in: `#error.mailTo#`.
Exception	Type of exception. Required if type = exception or type = monitor.

Though you can call it from anywhere, one generally includes the <CFERROR> tag in the Application.cfm file. First, you create a page to handle your errors. Then you can specify the relative path to this template in the <CFERROR> tag. For instance, let's create a folder off the application root called "Errors"; it will hold a template for handling request errors. I generally prefix error-handling templates with "err_". Then I create a simple HTML page that matches the design of the site I'm working on to display the contents of the error.

When the <CFERROR> tag generates an error page, there are several error variables available to you if you specified "Request," "Exception," or "Validate" as the value for the TYPE attribute. These are as follows:

```
Error.Diagnostics
Error.MailTo
Error.DateTime
Error.Browser
Error.GeneratedContent
Error.RemoteAddress
Error.HTTPReferer
Error.Template
Error.QueryString
```

These are referenced in the "error" scope, as shown in Listing 14.5.

Listing 14.5 Err_Request.cfm

```
<table width="%80">
        <tr align="right">
                <td bgcolor="silver">
                        <p>
<h2><font face="Verdana">Canyon WebWorks</font></
h2>  
</p>
                        <p align="center">
<h3>A request exception (error) has been thrown  
</h3>
                </td>
                <td bgcolor="white">
```

```
                          <img src="http://www.canyon.net/images/
cwwlogo2.gif" width=104 height=108 border=0 alt="Canyon Web-
Works and Multimedia">
               <td>
        </tr>
 <tr>
        <td>
               <p>
            An error occurred when you requested this page.
<br>
               Please email the <A
HREF="mailto:#Error.MailTo#">Administrator</A> with
              the contents of the diagnostics below, and we
will work to
           correct the problem as quickly as possible. <br>
               We apologize for the inconvenience.
               </p>

               <p>
<!----output information about this error----->
               <u>Error Diagnostics</u>:<br>
               Query String: <strong>#ERROR.querystring#</
strong><br>
               Referer Template: <strong>#ERROR.HTTPRef-
erer#</strong><br>
               Exception Data:<br> <strong>#ERROR.diagnos-
tics#</strong>
               </p>
               <p>

<!----output information about this request for reference---->
               <u>User Information</u>:<br>
         The error occurred at <B>#ERROR.DateTime#</B><br>
         You browser is #ERROR.Browser#</B><BR>
                Remote IP Address: <b>#ERROR.RemoteAddress#</
b><br>
           You were attempting to access<B>#ERROR.Tem-
plate#</B><br>
               </p>
        </td>
 <tr bgcolor="Silver">
        <td>
               Thank you.
        </td>
 </tr>
  </tr>
</table>
```

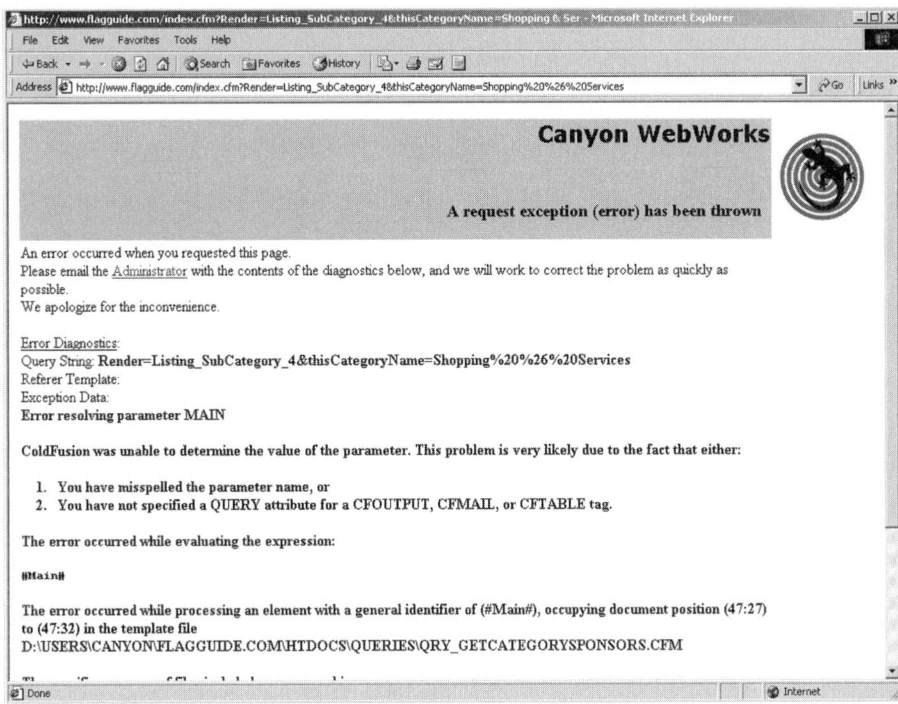

Figure 14.3 A custom error page.

If I force an error in my browser, the output looks like Figure 14.3.

You can specify "request," "exception," "monitor," and "validation" values for this tag. Here is a sample implementation in the Application.cfm file:

```
<cferror mailto="admin@mysite.com"
                              type="EXCEPTION"
                              template="Errors/err_Except.cfm">
```

Logging Site Information with <CFLOG>

There are a couple of different ways you can write information about the current state of your log file. One way is to use the "Write" attribute of the <CFFILE> tag, which we do in the e-commerce example at the end of the book. Now with ColdFusion 5, you can use the new <CFLOG> tag to write log information about your applications.

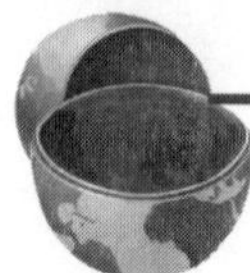

<NOTE>

Do not write your log file to a location within your Web server if you use CFFILE. Anyone who knows the URL could then download and view your log file. The same thing is true for your database. Never keep a database in the Web server path.

The <CFLOG> tag lets you write custom messages to log files. You can specify a log file to write to; if you do so, you must name it with a .log extension, and it must be located in the ColdFusion log directory. You may use ColdFusion expressions within the log. Table 14.5 shows the attributes of the new tag.

Table 14.5 <CFLOG> Tag Attributes

Attribute	*Description*
Text	Required. The message text to log.
Log	Optional. If you omit the FILE attribute, specifies the standard log file in which to write the message. Ignored if you specify a FILE attribute. Valid values are: • Application. Writes to the Application.log file, normally used for application-specific messages. • Scheduler. Writes to the Scheduler.log file, normally used to log the execution of scheduled tasks.
File	Optional. Name of the message file. Log files must have the suffix.log. Specify only the main part of the file name, without the suffix. The file must be located in the default log directory and is created if it does not exist.
Type	Optional. The severity of the message. Valid values are: • Information (default) • Warning • Error • Fatal Information
Thread	Optional. Specifies whether to log the thread ID. Yes / No
Date	Optional. Specifies whether to log the system date. Yes / No
Time	Optional. Specifies whether to log the system time. Yes / No
Application	Optional. Specifies whether to log the name of the application if one has been specified in the <CFAPPLICATION> tag. YES is the default.

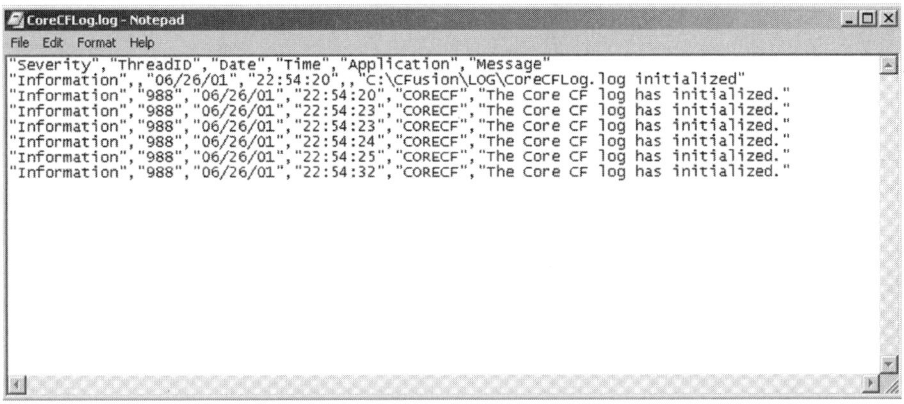

CoreCFLog.log - Notepad

File Edit Format Help

```
"Severity","ThreadID","Date","Time","Application","Message"
"Information",,"06/26/01","22:54:20",,"C:\CFusion\LOG\CoreCFLog.log initialized"
"Information","988","06/26/01","22:54:20","CORECF","The Core CF log has initialized."
"Information","988","06/26/01","22:54:23","CORECF","The Core CF log has initialized."
"Information","988","06/26/01","22:54:23","CORECF","The Core CF log has initialized."
"Information","988","06/26/01","22:54:24","CORECF","The Core CF log has initialized."
"Information","988","06/26/01","22:54:25","CORECF","The Core CF log has initialized."
"Information","988","06/26/01","22:54:32","CORECF","The Core CF log has initialized."
```

Figure 14.4 The results of running the <CFLOG> tag.

Here is an example of how you might use the new <CFLOG> tag within your application:

Listing 14.6 Using <cflog>

```
<cflog application="YES"
              date="YES"
              thread="YES"
              text="The Core CF log has initialized."
              type="Information"
              file="CoreCFLog">
```

If I open the CoreCFLog.log file under the ColdFusion Log directory, I see the output as shown in Figure 14.4.

Creating a Personalized Web Page

The last chapter of this book is devoted to creating a complete e-commerce site. In that application, we'll use session variables to keep track of the items in a user's shopping cart. In the administrative area of the store, where merchants can retrieve their orders, we use a cookie to make sure that the user is logged in properly, and check for the presence of that cookie on each protected page. Because you can see in greater depth how to use these variables in that section, here we'll quickly look at creating a personalized Web page using client variables. This will demonstrate many of the application framework topics we have covered throughout this chapter.

Listing 14.7 Application.cfm

```
<!---initialize the app. store client variables in the
CoreCFDB database, which has been set up as a DSN in the
Administrator------->
<cfapplication name="CoreCF"
               clientmanagement="Yes"
               clientstorage="CF5DB">

<!---set an applicationwide font definition------->
<cflock scope="APPLICATION" type="EXCLUSIVE" timeout="20">

<!---since we have a lot of cfsets in a row, let's use
CFSCRIPT since that will be faster------->
<cfscript>

// set a datasource in the application scope
application.datasource = "MyDatabaseName";
// used in the HTML title tag--->
application.title = "Core CF";

application.defaultFace = "Verdana, Arial, Helvetica";
application.defaultColor = "Red";
application.defaultSize = "+3";
</cfscript>

</cflock>
```

Listing 14.8 is the Index.cfm file, which is a very simple self-posting form. It uses conditional logic to test for the presence of client variables. If they exist already, the user is redirected to the menu page. If they don't exist, the user fills out a short form specifying personalization preferences.

Listing 14.8 Index.cfm

```
<html>
<head>

<!-------use our application variables. ------->
       <title>
       <cflock scope="APPLICATION" type="READONLY" time-
out="20">
       <cfoutput>#application.title#</cfoutput>
       </cflock>
```

```
        </title>
</head>

<body>

<!---if they have not been to the site before, have them
fill out this form to personalize the fonts and colors they
see
------->
<cfif NOT isDefined("Client.MyName")>
<cfoutput>
        <cflock scope="APPLICATION" type="READONLY" time-
out="20">
<font face="#application.defaultFace#">
        </cflock>
Welcome to our site. Please personalize your experience with
us:
</font>
<br>
</cfoutput>

<!---embedded logic: if the form has been submitted, set the
client variable------->
<cfif isDefined("FORM.MyName")>

<!---set client variables to reference on menu.cfm------->
<cfoutput>
        <cfset client.MyName = "#FORM.MyName#">
        <cfset client.color = "#FORM.color#">
        <cfset client.face = "#FORM.face#">
</cfoutput>

<!---now that we have their preferences, redirect them to the
personalized menu page.------->

<cflocation url="menu.cfm">

<!---we haven't posted the form yet, so show it.------->
<cfelse>
<form action="index.cfm" method = "post">

Please enter your name so we can remember you:<br>
<input type="text" size="25" name="MyName"><br><br>

<!---these should probably be select menus, and you
should require all of them.------->
Please enter the font face you like most:<br>
<input type="text" size="25" name="face"><br><br>

Please enter your favorite color:<br>
```

```
<input type="text" size="25" name="color"><br>
<input type="Submit" value="Submit">
</form>

<!---end form defined check------->
</cfif>

<cfelse>
<!---client variables already defined, redirect.------->
<cflocation url="menu.cfm">

<!---end the client.MyName check------->
</cfif>
</body>
</html>
```

Listing 14.9 Menu.cfm

```
<!---this is the menu page. it displays
      different things based on user preference------->

<cfoutput>
<table>

<tr>
<!---set from user preference---->
<td bgcolor="#client.color#">

<!---use the application settings here so they are uniform
across all personal pages------->
      <cflock scope="APPLICATION" type="READONLY" time-
out="20">
<font face="#application.defaultFace#" size="#application.
defaultSize#">
</cflock>
#client.MyName#'s personal page
</font>
</td>
</tr>
<tr>
<td>You have visited this page #client.HitCount# times.</td>
</tr>
<tr>
<td>Your last visit was on #DateFormat(client.lastvisit,
"mmmm dd")#
</td>
```

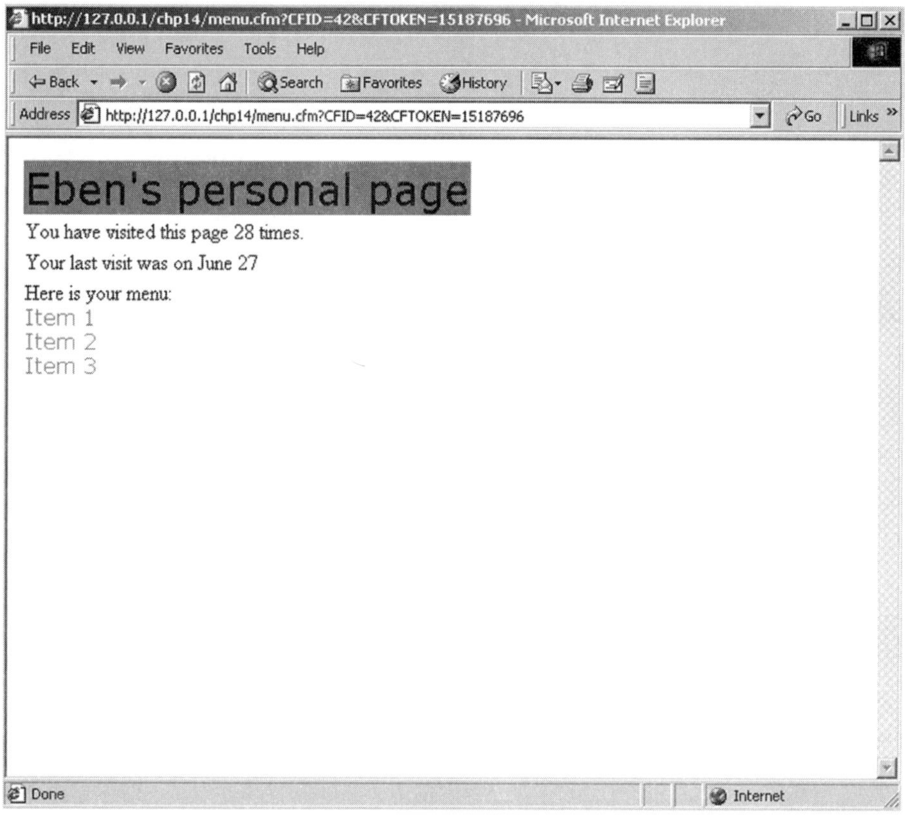

Figure 14.5 Using client variables to create personalized user experiences.

```
</tr>
<tr>
<td>Here is your menu:<br>
<font face="#client.face#" color="#client.color#">Item 1<br>
Item 2<br>
Item 3</font>
<br>
</td>
</tr>
</table>

</cfoutput>
```

Figure 14.5 shows the result of the finished application. You can use these variables as the building blocks for very complex, personalized sites and compelling user experiences.

GRAPHING WITH COLDFUSION

Topics in This Chapter

- ColdFusion's new graphing feature
- Making a simple graph
- Graphing a query
- Speeding load time with <CFSAVECONTENT>
- Setting the appearance of graphs
- A complete data drill-down graph application

Chapter 15

A new and exciting feature of ColdFusion 5 is perhaps a result of Allaire's merger with Macromedia. The new release not only expands the underlying architecture of ColdFusion by integrating processes with the Java Server JRun, it has enhanced the presentational power of ColdFusion as well. ColdFusion is now also integrated with a limited-functionality version of the Macromedia Generator server. ColdFusion leverages the power of both of these servers, versions of which install with ColdFusion. Generator creates and delivers dynamic graphics on the fly in Flash, .gif, or .jpg formats. With two new ColdFusion tags, <CFGRAPH> and <CFGRAPHDATA>, you can compose bar charts, line charts, and pie charts dynamically. This should be a lot of fun.

<NOTE>

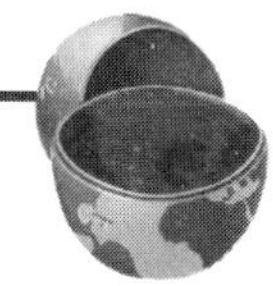

You must have chosen to install support for CFGRAPH when you installed ColdFusion in order to create graphs.

In the past when ColdFusion developers needed to represent data in a horizontal line graph, they had to dynamically set the "width" attribute of the HTML <img> tag based on data received from a query. They'd perform some calculation to keep the image from going out of control, and could then "fake" a bar graph, kind of like this:

```
<!---run a query called GetResponse ---->
<cfset imgwid=GetResponse.recordcount/10>

<!----The width of the bargraph.gif picture, which is a one-
pixel-wide plain image, is dynamically set based on the number
of answers in the column--->

<img src="images/bargraph.gif" width=#imgwid# height=10
      border=0>
```

This worked pretty well. But it wasn't very flexible or scalable, and it wasn't very pretty. This chapter will examine how you can create compelling graphs from your data using two new ColdFusion tags. Here are the types of graphs you can now create:

- Bar
- Horizontal
- Line
- Area
- Pie

Making a Simple Graph

You make graphs in ColdFusion 5 using the <CFGRAPH> tag, which encapsulates all of the work for you. The full list of <CFGRAPH> attributes is very long, since the tag takes different attributes depending on which type of graph you want to make. We will therefore start with four attributes (Table 15.1).

Table 15.1 Some <CFGRAPH> Tag Attributes

Attribute	*Description*	*Value*
Type	Specifies the type of graph to create.	Bar, HorizontalBar, Pie, or Line are acceptable values
Query	The query containing the data to be graphed.	QueryName
ValueColumn	The query column whose values you want to graph.	ColumnName

Table 15.1 Continued

Attribute	*Description*	*Value*
ItemColumn	The query column containing the description for this data point. This appears on the horizontal axis of bar and line graphs, and in pie charts.	ColumnName

Let's say we've got a query that returns the names of products and their prices. Note that, using <CFGRAPH>, you may graph only integers or real numbers. Therefore, you must convert date-time values or currency values before you can use them. Listing 15.1 shows the syntax of the <CFGRAPH> tag in conjunction with a query to create a horizontal bar graph.

Listing 15.1 A Simple Bar Graph

```
<!---prices and products from database ------->

<cfquery name="getPrices" datasource="CoreStore">

SELECT ProductName, Price
FROM Products
</cfquery>

<!----"Price" is stored as datatype "Money" in an SQL Server.
You don't need to convert it.------->

<cfgraph type = "horizontalbar"
        query = "getPrices"
        valueColumn = "Price"
        itemColumn = "ProductName"
        title = "Our Products Listed by price"
        >
</cfgraph>
```

This graph displays the values of the Price column with the ProductName as the item label. The value of the "title" attribute is displayed above the graph. The results of Listing 15.1 are shown in Figure 15.1.

This template is run through ColdFusion, SQL Server, JRun, and Generator, and returned to the browser. The entire process takes 1/25 of a second. You could create a vertical bar graph in just the same way by specifying Type="bar".

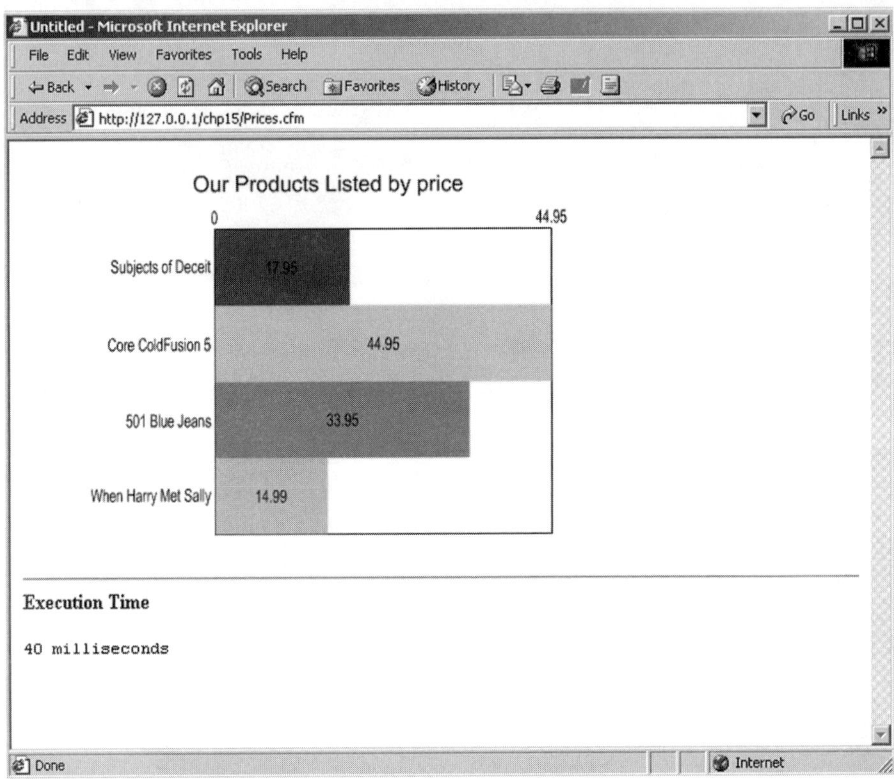

Figure 15.1 A simple graph dynamically generated from a query.

Table 15.2 Shared <CFGRAPH> Tag Attributes

Attribute	*Description*	*Value*
Title	A title for your graph.	String
TitleFont	Font to use for title display.	Font face
FileFormat	Specifies which file format to create the graph in.	Flash, .gif, or .jpg. Default is Flash
GraphWidth	Graph width in pixels.	Number in pixels
GraphHeight	Graph height. The width and height together define the entire graph area including legend and background area.	Number in pixels

Attribute	*Description*	*Value*
BackgroundColor	Specifies the background color to use for the *entire* graph area, including legends and margins.	Standard 256 web colors, or any valid HTML color format. You must escape pound signs if you use a hexadecimal, i.e.: ##336699.
BorderWidth	Width of the border surrounding the graph.	Number in pixels.
BorderColor	Color of the border surrounding the graph.	Any valid HTML color format. Value of 0 means no border.
Depth	The depth of the shading that gives the graph a three-dimensional appearance.	Number in pixels. Value of 0 means no 3D effect.

Table 15.2 lists the attributes of the <CFGRAPH> tag that are shared among all types of graphs. We will examine individual type attributes as we come to them.

<NOTE>

You cannot use just one of the graphWidth and graphHeight attributes to change the width-height ratio of the data area. Use them both together to change the overall size.

Horizontal and Bar Graphs

In addition to the shared graph attributes, you can specify certain attributes that pertain only to horizontal and bar graphs. These are listed in Table 15.3.

Table 15.3 Horizontal and Bar <CFGRAPH> Tag Attributes

Attribute	*Description*	*Value*
showValueLabel	Labels that display the numeric value being graphed.	Yes/No
valueLabelFont	Font type of the value label.	A valid web 256 font
valueLabelSize	Size of the value label.	Numeric

Table 15.3 Continued

Attribute	*Description*	*Value*
valueLocation	Location of the data value.	OnBar or OverBar
scaleFrom	Minimum point on the data axis (vertical for bar charts, horizontal bar charts).	Numeric; default is 0
scaleTo	The maximum point on the data axis.	Numeric; default is the maximum represented value
gridLines	The number of grid lines between the minimum and maximum values of the graph.	Numeric
showItemLabel	Labels to show on the second axis of the chart.	Yes/No
itemLabelFont	Font face for the item label.	Times, Arial, Courier
itemLabelSize	Size for the item labels.	Size in points
itemLabelOrientation	Orientation of the item label.	Horizontal or vertical
colorList	Comma-separated list of colors to use for each bar. If you specify fewer colors than datapoints, the colors repeat. If you specify more colors than datapoints, the extra colors are not used.	You can use any of the 256 standard web colors. You must escape pound signs when using hexadecimal.
barSpacing	Space between bars. Any 3D shadow specified by the depth attribute appears in this space, so if you want the background to appear between all bars, make the barSpacing value greater than the depth value.	Number in pixels

One thing to note about these attributes is that the gridlines attribute will automatically display numeric values that represent each incremental point along the value axis. For instance, if you've got a graph with ScaleFrom=0 and ScaleTo=50, you might initially think that you would want to specify gridlines=5 to define your graph with background segments of 10 each for reference. However, a line creates a segment on both sides of itself. Therefore, you want to specify gridlines=4 to get 5 segments. This, along with many of the other bar attributes, is shown in Listing 15.2. Here we have used the same query as before and simply modified the appearance of the bar chart.

Listing 15.2 Bar Chart with Enhanced Appearance

```
<!---prices and products from database ------->
<cfquery name="getPrices" datasource="CoreStore"
username="coldfusion" password="c5y4n2sql">
SELECT ProductName, Price
FROM Products
</cfquery>

<!-----you can have your users specify these
       attributes dynamically, for instance, by
       filling out a form.------->

<cfgraph type="bar"
       query="getPrices"
       valueColumn="Price"
       itemColumn="ProductName"
       title="Our Products Listed by price"
       TitleFont = "Courier"
       FileFormat="Flash"
       GraphWidth="400"
       GraphHeight="400"
       BackgroundColor="##CCCCCC"
       BorderWidth="5"
       BorderColor="Green"
       Depth="15"
       ShowValueLabel="Yes"
       valueLabelFont="Courier"
       valueLabelSize="25"
       valueLocation="OverBar"
       scaleFrom="0"
       scaleTo="50"
```

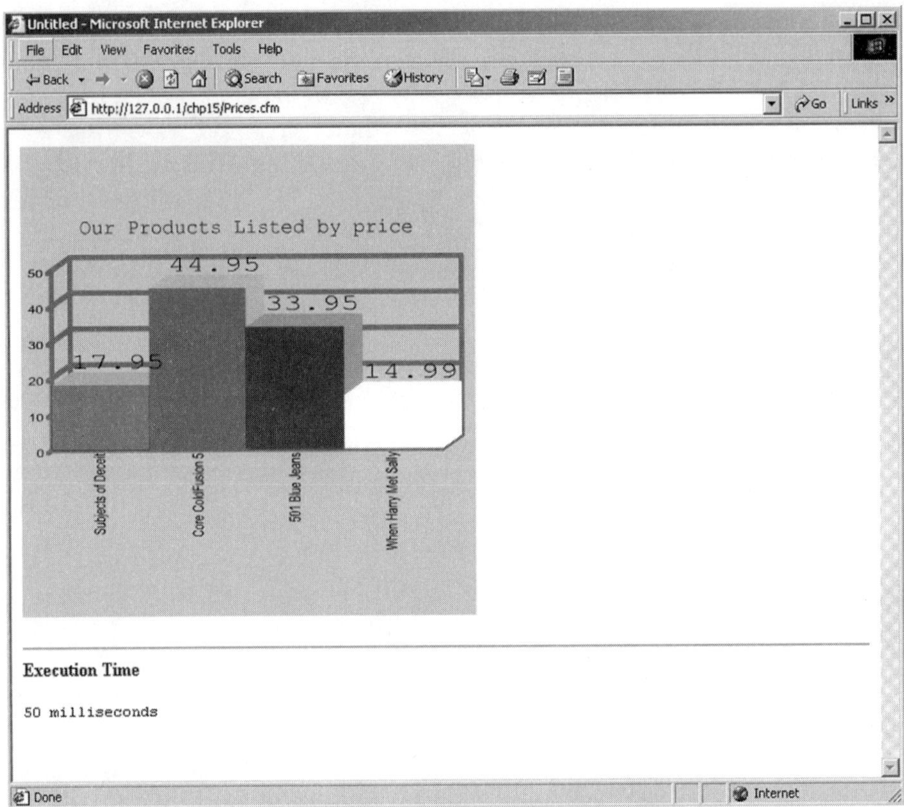

Figure 15.2 The enhanced graph takes advantage of presentation parameters.

```
        gridlines="4"
        itemLabelOrientation="vertical"
        colorList="Red, Green, Blue, White, Black"
        >
</cfgraph>
```

Figure 15.2 shows the result of running this code. Notice that the "Black" color never appears as a bar, since there are more colors in the colorList than columns returned from the query.

It's probably a good idea at this point to play around with a simple graph in this way so you get a feel for the parameters. It's not entirely intuitive, and a bit of lingo is involved in using them. So you will likely feel more at home if you simply pull a relatively simple result set and modify the gridlines parameters (for instance) to see what happens. Then try adding an aggregate function, maybe an AVG, and a GROUP BY statement into your SQL and see what happens.

Next, we'll look at how to create a simple pie graph.

Pie Graphs

As with bar graphs, a number of additional attributes are specific to pie graphs. These help you enhance the presentation of your pie graphs. They are listed in Table 15.4.

Table 15.4 <CFGRAPH> Tag Attributes for Pie Graphs

Attribute	*Description*	*Value*
showValueLabel	Labels that display the numeric value being graphed.	Yes/No
valueLabelFont	Font type of the value label.	A valid web 256 font
valueLabelSize	Size of the value label.	Numeric
valueLocation	Location of the data value.	OnBar or OverBar
showLegend	A legend relating the pie slice colors to the data point Item descriptions from the itemColumn attribute or cfgraphdata tag ItemColumn attribute.	By default the legend appears to the left of the chart. You can also specify above, below, right, and none. You can specify the font type as Arial (default), Courier, or Times.
legendFont		
colorList	Comma-separated list of colors to use for each bar. If you specify fewer colors than datapoints, the colors repeat. If you specify more colors than datapoints, the extra colors are not used.	You can use any of the 256 standard web colors. You must escape pound signs when using hexadecimal.

Note that value labels are on by default. If you are displaying your graph in Flash format, you can have the labels appear as mouse-overs (see Figure 15.3).

One neat feature of all Flash charts is that you can zoom in on them and move them around. You do this by right-clicking anywhere on the graph and then choosing “Zoom In.” You can then click and hold to drag the graph around within its frame.

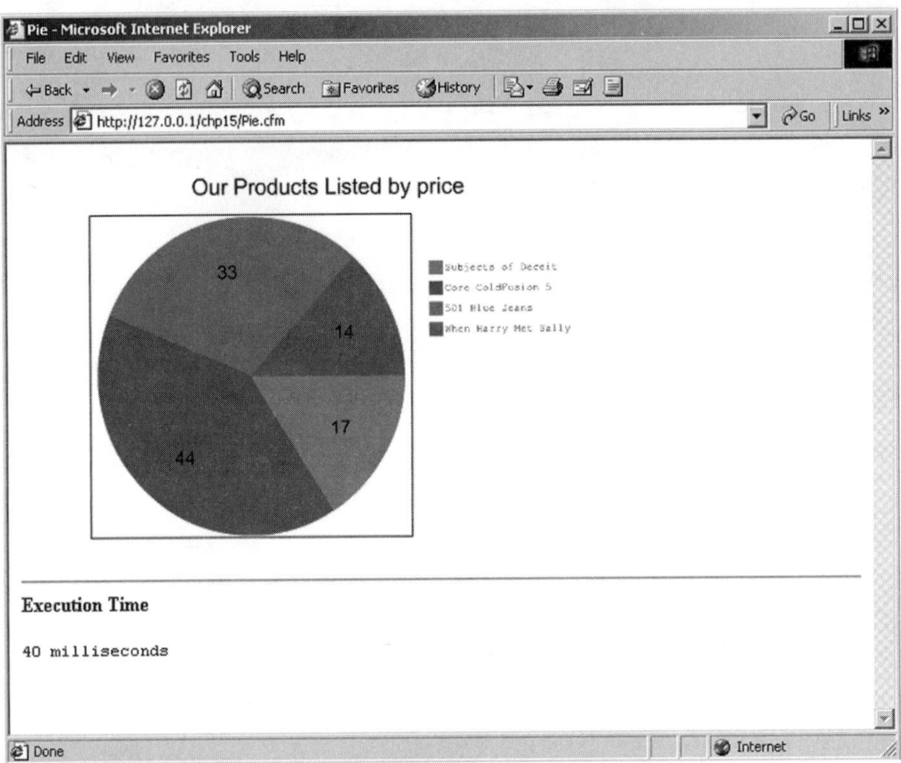

Figure 15.3 A pie chart generated from the same products query.

Line and Area Graphs

A line graph is perhaps what you're used to seeing in the stock market reports, since they are most often used to represent a change over time. An area graph is simply a "filled-in" line graph. These graphs also have a set of attributes to be used specifically with them, as listed in Table 15.5.

Table 15.5 <CFGRAPH> Tag Attributes for Line and Area Graphs

Attribute	*Description*	*Value*
showItemLabel	Labels that show on the horizontal axis of the chart.	By default, item labels are on if you specify an ItemColumn (or, for cfgraphdata tags, item) attribute.

Attribute	*Description*	*Value*
itemLabelFont	Font type of the item label.	A valid web 256 font
itemLabelSize	Size of the item label.	Numeric
itemLabelOrientation	Orientation of the label.	Horizontal or vertical
lineColor	Color of the line.	By default the legend appears to the left of the chart. You can also specify above, below, right, and none. You can specify the font type as Arial (default), Courier, or Times.
lineWidth	Width of the line.	Number in pixels; default is 1.
fill	Specifies whether to fill the area below the line with the line color to create an area graph.	Yes/No; default is No.
gridLines	The number of grid lines between the top area and bottom area of the graph. The value of each grid line appears along the value axis. The cfgraph tag displays horizontal grids only.	Numeric. A value of 0 means no grid lines.

Since we have seen two examples of how to create and enhance the appearance of two different kinds of graphs, let us make things a bit more complex. In this section we will create an area graph that shows product sales over time. This example assumes the existence of a database with a table called "Orders," which holds placed orders; "Products," which contains information about individual products; and "OrdersProducts," which joins an OrderID with the ProductIDs in that order. Finally, a Customer's table holds billing and shipping information about customers who place orders.

We will use the query shown in Listing 15.3 to create the e-commerce site in Chapter 22. This query, called GetOrders, is used in the administrative area of the store to allow merchants to retrieve orders from the database. We can use this query, slightly modified, to pull all of this order information into memory. It's a long query with a few joins, so it is a good candidate to serve as the source for later queries. We will use this as the building block for making a complete reporting application. Let's go to the code.

Listing 15.3 Retrieving a Complex Query Result and Graphing It Using Query of Queries

```
<!---select data about orders------->

<cfquery name="getOrders" datasource="CoreStore">
SELECT

O.orderconfirmation, O.CustomerID, O.SubTotal,
O.Shipping, O.Tax, O.GrandTotal,
O.OrderDate, O.Processed,

OP.ProductID, OP.Qty,

C.billFirstName, C.billLastName,
C.billAddress, C.billCity,
C.billState, C.billZipCode,
C.billCountry, C.billPhone,
C.billEmail, C.shipFirstName,
C.shipLastName, C.shipAddress,
C.shipCity, C.shipState,
C.shipZipCode, C.shipCountry,
C.shipPhone, C.shipEmail,
C.shipMethod, C.creditName,
C.creditNumber, C.creditExpDate,

P.ProductName,
P.Price

FROM orders O

INNER JOIN OrdersProducts OP
       ON O.OrderConfirmation = OP.OrderConfirmation

INNER JOIN Customers C
       ON O.CustomerID = C.CustomerID

LEFT JOIN Products P
       ON. OP.ProductID = P.ProductID
```

```
</cfquery>


<!---convert date to number by looping over the result set
        once for each record therein------->
<cfloop index="idx" from ="1" to="#GetOrders.RecordCount#">

<!---set the OrderDate into a number so we can use
the date in the graph------->

<cfset
GetOrders.OrderDate[idx]=NumberFormat(DatePart("yyyy",
GetOrders.OrderDate[idx] ),9999)>
</cfloop>

<!---query previous query to get avg orders --->

<cfquery name="avgOrders" dbtype="query">
SELECT OrderDate, AVG(GrandTotal) AS AvgTotal
FROM getOrders
GROUP BY OrderDate
</cfquery>

<html>
<head>
        <title>Area graph</title>
</head>

<body>

<!---set the query of queries into a graph. ---->
<cfgraph type="line"
        fill="yes"
        graphwidth=400
        backgroundcolor="##CCCC00"
        depth=10
        linecolor="tan"
        query="avgOrders"
        valueColumn="AvgTotal"
        itemColumn="OrderDate"
        title="Average Order Total by Order Placement Year"
        >
        </cfgraph>

</body>
</html>
```

As you can see, this is a complex query. It is slow to load the first time and gets successively faster. The first time I load Listing 15.3, it executes in 931 milliseconds, which is pretty slow. We can forgive this lengthy load time because of the complexity of the query, the number of records returned, and the complexity involved in creating the graph. Also, we can justify retrieving a more complex record set than we initially need so that we can use the remaining data to create other graphs. However, we can still load this page much faster. We could cache the entire page, using the <CFCACHE> tag. However, this solution is not very flexible. Instead, we can use a new tag with ColdFusion 5, <CFSAVECONTENT>, to cache the graph creation process, and use the cached within attribute of the <CFQUERY> tag to cache the query. This allows us to refer to each item in a separate memory pool, which gives us greater flexibility. So let's take a quick detour to see how the relatively simple <CFSAVECONTENT> tag works, so we can start taking advantage of it.

Speeding Load Time with <CFSAVECONTENT>

<CFSAVECONTENT> is a new tag in ColdFusion 5. It saves the generated content of the code inside its body into a variable. It saves all results of the code inside its body, including evaluating expressions and executing custom tags. This tag has only one attribute, "variable." This attribute is required, and it specifies the name of the variable in which to save the generated content.

Let's put this to work on our complex query and graphing example from Listing 15.3. Remember that the first run of this listing executed in 931 milliseconds. All we have to do is wrap the <CFSAVECONTENT> tag around the graph and cache the query, and we will vastly improve the performance of this page. Remember that we need to throw in a little conditional logic to see if the <CFSAVECONTENT> tag has already run. Otherwise, we would resave the graph every time the page ran, which would defeat the purpose of setting it into memory.

<NOTE>

You can see how the tables in this query were created by referring to Chapter 21, "Creating a Complete E-Commerce Application."

Listing 15.4 Area3.cfm

```
<!---select data about orders------->

<!----cache query for two hours. use the
SQL CAST command to change the Orderdate value
       into a character data type. Because we cannot
       modify a cached query, we move this operation into
the database------->

<cfquery name="getOrders" datasource="CoreStore"
       cachedwithin="#CreateTimeSpan(0,2,0,0)#"

SELECT

O.orderconfirmation, O.CustomerID, O.SubTotal,
O.Shipping, O.Tax, O.GrandTotal,

"OrderDate"=RIGHT(CAST(O.OrderDate AS char(12)), 5),

O.Processed,

OP.ProductID, OP.Qty,

C.billFirstName, C.billLastName, C.billAddress,
C.billCity, C.billState,
C.billZipCode, C.billCountry,
C.billPhone, C.billEmail, C.shipFirstName,
C.shipLastName, C.shipAddress, C.shipCity,
C.shipState, C.shipZipCode, C.shipCountry,
C.shipPhone, C.shipEmail, C.shipMethod,
C.creditName, C.creditNumber, C.creditExpDate,

P.ProductName,
P.Price

FROM orders O

INNER JOIN OrdersProducts OP
       ON O.OrderConfirmation = OP.OrderConfirmation

INNER JOIN Customers C
       ON O.CustomerID = C.CustomerID

LEFT JOIN Products P
       ON OP.ProductID = P.ProductID

</cfquery>
```

```
<!---we no longer need the loop that recasts the data. We
do it in the SQL statement---->


<!---query previous query to get avg salary by start year--->
<cfquery name="avgOrders" dbtype="query">
SELECT OrderDate, AVG(GrandTotal) AS AvgTotal
FROM getOrders
GROUP BY OrderDate
</cfquery>

<html>
<head>
       <title>Area graph</title>
</head>

<body>

<!----if the variable "savGetOrders" is not defined, we have
       not loaded this page yet, so run the graph normally and
save the content of the graph into a variable------->

<!----normally you would want to put a cflock around any
       reference to variables in the application scope---->

<cfif NOT isDefined("application.savgetOrders")>
<cfsavecontent variable="application.savGetOrders">
<cfgraph type="line"
       fill="yes"
       graphwidth=400
       backgroundcolor="##CCCC00"
       depth=10
       linecolor="tan"
       query="avgOrders"
       valueColumn="AvgTotal"
       itemColumn="OrderDate"
       title="Average Order Total by Order Placement Year"
       >
       </cfgraph>
</cfsavecontent>
</cfif>
      <!---we've got the savecontent variable now, so simply
output the "saved" graph from server memory------->

      <cfoutput>#application.savGetOrders#</cfoutput>


</body>
</html>
```

You'll notice we've made a few changes to increase performance here. First, we remove the loop that cast the datetime datatype into character. That's because once we have cached the query, we cannot modify the values in that query. Therefore, we forget about the loop and use the SQL CAST function inside the SQL statement. In general, it is best to make data manipulation inside your SQL statement if possible. Databases are optimized for those sorts of operations, and your ColdFusion templates will execute faster. The second thing we do to increase performance here is cache the first query for two hours. Finally, we use <CFSAVECONTENT> to create a memory-resident copy of the <CFGRAPH>.

Our initial page load is slower, because of the conversion. However, every subsequent loading of the page is 0 ms. You can't really beat that for a few minutes work, considering the tremendous load this template places on the ColdFusion server and the dataserver (see Figure 15.4).

Figure 15.4 Using <CFSAVECONTENT> can increase your performance.

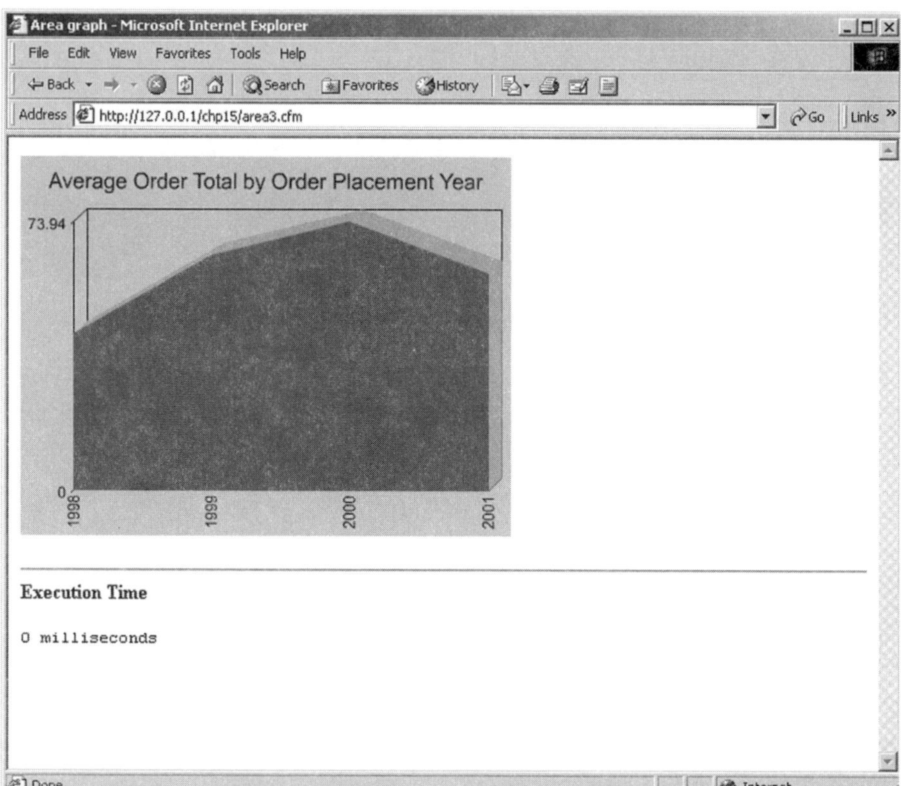

There are a number of questions to ask yourself when implementing caching and using the <CFSAVECONTENT> tag: How many unique page views do I expect for this page? How often does this data get modified? How recent do my users expect this data to be? Use the answers to these questions to determine where and how to implement performance tuning for your graphs and other ColdFusion actions.

That said, let's return to graphing and learn how to create data points and dynamic links.

Using <CFGRAPHDATA>

You can use the <CFGRAPHDATA> tag to specify a data point to be created by <CFGRAPH>. While you can use data from a query to populate a graph, there are many occasions when you might want specify values from other sources in the same graph. For instance, you might want to have a base query that retrieves records and then allows users to choose from a list of other items to view in the graph. <CFGRAPHDATA> allows you to do just that (see Table 15.6).

Table 15.6 <CFGRAPHDATA> Tag Attributes

Attribute	*Description*	*Value*
value	Required. Value that the data point represents.	Value
item	Optional. The item label for the data point.	A valid web 256 font
color	Optional. Color to use for the data point.	Web 256 color. The default is to use values from the <cfgraph> color list, if specified, or the built-in color list.
URL	Optional. A URL to load when the user clicks a data point. Works with Pie, Bar, and HorizontalBar charts only. The graph must be in the Flash file format.	URL to be loaded

Listing 15.5 shows you how to put it in action.

Listing 15.5 Use of <CFGRAPHDATA>

```
<body>

<!----say we're passed the "Shirt" param from a URL------->
<cfparam name="URL.Shirt" default= "49">

<!---prices and products from database ------->
<cfquery name="getPrices" datasource="corestore">

SELECT ProductName, Price
FROM Products
</cfquery>

<cfgraph type="Pie"
        fileformat="Flash"
        query="getPrices"
        valueColumn="Price"
        itemColumn="ProductName"
        title="Our Products Listed by price"
        TitleFont = "Arial"
        ShowLegend="Right"
        legendFont="Courier"
        colorList="Red, Brown, Green, ##336699, yellow"
        >

        <!----use cfgraph data to add hard-coded data or
                data from another source------->
<cfgraphdata item="Shirts"  value="#URL.Shirt#"
color="##00ffff">
<cfgraphdata item="Customers"  value="30">

</cfgraph>


</body>
```

Note that <CFGRAPHDATA> is a subtag of <CFGRAPH> and will work only when nested inside a <CFGRAPH> parent tag. In the next section we will look at how to make drill-down data graphs by applying dynamic hyperlinks to your graphs.

A Complete Data Drill-Down Graph Application

The new graphing engine allows you to create links from your graphs to create data drill-down applications. For instance, you could retrieve information about sales by department, and have each bar (data point) have a link to another page that shows more detailed information about that department.

In this example, we'll build on what we've learned so far and create a quick data drill-down application. This will display a graph that lists all of the orders in the database, and then create a link for each bar on the graph. When the user clicks the link, the detail query is run, and information about which products were sold in that particular order is displayed (Figure 15.5).

Figure 15.5 Clicking the dynamic URLs in the graph displays order detail information.

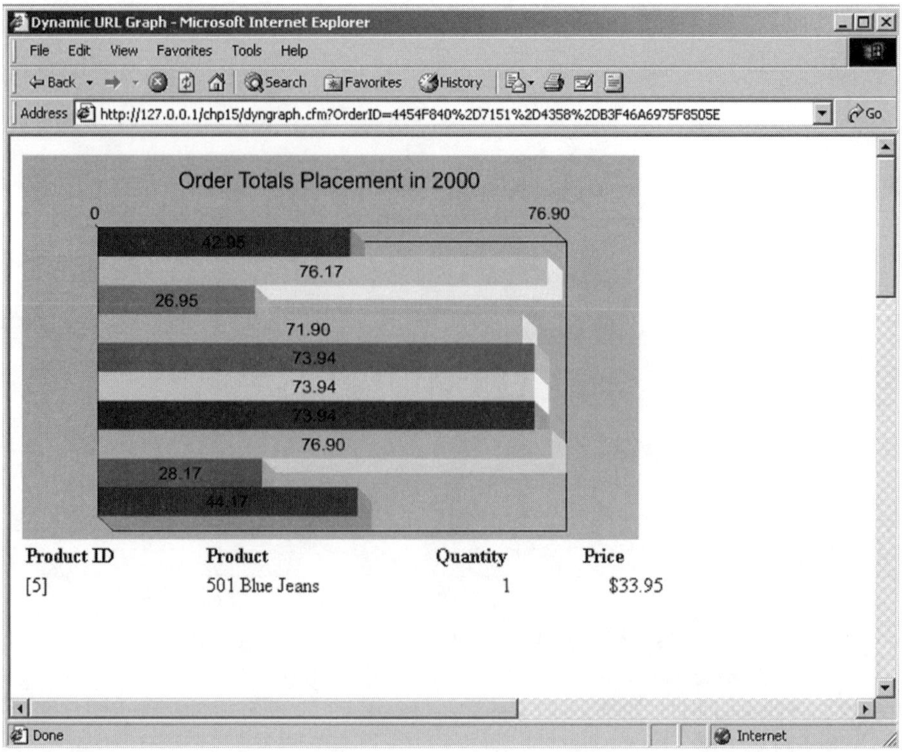

Listing 15.6 dynGraph.cfm

```
<cfset thisPage = cgi.Script_name>

<!---select data about orders------->
<cfquery name="getOrders" datasource="CoreStore">
SELECT GrandTotal, OrderConfirmation
FROM Orders
</cfquery>

<html>
<head>
	<title>Dynamic URL Graph</title>
</head>
<body>

<!---specify the URL attribute to pass the orderID so that
the user can see product info for a particular order--->

<cfgraph type="HorizontalBar"
	backgroundcolor="tan"
	depth=10
	query="getOrders"
	valueColumn="GrandTotal"
	title="Order Totals Placement in 2000"
	URL="#thisPage#?OrderID="
	URLColumn="OrderConfirmation"
	>
	</cfgraph>

	<!----self-post for details
		This will show the graph every time
		------->
<cfif isDefined("URL.OrderID")>

<!----get the details of the passed order ID, which
	is a datatype UUID (Universally Unique ID)------>

<cfquery name="getDetails" datasource="CoreStore">

select OP.OrderConfirmation, OP.ProductID, OP.Qty,
	P.ProductName, P.Price
from ordersproducts OP

inner join Products P
	on P.ProductID = OP.ProductID
```

```
where OrderConfirmation = '#URL.OrderID#'


</cfquery>

<cfif Len(getDetails.RecordCount) neq 0>

<!---output the detail information----->
<cfoutput>

<table width="80%">
<tr>
<td><b>Product ID</b></td>
<td><b>Product</b></td>
<td><b>Quantity</b></td>
<td><b>Price</b></td>
</tr>

<tr>
<td>[#getDetails.ProductID#]<br></td>

<td>#Trim(getDetails.ProductName)#<br></td>

<td align="center" valign="top">#getDetails.Qty#<br></td>

<td align="center" valign="top">#DollarFormat(getDe-
tails.Price)#<br></td>
</tr>

</table>
</cfoutput>

               <cfelse>
<br><br>
I'm sorry. I do not have any further information about that
order.

       <!-----end check for recordset length 0------->
       </cfif>

       <!----end check for is URL param defined------->
</cfif>

</body>
```

I hope that you find the new graphing engine fun and useful. These tags have so many different attributes that it can be daunting to use them at first. Also, some of the functionality is not entirely intuitive. For instance, I find it strange that you cannot pass parameters in the URL without unpredictable results: you have to use the URLColumn attribute to do the job right. It's a little bit to get used to. But once you do, you'll have a delightful time. I do urge you to carefully look at your data results as you start using these tags. ColdFusion will do everything in its power to output something to the browser. It is your job to make sure that the information you specify in your queries and the attributes of the tags is correct. And remember to use the new <CFSAVECONTENT> tag where possible to speed load time of your applications.

SENDING AND RECEIVING EMAIL WITH COLDFUSION

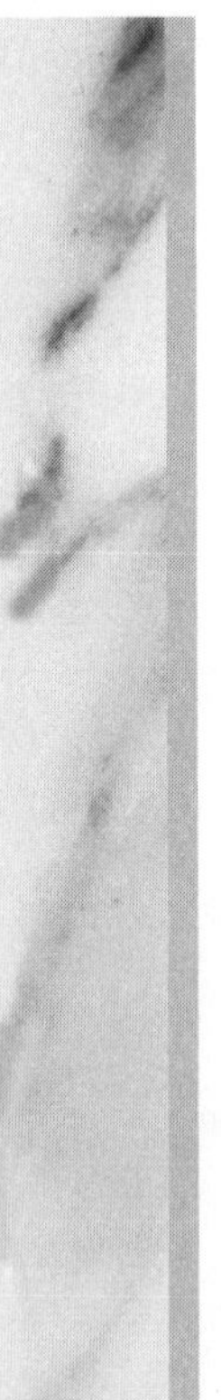

Topics in This Chapter

- Sending email from ColdFusion
- Sending the contents of a form via email
- Sending email from a query
- Sending attachments with <CFMAILPARAM>
- Sending HTML email

Chapter 16

If you are used to working with other development languages, you will be delighted to discover how easy it is to send and receive email through ColdFusion. This chapter will show you how to do so from an SMTP server.

Sending Email

In order to send email with ColdFusion, you use the <CFMAIL> tag. This tag allows you to easily send not only a regular email message, but also the contents of an HTML form via email. You can specify to send a plain text message or a fancier message with HTML embedded and images embedded in it. You can send and receive attachments of any MIME type. All you need in ColdFusion to create this core functionality is three tags: <CFMAIL>, <CFMAILPARAM>, and <CFPOP>. We'll examine all this here, and you'll come away with some good working examples that you can integrate into your websites.

ColdFusion does not ship with its own SMTP (Simple Mail Transfer Protocol) Server. You must have a valid email account already with an email provider. While you can use ColdFusion to interface with IMAP mail servers such as Microsoft Exchange, you do this via COM objects, which are not covered here. Consult the online documentation for more information, or take a look at www.cfcomet.com.

Before you can send email with ColdFusion, you must specify the name of a valid SMTP server, either with the "SERVER" attribute of the <CFMAIL> tag or in the ColdFusion Administrator. To do so in the Administrator, just login and click the Mail/Mail Logging link in the Server menu. In the Mail Server field, you may type the IP address or domain of your mail server.

Using the <CFMAIL> tag to send email is straightforward indeed. Its attributes are familiar from regular email clients; you will be sending email via ColdFusion in no time. Table 16.1 lists the attributes of the <CFMAIL> tag.

Table 16.1 <CFMAIL> Tag Attributes

Attribute	*Description*
to	Required. The name of the email message recipient(s). This can be either a static address, a variable that contains an address, or the name of a query column that contains address information. In the last case, one email is sent for each row returned by the query.
from	Required. The sender of the message. This attribute may either be static or dynamic.
cc	Optional. Carbon Copy indicates addresses to copy the email message to.
bcc	Optional. Blind Carbon Copy indicates message recipients without listing them in the header.
subject	Required. The subject of the email message. This field can be static or dynamic.
type	Optional. Specifies extended type of attributes for the message. The only valid value for this field is "HTML." This allows you to send a message with embedded HTML code in the message body, including images, links, colors, and fonts.
maxRows	Optional. Specifies the maximum number of email messages to send.
MIMEAttach	Optional. Specifies the path of the file to be attached to the message. The attached file is MIME-encoded.

Attribute	*Description*
Query	Optional. The name of the cfquery from which to retrieve data for messages. You can use this attribute to send email to multiple recipients, or to include query results in the body of an email.
group	Optional. Specifies the query column to use when you group sets of records together to send as an email message. The group attribute is case sensitive.
groupCaseSensitive	Optional. Boolean, indicating whether to group with regard to case or not. The default is YES. If the query attribute specifies a query object that was generated by a case-insensitive query, set this attribute to NO to keep the recordset intact.
startRow	Optional. Specifies the row in the query to start from.
Server	Required. The address of the SMTP server to use for sending messages. If none is provided, the mail server name specified in the ColdFusion Administrator is used.
port	The TCP/IP port number for your SMTP server (usually 25).
mailerID	Optional. Specifies a mailer ID to be passed in the X-Mailer SMTP header, which identifies the mailer application. (ColdFusion Application Server is the default.)
timeout	Optional. The number of seconds to wait before timing out the connection to the SMTP server.

Let us look now at how to send an email from ColdFusion.

Listing 16.1 Simple.cfm

```
<!---the email will be sent as soon as
                      this page is called----->

<!---the SMTP server has been specified in the ColdFusion
       Administrator in this form: Mail.Domain.Com------->

<cfmail to="eben@canyon.net"
              from="info@cybertrails.com"
              subject="This is a message from ColdFusion!"
              >
```

```
This is the content of the message. One must
be careful when sending mail from ColdFusion because
it is sensitive to tabs and spacing.

                                        Have fun!

                    </cfmail>

<!---output a status message to the browser------->

The message has been sent.
```

As you can see, it is a rather simple task to send mail from ColdFusion. Most of your job is simply specifying things you would have to specify sending mail from a regular email client such as Eudora or Outlook. However, there are a couple of important things to note. First, there is the matter of spacing. ColdFusion will honor the spacing and tabulation you specify between the opening and closing <CFMAIL> tags. Notice in Figure 16.1 that the words “Have fun!” are over to the right of the email message, exactly as written in Listing 16.1. You can use this to your advantage in making creative emails, but you must be aware of it as you send messages in a schedule. Sending mail with ColdFusion is fast, too—the above example clocks in at about 1/100 of a second.

Figure 16.1 An email message sent from ColdFusion.

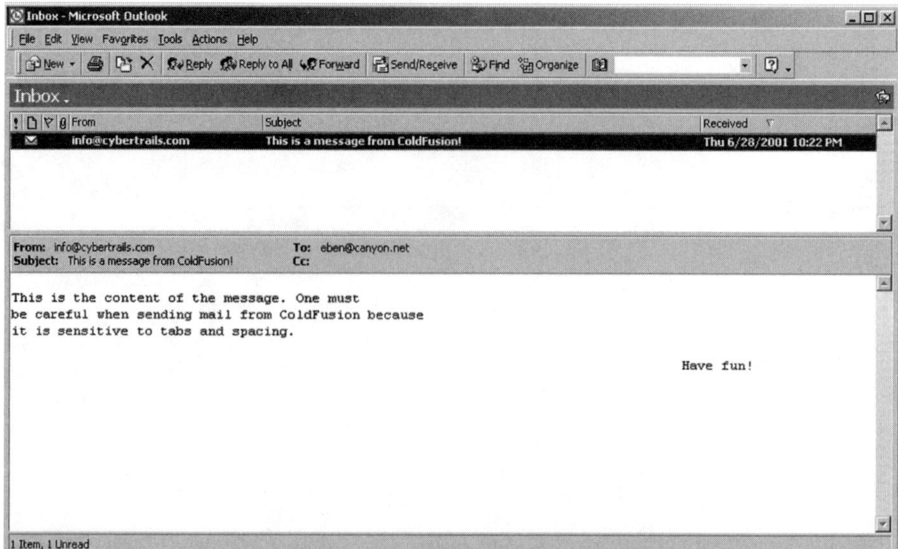

Sending Email from an HTML Form

It is often the case that you'll need to email newsletter subscribers, mail the contents of a form to a site administrator or support desk, or send an order confirmation to a user after a form has been filled out.

<NOTE>

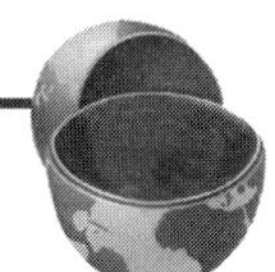

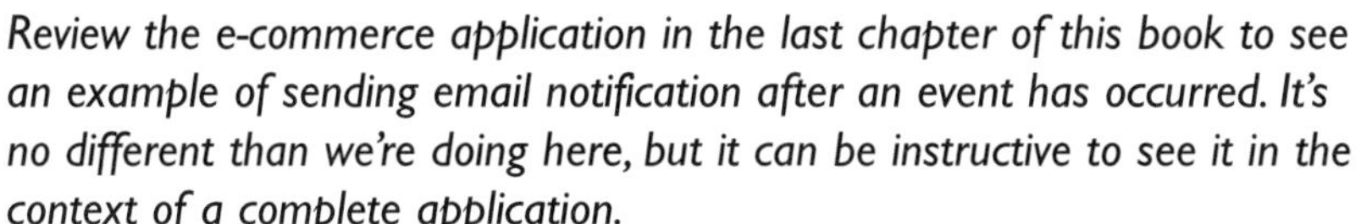

Review the e-commerce application in the last chapter of this book to see an example of sending email notification after an event has occurred. It's no different than we're doing here, but it can be instructive to see it in the context of a complete application.

Let's create a simple form to see how we send the contents by referencing the variables inside the body of the email. We don't need to use <CFOUTPUT> inside the message body, as it is assumed. If we create a simple feedback form, you can see how the results will look in Figure 16.2.

Listing 16.2 Sending Form Data via Email

```
<html>
<head>
        <title>Untitled</title>
</head>

<body>

<!---define thisPage for self-posting form------->

<cfset thisPage = cgi.script_name>

<cfif isDefined("FORM.Submit")>

<cfmail to="#FORM.Email#"
                    from="Ted@cybertrails.com"
                    subject="Thanks, #FORM.FirstName#!"
                    >
Thank you for filling out our form.

We hope you had a swell time at our site—we're sure you'll
hear even more about us from the #FORM.HowHeard#.
```

```
We're glad you like the "#FORM.FaveThing#"--it's just for you!

                        </cfmail>

<!----we've mailed a message to the user, but they need to see
          a confirmation too. We need a cfoutput since we're
          referencing form variables------->

          <cfoutput>
          Thank you for filling out our survey, #FORM.First-
Name#!
          <br>
          We appreciate your feedback.
          <br>
          </cfoutput>

<cfelse>
<!---form has not been submitted, so display it------->

<!---use cfoutput for the "thisPage" variable------->
<cfoutput>
<form action="#thisPage#" method="post">
How did you hear about our site? 
<select name="HowHeard">
<option name="News" value="newspaper"> Newspaper
<option name="News" value="radio"> Radio
<option name="News" value="little elf"> Little Elf
</select>
<br><br>
What is your favorite thing about our site?<br>
<input type="Radio" name="Favething" Value="Graphics"> Kewl
Graphics<br>
<input type="Radio" name="Favething" Value="CF"> Kewl CF<br>
<input type="Radio" name="Favething" Value="spell">
Innovative Spelling<br>
<input type="Radio" name="Favething" Value="cliche"> Lack of
Cliches<br>
<br><br>
What is your first name?<br>
<input type="text" size="25" maxlength="75"
name="FirstName">
<br>
<br>
What is your email address?<br>
<input type="text" size="25" maxlength="75" name="Email">
<br>
<input type="Submit" name="Submit">
```

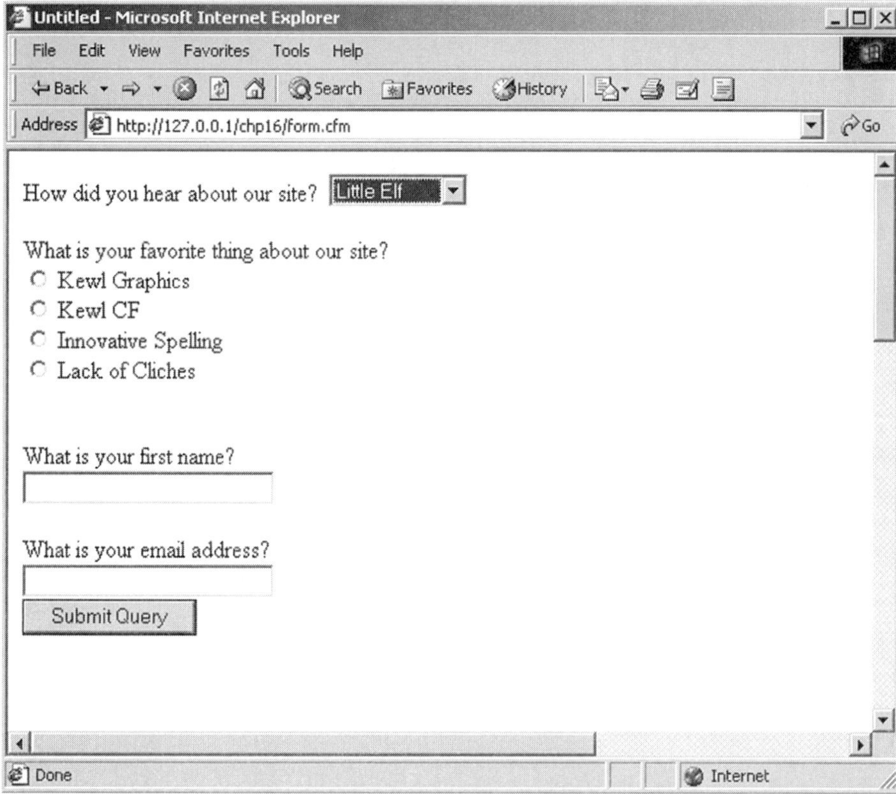

Figure 16.2 The form for users to fill out that will be submitted via email.

```
</form>
</cfoutput>
</cfif>
</body>
</html>
```

Below is what is displayed on the form action page once the user clicks the "Submit Query" button:

```
Thank you for filling out our survey, Jimmy!
We appreciate your feedback.
```

The FORM.FirstName variable is automatically evaluated, resulting, in this case, in "Jimmy." Figure 16.3 shows what is emailed to the user.

As you can see, it is easy to include dynamic variables in every part of an email sent via <CFMAIL>.

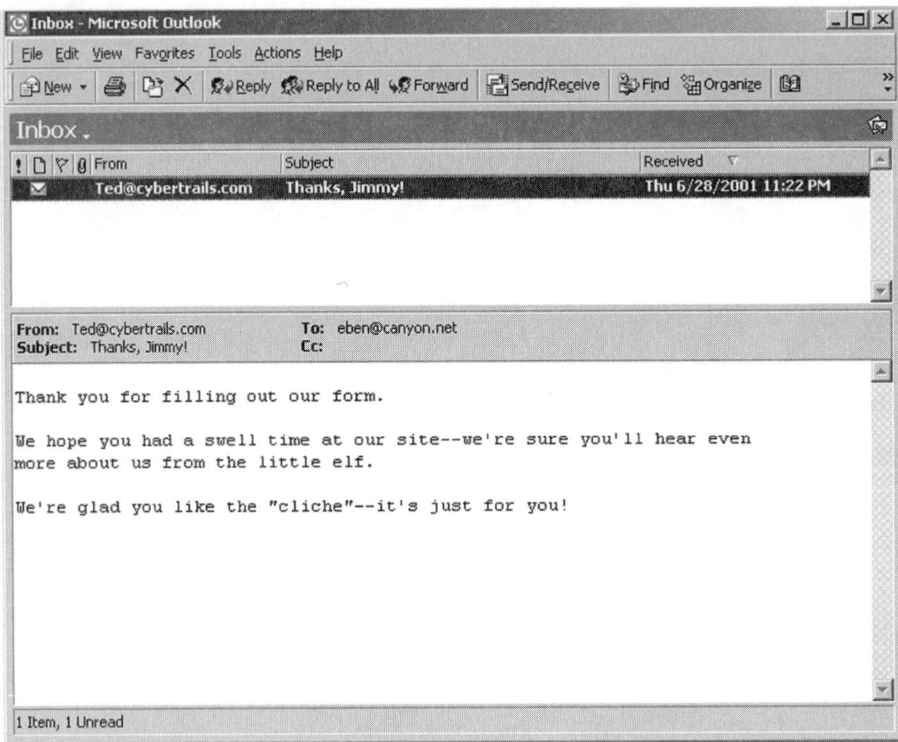

Figure 16.3 The email as sent to the user.

Next we will look at how to include the contents of a query in an email body, and how to send email to multiple recipients.

Sending Email from a Query

Often you'll want to send email to a list of recipients stored in a database, or to have the contents of a query output into the body of the email message. Below is an example of how you could make a form for users who have forgotten their login to your website. An embarrassing number of times I have been grateful for this feature at websites.

It's pretty straightforward: make a form that accepts an email address, and use that passed form variable to query the database and retrieve the password associated with that username. In this example, the username for the website is a valid email address. If you wanted to set it up otherwise, that would be short work.

Listing 16.3 Forgot.cfm

```
<!----User forgot password. Have them type their user name
and mail it to them.---->

<!---If form.username is defined, then process the form.---->
<cfif isDefined("FORM.Username")>


<!---Get the password associated with this query user--->

<cfquery datasource="DirectoryDB" name="GetPassword"
        dbtype="ODBC">

SELECT Username, Password, Firstname
FROM Users
WHERE Username = '#Username#'

</cfquery>

<!---Send the user the password via email--->
<cfmail query="GetPassword" from="Users at CyberTrails"
        to="#GetPassword.Username#"  maxrows="1"
        subject="Your password for Rutabagas.com.">
Someone (probably you) recently requested your password for
CyberTrails' premier rutabaga portal.

Here is your username: #GetPassword.Username#
Here is your password: #GetPassword.Password#

Thanks, from your number one information source on thick,
bulbous roots and livestock feed!
</cfmail>

<!----output the firstname we got from the query so we can
personalize the message------>
<cfset Request.FirstName = GetPassword.FirstName>

<!-----Let the user know the status--->
<!-----set all this as the message so we don't
                have to format a page------->
<cfoutput>
<font face="Verdana, Arial, Helvetica">
An email containing your password was sent to: <b>#Username#
</b>.
```

```
<br>Thanks, #Request.Firstname#!<br>
</font>
</cfoutput>

<!---They have not entered their username yet, so display
the form for them to do so.--->

<cfelse>
<cfoutput>
<font face="Verdana, Arial, Helvetica">
Type your current email address into the form below. You
will automatically<br>
be emailed your password. Your email address must match your
username for this site.<br>
</font>
<p>
<!----Form for user to enter their username. Processes
through this tag--->
<form action="forgot.cfm" method="post">
<tr>
<td align="right"><font face="Verdana, Arial, Helvetica"
size="3<f"Courier"z9.5>>Username:</font></td>
<td><input type="Text" name="Username" size="25"
value="me@somesite.com">
<br></td>
</tr>
<tr>
<td align="right"> </td>
<td><input type="Submit" value="Submit" align="right"></td>
      </tr>
</form>
</cfoutput>
</cfif>
```

Figure 16.4 shows the results. I have left debugging output on, so that you can see the statement that ColdFusion builds, and the form variables that get passed.

<NOTE>

Remember that you can turn on debugging output, which shows you passed form and CGI variables, as well as query information, in the ColdFusion Administrator. Just click on "Debugging Options." This is an invaluable tool for speeding your development. I just leave mine on all the time.

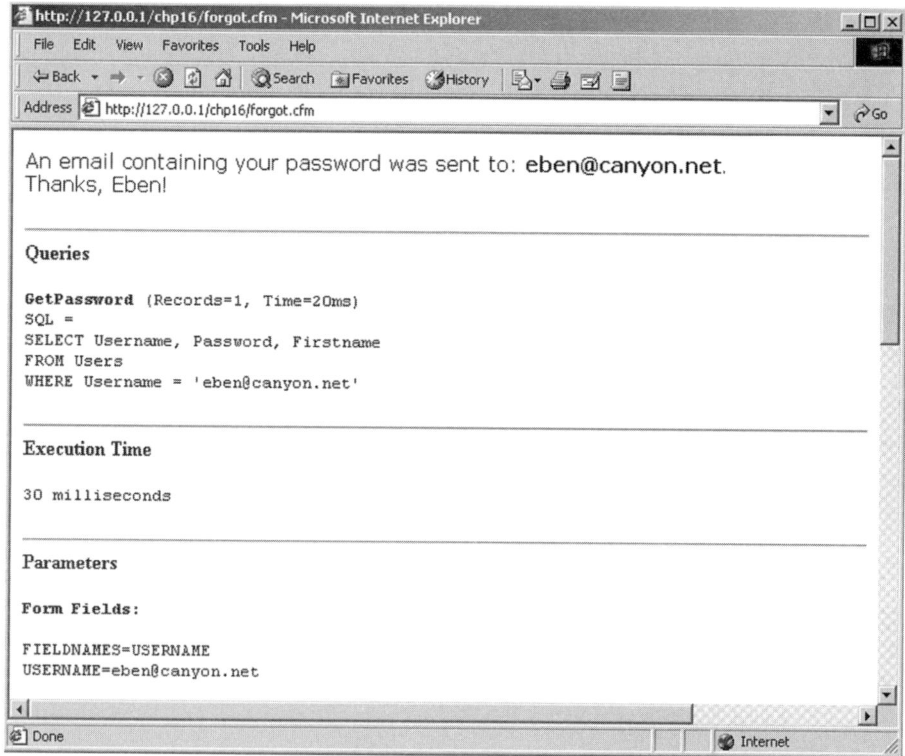
http://127.0.0.1/chp16/forgot.cfm - Microsoft Internet Explorer
File Edit View Favorites Tools Help
Address http://127.0.0.1/chp16/forgot.cfm
An email containing your password was sent to: eben@canyon.net.
Thanks, Eben!
Queries
GetPassword (Records=1, Time=20ms)
SQL =
SELECT Username, Password, Firstname
FROM Users
WHERE Username = 'eben@canyon.net'
Execution Time
30 milliseconds
Parameters
Form Fields:
FIELDNAMES=USERNAME
USERNAME=eben@canyon.net
Done
Internet

Figure 16.4 The email containing the user's password is sent, and a thank you page is displayed with debugging output.

Sending Attachments with Email

It is easy to send attachments with your email as well. The main thing you've got to do is create a regular HTML form and specify the TYPE attribute of the form tag as "File." This will automatically create a Browse feature that allows the user to navigate through the files on her local machine. Then you use the <CFMAILPARAM> tag to hold the attachment. <CFMAILPARAM> is a tag that you always nest inside a <CFMAIL> tag. All you need to do is specify a file to attach to the message in the "file" attribute. For instance, you could create a form that allows users to choose a file to attach to a message, specify the contents of the message, and send it off. This would be very useful for allowing business users to send weekly reports over a corporate website, or for creating a webmail client. By using ColdFusion to do this instead of a regular client, you could log all manner of information about the process, using

<CFLOG>, for instance. You could also use the code in Listing 16.4 to send a newsletter to users subscribed in a database.

Listing 16.4 Attach.cfm

```
<!---you would probably want to add form validation
       to make sure user entered info. Look into the
       <CFFORM> tags, such as CFINPUT, that do automatic
       JavaScript validation for you------->

<!---If form.username is defined, then process the form.---->
<cfif isDefined("FORM.Body")>

<!---Send the user the password via email Blind Copy yourself-
-->
<cfmail from="eben@Site.com" to="#FORM.To#"
bcc="eben@Site.com" subject="#FORM.Subject#">

       <!-----use conditional logic to test for the existence
of the attachment so that our app doesn't break if
none is specified------->

              <cfif IsDefined("FORM.MyAttachment")>
                     <cfmailparam file="#FORM.MyAttachment#">
              </cfif>
       <!------message body here------->
#FORM.Body#

Thank you,
Betty
</cfmail>


<!----log info that the mail was sent------->
<cflog date="YES" time="YES" file="ReportMailLog" text="Betty
sent the report.">

<!----Let the user know the status--->

<font face="Verdana, Arial, Helvetica">
Your message was sent to the following recipients:</font>
<br>
<cfoutput>#FORM.To#</cfoutput>
```

```
<!---Show the form----->
<cfelse>
<cfoutput>
<font face="Verdana, Arial, Helvetica">
Please select the appropriate parameters for your message.
</font>
<p>
<!----The form allows admin to choose multiple email recipi-
ents for the message---->
<form action="attach.cfm" method="post">
Recipients:
<br>
<!----you could pull these name and email values out of a
        database and loop over them to create a dynamic
        select------->
<select name="To" multiple>
<option name="Recipient" value="ted@site.com"> Teddy
<option name="Recipient" value="fred@site.com"> Freddy
<option name="Recipient" value="ed@site.com"> Eddie
<option name="Recipient" value="Joan@AnotherSite.com"> Joan
<option name="Recipient" value="Jane@ThirdSite.com"> Jane
</select>
<br>
<br>

<!---we'll use this for the subject of the email------->
Subject:
<input type="Text" name="Subject" size="25" value="Weekly
meeting">
<br>
<br>
<textarea name="Body" cols="40" rows="10" wrap="virtual">Type
your message text here.</textarea>
<br>
<br>

 <!---let user specify an attachment for the report------->
Attach Report:
<input type="File" name="MyAttachment">
<br>
<br>
<input type="Submit" value="Submit" align="right"></td>

 </form>
</cfoutput>
</cfif>
```

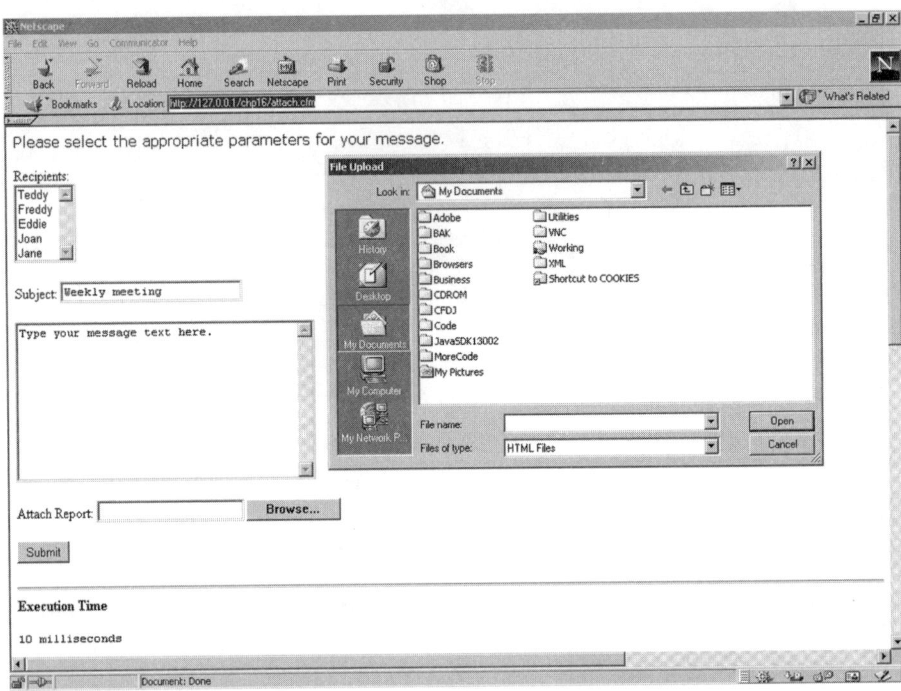

Figure 16.5 A form allowing a user to attach and send an email message to multiple recipients.

When we open Listing 16.4 in a browser, we see the form for us to fill out, and the user can click the browse button to browse her hard drive to attach a file. The user can specify the recipients for the select list, and type a subject and message body. When the user hits submit, the file is attached, the message is sent to all recipients in the list, and the transaction is logged in the Log directory as a text file called "ReportMailLog.log." Then the user is shown who the recipients of her message were. Also note that we use the BCC field here to blind copy the user. The form is shown in Figure 16.5.

For a good exercise, try pulling the recipient names out of a table in a database and using <CFOUTPUT> to populate the select box instead of having them hard coded.

<NOTE>

If you installed the example applications that ship with ColdFusion, you will find that a complete email client is one of them. The Crazy Cab application has been with ColdFusion for years and actually works quite well. Take a look at this application to see how a complete email client works. It includes limited attachment handling with the <CFCONTENT> tag, and *illustrates all of the concepts you need in order to understand <CFPOP>. <CFPOP> is the tag used for Post Office Protocol communications. If you decide to play around with it, try to add the ability to save messages to a database, and allow users to retrieve them at a later time.*

Sending HTML Email

ColdFusion allows you to easily put HTML code right into the body of your email message. All you need to do is set the TYPE attribute to HTML and put the code into your message. For instance, consider the code in Listing 16.5. Say we've got an application that allows users to sign a guestbook. We don't want to display any user entry on our site without its being approved first by a content administrator. So we can schedule a template to run that will pull all unapproved guestbook entries out of the database and output them into an HTML email that gets sent to the site content admin. This way, we can put dynamic links next to each entry: Clicking "Approve" *right in the email* launches a browser and go to another ColdFusion page that updates the "Approved" bit value in the database. It will automatically appear on the site. Alternatively, clicking the "Delete" link next to an entry will launch a browser and run the ColdFusion template at that URL, which just deletes the entry and returns a message to the admin like "The entry was deleted."

Listing 16.5 Guestbook Approver

```
<!----get the unapproved entries---->
<cfquery name="GetEntryForApproval" datasource="#datasource#">

        SELECT GuestEntryID, GuestEntryDate, GuestEntryText
        FROM Guestbook
        WHERE SiteID = #Request.App.SiteID#
                AND Approved = 0

</cfquery>

<!----Mail the CONTENT ADMIN proposed entries
        for approval. Email address of content admin
        is set in Application.cfm and copied into the
        Request scope.----->

<!---make sure to specify type="HTML"---->
```

```
<cfmail from="Guestbook at Your site"
        subject="A new Guestbook Entry Awaits your Approval"
        to="#Request.App.ContentAdmin#"
        type="HTML">

<!---the email has a ColdFusion loop, colors, a graphic, an
HTML table, fonts, and links: just about everything you can
do in a web page. --->

<img src="http://www.canyon.net/graphics/canyonlogo.gif">
<p>
<font face="Verdana, Arial, Helvetica" size="2">

<p>A new guestbook entry awaits your approval.</p>
<p>Click on the Entry ID to the <strong>left</strong> to
<strong>approve</strong> an entry.</p>

<p>Click on the Entry ID to the <strong>right</strong> to
<strong>delete</strong> an entry.</p>

<p>*Note that you may not see your new entry <I>immediately</
I> since the query is cached.</p>
</font>
<p>
      <table border="1" bordercolor="Gray" cols="4" cellpadd-
ing="3" cellspacing="3">
              <cfloop query="GetEntryforApproval">
              <tr><th>Approve</th><th>Entry Date</
th><th>Entry Text</th><th>Delete</th></tr>
              <tr>
<td>

<!---Request.App.SitePath is something like "http://
www.mysite.com/"----->
<a href="#Request.App.SitePath#index.cfm?Render=Guestbook_
EntryApprove&ItemID=#GetEntryforApproval.GuestEntryID#">
#GetEntryForApproval.GuestEntryID#
</a>

</td>

<!---show the date----->

<td>#DateFormat(GetEntryForApproval.GuestEntryDate)#</td>

<td>#GetEntryForApproval.GuestEntryText#</td><td>
```

```
<!---show link to delete---->
<a
href="#Request.App.SitePath#index.cfm?Render=Guestbook_EntryD
elete&ItemID=#GetEntryforApproval.GuestEntryID#">
#GetEntryForApproval.GuestEntryID#</a>
</td>
               </tr>
               </cfloop>
        </table>
</cfmail>
```

Figure 16.6 shows the results. Pretty catchy.

Figure 16.6 You can send email messages with embedded HTML from ColdFusion.

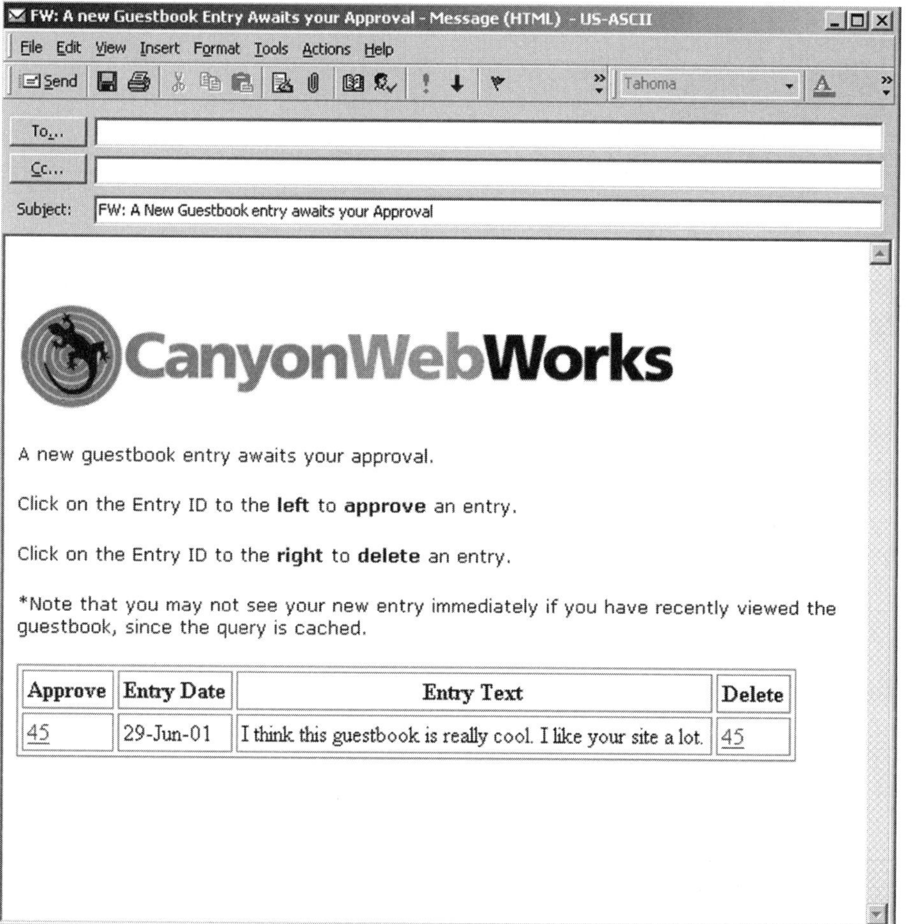

Conclusion

You can use the <CFPOP> tag to retrieve email messages from any POP server where you have a valid email account. Since ColdFusion ships with a complete webmail client in its example applications, I urge you to examine that code, written by the people who make ColdFusion, to see it in action. This chapter on <CFMAIL> should help you perform routine email tasks to help make your applications more interactive for your site administrators and users.

<NOTE>

Occasionally you will notice ColdFusion dropping email messages. This was common in version 4.0, that not all messages would be sent all the time. If this happens to you, look in the Cfusion\Mail directory, and in the ColdFusion Administrator log files. If messages have not been sent by ColdFusion, you can simply copy and paste the messages in the "UnDelivr" folder into the "Spool" folder. ColdFusion will check for messages in that folder every minute or so and try to send them again.

FILE AND DIRECTORY MANAGEMENT

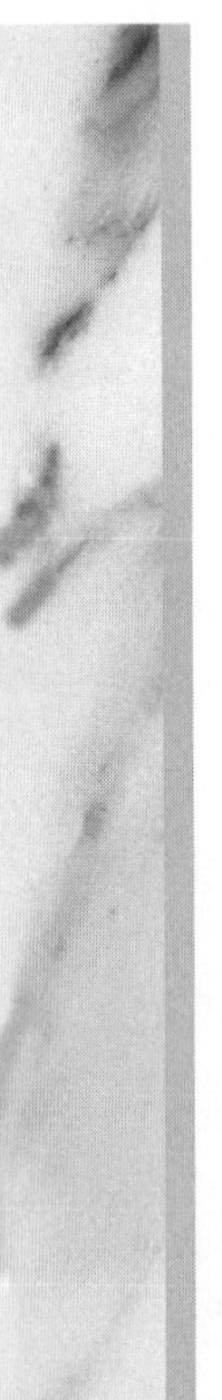

Topics in This Chapter

- Using <CFFILE>
- Uploading files
- Retrieving information about a file upload
- Reading a file
- Writing to a file and appending a file
- Copying, moving, and deleting a file
- Reading a directory file list
- Querying the directory object

Chapter 17

This chapter will introduce you to two new tags that make it easy to perform file and directory management operations.

The <CFFILE> tag lets you work with server files in myriad ways. You can read, write, delete, move, copy, rename, append, and upload files—all with this one tag. Its attributes are different, depending on what action you want to perform, so we will look at these actions one at a time.

The <CFDIRECTORY> tag allows you to retrieve file information from a specific directory and to create, delete, and rename directories.

<CFFILE> and <CFDIRECTORY> are two of the tags that can be disallowed in the ColdFusion Administrator. Because these tags give you the ability to create, move, and delete files and directories, they must be used with caution. It is potentially dangerous to your server to allow anonymous developers use of these tags. To disallow processing of these and other potentially dangerous tags, such as <CFREGISTRY> (which allows you to view and delete server registry keys), go to the ColdFusion Administrator, click "Security," and then click "Tag Restrictions." Uncheck boxes next to tags you want to turn off.

If a tag is turned off in the Administrator, ColdFusion will abort processing and throw an error any time it encounters one of them. If you have a shared hosting environment and want to allow these tags, you can configure Sandbox security to contain their use.

<CFFILE>

This is a complex tag with a great number of attributes. As with the <CFGRAPH> tag, the attributes are different, depending on what action you're performing. Actually the *Action* attribute defines not only what the tag will do and what the other attributes you may use in that instance of the tag are, but also what some of those attributes even mean. So we will work through a number of examples of how to take advantage of the rich operations this tag affords you, examining the different attributes along the way.

Uploading Files

This tag is probably most frequently used for uploading files to a directory on the Web server. This is a pretty straightforward process. Let's create a simple form that allows a user to browse for a file to upload, and then upload it (see Figure 17.1).

In order to use the <CFFILE> tag to upload files, you need to use a specific combination of attributes. These are shown in Table 17.1.

Figure 17.1 A simple form that accepts file names.

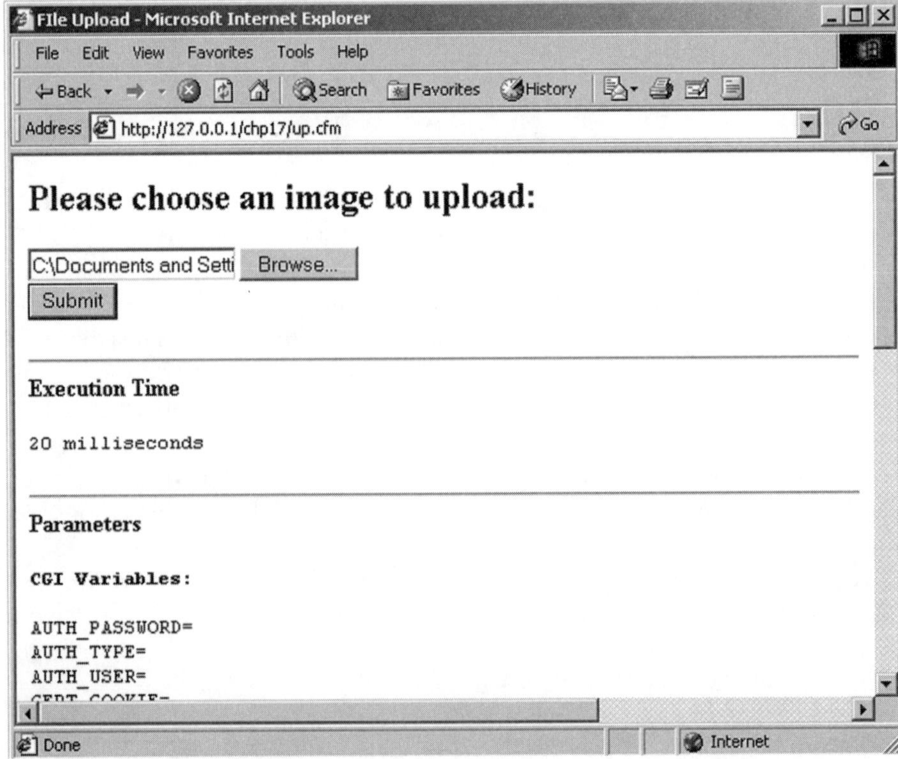

Table 17.1 <CFFILE> Tag Attributes When Action = "Upload"

Attribute	*Description*
FileField	Required. The name of the form field used to select the file. Do not use pound signs to specify the field name.
Destination	Required. The full path name of the destination directory or full path name of the file on the Web server where the file is saved. A trailing slash must follow the directory name. The target directory need not be under the web root.
NameConflict	Optional. Determines action to take if the file name conflicts with the name of a file already on the server directory. Possible values are: • Error. Default. File is not saved. ColdFusion aborts processing and returns an error. • Skip. Neither saves the file nor throws an error. • Overwrite. Replaces an existing file if it has the same name as the cffile destination file. • MakeUnique. Generates a unique file name for the upload. The name is stored in the file object variable ServerFile. You can use this variable to record the name used when the file was saved.
Accept	Optional. Allows you to limit the file types to accept. Possible values are any comma-delimited MIME type.
Mode	Optional. Defines permissions for an uploaded file on UNIX. Option values correspond with octal values of the UNIX chmod command.
Attributes	Optional. A comma-delimited list of file attributes to be set on the file being uploaded. Possible values are: • ReadOnly • Temporary • Archive • Hidden • System • Normal If the "Attributes" attribute is not specified in the tag, the file's attributes are maintained.

It is common that developers want to limit the kind of files they want to accept with a <CFFILE> upload. Therefore, here is a list of some of the MIME types you are likely to want to specify in the "Accept" attribute:

HTML	text/html
A plain text (.txt) file	text/plain
Microsoft Word	application/msword
Microsoft Excel	application/msexcel
.gif image	image/gif
.jpg image	image/jpg or image/pjpeg

You can find a more complete listing of MIME types at this website: http://www.ltsw.se/knbase/internet/mime.htp.

Having examined the attributes needed for uploading a file, let's make a form and an action page that upload a file. Listing 17.1 shows you how to do it.

Listing 17.1 Up.cfm

```
!DOCTYPE HTML PUBLIC "-//W3C//DTD HTML 4.0 Transitional//EN">
<html>
<head>
       <title>File Upload</title>
</head>

<body>
<!----create a self-posting form by checking for the
       existence of a form variable. If it doesn't exist,
       show the form. If it does exist, process the passed
       info. You could also make this two separate pages,
       a form and an action page.------->

<cfif isDefined("FORM.MyFile")>

<!----the local file name was passed, so upload it------>
<cffile action="UPLOAD"
       filefield="MyFile"
       destination="C:\CoreImages\"
       accept="image/*"
       nameConflict="MakeUnique"
                  >
```

```
        <!----note our use of the wildcard character (*)
                 to tell ColdFusion to any file as long as it
                 is some kind of image------>
        <br>

<!----use the automatically created CFFILE file status vari-
ables to show a different message depending on the success or
failure of the operation------>

        <cfif CFFILE.FileWasSaved is "YES">
                <h2>Your file was uploaded!</h2>
        <cfelse>
                <h2>The file was not saved. :(</h2>
        </cfif>

        <cfelse>
        <!----form variable was not passed yet, so show form.
                Make the action page the same name as this
                page to self-post------>

                <h2>Please choose an image to upload:</h2>

<form action="up.cfm" method="post"
                enctype="multipart/form-data">

<!---notice that we have specified the form attribute
"enctype", and that the input type="file" is used to allow
for automatic browsing abilities------->

        <input type="File" name="MyFile">
<br>
<input type="Submit" value="Submit">

</cfif>

</body>
</html>
```

I'll use this template to upload an image named "TheCanyonLogo.gif" to the C:\CoreImages directory. Figure 17.2 shows the results in the browser.

Notice the debugging output at the bottom of the screen, which shows us passed variables and other information. ColdFusion renamed the file and sent it to the TEMP directory before placing it in the proper directory with the proper name. The temp file is then removed.

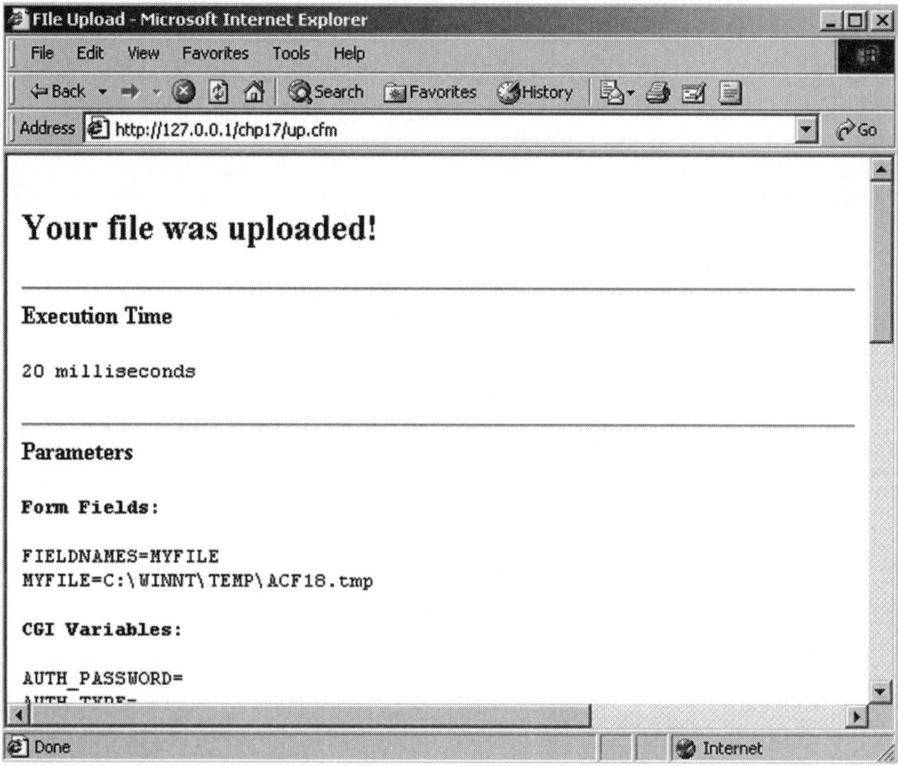

Figure 17.2 The file was uploaded to a directory on the ColdFusion server.

<NOTE>

As an aside, if you chose to install ColdFusion Application Manager, look in your Temp directory. ColdFusion will have placed an interesting file there called Install_CFAM.log. It contains a number of registry key settings that ColdFusion modifies and a complete list of files created in the installation process.

That's all there is too it. Be aware that certain versions of Internet Explorer on the Macintosh may need their default settings modified for uploading to work properly.

Retrieving Information about a File Upload

ColdFusion automatically creates several variables during the file upload process. They include information about the upload attempt, and the result of the operation. You can use these variables to output more complete information to your users, or in conditional logic to handle certain events. Table 17.2 lists the File Status variables and their descriptions.

Table 17.2 File Status Variables

Attribute	*Description*
AttemptedServerFile	Name of the file that ColdFusion initially attempted to save it as.
ClientDirectory	Client directory from which file was uploaded.
ClientFile	Full name of the source file on the client's system from which the file was uploaded, including the extension. For instance, SomeFile.gif.
ClientFileName	Name of the source file with no extension. For instance, SomeFile.
ClientFileExt	Extension of the source file without a dot. For instance, gif.
ContentSubType	MIME content subtype of the saved file. For instance, an uploaded gif image returns gif.
ContentType	MIME content type of the saved file. For instance, an uploaded gif image returns image/gif.
DateLastAccessed	Date that the uploaded file was last accessed.
FileExisted	Returns YES or NO depending on whether the file already existed on the server with the same path.
FileSize	Size of uploaded file.
FileWasAppended	Returns YES or NO whether ColdFusion appended the uploaded file to an existing file.
FileWasOverwritten	Returns YES or NO whether ColdFusion overwrote a file.
FileWasRenamed	Returns YES or NO whether ColdFusion renamed the file to avoid a naming conflict.
FileWasSaved	Returns YES or NO whether ColdFusion overwrote a file.

Table 17.2 Continued

Attribute	*Description*
OldFileSize	Size of the overwritten file. If no file was overwritten, this is an empty value.
ServerDirectory	Directory where the file was saved to on the server.
ServerFile	Full name of the file saved on the server with the file extension.
ServerFileName	Full name of the file saved on the server without the file extension.
ServerFileExt	The extension of the file saved on the server.
TimeCreated	Date and time the uploaded file was created.
TimeLastModified	Date and time of the last modification to the uploaded file.

As you can see, a good deal of information is available to us about the status of the file on the server in an upload operation. File Status variables are read-only, and they report only the most recent file upload operation results for your server. You reference these variables with a "CFFILE." prefix. While it is acceptable to reference the variables with "FILE.," this syntax is deprecated. You will likely come across it in code you inherit, however.

Renaming a File

In a production environment, you're probably going to want to add a little bit of functionality to your file upload application to make it complete. For instance, what happens when someone tries to upload a file with special characters in it? We should add a bit of handling for such an event to clean up the file name. Also, let's say that we're using CFFILE in a business application. It would be polite to return some information about the file upload. We'll learn now how to do this and make our upload into something more like a real application than just an example.

Let us improve our upload application a bit by reporting file status information back to the user. Also, let's use the `ListReplace()` function to clean up the file name in case it contains special characters that might make it difficult to work with. Then we'll use the <CFFILE> tag with the RENAME action to rename the uploaded file using the new, cleaned-up file name.

Here are the attributes you use to rename a file:

```
<CFFILE Action="RENAME"
        Source="C:\MyDocuments\DEVELOPMENT\OldFile.html"
        Destination="C:\MyDocuments\PRODUCTION\NewFile.html">
```

<NOTE>

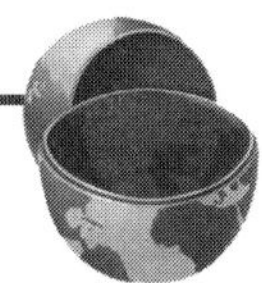

To save space, we won't list in detail all of the different attributes of the CFFILE tag when different actions are specified. You can refer to Appendix A, "ColdFusion Tag Reference," to see them all.

We can use both the RENAME and the UPLOAD actions in different CFFILE calls to perform the sort of application clean-up referred to earlier. Say we've got a file named "TheC@nyonLogo.gif." Listing 17.2 will upload the file to the server and replace any special characters, such as the @ sign, with an empty string. Then it will output information about the process to the user.

Listing 17.2 ImprovedUp.cfm

```
<!DOCTYPE HTML PUBLIC "-//W3C//DTD HTML 4.0 Transitional//EN">

<html>
<head>
        <title>File Upload</title>
</head>

<body>

<cfif isDefined("FORM.MyFile")>

<!----the local file name was passed, so upload it------->
<cffile action="UPLOAD"
        filefield="MyFile"
        destination="C:\CoreImages\"
        accept="image/*"
        nameConflict="Overwrite"
        >

        <cfif CFFILE.FileWasSaved is "YES">

<!----set variables to work with for renaming---->
                <cfset thisFile=CFFILE.serverfile>
                <cfset thisDirectory=CFFILE.serverdirectory>
```

```
        <!---Rename the file without special characters or
spaces---->

        <cfset newName=ReplaceList("#thisFile#",
                                " ,!,&,%,\,/,^,@,*","-")>

                <!----use dynamically set attribute values
for renaming the file using CFFILE------->

        <cffile action="RENAME"
                source="#thisDirectory#/#thisFile#"
                destination="#thisDirectory#/#NewName#">

<h2>Your file was uploaded!</h2>

                Below is information about the upload process:
                <br>

<!----you must use cfoutput as with any other variable----->
                <cfoutput>
                Originating client directory: <b>#CFFILE.Cli-
entDirectory#</b>
                <br>
                Original client file: <b>#CFFILE.ClientFile#</
b>
                <br>
                <br>
                What is the NEW file name? <b>#NewName#</b>
                <br>
                What is the NEW Directory name?
<b>#CFFILE.ServerDirectory#</b>
                <br>
                Date and Time Modified: <b>#CFFILE.timeLast-
Modified#</b>
                <br>

        <!----CFFILE.FileSize outputs the size in bytes. We
can do a bit of hocus-pocus to get the size in KB------>

        <cfset thisSize = CFFILE.FileSize / 1024 & " K">
                Uploaded File Size: <b>#thisSize#</b>

<br>
                </cfoutput>

        <cfelse>
                <h2>The file,
```

```
        <cfoutput>#cffile.attemptedServerFile#</cfoutput>
                was not saved. :(
</h2>

        </cfif>


        <!----form variable was not passed yet, so show form.
                Make the action page the same name as this
                page to self-post------->
        <cfelse>

                <h2>Please choose an image to upload:</h2>

<!----remember you must use MULTIPART/FORM-DATA
                                or it won't work------->

<form action="ImprovedUp.cfm"
                method="post" enctype="multipart/form-data">

        <input type="File" name="MyFile">
<br>
<input type="Submit" value="Submit">
</form>

</cfif>

</body>
</html>
```

This kind of functionality is great if you have anonymous users uploading files to your site and you cannot ensure that they have named their files according to your conventions. Figure 17.3 shows the result of running the code in Listing 17.2.

Deleting, Moving, and Copying Files

Deleting, moving, and copying files are very simple forms of the CFFILE tag that require few attributes. We'll look at those quickly.

To Delete a File

```
<cffile action = "Delete"
        file="C:\MyDocuments\SomeFileName.doc">
```

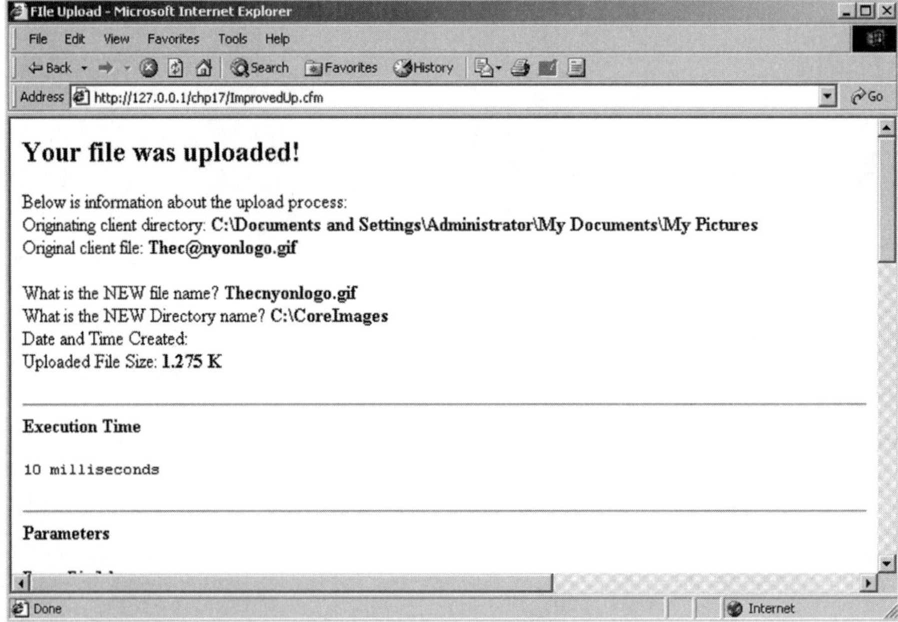

Figure 17.3 The CFFILE operation automatically creates several variables.

To Copy a File

```
<cffile action="Copy"
        source="C:\MyDocuments\CurrentBudget.xls"
        destination = "Z:\Backups\CurrentBudget.xls">
```

To Move a File

```
<cffile action="Move"
        source="C:\MyDocuments\CurrentBudget.xls"
        destination = "Z:\Backups\JulyBudget.xls">
```

Now, let's look at other key uses of the CFFILE tag.

Reading a File

You can read an entire file into a local variable using CFFILE Action="Read." This is a simple way to make files available for processing in your templates. Here's how you do it:

```
<cffile action="read"
        file="#FORM.FileName"
        variable="MyVariableName">

<cfoutput>#MyVariableName#</cfoutput>
```

There are a number of uses for this. Typically, people use the <CFFILE> tag with a READ action to view log files in a browser. You could also read a file, parse its contents using regular expressions, and send it into a database. Or you could create a plain text licensing agreement for something sold at a website, output the file variable into a <textarea> of an HTML form, and then allow users to click "Accept" or "Do Not Accept" on the form to proceed.

You can also read binary objects using Action="ReadBinary."

Writing a File

You can use CFFILE to write a plain text or static HTML file. The file will be created if it doesn't exist. You use the following attributes to do so:

```
<cffile action="Write"
        file="C:\Logs\MyLog.txt"
        output: Page accessed on "#CreateTimeSpan(Now())#"
by
        #SESSION.UserID#>
```

Now that you are familiar with the sorts of things you can accomplish using the <CFFILE> tag, let us turn to a related tag, <CFDIRECTORY>.

<CFDIRECTORY>

This tag lets you get file information from a specified directory. You can also create, rename, and delete directories. Let's create a simple example that gets directory information and outputs the values of all the variables available to us.

Listing 17.3 DirList.cfm

```
<h2>Please choose a directory:</h2>

<!---form to choose directory------->
<form action="DirList.cfm" method="post">
<input type="Text" name="MyDir" size="75"
```

```
        value="C:\Documents and Settings\Administrator\
        My Doc-uments\">
<br>
<input type="Submit" value="Submit">
</form>

<BR><BR>
<!---get directory info ------->
<cfif isDefined("FORM.MyDir")>

<cfdirectory
        directory = "#FORM.MyDir#"
        name = "MyDir"
        sort="size ASC, name DESC, datelastmodified">

<!----because <CFDIRECTORY> returns a query object, you use
        the query attribute to output using the name
        value of the CFDIRECTORY tag. Don't the values
        for the "sort" attribute look weirdly like SQL
        ORDER BY statements? ---->

<h2>Here is your info:</h2>
<cfoutput query="MyDir">
Name: <b>#MyDir.NAME#</b><br>
Size: <b>#MyDir.SIZE#</b><br>
Type: <b>#MyDir.Type#</b><br>
Last Modified: <b>#MyDir.datelastModified#</b><br>
Attributes: <b>#MyDir.name#</b><br>
</cfoutput>

<!---in UNIX, you can specify the MODE column instead
        of ATTRIBUTES. If you accidentally use MODE on
        Windows, you won't get an error, it will just
        be empty------->

</cfif>
</body>
</html>
```

Figure 17.4 shows the outputs. What you probably notice is that the first two entries aren't files in the MyPictures directory—they are directory information. The "." represents the current directory and the ".." the parent directory. The two lines are always returned at the beginning of a query object. In order to skip these in the output so that we have more predictable behavior, let's query the object.

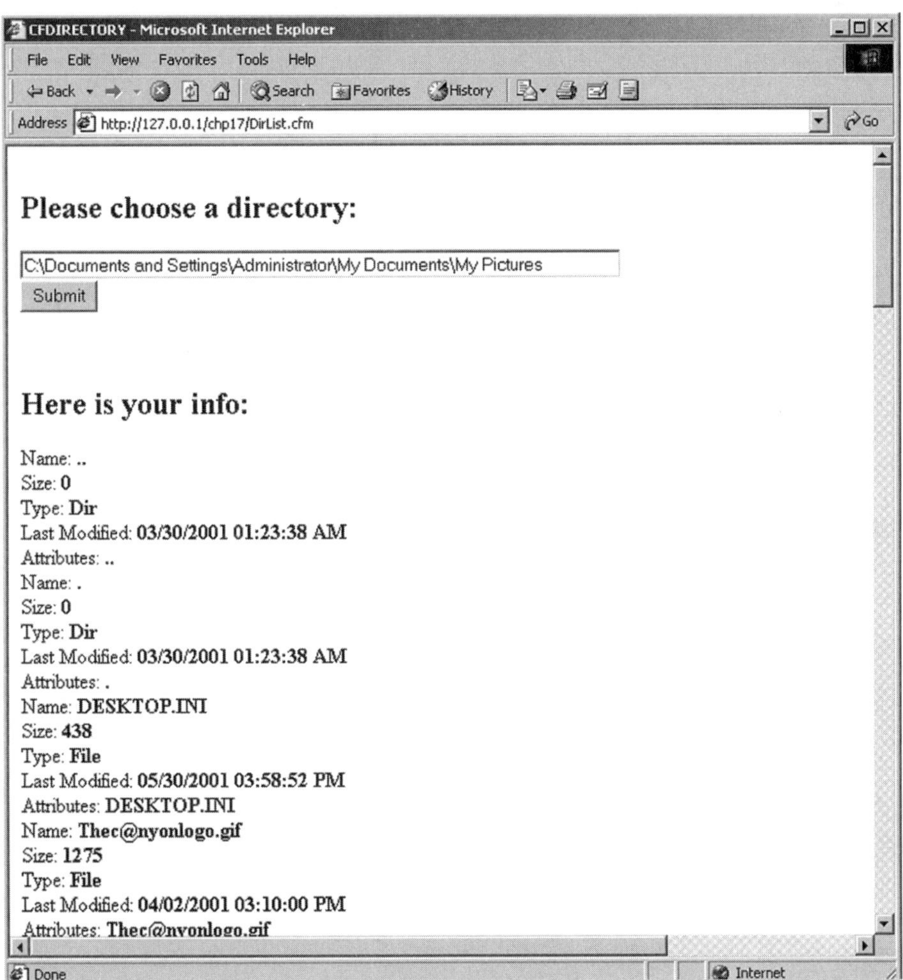

Figure 17.4 The directory listing output.

Querying the Directory Object

The <CFDIRECTORY> operation returns a query object, and with the new query-of-queries capability with ColdFusion 5, you can reference and manipulate information returned from CFDIRECTORY operations as if the CFDIRECTORY were a query to a database. This allows you to do more than sort and filter data. You can use such query variables as RecordCount, and such CFQUERY attributes as "CachedWithin."

Listing 17.4 DirList.cfm

```
<html>
<head>
        <title>CFDIRECTORY</title>
</head>
<body>
<br>
<h2>Please choose a directory:</h2>

<!---form to choose directory------->
<form action="DirList.cfm" method="post">

        <input type="Text" name="MyDir" size="75"
                value="C:\Documents and Settings\
                Administrator\My Documents\">
<br>
<input type="Submit" value="Submit">
</form>

<BR><BR>
<!---get directory info ------->
<cfif isDefined("FORM.MyDir")>

<cfdirectory
        directory = "#FORM.MyDir#"
        name = "MyDir"
        sort="size ASC, name DESC, datelastmodified">

<!---query the dir object
        Retrieve only files that start with "fav_",
        which are our favorites------->
<cfset thedate = "getdate()">
<cfquery dbtype="query" name="qDir">
SELECT *
FROM MyDir
WHERE name like 'fav_%'
</cfquery>

<!---use RECORDCOUNT variable------->
<h2>Your query returned <cfoutput>#qDir.RecordCount#</
cfoutput> records:</h2>

<cfoutput query="qDir">
<!---use startrow attribute to skip the dots------->
Name: <b>#qDir.NAME#</b><br>
Size: <b>#qDir.SIZE#</b><br>
Type: <b>#qDir.Type#</b><br>
```

```
Last Modified: <b>#qDir.datelastModified#</b><br>
Attributes: <b>#qDir.name#</b><br>
</cfoutput>

<!---in UNIX, you can specify the MODE column instead
       of ATTRIBUTES. If you accidentally use MODE on Windows,
       you won't get an error, it will just be empty------->

</cfif>
</body>
</html>
```

Figure 17.5 shows our output.

Figure 17.5 The directory listing output.

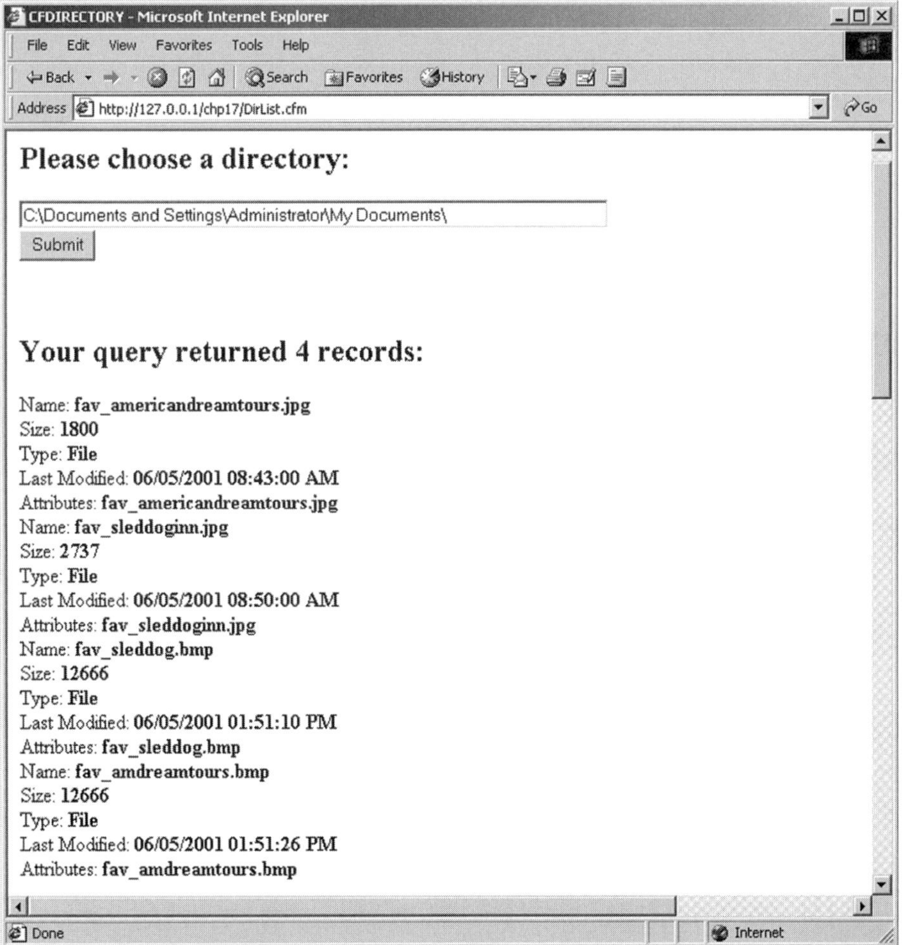

Note that you can use two functions as you work with directories: DirectoryExists() and GetDirectoryFromPath(), which extracts the directory with a backslash from a fully specified path. Remember, too, that you can turn off the CFDIRECTORY tag in the ColdFusion Administrator.

WRITING CUSTOM TAGS

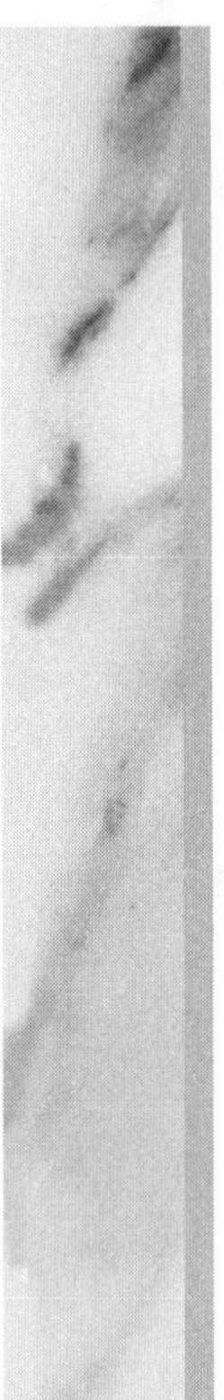

Topics in This Chapter

- Introduction to custom tags
- Creating a simple custom tag
- Attributes and the caller scope
- Calling and storing custom tags
- ThisTag scope and paired custom tags
- Child and parent tags and <CFASSOCIATE>
- Utilities and applications in custom tags

Chapter 18

Custom tags are a fabulous feature of ColdFusion. You may be used to writing custom functions in PHP or custom tags in JSP. ColdFusion custom tags are very similar. They allow you to encapsulate functionality and simplify the reuse of code. They are ColdFusion tags that you write yourself to extend the language and modularize your code. It is easy to get started writing them. In this chapter we will discuss everything you need to know about custom tags to start writing them yourself. This is going to be really fun.

There are a lot of reasons to write custom tags. Generally, they fall into two categories: utility tags and application tags. A utility tag performs some small function that helps you get along in creating applications. For instance, you might write a custom tag that sorts a three-dimensional array or sends form variables into URL variables. Application tags encapsulate entire applications within one tag. For instance, there are a number of custom tag calendars, guestbooks, and the like. You can download from the Developer's Exchange a custom tag called <CF_Classifieds> that is a complete Classified Ads application. It is free and open source and all.

But the distinction between utility and application tags is sort of arbitrary, too. I'm just trying to give you a sense of when you might want to make a custom tag; ColdFusion doesn't care how we classify them.

<TIP>

Before writing a custom tag, check in the Developer's Exchange to see if someone has already written a tag that does what you're looking for. The ColdFusion community is exceptionally generous, and you may not have to write it yourself if someone else already has. Also, as you're learning ColdFusion, it's hard to keep all of the tags and functions in the language in your head at once: ColdFusion itself might have what you need already. Since I don't seem to be above telling marginally embarrassing stories about myself, I once spent four hours writing a custom tag 50 lines long to do something that can be done natively in ColdFusion in one <CFSET> statement. Check around before you expend the energy and time.

So throughout this chapter we will explore how to write simple and complex custom tags, and we'll pick up a few new ColdFusion tags along the way. First let's look at a few of the advantages and disadvantages in using custom tags in your applications.

Advantages of Custom Tags

- Can be easily reused
- Encapsulate complex processing to keep your code easy to maintain and read
- Can be used simultaneously in multiple applications on a server
- Help make your applications flexible
- Help keep your code organized and streamlined
- Can be encrypted to protect or hide your work

Disadvantages of Custom Tags

- Can be very complex to write
- Load somewhat slower than "regular" code

Let's just dive in and make a simple custom tag. It's really too fun to put off longer.

Creating a Simple Custom Tag

You write custom tags when you've looked around and haven't found the functionality you need for your application. To write a custom tag, you write regular ColdFusion code and save your template normally. You then call the template as a custom tag by prefixing "CF_" to the name of the template. To demonstrate, let's write some text into a file, save it as a .cfm template, and call it as a custom tag.

Listing 18.1 A Simple Custom Tag

```
<h3>Hello! I'm your custom tag!</h3>
```

That's all the code—no <html> or <body> tags or like that. And, for now, no ColdFusion. Save this template as "HelloWorld.cfm." That way we can reference it as <CF_HelloWorld> to call it from another template. Note that custom tag names are, like most things in ColdFusion in Windows, case insensitive.

<NOTE>

In UNIX, custom tag names must be lowercase.

Listing 18.2 The Page That Calls the Custom Tag

```
<html>
<head>
        <title>Caller</title>
</head>
<body>
<h2>
I am the page that calls the custom tag, "caller.cfm"
</h2>

<!---call the custom tag, "CF_HelloWorld"------->
<cf_HelloWorld>

</body>
</html>
```

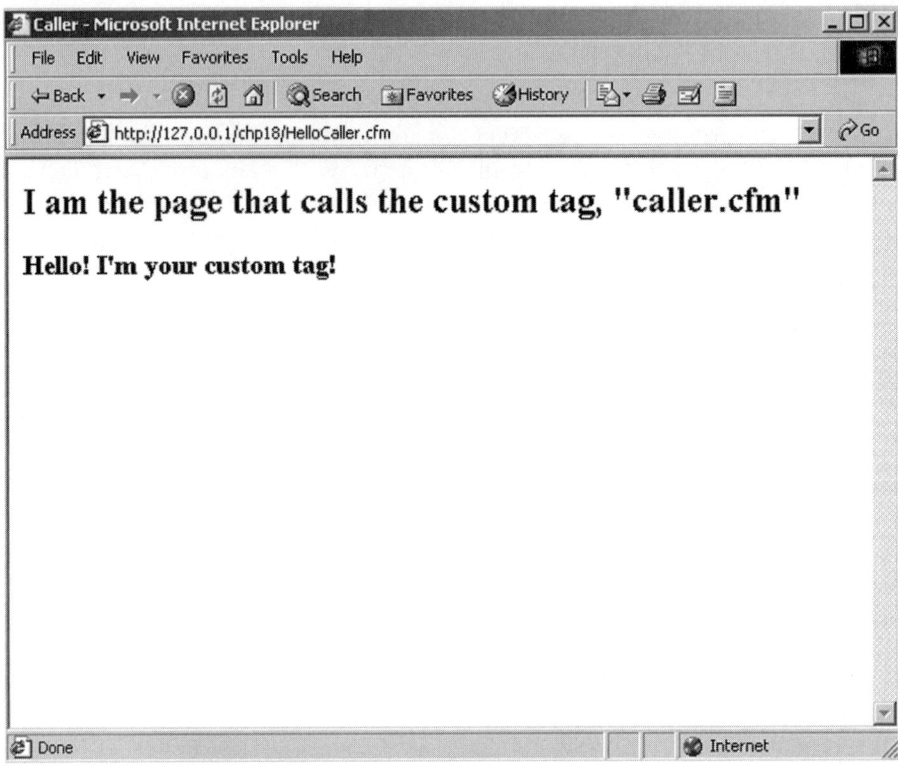

Figure 18.1 The called custom tag.

Listing 18.2 shows how to call the custom tag, and Figure 18.1 shows the result.

Where to Put Custom Tags

When you write code into a template and save it with a .cfm extension, you can call it as a custom tag. However, you have only three options of where to store a custom tag. You can store it in the same directory that it is called from. However, this becomes problematic if you want to share the tag between applications or even between different directories in the same application. Another option is to store all your custom tags in the CFusion CustomTags directory, or a subdirectory of that directory. With ColdFusion 5 you can specify other directories in which to store shared tags. You do this in the ColdFusion Administrator by following the Custom Tag Paths link on the Extensions menu. In this screen you will see the paths that you have assigned for custom tags, and you can specify new folders in which you would like to

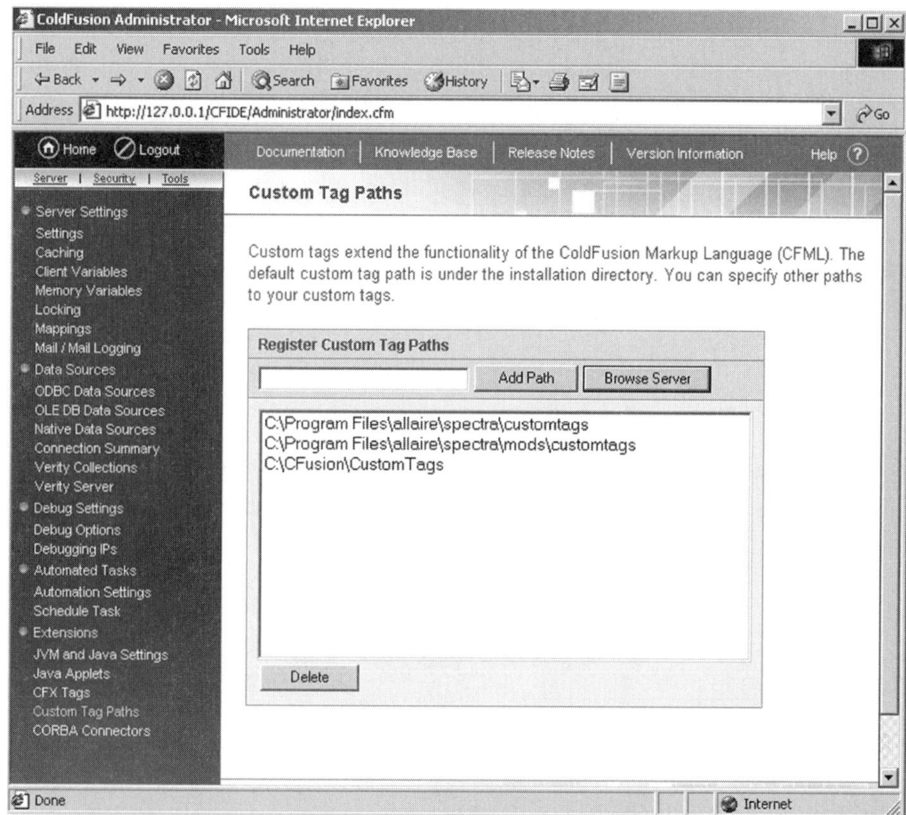

Figure 18.2 Custom tag paths in the administrator.

store custom tags. This is a convenience of ColdFusion 5. Before this release, one could specify custom tag paths other than the default only by editing the registry directly. Figure 18.2 shows three paths: the third is the default, and the first two are custom paths installed by Macromedia Spectra (which is made up of about 450 custom tags).

You can browse the server to register new custom tag paths.

Passing Values into and out of Custom Tags

Using a custom tag is not the same as using <CFINCLUDE>. It may look that way from the <CF_HelloWorld> tag, because it just prints the text on the page. Any text (not code) that you've got inside a custom tag will be output somewhere on the calling page unless you account for it. We began with such a simple example because custom tags act as a "black box"—you must be very specific about how you get information into and out of them.

Variables are *not* automatically shared between calling pages and custom tags. If this were the case, you would be in constant danger of overwriting variables or data. So custom tags are protected. You get data into them by specifying *attributes.* You get data out of them by using the *Caller* scope. We will examine each of these in turn.

Attributes

In general, tags have attributes. The <CFQUERY> tag has an attribute called "Datasource," with which you can tell the query where to look for data. The HTML anchor tag, which makes a link, has an "href" attribute that specifies the precise location of the resource to link to. On the other hand, the HTML <br> tag takes no attributes; there's no way to modify or be more specific about a break. It's just a break. ColdFusion custom tags are just like that. They can take attributes or not. And in order to pass data into a custom tag, you need to specify its attributes.

In order to create attributes for your custom tags, you have to do a few things. First, you have to determine what attributes you'll really need. Ask yourself what in the tag stays the same, and what is different each time it's called. If something could be different, it is a good candidate for an attribute. If you're creating a tag that displays something, do you need a "width" attribute, or a font face? Once you have determined what you'll need, you need to pass attributes into the tag, and your tag needs to accept them.

You pass attributes into custom tags exactly as you do with any other tag. The attribute values can be static or dynamic—like this:

```
<CF_MakeTable
        caption = "#FORM.TableName#"
        width = "300"
        height = "100">
```

The custom tag needs to accept these passed values as attributes. Generally one does this inside the tag using <CFPARAM>. By specifying a value for the "Default" attribute of <CFPARAM>, you can make an attribute of your custom tag optional. Even if no value is passed to the tag, you could still perform conditional processing based on the default action. Listing 18.3 illustrates this. We'll create a custom tag called "<CF_Att>," which accepts one attribute, Action. The tag will produce a different result based on the action specified.

Listing 18.3 Att.cfm

```
<cfparam name="attributes.action" default="normal">

<cfif attributes.Action is "Big">
        <h1>Your action is display big</h1>

<cfelseif attributes.Action is "normal">
        Your action is display normal.

<cfelse>
        You want to do something else.

</cfif>
```

Create a page that calls this custom tag. Try specifying different values for the attribute.

The Caller Scope

A special scope is reserved for use within custom tags called the caller scope. We aren't really returning data from the custom tag here; the browser is displaying the HTML and text it encounters within the conditional processing. Let's modify the tag to actually do some work. We will set a regular local variable inside it. I've saved this tag as "Att2.cfm" this time.

```
<!---call the tag which sets local variable
        "FavoriteColor"------->
<cf_att2 action = "big">

<!---output the value------->
<cfoutput>#FavoriteColor#</cfoutput>
```

The modified tag, which sets a variable, is shown in Listing 18.4.

Listing 18.4 Improperly Scoped Return Variable

```
<cfparam name="attributes.Action" default="normal">

<cfif attributes.Action is "Big">
```

```
<!---set a local variable inside the tag------->
      <cfset FavoriteColor = "Red">

      <cfelseif attributes.Action is "normal">
      Your action is display normal.

      <cfelse>
      You want to do something else.

</cfif>
```

ColdFusion throws an error saying it can't determine the value of the variable "FavoriteColor" when you run this code. That's because the custom tag is protected so that you don't overwrite variables in either the tag or the caller. You can hang around writing variables all day; if you don't specifically send the page to the calling template, ColdFusion doesn't know about them. You do this by prefixing your variable inside your tag with "Caller." Modifying the previous listing as shown below takes care of things.

```
<cfset caller.FavoriteColor = "Red">
```

Of course, the variable is set only in the case that Action = "Big." Otherwise it doesn't get set, and ColdFusion will throw an error because that code wasn't executed.

<NOTE>

You can write custom tags in more than just ColdFusion. You can use Java and C++ to do it, too. For instance, ColdFusion Enterprise ships with a custom tag called "CFX_GETLDINFO." It is written as a .dll and is used by the Administrator to interface with the Cisco Local Director to get load balancing information. In this chapter we're going to focus on writing custom tags in ColdFusion.

Passing Attributes in Structures

Now that we're passing data around, let's get a little fancier. You can pass entire sets of attributes to custom tags if you have them defined as a structure. You can do this in any custom tag by specifying a reserved attribute called attributeCollection. The value of attributeCollection must be a valid structure. It has just the same function as specifying each attribute individually; it is just more convenient on occasion. You can specify other attributes in the same call in which you use attributeCollection.

An example is shown in Listing 18.5, below. We set some variables as if they had been passed via an HTML form. Then we set those into a structure and pass them all off to the custom tag as attributes via the attributeCollection. The tag <cf_MakeTable>, shown in Listing 18.6 immediately following, accepts the key-value pairs in the structure as if they were specified normally and uses the values to make an HTML table, which is output to the browser.

Listing 18.5 AttCollection.cfm

```
<html>
<head>
	<title>Make Table Caller</title>
</head>

<body>
<cfset FORM.Width = "400">
<cfset FORM.Height = "200">
<cfset FORM.bgcolor = "green">

<cfscript>
// new structure holds values passed from form.
strTable = StructNew();
strTable.width = "#FORM.Width#";
strTable.height = "#FORM.height#";
strTable.bgcolor = "#FORM.bgcolor#";
</cfscript>

<!----notice the pound signs around struct name------->
<cf_MakeTable attributeCollection = "#strTable#">

</body>
</html>
```

Listing 18.6 MakeTable.cfm (Custom Tag)

```
<!---I am <CF_MakeTable>.
      I make an HTML table from passed attribs------->

<!---set up attributes with default values------->
<cfparam name="attributes.width" default="100">
<cfparam name="attributes.height" default="100">
<cfparam name="attributes.bgcolor" default="silver">
<cfparam name="attributes.border" default="4">
```

```
<!----notice we don't specify border, so
              default will be used------->

<cfoutput>
<table width = "#attributes.width#"
                     height = "#attributes.height#"
                     bgcolor = "#attributes.bgcolor#"
                     border = "#attributes.border#">

       <tr>
       <td>
              <font color = "white">
                     Hi from the tag
              </font>
       </td>
       </tr>
</table>
</cfoutput>
```

The Request Scope

The request scope is another special ColdFusion scope. You can use it outside of custom tags, but it was made for getting data to and from nested custom tags easily. The request scope is little documented, for reasons I fail to see because it's really useful. It was introduced in version 4.0.1 of ColdFusion, at the request of the team at Allaire then creating Spectra. Spectra is comprised of hundreds of custom tags, some nested deeply. A variable that is present in the request scope is available to an *entire* HTTP request. A variable in the request scope is not persistent across requests, but unlike a regular local variable, it is exposed to nested tags. You can store any kind of variable in the request scope: structures, arrays, queries, or regular variables. That is why you'll see it used in applications that employ a lot of custom tags.

Let's test out the power of this scope. Create a calling page with the following code:

Listing 18.7 doRequest.cfm (Custom Tag)

```
<cfset Request.FromTag = "I'm a request-scoped var set in the
tag.">

<!---modify the variable passed to the tag------->
<cfset Request.NewVar = Request.Var>
```

Listing 18.8 Request Caller

```
<!----set a variable in the Request scope--->
<cfset Request.Var = "I am a request-scoped variable.">

<!---call custom tag to see if variable is exposed.------->
<cf_doRequest>

Can I see data FROM the tag?<br>
<cfoutput>#Request.FromTag#</cfoutput>
<br>
<br>
Can the tag see CALLER data?<br>
<cfoutput>#Request.NewVar#</cfoutput>
```

The answer to the questions posed in the request caller is yes. That does not necessarily mean that it's necessarily smart to go around willy-nilly specifying the request scope all over the place. If you're not using tags, you can still write variables to the request scope, but you don't get anything for it. You might as well write them locally, since they don't persist. It's not going to hurt you, but as with writing in any language, why force your preprocessor to do a load of work it doesn't have to?

Anyway, the request scope is really meant for nested tags, so we will revisit it when we look at parent and child tags.

<NOTE>

Data that pertains directly to the current request is visible to the custom tag. This includes FORM, CGI, URL, server, application, session, and client variables as well as cookies and variables in the request scope. You may want to write these variables into the request scope on occasion for organizational purposes.

Making a Banner Ad Custom Tag

So far we have been using very simple examples in order to demonstrate fundamental concepts. It is also important to see what kinds of things you might really want to do in a custom tag. Listing 18.9 calls the custom tag <CF_MakeBanner>, which displays banner ads on a website. Listing 18.10 is a complete custom tag that gets passed attribute values, performs database queries and other processing, and returns data to the calling template. Listing 18.11 displays the ad.

Listing 18.9 MakeBannerCaller.cfm

```
<!-----set the banner action for custom tag.
Though use of IIF is not always recommended
for performance reasons, it is good to see it in
use. Try writing an if/else statement that does
the same thing.------->

<cfset banner.action
              = #iif(IsDefined("URL.AdAction"), DE("click"),
DE("display"))#>


<!-----randomly get a banner for display,
hit the database, and display it.
Show or relocate based on action------->

<cf_makeBanner action=#banner.action#>
```

Listing 18.10 MakeBanner (Custom Tag)

```
<!---- <cf_makebanner> handles retrieval, display, and log-
ging of banner ad ------->
<cfsetting enablecfoutputonly="Yes">

<cfparam name="attributes.action" default="display">

<cfswitch expression="#attributes.action#">
<cfcase value="display">
<!---get all the bannerids------->
<cfquery name="getBannerIDs" datasource="#Request.App.Data-
source#">
SELECT BannerID
FROM BannerAds;
</cfquery>

<!----choose a random banner from known ids ------->

<cfset VARIABLES.RandomID = RandRange(1, getBannerIDs.Record-
Count)>
```

```
<cfset VARIABLES.thisBannerID = ListGetAt((ValueList(getBan-
nerIDs.BannerID)), VARIABLES.RandomID)>

<!----Get a banner ad with that ID --->
<cfquery name="getOneBanner" datasource="#Request.App.Data-
source#">
        SELECT BannerID, ImagePath, AltText, WebsiteURL
        FROM BannerAds
        WHERE BannerID = #VARIABLES.thisBannerID#;
</cfquery>


<!---return ad to caller for display----->
<cfscript>
caller.strBanner = StructNew();
caller.strBanner.BannerID = getOneBanner.BannerID;
caller.strBanner.ImagePath = getOneBanner.ImagePath;
caller.strBanner.AltText = getOneBanner.AltText;
caller.strBanner.WebsiteURL = getOneBanner.WebsiteURL;
</cfscript>

<!----update times displayed------->
<cfquery name="UpdateBanners" datasource="#Request.App.Data-
source#">
        UPDATE BannerAds
        SET TimesDisplayed = TimesDisplayed + 1
        WHERE BannerID = #VARIABLES.thisBannerID#;
</cfquery>

</cfcase>

<cfcase value="click">
<!----update click thrus. ------->
<cfquery name="UpdateBanners" datasource="#Request.App.Data-
source#">
        UPDATE BannerAds
        SET ClickThrus = ClickThrus + 1
        WHERE BannerID = #URL.BannerID#;
</cfquery>

<!----and redirect------->
<cflocation url="#URL.thisURL#">
<cfabort>
</cfcase>
</cfswitch>

<cfsetting enablecfoutputonly="No">
```

Listing 18.11 ShowBanner

```
<!---the only job of this code is to display a banner
anywhere on the site that has access to the results
of the <CF_MakeBanner> custom tag------->

<cfoutput>
<a href="index.cfm?AdAction=Click&thisURL=#strBanner.Web-
siteURL#&BannerID=#strBanner.BannerID#"
        target="_blank">

<!---the image, alt text, and URL are stored in the
        database--->

<img src="images/banners/#strBanner.ImagePath#"
        alt="#strBanner.AltText#"
        width="468" height="60" border="0"></a>
</cfoutput>
```

We use the code in "ShowBanner.cfm" to process the results of the custom tag operation. This file can be included. We won't examine this further here, since it is used in the e-commerce site we make in the last chapter. But you can start using this tag and accompanying code on your site. You just need to set up the appropriate columns and table in your database.

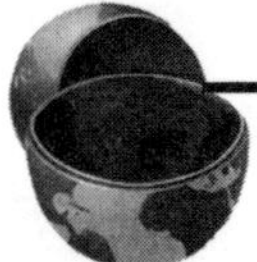

<NOTE>

In the above code, we use a tag called <CFSETTING>. This is a processing tag that, in this case, prevents the output of HTML that resides outside of <CFOUTPUT> tags.

How ColdFusion Finds Custom Tags

When you call a custom tag, ColdFusion immediately starts looking for it in the current directory. It will load the first instance of a tag that it finds. It is therefore imprudent to have different copies of a tag with the same name in different locations. You may get unpredictable results.

The next place ColdFusion looks is in any shared Custom Tags directories under CFusion\CustomTags. It will step down through any subdirectories looking for a matching template name.

As an alternative to using the standard syntax to call a custom tag, you can use <CFMODULE> to call your tag. It lets you specify the exact path of the tag you want to call, which helps you out in two ways. First, it means that you can resolve possible naming conflicts with other tags; it also gives you a bit of a performance boost, because ColdFusion doesn't have to go looking all over the server for your tag. Table 18.1 shows the attributes of <CFMODULE>.

Table 18.1 <CFMODULE> Tag Attributes

Attribute	*Description*
template	Used in place of name, defines a path to the custom tag template. Relative paths are expanded using ColdFusion mappings, which you can specify in the Administrator.
name	Used in place of template, defines the name of the custom tag in the form "Name.Name.Name...". Identifies a subdirectory that contains the custom tag page under the root directory for custom tags.
attributeCollection	Optional. A structure that contains a collection of key-value pairs that represent attribute names and their values.
Attribute_name	Optional. Attributes for a custom tag to use. You can use as many attributes as needed to specify the parameters of a custom tag.

<NOTE>

If you have created your own locations for custom tags outside of the CFusion directory, you need to restart, since the Administrator modifies registry keys.

Nested Custom Tags

The CFGRAPH and CFHTTP tags both can make use of subtags (<CFGRAPHDATA> or <CFHTTPPARAM>). Subtags are separate tags that depend on a parent tag. For instance, the <TR> and <TD> tags are not meaningful outside of an HTML <table> tag. With ColdFusion you can nest custom tags. You might also nest custom tags because you need to return a result to the "outside" tag so it can continue processing.

You have nested custom tags any time a custom tag calls another custom tag. A tag that calls another tag is called a parent tag. It is also known as a base tag or ancestor tag. The nested tag is referred to respectively as the child tag, subtag, or descendant tag. The parent-child and ancestor-descendant relationships are synonymous. There is one difference between these and base-subtag references: a base tag is an ancestor that is explicitly associated with a subtag with the <CFASSOCIATE> tag. Let's take a brief detour to look at this tag.

The <CFASSOCIATE> Tag

The <CFASSOCIATE> tag allows subtag data to be saved with the base tag. You use this tag only with custom tags. Table 18.2 lists its attributes.

Table 18.2 <CFASSOCIATE> Tag Attributes

Attribute	*Description*
baseTag	Required. Name of the base tag.
dataCollection	Optional. The name of the structure in which the base tag stores subtag data.

Subtag attributes are saved into a structure called AssocAttribs by default. You can change the name of this collection with the DataCollection attribute. Let's say you've got a base tag called <CF_Header> and you nest inside it a tag called <CF_Metatags>. You would use the following syntax to associate the two from inside <CF_Metatags>:

```
<!----retrieve attribute tag data from parent------->
        <cfassociate basetag="cf_header">
```

Because you can nest tags as deeply as you like, any subtag that calls another custom tag is automatically the base tag for that called tag. When ColdFusion finds a <CFASSOCIATE> tag in a subtag, it saves the attributes of the subtag in the base tag. The attributes are stored in a structure, which is appended to an array called "thisTag.CollectionName."

Getting Base Tag Data

There are two functions available to you for gaining access to the data that exists in a base tag. From the subtag, you can get the structure object that contains all of the base tag data using GetBaseTagList() and GetBasetagData().

`GetBaseTagList()` Returns a comma-delimited list of ancestor tag names in uppercase. If the current tag is not nested, it returns an empty string. The first element listed is always the parent.

`GetBaseTagData(TagName, InstanceNumber)` Returns an object containing all of the variables of the *n*th ancestor with a given name. The closest ancestor is returned by default. If there is no ancestor or the ancestor doesn't expose any data, an exception is thrown.

Processing Modes

There are three possible modes in which ColdFusion tags can be at any given moment. You can refer to these states using the thisTag.ExecutionMode variable. Possible values are Start, End, and Inactive. These are described in Table 18.3.

Table 18.3 thisTag.ExecutionMode

Attribute	*Description*
Start	When the base tag is processed for the first time.
Inactive	During this time, no processing occurs in the base tag. Any subtags or other code are processed at this time.
End	When ColdFusion reaches the custom tag's end tag, the tag is processed for a second time.

You can control the flow of processing using <CFIF> or <CFSWITCH>. For instance,

```
<cfswitch expression = "#thisTag.ExecutionMode#">
        <cfcase value = "Start">
                Do something
        </cfcase>

        <cfcase value = "End">
                Do something else
        </cfcase>
</cfswitch>
```

We'll put this to work in the next sections.

<CFEXIT>

You can end the processing of a custom tag using the <CFEXIT> tag. It acts much like <CFABORT> but is meant specifically for custom tags. It gives you the flexibility to stop processing entirely, have the calling page continue processing after the end tag, or continue processing from the first child in the body. See Appendix A for more information.

Let's look at how you might nest custom tags. For clarity, we'll create a tag called <CF_Header> and a tag called <CF_Metatags>. <CF_Metatags> will be nested inside the <CF_Header> tag. We will make an "Index.cfm" page to call <CF_Header>. While it may seem excessive to use custom tags for such functions, it works well because you can create one header and pass to it a path attribute depending on where you are in the directory structure.

Listing 18.12 Index.cfm

```
<!-------call header tag. pass path info to it------->
<cf_header imagePath="../">

<h2>I am index.</h2>

</body>
</html>
```

Listing 18.13 Header.cfm (Custom tag)

```
<!-----------
  template: custom tag <cf_header>
  use: displays the default header which includes the header
title.
         calls <cf_metatags> to display meta info.
  attributes: imagePath specifies path steps depending on
what directory you're in,
         for instance "../"

------------>

<cfparam name="attributes.imagePath" default="">

<html>
<head>
     <!---call the meta tag struct for this document----->
     <cf_metatags>
```

```
</head>
<body bgcolor="#FFFFFF" leftmargin="0" topmargin="0"<cfoutput>
background="#attributes.imagePath#images/bg.jpg" </cfoutput>
link="#484826" vlink="#000000" alink="#484826">

<!--- header title --->

<table width="100%" border="0" align="center" cellpadding="0"
cellspacing="0">
  <tr> <cfoutput>
    <td background="#attributes.imagePath#images/
bg_header.jpg" height="108">
      <p><img src="#attributes.imagePath#images/spacer.gif"
width="10" height="108" align="absmiddle">
        <a href="#attributes.imagePath#index.cfm" >
        <img src="#attributes.imagePath#images/
headers_home.gif" border="0" width="661" height="55"
align="absmiddle"></a></p>
       </td> </cfoutput>
  </tr>
  <tr>
  <cfoutput><td background="#attributes.imagePath#images/
bg_nav.jpg" height="27"></cfoutput>
    </td>
  </tr>
 </table>
<!--- end include header --->
```

Listing 18.14 Metatags.cfm (Custom Tag)

```
<!-----------
      template: <cf_metatags>
      purpose: invoke metatags for HTML head.
      use: called from <CF_Header>
------------->
<!---surpress output----->
<cfsetting enablecfoutputonly="yes">
<!----Create the metatag structure and populate----->
<cfset strMetatags = structNew()>
<cfset strMetatags["title"] ="Core ColdFusion Site">
<cfset strMetatags["keywords"] ="icy cold beverages">
<cfset strMetatags["description"] ="">
<cfset strMetatags["resource-type"] ="document">
<cfset strMetatags["copyright"] ="Copyright me 2001">
```

```
<cfset strMetatags["revisit-after"] ="all">
<cfset strMetatags["distribution"] ="global">

<!---output metatags----->

<cfset strKeyArr = StructKeyArray(strMetaTags)>

<cfloop from="1" to="#ArrayLen(strKeyArr)#" index="idx">
       <cfoutput>
<meta name=#Lcase(strKeyArr[idx])#
       content="#structfind(strMetaTags, strKeyArr[idx])#">
</cfoutput>
</cfloop>
<cfsetting enablecfoutputonly="no">

<!----retrieve attribute tag data from parent----->
       <cfassociate basetag="cf_header">
    <cfset parentdata = GetBaseTagData("cf_header")>

<cfoutput>
<!---link the stylesheet to the appropriate imagepath
              as specified in parent----->
<link rel="stylesheet" type="text/css" href="#parent
data.attributes.ImagePath#scripts/myStyle.css">
</cfoutput>
```

Executing Custom Tags

You can write simple custom tags and paired custom tags. A simple tag is like an HTML <BR> tag—there's no paired or ending </BR> tag. It wouldn't make any sense to have the "end" of a break; it's just a break. Same for <HR>. A paired tag is something like <TABLE>, which requires an accompanying </TABLE> tag. Everything in between the start and end tags will be considered part of the table. So it is with creating ColdFusion custom tags.

The ability to write custom tags that have end tags was introduced in ColdFusion 4.0. You can use end tags when you need to encompass data with a custom tag. For instance, you might make a custom tag that formats text or a table. These would be good candidates for paired tags.

Let's create a paired custom tag that requires an end tag but does not encompass any data between the start tag and end tag. We'll call it <CF_Lookup>. It accepts an IP address, uses the regular ColdFusion tag <CFEXECUTE> to execute the server process nslookup on the command line, and returns the name of the associated with that IP. First we'll create the page that displays a form for a user to enter an IP and then calls the custom tag <CF_Lookup> when the IP is passed. The tag takes one attribute: the IP address to pass to the command line.

Listing 18.15 LookUpCall.cfm

```
<html>
<head>
        <title>An NSLookup Utility</title>
</head>
<body>
<cfset thisPage = cgi.script_name>

<h2>Here is your NSLookUp utility.</h2>

<!---display a form for user to enter IP address------->
Please enter the IP Address you wish to look up:
<br><br>
<cfoutput>
        <form action="#thisPage#" method="post">
</cfoutput>
        <input type="text" size = "25" name="Site">
        <input type="Submit" name="Submit">
</form>
<br><br>

<cfif isDefined("FORM.Submit")>
        <br>

        <!----pass the address into the custom tag
                to get the result. ------->

        <cf_Lookup
                site="#FORM.Site#"></cf_Lookup>

<!---output the info generated by the tag------->
<br>
<cfoutput>#rsite#</cfoutput>

</cfif>
</body>
</html>
```

Listing 18.16 NsLookUp.cfm (Custom Tag)

```
<cfsetting enablecfoutputonly="Yes">
<cfparam name="attributes.site">

<cfswitch expression="#thisTag.ExecutionMode#">
<cfcase value="start">
<CFEXECUTE timeout="7" name="C:\WinNT\System32\nsLookup.exe"
               arguments="#attributes.site#"
               outputfile="C:\NsLookup.txt"/>
</cfcase>

<cfcase value="end">
<cffile action="read" file="C:\NsLookup.txt"
               variable="caller.rSite">
</cfcase>
</cfswitch>
<cfsetting enablecfoutputonly="No">
```

This may seem strange, to have a paired tag with no data between the start and end tags. But this is somewhat common. In this case, we do not have any other tags or data to be processed inside the <CF_Lookup> tags. Why do we need it, then? What we really need is some time to let the nslookup process end. If we try reading the file immediately after the <CFEXECUTE> spawns the process, ColdFusion will throw an error, telling us that we can't read the file because another process is currently modifying it. We have to wait a moment. So we put the file read into the end mode of the tag, which gives us enough time to slip through.

ThisTag.GeneratedContent

"Generated Content" is the result of processing the body of a custom tag. All text, code, evaluated variables, expressions, and functions are included in this result. The result is held in a variable called thisTag.GeneratedContent.

When thisTag.ExecutionMode = "Start," the variable is empty. Even if there is output generated in the start of a tag's processing, it won't be present in this variable.

ThisTag.HasEndTag

The final variable available to us as tag instance data is thisTag.HasEndTag. It is used primarily for code validation, letting you know if a tag is called with or without an end tag. Returns a Boolean.

Encrypting Custom Tags

You can encrypt your custom tags so that they cannot be read by others. ColdFusion can still run them normally, but this secures them. Often developers will sell custom tags or applications in encrypted and unencrypted versions for different prices.

To encrypt your templates (any template, not just custom tags), you use a command-line utility called cfencode. This utility is installed in the CFusion/Bin directory. You call it with the following syntax:

```
cfencode infile outfile [/r /q]  [/h "message]  /v"2"
```

Table 18.4 describes the different options.

Table 18.4 cfencode Utility Options

Attribute	*Description*
`infile`	Name of the file to encode.
`outfile`	Path and file name of the output file. If you do not specify an output file, you will be asked if you want to continue. If you do, the source file will be overwritten by the encoded file.
`/r`	Recursive. When used with wildcards, the encoding utility recourses through subdirectories, encoding all found files.
`/q`	Suppresses warning messages.
`/h`	Header; allows a custom header to be written to the top of the encoded file(s).
`/v`	Required. Parameter that allows encoding using a specified version number. Possible values are "1" for tags that you want to be able to run on version 3.x of ColdFusion, or "2" for tags you want to run only on version 4.0 and later.

Conclusion

Creating custom tags is a really fun aspect of ColdFusion. Just remember to document everything carefully. You can easily lose track of what tag is called where, and why, and what data is passed to it and from it—especially when you start nesting custom tags. Please document all of these things. You'll be glad you did later, and so will everyone you work with.

In the next chapter we'll take a look at how you can incorporate WDDX, an application of XML, into your ColdFusion work.

XML AND COLDFUSION

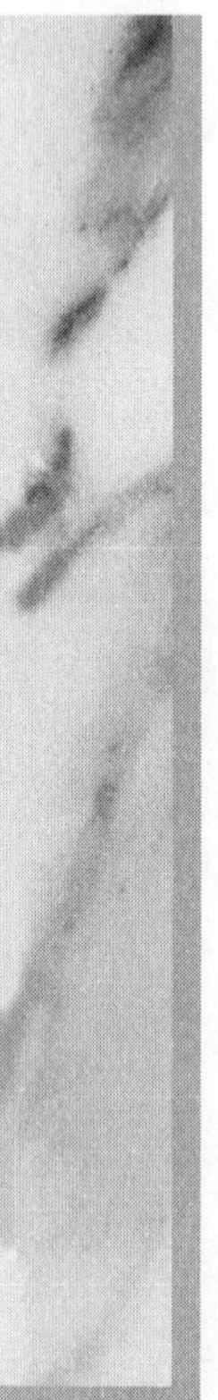

Topics in This Chapter

- Introduction to WDDX
- XML
- Serializing and deserializing data
- WDDX in action

Chapter 19

WDDX stands for Web Distributed Data eXchange. A standard XML 1.0 vocabulary created in 1998 by Allaire Corporation, it is the easiest way to incorporate generic data descriptions into your applications. WDDX is not proprietary like ColdFusion, nor is it a subset of ColdFusion. It is an open standard set that allows communication between a wide range of server and programming platforms. You can leverage WDDX to exchange data between your ColdFusion applications and many other platforms, including ASP, PHP, JavaScript, Perl, Java, Python, COM, and Macromedia Flash. You can exchange data with any of these application types using WDDX as the interpreter. This makes it exciting to work with as we enter the era of Web services and distribution.

In this chapter we will look how you can move not only strings, but complex data such as arrays, structures, and record sets using WDDX.

It is important to understand how to use WDDX for a number of reasons. As businesses move into really relying on the Web for their core operations, they need to incorporate existing data and software processes with their Web applications. Nobody is going to start over from scratch just because the Web is "pretty neat." A tremendous number of government agencies and organizations still, at the end of 2001, use DOS programs with frequency. The truly powerful application is the one that can communicate openly, have its generated content understood by other applications, and bring data from other applications into itself. If you can describe data generically, you can do this. That's where WDDX comes in.

<NOTE>

A Macromedia Spectra 1.5 30-day evaluation is included on the CD-ROM accompanying this book. Spectra is an application framework for developing e-commerce sites, personalization, and content management. It is a staggering undertaking, written entirely in ColdFusion. It is made up of about 450 custom ColdFusion tags, and it stores all of its internal data as WDDX. If nothing else, taking a look at how Spectra is put together will really inspire your work with custom tags and WDDX. Check it out.

In the following sections we will see how to use WDDX with ColdFusion applications. Before we do so, let's take a brief look at XML itself, in case you are not familiar with it.

XML

The eXtensible Markup Language is a specification of the W3C (World Wide Web Consortium). It was defined to allow flexibility in the representation of data and the structure of documents. HTML is about the presentation of documents. When you view an HTML page in a browser, the code that creates it (with the exception of comments and other meta data) is intended for display. XML, on the other hand, is about the structural representation of data. So, too, is WDDX.

<NOTE>

WML, the Wireless Markup Language, is another application of XML. In the Appendices you will learn more about XML, and how to create a dynamic ColdFusion application that is viewable on Web-enabled cell phones. We will cover XML in greater depth there.

Because WDDX is XML, it conforms with an XML DTD. So, once you send data into WDDX, you can transfer it over FTP, HTTP, email, or any transfer protocol capable of sending and receiving XML. The data structure sent and received will be exactly the same on either end of the transfer, regardless of platform.

There are a few specific things to keep in mind as you work with WDDX. WDDX has no provision whatsoever for security. It isn't meant to. You need to handle security programmatically, as WDDX is simply a generic way of describing the contents of a document. WDDX is not a facility for remote procedure calls; in WDDX alone you cannot invoke a server function. All it does is describe data. Therefore, let's take a look at how it does that.

WDDX Datatypes

ColdFusion is generally referred to as a typeless language. However, WDDX supports several datatypes. These are:

- Booleans (`bool`)
- Strings (`string`)
- Date/time values (`dateTime`)
- Numbers (`number`)
- Arrays (`array`)
- Structures and associative arrays (`struct`)
- Collections of structures, data retrieved from a database (`recordset`)
- Binary objects (`binary`)
- Null values (`null`)

Serializing and Deserializing Data

If you've worked with PHP before, you may be familiar with several functions available to you for handling WDDX. In order to *serialize* a packet (that is, set it into WDDX), you can invoke the wddx_serialize_value() function, like this:

```
$somevar = "I am a regular string.";
print(wddx_serialize_value($somevar, "I am a comment"));
```

To deserialize the packet back into PHP, you use, not surprisingly, the wddx_deserialize() function. In ASP, one uses a COM component to serialize and deserialize data for WDDX. In ColdFusion, things are easy. You use the

<CFWDDX> tag to serialize and deserialize packets. Its attributes are shown in Table 19.1.

Table 19.1 <CFWDDX> Tag Attributes

Attribute	*Description*
Action	The action to be taken by CFWDDX tag. Possible values are: • CFML2WDDX (Serialize CFML to WDDX) • WDDX2CFML (Deserialize WDDX to CFML) • CFML2JS (Serialize CFML to JavaScript) • WDDX2JS (Deserialize WDDX to JavaScript)
Input	Required. The value to be processed.
Output	The name of the variable to hold the output of the operation. Required for action = "WDDX2CFML." For all other actions, if this attribute is not provided, the result of the WDDX processing is output in the HTML stream.
topLevelVariable	Required if action = "WDDX2JS" or "CFML2JS." The name of the top-level JavaScript object in the deserialization. Applies only when working with JavaScript and is ignored otherwise. The object created is an instance of the WddxRecordSet object.
UseTimeZoneInfo	Optional. Indicates whether to output time zone information when serializing CFML to WDDX. If time zone info is taken into account, the hour–minute offset is calculated in the date–time output, formatted according to ISO8601. Otherwise the local time is output. Default is "Yes."
validate	For the WDDX2CFML or WDDX2JS actions, validate = "Yes" tells ColdFusion to process the WDDX input by a validating XML parser using the WDDX DTD. If the parser processes the packet without error, the packet is deserialized. If the packet is not well-formed, an error is thrown. Default is "No."

In this chapter we will focus on how to use WDDX with ColdFusion.

WDDX in Action

This section will show you how to use WDDX in your applications. It is often useful to transfer WDDX internally within one ColdFusion application. A good use of this, for example, is when creating multipart forms or Web wizards. You can serialize the data passed in each step of the form as a WDDX packet and set it into a client variable, outputting it to a structure, and add to it in subsequent steps of the form.

Here we'll see how you could communicate with an external application by exposing your data for content syndication. A website such as www.moreover.com features hundreds of third-party news headlines posted in generic XML formats. One of these is WDDX. You can send an intelligent agent to this website with CFHTTP, retrieve the data, and then locally deserialize the packet for display on your own website. It doesn't matter what language www.moreover.com is written in itself; because the standard is open, your sites can talk to each other. In the next chapter we'll see how to do that. For now, let's see how to get data in and out of WDDX.

<NOTE>

There is a new function in ColdFusion 5: IsWDDX(). *This function returns YES if the variable is a valid WDDX packet, NO if it is not.*

A Simple Example

Let us get familiar with the basic input and output of working with WDDX. In Listing 19.1 we take a basic string and serialize it, then we deserialize it again so you can see how the transformation works.

Listing 19.1 Simple.cfm

```
<html>
<head>
      <title>WDDX</title>
</head>

<body>

<!---create a string------->

<cfset FullName = "Groucho" & " " & "Marx">
<br>
The string is: <cfoutput>#FullName#</cfoutput>

<!---serialize the string into a wddx packet------->
<cfwddx
```

```
        action="CFML2WDDX"
        input="#FullName#"
        output="wddxString">
<br>
<br>

<!---output the raw wddx. The deprecated <XMP>
        tag, a Microsoft extension to HTML, displays examples
in a fixed-width font.
        It is used only show that the entire packet outputs
to the browser. You could
        just as easily output the packet without it and view
the source.------->

The serialized string is: <xmp><cfoutput>#wddxString#</cfout-
put></xmp>
<br>
<!----deserialize the wddx packet back into its original for-
mat------->
<cfwddx
        action="WDDX2CFML"
        input="#wddxString#"
        output="NewFullName">

        <!----output the deserialized packet------->
The deserialized string: <cfoutput>#NewFullName#</cfoutput>

</body>
</html>
```

Here is the output to Internet Explorer:

```
The string is: Groucho Marx

The serialized string is:
<wddxPacket version='1.0'><header></header><data>
<string>Groucho Marx</string></data></wddxPacket>

The deserialized string: Groucho Marx
```

Instead of using the <xmp> tag, we could have used the ColdFusion HTMLEditFormat() function, which returns an HTML-escaped string. You can have a lot of fun this way. For instance, try reading a file into a variable and outputting its contents as WDDX. You could do something like this:

```
<!---read the file into a variable----->
<cffile action = "read" file="C:\nslookup.txt" variable =
"fileLog">
```

```
<!----serialize log file------->

<cfwddx action="CFML2WDDX" input="#fileLog#" output="wddxLog">

<!---expose it for an agent------->
<cfoutput>#HTMLEditFormat(wddxLog)#</cfoutput>
```

While the idea is exactly the same, let's just create a more complex data set to serialize so that you can see how it looks.

Listing 19.2 Complex.cfm

```
<body>
<!----use cfscript because we're setting
       several variables at one time------->
<cfscript>
// create structure
strComedians = StructNew();
strComedians.from1980s = "Robin Williams";
strComedians.from1960s = "Bill Cosby";

// create array in structure
strComedians.from1940s = ArrayNew(1);
arrayAppend(strComedians.from1940s, "Groucho");
arrayAppend(strComedians.from1940s, "Harpo");
arrayAppend(strComedians.from1940s, "Chico");
</cfscript>

<!----serialize data------>
<cfwddx action="CFML2WDDX" input="#strComedians#"
output="wddxComedians">

<!---here you could set the data into the session or client
scope,
      write it to a file, or pass it in a hidden form field.
------>

       <cfoutput>#HTMLEditFormat(wddxComedians)#</cfoutput>

</body>
```

Here is the result. It is modified only in that I've added spacing and line breaks for readability. It's output as one long line.

```
<wddxPacket version='1.0'>
<header></header>
<data>
```

```
        <struct>
               <var name='FROM1940S'>
                      <array length='3'>
                             <string>Groucho</string>
                             <string>Harpo</string>
                             <string>Chico</string>
                      </array>
               </var>

               <var name='FROM1960S'>
                      <string>Bill Cosby</string>
               </var>

               <var name='FROM1980S'>
                      <string>Robin Williams</string>
               </var>
        </struct>
</data>
</wddxPacket>
```

We could also do a database query and expose the data for syndication by intelligent agents. You might make strong partnerships by exposing the product information in your database and then posting it as XML in a private area of your site to allow site partners to work more easily with you. Listing 19.3 shows you how to do it.

Listing 19.3 ExposeQuery.cfm

```
<!---query database to get our Product info------->

<cfquery datasource="CoreStore" name="qryProducts">
      SELECT ProductID, ProductName, Price, ShortDescription
      FROM Products
</cfquery>

<!----serialize query------>
<cfwddx action="CFML2WDDX"
      input="#qryProducts#" output="wddxProducts">

<!---write it to a file------->

<cffile action="write"
      file="C:mlProducts.xml" output="#wddxProducts#">

<h2>Exposure Complete.</h2>
```

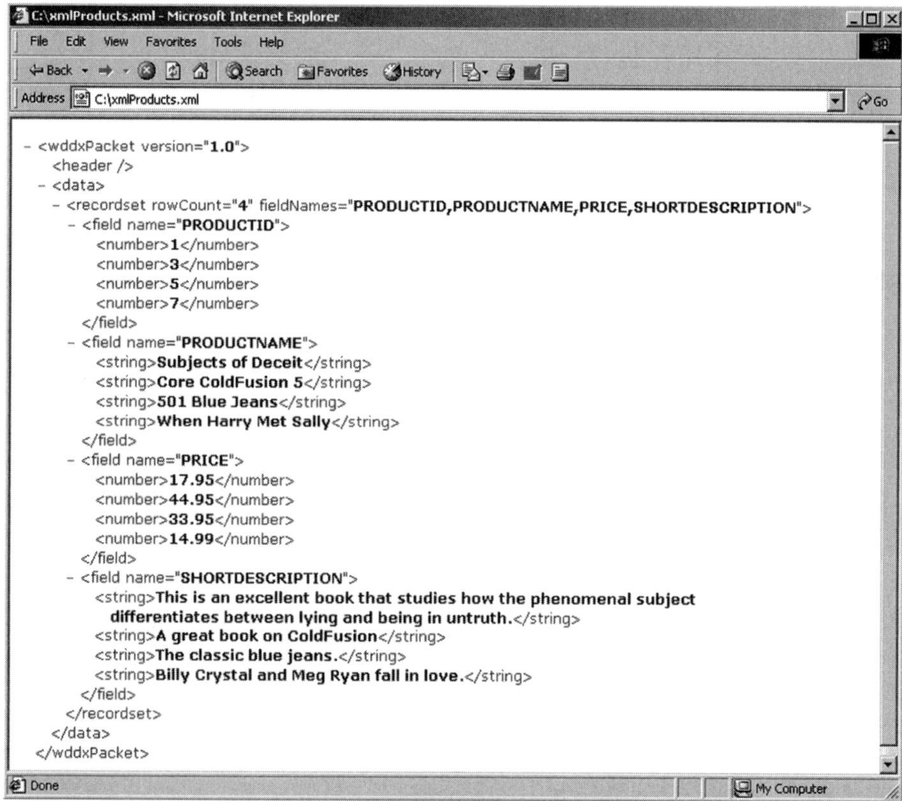

```
- <wddxPacket version="1.0">
  <header />
  - <data>
    - <recordset rowCount="4" fieldNames="PRODUCTID,PRODUCTNAME,PRICE,SHORTDESCRIPTION">
      - <field name="PRODUCTID">
          <number>1</number>
          <number>3</number>
          <number>5</number>
          <number>7</number>
        </field>
      - <field name="PRODUCTNAME">
          <string>Subjects of Deceit</string>
          <string>Core ColdFusion 5</string>
          <string>501 Blue Jeans</string>
          <string>When Harry Met Sally</string>
        </field>
      - <field name="PRICE">
          <number>17.95</number>
          <number>44.95</number>
          <number>33.95</number>
          <number>14.99</number>
        </field>
      - <field name="SHORTDESCRIPTION">
          <string>This is an excellent book that studies how the phenomenal subject
            differentiates between lying and being in untruth.</string>
          <string>A great book on ColdFusion</string>
          <string>The classic blue jeans.</string>
          <string>Billy Crystal and Meg Ryan fall in love.</string>
        </field>
      </recordset>
    </data>
</wddxPacket>
```

Figure 19.1 A query from our store database exposes product information as XML for retrieval by intelligent agents.

Figure 19.1 shows the output to Internet Explorer. As we develop, we can just navigate to the file with the browser, but in production you would place this file somewhere under your Web root.

It looks just like the headlines at Moreover.com, because that's how Internet Explorer outputs XML. It uses its own internal style sheet to display the data. Now any agent from a CGI, PHP, ASP, Java, or JSP website can bring your exposed data into its own website and display it there. I'll refrain from evangelizing too much. I think you can quickly see how cool this is, and what the opportunities are for your own sites.

Perhaps your product list changes often. Look up the CFSCHEDULE tag in Appendix A to see how to have ColdFusion execute the serialization page (or any page) for you at regular intervals. That way you never have to see it.

There is, as described briefly above, a lot more you can do with this. If you are very familiar with JavaScript, you will have fun exploring that aspect of working with WDDX.

In the next chapter you will discover how to create an intelligent agent to retrieve packet data in an automated process and incorporate it into your own site. This will be very exciting indeed.

Conclusion

Keep your eye on Web Services. This is an exciting new area of Web development that will help realize the true vision of the Web. Take a look at emerging technologies such as Simple Object Access Protocol (SOAP), Web Service Description Language (WSDL), and Universal Description, Discovery, and Integration (UDDI). Using WDDX and ColdFusion, you can perform actions complementary to what you'll find available in Web Services. To find out more about the WDDX specification, I urge you to visit the website. It used to be located at www.wddx.org, but public perception seemed to be that WDDX was some kind of corporate or proprietary technology, and so Allaire changed the website to www.OpenWDDX.org, in order to persuade developers that it is meant as an open, community project. At the website you can download a free SDK, visit the forums, and review a wide range of resources to help you understand this vocabulary and put it to work.

CREATING INTELLIGENT AGENTS

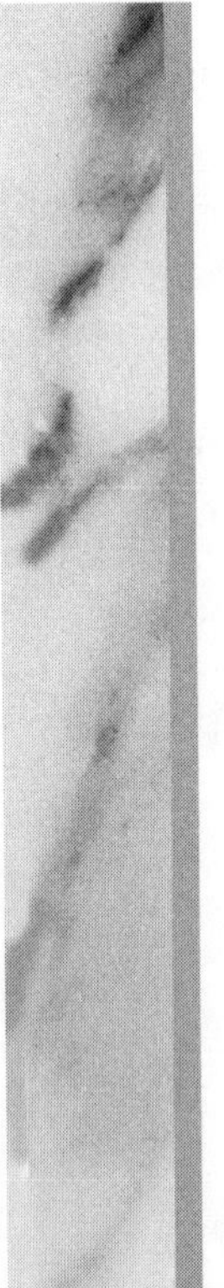

Topics in This Chapter

- Creating an intelligent agent
- CFHTTP
- CFHTTPPARAM

Chapter 20

The dot-com gold rush is over. In order to survive in this economy, businesses are not so willing to depend on advertising for their main revenue stream. As they turn away from advertising, they look increasingly to partnerships to provide them with stability and flow. One way of doing this is *content syndication*. You may have heard of television shows that are "syndicated." TV networks resell the right to broadcast certain popular shows, which is the reason you might see the same show on different channels on the same week. I have not watched television in several years, so I hope that I am not abusing this concept. The idea is the same on the Web. Content syndication is the process of serializing the content of your site, making it available to others in some form that they can retrieve automatically. Businesses can enter into meaningful partnerships that automate the process of sharing their content.

In this chapter you will learn how to leverage ColdFusion to create intelligent agents. We will make an application that goes out to an external website, retrieves the headlines in WDDX format, and processes the result for display on your website.

CFHTTP

This tag allows you to get data from and post data to any website. This is a very powerful tag in ColdFusion. Using the post action, you can post information to an external website; using the get action, you can retrieve the entire contents of a Web page into a local variable or a file.

Table 20.1 shows the attributes for using the <CFHTTP> tag.

Table 20.1 <CFHTTP> Tag Attributes

Attribute	*Description*
URL	Required. Full URL of the host name or IP address of the server that hosts the file. The URL must be absolute and include the protocol and host name. You may include port number if applicable; a port specified in the URL will override any value in the port attribute.
Port	Optional. The port number on the server from which the object is requested. Default is 80.
Method	Required. GET or POST. Use GET to download a text or binary file or to create a query from the contents of a text file. Use POST to send information to a server for processing. POST requires use of CFHTTPPARAM tag.
Username	Optional. A valid username when the server requires it.
Password	Optional. A valid password when the server requires it.
Name	Optional. The name to use for a query if you create a query from a file.
Columns	Optional. Specifies the column names for a query when creating a query as a result of CFHTTP get. By default, the first column of a text file is interpreted as column headings. If there are column headings in the text from which to draw the query, do not specify this attribute unless you want to overwrite them. If there are no column headers in the text file, or if you want to overwrite them, you specify the columns attribute. ColdFusion never treats the first row of a file as data.
Path	Optional. Path to the directory in which a file is to be stored. If a path is not specified in a POST or GET operation, a variable is created that you can use to display the results of the POST operation using CFOUTPUT. That variable is cfhttp.FileContent.

Attribute	*Description*
File	Required for Method=POST if a path is specified. The filename to be used for the file that is accessed. For GET operations, this defaults to the name specified in the URL attribute.
Delimiter	Required for creating a query. Default is comma. The other option is TAB.
TextQualifier	Required for creating a query. Indicates the start and end of a column. Should be escaped when embedded in a column. Default is double quotation mark (").
ResolveURL	Optional. YES or NO. For GET and POST operations, if YES, page reference returned into the fileContent variable has its internal URLs fully resolved so that links remain intact. This includes images, form actions, a hrefs, framesources, and other objects that can contain links.
ProxyServer	Optional. Name or IP of a proxy server.
ProxyPort	Optional. The port number on the proxy server from which the object is requested. When used with ResolveURL, the URLs of retrieved documents that specify a port number are automatically resolved to preserve links in the retrieved document. Default is 80.
UserAgent	Optional. User agent info to write to the request header.
ThrowOnError	Optional. Boolean indicating whether to throw an exception that can be caught by using the CFTRY and CFCATCH tags. Default is NO.
Redirect	Optional. Boolean indicating whether to redirect execution or stop execution. Default is YES.
Timeout	Optional. Value in seconds. When a URL timeout is specified in the browser, the timeout attribute setting takes precedence over the ColdFusion Administrator timeout. The ColdFusion server then uses the lesser of the URL timeout and the timeout passed in the timeout attribute, so that the request always times out at the same time or before when the page times out. If there is no timeout set on the URL in the browser, the Administrator, or this attribute, ColdFusion waits indefinitely for the request.

The GET Method

You generally use the GET method of the <CFHTTP> tag to retrieve an object from a remote server. Using this method, you can only send information right in the URL.

Now let's create a simple news agent that goes out to moreover.com and retrieves the headlines for the Phoenix, Arizona area. We do this by first going to moreover.com and browsing the many categories of information they make available.

Listing 20.1 NewsAgent.cfm

```
<!---retrieve the headlines from moreover.com's
       free news headline service------->
 <cfhttp
       method="get"
       url="http://p.moreover.com/cgi-local/page?c=Phoe-
nix%20news&o=cf"
       resolveURL="Yes">

<!---deserialize the retrieved content---->
<cfwddx
       action="wddx2cfml"
       input="#cfhttp.FileContent#"
       output="PhoenixHeadlines">

<h3>Today's Headlines in Phoenix</h3>
<!---notice that we can output the packet as a query----->
<cfoutput query="PhoenixHeadlines" maxrows="5">

<!---use format, and output 5 headlines---->
<font face="verdana, arial, Helvetica">
<a href="#PhoenixHeadlines.Document_URL#" target="_blank">
#PhoenixHeadlines.headline_text#</a>,<br></font>
</cfoutput>
```

Figure 20.1 shows how the data looks deserialized back on your own site.

Moreover.com asks that developers respect their wishes as they provide this free service. That means retaining the absolute links to the originating news sources, and not modifying the content of the headlines themselves.

In the above example, we retrieved a Web page and resolved the URLs so that links and images would still work. The file was set into a variable called CFHTTP.FileContent, which we then displayed with CFOUTPUT. ColdFusion automatically creates this and other variables during the CFHTTP operation. These variables are shown in Table 20.2.

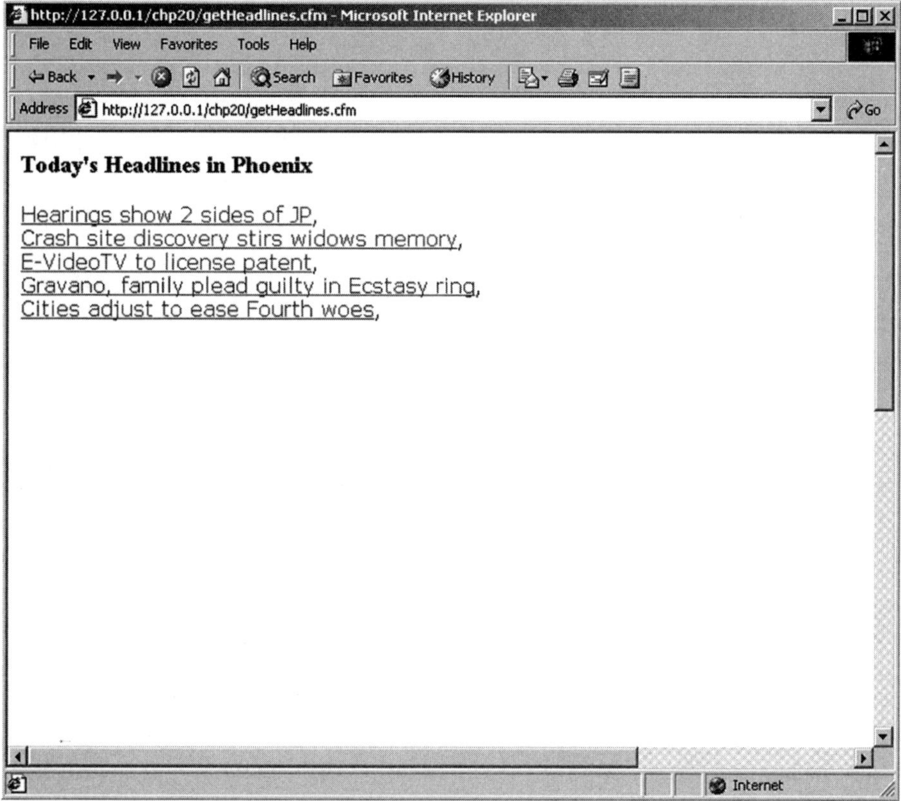

Figure 20.1 CFHTTP retrieves the entire Web page and brings it back for display on your site.

CFHTTP Variables

There are several variables returned during a CFHTTP operation that you can use with your applications.

Table 20.2 Variables Returned by CFHTTP

Attribute	*Description*
#CFHTTP.FileContent#	Returns the contents of the file for text and MIME files.
#CFHTTP.MIMEType#	Returns MIME type.
#CFHTTP.Header	Returns the raw response header as a simple text variable.

(continued)

Table 20.2 Continued

Attribute	*Description*
#CFHTTP.StatusCode	Returns the HTTP error code and associated error string if throwOnError is NO.
#CFHTTP.ResponseHeader#	Returns the HTTP error code and associated error string. For instance, "200 Okay" or "404 File Not Found."

You can use these in a manner similar to our use of CFFILE variables when we uploaded a file in Chapter 17.

Saving a Page to a File

Instead of displaying the Web page contents retrieved immediately, we can instead save it to a file for processing later. To do this, you use the PATH and FILE attributes of the tag. Listing 20.2 shows how we could retrieve and save the XML headlines page we viewed earlier.

Listing 20.2 saveFile.cfm

```
<body>
<!---retrieve the headlines from moreover.com's
        free news headline service------->
 <cfhttp
        method="get"
        url="http://p.moreover.com/cgi-local/page?c=Phoe-
nix%20news&o=cf"
        resolveURL="Yes"
        path = "C:\Partners"
        file = "Headlines_#DateFormat(Now())#.xml">

<h2>Done.</h2>
</body>
```

<NOTE>

When you specify a file path, the CFHTTP.FileContent *variable is not available. ColdFusion will throw an error if you try to access it.*

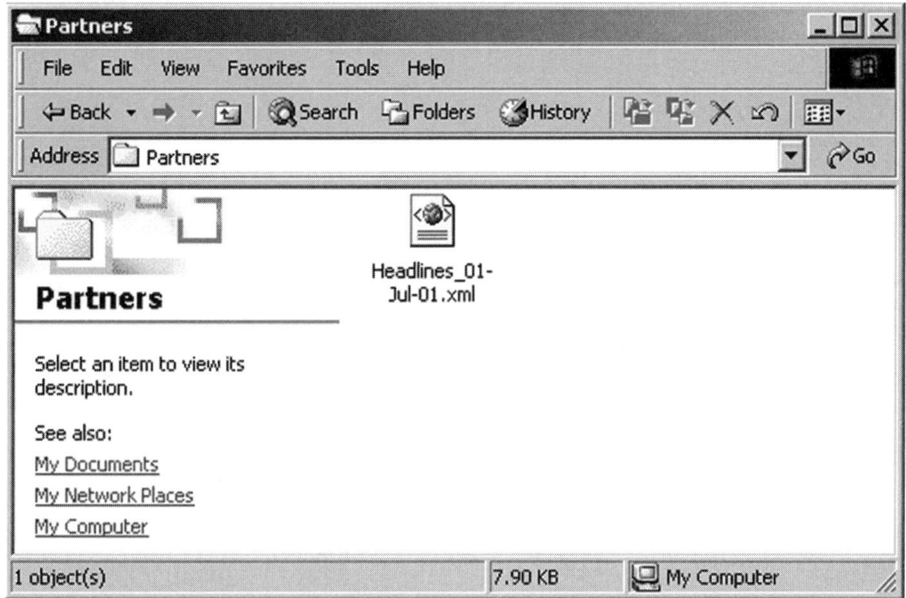

Figure 20.2 The results of saving an external file via CFHTTP.

Notice that here we have specified part of the file name dynamically using ColdFusion date functions. As we can see in Figure 20.2, the file is correctly named and saved to the appropriate directory.

Saving Binary Files

You can save binary files in addition to plain text and HTML files. Here's how you do it:

```
<CHTTP method = "GET"
       URL = "http://www.CyberTrails.com/MP3s/MySharona.mp3"
       PATH = "C:\ImportantFiles"
       FILE = "MySharona.mp3"
       >
```

The POST Method

Besides retrieving external Web pages, you can use CFHTTP to POST data to a website. This data can include form, URL, and CGI variables or cookies. Using CFHTTPPARAMs inside your CFHTTP operation, you could create a gateway that requires the presence of a cookie or username and password for your site partners. Once a partner has paid for your service, you could set up a form that accepts a username and password or product serial number. You could then create an agent that posts this information to retrieve the protected resources. Let's take a look at this new tag for a moment.

CFHTTPPARAM

The <CFHTTPPARAM> tag is required for POST operations of the CFHTTP tag. You use it to specify the parameters you want to post. It is a subtag of CFHTTP, just as CFGRAPHDATA is a subtag of CFGRAPH. It is therefore used only inside a CFHTTP call. Table 20.3 shows the attributes of this tag.

Table 20.3 Attributes of the <CFHTTPPARAM> Tag

Attribute	*Description*
Name	Required. A variable name for the data being passed.
Type	Required. The transaction type. Valid entries are: • `URL` (The server will receive the data as if it had been appended to the URL as a standard parameter) • `FormField` (The server will interpret the data as if it had been entered into a form field) • `Cookie` (The server will interpret the data if the browser had sent a cookie) • `CGI` (The server will make the posted data available as a CGI environment variable) • `File` (The server will receive the file as an uploaded file)
Value	Optional for type = "file." Specifies the value of the variable being passed.
File	Returns the HTTP error code and associated error string if throwOnError is NO.

Using this new tag, you can post information to an external website and bypass the usual navigation and forms. You can use these parameters to let users enter information into a form in the manner that the external site expects, and then post the data to the site via an http call.

Listing 20.3 Post.cfm

```
<!---post to the external site------->
<cfhttp method="POST"
        url="http://www.MyBigSite.com"
        resolveURL = "YES"
        >

<!---post a variable called "SearchTerms", since this is what
        the site expects. ------->
<cfhttpparam type="FORMFIELD" name="SearchTerms" value="Cold-
Fusion">

<!----pass cookie so we don't get interrupted------->
<cfhttpparam type="COOKIE" name="IsMember" value="1">
        </cfhttp>

<!---output the variables created by CF------->
<cfoutput>
Response Status Code: #cfhttp.statusCode#
<br>
Response MIME Type: #cfhttp.mimetype#
<br>
Response Length: #len(cfhttp.filecontent)#
<br>
Response Content: #HTMLCodeFormat(cfhttp.filecontent)#
<br>
</cfoutput>
```

In this chapter we've seen how to create agents to automate certain processes for us. You can do a lot more with these tags, too. You must consider copyright issues when you use them. It is possible, for instance, to use CFHTTP to retrieve the weather forecast or a dynamic map from an external website, clean up the contents of the returned file using regular expression parsing, and include it on your own site. The Developer's Exchange has many such tags that show you how to do this. It's a great way to learn regular expressions if you're not comfortable with them. However, many of these tags are intended for development purposes only; many websites charge for use of their news, maps, or other content, so it's important to observe this when implementing agents.

What Do We Do Now?

In the next and final chapter we will learn how to create a complete online store. This will put a lot of the work we've done into action, all in one large application. ColdFusion is a very extensive language, however, and there is a lot more to learn. I have tried to include in this limited space the aspects of the language that you are most likely to use in your day-to-day development. I have tackled the core facets of ColdFusion, and the new features of ColdFusion 5, so you can start developing real-world applications right now. There are a number of infrequently used tags (for instance, <CFSLIDER>, <CFTABLE>) that I didn't cover, so that I could pack in more real code instead.

You now have a solid foundation in the syntax and usage of ColdFusion and can discover additional exciting aspects of the language yourself with ease. A number of "enhanced forms" tags available in ColdFusion, for instance, create Java applet forms that let you manipulate data graphically, or perform form validation for you. There is a world of interactivity that ColdFusion can perform with external COM and Java objects, FTP, and POP servers, too. Check out the complete reference in the back of this book for the complete language—all of the tags and functions—and enjoy making your own ColdFusion applications using this extended functionality. Take a look at applications on the Developer's Exchange, hang around on lists like the ColdFusion Developer's Journal or the forums, and discuss your applications with other developers. I hope you have a really good time.

A COMPLETE E-COMMERCE APPLICATION

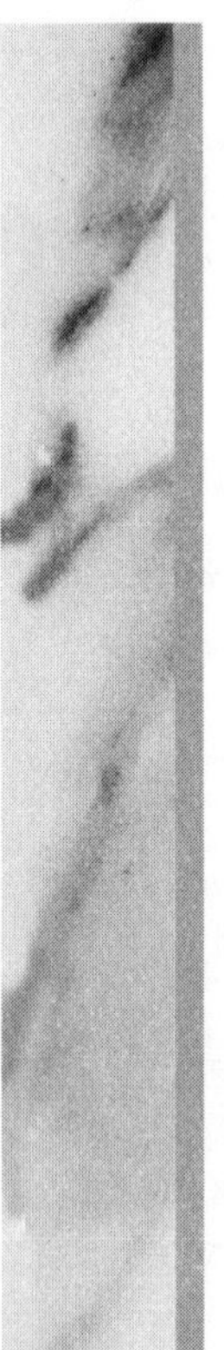

Topics in This Chapter

- All of the ColdFusion templates you need to create the store
- The database tables creation script
- More custom tags, user-defined functions, and query-of-queries

Chapter 21

This chapter is devoted entirely to the code base for a complete, working, ready-to-use e-commerce application. My aim here is not necessarily concision; I want you to have something you can use so that you can *change it,* which is, in my view, a good way to learn.

With that in mind, I have broken things up quite a bit. There are 52 files here, including the database script. That may sound like a lot, but many of them are only a few lines of code—and a lot of the code is actually comments. The structure of the application is similar to the "switchbox" search application we worked on earlier—and you will recognize some of the code. We start with the database script, which creates the tables and then alters them to create the foreign key relationships. It is written for Microsoft SQL Server but should work on Oracle or Access with little modification. The remainder of the chapter consists of all the template listings and a few screen shots that give you an idea of how it flows together.

This example application really includes everything you need to make a working e-commerce site. You have categories of products, each of which can be in a product subcategory. In my example there is a main category: Books, and it has the subcategories Non-Fiction and Philosophy. It has a search function and makes use of the query-of-queries feature new with ColdFusion 5. It creates its own log file that records information about users' habits and IP and such. The store also features a complete rotating Banner Ad system that records ad displays and click-throughs. The system is a custom tag that you can transfer with ease to other applications. User-defined functions take care of the heavy work such as calculation and program flow. Also, you can specify specials for display on the main page of your store. There is email notification and a password-protected administration area where you can log in to view the orders placed.

This store is written with several specific things in mind. First, you can add to it and modify it easily, which you certainly need to be able to do. I have tried to separate the logic layer from the presentation as much as possible. Admittedly there isn't much in the way of "presentation layer" in this particular version; most of the site is included inside one or two pages that the user actually sees. That means that you have to put the search code and the menu and so forth on only one page. That makes it easy. Second, the application makes use of a lot of the concepts we have discussed throughout the book. I have tried to focus on things that you will most need to know, such as structures, session variables, cookies, lists, custom tags, and user-defined functions. Third, the application is loaded with comments throughout, and each functional aspect of the site is broken into a template where possible, so that you can study how it works in a focused manner. Fourth, the application totals over 2500 lines of code that *work together* and incorporates many different aspects of ColdFusion. You can see how everything you have learned fits together.

There are a number of changes you could make to this application to improve it. You could create a table that holds product options (for instance, "large," "small," or "medium") and allow users to specify options for products they buy. You could use <CFGRAPH> to create Flash-based reports in the administration area. You might try using client variables instead of session variables in some places. Another good idea is to create links in the administrative area that allow you to add, edit, and delete product information. An obvious change you might make is to allow real-time processing, instead of batch processing, of credit cards. You can do this using custom CFX tags provided by Macromedia and various other vendors. Usually these tags are free, and they allow you to integrate with the processing system.

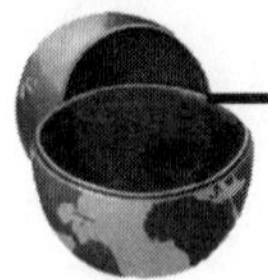

<NOTE>

You will notice that this store doesn't have the most compact code in the world. Partly that's because I want to put all you've learned into action. It's also because if you spend every day making websites, you want to make your components as modular as possible so you can move them around, easily make changes to sites, and reuse the same code base in an entirely new graphic design with little or no modification to the logic layer.

Remember, too, that this application was designed to grow, and for you to add your own components easily.

My example uses familiar products like books and movies so that it will be easy for you to populate your database. There is minimal formatting so that a style sheet can be applied with little effort. Type in the code as listed below, naming the files exactly as listed in the folders. The main folder, "Store," holds a number of files such as application.cfm. Then there are several sub-folders. Each heading below represents a folder. Have fun!

Store

Listing 21.1 CreateTables.sql

```
/**** Run this script in your text-based interface for your
database (such as SQL Server Query Analyzer, or create the
tables according to this specification*******/

/****** Object: Table [dbo].[BannerAds]
Script Date: 6/24/2001 4:44:35 PM ******/

CREATE TABLE [dbo].[BannerAds] (
        [BannerID] [int] IDENTITY (1, 1) NOT NULL ,
        [ImagePath] [varchar] (75) NULL ,
        [WebsiteURL] [varchar] (100) NULL ,
        [AltText] [varchar] (100) NULL ,
        [TimesDisplayed] [int] NULL ,
        [ClickThrus] [int] NULL
) ON [PRIMARY]
GO


/****** Object: Table [dbo].[Categories]
Script Date: 6/24/2001 4:44:36 PM ******/

CREATE TABLE [dbo].[Categories] (
        [CategoryID] [int] IDENTITY (1, 1) NOT NULL ,
        [CategoryName] [varchar] (100) NOT NULL
) ON [PRIMARY]
GO


/****** Object: Table [dbo].[Customers]
```

```
Script Date: 6/24/2001 4:44:36 PM ******/

CREATE TABLE [dbo].[Customers] (
	[CustomerID] [int] IDENTITY (1, 1) NOT NULL ,
	[billFirstName] [varchar] (100) NULL ,
	[billLastName] [varchar] (100) NULL ,
	[billAddress] [varchar] (255) NULL ,
	[billCity] [varchar] (50) NULL ,
	[billState] [varchar] (5) NULL ,
	[billZipCode] [varchar] (10) NULL ,
	[billCountry] [varchar] (100) NULL ,
	[billPhone] [varchar] (50) NULL ,
	[billEmail] [varchar] (100) NULL ,
	[shipFirstName] [varchar] (50) NULL ,
	[shipLastName] [varchar] (100) NULL ,
	[shipAddress] [varchar] (255) NULL ,
	[shipCity] [varchar] (50) NULL ,
	[shipState] [varchar] (5) NULL ,
	[shipZipCode] [varchar] (10) NULL ,
	[shipCountry] [varchar] (100) NULL ,
	[shipPhone] [varchar] (50) NULL ,
	[shipEmail] [varchar] (100) NULL ,
	[shipMethod] [varchar] (50) NULL ,
	[creditNumber] [varchar] (50) NULL ,
	[creditName] [varchar] (100) NULL ,
	[creditExpDate] [varchar] (50) NULL
) ON [PRIMARY]
GO


/****** Object: Table [dbo].[Orders]
Script Date: 6/24/2001 4:44:36 PM ******/

CREATE TABLE [dbo].[Orders] (
	[OrderConfirmation] [varchar] (50) NOT NULL ,
	[CustomerID] [int] NULL ,
	[SubTotal] [money] NULL ,
	[Shipping] [money] NULL ,
	[Tax] [money] NULL ,
	[GrandTotal] [money] NULL ,
	[OrderDate] [datetime] NULL ,
	[Processed] [bit] NOT NULL
) ON [PRIMARY]
GO

/*******In Access, the "BIT" datatype is "Yes/No" *******/
```

```
/****** Object: Table [dbo].[OrdersProducts]
Script Date: 6/24/2001 4:44:36 PM ******/

CREATE TABLE [dbo].[OrdersProducts] (
        [OrderConfirmation] [varchar] (50) NULL ,
        [ProductID] [int] NULL ,
        [Qty] [int] NULL
) ON [PRIMARY]
GO


/****** Object: Table [dbo].[Products]
Script Date: 6/24/2001 4:44:37 PM ******/

CREATE TABLE [dbo].[Products] (
        [ProductID] [int] IDENTITY (1, 1) NOT NULL ,
        [ProductName] [varchar] (75) NOT NULL ,
        [Price] [money] NOT NULL ,
        [ShortDescription] [varchar] (150) NOT NULL ,
        [LongDescription] [text] NOT NULL ,
        [SmallImage] [varchar] (100) NOT NULL ,
        [LargeImage] [varchar] (100) NOT NULL ,
        [IsSpecial] [bit] NOT NULL
) ON [PRIMARY] TEXTIMAGE_ON [PRIMARY]
GO


/****** Object: Table [dbo].[ProductsCategories]
Script Date: 6/24/2001 4:44:37 PM ******/

CREATE TABLE [dbo].[ProductsCategories] (
        [ProductID] [int] NOT NULL ,
        [CategoryID] [int] NOT NULL ,
        [SubCatID] [int] NOT NULL
) ON [PRIMARY]
GO


/****** Object: Table [dbo].[SubCategories]
Script Date: 6/24/2001 4:44:37 PM ******/

CREATE TABLE [dbo].[SubCategories] (
        [SubCatID] [int] IDENTITY (1, 1) NOT NULL ,
        [SubCatName] [varchar] (100) NOT NULL
) ON [PRIMARY]
GO
```

Listing 21.2 Application.cfm

```
<!---initialize application and set
session timeout to 25 minutes--->

<cfapplication
       name="CoreStore"
       sessionmanagement="Yes"
       sessiontimeout="#CreateTimeSpan(0,0,25,0)#"
       applicationtimeout="#CreateTimeSpan(0,1,0,0)#">

<!---initialize global variables.--->
<cfparam name="title" default="Core CF Store">

<!---set sitewide variables.
datasource username and password set in
ColdFusion Administrator--->

<cflock scope="Application" timeout="20">

<cfscript>
application.datasource = "CoreStore";
application.logfile = "C:\CoreStore.log";
application.AdminEmail = "eben@canyon.net";
</cfscript>

</cflock>
<cfset Store.fromEmail = "Orders at Core CF Store">

<!----set this to the merchant email address------>
<cfset Store.adminEmail = "Me@SomeSite.net">

<!---copy the application & session variables
structures into the request scope so we don't
have to lock them everywhere--->

<cflock scope="Application" type="ReadOnly" timeout="20">

       <cfset Request.App = StructCopy(Application)>

</cflock>

<cflock scope="Session" type="ReadOnly" timeout="20">

       <cfset Request.Ses = Duplicate(Session)>

</cflock>
```

Listing 21.3 OnRequestEnd.cfm

```
<!----copy request.Ses variables
back into SESSION scope in case they have changed.
Duplicate will copy the entire Structure.
------->
<cflock timeout="30" name="ReqSes">
      <cfset Session = Duplicate(Request.Ses)>
</cflock>

<!----for development only
<cfdump var=#StoreStruct#>
<cfdump var=#session#>---->
```

Listing 21.4 Index.cfm

```
<!---include library so that
custom functions are available
------->
<cfinclude template="Library.cfm">

<!---include header------->
<cfinclude template="header.cfm">

<!----call custom function to handle flow------->
<cfset SwitchHandler()>

<!---include log file handler.
do it here in case we do a cflocation------->

<cf_makelog thisPage="#StoreStruct.thisPage#">

<!-----set the banner action for custom tag.
Though use of IIF is not always recommended
for performance reasons, it is good to see it in
use. Try writing an if/else statement that does
the same thing.------->

<cfset banner.action = #iif(IsDefined("URL.AdAction"),
DE("click"), DE("display"))#>
```

```
<!-----randomly get a banner for display,
hit the database, and display it.
Show or relocate based on action------->

<cf_makeBanner action=#banner.action#>


<cfif StoreStruct.action neq "Checkout">

<!----put category queries
inside the "Shop" switch so that
we aren't running queries unnecessarily in the
"Checkout" process------->

<!---categories for display------->
<cfinclude template="Queries/qry_getCategories.cfm">

<!---include catalog of categories
and each product therein. That way we
can speed things up by requerying the
query, not the database------->
<cfinclude template="Queries/qry_getCatalog.cfm">

</cfif>


<!---switch against structure to perform appropriate store
action------->
<cfswitch expression="#StoreStruct.Action#">

<cfcase value="Shop">


        <cfswitch expression="#StoreStruct.thisPage#">

        <!----Browsing------->
                <cfcase value = "SubCat">
                <!----they want to see subcategories within a
category, and the products therein------->

<cfinclude template="Queries/qry_getSubCats.cfm">

<cfinclude template="display.cfm">
                </cfcase>

                <cfcase value = "Detail">
```

```
<cfinclude template="Queries/qry_getProductDetail.cfm">
<cfinclude template="display.cfm">
            </cfcase>

        <!----Shopping Basket interactions------->
            <cfcase value = "Basket">

        <!---this template calculates what needs to get passed
to <CF_Basket> custom tag)------->

        <cfinclude template="MakeBasketParams.cfm">
                    <!----pass to custom tag------->

        <cf_basket action = #basket.action#
            idx = #Request.idx#
            thisProduct = #basket.ProductID#>

        <!---set thisPage var to pass to display switch, since
it won't really be in the URL; this displays
the basket after each transaction with it, and when My Basket
is clicked------->

                    <cfif not isDefined("URL.thisPage")>
                        <cfset URL.thisPage = "basket">
                    </cfif>

                    <cfinclude template="display.cfm">

            </cfcase>
        </cfswitch>
</cfcase>




<cfcase value="Checkout">

<!---make sure their basket has not expired before every
checkout action------->

<cfinclude template="Checkout/CheckBasket.cfm">

        <!----handles the checkout process------->
        <cfswitch expression = "#StoreStruct.thisPage#">
```

```
        <!---which step of the checkout process are we in?--->

                <cfcase value="billinfo">
                <!----show the billing form------->
        <cfinclude template = "Checkout/ShowBilling.cfm">
                </cfcase>

                <cfcase value="shipinfo">
        <!---include the query that inserts billing info---->
        <cfinclude template="Checkout/PutBillInfo.cfm">

<!----show the billing form, since conditional logic allows us
to reuse it as the shipping form too------->

        <cfinclude template = "Checkout/ShowBilling.cfm">
                </cfcase>

                <cfcase value="creditinfo">
        <!----include put ship info from last step------->

        <cfinclude template="Checkout/PutShipInfo.cfm">
        <!---show form for entering credit info------->
        <cfinclude template = "Checkout/ShowCreditInfo.cfm">

                </cfcase>

                <cfcase value="confirmOrder">

        <!----include put credit info from last step------->
        <cfinclude template="Checkout/PutCreditInfo.cfm">

        <cfinclude template="Checkout/Confirmation.cfm">

                </cfcase>

                <cfcase value="Complete">

                <!---insert data into database------->
                <cfinclude template="Checkout/putOrder.cfm">

                <!---notify admin and customer of order by
email, and display thank you page------->

<cfinclude template="Checkout/complete.cfm">
                </cfcase>

                <cfdefaultcase>
```

```
<cfthrow message="No checkout step has been
               defined.<br>Please notify the site admin.">
               </cfdefaultcase>

       </cfswitch>
</cfcase>


<cfcase value="Search">

       <!---user wants to search the products------->
       <cfinclude template="display.cfm">

</cfcase>

<cfdefaultcase>

       <!----Action=default display page with
       categories and specials------->
       <cfinclude template="display.cfm">

</cfdefaultcase>

</cfswitch>

<!---call footer, which is a custom tag only so you can pass a
"path" attribute (such as "../") if your site gets large------
->
<cf_footer>
```

Listing 21.5 Header.cfm

```
<!------Header will always be included------>
<html>
<head>
<!---link to stylesheet, metatags here------->
<cfoutput><title>#title#</title></cfoutput>
</head>

<body bgcolor="#FFFFFF">

<h1><a href="index.cfm">Core CF Store</a></h1>

<!---table for view cart link and search form------->
<table border="0" align="right">
```

```
<tr align="right">
<td>
<a href="index.cfm?action=Shop&do=View&thisPage=Basket">
My Basket</a>
</td>
</tr>
<tr>
<td align="right">

<!---search form. Try moving this to the main body so that it
doesn't show during the checkout process. ------->

<cfform action="index.cfm?thisPage=search">

<cfinput type="Text" name="SearchTerms">
<!---you can use an image here instead------->
<input type="submit" value="Search">

</cfform>

</td>
</tr>
</table>
```

Listing 21.6 Footer.cfm

```
<!----use thisPath attribute so that
you can easily specify different image paths
depending on where you are in the directory
structure ------->

<cfparam name="attributes.thisPath" default="">
<br>
<br>
<br>
<hr width="60%" align="right">
<br>

<table border="0" align="center">
<tr><td>contact | <a href="index.cfm"<home</a> | about us >/
td></tr>
</table>

<!----end the HTML---->
<br>
```

```
<br>
</body>
</html>
```

Listing 21.7 Display.cfm

```
<!---display.cfm
presentation layer------->

<!---include code to show banner ad.
We include it so that it can be included
on other presentation pages (like in checkout),
too, that don't use this page------->
<cfinclude template="ShowBanner.cfm">


<!-----content areas------->
<table border=0 width="98%">
<!----left side------->
<tr><td width="20%">
<!----make tables and graphics here------->
<br>
<!----output categories------->
<cfloop query="getcategories" >
<cfoutput>
<a href="index.cfm?action=Shop&thisPage=SubCat&catID=#get-
categories.CategoryID#">
<h2>#getcategories.CategoryName#</h2></a><br></cfoutput>
</cfloop>
<br>
</td>
<!----middle------->
<td>
<!---show default page or a store page------->
<cfif not isDefined("URL.thisPage")>
<!---only show specials on the default page,
don't run the query if we don't need to.------->
        <cfinclude template = "Queries/qry_getSpecials.cfm">
        <cfinclude template = "middle.cfm">
<cfelse>
<!----thisPage IS defined, so do specified action------->
<cfswitch expression = "#thisPage#">

<cfcase value="SubCat">
<!---show the products in this subcategory------->
```

```
<cfinclude template="Shop/ShowProducts.cfm">

</cfcase>

<cfcase value="Detail">
        <!---show product detail info------->
        <cfinclude template="Shop/ShowDetail.cfm">
<br>
</cfcase>

<cfcase value="Basket">
<!-----this case displays the cart after any interaction with
it (adding, removing, updating qty)------->

<cfinclude template="Shop/ShowBasket.cfm">

</cfcase>

<cfcase value="Search">
        <!---query to get products included in index------->
        <cfinclude template="Queries/qry_SearchProducts.cfm">
        <cfinclude template="Shop/Search.cfm">

</cfcase>

<!----end thisPage switch------->
</cfswitch>
</cfif>
</td>

<!----right side column------->
<td>
<cfinclude template="ShowRight.cfm">
</td>
</tr>
</table>
```

Figure 21.1 shows the store page that greets the user.

Listing 21.8 Middle.cfm

```
<!-----default content for middle section------->
I am the middle content area.
<br>
At this store you can buy some things.
```

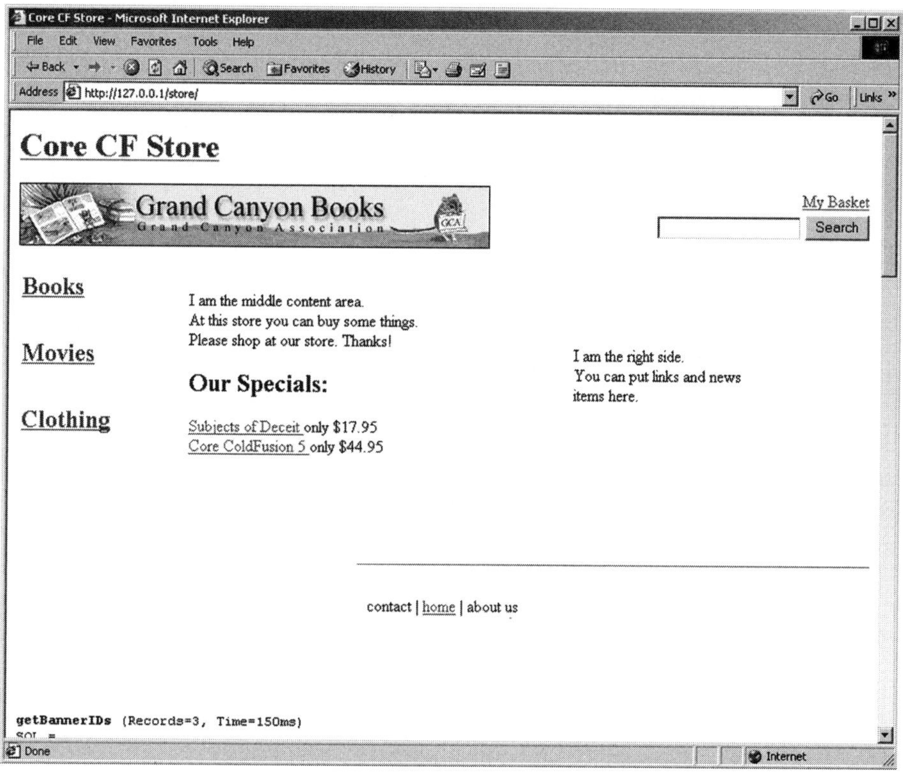

Figure 21.1 The main page of the store when the user enters.

```
<br>
Please shop at our store. Thanks!
<br>
<h2>Our Specials:</h2>

<!----Display a special here. Specials are marked in the
database. Query is run in
index------->
<cfloop query="getSpecials">
        <cfoutput>
        <a href="index.cfm?action=Shop&thisPage=Detail&this-
Product=#getSpecials.ProductID#">
        #getSpecials.ProductName#
        </a>
        only #DollarFormat(getSpecials.Price)#<br>
        </cfoutput>
</cfloop>
```

Listing 21.9 ShowRight.cfm

```
<!---here is the content for the
right-hand column.
you can put links, ads, or news here
------->

I am the right side.<br>
You can put links and news <br> items here.<br>
```

Listing 21.10 ShowBanner.cfm

```
<!---the only job of this code is to display a banner any-
where on the site that has access to the results of the
<CF_MakeBanner> custom tag------->

<cfoutput>
<ahref="index.cfm?AdAction=Click&thisURL=#strBanner.Web
siteURL#&BannerID=#strBanner.BannerID#"
        target="_blank">

<!---the image, alt text, and URL are stored in the
        database--->

<img src="images/banners/#strBanner.ImagePath#"
        alt="#strBanner.AltText#"
        width="468" height="60" border="0"></a>
</cfoutput>
```

Listing 21.11 Library.cfm

```
<!-----site library------->

<!-----SwitchHandler defines a structure
to pass the current page and actions to. It accepts URL and
form variables that are used in Index.cfm for processing
control.

The chief benefits are speed and separating the
logic layer from the presentation layer, and it
encapsulates the backbone of the
site for readability
```

```
------->
<cfscript>
function SwitchHandler() {

        // create global structure 'StoreStruct'
        // for site variables that
        // tell the switchbox what to do or display

        StoreStruct = StructNew();

        // create StoreStruct variables.
        if (IsDefined("URL.thisPage"))
                StoreStruct.thisPage = URL.thisPage;

        // basket uses form to pass thisPage variable
        else if (IsDefined("FORM.thisPage"))
                StoreStruct.thisPage = FORM.thisPage;
        else
                StoreStruct.thisPage = "Default";

        if (IsDefined("URL.Action"))
                StoreStruct.Action = URL.Action;
        else if (IsDefined("FORM.Action"))
                StoreStruct.Action = FORM.Action;
        else StoreStruct.Action = "Default";

        }
</cfscript>

<!-----remember that in many cases using script is faster
than using <cfset>---->
```

Listing 21.12 MakeBanner

```
<!----
<cf_makebanner> custom tag that
handles retrieval, display, and logging of banner ads
------->
<cfsetting enablecfoutputonly="Yes">

<cfparam name="attributes.action" default="display">

<cfswitch expression="#attributes.action#">
<cfcase value="display">
```

```
<!---get all the banner ids------->

<cfquery name="getBannerIDs" datasource="#Request.App.Data
source#">

SELECT BannerID
FROM BannerAds;

</cfquery>

<!----choose a random banner from known ids ------->

<cfset VARIABLES.RandomID = RandRange(1, getBannerIDs.Record-
Count)>

<cfset VARIABLES.thisBannerID = ListGetAt((ValueList(getBan-
nerIDs.BannerID)), VARIABLES.RandomID)>

<!----Get a banner ad with that ID --->

<cfquery name="getOneBanner"  datasource="#Request.App.Data-
source#">
        SELECT BannerID, ImagePath, AltText, WebsiteURL
        FROM BannerAds
        WHERE BannerID = #VARIABLES.thisBannerID#;
</cfquery>


<!---return ad to calling template for display------->

<cfscript>
caller.strBanner = StructNew();
caller.strBanner.BannerID = getOneBanner.BannerID;
caller.strBanner.ImagePath = getOneBanner.ImagePath;
caller.strBanner.AltText = getOneBanner.AltText;
caller.strBanner.WebsiteURL = getOneBanner.WebsiteURL;
</cfscript>

<!----update times displayed------->
<cfquery name="UpdateBanners" datasource="#Request.App.Data-
source#">
        UPDATE BannerAds
        SET TimesDisplayed = TimesDisplayed + 1
        WHERE BannerID = #VARIABLES.thisBannerID#;
</cfquery>
```

```
</cfcase>

<cfcase value="click">

<!----update click-throughs. You must make sure
database does not have NULL values for these columns,
or it won't update. Set a default value of 0.------->

<cfquery name="UpdateBanners" datasource="#Request.App.Data
source#">
        UPDATE BannerAds
        SET ClickThrus = ClickThrus + 1
        WHERE BannerID = #URL.BannerID#;
</cfquery>

<!----and redirect------->
<cflocation url="#URL.thisURL#">
<cfabort>
</cfcase>
</cfswitch>

<cfsetting enablecfoutputonly="No">
```

Listing 21.13 MakeLog.cfm

```
<!---creates a plain text log file. Try using the new <CFLOG>
tag instead, or customizing the output.------->

<cfparam name="attributes.thisPage" default="Default"
type="string">
<cfparam name="attributes.theTime" default="#Now()#"
type="date">

<!---write the log. Put your output on one line
or ColdFusion will honor the line breaks------->
<cffile action="append"  file="#Request.App.Logfile#"
        output="#attributes.thisPage#, #cgi.query_string#,
        #cgi.remote_addr#, #cgi.http_referer#,
        #cgi.http_user_agent#,
        #attributes.theTime#">

<!----the log will be automatically created if
it doesn't exist ------->
```

Listing 21.14 MakeBasketParams.cfm

```
<!---
called from index.cfm?action=shop&thisPage=Basket

this template calculates necessary
parameters to pass to the custom tag.------->

<!---get the action from the URL in the  "Add to Cart"
link------->
<cfparam name="basket.action" default="#URL.do#">

<!---you can only add or delete or update a particular prod-
uct.
so the URL.ProductID should always get passed.------->
<cfparam name="URL.thisProduct" default="">
<cfparam name="basket.ProductID" default="#URL.thisProduct#">

<cflock scope="SESSION" timeout="30" type="EXCLUSIVE">

        <cfscript>
        // create basket if it doesn't exist
        if (not isDefined("Session.arrBasket")) {
                Session.arrBasket = ArrayNew(2);
                }
        // create a new length so we don't overwrite anything
        // remember ColdFusion arrays start at one, not zero
        if (isDefined("URL.thisidx")) {
                Request.idx = URL.thisidx;
        }
        // check for URL param in case action is remove item
        else {
                Request.idx = ArrayLen(Session.arrBasket) + 1;
        }
        </cfscript>
</cflock>
```

Listing 21.15 Basket.cfm

```
<!----<CF_Basket>
creates a shopping cart if it does not already exist
use after <CF_MakeBasketParams>
add an item
remove an item
```

```
------->
<cfsetting enablecfoutputonly="Yes">
<cfparam name="attributes.action" default="">
<cfparam name="attributes.thisProduct" default="">
<cfparam name="attributes.Qty" default="1">


<cfswitch expression="#attributes.action#">

<cfcase value="add">
<!----- get product name and price,
which we need to display to the user.
don't pass the info so user cannot modify it.
also, it's easier to handle and maintain.------->

<!----add item to basket------->

<cfquery name="getProductInfo" datasource="#Request.App.data
source#">
        SELECT ProductID, ProductName, Price
        FROM Products
        WHERE ProductID = #attributes.thisProduct#;
</cfquery>

<cflock scope="SESSION" timeout="30" type="EXCLUSIVE">

<cfscript>
// set ProductID
        Session.arrBasket[Request.idx][1] = "#attributes.this
Product#";
// set product name
        Session.arrBasket[Request.idx][2] = "#getProduct
Info.ProductName#";
// set price
        Session.arrBasket[Request.idx][3] = "#getProduct
Info.Price#";
// set quantity
        Session.arrBasket[Request.idx][4] =
"#attributes.qty#";
</cfscript>
</cflock>


</cfcase>

<cfcase value="remove">
<!----take one item out of the basket------->
```

```
<cfset ArrayDeleteAt(Session.arrBasket, "#Request.idx#")>
</cfcase>

<!---update basket quantities--->
<cfcase value="update">
<cflock scope= "SESSION" timeout="30" type= "EXCLUSIVE">
<cfscript>
      //set qty
      for (i=1; lte arraylen(session.arrBasket); i=i+1)
{session.arrBasket[i]} [4] = evaluate ("form.Quantity_"&i);
{
</cfscript>
</cflock>
</cfcase>
</cfswitch>

<cfsetting enablecfoutputonly="No">
```

Shop

Now make a folder within the store folder called "Shop." It contains files related to users browsing your store, selecting items, and adding them to their shopping basket.

Listing 21.16 Search.cfm

```
<!--- displays Search results from form in header
       included from display.cfm--->

<table cellspacing="0" cellpadding="2" border="0"
width="100%">
<tr>
<td>

<p>
<cfoutput>
Your search for <b>#FORM.SearchTerms#</b> returned

<cfif SearchProducts.RecordCount eq "1">
#SearchProducts.RecordCount# result.
<cfelse> <b>#SearchProducts.RecordCount#</b> results.
</cfif>
```

```
</cfoutput>

<p>
</td></tr><tr><td>
<table border=0 cellpadding="5" cellspacing="5">
<tr><td colspan=2><p> </p></td>
</tr>

<!---output the results. We really should query the catalog
query here, which already has all the info we need.

The only problem is that the query object is case sensitive.
The way around this is to set the user-provided search terms
into caps, query the query with the modified string, and then
return. That's a good exercise to try.
------>
<tr>
<cfoutput query="SearchProducts">
<td valign="top"<<b>
<ahref="index.cfm?action=Shop&thisPage=Detail&thisProduct=
#SearchProducts.ProductID#">
#ProductName#</a>
</b>
</td>


<!----show short description------->
<td valign="top">#SearchProducts.ShortDescription#...
</td>
<td valign="top">#DollarFormat(Price)#
</td></tr>
</cfoutput>
</table>
</td>
</tr>
</table>
```

Figure 21.2 shows our search results.

Listing 21.17 ShowProducts.cfm

```
<!----show products in
specified subcategory------->

<cfloop query="getSubCats">
<cfoutput><h2>#getSubCats.SubCatName#</h2>
```

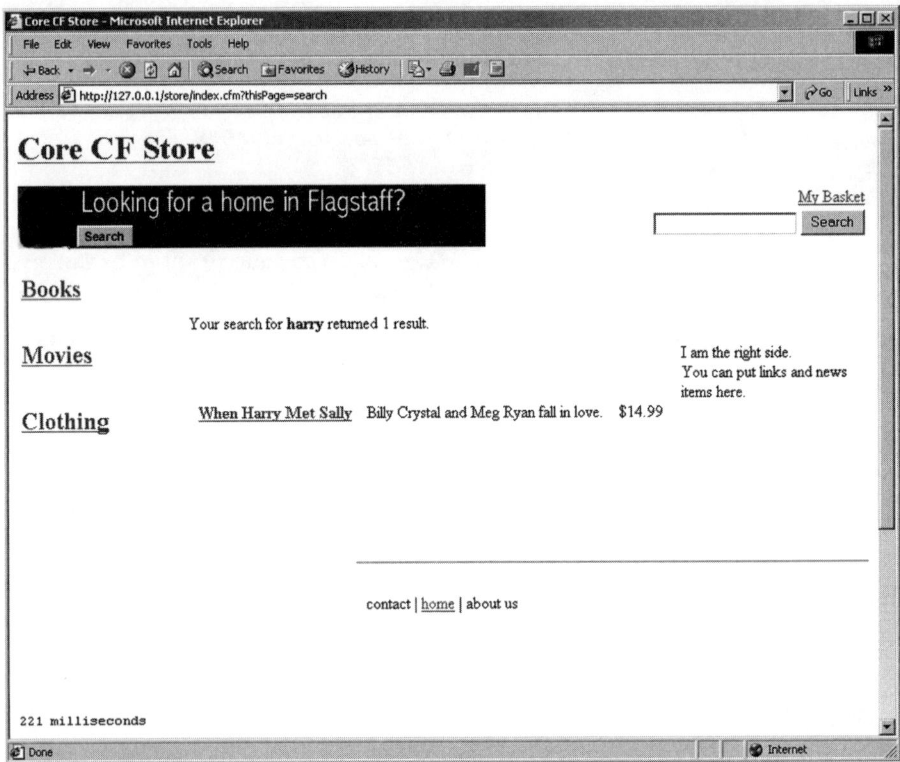

Figure 21.2 Results of a keyword search.

```
<table border="0" width="60%">
<tr><td>
<ahref="index.cfm?action=Shop&thisPage=Detail&thisProduct=
#getSubCats.ProductID#">
<img src="images/products/#getSubCats.SmallImage#" bor-
der="0"</a>
</td>
<td>
<b>
<a href="index.cfm?action=Shop&thisPage=Detail&thisProd-
uct=#getSubCats.ProductID#">
#getSubCats.ProductName#</a>
</b>
</td>
</tr>
<tr><td> </td>
<td>#DollarFormat(getSubCats.Price)#</td></tr>
<tr><td> </td>
<td>#getSubCats.ShortDescription#</td></tr>
```

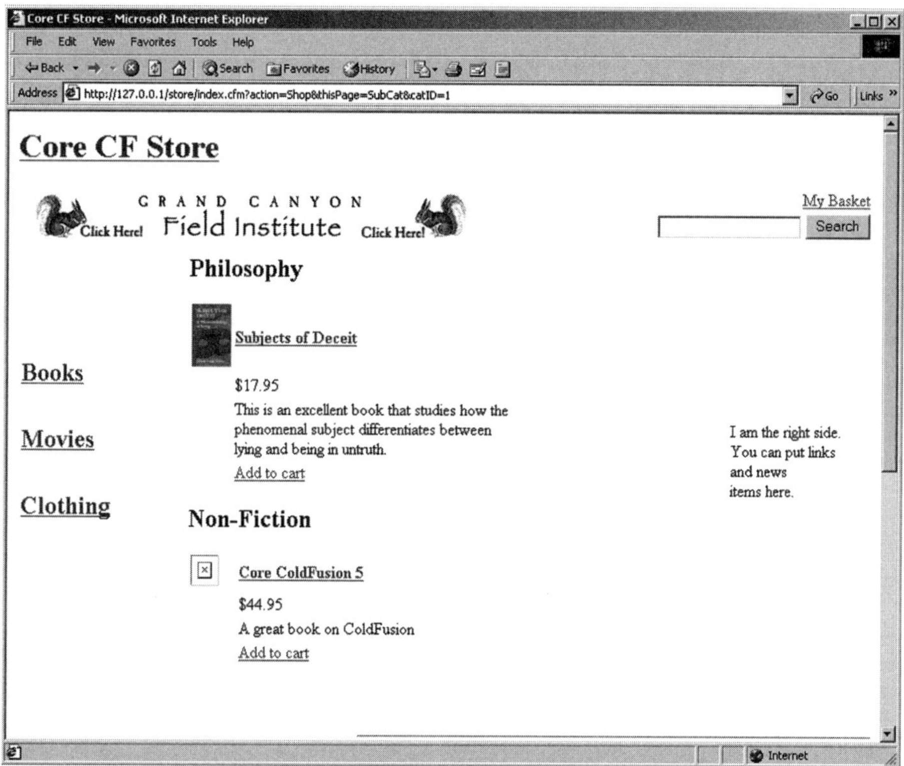

Figure 21.3 Product listings in a particular subcategory.

```
<tr><td> </td>
<td>
<a href="index.cfm?action=Shop&thisPage=Basket&do=Add&this-
Product=#getSubCats.ProductID#">
Add to cart</a>
</td>
</tr>
</table>
</cfoutput>
</cfloop>
```

Figure 21.3 shows our subcategory product listings.

Listing 21.18 ShowDetail.cfm

```
<!----displays product detail------->
<cfoutput>
<br>
```

```
<table border="0">
<tr>
<td>
<img src="images/products/#getProductDetail.LargeImage#">
</td>
<td>
<b>#getProductDetail.ProductName#</b>
</td></tr>
<tr>
<td> </td>
<td>#DollarFormat(getProductDetail.Price)#</td></tr>
<tr>
<td> </td>
<td>#getProductDetail.LongDescription#</td></tr>
<tr><td> </td>
<td>
<a href="index.cfm?action=Shop&thisPage=Basket&do=Add&this-
Product=#getProductDetail.ProductID#">
Add to cart
</a></td></tr>
</table>
</cfoutput>
```

Figure 21.4 displays product detail.

Listing 21.19 ShowBasket.cfm

```
<!---displays the current basket contents------->

<cfif ArrayLen(Session.arrBasket) neq 0>

<!---show products added to basket if there are any in it---
---->

<!----table headers--->
<table border="0" width="80%">
<tr>
<td align="center"><b>Item</b><br></td>
<td align="center"><b>Qty.</b><br></td>
<td align="center"><b>Price</b><br></td>
<td align="center"><b>Total</b><br></td>
<td> </td>
</tr>
<form name="basket" action="index.cfm?action=Shop&this-
Page=Basket&do=update"method=post>
<!----loop over basket and
```

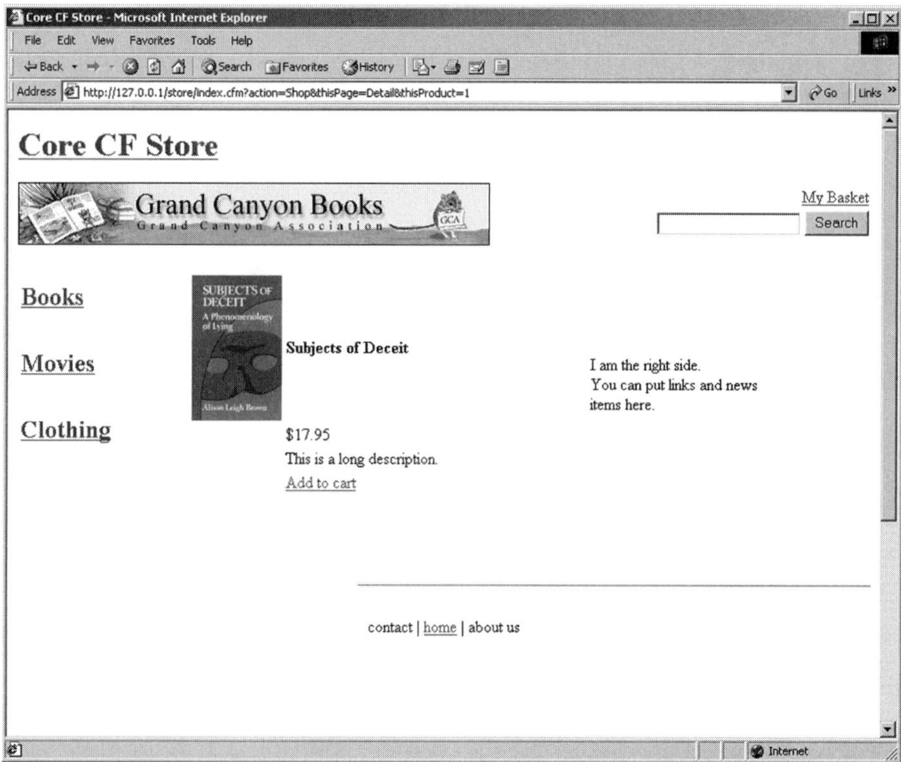

Figure 21.4 A product in detail has a longer description and a bigger picture.

```
output each item's values (name, price, qty)------->
<cfloop from="1" to = "#ArrayLen(Session.arrBasket)#" index =
"Request.idx">
<cfoutput>

<!----set array into local variables for ease of use------->

<cflock scope="SESSION" type="EXCLUSIVE" timeout="30">

<cfscript>
        NumberItems = ArrayLen(Session.arrBasket);
        ProductID = Session.arrBasket[Request.idx][1];
        ProductName = Session.arrBasket[Request.idx][2];
        Price = Session.arrBasket[Request.idx][3];
        Qty = Session.arrBasket[Request.idx][4];
</cfscript>

</cflock>
```

```
<tr>
<td>
<a href="index.cfm?action=Shop&thisPage=Detail&thisProd-
uct=#ProductID#">
#ProductName#</a>

</td>

<!---quantity------->
<td align="center">

<!---quantity------->
<td align="center">

<input type="Text" name="Quantity_#Request.idx#"
      value="#Qty#" size="2" maxlength="2">

<br></td>

<td align="right">#DollarFormat(Price)#<br></td>

<!----- product price times quantity------>
<td align="right">#DollarFormat(Price * Qty)#<br></td>

<td align="center">


<!----use thisIdx variable with the value of current loop
iteration
as the position holder for this
element in the array so that it can be removed. ------->

<a href="index.cfm?action=Shop&thisPage=Bas-
ket&do=Remove&thisProduct=#ProductID#&thisidx=#Request.idx#">
</cfoutput>
<font size="-1">remove</font></a>
<br></td>
</tr>

<!----create subtotal------->
<cfparam name = "Basket.SubTotal" default = 0>
<!------------>

<cfscript>
Basket.SubTotal = (evaluate(Basket.SubTotal + (Session.arr
Basket[Request.idx][3] * qty)));
</cfscript>
```

```
</cfloop>
<tr><td colspan="2" align="left"><input type="submit"
value="update"></form></td>

<!----output the subtotal (qty * price for each item)---->
<tr>
<td colspan="3" align="right">
<b>SubTotal </b><br></td>

<td align="right">
<cfoutput>#DollarFormat(Basket.SubTotal)#</cfoutput><ltd>

</tr>
<tr>
<td> </td>
<td>
<a href="index.cfm?action=Checkout&thisPage=billinfo">
Checkout</a>
</td>
</tr>

</table>

<cfelse>

There are no items in your basket.

</cfif>
```

Figure 21.5 shows our basket contents.

Images

The images folder has other folders in it: one for Banner ads, called "Banners," and another for small and large Product images called "Products." You can create other folders here as needed.

Queries

This folder holds templates that have only queries on them. These queries are then included within or before other templates. This allows for better code

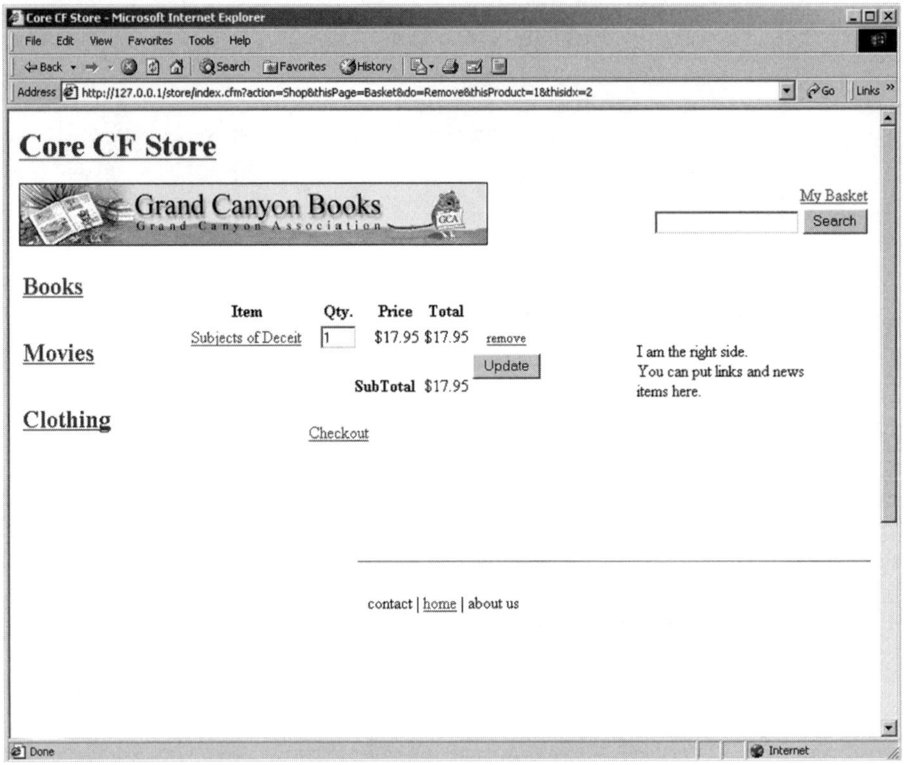

Figure 21.5 The shopping basket displayed.

readability, debugging, and maintenance. It has worked well for me. Remember that using the query-of-queries feature in this way, which brings the catalog into memory, works just fine for small to medium-sized sites. It will mean that a user's initial page load is a bit slow, and then the rest of the site will load very fast.

Listing 21.20 qry_getCatalog.cfm

```
<!----this query retrieves all of the
related category, subcategory, and product info
so that the entire catalog can be displayed
without hitting the database again.
This will enhance speed and network traffic.
------->

<cfquery name="getcatalog"
       datasource="#Request.App.datasource#">
```

```
SELECT PC.CategoryID, C.CategoryName, PC.SubCatID,
PC.ProductID, SC.SubCatName, P.ProductName,
P.ShortDescription, P.LongDescription, P.Price,
P.SmallImage, P.LargeImage

FROM ProductsCategories PC

LEFT JOIN Categories C
ON  C.CategoryID = PC.CategoryID

LEFT JOIN SubCategories SC
ON  SC.SubCatID = PC.SubCatID

LEFT JOIN Products P
ON  P.ProductID = PC.ProductID

</cfquery>
```

Listing 21.21 qry_getCategories.cfm

```
<!----this query gets the categories for
output------->

<cfquery name="getCategories">
       datasource="#Request.App.datasource#">

SELECT CategoryID, CategoryName
FROM Categories

</cfquery>
```

Listing 21.22 qry_GetSubCats.cfm

```
<!----choose the products in a
       selected subcategory------->

<cfquery name="getSubcats" dbtype="query">

SELECT SubCatName, ProductID, ProductName,
              Price, ShortDescription, SmallImage

FROM getCatalog
```

```
WHERE CategoryID = #URL.catID#

</cfquery>
```

Listing 21.23 qry_GetProductDetail.cfm

```
<!----get product details from the catalog query------->

<cfquery name="getProductDetail" dbtype="query">

SELECT ProductID, ProductName, Price,
       LongDescription, LargeImage

FROM getCatalog

WHERE ProductID = #URL.thisProduct#

</cfquery>
```

Listing 21.24 qry_GetSpecials.cfm

```
<!----get items that are on
      special for default page
      cached for one day. It's probably a good idea to cache
some of these other queries--------->

<cfquery name="getSpecials"
       datasource="#Request.App.datasource#"
       cachedwithin="#CreateTimeSpan(0,1,0,0)#"

SELECT *
FROM Products
WHERE IsSpecial = 1;

</cfquery>
```

Listing 21.25 qry_SearchProducts.cfm

```
<!---search the catalog query.
We're going back to the database
for this, since a query of queries is
```

```
case sensitive. Rewrite this so it queries the query as
explained in the opening of this chapter. ------->

<cfquery datasource="#Request.App.datasource#" name="Search
Products">

SELECT       ProductID, ProductName, ShortDescription, Price

FROM         Products

WHERE        (ProductName like '%#form.searchTerms#%'
       OR ShortDescription like '%#form.searchTerms#%')

ORDER BY     ProductName

</cfquery>
```

Checkout

The Checkout folder contains all of the templates related to the checkout process. Once a user clicks "checkout," we're routed to that case in the switch. The process has several steps. First, the customer enters her billing information. She chooses what kind of shipping she wants and whether or not the order will be shipped to the same person it is billed to. These two "pages" are actually one template, whose form fields, and the information in them, are dynamically generated. This is a good example of how to reuse code and keep the number of templates in your application down. These forms use enhanced ColdFusion forms, which perform JavaScript form validation. Using the <CFFORM> tag instead of the regular HTML form tag allows you to enter a message that will appear in a JavaScript alert if a form field is left empty or the data entered is improper. See Appendix A for more information on this tag.

Once the billing and shipping information has been entered, the user enters her credit card information in a separate step, and then is presented with all of the order information on one complete page. This can be printed as a mail-in invoice but is used here as a confirmation step, so that the user is certain that all provided information and product information is correct. At that point, the user hits the "Place Order" button, and the order is sent to the database. An email confirmation is sent to the user, and an email notification that a new order has been placed is sent to the site merchant (as specified in application.cfm).

We'll start with "ShowBilling.cfm," since it is the first step in the Checkout process. Remember that the index.cfm switch one folder above is still doing the program flow work.

Listing 21.26 ShowBilling.cfm

```
<!----in order to reduce the number
of pages we have to use, and the amount
of code to be written, we will use the same page
for the shipping info as for the billing info.
We just set the variables we need based on what step
we're in. But not only does the billing page get reused
as the shipping page, if the user checks that
the shipping and billing are the same, the
shipping form is automatically populated with
data, and displayed only for confirmation.
------->


<!---if this button has not been passed, we need to show
billing info, since it comes first.------->

<cfscript>

if (isDefined("FORM.ShippingSame")) {
// post it to a different page depending on what step we're in
thisStep = "ship";

// this will appear as "creditinfo" in a hidden field on the
//form
nextStep = "credit";



pagetitle = "Shipping Information";

/* if the shipping address is not the same
       as the billing address, set these fields to blank
       for the Shipping form */

if (FORM.ShippingSame is "Yes") {
       firstname = "#FORM.billfirstname#";
       lastname = "#Form.billLastName#";
       Address = "#FORM.billAddress#";
       City = "#FORM.billCity#";
```

```
        State = "#FORM.billState#";
        ZipCode = "#FORM.billZipCode#";
        Country = "#FORM.billCountry#";
        Phone = "#FORM.billPhone#";
        Email = "#FORM.billEmail#";
        }
        else {
        firstname = "";
        lastname = "";
        Address = "";
        City = "";
        State = "";
        ZipCode = "";
        Country = "";
        Phone = "";
        Email = "";
        }
}
else {
thisStep = "bill";
nextStep = "ship";
pagetitle = "Billing Information";
        firstname = "";
        lastname = "";
        Address = "";
        City = "";
        State = "";
        ZipCode = "";
        Country = "";
        Phone = "";
        Email = "";
}

</cfscript>

<!---include code to show banner ad.
We include it so that it can be included
on other presentation pages (such as checkout),
too------->
<cfinclude template="../ShowBanner.cfm">

<cfoutput>
<p><h2>#pageTitle#</h2></p>
</cfoutput>

<cfform name="PersonalInfo" method="post" action="index.cfm">
<cfoutput>
```

```
<!---pass these params to the switchbox------->
<input type = "hidden" name="action" value = "Checkout">
<input type = "hidden" name="thisPage"
value = "#nextstep#Info">

<cfif nextStep is "Credit">
      <input type="hidden" name="CustomerID" value="
#GetLas tID.CustomerID#">
      <input type="hidden" name = "ShipMethod"
value="#FORM.ShipMethod#">
</cfif>

<table width="50%" align="center">
<tr>
<td colspan="2" align="center"><b>#pageTitle#</b><br></td>
</tr>

<!---the "message" attribute of the cfinput tag, which must
always be inside a cfform tag, lets you specify a JavaScript
alert message if no data is entered in that form control.--->


<tr><td align="left" width="110">First Name<br></td>
<td>
<cfinput name="#thisStep#FirstName" size="25" maxlength="100"
required="yes"
message="You must enter the First Name."
value="#FirstName#"><br>
</td>
</tr>

<tr><td align="left" width="110"Last Name<br></td>
<td>
<cfinput name="#thisStep#LastName" size="25" maxlength="100"
required="yes"
message="You must enter the Last Name."
value="#LastName#"><br>
</td>
</tr>

<tr><td align="left" align="top"Address<br></td>
<td>
<textarea cols=23 rows=2 wrap="virtual"
name="#thisStep#Address">
#Address#
</textarea>
```

```
<br></td>
</tr>

<tr>
<td align="left">City<br></td>
<td>
<cfinput name="#thisStep#City" size="25" maxlength="50"
required="yes"
message="You must enter the City." value="#City#"<<br>
</td>
</tr>
<tr>
<td align="left"State<br></td>
<td>
<SELECT NAME="#thisStep#State" SIZE="1">
<cfinclude template="StateList.cfm"<<br>
</td>
</tr>
<tr>
<td align="left">Zip Code<br></td>
<td>
<cfinput name="#thisStep#ZipCode" size="25" maxlength="10"
required="yes"
message="You must enter the Zip Code." value="#Zip
Code#"<br></td>
</tr>
<tr>
<td align="left">Country<br></font></td>
<td>
<cfinput name="#thisStep#Country" size="25" maxlength="100"
required="yes"
message="You must enter the Country." value="#Country#"<<br>
</td>
</tr>
<tr>
<td align="left"Phone<br></font></td>
<td>
<cfinput name="#thisStep#Phone" size="25" maxlength="50"
required="yes"
message="You must enter the Phone Number."
value="#Phone#"<<br></td>
</tr>
<tr>
<td align="left">E-mail<br></td>
<td>
```

```
<cfinput name="#thisStep#Email" size="25" maxlength="100"
required="yes"
message="You must enter the E-mail Address."
value="#Email#"<<br>
</td>
</tr>

<cfif thisStep is "bill">

<tr>
<td colspan="2" align="center"><b>Shipping Information</b>
<br></td>
</tr>

<!---only ask for this info if they are in the billing step.
Otherwise, leave it out.------->
<tr>
<td>
<!----if different shipping address, display it on next
step------->
Ship to same address<br>as billing address?<br>
</td><td>
<input type="radio" name="ShippingSame" value="Yes" checked>
Yes
<input type="radio" name="ShippingSame" value="No"> No<br>
</td>
</tr>
<tr>
<td align="left" valign="top">Ship Method<br></td><td>

<input type="radio" name="ShipMethod" value="Ground" checked>
Ground
<input type="radio" name="ShipMethod" value="Express>"
Express<br>
<input type="radio" name="ShipMethod" value="International">
International<br>

</td>
</tr>
</cfif>
<tr>
<td colspan="2" align="right">

<!---next step is CONFIRMATION------->
<input type="submit" value="Go to the Next Step">
</td>
</tr>
```

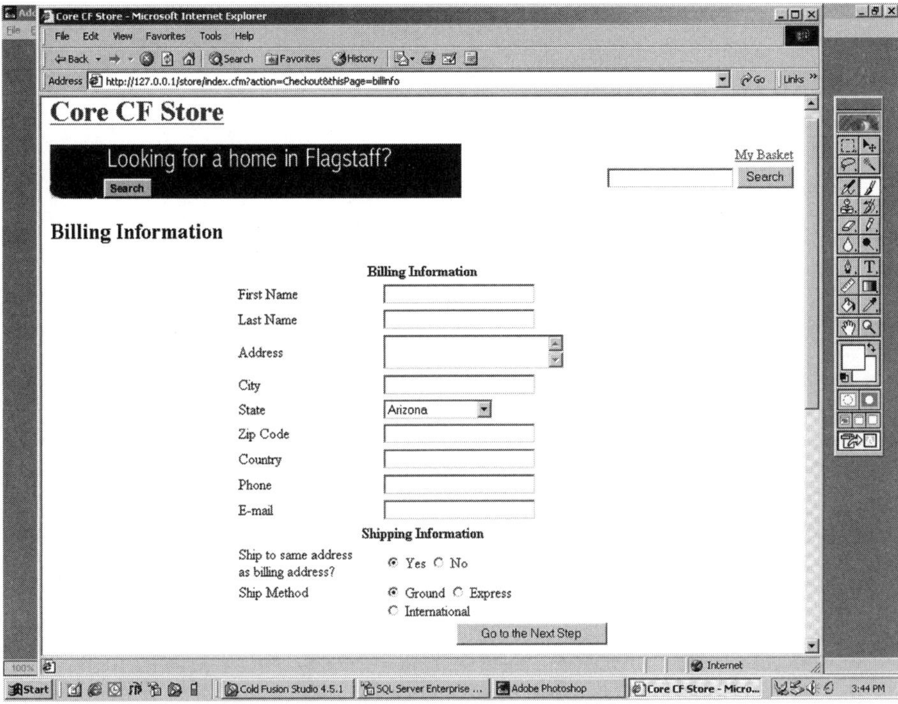

Figure 21.6 Billing information page.

```
</table>
</cfoutput>
</cfform>
</center>
```

Figure 21.6 shows the billing information page.

Listing 21.27 PutBillInfo

```
<!----this template inserts the billing information
into the Customers table------->

<cftransaction isolation="READ_COMMITTED">

<cfquery name="PutBillInfo" datasource="#Request.App.data-
source#">

INSERT INTO Customers
```

```
        (billFirstName, billLastName, billAddress,
        billCity, billState, billZipCode, billCountry,
        billPhone, billEmail)
VALUES
        ('#FORM.billFirstName#', '#FORM.billLastName#',
         '#FORM.billAddress#', '#FORM.billCity#',
         '#FORM.billState#', '#FORM.billZipCode#',
         '#FORM.billCountry#', '#FORM.billPhone#',
         '#FORM.billEmail#')

</cfquery>

<!----get this customer's newly created ID number to
pass to the rest of the forms.------->

<cfquery name="GetLastID"
datasource="#Request.App.datasource#">

SELECT MAX (CustomerID) AS CustomerID
FROM Customers;

</cfquery>

</cftransaction>
```

Figure 21.7 shows the shipping information page.

Listing 21.28 PutShipInfo.cfm

```
<!----this template inserts the billing information
into the Customers table------->

<cfquery name="PutShipInfo"
datasource="#Request.App.datasource#">

UPDATE Customers SET

shipFirstName = '#FORM.shipFirstName#',
shipLastName = '#FORM.shipLastName#',
shipAddress =  '#FORM.shipAddress#',
shipCity = '#FORM.shipCity#',
shipState = '#FORM.shipState#',
shipZipCode =  '#FORM.shipZipCode#',
shipCountry = '#FORM.shipCountry#',
shipPhone =  '#FORM.shipPhone#',
shipEmail =  '#FORM.shipEmail#',
```

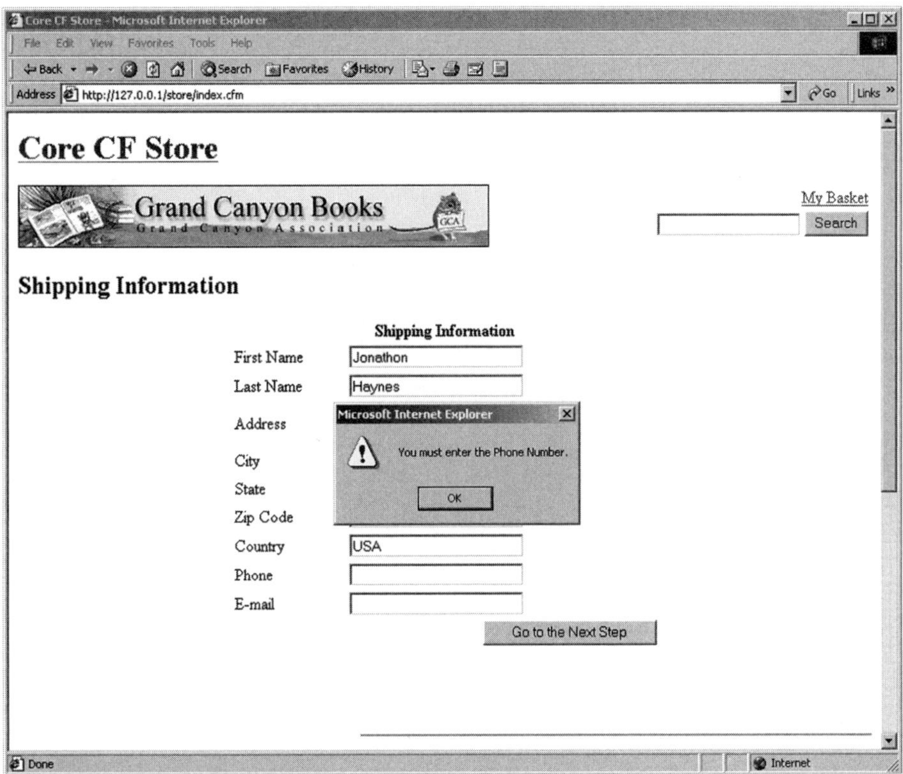

Figure 21.7 Shipping information page with the JavaScript alert function from the <CFINPUT> tag.

```
shipMethod = '#FORM.ShipMethod#'

WHERE CustomerID = #FORM.CustomerID#

</cfquery>
```

Listing 21.29 CheckBasket.cfm

```
<!----make sure user's basket has not timed out
before allowing them to proceed with checkout.------->


<cfif NOT IsDefined("session.arrBasket")>

Your shopping basket has expired due to inactivity.<br>
```

```
Please <a href="index.cfm">return to the store</a> and
select your items again.<br>
<cfabort>

</cfif>
```

Listing 21.30 StateList.cfm

```
<!----holds list of states
               for billing and shipping forms------->

<OPTION VALUE="AL">Alabama</OPTION>
<OPTION VALUE="AK">Alaska</OPTION>
<OPTION VALUE="AZ" SELECTED>Arizona</OPTION>
<OPTION VALUE="AR">Arkansas</OPTION>
<OPTION VALUE="CA">California</OPTION>
<OPTION VALUE="CO">Colorado</OPTION>
<OPTION VALUE="CT">Connecticut</OPTION>
<OPTION VALUE="DE">Delaware</OPTION>
<OPTION VALUE="FL">Florida</OPTION>
<OPTION VALUE="GA">Georgia</OPTION>
<OPTION VALUE="HI">Hawaii</OPTION>
<OPTION VALUE="ID">Idaho</OPTION>
<OPTION VALUE="IL">Illinois</OPTION>
<OPTION VALUE="IN">Indiana</OPTION>
<OPTION VALUE="IA">Iowa</OPTION>
<OPTION VALUE="KS">Kansas</OPTION>
<OPTION VALUE="KY">Kentucky</OPTION>
<OPTION VALUE="LA">Louisiana</OPTION>
<OPTION VALUE="ME">Maine</OPTION>
<OPTION VALUE="MD">Maryland</OPTION>
<OPTION VALUE="MA">Massachusetts</OPTION>
<OPTION VALUE="MI">Michigan</OPTION>
<OPTION VALUE="MN">Minnesota</OPTION>
<OPTION VALUE="MS">Mississippi</OPTION>
<OPTION VALUE="MO">Missouri</OPTION>
<OPTION VALUE="MT">Montana</OPTION>
<OPTION VALUE="NE">Nebraska</OPTION>
<OPTION VALUE="NV">Nevada</OPTION>
<OPTION VALUE="NH">New Hampshire</OPTION>
<OPTION VALUE="NJ">New Jersey</OPTION>
<OPTION VALUE="NM">New Mexico</OPTION>
<OPTION VALUE="NY">New York</OPTION>
<OPTION VALUE="NC">North Carolina</OPTION>
<OPTION VALUE="ND">North Dakota</OPTION>
```

```
<OPTION VALUE="OH">Ohio</OPTION>
<OPTION VALUE="OK">Oklahoma</OPTION>
<OPTION VALUE="OR">Oregon</OPTION>
<OPTION VALUE="PA">Pennsylvania</OPTION>
<OPTION VALUE="RI">Rhode Island</OPTION>
<OPTION VALUE="SC">South Carolina</OPTION>
<OPTION VALUE="SD">South Dakota</OPTION>
<OPTION VALUE="TN">Tennessee</OPTION>
<OPTION VALUE="TX">Texas</OPTION>
<OPTION VALUE="UT">Utah</OPTION>
<OPTION VALUE="VT">Vermont</OPTION>
<OPTION VALUE="VA">Virginia</OPTION>
<OPTION VALUE="WA">Washington</OPTION>
<OPTION VALUE="DC">Washington D.C.</OPTION>
<OPTION VALUE="WV">West Virginia</OPTION>
<OPTION VALUE="WI">Wisconsin</OPTION>
<OPTION VALUE="WY">Wyoming</OPTION>
<OPTION VALUE="PR">Puerto Rico</OPTION>
<OPTION>International</OPTION>
</SELECT>

<!---obviously one would want to expand the options for inter-
national here.---->
```

Listing 21.31 ShowCreditInfo.cfm

```
<!----for entering credit card info--->

<center>
<cfform name="CreditInfo" method="post" action="index.cfm">

<!---pass these params to the switchbox so we can
go to the next step------->

<input type = "hidden" name="action" value = "Checkout">
<input type = "hidden" name="thisPage" value =
"ConfirmOrder">
<cfoutput>
<input type = "hidden" name="CustomerID"
value = "#FORM.CustomerID#">
</cfoutput>

<table width="449" align="center">
<tr>
<td colspan="2" align="center">
```

```
<b>Credit Card Information</b></td>
</tr>

<tr>
<td>Name<br></td>
<td>

<cfinput name="creditName" size="30" required="yes"
message="Please enter the name as it appears on your card.">
<br></td>
</tr>
<tr>

<!---we don't check for card type, because
you can always differentiate them, given their
first number. Also, we're going to hash the stored
number anyway------->

<td>Card Number<br></td>

<!----using the "creditcard" value for the "validate"
attribute causes ColdFusion to check the number entered
against the MOD 10 algorithm. For development, you can use
the number 4111 1111 1111 1111 to pass ColdFusion's test.
------->

<td>
<cfinput name="creditNumber" size="30" required="yes"
message="Please enter a valid credit card number." vali-
date="creditcard"<<br></td>
</tr>
<tr>
<td>Expiration Date<br></td>
<td>

<!----they have to type something, but we don't validate this
field using the "date" value of the validate attribute, since
different cards have different date methods------->

<cfinput name="creditExpDate" size="10" required="yes"
message="Please enter an expiration date."<<br></td>
</tr>
<tr>
<td colspan="2" align="right">
<input type="submit" value="Confirm Order">
</td>
</tr>
```

```
</table>
</cfform>

</center>
```

Listing 21.32 PutCreditInfo.cfm

```
<!----this template inserts the billing information
into the Customers table. This is an UPDATE
statement rather than an INSERT, because we are
not creating a new row, but rather updating the
row that already exists for this customer------->

<cfquery name="PutCreditInfo"
datasource="#Request.App.datasource#">

UPDATE Customers SET

creditNumber = '#FORM.creditNumber#',
creditName = '#FORM.creditName#',
creditExpDate = '#FORM.creditExpDate#'

WHERE CustomerID = #FORM.CustomerID#

</cfquery>
```

Figure 21.8 shows the page for credit card information.

Listing 21.33 Confirmation.cfm

```
<!----call custom tag that
       sets the customer values into session variables.
       That way, we can simply reference them in this
       step and the final step (Complete.cfm) without
       having to requery or worry about hidden fields
       ------->

<cf_Query2Session
               QueryName = "getConfirm"
               table = "Customers"
               columns = "*"
               where = "CustomerID"
               condition = #FORM.CustomerID#
               >
```

Figure 21.8 The credit card information page.

```
<!----displays order to the user as
merchant will see it, so that they can confirm
everything is correct, or print out for records.--->

<h2>Order Confirmation</h2><br></font>

<table width="440">
<tr>
<td width="50%">
<h3>Billing Information</h3><br></td>
<td width="50%">
<h3>Shipping Information</h3><br></td>
</tr>
<tr>
<td valign="top">

<!---hereafter this info will be copied into the
       request scope, and we won't have to lock it
```

```
        ------->

<cflock scope="SESSION" timeout="30">
<cfoutput>
#SESSION.strgetConfirm.billFirstName#
#SESSION.strgetConfirm.billLastName#<br>
#Replace(SESSION.strgetConfirm.billAddress, Chr(10),
"<br>")#<br>
#SESSION.strgetConfirm.billCity#, #SESSION.strgetConfirm.
billState# #SESSION.strgetConfirm.billZipCode#<br>
#SESSION.strgetConfirm.billCountry#<br>
Phone: #SESSION.strgetConfirm.billPhone#<br>
Email: #SESSION.strgetConfirm.billEmail#<br>
<br><br>
</cfoutput>

</td>

<td valign="top">
<cfoutput>
#SESSION.strgetConfirm.shipFirstName# #SESSION.strgetConfirm
.shipLastName#<br>
#Replace(SESSION.strgetConfirm.shipAddress, Chr(10),
"<br>")#<br>
#SESSION.strgetConfirm.shipCity#, #SESSION.strgetConfirm
.shipState#
#SESSION.strgetConfirm.shipZipCode#<br>
#SESSION.strgetConfirm.shipCountry#<br>
Phone: #SESSION.strgetConfirm.shipPhone#<br>
</cfoutput>

</cflock>

</td>
</tr>
</table>



<!---You will notice much of this code from
        ShowBasket.cfm, but it's just different enough
        that we don't save any space trying to combine
        the functionality of this template and that into
        one.------->

<cfif ArrayLen(Session.arrBasket) neq 0>
```

```
<!---show products added to basket if there are any in it-----
-->

<!----table headers--->
<table border="0" width="80%">
<tr>
<td align="center"><b>Item</b><br></td>
<td align="center"><b>Qty.</b><br></td>
<td align="center"><b>Price</b><br></td>
<td align="center"><b>Total</b><br></td>
<td> </td>
</tr>

<!----loop over basket and
output each item's values (name, price, qty)------->
<cfloop from="1" to = "#ArrayLen(Session.arrBasket)#" index =
"Request.idx">


<!----set array into local variables for ease of use------->

<cflock scope="SESSION" type="EXCLUSIVE" timeout="30">
<cfscript>
NumberItems = ArrayLen(Session.arrBasket);
ProductID = Session.arrBasket[Request.idx][1];
ProductName = Session.arrBasket[Request.idx][2];
Price = Session.arrBasket[Request.idx][3];
Qty = Session.arrBasket[Request.idx][4];
</cfscript>
</cflock>

<cfoutput>
<tr>
<td>#ProductName#</td>

<!---quantity------->
<td align="center"<#Qty#<br></td>

<td align="right"<#DollarFormat(Price)#<br></td>

<!----- product price times quantity------>
<td align="right"<#DollarFormat(Price * Qty)#<br></td>

<td align="center">

<!---remove------->
</td>
```

```
</tr>

<!----create subtotal------->
<cfparam name = "Basket.SubTotal" default = 0>
<!------------>

<cfscript>
Basket.SubTotal = (evaluate(Basket.SubTotal + (Session.
arrBasket[Request.idx][3] * qty)));
</cfscript>
</cfoutput>
</cfloop>


<!----output the subtotal ( qty * price for each item)
------->
<tr>
<td colspan="3" align="right">
<b>SubTotal </b><br></td>
<td align="right">
<cfoutput>#DollarFormat(Basket.SubTotal)#
</cfoutput>
<br></td>
<td align="center" valign="top"></td>
</tr>


<!-----calculate Shipping Price,
               tax depending on state, and Grand Total------->


<cfinclude template="CalculateTotal.cfm">

<cfoutput>
        <tr><td><b>Sales Tax:</b></td><td>#DollarFormat
(Basket.SalesTax)#</td></tr>
        <tr><td><b>Shipping:</b></td><td>#DollarFormat
(Basket.ShipAmount)#</td></tr>
        <tr><td><b>Grand Total:</b></td><td><b>#DollarFormat
(GrandTotal)#</b></td></tr>
</cfoutput>

<form method="post" action="index.cfm">

<input type = "hidden" name="action" value = "Checkout">
<input type = "hidden" name="thisPage" value = "Complete">
```

```
<cfoutput>
<input type="hidden" name="CustomerID" value=
"#FORM.CustomerID#">
</cfoutput>
<!---put all of the money info into the structure so we
can insert it in the next step into the database------->


<cfset StructInsert(session.strGetConfirm, "SubTotal",
Basket.SubTotal)>
<cfset StructInsert(session.strGetConfirm, "SalesTax",
Basket.SalesTax)>
<cfset StructInsert(session.strGetConfirm, "ShipAmount",
Basket.ShipAmount)>
<cfset StructInsert(session.strGetConfirm, "GrandTotal",
GrandTotal)>

<tr>
<td> </td>
<td><input type="Submit" value="Place Order"></td>
</tr>
<tr></tr>
</form>

</table>

<cfelse>
<!----their basket may have expired; tell them so.------->
<cfinclude template = "CheckBasket.cfm">
</cfif>

<!----development only
<cfdump var = #REQUEST.SES.STRGETCONFIRM#>
------->
```

Listing 21.34 Query2Session.cfm

```
<!-----NOTE: use of this custom tag is ENTIRELY UNNECESSARY.
       You can accomplish everything that this does (set-
ting a query
       into the session scope, like this:

       <cfset session.MyQuery = MyQuery>
```

```
        and then reference column values like this:

        <cfoutput>#session.MyQuery.MyColumnName#</cfoutput>

        I have included this because I find that developers
often need to do this sort of looping and assignment, espe-
cially with form fields.
        ------->


<!---<CF_Query2Session>

<!---this custom tag queries the database
        and sets retreived records into a structure
        in the session scope. This is one way to
        save us from having to pass everything in
        hidden fields, which can be insecure
        and cumbersome.------->

takes three attributes:
TABLE: the name of the table to query,
COLUMN: the column for the conditional,
CONDITION: the column criteria.

Ex: <cf_Query2Session
                table = Customers
                columns = CustomerID, billName
                condition = #FORM.CustomerID#
                >

this tag can be expanded to accept more attributes for
the SQL statement
------->

<cfsetting enablecfoutputonly="Yes">

<cfparam name = "attributes.QueryName" default="doQuery">
<!---default columns to select is * ------->
<cfparam name = "attributes.columns" default="*">
<cfparam name = "attributes.table" default="">
<cfparam name = "attributes.condition" default="">
<cfparam name = "attributes.where" default="">

<cftry>

<cfquery name="#attributes.QueryName#"
datasource="#Request.App.datasource#">
```

```
        SELECT #attributes.columns#
        FROM #attributes.table#
        WHERE #attributes.where# = #attributes.condition#
</cfquery>

<!---remember that any time you use SESSION, SERVER, or
APPLICATION
        variables, wrap a cflock around them------->

<!---transfer query results into session scope------->

<cfscript>
/* create a struct to hold values.*/

strget = StructNew();

// we have to do it this way in case the tag passes a
//wildcard

QueryColumns = (Evaluate("#attributes.QueryName#" & "." &
"ColumnList"));

// ColumnValues = ValueList("#attributes.QueryName#" & "." &
"ColumnList");

for (idx = 1;
        idx LTE Val(ListLen(QueryColumns));
        idx = idx + 1)
        {
        // set each column name into a struct key
        thisKey = ListGetAt(QueryColumns, idx);

/* set each column value into the value for the struct
key we just created */
        thisValue = "getConfirm" & "." & thisKey;
        thisValue = Evaluate(thisValue);

        // insert the new key-value pair into the structure
        StructInsert(#strget#, "#thisKey#", thisvalue);
        }
</cfscript>


<!----
then prepend the "session." for scope.
rename the structure by prepending "str" for consistency.
```

```
so if the query name is "getConfirm", the resulting structure
in the session scope will be "SESSION.strgetConfirm"------->

<cfset temp = "SESSION.str">

<cfset temp = temp & attributes.QueryName>

<!---by setting the structure into the session scope outside
the script block, we don't need to lock the entire operation
------->

<cflock scope="SESSION" timeout="30" type="EXCLUSIVE"
throwontimeout="Yes">
        <cfset "#temp#" = StructCopy(#strget#)>
</cflock>

<cfcatch type="Database">
        <cfthrow message="The database attributes of the
custom tag were incorrectly specified.">
</cfcatch>

</cftry>
<cfsetting enablecfoutputonly="No">
```

Listing 21.35 CalculateTotal.cfm

```
<!----CalculateTotal()

User-defined function to calculate shipping, billing------->

<cfscript>
// refresh taxrate
TaxRate = 0;

// determine if we are shipping to the billing address

if (session.strGetConfirm.billState eq session.strGetCon
firm.shipState )
         thisState = session.strGetConfirm.shipState;
else
        thisState = session.strGetConfirm.billState;
// add sales tax if state is ship state
// change tax rate to appropriate value
```

```
if (thisState is "AZ")
       TaxRate = 0.068;

// set sales tax
Basket.SalesTax = basket.SubTotal * TaxRate;

// charge more for shipping depending on shipping method
if (session.strgetConfirm.ShipMethod is "Express")
       Basket.ShipAmount = 9;
else if (session.strgetConfirm.ShipMethod is "International")
       Basket.ShipAmount = 14;
else
       Basket.ShipAmount = (SubTotal * 0.017);
// expand this algorithm to make it really useful

GrandTotal = Basket.SubTotal + Basket.SalesTax + Basket.Ship
Amount;
</cfscript>
```

Figure 21.9 shows the order confirmation.

Listing 21.36 Complete.cfm

```
<!--- COMPLETE CHECKOUT PROCESS
display the confirmation/thank you
message and their confirmation number --->

<!---use pointer copy of session scope
that we're storing in the REQUEST scope
so we don't have to lock everything------->

<p>
<center>
<p>
<b>
Thank you <cfoutput>#Request.Ses.strgetConfirm.billFirst
Name# #Request.Ses.strgetConfirm.billLastName#</cfoutput>!
</b>
</p>
<p>
We appreciate your order.</p>
Your confirmation number is
<cfoutput>
<b>#Request.Ses.OrderID#
</cfoutput></b>.
<br>
```

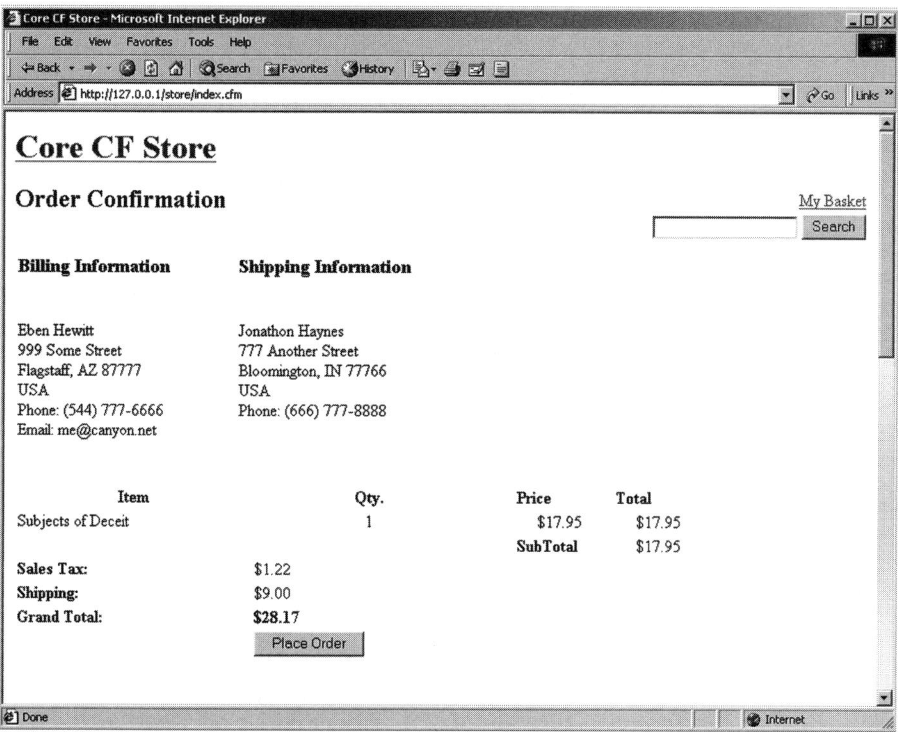

Figure 21.9 Order confirmation.

```
Please write this number down or print this page
out for future reference.
</p>
<p>
A confirmation email has been sent to
<cfoutput>#session.strgetConfirm.billEmail#</cfoutput>.</p>

</td>
</tr>
</center>

<!--- email the user order confirmation --->
<cfmail
        to="#session.strgetConfirm.billEmail#"
        from="#Store.fromEmail#"
        subject="Order confirmation">

Thanks for placing an order at our website!
```

```
Your confirmation number is #Request.Ses.OrderID#.

Billing info:
#session.strgetConfirm.billFirstName#
#session.strgetConfirm.billLastName#
#session.strgetConfirm.billAddress#
#session.strgetConfirm.billCity#,
#session.strgetConfirm.billState#
#session.strgetConfirm.billZipCode#
#session.strgetConfirm.billCountry#

Shipping info:
#session.strgetConfirm.shipFirstName#
#Request.Ses.strgetConfirm.shipLastName#
#session.strgetConfirm.shipAddress#
#session.strgetConfirm.shipCity#,
#session.strgetConfirm.shipState#
#session.strgetConfirm.shipZipCode#
#session.strgetConfirm.shipCountry#


- - - - - - - - - - - - - -

Sub Total    #DollarFormat(session.strGetConfirm.SubTotal)#
Shipping     #DollarFormat(session.strGetConfirm.ShipAmount)#
Tax          #DollarFormat(session.strGetConfirm.SalesTax)#
Total        #DollarFormat(session.strGetConfirm.GrandTotal)#

Thank you, and visit our site again soon!
</cfmail>

<!-----Notify Site Administrator------->

<cfmail to="#Store.adminEmail#"
        from="#Store.fromEmail#"
        subject="An online order has been placed"

An online order has been placed.

Please check the website's administrative area to
retrieve your new order.
</cfmail>


<!---delete basket------->
<cfset session.OrderID = "">
<cfset StructClear(SESSION)>
```

Listing 21.37 PutOrder.cfm

```
<!---this template puts the order information
into the database.
Since it is already in the customers table,
use a unique ID to get the job done.------->

<cfset Request.Ses.OrderID = CreateUUID()>

<!----both OrderDate and Processed will use
the default values set in the database------->

<cftransaction isolation="SERIALIZABLE">
<cfquery name="PutOrder" datasource="#Request.App.
datasource#">

INSERT INTO Orders
        (OrderConfirmation,
        CustomerID,
        SubTotal,
        Shipping,
        Tax,
        GrandTotal,
        Processed
        )
VALUES
        ('#Request.Ses.OrderID#',
         '#FORM.CustomerID#',
         #session.strGetConfirm.SubTotal#,
         #session.strGetConfirm.ShipAmount#,
         #session.strGetConfirm.SalesTax#,
         #session.strGetConfirm.GrandTotal#,
         DEFAULT
        )
</cfquery>

<!---
Now insert order into productsOrders join table
------->
<cfloop from ="1" to ="#ArrayLen(session.arrBasket)#"
index="Request.idx">

<cfquery name="PutProductsOrders"
datasource="#Request.App.datasource#">

INSERT INTO OrdersProducts
```

```
        (OrderConfirmation,
        ProductID,
        Qty
        )
VALUES
        ('#Request.Ses.OrderID#',
         #session.arrBasket[Request.idx][1]#,
         #session.arrBasket[Request.idx][4]#
        )
</cfquery>

</cfloop>
</cftransaction>
```

Admin

In the password-protected administration area, the merchant can retrieve and process new orders. In this example I have used the username "Admin" and the password "p0l@ri$." You can change these in LoginPost.cfm to whatever you like. It would be more scalable and secure to query a database for a match of username and password, and set a cookie if record-count is 1.

Listing 21.38 Index.cfm

```
<!---administration area------->
<cfscript>
        // Create struct to hold thisPage variables
        StoreAdmin = StructNew();

        if (IsDefined("Form.thisPage"))
                StoreAdmin.thisPage = Form.thisPage;
        else if (IsDefined("URL.thisPage"))
                StoreAdmin.thisPage = URL.thisPage;
        else
                StoreAdmin.thisPage = "Default";

        /* make sure the thisPage variable has at least 2
         positions just in case we are using the ListGetAt()
         function */
        while (ListLen(StoreAdmin.thisPage,"_") LT 2)
```

```
                StoreAdmin.thisPage = StoreAdmin.thisPage &
"_Default";

</cfscript>

<!---
this format is certainly excessive at this point,
since the only thing we can do here now is process
orders. However, I've set it up this way because
it will let you easily add your own templates to
allow adding, deleting, and updating of product info,
or reporting using CFGRAPH, or searching for past orders,
etc.
------->

<!---this is the exact same idea as the switch in the
public part of the store. Here we just illustrate another
technique. Using the list function "ListGetAt", we
can find segments of parameters passed in form or url
variables. For instance, on the ShowOrders page,
we pass the form variables "Orders_Process". It gets
sent to the structure when the "Process Order" button
is clicked. The list function interprets the passed
variables as a list with two elements, with a "_" as the
delimiter. So the switch will execute the code in the
"Process" case.

We don't do this in the main store because
list functions aren't lightning fast.------->

<cfswitch expression=
"#ListGetAt(StoreAdmin.thisPage,1,"_")#">

<cfcase value="Orders">
<cfswitch expression=
"#ListGetAt(StoreAdmin.thisPage,2,"_")#">

<!-----mark order as "processed"------->
        <cfcase value="Process">
                <cfinclude template="actProcess.cfm">
                <cfinclude template="qryGetOrders.cfm">
                <cfinclude template="ShowOrders.cfm">
        </cfcase>

        <cfdefaultcase>
        <!---display current orders------->
                <cfinclude template="qryGetOrders.cfm">
```

```
                <cfinclude template="ShowOrders.cfm">
        </cfdefaultcase>

</cfswitch>
</cfcase>

<!----the default case includes the menu of links
to administer the store. That page checks for the
presence of a cookie. If it doesn't exist, the
user is redirected to the login.cfm page.------->

<cfdefaultcase>
        <cfinclude template="menu.cfm">
</cfdefaultcase>

</cfswitch>
```

Listing 21.39 Login.cfm

```
<!---If they already have logged in, redirect them to the
menu--->
<cfif isDefined("cookie.password")>

<!----we can use cflocation here, since
cookie is already set.------->
<cflocation url="menu.cfm">

<cfelse>
<!--- They haven't logged in, so have them submit the form--
->
<cfform action="loginpost.cfm" method="POST">
<p>
Login
</p>
<br>
<table border="0">
<tr>
        <td>Username:</font> </td>
        <td><input type="Text" name="username"
size="20"<br></td>
</tr>
<tr>
        <td>Password:</font></td>
        <td> <input type="password" name="password"
size="20"<br></td>
```

```
</tr>
<tr>
<td> </td>
<td><input type="Submit" value="submit"</td>
</tr>
</table>

</cfform>

</center>
</BODY>
</HTML>

<!--- end cookie check--->
</cfif>
```

Listing 21.40 LoginPost.cfm

```
<!----Check for username and password----->

<!----You can modify these values to
whatever you want. Try storing them in a database,
running a query to retrieve them, and setting the
cookie only if the passed form variables match
any records in the database.------->
<cfif #form.username# is "admin" and #form.password# is
"p01@ri$">

<cfcookie name="password" value="password">

<!----cannot use cflocation as it does not
send data back to client. Use javascript instead.------->

<script language="JavaScript">
location.replace('menu.cfm')
</script>

<!----they entered password incorrectly------->
<cfelse>

<html>
<head><title>Password Incorrect</title></head>

<center>
<h2>That username and password combination is incorrect.</h2>
```

```
</center>
<br>
<a href="login.cfm"Back to Login</a></font></center>
</body>
</html>
<!---end check for correct username and password------->
</cfif>
```

Listing 21.41 Menu.cfm

```
<!---holds menu items for admin------->
<cfif isDefined("cookie.password")>

<html>
<head></head>
<body bgcolor="white">
<p>
<center>

<font face="Arial" size="4">Store Administration</font>
</center>

<a href="index.cfm?thisPage=Orders">Retrieve new
orders</a><br>
<!----this is a separate page so that you can add
other links of your own.------->

</body>
</html>

<cfelse>
<!---if cookie is not set, relocate user to login.------->
<cflocation url="login.cfm">
</cfif>
```

Listing 21.42 qryGetOrders.cfm

```
<!---get all unprocessed orders------->

<cfquery name="getNewOrders" datasource="#Request.App.
datasource#">
```

```
SELECT

O.orderconfirmation, O.CustomerID, O.SubTotal,
O.Shipping, O.Tax, O.GrandTotal,
O.OrderDate, O.Processed,

OP.ProductID, OP.Qty,

C.billFirstName,
C.billLastName,
C.billAddress,
C.billCity,
C.billState,
C.billZipCode,
C.billCountry,
C.billPhone,
C.billEmail,
C.shipFirstName,
C.shipLastName,
C.shipAddress,
C.shipCity,
C.shipState,
C.shipZipCode,
C.shipCountry,
C.shipPhone,
C.shipEmail,
C.shipMethod,
C.creditName,
C.creditNumber,
C.creditExpDate,

P.ProductName,
P.Price

FROM orders O

INNER JOIN OrdersProducts OP
       ON O.OrderConfirmation = OP.OrderConfirmation

INNER JOIN Customers C
       ON O.CustomerID = C.CustomerID

LEFT JOIN Products P
       ON. OP.ProductID = P.ProductID

WHERE O.Processed = 0
```

```
ORDER BY O.OrderDate ASC

</cfquery>

<!---show orders descending by date so
orders placed first show up first.------->
```

Listing 21.43 ShowOrders.cfm

```
<!----display any unprocessed
orders so merchant can run credit card
------->
<cfif isDefined("cookie.password")>

<cfif getNewOrders.RecordCount gt 0>
<h2>New Orders</h2>

<cfoutput query="getNewOrders" group="OrderConfirmation">

<!---billing and shipping------->
<table width="60%">
<tr>
<th>Billing Information</th>
<th>Shipping Information</th>

</tr>
<tr>
<!----display billing info------->
<td valign="top">
#getNewOrders.billFirstName# #getNewOrders.billLastName#<br>
#Replace(Trim(billAddress), Chr(10), "<br>")#<br>
#billCity#, #billState# #billZipCode#<br>
#billCountry#<br>
Phone: #billPhone#<br>
Email: #billEmail#<br>
</td>

<td valign="top">
#shipFirstName# #shipLastName#<br>
<!-----replace function with chr function
        leaves address breaks intact------->
#Replace(shipAddress, Chr(10), "<br>")#<br>
#shipCity#, #shipState# #shipZipCode#<br>
#shipCountry#<br>
Phone: #shipPhone#<br>
</td>
```

```
</tr>
</table>

<!----credit info------->
<table width="60%">
<tr>
<th>Credit Card Info</th>
</tr>
<tr>
<td>Name</td>
<td>#creditName#</td>
</tr>
<tr>
<td>Number</td>
<td>#creditNumber#</td>
</tr>
<tr>
<td>Exp. Date</td>
<td>#creditExpDate#</td>
</tr>

<tr><td> </td></tr>
<tr>
<td><b>Order Date:</b></td>
<td>#DateFormat(OrderDate, "dddd, mmmm dd, yyyy")#
#TimeFormat(OrderDate, "h:mm:ss tt")#</td></tr>
</table>

<table width="80%">

<tr>
<td><b>Product ID</b></td>
<td><b>Product</b></td>
<td><b>Quantity</b></td>
<td><b>Price</b></td>
</tr>

<tr>
<td>[#getNewOrders.ProductID#]<br></td>

<td>#Trim(getNewOrders.ProductName)#<br></td>

<td align="center" valign="top">#getNewOrders.Qty#<br></td>

<td align="center" valign="top">#DollarFormat(getNe-
wOrders.Price)#<br></td>
```

```
</tr>
<tr><td> </td></tr>

<tr>
<td colspan="3" align="right"><b>Sub Total</b></font></td>
<td align="right">#DollarFormat(getNewOrders.SubTotal)#</
font><br></td>
</tr>
<tr>
<td colspan="3" align="right"><b>Shipping</b></td>
<td align="right">#DollarFormat(getNewOrders.Shipping)#<br>/
</td>
</tr>
<tr>
<td colspan="3" align="right"<<b>Tax</b></td>
<td align="right">#DollarFormat(getNewOrders.Tax)#<br></td>
</tr>
<tr>
<td colspan="3" align="right"<<b>Total</b></td>
<td align="right">#DollarFormat(getNewOrders.GrandTotal)#
<br></td>
</tr>
</table>

<!---nothing is really "processed" here, but the
database is updated so that the merchant does
not see this order again. But it's still there
if needed later.------->

<form action="index.cfm" method="post">

<input type="hidden" name="thisPage" value="Orders_Process">
<input type="hidden" name="thisOrder"
value="#OrderConfirmation#">

<input type="submit" value="Process Order">
</form>

<HR>
</cfoutput>

<cfelse>
<p>There are no new orders.</p>

</cfif>

<cfelse>
```

```
<!---password not defined, relocate------->
<cflocation url="login.cfm">
</cfif>
```

Listing 21.44 actProcess.cfm

```
<!---update the creditnumber now the
order has been processed so that
customers' info is more secure.
This also makes a nice demonstration
of how you can update one table
with data from multiple tables.------->


<!---the hash function, present in previous versions of Cold-
Fusion,
but undocumented until now, converts a variable-length string
to
a 32-byte hexadecimal string using the MD5 algorithm. You
may want to do this differently, for instance, by
marking the first 12 digits as X's and leaving the last four.
-------->

<cfset hashString = hash(randrange(999, 99999))>

<cfquery name = "getCredit" datasource="#Request.App.
datasource#">
UPDATE Customers
        SET CreditNumber = '#hashString#'
        FROM Customers C, Orders O
        WHERE O.OrderConfirmation = '#FORM.thisOrder#'
        AND O.CustomerID = C.CustomerID

</cfquery>


<!-----
set the Downloaded bit to 1 so we don't see
this order again, but it is still in the database
if we need to find it later. This is
sometimes called a "soft delete"---->

<cfquery name="ProcessOrder" datasource="#Request.App.
datasource#">
        UPDATE Orders
```

```
        SET Processed = 1
        WHERE OrderConfirmation = '#FORM.thisOrder#';
</cfquery>
```

Conclusion

As mentioned above, there are a number of modifications and improvements you can and should make to this store. It is intended primarily to demonstrate how large applications can scale when each component is modularly defined, and to show you how a number of the topics we have covered can all work together. Please visit www.corecoldfusion.com for updates.

I hope that your continued work in ColdFusion is fun and engaging.

Appendix A

ColdFusion 5 Tag Reference

This appendix describes the tags that make up the ColdFusion 5 language. You will find a list of tags that are new to ColdFusion 5, and a list of all of the tags divided into logical categories. Then you will find complete descriptions of each tag and accompanying attributes to use as a reference.

New Tags in ColdFusion 5

cfflush, cfgraph, cfgraphdata, cflog, cfsavecontent, cfdump

Tags in Logical Divisions

ColdFusion Forms Tags

cfapplet, cfform, cfgrid, cfgridcolumn, cfgridrow, cfgridupdate, cfinput, cfselect, cfslider, cftextinput, cftree, cftreeitem

Database Manipulation Tags

cfinsert, cfprocparam, cfprocresult, cfquery, cfqueryparam, cfstoredproc, cftransaction, cfupdate

Data Output Tags

cfcol, cfcontent, cflog, cfoutput, cfprocessingdirective, cftable

Exception Handling Tags

cferror, cfrethrow, cfthrow, cftry/cfcatch

Extensibility Tags

cfcollection, cfexecute, cfgraph, cfindex, cfobject, cfreport, cfsearch, cfservlet, cfservletparam, cfwddx

File Management Tags

cfdirectory, cffile

Flow-Control Tags

cfabort, cfbreak, cfexecute, cfexit, cfif cfelseif cfelse, cflocation, cfloop, cfrethrow, cfswitch cfcase cfdefaultcase, cfthrow, cftry/cfcatch

Internet Protocol Tags

cfftp, cfhttp, cfhttpparam, cfldap, cfmail, cfmailparam, cfpop

Java Servlet and Java Object Tags

cfobject, cfservlet, cfservletparam

Page Processing Tags

cfcache, cfflush, cfheader, cfhtmlhead, cfinclude, cfsetting, cfsilent

Variable Manipulation Tags

cfcookie, cfdump, cfparam, cfregistry, cfsavecontent, cfschedule, cfset

Web Application Framework Tags

cfapplication, cfassociate, cfauthenticate, cfimpersonate, cflock, cfmodule, cfscript

Alphabetical Listing of ColdFusion 5 Tags

CFABORT	Stops processing of a ColdFusion template at the tag location.
CFAPPLET	Embeds Java applets in a CFFORM.
CFAPPLICATION	Defines an application name, and activates client variables.
CFASSOCIATE	Enables subtag data to be saved with the base tag.
CFAUTHENTICATE	Authenticates a user and sets a security context for an application.
CFBREAK	Breaks out of a CFML looping construct.
CFCACHE	Caches ColdFusion templates.
CFCOL	Defines a table column header, width, alignment, and text.
CFCOLLECTION	Creates and administers Verity 8.0 collections.

CFCONTENT	Defines the content type and, optionally, the filename of a file to be downloaded by the current template.
CFCOOKIE	Defines and sets cookie variables.
CFDIRECTORY	Performs typical directory-handling tasks from within your ColdFusion application.
CFERROR	Displays customized HTML error pages when errors occur.
CFEXECUTE	Executes any developer-specified process on the server machine.
CFEXIT	Aborts processing of any currently executing CFML custom tag.
CFFILE	Performs typical file-handling tasks from within your application.
CFFLUSH	The CFFLUSH tag flushes the current ColdFusion output buffer to the Web server, which then sends it back to the client.
CFFORM	Builds an input form and performs client-side input validation.
CFFTP	Permits FTP file operations.
CFGRID	Used in CFFORM to create a grid control for tabular data.
CFGRIDCOLUMN	Used in CFGRID to define the columns in a CFGRID.
CFGRIDROW	Used with CFGRID to define a grid row.
CFGRIDUPDATE	Performs updates directly to an ODBC data source from edited grid data.
CFHEADER	Generates HTTP headers.
CFHTMLHEAD	Writes text, including HTML, to the HEAD section of a specified page.
CFHTTP	Used to perform GET and POST to upload files or post a form,

	cookie, query, or CGI variable directly to a specified server.
CFHTTPPARAM	Used with CFHTTP to specify parameters necessary for a CFHTTP POST operation.
CFIF/CFELSE/CFELSEIF	Used to create conditional logic constructs.
CFIMPERSONATE	Allows you to impersonate a user defined in a security context defined in Advanced Security.
CFINCLUDE	Embeds ColdFusion pages at the place of the tag call.
CFINDEX	Used to create Verity search engines.
CFINPUT	Used in CFFORM to create input elements such as radio buttons, checkboxes, and text entry boxes.
CFINSERT	Inserts records in an ODBC data source.
CFLDAP	Provides access to LDAP directory servers.
CFLOCATION	Opens a ColdFusion page or HTML file.
CFLOCK	Ensures data integrity and synchronizes the execution of CFML code.
CFLOG	Logs custom messages to standard or custom log files.
CFLOOP	Repeats a set of instructions based on a set of conditions.
CFMAIL	Assembles and posts an email message.
CFMAILPARAM	Attaches a file or adds a header to an email message.
CFMODULE	Invokes a custom tag for use in your ColdFusion application pages.
CFOBJECT	Creates and uses COM, CORBA, or JAVA objects.

CFOUTPUT	Displays output of a database query or another operation.
CFPARAM	Defines a parameter and its initial default values.
CFPOP	Retrieves messages from a POP mail server.
CFPROCESSING-DIRECTIVE	Suppresses extraneous whitespace and other output.
CFPROCPARAM	Specifies parameter information for a stored procedure.
CFPROCRESULT	Specifies a result set name that other ColdFusion tags use to access the result set from a stored procedure.
CFQUERY	Passes SQL statements to a data source.
CFQUERYPARAM	Checks the data type of a query parameter.
CFREGISTRY	Reads, writes, and deletes keys and values in the system registry.
CFREPORT	Embeds a Crystal Reports object.
CFRETHROW	Rethrows the currently active exception.
CFSAVECONTENT	The CFSAVECONTENT tag saves everything in the body of the CFSAVECONTENT tag (including the results of evaluating expressions and executing custom tags) in the specified variable.
CFSCRIPT	Encloses a set of CFScript statements.
CFSEARCH	Executes searches against data indexed in Verity search collections using CFINDEX.
CFSELECT	Used in CFFORM to create a drop-down list box form element.
CFSERVLET	Executes a Java servlet on a JRun engine.

CFSERVLETPARAM	Used to pass data to the Java servlet. CFSERVLETPARAM is a child tag of CFSERVLET.
CFSET	Defines a variable.
CFSETTING	Defines and controls a variety of ColdFusion settings.
CFSILENT	Suppresses all output that is produced by the CFML within the tag's scope.
CFSLIDER	Used in CFFORM to create a slider control element.
CFSTOREDPROC	Specifies database connection information and identifies the stored procedure to execute.
CFSWITCH/CFCASE/ CFDEFAULTCASE	Evaluates a passed expression and passes control to the CFCASE tag that matches the expression result.
CFTABLE	Builds a table.
CFTEXTINPUT	Places a single-line text entry box in a CFFORM.
CFTHROW	Raises a developer-specified exception.
CFTRANSACTION	Groups CFQUERYs into a single transaction; performs rollback processing.
CFTREE	Used in a CFFORM to create a Java tree control element.
CFTREEITEM	Used with CFTREE to populate a tree control element in a CFFORM.
CFTRY/CFCATCH	Allows developers to catch and process exceptions in ColdFusion pages.
CFUPDATE	Updates rows in a database data source.
CFWDDX	Serializes and deserializes CFML data structures to the XML-based WDDX format.

ColdFusion 5 Tags and Their Descriptions

Listed below is the ColdFusion 5.0 language set, complete with attributes and descriptions.

CFABORT

The CFABORT tag stops processing of the current template in the tag location. ColdFusion simply returns everything that was processed before the CFABORT tag. CFABORT is often used with conditional logic to stop processing of a page because of the presence of a particular condition.

Syntax

```
<CFABORT showerror="text">
```

Attributes

SHOWERROR (optional). Specify the error you want to display when CFABORT executes. This error message appears in the standard ColdFusion error page.

Usage

When combining CFABORT and CFERROR, remember that CFERROR is meant to redirect output to a specified page. CFABORT is intended to halt processing immediately.

If the CFABORT tag does not contain a SHOWERROR attribute value, processing stops immediately and the page contents are shown all the way up to the line containing the CFABORT tag.

When using CFABORT with SHOWERROR all by itself (that is, without defining an error page using CFERROR), page processing stops once the CFABORT tag is reached, and the message defined in SHOWERROR is displayed to the client.

If you have a page in which you've defined both an error page using CFERROR and a CFABORT tag using the SHOWERROR attribute, ColdFusion redirects output to the error page specified in the CFERROR tag.

CFAPPLET

Used in a CFFORM, CFAPPLET allows you to reference custom Java applets that have been previously registered using the ColdFusion Administrator.

To register a Java applet, open the ColdFusion Administrator and click the 'Java Applets' button.

Syntax

```
<CFAPPLET APPLETSOURCE="applet_name"
NAME="form_variable_name"
HEIGHT="pixels"
WIDTH="pixels"
VSPACE="pixels"
HSPACE="pixels"
ALIGN="alignment"
NOTSUPPORTED="text"
Param_1="value"
Param_2="value"
Param_n="value">
```

Attributes

APPLETSOURCE (required). The name of the registered applet.

NAME (required). The form variable name for the applet.

HEIGHT (optional). The height in pixels.

WIDTH (optional). The width in pixels.

VSPACE (optional). Space above and below the applet in pixels.

HSPACE (optional). Space on each side of the applet in pixels.

ALIGN (optional). Alignment. Valid entries are:

- Left
- Right
- Top
- Bottom
- TextTop
- Middle
- AbsMiddle
- Baseline
- AbsBottom

NOTSUPPORTED (optional). The text you want to display if the page containing a Java-applet based CFFORM control is opened by a browser that does not support Java or has Java support disabled.

PARAM_n (optional). The valid name of a registered parameter for the applet. Specify a parameter only if you want to override parameter values already defined for the applet using the ColdFusion Administrator.

Usage

Since Java applets must be preregistered, the CFAPPLET tag can be very simple, taking the default parameter values as they were registered in the ColdFusion Administrator. You can also override parameters by invoking them directly in the CFAPPLET tag.

CFAPPLICATION

Defines scooping for a ColdFusion application, enables or disables storing client variables, and specifies a client variable storage mechanism. By default, client variables are disabled. Used also to enable session variables and to set timeouts for both session and application variables. Session and application variables are stored in server memory.

Syntax

```
<CFAPPLICATION NAME="name"
CLIENTMANAGEMENT="Yes|No"
CLIENTSTORAGE="Storage Type"
SETCLIENTCOOKIES="Yes|No"
SESSIONMANAGEMENT="Yes|No"
SESSIONTIMEOUT=#CreateTimeSpan(days, hours, minutes,
seconds)#
APPLICATIONTIMEOUT=#CreateTimeSpan(days, hours, minutes,
seconds)#
SETDOMAINCOOKIES="Yes|No">
```

Attributes

NAME (required). The name you want to give your application. This name can be up to 64 characters long. Required in order for application and session variables to work. Optional for client variables.

CLIENTMANAGEMENT (required). Yes or No. Default is No. Enables client variables.

CLIENTSTORAGE (optional). Specifies the mechanism for storing client variables:

- datasourcename—ColdFusion stores client variables in the specified ODBC or native data source. To use this option you must create a client variable storage repository using the Variables page of the ColdFusion Administrator.
- Registry—ColdFusion stores client variables in the system registry. This is the default.
- Cookie—ColdFusion stores client variables on the client machine in a cookie. Storing client data in a cookie is scalable to large numbers of clients, but this storage mechanism has some limitations. Chief among them is that if the client turns off cookies in the browser, client variables won't work.

SETCLIENTCOOKIES (optional). Yes or No. Yes enables client cookies. Default is Yes. If you set this attribute to "No," ColdFusion does not automatically send the CFID and CFTOKEN cookies to the client browser; you must manually code CFID and CFTOKEN on the URL for every page that uses Session or Client variables.

SESSIONMANAGEMENT (optional). Yes or No. Yes enables session variables. Default is No.

SESSIONTIMEOUT (optional). Enter the CreateTimeSpan function and the values you want in days, hours, minutes, and seconds, separated by commas to specify the lifespan of any session variables that are set. The default value is specified in the Variables page of the ColdFusion Administrator.

APPLICATIONTIMEOUT (optional). Enter the CreateTimeSpan function and the values you want in days, hours, minutes, and seconds, separated by commas to specify the lifespan of any application variables that are set. The default value is specified in the Variables page of the ColdFusion Administrator.

SETDOMAINCOOKIES (optional). Yes or No. Sets the CFID and CFTOKEN cookies for an entire domain, not just a single host. Applications that are running on clusters must set this value to Yes. The default is No.

Usage

Cfapplication is typically used in the Application.cfm file to set defaults for a specific ColdFusion application. Cfapplication enables application variables unless they have been disabled in the ColdFusion Administrator. Using the sessionManagement attribute to enable session variables is also overridden by the Administrator. See *Administering ColdFusion Server* for information about the ColdFusion Administrator.

Server, Application, and Session Variables

Whenever you display, set, or update variables in the server, application, and session scopes, you should use the cflock tag with the scope attribute. For server variables, specify the "Server" scope. For application variables, specify the "Application" scope. For session variables, specify the "Session" scope. See cflock for information about locking server, application, and session scopes.

If you are running ColdFusion on a cluster, you must specify either Cookie or a data source name for clientStorage; you cannot specify Registry.

CFAUTHENTICATE

The cfauthenticate tag authenticates a user, setting a security context for the application. See the descriptions of the functions IsAuthenticated and AuthenticatedContext.

Syntax

```
<cfauthenticate securityContext = "security_context"
  username = "user_ID"
  password = "password"
  setCookie = "Yes" or "No"
  throwOnFailure = "Yes" or "No"
  authType = "Basic" or "X509">
```

Attributes

SECURITYCONTEXT (required). Security context with which the specified user is authenticated. This context must have been previously defined in the security system.

USERNAME (required). User to be authenticated.

PASSWORD (required). Password for the user.

SETCOOKIE (optional). Default is Yes. Indicates whether ColdFusion sets a cookie to contain authentication information. This cookie is encrypted, and its contents include user name, security context, browser remote address, and the HTTP user agent.

THROWONFAILURE (optional). Default is Yes. Indicates whether ColdFusion throws an exception (of type SECURITY) if authentication fails.

AUTHTYPE (optional). Indicates the type of authentication ColdFusion should use. Setting the value to Basic indicates that authentication will be accomplished using username/password. Setting the value to X509 indicates that authentication will be done using X.509 client certificates that are passed to the Web server from a browser using SSL. The default is Basic.

Usage

Code this tag in the Application.cfm file to set a security context for your application. Call the IsAuthenticated function to determine if the user has been authenticated. If you specify No for setCookie, you must call cfauthenticate for every page in the application (perhaps in an Application.cfm file). If you specify throwOnFailure = "Yes," you can enclose cfauthenticate in a cftry/cfcatch block to handle possible exceptions programmatically.

CFBREAK

Used to break out of a CFLOOP.

Syntax

```
<cfbreak>
```

Attributes

None.

Usage

```
<H1>cfbreak Example</H1>
<P>This example uses cfloop to cycle through a query to find
a desired value (in our example, a list of values
corresponding to courses in the cfsnippets datasource).
```

```
When the conditions of the query are met, cfbreak stops the
loop.

<!--- loop through the query until desired value is found,
  then use cfbreak to exit the query --->
<cfloop query = "GetCourses">
  <cfif GetCourses.Course_Num is form.courseNum>
  <cfoutput>
  <H4>Your Desired Course was found:</H4>
  <PRE>#Number#  #Descript#</PRE></cfoutput>
  <cfbreak>
  <cfelse>
    <BR>Searching...
  </cfif>
</cfloop>
</cfif>
```

CFCACHE

Cfcache allows you to speed up pages considerably in cases where the dynamic content doesn't need to be retrieved each time a user accesses the page. To accomplish this, it creates temporary files that contain the static HTML returned from a particular run of the ColdFusion page.

Syntax

```
<cfcache
  action = "cache" or "flush" or "clientCache" or "optimal"
  username = "username"
  password = "password"
  protocol = "protocol_name"
  timeout = "#DateAdd(datepart, number, date)#"
  directory = "directory_name_for_map_file"
  cacheDirectory = "directory_name_for_cached_pages"
  expireURL = "wildcarded_URL_reference"
  port = "port_number">
```

Attributes

ACTION (optional). Specifies one of the following:

- cache—Specifies server-side caching. The default is cache.
- flush—Refresh the cached page. If you specify flush, you can also specify the directory and expireURL attributes.

- clientCache—Specifies browser caching.
- optimal—Specifies optimal caching through a combination of server-side and browser caching.

USERNAME (optional). When required for basic authentication, a valid username.

PASSWORD (optional). When required for basic authentication, a valid password.

PROTOCOL (optional). Specifies the protocol used to create pages from cache. Specify either http:// or https://. The default is http://.

TIMEOUT (optional). DateTime that specifies the oldest acceptable cached page. If the cached page is older than the specified datetime, ColdFusion refreshes the page. By default, ColdFusion uses all cached pages. For example, if you want a cached file to be no older than 4 hours, code the following:

```
<cfcache timeout = "#DateAdd("h", "-4", Now() )#">
```

DIRECTORY (optional). Used with action = "flush." Specifies the fully qualified path of a directory containing the cfcache.map to be used when action = "flush." The default is the directory of the current page.

DIRECTORY (optional). Used with action = "flush." Specifies the fully qualified path of a directory containing the cfcache.map to be used when action = "flush." The default is the directory of the current page.

CACHEDIRECTORY (optional). Specifies the fully qualified path of the directory where the pages are to be cached. The default is the directory of the current page.

EXPIREURL (optional). Used with action = "flush." ExpireURL takes a wildcarded URL reference that ColdFusion matches against all mappings in the cfcache.map file. The default is to flush all mappings. For example, "foo.cfm" matches "foo.cfm"; "foo.cfm?*" matches "foo.cfm?x = 5" and "foo.cfm?x = 9."

PORT (optional). The port number of the Web server from which the page is being requested. The port number defaults to 80. The port number is useful because the cfcache code calls cfhttp. If the port number is specified correctly in the internal call to cfhttp, the URL of each retrieved document is resolved to preserve links.

Usage

In its simplest form, all you need to do is code cfcache at the top of a page for the page to be cached.

With the action attribute, you can specify server-side caching, browser caching, or a combination of server-side and browser caching. The advantage of browser caching is that it takes no ColdFusion resources, because the browser stores the pages in its own cache, thus improving performance. The advantage of using a combination of the two forms of caching is that it optimizes performance; if the browser cache times out, the server can retrieve the cached data from its own cache.

In addition to the cached files themselves, cfcache uses a mapping file to control caching. It is named cfcache.map and uses a format similar to a Windows INI file. The mapping of a URL with parameters is stored as follows. Assume a directory c:\netPub\wwwroot\dir1 that has a CFM file called foo.cfm, which can be invoked with or without URL parameters. The cfcache.map file entries for foo.cfm will look like this:

```
[foo.cfm]
Mapping = C:\InetPub\wwwroot\dir1\CFCBD.tmp
SourceTimeStamp = 08/31/1999 08:59:04 AM
[foo.cfm?x=5]
Mapping = C:\InetPub\wwwroot\dir1\CFCBE.tmp
SourceTimeStamp = 08/31/1999 08:59:04 AM
[foo.cfm?x=9]
Mapping = C:\InetPub\wwwroot\dir1\CFCBF.tmp
SourceTimeStamp = 08/31/1999 08:59:04 AM
```

The cfcache.map file in a given directory stores mappings for that directory only. Whenever the timestamp of the underlying page changes, ColdFusion updates the cache file for that URL only. ColdFusion uses the SourceTimeStamp field to determine if the currently cached file is up to date or needs to be rebuilt.

You can refresh the cache in the following ways:

- timeout attribute—ColdFusion tests the timestamp of the cached file against the timeout attribute. If the cached file's timestamp is older than timeout, the old file is deleted and a new one created. You can use fixed dates if necessary, but it's preferable to use relative dates. This is the preferred technique, and it works for seconds, hours, days, weeks, years, etc.
- action = "flush"—You use action = "flush" to force the cleanup of cached files. It can take two attributes, directory and expireURL.
- Manually—Manually or programmatically (using cffile) delete the .tmp files. This is not recommended.

Note

Cfcache requires that ColdFusion Server "simultaneous requests" be greater than 1. When a cache file is generated, the requested page requires two connections to satisfy the request. When a cached file is found, only one request is required.

Debug settings have no effect on cfcache unless the template explicitly turns it on. When generating a cached file, cfcache uses cfsetting showDebugOutput = "No."

ColdFusion does not cache pages that are dependent on anything other than URL parameters.

To use cfcache with the Secure Sockets Layer (SSL), specify protocol = "http://."

If a template returns an error for any reason, the error page gets cached.

CFCOL

Defines table column header, width, alignment, and text. Only used inside a cftable.

Syntax

```
<cfcol header = "column_header_text"
  width = "number_indicating_width_of_column"
  align = "Left" or "Right" or "Center"
  text = "double_quote_delimited_text_indicating_type_of_text">
```

Attributes

HEADER (required). The text to use for the column's header.

WIDTH (optional). The width of the column in characters (the default is 20). If the length of the data displayed exceeds the width value, the data is truncated to fit.

ALIGN (optional). Column alignment, Left, Right, or Center.

TEXT (optional). Double-quote delimited text that determines what displays in the column. The rules for the text attribute are identical to those for cfoutput sections, meaning that it can consist of a combination of literal text, HTML tags, and query record set field references. This means you can embed hyperlinks, image references, and even input controls within table columns.

CFCOLLECTION

The cfcollection tag allows you to create and administer Verity collections.

Syntax

```
<cfcollection action = "create" or "repair" or
    "delete" or "optimize" or "map"
  collection = "collection_name"
  path = "path_of_verity_directory"
  language = "English" or "German" or "Finnish" or "French"
or "Danish"
  or "Dutch" or "Italian" or "Norwegian" or "Portuguese" or
"Spanish"
  or "Swedish">
```

Attributes

ACTION (required). Specifies the action to perform:

- create—Creates a new collection using the specified path and optionally specified language.
- repair—Fixes data corruption in the collection.
- delete—Destroys the collection.
- optimize—Purges and reorganizes data for efficiency.
- map—Assigns an alias to an existing Verity collection.

COLLECTION (required). Specifies a collection name or an alias if the action = "map."

PATH (required for create and map). Specifies a path to the Verity collection. The effect of the path attribute depends on the action that you specify:

- The create action creates a directory for the use of Verity. The directory path is composed of the directory path specified in the path attribute with the name specified in the collection attribute appended to it. Thus, the full directory path is "path_name\collection_name\". For example, if the path name is "C:\Col\", and the collection name is "myCollection," the full directory path is "C:\Col\myCollection\".

- The map action provides a name with which ColdFusion can reference an existing collection. This name is specified with the collection attribute. It is an alias for the collection, which can be used in cfindex and to reinstate a collection after you have reinstalled ColdFusion. The directory path specified with the path attribute is the full path name of the Verity directory. Therefore, to reference the directory created in the previous example, specify "C:\Col\myCollection\."

LANGUAGE: Optional for create. To use the language attribute you must have the ColdFusion International Search Pack installed. Valid entries are:

- English (default)
- German
- Finnish
- French
- Danish
- Dutch
- Italian
- Norwegian
- Portuguese
- Spanish
- Swedish

Usage

cfcollection works at the collection level only. To add content to a collection, use cfindex.

Note the following regarding mapped collections:

- Mapping allows you to assign an alias to a Verity collection created by a tool other than ColdFusion.
- The action, collection, and path attributes are required.
- The path must point to a valid Verity collection; mapping does not validate the path.
- Deleting a mapped collection unregisters the alias; the base collection is not deleted.

CFCONTENT

Defines the MIME type returned by the current page. Optionally, allows you to specify the name of a file to be returned with the page.

Note

The ColdFusion Server Basic security settings may prevent cfcontent from executing. These settings are managed using the ColdFusion Administrator Basic Security page. In order for cfcontent to execute, it needs to be enabled on the Basic Security page. Please refer to *Administering ColdFusion Server* (part of the Allaire Documentation set) for more information about securing ColdFusion tags.

Syntax

```
<cfcontent type = "file_type"
  deleteFile = "Yes" or "No"
  file = "filename"
  reset = "Yes" or "No">
```

Attributes

TYPE (required). Defines the File/ MIME content type returned by the current page.

DELETEFILE (optional). Yes or No. Yes deletes the file after the download operation. Defaults to No. This attribute applies only if you are specifying a file with the file attribute.

FILE (optional). Denotes the name of the file retrieved.

LANGUAGE (optional). Yes or No. Yes discards any output that precedes the call to cfcontent. No preserves the output that precedes the call. Default to yes. The reset and file attributes are mutually exclusive. If you specify a file, the reset attribute has no effect.

Note

You should consider setting reset to No if you are calling cfcontent from a custom tag and do not want the tag to have the side effect of discarding the current page whenever it is called from another application or custom tag.

CFCOOKIE

Defines cookie variables, including expiration and security options. See the Usage section for important details.

Syntax

```
<cfcookie name = "cookie_name"
  value = "text"
  expires = "period"
  secure = "Yes" or "No"
  path = "url"
  domain = ".domain">
```

Attributes

NAME (required). The name of the cookie variable.

VALUE (optional). The value assigned to the cookie variable.

EXPIRES (optional). Schedules the expiration of a cookie variable. Can be specified as a date (as in, 10/09/97), number of days (as in, 10, 100), "Now," or "Never." Using Now effectively deletes the cookie from the client browser.

SECURE (optional). Yes or No. Indicates that the variable has to transmit securely. If the browser does not support Secure Socket Layer (SSL) security, the cookie is not sent.

PATH (optional). Specifies the subset of URLs within the specified domain to which this cookie applies. If you need to specify more than one URL, you need to use multiple cfcookie tags.

```
path = "/services/login"
```

If you specify a path, you must also specify a value for the `domain` attribute.

DOMAIN (optional). Specifies the domain for which the cookie is valid and to which the cookie content can be sent. An explicitly specified domain must always start with a dot. This can be a subdomain, in which case the valid domains will be any domain names ending in this string.

For domain names ending in country codes (such as .jp, .us), the subdomain specification must contain at least three periods—for example, .mongo.stateu.us. In the case of special top-level domains, only two periods are needed, as in .allaire.com.

When specifying a path value, you must include a valid domain. Separate multiple entries with a semicolon (;).

Usage

Cookies written with cfcookie do not get written to the cookies.txt file until the browser session ends. Until the browser is closed, the cookie resides in memory. If you do not have an expires attribute in a cfcookie, the cookie set exists only as long as the client browser is open. When the browser is closed, the cookie expires. It is never written to the cookies.txt file.

Warning

Do not set a cookie variable on the same page where you use the cflocation tag. If you do, the cookie is never saved on the browser; therefore, it is of no value.

CFDIRECTORY

Performs typical directory-handling tasks from within your ColdFusion application.

Note

The ColdFusion Server Basic security settings may prevent cfdirectory from executing. These settings are managed using the ColdFusion Administrator Basic Security page. In order for cfdirectory to execute, it needs to be enabled on the Basic Security page.

Syntax

```
<cfdirectory action = "directory action"
  directory = "directory name"
  name = "query name"
  filter = "list filter"
  mode = "permission"
  sort = "sort specification"
  newDirectory = "new directory name">
```

Attributes

ACTION (optional). Defines the action to be taken with directory(ies) specified in directory. Valid entries are:

- list (default)
- create
- delete
- rename

DIRECTORY. Required for all actions. The name of the directory you want the action to be performed against.

NAME. Required for action = "list." Ignored for all other actions. Name of output query for directory listing.

FILTER. Optional for action = "list." Ignored for all other actions. File extension filter to be applied to returned names—for example: *.cfm. Only one mask filter can be applied at a time.

MODE (optional). Used with action = "Create" to define the permissions for a directory on UNIX and Linux platforms. Ignored in Windows. Valid entries correspond to the octal values (not symbolic) of the UNIX chmod command. Permissions are assigned for owner, group, and other, respectively. For example:

- mode = "644"—Assigns all owner read/write permissions, group and other read/write permissions.
- mode = "666"—Assigns read/write permissions for owner, group, and other.
- mode = "777"—Assigns read, write, and execute permissions for all.

SORT. Optional for action = "list." Ignored for all other actions. List of query columns to sort directory listing by. Any combination of columns from query output can be specified in comma-separated list. ASC or DESC can be specified as qualifiers for column names. ASC is the default. For example:

```
sort = "dirname ASC, filename2
  DESC, size, datelastmodified"
```

NEWDIRECTORY. Required for action = "rename." Ignored for all other actions. The new name of the directory specified in the directory attribute.

Usage

When using the action = "list," cfdirectory returns five result columns you can reference in your cfoutput:

- name—Directory entry name.
- size—Size of directory entry.
- type—File type: File or Dir for File or Directory.
- dateLastModified—Date an entry was last modified.
- attributes—File attributes, if applicable.
- mode (UNIX and Linux only)—The octal value representing the permissions setting for the specified directory. For information about octal values, refer to the UNIX man pages for information about the chmod shell command.

You can use the following result columns in standard CFML expressions, preceding the result column name with the name of the query:

```
#mydirectory.name#
#mydirectory.size#
#mydirectory.type#
#mydirectory.dateLastModified#
#mydirectory.attributes#
#mydirectory.mode#
```

CFERROR

Provides the ability to display customized HTML pages when errors occur. This allows you to maintain a consistent look and feel within your application, even when errors occur.

Syntax

```
<cferror type = "request" or "validation" or
    "monitor" or "exception"
  template = "template_path"
  mailTo = "email_address"
  exception = "exception_type">
```

Attributes

TYPE (required). The type of error that this custom error page is designed to handle. For information about the variables and other constructs available from the templates used to handle each type of error, see the table in the Usage section.

TEMPLATE (required). The relative path to the custom error handling page. For a description of the template for each type of error, see the table in the Usage section.

MAILTO (optional). The email address of the administrator who should be notified of the error. This value is available to your custom error page using the MailTo property of the error object, such as #error.mailTo#.

EXCEPTION (required). Type of exception. Required if type = "exception" or monitor.

Usage

Use the cferror tag to customize the error messages for all the pages in an application. You generally embed the cferror tag in the Application.cfm file. For more information about the Application.cfm file, see *Developing Web Applications with ColdFusion* (part of the Allaire Documentation set).

To ensure that error pages display successfully, do not encode pages that include cferror with the cfencode utility.

CFEXECUTE

Enables ColdFusion developers to execute any process on the server machine.

Syntax

```
<cfexecute
  name = " ApplicationName "
  arguments = "CommandLine Arguments"
  outputFile = "Output file name"
  timeout = "Timeout interval in seconds">
  ...
</cfexecute>
```

Attributes

On UNIX, the elements of the NAME (required). The full path name of the application that is to be executed.

Note: On Windows systems, you must specify the extension—for example, .exe—as part of the application's name.

ARGUMENTS (optional). Any command-line arguments that should be passed to the program.

If arguments is specified as a string, it is processed as follows:

- On Windows systems, the entire string is passed to the Windows process control subsystem for parsing.
- On UNIX, the string is tokenized into an array of arguments. The default token separator is a space; arguments with embedded spaces may be delimited by double quotes.

If arguments is passed as an array, it is processed as follows:

- On Windows systems, the array elements are concatenated into a string of tokens, separated by spaces. This string is then passed to the Windows process control subsystem as above.
- The arguments array is copied into a corresponding array of exec() arguments.

OUTPUTFILE (optional). The file where the output of the program is to be directed. If this is not specified, the output appears on the page from which it was called.

TIMEOUT (optional). Indicates how long in seconds the ColdFusion executing thread will wait for the spawned process. Indicating a timeout of 0 is equivalent to the nonblocking mode of executing. A very high timeout value is equivalent to a blocking mode of execution. The default is 0; therefore, the ColdFusion thread spawns a process and immediately returns without waiting for the process to terminate.

If no output file is specified, and the timeout value is zero, then the program's output will be directed to the bit bucket.

Usage

Cfexecute is available on Windows NT 4.0 and UNIX platforms. Do not put any other ColdFusion tags or functions between the start and the end tags of cfexecute. Also, cfexecute tags cannot be nested.

EXCEPTIONS. Cfexecute throws the following exceptions:

- If the application name is not found, an Application File Not Found exception will be thrown.
- If the output file cannot be opened, an Output File Cannot be Opened will be thrown.
- If the effective user of the ColdFusion executing thread does not have permission to execute the process, a security exception will be thrown.
- The time out values must be between 0 and some high number (to be determined).

CFEXIT

Is used to

- Abort the processing of the currently executing CFML custom tag.
- Exit the template within the currently executing CFML custom tag.
- Reexecute a section of code within the currently executing CFML custom tag.

Syntax

```
<cfexit method = "method">
```

Attributes

METHOD (optional). Specifies one of the following:

- exitTag (default)—Aborts processing of the currently executing CFML custom tag.
- exitTemplate—Exits the template of the currently executing CFML custom tag.
- loop—Reexecutes the body of the currently executing CFML custom tag.

Usage

If a cfexit tag is encountered outside the context of a custom tag, for example in the base page or an included page, it acts exactly like cfabort. The cfexit tag can help simplify error checking and validation logic in custom tags.

Cfexit behaves differently depending on location and execution mode:

ExitTag	Base template	Terminate processing
	Execution mode = Start	Continue after end tag
	Execution mode = End	Continue after end tag
ExitTemplate	Base template	Terminate processing
	Execution mode = Start	Continue from first child in body
	Execution mode = End	Continue after end tag
Loop	Base template	Error
	Execution mode = Start	Error
	Execution mode = End	Continue from first child in body

CFFILE

Enables ColdFusion developers to execute any process on the server machine. Use the cffile tag to handle all interactions with files. The attributes you use with cffile depend on the value of the action attribute. For example, if the action = "write," ColdFusion expects the attributes associated with writing a text file. See the individual cffile topics below for details about which attributes apply to which actions.

Note

The Basic Security settings may prevent cffile from executing. These settings are managed using the Basic Security page in the ColdFusion Administrator. In order for cffile to execute, it needs to be enabled on the Basic Security page.

If you write ColdFusion applications designed to run on a server that is used by multiple customers, you need to consider the security of the files that could be uploaded or otherwise manipulated by cffile. See Administering ColdFusion Server (part of the Allaire Documentation Set) for more information about securing ColdFusion tags.

Syntax

See attribute sections below.

CFFILE ACTION="UPLOAD"

Use cffile with the upload action to upload a file specified in a form field to a directory on the Web server.

Note

The mode attribute applies to ColdFusion on Solaris and HP-UX, only.

Syntax

```
<cffile action = "upload"
  fileField = "formfield"
  destination = "full_path_name"
  nameConflict = "behavior"
  accept = "mime_type/file_type"
  mode = "permission"
  attributes = "file_attributes">
```

Attributes

DESCRIPTION (required). The name of the form field that was used to select the file.

Note

Do not use pound signs (#) to specify the field name.

NAMECONFLICT (required). The full path name of the destination directory on the Web server where the file should be saved. A trailing slash must be included in the target directory when uploading a file. Use the backward slash (\) on Windows ; use the forward slash (/) on UNIX.

Note

The directory does not need to be beneath the root of the Web server document directory.

ACCEPT (optional). Default is error. Determines how the file should be handled if its name conflicts with the name of a file that already exists in the directory. Valid entries are:

Error—Default. The file will not be saved, and ColdFusion will stop processing the page and return an error.

Skip—Neither saves the file nor throws an error. This setting is intended to allow custom behavior based on inspection of file properties.

Overwrite—Replaces an existing file if it shares the same name as the cffile destination.

MakeUnique—Automatically generates a unique filename for the upload. This name will be stored in the file object variable serverFile. You can use this variable to record what name was used when the file was saved.

ACCEPT (optional). Use to limit what types of files will be accepted. Enter one or more MIME types, each separated by comma, of the file types you want to accept. For example, to allow uploads of GIF and Microsoft Word files, enter:accept = "image/gif, application/msword." Note that the browser uses the file extension to determine file type.

MODE (optional). Defines permissions for an uploaded file on UNIX and Linux platforms. Ignored in Windows. Valid entries correspond to the octal values (not symbolic) of the UNIX chmod command. Permissions are assigned for owner, group, and other, respectively. For example:

- mode = "644"—Assigns the owner read/write permissions and group/other read permission.
- mode = "666"—Assigns read/write permissions for owner, group, and other.
- mode = "777"—Assigns read, write, and execute permissions for all.

ATTRIBUTES (optional). A comma-delimited list of file attributes to be set on the file being uploaded. The following file attributes are supported:

- readOnly
- temporary
- archive
- hidden
- system
- normal

If attributes is not used, the file's attributes are maintained. If normal is specified as well as any other attributes, normal is overridden by whatever other attribute is specified. Individual attributes must be specified explicitly. For example, if you specify just the readOnly attribute, all other existing attributes are overwritten.

The following example will create a unique filename if there is a name conflict when the file is uploaded on Windows:

```
<cffile action = "upload"
  fileField = "FileContents"
  destination = "c:\web\uploads\"
  accept = "text/html"
  nameConflict = "MakeUnique">
```

CFFILE ACTION="MOVE"

Use cffile with the upload action to upload a file specified in a form field to a directory on the Web server.

Note

The mode attribute applies to ColdFusion on Solaris and HP-UX only.

Syntax

```
<cffile action = "move"
  source = "full_path_name"
  destination = "full_path_name"
  attributes = "file_attributes">
```

Attributes

DESCRIPTION SOURCE (required). The full path name of the file to move.

DESTINATION (required). The full path name of the directory to which the file will be moved. If you do not specify the file name, a trailing slash must be included in the target when moving a file. Use the backward slash (\) on Windows; use the forward slash (/) on UNIX.

ATTRIBUTES (optional). A comma-delimited list of file attributes to be set on the file being moved. The following file attributes are supported:

- readOnly
- temporary
- archive
- hidden
- system
- normal

If attributes is not used, the file's attributes are maintained. If normal is specified as well as any other attributes, normal is overridden by whatever other attribute is specified. Individual attributes must be specified explicitly. For example, if you specify just the readOnly attribute, all other existing attributes are overwritten.

The following example moves the keymemo.doc file from the c:\files\upload\ directory to the c:\files\memo\ directory on Windows:

```
<cffile action = "move"
  source = "c:\files\upload\keymemo.doc"
  destination = "c:\files\memo\">
```

Note

On Windows, you must include the backward slash (\) after the destination directory name if you do not specify a file name. In this example, the specified destination directory is "memo."

CFFILE ACTION="RENAME"

Use cffile with the rename action to rename a file that already exists on the server.

```
<cffile action = "rename"
  source = "full_path_name"
  destination = "full_path_name"
  attributes = "file_attributes">
```

Attributes

SOURCE (required). The full path name of the file to rename.

DESTINATION (required). The full path name, including the new name, of the file.

ATTRIBUTES (optional). A comma-delimited list of file attributes to be set on the file being renamed. The following file attributes are supported:

- rcadOnly
- temporary
- archive
- hidden
- system
- normal

If attributes is not used, the file's attributes are maintained. If normal is specified as well as any other attributes, normal is overridden by whatever other attribute is specified. Individual attributes must be specified explicitly. For example, if you specify just the readOnly attribute, all other existing attributes are overwritten.

The following example renames the file keymemo.doc to oldmemo.doc:

```
<cffile action = "rename"
  source = "c:\files;memo\keymemo.doc"
  destination = "c:\files\memo\y\ldmemo.doc">
```

CFFILE ACTION="COPY"

The cffile tag can be used to copy a file from one directory to another on the server.

```
<cffile action = "copy"
  source = "full_path_name"
  destination = "full_path_name"
  attributes = "file_attributes">
```

Attributes

SOURCE (required). The full path name of the file to copy.

DESTINATION (required). The full path name of the directory where the copy of the file will be saved. If you do not specify a file name, you must include the trailing slash. On Windows, use the backward slash (\). On UNIX, use the forward slash (/).

ATTRIBUTES (optional). A comma-delimited list of file attributes to be set on the file being renamed. The following file attributes are supported:

- readOnly
- temporary
- archive
- hidden
- system
- normal

If attributes is not used, the file's attributes are maintained. If normal is specified as well as any other attributes, normal is overridden by whatever other attribute is specified. Individual attributes must be specified explicitly. For example, if you specify just the readOnly attribute, all other existing attributes are overwritten.

On Windows, you must include the backward slash (\) after the destination directory name if you do not specify a file name. In this example, the specified destination directory is "backup."

The following example saves a copy of the keymemo.doc file in the c:\files\backup\ directory:

```
<cffile action = "copy"
  source = "c:\files\upload\keymemo.doc"
  destination = "c:\files\backup\">
```

CFFILE ACTION="DELETE"

The cffile tag can be used to delete a file on the server.

```
<cffile action = "delete"
  file = "full_path_name">
```

FILE (required). The full path name of the file to delete.

On Windows, you must include the backward slash (\) after the destination directory name if you do not specify a file name. In this example, the specified destination directory is "backup."

The following example permanently deletes the specified file:

```
<cffile action = "delete"
  file = "c:\files\upload\#Variables.DeleteFileName#">
```

CFFILE ACTION="READ"

You can use the cffile tag to read an existing text file. The file is read into a dynamic parameter you can use anywhere in the page like any other dynamic parameter. For example, you could read a text file and then insert its contents into a database. Or you could read a text file and then use one of the find-and-replace functions to modify its contents.

Note

Using cffile action = "READ" reads the entire text file into memory. Therefore, it is not intended for use with extremely large files, such as log files, because they can bring down the server.

```
<cffile action = "read"
  file = "full_path_name"
  variable = "var_name">
```

Attributes

FILE (required). The full path name of the text file to be read.

VARIABLE (required). The name of the variable that will contain the contents of the text file after it has been read.

The following example creates a variable named “Message ” that will contain the contents of the file message.txt.

```
<cffile action = "read"
  file = "c:\web\message.txt"
  variable = "Message">
```

The variable “Message” could then be used in the page. For example, you could display the contents of the message.txt file in the final Web page:

```
<cfoutput>#Message#</cfoutput>
```

ColdFusion supports a number of powerful functions for manipulating the contents of text files. You can also use the variable created by a cffile action = “read” operation in ArrayToList and ListToArray functions.

See String Functions and Array Functions for more information about working with strings and arrays.

CFFILE ACTION=“READBINARY”

You can use the cffile tag to read an existing binary file, such as an executable or image file. The file is read into a binary object parameter you can use anywhere in the page like any other parameter. If you would like to send it through one of the Web protocols, such as HTTP or SMTP, or store it in a database, you should first convert it to Base64 (see ToBase64).

```
<cffile action = "readBinary"
  file = "full_path_name"
  variable = "var_name">
```

Attributes

FILE (required). The full path name of the file to be read.

VARIABLE (required). The name of the variable that will contain the contents of the binary file after it has been read. You can then convert the binary file to Base64 so that you could FTP it to another site for upload.

The following example creates a variable named "aBinaryObj" that will contain the ColdFusion Server executable.

```
<cffile action = "readBinary"
  file = "c:\cfusion\bin\cfserver.exe"
  variable = "aBinaryObj">
```

CFFILE ACTION="WRITE"

You can use the cffile tag to write a text file based on dynamic content. For example, you could create static HTML files from this content or log actions in a text file.

```
<cffile action = "write"
  file = "full_path_name"
  output = "content"
  mode = "permission"
  addNewLine = "Yes" or "No"
  attributes = "file_attributes">
```

Attributes

FILE (required). The full path name of the file to be created.

OUTPUT (required). The content of the file to be created.

MODE (optional). Defines permissions for a file on Solaris or HP-UX. Ignored in Windows. Valid entries correspond to the octal values (not symbolic) of the UNIX chmod command. Permissions are assigned for owner, group, and other, respectively. For example:

- mode = "644"—Assigns the owner read/write permissions and group/other read permission.
- mode = "666"—Assigns read/write permissions for owner, group, and other.
- mode = "777"—Assigns read, write, and execute permissions for all.

AddNewLine (optional). Yes or No. If this attribute is set to Yes, a new line character is appended to the text that is written to the file. If this attribute is set to No, no new line character is appended to the text. The default value is Yes.

ATTRIBUTES (optional). A comma-delimited list of file attributes to be set on the file being written. The following file attributes are supported:

- readOnly
- temporary
- archive
- hidden
- system
- normal

If attributes is not used, the file's attributes are maintained. If normal is specified as well as any other attributes, normal is overridden by whatever other attribute is specified. Individual attributes must be specified explicitly. For example, if you specify just the readOnly attribute, all other existing attributes are overwritten.

The following example creates a file with the information a user entered into an HTML insert form:

```
<cffile action = "write"
  file = "c:\files\updates\#Form.UpdateTitle#.txt"
  output = "Created By: #Form.FullName#
  Date: #Form.Date#
  #Form.Content#">
```

If the user submitted a form where:

UpdateTitle = "FieldWork"

FullName = "World B. Frueh"

Date = "07/30/01"

Content = "We had a wonderful time in Cambridgeport."

ColdFusion would create a file named FieldWork.txt in the c:\files\updates\ directory and the file would contain the text:

Created By: World B. Frueh

Date: 07/30/01

We had a wonderful time in Cambridgeport.

The following examples show the use of the mode attribute for UNIX. The first creates the file /tmp/foo with permissions defined as rw_r_ _ r_ _ (owner = read/write, group/other = read).

```
<cffile action = "write"
  file = "/tmp/foo"
  mode = 644>
```

This example appends to the specified file and makes permissions read/write (rw) for all.

```
<cffile action = "append"
  destination = "/home/tomj/testing.txt"
  mode = 666
  output = "Is this a test?">
```

The next example uploads a file and gives it rwx_rw_rw permissions (owner/group/other = read/write).

```
<cffile action = "upload"
  fileField = "fieldname"
  destination = "/tmp/program.exe"
  mode = 755>
```

CFFILE ACTION="APPEND"

Use cffile with the append action to append additional text to the end of an existing text file, for example, when creating log files.

```
<cffile action = "append"
  file = "full_path_name"
  output = "string"
  attributes = "file_attributes">
```

Attributes

FILE (required). The full path name of the file to which the content of the output attribute is appended.

OUTPUT (required). The string to be appended to the file designated in the destination attribute.

AddNewLine (optional). Yes or No. If this attribute is set to Yes, a new line character is appended to the text that is written to the file. If this attribute is set to No, no new line character is appended to the text. The default value is Yes.

ATTRIBUTES (optional). A comma-delimited list of file attributes to be set on the file being written. The following file attributes are supported:

- readOnly
- temporary
- archive
- hidden
- system
- normal

If attributes is not used, the file's attributes are maintained. If normal is specified as well as any other attributes, normal is overridden by whatever other attribute is specified. Individual attributes must be specified explicitly. For example, if you specify just the readOnly attribute, all other existing attributes are overwritten.

The following example appends the text string "But Davis Square is the place to be." to the file fieldwork.txt which was created in the previous example:

```
<cffile action = "append"
  file = "c:\files;updates\fieldwork.txt"
  output = "<B>But Davis Square is the place to be.</B>">
```

CFFLUSH

Flushes currently available data to the client.

Category

Page Processing Tags.

Syntax

```
<cfflush
  interval = integer number of bytes>
```

Attributes

INTERVAL (optional). Tells ColdFusion to flush the output each time at least the specified number of bytes become available. The HTML headers and any data that is already available when you make this call are not included in the count.

Usage

The first time you use the cfflush tag on a page, it sends back all of the HTML headers, and any other available HTML. Subsequent cfflush tags on the page send only the output that has been generated since the previous flush.

When you flush data, make sure that a sufficient amount of information is available, as some browsers may not respond if you flush only a very small amount. Similarly, set the interval attribute for a reasonable size, such as a few hundred bytes or more but not many thousands of bytes.

You should only use cfflush with the interval attribute when you know that a large amount of output will be sent to the client, such as in a cfloop or a cfoutput of a large query. Using this form globally (such as in the Application.cfm file) may cause unexpected errors when CFML tags which modify HTML headers are executed.

Caution

Once you have used the cfflush tag on a page, any CFML function or tag on the page that modifies the HTML header will cause an error. These include the cfcontent, cfcookie, cfform, cfheader, cfhtmlhead, and cflocation tags. You will also get an error if you use the cfset tag to set a cookie scope variable. All errors except cookie errors can be caught with a cfcatch type = "template" tag. Cookie errors can be caught with cfcatch type = "Any."

Note

Normally, cferror discards the current output buffer and replaces it with the contents of the error template. cfflush discards the current buffer. As a result, the Error.GeneratedContent variable resulting from a cferror tag after a cfflush will contain any contents of the output buffer that has not been flushed, and this content will not be sent to the client. The content of the error template will appear to the client after the bytes that have already been sent.

Example

The following example uses cfloop tags and the rand() random number generating function to artificially delay the generation of data for display. It simulates a situation where a page takes a while to retrieve its first data, and where additional information is generated slowly and can be displayed incrementally.

```
<html>
<head>
  <title>Your Magic numbers</title>
</head>

<body>
<H1>Your Magic numbers</H1>
<P>It will take us a little while to calculate your ten magic
numbers. It takes a lot of work to find numbers that truly
fit your personality. So relax for a minute or so while we do
the hard work for you.</P>
<H2>We are sure you will agree it was worth the short
wait!</H2>
<cfflush>

<cfflush interval=10>
<!--- Delay Loop to make it seem harder --->
<cfloop index="randomindex" from="1" to="200000" step="1">
  <cfset random=rand()>
</cfloop>

<!--- Now slowly output 10 random numbers --->
<cfloop index="Myindex" from="1" to="10" step="1">
  <cfloop index="randomindex" from="1" to="100000" step="1">
    <cfset random=rand()>
  </cfloop>

  <cfoutput>
    Magic number number #Myindex# is:  #RandRange(
100000, 999999)#<br><br>
  </cfoutput>
</cfloop>
</body>
</html>
```

CFFORM

<cfform> allows you to build a form with CFML custom control tags that provide much greater functionality than standard HTML form input elements.

Note

Cfform requires the client to download a Java applet. Downloading an applet takes time, so using cfform may be slightly slower than using a simple HTML form. In addition, browsers must be Java-enabled for cfform to work properly.

Syntax

```
<cfform name = "name"
  action = "form_action"
  preserveData = "Yes" or "No"
  enableCAB = "Yes" or "No"
  onSubmit = "javascript"
  target = "window_name"
  encType = "type"
  passThrough = "HTML_attributes">

...
</cfform>
```

Attributes

NAME (optional). A name for the form you are creating.

ACTION (required). The name of the ColdFusion page that will be executed when the form is submitted for processing.

PreserveData (optional). Enter "Yes" or "No." Specifies whether to display the data that was entered into cfform controls in the action page. Data is preserved in the cftext, cfselect, cfslider, cftextinput, cfgrid, and cftree controls. This attribute can be used only if the form and action are on a single page, or if the action page has a form that contains controls with the same names as the corresponding controls on the form page.

EnableCAB (optional). Yes or No. This attribute is deprecated and is no longer functional.

OnSubmit (optional). JavaScript function to execute after other input validation returns. Use this attribute to execute JavaScript for preprocessing data before the form is submitted. See *Developing ColdFusion Applications* for information on using JavaScript for form validation.

TARGET (optional). The name of the window or window frame where the form output will be sent.

EncType (optional). The MIME type used to encode data sent via the POST method. The default value is application/x-www-form-urlencoded. It is recommended that you accept the default value. This attribute is included for compatibility with the HTML form tag.

PassThrough (optional). HTML attributes that are not explicitly supported by cfform. If you specify an attribute and its value, the attribute and value are passed to the HTML code that is generated for the cfinput tag. See the Usage section for more information about specifying values.

Usage

The following custom control tags are available:

- cfinput—Creates a form input element (radio button, text box, or checkbox) and can validate form input.
- cfselect—Creates a drop-down listbox.
- cfslider—Creates a slider control.
- cftextinput—Creates a text input box.
- cftree—Creates a tree control.
- cfgrid—Creates a grid control for displaying tabular data in a ColdFusion form.
- cfapplet—Embeds a registered Java applet in a ColdFusion form. Applets are registered in the ColdFusion Administrator.

You can add standard and dynamic HTML form tag attributes and their values to the cfform tag by using the passThrough attribute. These attributes and values are passed directly through ColdFusion to the browser in creating a form.

If you specify a value in quotation marks, you must escape the quotation marks by doubling them—for example:

```
passThrough = "readonly = " "YES " " "
```

Incorporating HTML Form Tags

cfform allows you to incorporate standard HTML in two ways:

- You can add standard form tag attributes and their values to the cfform tag. These attributes and values are passed directly through ColdFusion to the browser in creating a form. For example, you can use form tag attributes like target to enhance your cfform features.

- HTML tags that can ordinarily be placed within an HTML form tag can also be placed between <cfform> and </cfform> tags. For example, you use a standard HTML input tag to create a submit button in a cfform:

```
<cfform>
  <input type = "Submit" value = " update... ">
</cfform>
```

CFFTP

Allows users to implement File Transfer Protocol operations.

Usage

Use the cfftp tag to move files between a ColdFusion server and an FTP server. cfftp cannot move files between a ColdFusion server and a browser (client). Use cffile action = "upload" to transfer files from the client to a ColdFusion server; use cfcontent to transfer files from a ColdFusion server to the browser.

See Also

cfhttp, cfldap, cfmail, cfpop

Security Settings

The ColdFusion Server Basic security settings can prevent cfftp from executing. If you write ColdFusion applications designed to run on a server that is used by multiple customers, you need to consider the security of the files that the customer can move. You manage the security settings using the ColdFusion Administrator Basic Security page. For more information about securing ColdFusion tags, see *Administering ColdFusion Server*.

Attributes

You can use the cfftp attributes in various ways to accomplish different operations:

- Connecting to an FTP server—Establish a connection with an FTP server.

- cfftp: Connection caching—Use the cached connection with the FTP server to perform additional FTP operations.
- Connection: File and directory operations—Perform file and directory operations.
- Action (cfftp.ReturnValue variable)—Determine the results of the action attribute.
- cfftp action = "listDir"—Access the columns in a query object.

CFGRAPH

Displays a graphical representation of data. CFGraph is an extensibility tag.

See Also

cfcollection, cfexecute, cfindex, cfobject, cfreport, cfsearch, cfservlet, cfwddx

Usage

The cfgraph tag requires a terminating </cfgraph> end tag, even if the tag body is empty.

Only cfgraphdata tags are allowed inside the cfgraph tag body. The cfgraphdata tag allows you to graph data that does not come from a query. You can combine data from a query and cfgraphdata tags.

To use the cfgraph tag, you must have Macromedia Generator running on a JRun server. If the JRun server that hosts Macromedia Generator is not listening on the default port on your localhost, you must use ColdFusion Administrator to specify the host address and port. For more information on installing and configuring MacroMedia Generator server, see *Installing and Configuring ColdFusion Server.*

cfgraph Topics

- cfgraph type = "bar" or type = "horizontalBar"
- cfgraph type = "line" (includes area graphs)
- cfgraph type = "pie"

CFGRAPHDATA

Specifies a single data point to be displayed by a cfgraph tag. <cfgraphdata> is an extensibility tag.

Syntax

```
<cfgraphdata item = "data item"
  value = data value
  item = "label string"
  color = "Web color"
  URL = "URL string">
```

See Also

cfgraph, cfcollection, cfexecute, cfindex, cfobject, cfreport, cfsearch, cfservlet, cfwddx

Attributes

VALUE (required). Value to be represented by this data point.

ITEM (optional). The item label for this data point. The item labels appear on the horizontal axis of Line and Bar charts, on the vertical axis of Horizontal Bar charts, and in the legend of Pie charts.

COLOR (optional). The color to use when graphing this data point. The default is to use the values from the cfgraph tag colorlist attribute or the built-in default list of colors. Line graphs ignore this attribute.

URL (optional). A URL to load when the user clicks the data point. This attribute works with Pie, Bar, and HorizontalBar charts. This attribute has an effect only if the graph is in Flash file format.

Usage

The cfgraph tag enables you to graph data that is not from a query. You can use hard-coded data, variables, and other dynamically generated data. You can combine these data points with query data in a single graph by including cfgraphdata tags in a cfgraph tag that specifies a query.

CFGRID

Used inside cfform, cfgrid allows you to place a grid control in a ColdFusion form. A grid control is a table of data divided into rows and columns. Cfgrid column data is specified with individual cfgridcolumn tags. CFGrid is a ColdFusion Forms Tag.

Syntax

```
<cfgrid name = "name"
  height = "integer"
  width = "integer"
  vSpace = "integer"
  hSpace = "integer"
  align = "value"
  query = "query_name"
  insert = "Yes" or "No"
  delete = "Yes" or "No"
  sort = "Yes" or "No"
  font = "column_font"
  fontSize = "size"
  italic = "Yes" or "No"
  bold = "Yes" or "No"
  href = "URL"
  hrefKey = "column_name"
  target = "URL_target"
  appendKey = "Yes" or "No"
  highlightHref = "Yes" or "No"
  onValidate = "javascript_function"
  onError = "text"
  gridDataAlign = "position"
  gridLines = "Yes" or "No"
  rowHeight = "pixels"
  rowHeaders = "Yes" or "No"
  rowHeaderAlign = "position"
  rowHeaderFont = "font_name"
  rowHeaderFontSize = "size"
  rowHeaderItalic = "Yes" or "No"
  rowHeaderBold = "Yes" or "No"
  rowHeaderWidth = "col_width"
  colHeaders = "Yes" or "No"
  colHeaderAlign = "position"
  colHeaderFont = "font_name"
  colHeaderFontSize = "size"
```

```
    colHeaderItalic = "Yes" or "No"
    colHeaderBold = "Yes" or "No"
    bgColor = "color"
    selectColor = "color"
    selectMode = "mode"
    maxRows = "number"
    notSupported = "text"
    pictureBar = "Yes" or "No"
    insertButton = "text"
    deleteButton = "text"
    sortAscendingButton = "text"
    sortDescendingButton = "text">
</cfgrid>
```

See Also

cfapplet, cfform, cfinput, cfselect, cfslider, cftextinput, cftree, cfgridcolumn, cfgridrow, cfgridupdate

Attributes

NAME (required). A name for the grid element.

HEIGHT (optional). Height value of the grid control in pixels.

WIDTH (optional). Width value of the grid control in pixels.

VSpace (optional). Vertical margin spacing above and below the grid control in pixels.

HSpace (optional). Horizontal margin spacing to the left and right of the grid control in pixels.

ALIGN (optional). Alignment value. Valid entries are: Top, Left, Bottom, Baseline, Texttop, Absbottom, Middle, Absmiddle, Right.

QUERY (optional). The name of the query associated with the grid control.

INSERT (optional). Yes or No. Yes allows end users to insert new row data into the grid. Default is No.

DELETE (optional). Yes or No. Yes allows end users to delete row data in the grid. Default is No.

SORT (optional). Yes or No. When Yes, sort buttons are added to the grid control. When clicked, the sort buttons perform a simple text sort on the selected column. Default is No.

FONT (optional). Font name to use for all column data in the grid control.

FontSize (optional). Font size for text in the grid control, measured in points.

ITALIC (optional). Yes or No. Yes presents all grid control text in italic. Default is No.

BOLD (optional). Yes or No. Yes presents all grid control text in boldface. Default is No.

Href (optional). URL to associate with the grid item or a query column for a grid that is populated from a query. If href is a query column, then the href value that is displayed is populated by the query. If href is not recognized as a query column, it is assumed that the href text is an actual HTML href.

HrefKEY (optional). The name of a valid query column when the grid uses a query. The column specified becomes the Key no matter what the select mode is for the grid.

TARGET (optional). Target attribute for href URL.

AppendKey (optional). Yes or No. When used with href, Yes passes the cfgrid-key variable along with the value of the selected tree item in the URL to the application page specified in the cfform action attribute. Default is Yes.

HighlightHref (optional). Yes highlights links associated with a cfgrid with an href attribute value. No disables highlight. Default is Yes.

OnValidate (optional). The name of a valid JavaScript function used to validate user input. The form object, input object, and input object value are passed to the specified routine, which should return True if validation succeeds and False otherwise.

OnError (optional). The name of a valid JavaScript function you want to execute in the event of a failed validation.

GridDataAlign (optional). Enter Left, Right, or Center to position data in the grid within a column. Default is Left.

GRIDLINES (optional). Yes or No. Yes enables rules (lines) in the grid control. No suppresses row and column rules. Default is Yes.

rowHeight (optional). Enter a numeric value for the number of pixels to determine the minimum row height for the grid control. Used with cfgridcolumn type = "Image," you can use rowHeight to define enough room for graphics you want to display in the row.

RowHeader (optional). Yes or No. Yes displays row labels in the grid control. Defaults to Yes.

RowHeaderAlign (optional). Enter Left, Right, or Center to position data within a row header. Default is Left.

RowHeaderFont (optional). Font to use for the row label.

RowHeaderFontSize (optional). Size font for row label text in the grid control, measured in points.

RowHeaderItalic (optional). Yes or No. Yes presents row label text in italic. Default is No.

RowHeaderBold (optional). Yes or No. Yes presents row label text in boldface. Default is No.

RowHeaderWidth (optional). The width, in pixels, of the row header column.

colHeaders (optional). Yes or No. Yes displays column headers in the grid control. Defaults to Yes.

ColHeaderAlign (optional). Enter Left, Right, or Center to position data within a column header. Default is Left.

ColHeaderFont (optional). Font to use for the column header in the grid control.

ColHeaderFontSize (optional). Size font for column header text in the grid control, measured in points.

ColHeaderItalic (optional). Yes or No. Yes presents column header text in italic. Default is No.

ColHeaderBold (optional). Yes or No. Yes presents column header text in boldface. Default is No.

BgColor (optional). Background color value for the grid control. Valid entries are: black, magenta, cyan, orange, darkgray, pink, gray, white, lightgray, yellow. A hex value can be entered in the form: bgColor = "##xxxxxx" where x is 0–9 or A–F. Use either two pound signs or no pound signs.

selectColor (optional). Background color for a selected item. See bgColor for color options.

selectMode (optional). Selection mode for items in the grid control. Valid entries are:

- Edit—Users can edit grid data.
- Single—User selections are confined to the selected cell.
- Row—User selections automatically extend to row containing selected cell.
- Column—User selections automatically extend to column containing selected cell.
- Browse—(default) User can only browse grid data.

MaxRows (optional). Specifies the maximum number of rows you want to display in the grid.

NotSupported (optional). The text you want to display if the page containing a Java applet-based cfform control is opened by a browser that does not support Java or has Java support disabled. For example: notSupported = "<B> Browser must support Java to view ColdFusion Java Applets</B>". By default, if no message is specified, the following message appears: <B>Browser must support Java to
view ColdFusion Java Applets!</B>

PictureBar (optional). Yes or No. When Yes, image buttons are used for the Insert, delete, and Sort actions rather than text buttons. Default is No.

InsertButton (optional). Text to use for the Insert action button. The default is Insert.

DeleteButton (optional). Text to use for the delete action button. The default is delete.

SortAscendingButton (optional). Text to use for the Sort button. The default is "A -> Z."

SortDescendingButton (optional). Text to use for the Sort button. The default is "Z <- A."

Usage

You can populate a cfgrid with data from a cfquery. If you do not specify any cfgridcolumn entries, a default set of columns is generated. Each column in the query is included in the default column list. In addition, a default header for each column is created by replacing any hyphen (-) or underscore (_) characters in the table column name with spaces. The first character and any character after a space are changed to uppercase; all other characters are lowercase.

Note

Cfgrid requires the client to download a Java applet. Downloading an applet takes time, so using cfgrid may be slightly slower than using a simple HTML table. In addition, browsers must be Java-enabled for cfgrid to work properly.

Select Mode and Form Variables

Grid data is submitted in a cfform as form variables, depending on the value of the selectMode attribute, as follows:

- When selectMode = "Single," grid data is returned as grid_name.selectedname and the value of the selected cell.

- When selectMode = "Column," grid data is returned as a comma-separated list of all the values for the selected column.
- When selectMode = "Row," grid data is returned as grid_name.colum1_name and grid_name.column2_name and their respective values for the selected row.
- When selectMode = "Browse," no selection data is returned.
- Using selectMode = "edit."
- When selectMode = "edit," one-dimensional arrays are used to store data about changes to the grid cells.

For example, a one-dimensional array is used to store the type of edits made to grid cells:

```
gridname.RowStatus.Action [ value ]
```

where gridname is the name of the cfgrid and action is U, I, or D for update, insert, and delete, respectively.

ColdFusion also maintains both the value of the edited cell and the original value in one-dimensional arrays. You can reference this data in ColdFusion expressions as follows:

```
gridname.colname[ value ]
gridname.original.colname[ value ]
```

where gridname is the name of the cfgrid, colname is the name of the column, and value is the index position containing the grid data.

Using the href Attribute

When specifying a URL with grid items using the href attribute, the value of the selectMode attribute determines whether the appended key value is limited to a single grid item or whether it extends to a grid column or row. When a user clicks on a linked grid item, a cfgridkey variable is appended to the URL in the following form:

```
http://myserver.com?cfgridkey = selection
```

If the appendKey attribute is set to No, then no grid values are appended to the URL.

The value of selection is determined by the value of the selectMode attribute:

- When selectMode = "Single," selection is the value of the column clicked.

- When selectMode = "Row," selection is a comma-separated list of column values in the clicked row, beginning with the value of the first cell in the selected row.
- When selectMode = "Column," selection is a comma-separated list of row values in the clicked column, beginning with the value of the first cell in the selected column.

CFGRIDROW

<cfgridrow> allows you to define a cfgrid that does not use a query as source for row data. If a query attribute is specified in cfgrid, the cfgridrow tags are ignored. CFGRIDROW is a ColdFusion Form Tag.

Syntax

```
<cfgridrow data = "col1, col2, ...">
```

See Also

cfapplet, cfform, cfinput, cfselect, cfslider, cftextinput, cftree, cfgrid, cfgrid-column, cfgridupdate

Attributes

DATE (required). A comma-separated list of column values. If a column value contains a comma character, it must be escaped with a second comma character.

CFGRIDUPDATE

Used in a cfgrid, cfgridupdate allows you to perform updates to data sources directly from edited grid data. It provides a direct interface with your data source. Cfgridupdate first applies delete row actions followed by INSERT row actions and finally UPDATE row actions. Row processing stops if any errors are encountered. Cfgridupdate is a ColdFusion Forms Tag.

Syntax

```
<cfgridupdate grid = "gridname"
  dataSource = "data source name"
```

```
dbType = "type"
dbServer = "dbms"
dbName = "database name"
tableName = "table name"
connectString = "connection string"
username = "data source username"
password = "data source password"
tableOwner = "table owner"
tableQualifier = "qualifier"
provider = "COMProvider"
providerDSN = "datasource"
keyOnly = "Yes" or "No">
```

See Also

cfapplet, cfform, cfinput, cfselect, cfslider, cftextinput, cftree, cfgrid, cfgrid-column, cfgridrow

Attributes

GRID (required). The name of the cfgrid form element that is the source for the update action.

dataSource (required). The name of the data source for the update action. To connect to an ODBC data source that is not defined in the ColdFusion Administrator, specify __dynamic__. You must precede and follow the word dynamic with two underscore characters. When you use this attribute value, you must also specify all the ODBC connection information in a connect-string attribute.

dbType (optional). The database driver type: ODBC (default)—ODBC driver. Oracle73—Oracle 7.3 native database driver. Using this option, the ColdFusion Server computer must have Oracle 7.3.4.0.0 (or greater) client software installed. Oracle80—Oracle 8.0 native database driver. Using this option, the ColdFusion Server computer must have Oracle 8.0 (or greater) client software installed. Sybase11—Sybase System 11 native database driver. Using this option, the ColdFusion Server computer must have Sybase 11.1.1 (or greater) client software installed. Sybase patch ebf 7729 is recommended. OLEDB—OLE DB provider. If specified, this database provider overrides the driver type specified in the ColdFusion Administrator. DB2—DB2 5.2 native database driver. Informix73—Informix73 native database driver.

DbServer (optional). For native database drivers and the SQLOLEDB provider, specifies the name of the database server machine. If specified, dbServer overrides the server specified in the data source.

dbName (optional). The database name (Sybase System 11 driver and SQLOLEDB provider only). If specified, dbName overrides the default database specified in the data source.

tableName (required). The name of the table you want to update. Note the following: ORACLE drivers—This specification must be in uppercase. Sybase driver—This specification is case sensitive and must be in the same case as that used when the table was created.

connectString (optional). The contents of a connection string to send to the ODBC server. If you are connecting to a data source defined in the ColdFusion Administrator, you can use this attribute to specify additional connection details or to override connection information specified in the Administrator. If you are dynamically connecting to a datasource by specifying datasource = "__dynamic__," the connection string must specify all required ODBC connection attributes.

USERNAME (optional). If specified, username overrides the username value specified in the ODBC setup.

PASSWORD (optional). If specified, password overrides the password value specified in the ODBC setup.

tableOwner (optional). For data sources that support table ownership (such as SQL Server, Oracle, and Sybase SQL Anywhere), use this field to specify the owner of the table.

tableQualifier (optional). For data sources that support table qualifiers, use this field to specify the qualifier for the table. The purpose of table qualifiers varies across drivers. For SQL Server and Oracle, the qualifier refers to the name of the database that contains the table. For the Intersolv dBase driver, the qualifier refers to the directory where the DBF files are located.

provider (optional). COM provider (OLE-DB only).

ProviderDSN (optional). Data source name for the COM provider (OLE-DB only).

keyOnly (optional). Yes or No. Yes specifies that in the update action, the WHERE criteria are confined to just the key values. No specifies that in addition to the key values, the original values of any changed fields are included in the WHERE criteria. Default is Yes.

CFHEADER

<cfheader> generates custom http response headers to return to the client. CFHeader is a Page Processing Tag.

Syntax

```
<cfheader
  name = "header_name"
  value = "header_value">
```

or

```
<cfheader
  statusCode = "status_code"
  statusText = "status_text">
```

See Also

cfcache, cfflush, cfheader, cfhtmlhead, cfinclude, cfsetting, cfsilent

Attributes

NAME (required if you do not specify the statusCode attribute). A name for the header.

VALUE (optional). A value for the HTTP header. This attribute is used in conjunction with the name attribute.

statusCode (required if you do not specify the name attribute). A number that sets the HTTP status code.

statusText (optional). Text that explains the status code. This attribute is used in conjunction with the statusCode attribute.

CFHTMLHEAD

<cfhtmlhead> writes the text specified in the text attribute to the <head> section of a generated HTML page. Cfhtmlhead can be useful for embedding JavaScript code, or placing other HTML tags such as META, LINK, TITLE, or BASE in an HTML page header. Cfhtmlhead is a page-processing tag.

Syntax

```
<cfhtmlhead text = "text">
```

See Also

cfcache, cfflush, cfheader, cfheader, cfinclude, cfsetting, cfsilent

Attributes

TEXT. The text you want to add to the <head> area of an HTML page. Everything inside the quotation marks is placed in the <head> section.

CFHTTP

The <cfhttp> tag allows you to execute HTTP POST and GET operations on files. Using cfhttp, you can execute standard GET operations as well as create a query object from a text file. POST operations allow you to upload MIME file types to a server, or post cookie, formfield, URL, file, or CGI variables directly to a specified server. CFHTTP is an Internet Protocol Tag.

Syntax

```
<cfhttp url = "hostname"
  port = "port_number"
  method = "get_or_post"
  username = "username"
  password = "password"
  name = "queryname"
  columns = "query_columns"
  path = "path"
  file = "filename"
  delimiter = "character"
  textQualifier = "character"
  resolveURL = "yes" or "no"
  proxyServer = "hostname"
  proxyPort = "port_number"
  userAgent = "user_agent"
  throwOnError = "yes" or "no"
  redirect = "yes" or "no"
  timeout = "timeout_period">
</cfhttp>
```

See Also

cfftp, cfhttpparam, cfldap, cfmail, cfmailparam, cfpop

Attributes

URL (required). Full URL of the host name or IP address of the server on which the file resides. The URL must be an absolute URL, including the protocol (http or https) and hostname. It may optionally contain a port number. Any port number specified in the URL attribute will override the port attribute.

PORT (optional). The port number on the server from which the object is being requested. Default is 80. When used with resolveURL, the URLs of retrieved documents that specify a port number are automatically resolved to preserve links in the retrieved document. If a port number is specified in the url attribute, that port value will override the value of the port attribute.

METHOD (required). GET or POST. Use GET to download a text or binary file, or to create a query from the contents of a text file. Use POST to send information to a server page or a CGI program for processing. POST requires the use of a cfhttpparam tag.

USERNAME (optional). When required by a server, a valid username.

PASSWORD (optional). When required by a server, a valid password.

NAME (optional). The name to assign to a query when a query is to be constructed from a file.

COLUMNS (optional). Specifies the column names for a query when creating a query as a result of a cfhttp GET. If there are column headers in the text file from which the query is drawn, do not specify this attribute unless you need to overwrite the existing headers. If there are no column headers in the text file, you must specify the columns attribute, or you will lose the data in the first row.

PATH (optional). The path to the directory in which a file is to be stored. If a path is not specified in a POST or GET operation, a variable is created (cfhttp.fileContent) that you can use to present the results of the POST operation in a cfoutput.

FILE (required in a POST operation if path is specified). The filename to be used for the file that is accessed. For GET operations, defaults to the name specified in URL. Enter path information in the path attribute.

DELIMITER (required for creating a query). Valid characters are a tab or comma. Default is a comma (,).

TextQualifier (required for creating a query). Indicates the start and finish of a column. Should be appropriately escaped when embedded in a column. For example, if the qualifier is a quotation mark, it should be escaped as `"""`. If there is no text qualifier in the file, specify a blank space as `" "`. Default is the quote mark (`"`).

ResolveURL (optional). Yes or No. Default is No. For GET and POST operations, when Yes, any page reference returned into the fileContent internal variable will have its internal URLs fully resolved, including port number, so that links remain intact. The following HTML tags, which can contain links, will be resolved:

- img src
- a href
- form action
- applet code
- script src
- embed src
- embed pluginspace
- body background
- frame src
- bgsound src
- object data
- object classid
- object codebase
- object usemap

proxyServer (optional). Host name or IP address of a proxy server.

ProxyPort (optional). The port number on the proxy server from which the object is being requested. Default is 80. When used with resolveURL, the URLs of retrieved documents that specify a port number are automatically resolved to preserve links in the retrieved document.

UserAgent (optional). User agent request header.

ThrowOnError (optional). Boolean indicating whether to throw an exception that can be caught by using the cftry and cfcatch tags. The default is NO. See the Usage section for more information.

redirect (optional). Boolean indicating whether to redirect execution or stop execution. The default is YES. If set to NO and throwOnError = "yes," execution stops if cfhttp fails, and the status code and associated error message are returned in the variable cfhttp.statuscode. To see where execution would have been redirected, use the variable cfhttp.responseHeader[LOCATION]. The key LOCATION identifies the path of redirection. ColdFusion will follow up to five redirections on a single request. if this limit is exceeded, ColdFusion will behave as if redirect = "no."

TIMEOUT (optional). A value in seconds. When a URL timeout is specified in the browser, the timeout attribute setting will take precedence over the

ColdFusion Administrator timeout. The ColdFusion server then takes the lesser of the URL timeout and the timeout passed in the timeout attribute so that the request will always time out before or at the same time as the page times out. Likewise, if there is no URL timeout specified, ColdFusion takes the lesser of the ColdFusion Administrator timeout and the timeout passed in the timeout attribute. If there is no timeout set on the URL in the browser, no timeout set in the ColdFusion Administrator, and no timeout set with the timeout attribute, ColdFusion processes requests synchronously; thus, ColdFusion waits indefinitely for the cfhttp request to process.

Usage

Note that you must enable the timeout set in the ColdFusion Administrator in order for the ColdFusion Administrator timeout and the URL timeout to take effect. This setting is on the ColdFusion Administrator Server Settings page. Please refer to *Administering ColdFusion Server* for more information about ColdFusion settings.

Variables Returned by a Cfhttp Get Operation

Cfhttp returns data in a number of variables. For example, when you specify a URL that points to a text or binary file in a cfhttp method = "get" operation, the file is downloaded and stored in a ColdFusion variable or file.

- The fileContent variable is available for text and MIME file types.
- The mimeType variable is available for all file manipulations.
- And the Header and responseHeader variables allow you to see the response headers.

These variables can be accessed in the following manner:

```
#cfhttp.fileContent#
#cfhttp.mimeType#
#cfhttp.header#
#cfhttp.responseHeader [http_header_key] #
```

The responseHeader variable is returned as a CFML structure. The other variables are returned as strings. See the table at the end of this section for a summary of variables returned by cfhttp.

Building a Query from a Delimited Text File

To download a file in a ColdFusion page so that a query can be built using the file, the file must be either comma-separated or tab-delimited. Although risky, text qualification may be omitted. The file will be parsed and an appropriate query built from it. Columns may be specified in the attribute list so that the client can override the columns specified in the file. There is error checking within the tag that prevents a user from either entering an invalid column name or using an invalid column name that was specified in the original file. If such an illegal filename is encountered, the illegal characters are stripped. Such action could produce duplicate column names, so duplicate columns are renamed and inserted into the query header. The query has all of the functionality of a standard cfquery object.

- HTTP POST—cfhttpparam tags can be nested inside a cfhttp tag in a POST operation. The browser can be pointed to a URL specifying a CGI executable or a ColdFusion page. Since multiple cfhttpparam tags can be nested in one cfhttp tag, you can construct a multipart/form-data style post. A file content variable is created, and this can be used in a cfoutput tag. If path and file attributes are specified, the data returned from the server is saved to the specified location.
- Authentication—cfhttp supports Windows NT Basic Authentication for both GET and POST operations. However, Basic Authentication will not work if your Web server has enabled Windows NT Challenge/Response (Microsoft IIS).
- Encryption—cfhttp is capable of using Secure Sockets Layer (SSL) for negotiating secured transactions over the wire.
- cfhttp.statuscode—cfhttp provides the cfhttp.statuscode variable for access to the HTTP error string associated with the error if the throwOnError attribute is set to No (or not specified at all, since it defaults to "No"). See the following list for all the variables returned by cfhttp.

#cfhttp.fileContent# Returns the contents of the file for text and MIME files.

#cfhttp.mimeType# Returns the MIME type.

#cfhttp.responseHeader[http_hd_key]# Returns the response headers. If there is only one instance of a header key, then the value may be accessed as a simple type. If there is more than one instance, then the values are placed in an array within the responseHeader structure.

#cfhttp.header# Returns the raw response header.

#cfhttp.statuscode# Returns the HTTP error code and associated error string if throwOnError is NO. Terminate cfhttp method =

"post" operations with </cfhttp>. Termination is not required with cfhttp method = "get" operations.

CFHTTPPARAM

Required for cfhttp POST operations, cfhttpparam is used to specify the parameters necessary to build a cfhttp POST. CFHTTPPARAM is an Internet Protocol Tag.

Syntax

```
<cfhttpparam name = "name"
  type = "type"
  value = "transaction type"
  file = "filename">
```

See Also

cfftp, cfhttp, cfldap, cfmail, cfmailparam, cfpop

Attributes

NAME (required). A variable name for the data being passed.

TYPE (required). The transaction type. Valid entries are:

- URL
- FormField
- Cookie
- CGI
- File

VALUE (optional for type = "File"). Specifies the value of the URL, FormField, Cookie, File, or CGI variable being passed.

FILE (Required for type = "File").

CFIF, CFELSE, CFELSEIF

Used with cfelse and cfelseif, cfif lets you create simple and compound conditional statements in CFML. The value in the cfif tag can be any expression. These are Flow-Control Tags.

Syntax

```
<cfif expression>
  HTML and CFML tags
<cfelseif>
  HTML and CFML tags
<cfelse expression>
  HTML and CFML tags
</cfif>
```

See Also

cfabort, cfbreak, cfexecute, cfexit, cflocation, cfloop, cfswitch cfcase cfdefaultcase, cfthrow, cftry /cfcatch

Usage

Note that when testing for the return value of any function that returns a Boolean, you do not need to explicitly define the TRUE condition. The following code uses `IsArray` as an example:

```
<cfif IsArray(myarray)>
```

When successful, `IsArray` evaluates to YES, the string equivalent of the Boolean TRUE. This method is preferred over explicitly defining the TRUE condition:

```
<cfif IsArray(myarray) IS TRUE>
```

Note

On UNIX, there is a switch that provides fast date-time parsing. If you have enabled this switch, you must refer to dates in expressions in the following order: month, day, and year. For example:

```
<cfif "11/23/1998 " GT "11/15/1998 ">
```

CFIMPERSONATE

Allows you to impersonate a user defined in a security context defined in Advanced Security. ColdFusion Server enforces all the privileges and restrictions that have been set up for that user with the Advanced Security rules. cfimpersonate is a Web application framework.

Syntax

```
<cfimpersonate
  securityContext = "SecurityContext"
  username = "Name"
  password = "Password"
  type = "CF" or "OS">
  ...
  HTML or CFML code to execute
  ...
</cfimpersonate>
```

See Also

cfapplication, cfassociate, cfauthenticate, cferror, cflock, cfmodule

Attributes

securityContext(required). The security context in which the user should be authenticated. If the impersonation type is "CF," then you should specify a security context that has already been defined using the ColdFusion Administrator. If the impersonation type is "OS," then you should specify an NT domain as the security context.

USERNAME (required). The user name of the user you want to impersonate. You can create a rule within ColdFusion Advanced Security to restrict a user from being impersonated within a security context.

PASSWORD (required). The password of the user that you want to impersonate.

TYPE (required). The type of impersonation needed. This attribute can have the value "CF" for impersonation at the application level or "OS" for impersonation at the operating-system level. Operating-system-level impersonation means that the impersonation is of a user known to the operating system. Currently, this type of impersonation is available only for Windows NT and not for UNIX. When it is in effect, the operating system will automatically perform access control for access to any resources managed by the operating system such as files and directories. This is fast, since ColdFusion is not doing any extra checking; the OS is, but the OS is limited, since only resources that are protected by the operating system are protected. For example, the operating system cannot check for resource types such as application, data sources etc.

Usage

Cfimpersonate is typically used to run a block of code in a secure mode. For impersonation of type "CF," there is automatic enforcement of access control of ColdFusion resources such as files, data sources, and collections between the start and end tags of cfimpersonate. If CF type impersonation is turned on, the ColdFusion engine enforces the rules and policies specified for the user in the Advanced Security section of the ColdFusion Administrator. Therefore, there is no need to make multiple isAuthorized calls in the code to protect each resource.

CFINCLUDE

Cfinclude lets you embed references to ColdFusion pages in your CFML. If necessary, you can embed cfinclude tags recursively. For an additional method of encapsulating CFML, refer to the cfmodule tag, which is used to create custom tags in CFML. cfinclude is a page-processing tag.

Syntax

```
<cfinclude template = "template_name">
```

See Also

cfcache, cfflush, cfheader, cfhtmlhead, cfsetting, cfsilent

Attributes

TEMPLATE. A logical path to an existing page.

Usage

ColdFusion searches for included files as follows:

- Checks the directory in which the current page lives.
- Searches directories explicitly mapped in the ColdFusion Administrator for the included file.

CFINDEX

Use the cfindex tag to populate collections with indexed data. cfindex and cfsearch encapsulate the Verity indexing and searching utilities. Verity collections can be populated either from text files in a directory you specify or from a query generated by any ColdFusion query. Before you can populate a Verity collection, you need to create the collection using either the cfcollection tag or the ColdFusion Administrator. Use cfsearch to search collections you populate with cfindex. cfindex is an extensibility tag.

Syntax

```
<cfindex collection = "collection_name"
  action = "action"
  type = "type"
  title = "title"
  key = "ID"
  body = "body"
  custom1 = "custom_value"
  custom2 = "custom_value"
  URLpath = "URL"
  extensions = "file_extensions"
  query = "query_name"
  recurse = "Yes" or "No"
  external = "Yes" or "No"
  language = "language">
```

See Also

cfcollection, cfexecute, cfgraph, cfobject, cfreport, cfsearch, cfservlet, cfwddx

Attributes

COLLECTION (required). Specifies a collection name. If you are indexing an external collection (external = "Yes"), specify the collection name, including fully qualified path:

```
collection = "e:\collections\personnel"
```

You cannot combine internal and external collections in the same indexing operation.

ACTION (optional). Specifies the index action. Valid entries are:

- update—Updates the index and adds the key specified in key to the index if it is not already defined.

- delete—Deletes the key specified in key in the specified collection.
- purge—Deletes data in the specified collection, leaving the collection intact for repopulation.
- refresh—Clears data in the specified collection prior to repopulating it with new data.
- optimize—Optimizes the specified collection of files. This action is deprecated; use cfcollection instead.

TYPE (optional). Specifies the type of entity being indexed. Default is CUSTOM. Valid entries are:

- file—Indexes files.
- path—Indexes all files in specified path that pass extensions filter.
- custom—Indexes custom entities from a ColdFusion query.

TITLE (required when type = "Custom"). Specifies one of the following:

- A title for the collection.
- A query column name for any type and a valid query name.
- The title attribute allows searching collections by title or displaying a separate title from the actual key.

KEY (optional). A unique identifier reference that specifies one of the following:

- Document filename when type = "file."
- Fully qualified path when type = "path."
- A unique identifier when type = "custom," such as the table column holding the primary key.
- A query column name for any other type argument.

BODY (optional). ASCII text to index or a query column name. Required if type = "Custom." Ignored for type = "File" and type = "Path." Invalid if type = "delete." Specifies one of the following:

- The ASCII text to be indexed.
- A query column name when a valid query name is specified in query.

- Multiple columns can be specified in a comma-separated list: body = "employee_name, dept_name, location."

CUSTOM1 (optional). A custom field you can use to store data during an indexing operation. Specify a query column name for any type and a valid query name.

CUSTOM2 (optional). A second custom field you can use to store data during an indexing operation. Usage is the same as for custom1.

URLpath (optional). Specifies the URL path for files when type = "file" and type = "path." When the collection is searched with cfsearch, this path name will automatically be prepended to all file names and returned as the URL attribute.

EXTENSIONS (optional). Specifies the comma-separated list of file extensions that ColdFusion uses to index files when type = "path." Default is HTM, HTML, CFM, CFML, DBM, DBML. An entry of "*." returns files with no extension: extensions = ".htm, .html, .cfm, .cfml, *." Returns files with the specified extensions as well as files with no extension.

QUERY (optional). Specifies the name of the query against which the collection is being generated.

RECURSE (optional). Yes or No. Yes specifies that directories below the path specified in key when type = "path" will be included in the indexing operation.

EXTERNAL (optional). Yes or No. Yes indicates that the collection specified in collection was created outside of ColdFusion using native Verity indexing tools.

LANGUAGE (optional). To use the language attribute you must have the ColdFusion International Search Pack installed. Valid entries are:

- English (default)
- German
- Finnish
- French
- Danish
- Dutch
- Italian
- Norwegian
- Portuguese
- Spanish
- Swedish

CFINPUT

<cfinput> is used inside cfform to place radio buttons, checkboxes, or text boxes. Provides input validation for the specified control type. cfinput is a ColdFusion form tag.

Syntax

```
<cfinput type = "input_type"
  name = "name"
  value = "initial_value"
  required = "Yes" or "No"
  range = "min_value, max_value"
  validate = "data_type"
  onValidate = "javascript_function"
  pattern = "regexp"
  message = "validation_msg"
  onError = "text"
  size = "integer"
  maxLength = "integer"
  checked
  passThrough = "HTML_attributes">
```

See Also

cfapplet, cfform, cfgrid, cfselect, cfslider, cftextinput, cftree

Attributes

TYPE (optional). Valid entries are:

- text—(default) Creates a text entry box control.
- radio—Creates a radio button control.
- checkbox—Creates a checkbox control.
- password—Creates a password entry control.

NAME (required). A name for the form input element.

VALUE (optional). An initial value for the form input element.

REQUIRED (optional). Enter Yes or No. Default is No.

RANGE (optional). Enter a minimum-value, maximum-value range separated by a comma. Valid only for numeric data.

VALIDATE (optional). Valid entries are:

- date—Verifies U.S. date entry in the form mm/dd/yyyy.
- eurodate—Verifies valid European date entry in the form dd/mm/yyyy.
- time—Verifies a time entry in the form hh:mm:ss.
- float—Verifies a floating-point entry.
- integer—Verifies an integer entry.
- telephone—Verifies a telephone entry. Telephone data must be entered as ###-###-####. The hyphen separator (-) can be replaced with a blank. The area code and exchange must begin with a digit between 1 and 9.
- zipcode (U.S. formats only)—Number can be a 5- or 9-digit zip in the form #####-####. The hyphen separator (-) can be replaced with a blank.
- creditcard—Blanks and dashes are stripped and the number is verified using the mod10 algorithm.
- social_security_number—Number must be entered as ###-##-####. The hyphen separator (-) can be replaced with a blank.
- regular_expression—Match the input against the regular expression specified by the pattern attribute. Text that matches the regular expression pattern is valid.

OnValidate (optional). The name of a valid JavaScript function used to validate user input. The form object, input object, and input object value are passed to the specified routine, which should return true if validation succeeds and false otherwise. When used, the validate attribute is ignored.

PATTERN (optional). The JavaScript regular expression pattern to use to validate the input. Required only if you specify validate = "regular_expression."

MESSAGE (optional). Message text to appear if validation fails.

OnError (optional). The name of a valid JavaScript function you want to execute in the event of a failed validation.

SIZE (optional). The size of the input control. Ignored if type is Radio or Checkbox.

MaxLength (optional). The maximum length of text entered when type is Text.

CHECKED (optional). No arguments. Valid only if type = "radio" or checkbox. If present in the cfinput tag, causes the radio button or checkbox button to be prechecked.

PassThrough (optional). HTML attributes that are not explicitly supported by cfinput. If you specify an attribute and its value, the attribute and value are passed to the HTML code that is generated for the cfinput tag. See the Usage section for more information about specifying values.

Usage

You can add standard and dynamic HTML form tag attributes and their values to the cfinput tag by using the passThrough attribute. These attributes and values are passed directly through ColdFusion to the browser in creating a form.

If you specify a value in quotation marks, you must escape the quotation marks by doubling them—for example,

```
passThrough = "readonly = " "YES " " "
```

Cfinput supports the JavaScript onClick event in the same manner as the HTML input tag:

```
<cfinput type = "radio"
  name = "radio1"
  onClick = "JavaScript_function">
```

Note

Cfinput requires the client to download a Java applet. Downloading an applet takes time, so using cfinput may be slightly slower than using a simple HTML form. In addition, browsers must be Java-enabled for cfinput to work properly.

CFINSERT

<cfinsert> inserts new records in data sources. cfinsert is a Database Manipulation Tag.

Syntax

```
<cfinsert dataSource = "ds_name"
  dbType = "type"
  dbServer = "dbms"
  dbName = "database name"
  tableName = "tbl_name"
  connectString = "connection string"
  tableOwner = "owner"
  tableQualifier = "tbl_qualifier"
  username = "username"
```

```
password = "password"
provider = "COMProvider"
providerDSN = "datasource"
formFields = "formfield1, formfield2, ...">
```

See Also

cfprocparam, cfprocresult, cfquery, cfqueryparam, cfstoredproc, cftransaction, cfupdate

Attributes

DataSource (required). Name of the data source that contains your table.

To connect to an ODBC data source that is not defined in the ColdFusion Administrator, specify __dynamic__. You must precede and follow the word dynamic with two underscore characters. When you use this attribute value, you must also specify all the ODBC connection information in a connectstring attribute.

DbType (optional). The database driver type:

- ODBC (default)—ODBC driver.
- Oracle73—Oracle 7.3 native database driver. Using this option, the ColdFusion Server computer must have Oracle 7.3.4.0.0 (or greater) client software installed.
- Oracle80—Oracle 8.0 native database driver. Using this option, the ColdFusion Server computer must have Oracle 8.0 (or greater) client software installed.
- Sybase11—Sybase System 11 native database driver. Using this option, the ColdFusion Server computer must have Sybase 11.1.1 (or greater) client software installed. Sybase patch ebf 7729 is recommended.
- OLEDB—OLE DB provider. If specified, this database provider overrides the driver type specified in the ColdFusion Administrator.
- DB2—DB2 5.2 native database driver.
- Informix73—Informix73 native database driver.

DbServer (optional). For native database drivers and the SQLOLEDB provider, specifies the name of the database server machine. If specified, dbServer overrides the server specified in the data source.

dbName (optional). The database name (Sybase System 11 driver and SQLOLEDB provider only). If specified, dbName overrides the default database specified in the data source.

TableName (required). Name of the table you want the form fields inserted in. Note the following:

- ORACLE drivers—This specification must be in uppercase.
- Sybase driver—This specification is case sensitive and must be in the same case as that used when the table was created.

connectString (optional). The contents of a connection string to send to the ODBC server. If you are connecting to a data source defined in the ColdFusion Administrator, you can use this attribute to specify additional connection details or to override connection information specified in the Administrator. If you are dynamically connecting to a datasource by specifying datasource = "__dynamic__," the connection string must specify all required ODBC connection attributes.

tableOwner (optional). For data sources that support table ownership (such as SQL Server, Oracle, and Sybase SQL Anywhere), use this field to specify the owner of the table.

TableQualifier (optional). For data sources that support table qualifiers, use this field to specify the qualifier for the table. The purpose of table qualifiers varies across drivers. For SQL Server and Oracle, the qualifier refers to the name of the database that contains the table. For the Intersolv dBase driver, the qualifier refers to the directory where the DBF files are located.

USERNAME (optional). If specified, username overrides the username value specified in the ODBC setup.

PASSWORD (optional). If specified, password overrides the password value specified in the ODBC setup.

PROVIDER (optional). COM provider (OLE-DB only).

PROVIDERDSN (optional). Data source name for the COM provider (OLE-DB only).

FormFields (optional). A comma-separated list of form fields to insert. If this attribute is not specified, all fields in the form are included in the operation.

CFLDAP

Cfldap provides an interface to LDAP (Lightweight Directory Access Protocol) directory servers like the Netscape Directory Server. For complete examples of cfldap usage, refer to *Developing ColdFusion Applications.* Cfldap is an Internet Protocol Tag.

Syntax

```
<cfldap server = "server_name"
  port = "port_number"
  username = "name"
  password = "password"
  action = "action"
  name = "name"
  timeout = "seconds"
  maxRows = "number"
  start = "distinguished_name"
  scope = "scope"
  attributes = "attribute, attribute"
  filter = "filter"
  filterFile = "<file_name>,<stanza_name>"
  sort = "attribute[, attribute]..."
  sortControl = "nocase" and/or "desc" or "asc"
  dn = "distinguished_name"
  startRow = "row_number"
  modifyType = "REPLACE" or "ADD" or "delete"
  rebind = "Yes" or "No"
  referral = "number_of_allowed_hops"
  secure = "multi_field_security_string"
  separator = "separator_character"
  delimiter = "delimiter_character">
```

See Also

cfftp, cfhttp, cfmail, cfmailparam, cfpop

Attributes

SERVER (required). Host name ("biff.upperlip.com") or IP address ("192.1.2.225") of the LDAP server.

PORT (optional). Port defaults to the standard LDAP port, 389.

USERNAME (optional). If no user name is specified, the LDAP connection will be anonymous.

PASSWORD (optional). Password corresponds to user name.

ACTION (optional). Specifies the LDAP action. There are five possible values:

- query (default)—Returns LDAP entry information only. Requires name, start, attributes. See Usage for more information.
- add—Adds LDAP entries to the LDAP server. Requires attributes.
- modify—Modifies LDAP entries on an LDAP server with the exception of the distinguished name dn attribute. Requires dn attribute. See the modifyType attribute for additional controls.
- modifyDN—Modifies the distinguished name attribute for LDAP entries on an LDAP server. Requires dn attribute.
- delete—Deletes LDAP entries on an LDAP server. Requires dn.

NAME (required for action = "Query"). The name you assign to the LDAP query.

TIMEOUT (optional). Specifies the maximum amount of time in seconds to wait for LDAP processing. Defaults to 60 seconds.

MAXROWS (optional). Specifies the maximum number of entries for LDAP queries.

START (required for action = "Query"). Specifies the distinguished name of the entry to be used to start the search.

SCOPE (optional). Specifies the scope of the search from the entry specified in the Start attribute for action = "Query." There are three possible values:

- oneLevel (default)—Searches all entries one level beneath the entry specified in the start attribute.
- base—Searches only the entry specified in the start attribute.
- subtree—Searches the entry specified in the start attribute as well as all entries at all levels beneath it.

ATTRIBUTES (required for action = "Query," Add, ModifyDN, and Modify). For queries, specifies the comma-separated list of attributes to be returned for queries. For queries, you can also specify the wildcard "*" to get all the attributes associated with the entry. In addition, it can be used to specify the list of update columns for action = "Add" or modify. When used with action = "Add" and action = "Modify," separate multiple attributes with a semicolon. When used with action = "ModifyDN," ColdFusion passes attributes to the LDAP server without performing any syntax checking.

FILTER (optional). Specifies the search criteria for action = "Query." Attributes are referenced in the form: "(attribute operator value)." Example: "(sn =

Smith)." Default is "objectclass = *." If you also specify the filterFile attribute, the filter is considered to be a search string, not a filter.

filterFile (optional). Specifies the name of a filter file and the name of the stanza tag within that file that contains the LDAP filter string specification. You can specify either an absolute path name or a simple file name to identify the file. If you use a simple file name, cfldap looks for it in ColdFusion's default LDAP directory location. The default LDAP directory location for a user-installed LDAP directory is C:\cfusion\ldap. The filter file must be in LDAP filter file format as defined in RCF-1558.

SORT (optional). Indicates the attribute or attributes to sort query results by. Use a comma to separate attributes if more than one attribute is specified.

SORTCONTROL (optional). Specifies how to sort query results. Enter nocase for a. Enter one or more of the following values:

- nocase—Case-insensitive sort.
- asc (default)—Ascending case-sensitive sort.
- desc—Descending case-sensitive sort By default, sorts are case sensitive. You can enter a combination of sort types—for example, sortControl = "nocase, asc."

dn (required for action = "Add", Modify, ModifyDN, and delete). Specifies the distinguished name for update actions. Example: "cn = Barbara Jensen, o = Ace Industry, c = US."

startRow (optional). Used in conjunction with action = "Query." Specifies the first row of the LDAP query that is to be inserted into the ColdFusion query. The default is 1. See the Usage section for more information about the query object and query variables.

modifyType (optional). Indicates whether to add, delete, or replace an attribute within a multivalue list of attributes, as follows:

- add—Appends the new attribute to any existing attributes.
- delete—Deletes the specified attribute from the set of existing attributes.
- replace (default)—Replaces an existing attribute with the specified attribute or attributes. Note that you cannot add attributes that already exist or that are null.

REBIND (optional). Yes or No. If you set rebind to Yes, cfldap attempts to rebind the referral callback and reissue the query via the referred address using the original credentials. The default is No, which means referred connections are anonymous.

REFERRAL (optional). Specifies the number of hops allowed in a referral. Valid values for this are integers equal to or greater than zero. If you specify zero, you turn off cfldap's ability to use referred addresses; thus, no data is returned.

SECURE (optional). Identifies the type of security to employ, CFSSL_BASIC or CFSSL_CLIENT_AUTH, and additional information that is required by the specified security type. secure = "CFSSL_BASIC,certificate_db" or secure = "CFSSL_CLIENT_AUTH, certificate_db,certificate_name, key_db,key_password." These fields have the following values:

- certificate_db: The name of the certificate database file (in Netscape cert7.db format). You can specify either an absolute path or a simple file name.
- certificate_name: The name of the client certificate to send the server.
- key_db: Keyword database that holds the public/private keypair (in Netscape key3.db format). You can specify either an absolute path or a simple file name.
- keyword_db: The password to key database. If you use a simple file name for certificate_db or keyword_db, cfldap looks in the ColdFusion default LDAP directory location for a user-installed LDAP directory (C:\cfusion\ldap for Windows).

Refer to the Usage section for information about the differences between the two types of security: CFSSL_BASIC and CFSSL_CLIENT_AUTH types.

SEPARATOR (optional). Specifies the character that cfldap uses to separate attribute values in multivalue attributes. This character is used by the query, add, and modify action attributes, and is used by cfldap to output multivalue attributes. The default character is the comma (,). For example, if you set the value of separator to a dollar sign ($), the attribute could have the following value:"objectclass = top$person," where the first value of objectclass is "top" and the second is "person." Using an alternate character to separate different values of the same attribute eliminates confusion when the values themselves have commas in them.

DELIMITER (optional). Specifies the character that cfldap uses to separate multiple attribute name/value pairs when more than one attribute is specified in the attribute or when the attribute you want to use has the default delimiter character, which is the semicolon (;), such as mgrpmsgrejecttext;lang-en. The delimiter character is used by the query, add, and modify action attributes, and is used by cfldap to output multivalue attributes. For example, if you used a dollar sign ($), you could specify the following list of name-value pairs with attributes: "cn = Double Tree Inn$street = 1111 Newbury;Suite 100."

Usage

If you use the Query action, cfldap creates a query object, allowing you access to information in the three query variables as described below:

- queryname.recordCount—The total number of records returned by the query.
- queryname.currentRow—The current row of the query being processed by cfoutput.
- queryname.columnList—The list of the column names in the query.

The CFSSL_BASIC type of security provides V2 SSL, and the CFSSL_CLIENT_AUTH type of security provides V3 SSL. V2 SSL provides encryption and server authentication. V3 SSL adds to this certificate-based client authentication.

Both forms of security encrypt the conversation, and the server always sends a digital certificate to confirm that it is the right server.

For CFSSL_BASIC, you must also specify the cfldap attributes username and password to authenticate yourself. V2 then encrypts the password prior to transmission.

For CFSSL_CLIENT_AUTH, you do not send a user name and password; instead, you perform authentication by a digital certificate that you send to the server. CFSSL_CLIENT_AUTH is much more secure; however, it is difficult to administer, since all the clients must have certificates, which the server must be able to validate, and all the certificates must have keys associated with them and passwords to protect those keys.

CFLOCATION

Cflocation opens a specified ColdFusion page or HTML file. For example, you might use cflocation to specify a standard message or response that you use in several different ColdFusion applications. Use the addToken attribute to verify client requests. See Warning for information about the interaction between cookies and cflocation. cflocation is a flow-control tag.

Syntax

```
<cflocation url = "url" addToken = "Yes" or "No">
```

See Also

cfabort, cfbreak, cfexecute, cfexit, cfif cfelseif cfelse, cfloop, cfswitch cfcase cfdefaultcase, cfthrow, cftry /cfcatch

Attributes

URL. The URL of the HTML file or CFML page you want to open.

addToken (optional). Yes or No. clientManagement must be enabled (see cfapplication). A value of Yes appends client variable information to the URL you specify in the url attribute.

Warning

Do not set a cookie variable on the same page on which you use the cflocation tag. If you do, the cookie is never saved on the browser. Likewise, if you use a cookie to store a client variable, the client variable is never set.

CFLOCK

The cflock tag provides two types of locks to ensure the integrity of shared data:

- exclusive lock
- read-only lock

An exclusive lock single-threads access to the CFML constructs in its body. Single-threaded access implies that the body of the tag can be executed by at most one request at a time. A request executing inside a cflock tag has an "exclusive lock" on the tag. No other requests are allowed to start executing inside the tag while a request has an exclusive lock. ColdFusion issues exclusive locks on a first-come, first-served basis.

A read-only lock allows multiple requests to access the CFML constructs inside its body concurrently. Therefore, read-only locks should be used only when the shared data will only be read and not modified. If another request already has an exclusive lock on the shared data, the request will wait for the exclusive lock to be released before it can obtain it.

cflock is a Web application framework tag.

Syntax

```
<cflock timeout = "timeout in seconds "
  scope = "Application" or "Server" or "Session"
  name = "lockname"
  throwOnTimeout = "Yes" or "No"
  type = "readOnly/Exclusive ">
  <!--- CFML to be synchronized --->
</cflock>
```

See Also

cfapplication, cfassociate, cfauthenticate, cfmodule

Attributes

TIMEOUT (required). Specifies the maximum amount of time in seconds to wait to obtain a lock. If a lock can be obtained within the specified period, execution will continue inside the body of the tag. Otherwise, the behavior depends on the value of the throwOnTimeout attribute.

SCOPE (optional). Specifies the scope as one of the following: Application, Server, or Session. This attribute is mutually exclusive with the name attribute. See the Scope section for valuable information.

NAME (optional). Specifies the name of the lock. Only one request will be able to execute inside a cflock tag with a given name. Therefore, providing the name attribute allows for synchronizing access to the same resources from different parts of an application. Lock names are global to a ColdFusion server. They are shared between applications and user sessions, but not across clustered servers. This attribute is mutually exclusive with the scope attribute. Therefore, do not specify the scope attribute and the name attribute in the same tag. Note that the value of name cannot be an empty string.

throwOnTimeout (optional). Yes or No. Specifies how timeout conditions should be handled. If the value is Yes, an exception will be generated to provide notification of the timeout. If the value is No, execution continues past the </cflock> tag. Default is Yes.

TYPE (optional). readOnly or Exclusive. Specifies the type of lock: read-only or exclusive. Default is Exclusive. A read-only lock allows more than one request to read shared data. An exclusive lock allows only one request to read or write to shared data. See the following Note.

Note

Limit the scope of code that updates shared data. Exclusive locks are required to ensure the integrity of these updates, but they have a significant impact on performance. Read-only locks are faster. If you have a performance-sensitive application, you should substitute read-only locks for exclusive locks wherever it is possible, for example, when reading shared data.

Usage

ColdFusion Server is a multithreaded Web application server that can process multiple page requests at any given time. Use cflock to guarantee that multiple concurrently executing requests do not manipulate shared data structures, files, or CFXs in an inconsistent manner. Note the following:

- Using cflock around CFML constructs that modify shared data ensures that the modifications occur one after the other and not all at the same time.
- Using cflock around file-manipulation constructs can guarantee that file updates do not fail due to files being open for writing by other applications or ColdFusion tags.
- Using cflock around CFX invocations can guarantee that CFXs that are not implemented in a thread-safe manner can be safely invoked by ColdFusion. This usually applies only to CFXs developed in C++ using the CFAPI. Any C++ CFX that maintains and manipulates shared (global) data structures will have to be made thread-safe to safely work with ColdFusion. However, writing thread-safe C++ CFXs requires advanced knowledge. A CFML custom tag wrapper can be used around the CFX to make its invocation thread-safe.

Scope

Whenever you display, set, or update variables in one of the shared scopes, use the scope attribute to identify the scope as Server, Application or Session.

Within the ColdFusion Administrator, the Locking page, under the Server section, allows you to set different characteristics of the locking schema according to scope. The following table shows which features are available for Server, Application, and Session scope.

Features	*Server*	*Application*	*Session*
No automatic checking or locking	Yes	Yes	Yes
Full checking	Yes	Yes	Yes
Automatic read locking	Yes	Yes	Yes
Single-threaded sessions			Yes

Each feature that you select has tradeoffs.

- No automatic checking or locking: If you select this button, no reads or writes are locked or checked for correct protection. You should select this only after you have run with full checking and know that there are no errors to handle and that all locking is handled programmatically. Selecting this button provides the fastest performance.
- Full checking: If you select this button, all unlocked accesses will be detected. You should select this when you are in debug mode. Selecting this button slows performance.
- Automatic read locking: If you select this button, all reads are locked and unlocked writes cause an error. Selecting this button also slows down performance considerably.
- Single-threaded sessions: If you select this button, the whole request has to finish before another request for the same session is processed. Selecting this button may have an effect on performance, depending on the request pattern. For example, the total response time may increase if an application has multiple frames that can be refreshed at once, thus causing multiple requests to have to queue up and wait to be processed.

For an analysis of best practices with respect to locking, please refer to *Administering ColdFusion Server.*

If you create a lock with the name attribute, not with the scope attribute, and enable full lock checking in the ColdFusion Administrator, ColdFusion returns an error.

- If the named lock is in the application scope, do not specify full checking for the application scope.
- If the lock is in the session scope, do not specify full lock checking for the session scope.

- If the lock is in the server scope, do not specify full lock checking for the server scope.

Deadlocks

<cflock> uses kernel-level synchronization objects that are released automatically upon timeout and/or abnormal termination of the thread that owns them. Therefore, ColdFusion will never deadlock for an infinite period of time while processing a cflock tag. However, very large timeouts can block request threads for long periods of time and thus radically decrease throughput. Always use the minimum timeout value allowed.

Another cause of blocked request threads is inconsistent nesting of cflock tags and inconsistent naming of locks. If you are nesting locks, you and everyone accessing the locked variables must consistently nest cflock tags in the same order. If everyone accessing locked variables does not adhere to these conventions, a deadlock can occur. A deadlock is a state in which no request can execute the locked section of the page. Thus, all requests to the protected section of the page are blocked until there is a timeout. The following tables show two scenarios that cause deadlocks.

Deadlock Scenario with Two Users

User 1	*User 2*
Locks the session scope.	Locks the application scope.
Deadlock: Tries to lock the application scope, but it already is locked by User 2.	Deadlock: Tries to lock the session scope, but it already is locked by User 1.

Deadlock Scenario with One User

User 1
Locks the session scope with a read lock.
Attempts to lock the session scope with an exclusive lock.
Deadlock: Attempts to lock the session scope with an exclusive lock, but cannot because the scope is already locked for reading.

A deadlock scenario could take place if you tried to nest a write lock after a read lock, as in the following code:

```
<cflock timeout = "60" scope = "SESSION" type = "readOnly">
   ...............
```

```
  <cflock timeout = "60" scope = "SESSION" type =
"Exclusive">
  .........
  </cflock>
</cflock>
```

Once a deadlock occurs, neither of the users can do anything to break it, because the execution of their requests is blocked until the deadlock can be resolved by a lock timeout.

In order to avoid a deadlock, you and all who need to nest locks should do so in a well-specified order and name the locks consistently. In particular, if you need to lock access to the server, application, and session scopes, you must do so in the following order.

1. Lock the session scope. In the cflock tag, indicate the scope by specifying “Session” as the value of the scope attribute.
2. Lock the application scope. In the cflock tag, indicate scope by specifying “Application” as the value of the scope attribute.
3. Lock the server scope. In the cflock tag, indicate the scope by specifying “Server” as the value of the scope attribute.
4. Unlock the server scope.
5. Unlock the application scope.
6. Unlock the session scope.

Note

You can take out any pair of lock/unlock steps if you do not need to lock a particular scope. For example, you can take out steps 3 and 4 if you do not need to lock the server scope. Similar rules apply for named locks.

CFLOG

Writes a message to a log file. <cflog> is a data output tag.

Syntax

```
<cflog text = "text"
  log = "log type"
  file = "filename"
  type = "message type"
```

```
thread = "thread ID yes or no"
date = "date yes or no"
time = "time yes or no"
application = "application name yes or no">
```

See Also

cfcol, cfcontent, cfoutput, cftable

Attributes

TEXT (required). The text of the message to be logged.

LOG (optional). If you omit the file attribute, specifies the standard log file in which to write the message. Ignored if you specify a file attribute. Valid values are:

- Application—Writes to the Application.log file, normally used for application-specific messages.
- Scheduler—Writes to the Scheduler.log file, normally used to log the execution of scheduled tasks.

FILE (optional). The name of the file in which to log the message. All log files must have the suffix .log. You must specify only the main part of the file name, without the .log suffix. For example, to log to the Testing.log file, specify "Testing." The file must be located in the default log directory. You cannot specify a directory path. The file is created automatically if it does not exist.

TYPE (optional). The type (severity) of the message. Valid values are:

- Information (default)
- Warning
- Error
- Fatal Information

DATE (optional). Specifies whether to log the system date. Valid values are YES (default) and NO.

TIME (optional). Specifies whether to log the system time. Valid values are YES (default) and NO.

APPLICATION (optional). Specifies whether to log the application name if one has been specified in a cfapplication tag. Valid values are YES (default) and NO.

Usage

The cflog tag lets you log custom messages to standard of custom log files. You can specify your own files for the log message or send messages to either the default application or scheduler log. The log message can include ColdFusion expressions. All log files must have the suffix .log and must be located in the ColdFusion log directory.

Log entries are written as comma-delimited lists with these fields:

- type
- thread
- date
- time
- application
- text

Values are enclosed in double quotation marks. If you specify No for any of thread, date, time, or application, the corresponding entry in the list is empty.

You can disable cflog tag execution. See the ColdFusion Administrator, Basic Security page, for details.

CFLOOP

Looping is a very powerful programming technique that lets you repeat a set of instructions or display output over and over until one or more conditions are met. Cfloop supports five different types of loops: index loop, conditional loop, looping over a query, looping over a list, and looping over a com collection or structure.

Index Loop

An index loop repeats for a number of times determined by a range of numeric values. Index loops are commonly known as FOR loops, as in "loop FOR this range of values." An index loop is a flow-control tag.

Syntax

```
<cfloop index = "parameter_name"
  from = "beginning_value"
  to = "ending_value"
  step = "increment">
  ...
  HTML or CFML code to execute
   ...
</cfloop>
```

See Also

cfabort, cfbreak, cfexecute, cfexit, cfif cfelseif cfelse, cflocation, cfrethrow, cfswitch cfcase cfdefaultcase, cfthrow, cftry /cfcatch

Attributes

INDEX (required). Defines the parameter that is the index value. The index value will be set to the FROM value and then incremented by 1 (or the step value) until it equals the TO value.

FROM (required). The beginning value of the index.

TO (required). The ending value of the index.

STEP (optional). Default is 1. Sets the value by which the loop index value is incremented each time the loop is processed.

Usage

When coding an index loop, using anything other than integer values in the from and to attributes can product unexpected results. For example, if you increment through an index loop between 1 and 2 with a step of 0.1, ColdFusion outputs "1,1.1,1.2,...,1.9," but NOT "2." This is a well-known problem in programming languages that has to do with the internal representation of floating-point numbers.

Note

The TO value is a tag attribute that is evaluated only once when the cfloop tag is encountered. Therefore, any change within the loop's block to this value, or the expression that evaluates to this value, does not affect the number of times the loop is executed.

Conditional Loop

A conditional loop iterates over a set of instructions while a given condition is TRUE. To use this type of loop correctly, the instructions must change the condition every time the loop iterates until the condition evaluates as FALSE. Conditional loops are commonly known as WHILE loops, as in "loop WHILE this condition is true." It is a flow-control tag.

Syntax

```
<cfloop condition = "expression">
```

See Also

cfabort, cfbreak, cfexecute, cfexit, cfif cfelseif cfelse, cflocation, cfswitch cfcase cfdefaultcase, cfthrow, cftry /cfcatch

Attributes

CONDITION (required). Sets the condition that controls the loop. The loop will repeat as long as the condition evaluates as TRUE. When the condition is FALSE, the loop stops.

Looping Over a Query

A loop over a query repeats for every record in the query record set. The cfloop results are just like a cfoutput. During each iteration of the loop, the columns of the current row will be available for output. cfloop allows you to loop over tags that cannot be used inside cfoutput. It is a flow-control tag.

Syntax

```
<cfloop query = "query_name"
  startRow = "row_num"
  endRow = "row_num">
```

See Also

cfabort, cfbreak, cfexecute, cfexit, cfif cfelseif cfelse, cflocation, cfswitch cfcase cfdefaultcase, cfthrow, cftry /cfcatch

Attributes

QUERY (required). Specifies the query that will control the loop.

startRow (optional). Specifies the first row of the query that will be included in the loop.

endRow (optional). Specifies the last row of the query that will be included in the loop.

Looping Over a List

Looping over a list offers the option of walking through elements contained within a variable or value returned from an expression. In a list loop, the index attribute specifies the name of a variable to receive the next element of the list, and the list attribute holds a list or a variable containing a list. It is a flow-control tag.

Syntax

```
<cfloop index = "index_name"
  list = "list_items"
  delimiterS = "item_delimiter">
</cfloop>
```

See Also

cfabort, cfbreak, cfexecute, cfexit, cfif cfelseif cfelse, cflocation, cfswitch cfcase cfdefaultcase, cfthrow, cftry /cfcatch

Attributes

INDEX (required). In a list loop, the index attribute specifies the name of a variable to receive the next element of the list, and the list attribute holds a list or a variable containing a list.

LIST (required). The list items in the loop, provided directly or with a variable.

delimiterS (optional). Specifies the delimiter characters used to separate items in the list.

Looping Over a COM Collection or Structure

The cfloop collection attribute allows you to loop over a structure or a COM/DCOM collection object:

A COM/DCOM collection object is a set of similar items referenced as a group rather than individually. For example, the group of open documents in an application is a type of collection. A structure can contain either a related set of items or be used as an associative array. Looping is particularly useful when using a structure as an associative array.

Each collection item is referenced in the cfloop by the variable name that you supply in the item attribute. This type of iteration is generally used to access every object within a COM/DCOM collection or every element in the structure. The loop is executed until all objects have been accessed.

The collection attribute is used with the item attribute in a cfloop. In the example that follows, an item is assigned a variable called file2, so that with each cycle in the cfloop, each item in the collection is referenced. In the cfoutput section, the name property of the file2 item is referenced for display. The type of loop is determined by the attributes of the cfloop tag.

CFMAIL

<cfmail> allows you to send email messages via an SMTP server. cfmail is an Internet Protocol Tag.

Syntax

```
<cfmail to = "recipient"
  from = "sender"
  cc = "copy_to"
  Bcc = "blind_copy_to"
  subject = "msg_subject"
  type = "msg_type"
  maxRows = "max_msgs"
  MIMEAttach = "path"
  query = "query_name"
  group = "query_column"
  groupCaseSensitive = "Yes" or "No"
  startRow = "query_row"
  server = "servername"
  port = "port_ID"
  mailerID = "headerid"
  timeout = "seconds">
```

See Also

cfftp, cfhttp, cfldap, cfmailparam, cfpop

Attributes

TO (required). The name of the recipient(s) of the email message. This can be either a static address (as in, to = "support@allaire.com"), a variable that contains an address (such as, to = "#Form.Email#"), or the name of a query column that contains address information (such as, to = "#EMail#"). In the latter case, an individual email message is sent for every row returned by the query.

FROM (required). The sender of the email message. This attribute may be either static (e.g., from = "support@allaire.com") or dynamic (as in, from = "#GetUser.EMailAddress#").

CC (optional). Indicates additional addresses to copy the email message to; "cc" stands for "carbon copy."

BCC (optional). Indicates additional addresses to copy the email message without listing them in the message header. "bcc" stands for "blind carbon copy."

SUBJECT (required). The subject of the mail message. This field may be driven dynamically on a message-by-message basis. For example, if you want to do a mailing that updates customers on the status of their orders, you might use a subject attribute like subject = "Status for Order Number #Order_ID#".

TYPE (optional). Specifies extended type attributes for the message. Currently, the only valid value for this attribute is "HTML". Specifying type = "HTML" informs the receiving email client that the message has embedded HTML tags that need to be processed. This is only useful when sending messages to mail clients that understand HTML (such as Netscape 2.0 and above email clients).

maxRows (optional). Specifies the maximum number of email messages you want to send.

MIMEAttach (optional). Specifies the path of the file to be attached to the email message. Attached file is MIME encoded.

QUERY (optional). The name of the cfquery from which you want to draw data for message(s) you want to send. Specify this attribute to send more than one mail message, or to send the results of a query within a single message.

GROUP (optional). Specifies the query column to use when you group sets of records together to send as a single email message. For example, if you send a set of billing statements out to your customers, you might group on "Customer_ID." The group attribute, which is case sensitive, eliminates adjacent duplicates in the case where the data is sorted by the specified field. See the Usage section for exceptions.

groupCaseSensitive (optional). Boolean indicating whether to group with regard to case or not. The default value is YES; case is considered while grouping. If the query attribute specifies a query object that was generated by a case-insensitive SQL query, set the groupCaseSensitive attribute to NO to keep the recordset intact.

startRow (optional). Specifies the row in the query to start from.

SERVER (required). The address of the SMTP server to use for sending messages. The server name specified in the ColdFusion Administrator is used if no server is specified.

PORT. The TCP/IP port on which the SMTP server listens for requests. This is almost always 25.

mailerID (optional). Specifies a mailer ID to be passed in the X-Mailer SMTP header, which identifies the mailer application. The default is Allaire ColdFusion Application Server.

TIMER (optional). The number of seconds to wait before timing out the connection to the SMTP server.

CFMAILPARAM

cfmailparam can either attach a file or add a header to a message. If you use cfmailparam, it is nested within a cfmail tag. You can use more than one cfmailparam tags within a cfmail tag in order to attach one or more files and headers. cfmailparam is an Internet Protocol Tag.

Syntax

```
<cfmail
  to = "recipient"
  subject = "msg_subject"
  from = "sender"
  ...more attibutes...
>
  <cfmailparam
    file = "file-name"
  >
```

or

```
            <cfmailparam
              name = "header-name"
               value = "header-value"
          >
            ...
          </cfmail>
```

See Also

cfftp, cfhttp, cfldap, cfmail, cfpop

Attributes

FILE (required if you do not specify the name attribute). Attaches the specified file to the message. This attribute is mutually exclusive with the name attribute.

NAME (required if you do not specify the file attribute). Specifies the name of the header. Header names are case insensitive. This attribute is mutually exclusive with the file attribute.

VALUE (optional). Indicates the value of the header.

CFMODULE

Use cfmodule to invoke a custom tag for use in your ColdFusion application pages. cfmodule can help deal with any custom tag-name conflicts that might arise.

Use the template attribute to name a ColdFusion page containing the custom tag definition, including its path. Use the name attribute to refer to the custom tag, using a dot notation scheme indicating the location of the custom tag in the ColdFusion installation directory. <cfmodule> is a Web application framework tag.

Syntax

```
<cfmodule template = "template"
  name = "tag_name"
  attributeCollection = "collection_structure"
```

```
attribute_name1 = "value"
attribute_name2 = "value"
...>
```

See Also

cfapplication, cfassociate, cfauthenticate, cflock

Attributes

TEMPLATE. Used in place of name, defines a path to the application page (.cfm file) implementing the tag. Relative paths are expanded from the current page. Physical paths are not allowed. Absolute paths are expanded using the ColdFusion mappings.

NAME. Used in place of template, defines the name of the custom tag in the form "Name.Name.Name..." that uniquely identifies a subdirectory containing the custom tag page under the root directory for ColdFusion custom tags. For example: <cfmodule name = "Allaire.Forums40. GetUserOptions"> identifies the page GetUserOptions.cfm in the directory CustomTags\Allaire\Forums40 under the root directory of the ColdFusion installation.

attributeCollection (optional). A structure that contains a collection of key-value pairs that represent attribute names and their values. You can specify as many key-value pairs as needed. However, you can specify the attributeCollection attribute only once. See Usage for more information.

attribute_name (optional). Attributes that you want your custom tag to use. You can use as many attributes as needed to specify the parameters of a custom tag.

Usage

You can use attributeCollection and attribute in the same call.

Within the custom tag code, the attributes passed with attributeCollection are saved as independent attribute values with no indication that the attributes were grouped into a structure by the custom tag's caller.

Likewise, if the custom tag uses a cfassociate tag to save its attributes, the attributes passed with attributeCollection are saved as independent attribute values with no indication that the attributes are grouped into a structure by the custom tag's caller.

CFOBJECT

The cfobject tag allows you to call methods in COM, CORBA, and JAVA objects.

Note

ColdFusion administrators can disable the cfobject tag in the ColdFusion Administrator Basic Security page.

On UNIX, COM objects are not currently supported by cfobject.

CFOBJECT TYPES

- cfobject type = "com"
- cfobject type = "corba"
- cfobject type = "java"

CFOUTPUT

Displays the results of a database query or other operation. If you need to nest cfoutput tags, please read the "Usage" section. cfoutput is a data output tag.

Syntax

```
<cfoutput
  query = "query_name"
  group = "query_column"
  groupCaseSensitive = "Yes" or "No"
  startRow = "start_row"
  maxRows = "max_rows_output">
</cfoutput>
```

See Also

cfcol, cfcontent, cftable

Attributes

QUERY (optional). The name of the cfquery from which you want to draw data for the output section.

GROUP (optional). Specifies the query column to use when you group sets of records together. Use this attribute if you have retrieved a record set ordered on a certain query column. For example, if you have a record set that is ordered according to "Customer_ID" in the cfquery tag, you can group the output on "Customer_ID." The group attribute, which is case sensitive, eliminates adjacent duplicates in the case where the data is sorted by the specified field. See the groupCaseSensitive attribute for information about specifying a case-insensitive grouping.

groupCaseSensitive (optional). Boolean indicating whether to group with regard to case or not. The default value is YES; case is considered while grouping. If the query attribute specifies a query object that was generated by a case-insensitive SQL query, set the groupCaseSensitive attribute to NO to keep the recordset intact.

startRow (optional). Specifies the row from which to start output.

maxRows (optional). Specifies the maximum number of rows you want displayed in the output section.

Usage

In order to nest cfoutput blocks, you must specify the group and query attributes at the topmost level, and the group attribute for all inner blocks except for the innermost cfoutput block.

CFPOP

<cfpop> retrieves and deletes email messages from a POP mail server. cfpop is an Internet Protocol Tag.

Syntax

```
<cfpop server = "servername"
  port = "port_number"
  username = "username"
  password = "password"
  action = "action"
  name = "queryname"
  messageNumber = "number"
  attachmentPath = "path"
  timeout = "seconds"
  maxRows = "number"
```

```
startRow = "number"
generateUniqueFilenames = "boolean">
```

See Also

cfftp, cfhttp, cfldap, cfmail, cfmailparam

Attributes

SERVER (required). Host name (biff.upperlip.com) or IP address (192.1.2.225) of the POP server.

PORT (optional). Defaults to the standard POP port, 110.

USERNAME (optional). If no user name is specified, the POP connection is anonymous.

PASSWORD (optional). Password corresponds to user name.

ACTION (optional). Specifies the mail action. There are three possible values:

- getHeaderOnly (default)—Returns message header information only.
- getAll—Returns message header information, message text, and attachments if attachmentPath is specified.
- delete—Deletes messages on the POP server.

NAME (optional). The name you assign to the index query. Required for action = "getHeaderOnly" and action = "getAll."

messageNumber (optional). Specifies the message number(s) for the given action. messageNumber is required for action = "delete." If it is provided for action = "getHeaderOnly" or action = "getAll," only referenced messages will be retrieved. If it is omitted for action = "getHeaderOnly" or action = "getAll," all messages available on the server are returned. messageNumber can contain individual message numbers or a comma-separated list of message numbers. Invalid message numbers will be ignored.

attachmentPath (optional). Allows attachments to be written to the specified directory when action = "getAll." If an invalid attachmentPath is specified, no attachment files are written to the server.

TIMEOUT (optional). Specifies the maximum amount of time in seconds to wait for mail processing. Defaults to 60 seconds.

maxRows (optional). Sets the number of messages returned, starting with the number specified in the startRow attribute. This attribute is ignored if messageNumber is specified.

startRow (optional). Specifies the first row number to be retrieved. Default is 1. This attribute is ignored if messageNumber is specified.

generateUniqueFilenames (optional). Boolean indicating whether to generate unique file names for the files attached to an email message in order to avoid naming conflicts when the files are saved. The default is NO.

Usage

Note

Two retrieve options are offered to maximize performance. Message header information is typically short and therefore quick to transfer. Message text and attachments can be very long and therefore take longer to process. See the Message Header and Body Columns table, which follows the cfpop attribute descriptions, for information on retrieving header and body information from the query when you specify getHeaderOnly or getAll.

cfpop query variables

The following list describes the query variables that are returned by cfpop. The example illustrates their use.

queryname.recordCount	The total number of records returned by the query.
queryname.currentRow	The current row of the query being processed by cfoutput.
queryname.columnList	The list of the column names in the query.

Message Header and Body Columns

The following list describes the message header and body columns that are returned by cfpop when you specify the action attribute to be either getHeaderOnly or getAll. All of the columns are returned if you specify getAll, but only header information is returned when you specify getHeaderOnly.

Column Name	getHeaderOnly returns	getAll returns
queryname.date	yes	yes
queryname.from	yes	yes

Column Name	getHeaderOnly returns	getAll returns
queryname.messagenumber	yes	yes
queryname.replyto	yes	yes
queryname.subject	yes	yes
queryname.cc	yes	yes
queryname.to	yes	yes
queryname.body	not available	yes
queryname.header	not available	yes
queryname.attachments	not available	yes
queryname.attachmentfiles	not available	yes

To create a ColdFusion date/time object from the date-time string that is extracted from a mail message in the queryname.date column, here is how to do it. For the English (US) locale, use the ParseDateTime function and specify the POP attribute, which converts the date-time value to Greenwich Mean Time. For other locales, extract the date portion of the string and pass it to the LSParseDateTime function, then add or subtract the conversion time, depending on the locale.

See Also

The description of the SetLocale function. For complete usage information on cfpop, see *Developing ColdFusion Applications.*

CRPROCESSINGDIRECTIVE

Suppresses extraneous white space, and other output, produced by the CFML within the tag's scope. cfprocessingdirective is a data output tag.

Syntax

```
<cfprocessingdirective
  suppressWhiteSpace = "Yes" or "No">
... any CFML tags here ...
</cfprocessingdirective>
```

See Also

cfcol, cfcontent, cfoutput, cftable

Attributes

SuppressWhiteSpace (required). Boolean indicating whether to suppress the whitespace and other output generated by the CFML tags within the cfprocessingdirective block.

Usage

If a cfprocessingdirective tag's scope includes another cfprocessingdirective tag, then the inner tag's settings override the enclosing tag's settings within the body of the inner tag, where they differ. If the enclosing tag specifies settings that the inner tag does not, those settings remain in effect within the inner tag's scope.

Cfprocessingdirective settings do not apply to templates included via cfinclude, cfmodule, custom tag invocation, etc.

CFPROCPARAM

The <cfprocparam> tag is nested within a cfstoredproc tag. You use it to specify parameter information, including type, name, value, and length. cfprocparam is a database manipulation tag.

Syntax

```
<cfprocparam type = "IN or OUT or INOUT"
  variable = "variable name"
  dbVarName = "DB variable name"
  value = "parameter value"
  CFSQLType = "parameter datatype"
  maxLength = "length"
  scale = "decimal places"
  null = "Yes" or "No">
```

See Also

cfinsert, cfprocresult, cfquery, cfqueryparam, cfstoredproc, cftransaction, cfupdate

Attributes

TYPE (optional). Indicates whether the passed variable is an input, output, or input/output variable. Default is IN.The value IN passes the paramater by value. Values OUT and INOUT pass parameters as bound variables.

VARIABLE (required for OUT and INOUT parameters). This is the ColdFusion variable name that you use to reference the value that the output parameter represents after the call is made to the stored procedure.

dbVarName (required if named notation is desired). This is the parameter name. It corresponds to the name of the parameter in the stored procedure.

VALUE (required for IN and INOUT parameters). This corresponds to the actual value that ColdFusion passes to the stored procedure.

CFSQLType (required). This is the SQL type that the parameter (any type) will be bound to. The CFSQLTypes are as follows:

- CF_SQL_BIGINT
- CF_SQL_BIT
- CF_SQL_CHAR
- CF_SQL_DATE
- CF_SQL_DECIMAL
- CF_SQL_DOUBLE
- CF_SQL_FLOAT
- CF_SQL_IDSTAMP
- CF_SQL_INTEGER
- CF_SQL_LONGVARCHAR
- CF_SQL_MONEY
- CF_SQL_MONEY4
- CF_SQL_NUMERIC
- CF_SQL_REAL
- CF_SQL_REFCURSOR
- CF_SQL_SMALLINT
- CF_SQL_TIME
- CF_SQL_TIMESTAMP

- CF_SQL_TINYINT
- CF_SQL_VARCHAR

maxLength (optional). Maximum length of the parameter.

SCALE (optional). Number of decimal places of the parameter.

NULL (optional). Specify Yes or No. Indicates whether the parameter is passed as a null. If you specify Yes, the tag ignores the value attribute.

Usage

Use this tag to identify stored procedure parameters and their data types. Code one cfprocparam tag for each parameter. The parameters you code vary based on parameter type and DBMS. Additionally, the order in which you code cfprocparam tags matters, depending on whether the stored procedure was coded using positional notation or named notation:

- Positional notation—Order is very important if the stored procedure was defined using positional notation. ColdFusion passes these parameters to the stored procedure in the order in which they are defined.
- Named notation—If named notation is used, the dbVarName for the parameter must correspond to the variable name in the stored procedure on the server.

Output variables will be scoped with the name of the variable attribute that was passed to the tag.

CFML supports Oracle 8's REFERENCE CURSOR type. A REFERENCE CURSOR allows you to pass a parameter by reference. Therefore, parameters that are passed by reference can by allocated and deallocated memory within the course of one application. See the example for an illustration of the use of REFERENCE CURSORS.

CFPROCRESULT

The <cfprocresult> tag is nested within a <cfstoredproc> tag. This tag's name parameter specifies a result set name that other ColdFusion tags, such as cfoutput and cftable, use to access the result set. It also allows you to optionally identify which of the stored procedure's result sets to return. cfprocresult is a database manipulation tag.

Syntax

```
<cfprocresult name = "query_name"
  resultSet = "1-n"
  maxRows = "maxrows">
```

See Also

cfinsert, cfprocparam, cfquery, cfqueryparam, cfstoredproc, cftransaction, cfupdate

Attributes

NAME (required). Name for the query result set.

resultSet (optional). Specify this parameter to identify the desired result set if the stored procedure returns multiple result sets. Default is 1.

maxRows (optional). Specifies the maximum number of rows returned in the result set. The default is to return all rows in the result set.

Usage

Specify one or more cfprocresult tags to enable access to data returned by the stored procedure.

ResultSet must be unique within the scope of the cfstoredproc tag. If you specify the same result set twice, the second occurrence overwrites the first.

CFQUERY

<cfquery> passes SQL statements for any purpose to your data source. Not limited to queries.

<cfquery> is a database manipulation tag.

Syntax

```
<cfquery name = "query_name"
  dataSource = "ds_name"
```

```
dbType = "type"
dbServer = "dbms"
dbName = "database name"
connectString = "connection string"
username = "username"
password = "password"
maxRows = "number"
blockFactor = "blocksize"
timeout = "milliseconds"
cachedAfter = "date"
cachedWithin = "timespan"
provider = "COMProvider"
providerDSN = "datasource"
debug>
```

SQL Statements go here...

```
</cfquery>
```

See Also

cfinsert, cfprocparam, cfprocresult, cfqueryparam, cfstoredproc, cftransaction, cfupdate

Attributes

NAME (required). The name you assign to the query. Query names must begin with a letter and may consist of letters, numbers, and the underscore character (spaces are not allowed). The query name is used later in the page to reference the query's record set.

dataSource (required for all dbType operations except for dbType = "query"). The name of the data source from which this query should retrieve data. To connect to an ODBC data source that is not defined in the ColdFusion Administrator, specify __dynamic__. You must precede and follow the word dynamic with two underscore characters. When you use this attribute value, you must also specify all the ODBC connection information in a connectstring attribute.

dbType (optional). The database driver type:

- query—Use the result set from an existing query as the data source. Do not specify a datasource attribute when using dbType = "query." Instead, use existing query names as table names.

- ODBC (default)—ODBC driver.
- Oracle73—Oracle 7.3 native database driver. Using this option, the ColdFusion Server computer must have Oracle 7.3.4.0.0 (or greater) client software installed.
- Oracle80—Oracle 8.0 native database driver. Using this option, the ColdFusion Server computer must have Oracle 8.0 (or greater) client software installed.
- Sybase11—Sybase System 11 native database driver. Using this option, the ColdFusion Server computer must have Sybase 11.1.1 (or greater) client software installed. Sybase patch ebf 7729 is recommended.
- OLEDB—OLE DB provider. If specified, this database provider overrides the driver type specified in the ColdFusion Administrator.
- DB2—DB2 5.2 native database driver.
- Informix73—Informix73 native database driver.

dbServer (optional). For native database drivers and the SQLOLEDB provider, specifies the name of the database server machine. If specified, dbServer overrides the server specified in the data source.

dbName (optional). The database name (Sybase System 11 driver and SQLOLEDB provider only). If specified, dbName overrides the default database specified in the data source.

connectString (optional). The contents of a connection string to send to the ODBC server. If you are connecting to a data source defined in the ColdFusion Administrator, you can use this attribute to specify additional connection details or to override connection information specified in the Administrator. If you are dynamically connecting to a datasource by specifying datasource = "__dynamic__," the connection string must specify all required ODBC connection attributes.

USERNAME (optional). If specified, username overrides the username value specified in the data source setup.

PASSWORD (optional). If specified, password overrides the password value specified in the data source setup.

maxRows (optional). Specifies the maximum number of rows you want returned in the record set. The maxRows attribute accepts an argument of −1, which causes cfquery to return all rows in the query object.

blockFactor (optional). Specifies the maximum number of rows to fetch at a time from the server. The range is 1 (default) to 100. This parameter applies to ORACLE native database drivers and to ODBC drivers. Certain ODBC drivers may dynamically reduce the block factor at runtime.

TIMEOUT (optional). Lets you specify a maximum number of milliseconds for the query to execute before returning an error indicating that the query has timed out. This attribute is not supported by most ODBC drivers. TIMEOUT is supported by the SQL Server 6.x or above driver. The minimum and maximum allowable values vary, depending on the driver.

cachedAfter (optional). Specify a date value (for example, 4/16/98, April 16, 1999, 4-16-99). ColdFusion uses cached query data if the date of the original query is after the date specified. Effective only if query caching has been enabled in the ColdFusion Administrator. To use cached data, the current query must use the same SQL statement, data source, query name, user name, password, and dbType. Additionally, for native drivers it must have the same dbServer and dbName (Sybase only). Years from 0 to 29 are interpreted as 21st century values. Years 30 to 99 are interpreted as 20th century values. When specifying a date value as a string, make sure it is enclosed in quotes.

cachedWithin (optional). Enter a timespan using the ColdFusion CreateTimeSpan function. Cached query data will be used if the original query date falls within the time span you define. The CreateTimeSpan function is used to define a period of time from the present backward. Effective only if query caching has been enabled in the ColdFusion Administrator. To use cached data, the current query must use the same SQL statement, data source, query name, user name, password, and dbType. Additionally, for native drivers it must have the same dbServer and dbName (Sybase only).

PROVIDER (optional). COM provider (OLE-DB only).

providerDSN (optional). Data source name for the COM provider (OLE-DB only).

DEBUG (optional). Used for debugging queries. Specifying this attribute causes the SQL statement submitted to the data source and the number of records returned from the query to be returned.

Usage

In addition to returning data from a ColdFusion data source, the cfquery tag also returns information about the query. Cfquery.ExecutionTime returns the time it took the query to execute in milliseconds.

Cfquery creates a query object, providing you information in three query variables as described in the following list.

query_name.recordCount: The total number of records returned by the query.

query_name.currentRow: The current row of the query being processed by cfoutput.

query_name.columnList: Returns a comma-delimited list of the query columns.

You can cache query results and execute stored procedures. For information about caching cfquery results, executing stored procedures, and displaying cfquery output, see Developing ColdFusion Applications.

CFQUERYPARAM

<cfqueryparam> checks the data type of a query parameter. The cfqueryparam tag is nested within a cfquery tag. More specifically, it is embedded within the query SQL statement. If you specify its optional parameters, cfqueryparam also performs data validation. <cfqueryparam> is a database manipulation tag.

Syntax

```
<cfquery name = "query_name"
  dataSource = "ds_name"
  ...other attributes...
>
  SELECT STATEMENT WHERE column_name =
  <cfqueryPARAM value = "parameter value"
    CFSQLType = "parameter type"
    maxLength = "maximum parameter length"
    scale = "number of decimal places"
    dbName = "database name"
    null = "Yes" or "No"
    list = "Yes" or "No"
    separator = "separator character">
  AND/OR ...additional criteria of the WHERE clause...
</cfquery>
```

See Also

cfinsert, cfprocparam, cfprocresult, cfquery, cfstoredproc, cftransaction, cfupdate

Attributes

VALUE (required). Specifies the actual value that ColdFusion passes to the right of the comparison operator in a where clause. See the Usage section for details.

CFSQL Type (optional). This is the SQL type that the parameter (any type) will be bound to. The default value is CF_SQL_CHAR. The CFSQL types are as follows:

- CF_SQL_BIGINT
- CF_SQL_BIT
- CF_SQL_CHAR
- CF_SQL_DATE
- CF_SQL_DECIMAL
- CF_SQL_DOUBLE
- CF_SQL_FLOAT
- CF_SQL_IDSTAMP
- CF_SQL_INTEGER
- CF_SQL_LONGVARCHAR
- CF_SQL_MONEY
- CF_SQL_MONEY4
- CF_SQL_NUMERIC
- CF_SQL_REAL
- CF_SQL_REFCURSOR
- CF_SQL_SMALLINT
- CF_SQL_TIME
- CF_SQL_TIMESTAMP
- CF_SQL_TINYINT
- CF_SQL_VARCHAR

maxLength (optional). Maximum length of the parameter. The default value is the length of the string specified in the value attribute.

SCALE (optional). Number of decimal places of the parameter. The default value is zero. Applicable for CF_SQL_NUMERIC and CF_SQL_DECIMAL.

NULL (optional). Specify Yes or No. Indicates whether the parameter is passed as a null. If you specify Yes, the tag ignores the value attribute. The default value is No.

LIST (optional). Specify Yes or No. Indicates that the parameter value of the value attribute is a list of values, separated by a separator character. The default value is No. See the separator attribute for details.

SEPARATOR (optional). Specifies the character that is to be used to separate the values in the list of parameter values specified by the value attribute. The default separator is a comma. If you specify a list of values for the value attribute, you must also specify the list attribute.

Usage

Note

For data, you must specify the maxlength attribute in order to ensure that maximum-length validation is enforced.

The cfqueryparam tag is designed to do the following things:

- Allows the use of SQL bind parameters.
- Allows long text fields to be updated from an SQL statement.
- Improves performance.

The ColdFusion ODBC, DB2, Informix, Oracle 7 and Oracle 8 drivers support SQL bind parameters. However, at present, the ColdFusion Sybase 11 driver and Sybase native driver do not support SQL bind parameters.

If a database does not support bind parameters, ColdFusion still performs validation and substitutes the validated parameter value back into the string. If validation fails, an error message is returned. The validation rules follow:

- For types CF_SQL_SMALLINT, CF_SQL_INTEGER, CF_SQL_REAL, CF_SQL_FLOAT, CF_SQL_DOUBLE, CF_SQL_TINYINT, CF_SQL_MONEY, CF_SQL_MONEY4, CF_SQL_DECIMAL, CF_SQL_NUMERIC, and CF_SQL_BIGINT, data values can be converted to a numeric value.
- For types CF_SQL_DATE, CF_SQL_TIME and CF_SQL_TIMESTAMP, data values can be converted to a date supported by the target data source.
- For all other types, if the maxLength attribute is used, data value cannot exceed the maximum length specified.

The SQL syntax generated by the ColdFusion server is dependent on the target database. For an ODBC, DB2, or Informix data source, the generated syntax of the SQL statement is as follows:

```
SELECT *
 FROM courses
 WHERE col1 = ?
```

For an Oracle 7 or Oracle 8 data source, the syntax of the SQL statement is as follows:

```
SELECT *
 FROM courses
 WHERE col1 = :1
```

For a Sybase11 data source, the syntax of the SQL statement is as follows:

```
SELECT *
 FROM courses
 WHERE col1 = 10
```

CFREGISTRY

The <cfregistry> tag reads, writes, and deletes keys and values in the system registry. cfregistry is supported on all platforms, including Linux, Solaris, and HP-UX.

Note

The ColdFusion Server Basic security settings may prevent cfregistry from executing. These settings are managed using the ColdFusion Administrator Basic Security page. In order for cfregistry to execute, it needs to be enabled on the Basic Security page. Please refer to *Administering ColdFusion Server* for more information about securing ColdFusion tags.

CFREGISTRY Actions

- cfregistry action = “getAll”
- cfregistry action = “get”
- cfregistry action = “set”
- cfregistry action = “delete”

CFREPORT

<cfreport> runs a predefined Crystal Reports report; it is an extensibility tag.

Syntax

```
<cfreport report = "report_path"
      orderBy = "result_order"
      username = "username"
      password = "password"
      formula = "formula">
</cfreport>
```

See Also

cfcollection, cfexecute, cfgraph, cfindex, cfobject, cfsearch, cfservlet, cfwddx

Attributes

REPORT (required). Specifies the path of the report. Store your Crystal Reports files in the same directories in which you store your ColdFusion page files.

orderBy (optional). Orders results according to your specifications.

USERNAME (optional). The username required for entry into the database from which the report is created. Overrides the default settings for the data source in the ColdFusion Administrator.

PASSWORD (optional). The password that corresponds to a username required for database access. Overrides the default settings for the data source in the ColdFusion Administrator.

FORMULA (optional). Specifies one or more named formulas. Terminate each formula specification with a semicolon. Use the following format: formula = "formulaname1 = 'formula1';formulaname2 = 'formula2';". If you need to use a semicolon as part of a formula, you must escape it by typing the semicolon twice (;;)—for example: formula = "Name1 = 'Val_1a;;Val_1b';Name2 = 'Val2';".

CFRETHROW

Rethrows the currently active exception. cfrethrow preserves the exception's cfcatch.type and cfcatch.tagContext information. Cfrethrow is an exception handling tag.

Syntax

```
<cfrethrow>
```

See Also

cferror, cfthrow, cftry /cfcatch

Usage

Use the cfrethrow tag within a cfcatch block. This tag is useful in error handling code when the error handler is not designed to handle an error that it catches. For example, if cfcatch type = "any" gets a DATABASE exception when the code is designed only to handle CFX exceptions, the handler should reraise the original exception with all detail intact, so that a higher-level handler can process the error information. If you used cfthrow in this case, you would lose the type and all relevant details of the original exception.

CFSAVECONTENT

Saves the generated content inside the tag body in a variable. <cfsavecontent> is a variable manipulation tag.

Syntax

```
<cfsavecontent variable = "variable name">
        content goes here...
</cfsavecontent>
```

See Also

cfcookie, cfparam, cfregistry, cfschedule, cfset

Attributes

VARIABLE (required). The name of the variable in which to save the generated content inside the tag.

Usage

This tag saves everything in the body of the cfsavecontent tag, including the results of evaluating expressions and executing custom tags, in the specified variable.

CFSCHEDULE

<cfschedule> provides a programmatic interface to the ColdFusion scheduling engine. You can run a specified page at scheduled intervals with the option to write out static HTML pages. This allows you to offer users access to pages that publish data, such as reports, without forcing them to wait while a database transaction is performed in order to populate the data on the page.

ColdFusion scheduled events are registered using the ColdFusion Administrator. In addition, execution of cfschedule can be disabled in the Administrator. Information supplied by the user includes the scheduled ColdFusion page to execute, the time and frequency for executing the page, and whether the output from the task should be published. If the output is to be published, then a path and file are specified.

The event submission and its success or failure status are written to the \cfusion\log\schedule.log file.

Cfschedule is a variable manipulation tag.

Syntax

```
<cfschedule action = "update"
  task = "taskname"
  operation = "HTTPRequest"
  file = "filename"
  path = "path_to_file"
  startDate = "date"
  startTime = "time"
  url = "URL"
  publish = "Yes" or "No"
  endDate = "date"
  endTime = "time"
  interval = "seconds"
  requestTimeOut = "seconds"
  username = "username"
  password = "password"
  resolveURL = "Yes" or "No"
  proxyServer = "hostname"
  port = "port_number"
  proxyPort = "port_number">

<cfschedule action = "delete" task = "TaskName">
<cfschedule action = "Run" task = "TaskName">
```

See Also

cfcookie, cfparam, cfregistry, cfsavecontent, cfset

Attributes

ACTION (required). Valid entries are:

- delete—Deletes task specified by task.
- update—Creates a new task if one does not exist.
- run—Executes task specified by task.

TASK (required). The name of the task to delete, update, or run.

OPERATION (required when creating tasks with action = "update"). Specify the type of operation the scheduler should perform when executing this task. For now only operation = "HTTPRequest" is supported for static page generation.

FILE (required with publish = "Yes"). A valid filename for the published file.

PATH (required with publish = "Yes"). The path location for the published file.

startDate (required when action = "update"). The date when scheduling of the task should start.

StartTime (required when creating tasks with action = "update"). Enter a value in seconds. The time when scheduling of the task should start.

URL (required when action = "update"). The URL to be executed.

PUBLISH (optional). Yes or No. Specifies whether the result should be saved to a file.

endDate (optional). The date when the scheduled task should end.

endTime (optional). The time when the scheduled task should end. Enter a value in seconds.

INTERVAL (required when creating tasks with action = "update"). Interval at which task should be scheduled. Can be set in seconds or as Once, Daily, Weekly, Monthly, and Execute. The default interval is one hour and the minimum interval is one minute.

requestTimeOut (optional). Customizes the requestTimeOut for the task operation. Can be used to extend the default timeout for operations that require more time to execute.

USERNAME (optional). Username if URL is protected.

PASSWORD (optional). Password if URL is protected.

proxyServer (optional). Host name or IP address of a proxy server.

resolveURL (optional). Yes or No. Specifies whether to resolve links in the result page to absolute references.

PORT (optional). The port number on the server from which the task is being scheduled. Default is 80. When used with resolveURL, the URLs of retrieved documents that specify a port number are automatically resolved to preserve links in the retrieved document.

proxyPort (optional). The port number on the proxy server from which the task is being requested. Default is 80. When used with resolveURL, the URLs of retrieved documents that specify a port number are automatically resolved to preserve links in the retrieved document.

Usage

You cannot use cfschedule and apply the Secure Sockets Layer (SSL) to your application.

CFSCRIPT

The cfscript tag encloses a code segment containing cfscript. It is a Web application framework tag.

Syntax

```
<cfscript>
 cfscript code goes here...
</cfscript>
```

See Also

cfapplication, cflock, cfassociate, cfmodule, cfauthenticate, cfimpersonate

Usage

Use cfscript to perform processing in cfscript instead of CFML. Note the following regarding cfscript:

- cfscript uses ColdFusion functions, expressions, and operators
- You can read and write ColdFusion variables inside of cfscript

One use of cfscript is to wrap a series of assignment functions that would otherwise require cfset statements.

Note

If you use cfscript around the cfloop tag, any test expressions used as values to cfloop attributes are reevaluated before each iteration of the loop, and if any part of the test expression is changed by code in the loop, it may affect the number of iterations that are executed by the loop.

For more information on cfscript, see Developing ColdFusion Applications.

CFSEARCH

Use the cfsearch tag to execute searches against data indexed in Verity collections. Collections can be created by calling the cfcollection tag, by using the ColdFusion Administrator, or through native Verity indexing tools. Collections are populated with data either with the cfindex tag, or externally, using native Verity indexing tools. Collections must be created and populated before any searches can be executed. cfsearch is an extensibility tag.

Syntax

```
<cfsearch name = "search_name"
  collection = "collection_name"
  type = "criteria"
  criteria = "search_expression"
  maxRows = "number"
  startRow = "row_number"
  external = "Yes" or "No"
  language = "language">
```

See Also

cfcollection, cfreport, cfexecute, cfgraph, cfservlet, cfindex, cfservletparam, cfobject, cfwddx

Attributes

NAME (required). A name for the search query.

COLLECTION (required). Specifies the logical collection name that is the target of the search operation or an external collection with fully qualified path. Collection names are defined either through the cfcollection tag or in the ColdFusion Administrator, Verity page. Multiple ColdFusion collections can be specified in a comma-separated list: collection = "CFUSER, CFLANG." If you are searching an external collection (external = "Yes"), specify the collection name, including fully qualified path: collection = "e:\collections;personnel." If multiple collections are specified in collection and external = "Yes," the specified collections must all be externally generated. You cannot combine internal and external collections in the same search operation.

TYPE (optional). Specifies the criteria type for the search. Valid entries are:

- simple—By default the STEM and MANY operators are used.
- explicit—All operators must be invoked explicitly.

CRITERIA (optional). Specifies the criteria for the search following the syntactic rules specified by type.

maxRows (optional). Specifies the maximum number of entries for index queries. If omitted, all rows are returned.

startRow (optional). Specifies the first row number to be retrieved. Default is 1.

EXTERNAL (optional). Yes or No. Yes indicates that the collection you are searching was created outside of ColdFusion using native Verity indexing tools. The default is No.

LANGUAGE (optional). To use the language attribute you must have the ColdFusion International Search Pack installed. Valid entries are:

- English (default)
- German
- Finnish
- French
- Danish
- Dutch
- Italian
- Norwegian
- Portuguese
- Spanish
- Swedish

Usage

In the criteria attribute, if you pass a mixed-case entry (mixed upper and lower case), case sensitivity is applied to the search. If you pass all upper or all lower case, case insensitivity is assumed.

Every search conducted with the cfsearch tag returns, as part of the record set, a number of result columns you can reference in your cfoutput.

cfsearch Result Columns

URL	Returns the value of the URLpath attribute defined in the cfindex tag used to populate the collection. This value is always empty when you populate the collection with cfindex when type = "custom."
KEY	Returns the value of the key attribute defined in the cfindex tag used to populate the collection.
TITLE	Returns whatever was placed in the title attribute in the cfindex operation used to populate the collection, including the titles of PDF and Office documents. If no title was provided in the title attribute, cfsearch returns CF_TITLE.
SCORE	Returns the relevancy score of the document based on the search criteria.
custom1custom2	Returns whatever was placed in the custom fields in the cfindex operation used to populate the collection.
SUMMARY	Returns the contents of the automatic summary generated by cfindex. The default summarization selects the best three matching sentences, up to a maximum of 500 characters.
recordCount	Returns the number of records returned in the record set.
currentRow	Returns the current row being processed by cfoutput.
columnList	Returns the list of the column names within the record set.
recordsSearched	Returns the number of records searched.

You can use these result columns in standard CFML expressions, preceding the result column name with the name of the query:

```
#DocSearch.url#
#DocSearch.key#
```

```
#DocSearch.title#
#DocSearch.score#
```

CFSELECT

Used inside <cfform>, <cfselect> allows you to construct a drop-down list box form control. You can populate the drop-down list box from a query, or using the option tag. Use option elements to populate lists. Syntax for the option tag is the same as for its HTML counterpart.

Syntax

```
<cfselect name = "name"
  required = "Yes" or "No"
  message = "text"
  onError = "text"
  size = "integer"
  multiple = "Yes" or "No"
  query = "queryname"
  selected = "column_value"
  value = "text"
  display = "text"
  passThrough = "HTML_attributes">
</cfselect>
```

See Also

cfapplet, cfinput, cfform, cfgrid, cfslider, cfgridcolumn, cftextinput, cfgridrow, cftree, cfgridupdate, cftreeitem

Attributes

NAME (required). A name for the form you are creating.

SIZE (optional). Size of the drop-down list box in number of entries.

REQUIRED (optional). Yes or No. If Yes, a list element must be selected when the form is submitted, and the size of the drop-down list must be at least two. Default is No.

MESSAGE (optional). Message that appears if required = "Yes" and no selection is made.

onError (optional). The name of a valid JavaScript function you want to execute in the event of a failed validation.

MULTIPLE (optional). Yes or No. Yes permits selection of multiple elements in the drop-down list box. The default is No.

QUERY (optional). Name of the query to be used to populate the drop-down list box.

SELECTED (optional). Enter a value matching at least one entry in value to preselect the entry in the drop-down list box.

VALUE (optional). The query column value for the list element. Used with the query attribute.

DISPLAY (optional). The query column displayed. Defaults to the value of value. Used with the query attribute.

passThrough (optional). HTML attributes that are not explicitly supported by cfselect. If you specify an attribute and its value, they are passed to the HTML code that is generated for the cfselect tag. See the Usage section for more information about specifying values.

Usage

Note

Cfselect requires the client to download a Java applet. Downloading an applet takes time, so using cfselect may be slightly slower than using a select element within an HTML form tag. In addition, browsers must be Java-enabled for cfselect to work properly.

You can add standard and dynamic HTML form tag attributes and their values to the cfselect tag by using the passThrough attribute. These attributes and values are passed directly through ColdFusion to the browser in creating a form.

If you specify a value in quotation marks, you must escape the quotation marks by doubling them, for example:

```
passThrough = "readonly = " "YES " " "
```

<cfselect> supports the JavaScript onClick event in the same manner as the HTML input tag:

```
<cfselect name = "dept"
  message = "You must select a department name"
  query = "get_dept_list"
  value = "dept_name"
  onClick = "JavaScript_function">
```

CFSERVLET

Executes a Java servlet on a JRun engine. This tag is used in conjunction with the cfservletparam tag, which passes data to the servlet. Cfservlet is a Java servlet and Java object tag.

Syntax

```
<cfservlet code = "class name of servlet"
  jrunProxy = "proxy server"
  timeout = "timeout in seconds"
  writeOutput = "Yes" or "No"
  debug = "Yes" or "No">
    <cfservletparam name = "parameter name"
      value = "value">
  ...
</cfservlet>
```

See Also

cfobject, cfservletparam

Attributes

CODE (required). The class name of the Java servlet to execute.

jrunProxy (optional). Specifies a remote machine where the JRun engine is executing. By default, the JRun engine is assumed to be on the host running ColdFusion. To indicate the name of a remote host, specify the IP address of the remote host followed by a colon and the port number at which JRun is listening. By default, for the JCP server, JRun 2.3.3 listens at port 8081; JRun 3.0 listens at port 51000.

TIMEOUT (optional). Specifies how many seconds JRun should wait for the servlet to complete before timing out.

writeOutput (optional). Boolean specifying if the text output of the tag should appear as inline text on the generated page or be returned inside a ColdFusion variable for further processing. The default value, Yes, means output is returned as text to appear inline on the generated page. Setting it to No means no visible text is returned but, instead, the text is returned as the value of the cfservlet.output variable. See the Usage section for more information.

DEBUG (optional). Boolean specifying whether additional information about the JRun connection status and activity is to be written to the JRun error log. For JRun 2.3.3, the error log is in: jrunhomedir/jsm-default/logs/stderr.log. For JRun 3.0, the error log is in: jrunhomedir/logs/jrunservername_event.log, where jrunservername can be default, admin, or the name of another JRun server that you are running on. Reading the log file is helpful for debugging server-side problems. The default is No.

Usage

The syntax of the cfservlet tag is designed to be consistent with the HTML markup servlet and param tags used by some Web servers to invoke Java servlets from .shtml pages in what is known as SSI (Server-Side Includes).

cfservlet.output

Inline text output of the servlet is directed to this structure if the writeOutput attribute is set to No.

cfservlet.servletResponseHeaderName

The cfservlet return structure also contains the values of any response headers returned by the servlet. To access a response header, specify its name in servletResponseHeaderName. The servlet must exist somewhere in the class path of the JRun engine executing the servlet. For JRun 2.23, the JRun servlets subdirectory is a good location, since it is already in the JRun class path and because classes in this directory are automatically reloaded by JRun if they change. For JRun 3.0, you can store servlets in the servlets subdirectory, or in jrun/servers/default/default-app/WEB-INF/classes.

CFSERVLETPARAM

The cfservletparam is a child of cfservlet. It is used to pass data to the servlet. Each cfservletparam tag within the cfservlet block passes a separate piece of data to the servlet. cfservletparam is a Java servlet and Java object tag.

Syntax

```
<cfservlet...>
  <cfservletparam name = "servlet parameter name"
    value = "servlet parameter value">
  ...
  <cfservletparam name = "servlet attribute name"
    variable = "coldfusion variable name"
```

```
    type = "INT" or "DOUBLE" or "BOOL" or "DATE" or "STRING">
  ...
</cfservlet>
```

See Also

cfobject, cfservlet

Attributes

NAME (required). If used with the value attribute, it is the name of the servlet parameter. If used with the variable attribute, it is the name of the servlet attribute. See the Usage section for details on passing parameters.

VALUE (optional). The value of a name-value pair to be passed to the servlet as a parameter.

VARIABLE (optional). The name of a ColdFusion variable, the value of which will appear in the servlet as an attribute. See the TYPE attribute for a way to pass data type information to the Java servlet.

TYPE (optional). The data type of the ColdFusion variable being passed. By default, ColdFusion usually passes variables as strings; however, to ensure that the data is correctly typed on the Java side, you can specify any of the following types: INT, DOUBLE, BOOL, DATE, or STRING. See the Data Types table under Usage for information about how these types map to Java object types.

Usage

There are two different ways that cfservletparam can be used to pass information to the servlet: by value or by reference. Depending on the method used, this information appears in the servlet either as a parameter (by value) or attribute (by reference).

The first passes name-value pairs by value. This method uses the attribute's name and value to pass a simple name-value string pair to the servlet. The name attribute represents the name of the servlet parameter from which the string specified in the value attribute can be retrieved. Although the servlet can use these parameters as input, it cannot change their values in the ColdFusion template.

The second passes a ColdFusion variable to the servlet by reference. This method uses the attribute variable to pass the specified ColdFusion variable by reference to the servlet. Within the servlet, the variable data is made available as servlet attributes in the form of Java objects. On the Java side, the data can be manipulated, even changed, and those changes will, in turn, change the value of the associated ColdFusion variable.

When used in this mode, the name attribute represents the name of the servlet attribute that will be created to hold the value of the ColdFusion variable. The variable attribute represents the name, not the #value#, of a ColdFusion variable. This ability to directly share ColdFusion variables with a servlet is a powerful extension to the servlet API, because it allows even complex ColdFusion objects such as structures and result sets to be directly accessed from Java.

Here is the mapping between ColdFusion data types (specified with the type attribute) and the corresponding Java objects.

Type	*in Java*
int	java.lang.Integer
double	java.lang.Double
bool	java.lang.Bool
date	java.util.Date
string	java.lang.String
array	java.util.Vector
structure	java.util.Hashtable
ColdFusion query result	com.allaire.util.RecordSet (a WDDX-supplied utility class)

Note

You need to have JRun 3.0 in order for the Name/Variable functionality to work. You can download the latest version of JRun at http://www.allaire.com/products/Jrun/.

In addition, in order to return a modified attribute to ColdFusion, thereby changing the value of the ColdFusion variable, you need to call the servlet API setAttribute method from the servlet to reset the value of the attribute.

CFSET

Use the <cfset> tag to define a ColdFusion variable. If the variable already exists, cfset resets it to the specified value. <cfset> is a variable manipulation tag.

Syntax

```
<cfset variable_name = expression>
```

See Also

cfcookie, cfparam, cfregistry, cfsavecontent, cfschedule

Usage

Arrays

The following example assigns a new array to the variable "months."

```
<cfset months = ArrayNew(1)>
```

This example creates a variable "Array_Length" that resolves to the length of the array "Scores."

```
<cfset Array_Length = ArrayLen(Scores)>
```

This example assigns to index position two in the array "months" the value "February."

```
<cfset months[ 2] = "February">
```

Dynamic Variable Names

In this example, the variable name is itself a variable.

```
<cfset myvariable = "current_value">
<cfset "#myvariable#" = 5>
```

COM Objects

In this example, a COM object is created. A cfset defines a value for each method or property in the COM object interface. The last cfset creates a variable to store the return value from the COM object's "SendMail" method.

```
<cfobject action = "Create"
  name = "Mailer"
  class = "SMTPsvg.Mailer">
<cfset MAILER.FromName = form.fromname>
<cfset MAILER.RemoteHost = RemoteHost>
<cfset MAILER.FromAddress = form.fromemail>
<cfset MAILER.AddRecipient("form.fromname",
"form.fromemail")>
<cfset MAILER.Subject = "Testing cfobject">
```

```
<cfset MAILER.BodyText = "form.msgbody">
<cfset Mailer.SMTPLog = "logfile">

<cfset success = MAILER.SendMail()>

<cfoutput> #success# </cfoutput>
```

CFSETTING

<cfsetting> is used to control various aspects of page processing, such as controlling the output of HTML code in your pages. One benefit of this option is managing whitespace that can occur in output pages that are served by ColdFusion.cfsetting is a page processing tag.

Syntax

```
<cfsetting enableCFoutputOnly = "Yes" or "No"
  showDebugOutput = "Yes" or "No"
  catchExceptionsByPattern = "Yes" or "No">
```

See Also

cfcache, cfflush, cfheader, cfhtmlhead, cfinclude, cfsilent

Attributes

enableCFoutputOnly (required). Yes or No. When set to Yes, cfsetting blocks output of all HTML that resides outside cfoutput tags.

ShowDebugOutput (optional). Yes or No. When set to No, showDebugOutput suppresses debugging information that would otherwise display at the end of the generated page. Default is Yes.

catchExceptionsByPattern (optional). Yes or No. When set to Yes, it overrides the structured exception handling introduced in ColdFusion Server 4.5. Default is No.

NoteStructured exception handling introduces a subtle upward incompatibility. In 4.0.x, an exception was handled by the first cfcatch block that could handle that type of exception. Since ColdFusion 4.5, the structured exception manager searches for the best-fit cfcatch handler.

Usage

When nesting cfsetting tags, you must match each enableCFoutputOnly = "Yes" setting with an enableCFoutputOnly = "No" setting in order for ordinary HTML text to be visible to a user. For example, if you have five enableCFoutputOnly = "Yes" statements, you must also have five corresponding enableCFoutputOnly = "No" statements for HTML text to be displayed again.

If at any point the output of plain HTML is enabled (no matter how many enableCFoutputOnly = "No" statements have been processed), the first enableCFoutputOnly = "Yes" statement will block output.

CFSILENT

<cfsilent> suppresses all output that is produced by the CFML within the tag's scope. cfsilent is a page processing tag.

Syntax

```
<cfsilent>
```

See Also

cfcache, cfflush, cfheader, cfhtmlhead, cfinclude, cfsetting

CFSLIDER

Used inside cfform, cfslider allows you to place a slider control in a ColdFusion form. A slider control is like a sliding volume control. The slider groove is the area over which the slider moves. cfslider is a ColdFusion form tag.

Syntax

```
<cfslider name = "name"
  label = "text"
  refreshLabel = "Yes" or "No"
  img = "filename"
  imgStyle = "style"
  range = "min_value, max_value"
  scale = "uinteger"
  value = "integer"
```

```
onValidate = "script_name"
message = "text"
onError = "text"
height = "integer"
width = "integer"
vSpace = "integer"
hSpace = "integer"
align = "alignment"
grooveColor = "color"
bgColor = "color"
textColor = "color"
font = "font_name"
fontSize = "integer"
italic = "Yes" or "No"
bold = "Yes" or "No"
notSupported = "text">
```

See Also

cfapplet, cfinput, cfform, cfselect, cfgrid, cfgridcolumn, cftextinput, cfgridrow, cftree, cfgridupdate, cftreeitem

Attributes

NAME (required). A name for the cfslider control.

LABEL (optional). A label that appears with the slider control, for example: label = "Volume %value%." You can use %value% to reference the slider value. If % is omitted, the slider value appears immediately following the label.

refreshLabel (optional). Yes or No. If Yes, the label is not refreshed when the slider is moved. Default is Yes.

IMG (optional). Filename of the image to be used in the slider groove.

imgStyle (optional). Style of the image to appear in the slider groove. Valid entries are:

- Centered
- Tiled
- Scaled (Default)

RANGE (optional). Determines the values of the left and right slider range. The slider value appears as the slider is moved. Separate values by a comma—for example: range = "1,100." Default is "0,100." Valid only for numeric data.

SCALE (optional). An unsigned integer.scale defines the slider scale within the value of range. For example, if range = 0,1000 and scale = 100, the incremental values for the slider would be 0, 100, 200, 300, and so on. Signed and unsigned integers in ColdFusion are in the range −2,147,483,648 to 2,147,483,647.

VALUE (optional). Determines the default slider setting. Must be within the values specified in range. Defaults to the minimum value specified in range.

onValidate (optional). The name of a valid JavaScript function used to validate user input—in this case, a change to the default slider value.

MESSAGE (optional). Message text to appear if validation fails.

onError (optional). The name of a valid JavaScript function you want to execute in the event of a failed validation.

HEIGHT (optional). Height value of the slider control, in pixels.

WIDTH (optional). Width value of the slider control, in pixels.

vSpace (optional). Vertical margin spacing above and below slider control, in pixels.

hSpace (optional). Horizontal margin spacing to the left and right of slider control, in pixels.

ALIGN (optional). Alignment value. Valid entries are:

- top
- left
- bottom
- baseline
- texttop
- absbottom
- middle
- absmiddle
- right

grooveColor (optional). Color value of the slider groove. The slider groove is the area in which the slider box moves. Valid entries are:

- black
- magenta
- cyan

- orange
- darkgray
- pink
- gray
- white
- lightgray
- yellow

A hex value can be entered in the form: grooveColor = "##xxxxxx," where x is 0-9 or A–F. Use either two pound signs or no pound signs.

bgColor (optional). Background color of slider label. See grooveColor for color options.

textColor (optional). Slider label text color. See grooveColor for color options.

FONT (optional). Font name for label text.

fontSize (optional). Font size for label text measured in points.

ITALIC (optional). Enter Yes for italicized label text, No for normal text. Default is No.

BOLD (optional). Enter Yes for bold label text, No for medium text. Default is No.

notSupported (optional). The text you want to display if the page containing a Java applet-based cfform control is opened by a browser that does not support Java or has Java support disabled. For example: notSupported = "<B> Browser must support Java to view ColdFusion Java Applets</B>." By default, if no message is specified, the following message appears: <B>Browser must support Java to <BR> view ColdFusion Java Applets!</B>

Note

<cfslider> requires the client to download a Java applet. Downloading an applet takes time; therefore, using cfslider may be slightly slower than using an HTML form element to retrieve or display the same information. In addition, browsers must be Java-enabled for cfslider to work properly.

CFSTOREDPROC

The <cfstoredproc> tag is the main tag used for executing stored procedures via an ODBC or native connection to a server database. It specifies database connection information and identifies the stored procedure. cfstoredproc is a database manipulation tag.

Syntax

```
<cfstoredproc procedure = "procedure name"
  dataSource = "ds_name"
  username = "username"
  password = "password"
  dbServer = "dbms"
  connectString = "connection string"
  dbName = "database name"
  blockFactor = "blocksize"
  provider = "COMProvider"
  providerDSN = "datasource"
  debug = "Yes" or "No"
  returnCode = "Yes" or "No">
```

See Also

cfinsert, cfqueryparam, cfprocparam, cfprocresult, cftransaction, cfquery, cfupdate

Attributes

PROCEDURE (required). Specifies the name of the stored procedure on the database server.

dataSource (required). The name of an ODBC or native data source that points to the database containing the stored procedure. To connect to an ODBC data source that is not defined in the ColdFusion Administrator, specify __dynamic__. You must precede and follow the word dynamic with two underscore characters. When you use this attribute value, you must also specify all the ODBC connection information in a connectstring attribute.

USERNAME (optional). If specified, username overrides the username value specified in the data source setup.

PASSWORD (optional). If specified, password overrides the password value specified in the data source setup.

dbServer (optional). For native database drivers, specifies the name of the database server machine. If specified, dbServer overrides the server specified in the data source.

connectString (optional). The contents of a connection string to send to the ODBC server. If you are connecting to a data source defined in the ColdFusion Administrator, you can use this attribute to specify additional connection details or to override connection information specified in the Administrator. If you are dynamically connecting to a datasource by specifying datasource = "__dynamic__," the connection string must specify all required ODBC connection attributes.

dbName (optional). The database name (Sybase System 11 driver only). If specified, dbName overrides the default database specified in the data source.

blockFactor (optional). Specifies the maximum number of rows to fetch at a time from the server. The range is 1 (default) to 100. The ODBC driver may dynamically reduce the block factor at runtime.

PROVIDER (optional). COM provider (OLE-DB only).

providerDSN (optional). Data source name for the COM provider (OLE-DB only).

DEBUG (optional). Yes or No. Specifies whether debug info will be listed on each statement. Default is No.

returnCode (optional). Yes or No. Specifies whether the tag populates cfstoredproc.statusCode with the status code returned by the stored procedure. Default is No.

Usage

Within a <cfstoredproc> tag, you code cfprocresult and cfprocparam tags as necessary.

If you set the returnCode parameter to "Yes," cfstoredproc sets a variable called cfstoredproc.statusCode, which indicates the status code for the stored procedure. Stored procedure status code values vary by DBMS. Refer to your DBMS-specific documentation for the meaning of individual status code values.

In addition to returning a status code, cfstoredproc sets a variable called cfstoredproc.ExecutionTime. This variable contains the number of milliseconds that it took the stored procedure to execute.

Stored procedures represent an advanced feature, found in high-end database management systems, such as Oracle 8 and Sybase. You should be familiar with stored procedures and their usage before implementing these tags.

CFSWITCH, CFCASE, CFDEFAULTCASE

Used with cfcase and cfdefaultcase, the cfswitch tag evaluates a passed expression and passes control to the cfcase tag that matches the expression result. You can optionally code a cfdefaultcase tag, which receives control if there is no matching cfcase tag value.

Cfswitch, cfcase, and cfdefaultcase are flow-control tags.

Syntax

```
<cfswitch expression = "expression">
  <cfcase value = "value" delimiters = "delimiters">
    HTML and CFML tags
  </cfcase>
  additional <cfcase></cfcase> tags
  <cfdefaultcase>
    HTML and CFML tags
  </cfdefaultcase>
</cfswitch>
```

See Also

cfabort, cfloop, cfbreak, cfrethrow, cfexecute, cfexit, cfthrow, cfif cfelseif cfelse, cftry /cfcatch, cflocation

Attributes

EXPRESSIONS (required). Any ColdFusion expression that yields a scalar value. ColdFusion converts integers, real numbers, Booleans, and dates to numeric values. For example, TRUE, 1, and 1.0 are all equal.

VALUE (required). One or more constant values that cfswitch compares to the specified expression (case-insensitive comparison). If a value matches the expression, cfswitch executes the code between the cfcase start and end tagsSeparate multiple values with a comma or an alternative delimiter, as specified in the delimiters parameter. Duplicate value attributes are not allowed and will cause a runtime error.

DELIMITERS (optional). Specifies the character that separates multiple entries in a list of values. The default delimiter is the comma (,).

Usage

Use cfswitch followed by one or more cfcase tags, optionally ending with a cfdefaultcase tag. The cfswitch tag selects the matching alternative from the specified cfcase and cfdefaultcase tags and jumps to the matching tag, executing the code between the cfcase start and end tags. There is no need to explicitly break out of the cfcase tag, as there is in some other languages.

You can specify only one cfdefaultcase tag within a cfswitch tag. cfcase tags cannot appear after the cfdefaultcase tag.

cfswitch provides better performance than a series of cfif/cfelseif tags, and the resulting code is easier to read.

CFTABLE

Builds a table in your ColdFusion page. Use the cfcol tag to define column and row characteristics for a table. cftable renders data either as preformatted text, or, with the HTML Table attribute, as an HTML table. Use cftable to create tables if you don't want to write your own HTML table tag code, or if your data can be well presented as preformatted text. See Usage for information about using the cfcol tag with the cftable tag.

Syntax

```
<cftable query = "query_name"
  maxRows = "maxrows_table"
  colSpacing = "number_of_spaces"
  headerLines = "number_of_lines"
  HTMLTable
  border
  colHeaders
  startRow = "row_number">
</cftable>
```

See Also

cfcol, cfoutput, cfcontent, cfprocessingdirective, cflog, cftable

Attributes

QUERY (required). The name of the cfquery from which you want to draw data.

maxRows (optional). Specifies the maximum number of rows you want to display in the table.

colSpacing (optional). Indicates the number of spaces to insert between columns (default is 2).

headerLines (optional). Indicates the number of lines to use for the table header (the default is 2, which leaves one line between the headers and the first row of the table).

HTMLTable (optional). Renders the table as an HTML 3.0 table.

BORDER (optional). Adds a border to the table. Use only when you specify the HTML Table attribute for the table.

colHeaders (optional). Displays headers for each column, as specified in the cfcol tag.

startRow (optional). Specifies the query row from which to start processing.

Usage

You can use the cfcol tag to align the data in the table, specify the width of each column, and provide column headers.

Note

<cfcol> is the only tag that you can nest within cftable.

CFTEXTINPUT

The cftextinput form custom control allows you to place a single-line text entry box in a cfform. In addition to input validation, the tag gives you control over all font characteristics. Cftextinput is a ColdFusion form tag.

Syntax

```
<cftextinput name = "name"
  value = "text"
  required = "Yes" or "No"
  range = "min_value, max_value"
  validate = "data_type"
  onValidate = "script_name"
  message = "text"
  onError = "text"
  size = "integer"
  font = "font_name"
  fontSize = "integer"
  italic = "Yes" or "No"
  bold = "Yes" or "No"
  height = "integer"
```

```
width = "integer"
vSpace = "integer"
hSpace = "integer"
align = "alignment"
bgColor = "color"
textColor = "color"
maxLength = "integer"
notSupported = "text">
```

See Also

cfapplet, cfinput, cfform, cfselect, cfgrid, cfslider, cfgridcolumn, cfgridrow, cftree, cfgridupdate, cftreeitem

Attributes

NAME (required). A name for the cftextinput control.

VALUE (optional). Initial value that appears in the text control.

REQUIRED (optional). Yes or No. If Yes, the user must enter or change text. Default is No.

RANGE (optional). Enter a minimum value, maximum value range separated by a comma. Valid only for numeric data.

VALIDATE (optional). Valid entries are:

- date—Verifies U.S. date entry in the form mm/dd/yy.
- eurodate—Verifies valid European date entry in the form dd/mm/yyyy.
- time—Verifies a time entry in the form hh:mm:ss.
- float—Verifies a floating-point entry.
- integer—Verifies an integer entry.
- telephone—Verifies a telephone entry. Telephone data must be entered as ###-###-####. The hyphen separator (-) can be replaced with a blank. The area code and exchange must begin with a digit between 1 and 9.
- zipcode (U.S. formats only)—Number can be a 5- or 9-digit zip in the form #####-####. The hyphen separator (-) can be replaced with a blank.
- creditcard—Blanks and dashes are stripped and the number is verified using the mod10 algorithm.

- social_security_number—Number must be entered as ###-##-####. The hyphen separator (-) can be replaced with a blank.

onValidate (optional). The name of a valid JavaScript function used to validate user input. The form object, input object, and input object value are passed to the specified routine, which should return TRUE if validation succeeds and FALSE otherwise. When used, the validate attribute is ignored.

MESSAGE (optional). Message text to appear if validation fails.

onError (optional). The name of a valid JavaScript function you want to execute in the event of a failed validation.

SIZE (optional). Number of characters displayed before horizontal scroll bar appears.

font (optional). Font name for text.

fontSize (optional). Font size for text.

italic (optional). Enter Yes for italicized text, No for normal text. Default is No.

bold (optional). Enter Yes for boldface text, No for medium text. Default is No.

height (optional). Height value of the control, in pixels.

width (optional). Width value of the control, in pixels.

vSpace (optional). Vertical spacing of the control, in pixels.

hSpace (optional). Horizontal spacing of the control, in pixels.

align (optional). Alignment value. Valid entries are:

- Top
- Left
- Bottom
- Baseline
- TextTop
- AbsBottom
- Middle
- AbsMiddle
- Right

BgColor (optional). Background color of the control. Valid entries are:

- black

- magenta
- cyan
- orange
- darkgray
- pink
- gray
- white
- lightgray
- yellow

A hex value can also be entered in the form: bgColor = "##xxxxxx," where x is 0–9 or A–F. Use either two pound signs or no pound signs.

textColor (optional). Text color for the control. See bgColor for color options.

maxLength (optional). The maximum length of text entered.

notSupported (optional). The text you want to display if the page containing a Java applet-based cfform control is opened by a browser that does not support Java or has Java support disabled. For example: notSupported = "<B> Browser must support Java to view ColdFusion Java Applets</B>." By default, if no message is specified, the following message appears: <B>Browser must support Java to <BR> view ColdFusion Java Applets!</B>.

Note

cftextinput requires the client to download a Java applet. Downloading an applet takes time; therefore, using cftextinput may be slightly slower than using an HTML form element to retrieve the same information. In addition, browsers must be Java-enabled for cftextinput to work properly.

CFTHROW

The cfthrow tag raises a developer-specified exception that can be caught with cfcatch tag having any of the following type specifications:

- cfcatch type = "custom_type"
- cfcatch type = "Application"
- cfcatch type = "Any"

<cfthrow> is an exception handling tag.

Syntax

```
<cfthrow
  type = "exception_type "
  message = "message"
  detail = "detail_description "
  errorCode = "error_code "
  extendedInfo = "additional_information ">
```

See Also

cferror, cfrethrow, cftry /cfcatch

Attributes

NAME (required). A name for the cftree control.

REQUIRED (optional). Yes or No. User must select an item in the tree control. Default is No.

DELIMITER (optional). The character used to separate elements in the form variable path. The default is "\".

completePath (optional). Yes passes the root level of the treename.path form variable when the cftree is submitted. If omitted or No, the root level of this form variable is not included.

appendKey (optional). Yes or No. When used with href, Yes passes the CFTREEITEMKEY variable along with the value of the selected tree item in the URL to the application page specified in the cfform action attribute. The default is Yes.

highlightHref (optional). Yes highlights links associated with a cftreeitem with a URL attribute value. No disables highlight. Default is Yes.

onValidate (optional). The name of a valid JavaScript function used to validate user input. The form object, input object, and input object value are passed to the specified routine, which should return true if validation succeeds and false otherwise.

MESSAGE (optional). Message text to appear if validation fails.

onError (optional). The name of a valid JavaScript function you want to execute in the event of a failed validation.

FONT (optional). Font name to use for all data in the tree control.

fontSize (optional). Font size for text in the tree control, measured in points.

ITALIC (optional). Yes or No. Yes presents all tree control text in italic. Default is No.

BOLD (optional). Yes or No. Yes presents all tree control text in boldface. Default is No.

HEIGHT (optional). Height value of the tree control, in pixels.

WIDTH (optional). Width value of the tree control, in pixels.

vSpace (optional). Vertical margin spacing above and below the tree control in pixels.

hSpace (optional). Horizontal spacing to the left and right of the tree control, in pixels.

ALIGN (optional). Alignment value. Valid entries are:

- Top
- Left
- Bottom
- Baseline
- TextTop
- AbsBottom
- Middle
- AbsMiddle
- Right

BORDER (optional). Places a border around the tree. Default is Yes.

hScroll (optional). Permits horizontal scrolling. Default is Yes.

vScroll (optional). Permits vertical scrolling. Default is Yes.

notSupported (optional). The text you want to display if the page containing a Java applet-based cfform control is opened by a browser that does not support Java or has Java support disabled. For example: notSupported = "<B> Browser must support Java to view ColdFusion Java Applets</B>." By default, if no message is specified, the following message appears: <B>Browser must support Java to
view ColdFusion Java Applets!</B>.

Note

Cftree requires the client to download a Java applet. Downloading an applet takes time; therefore, using cftree may be slightly slower than using an HTML form element to retrieve the same information. In addition, browsers must be Java-enabled for cftree to work properly.

CFTREEITEM

Use cftreeitem to populate a tree control created with cftree with individual elements. You can use the img values supplied with ColdFusion or reference your own icons. cftreeitem is a ColdFusion forms tag.

Syntax

```
<cftreeitem value = "text"
  display = "text"
  parent = "parent_name"
  img = "filename"
  imgopen = "filename"
  href = "URL"
  target = "URL_target"
  query = "queryname"
  queryAsRoot = "Yes" or "No"
  expand = "Yes" or "No">
```

See Also

cfapplet, cfform, cfgrid, cfgridcolumn, cfgridrow, cfgridupdate, cfinput, cfselect, cfslider, cftextinput, cftree

Attributes

VALUE (required). Value passed when the cfform is submitted. When populating a cftree with data from a cfquery, columns are specified in a comma-separated list: value = "dept_id,emp_id."

DISPLAY (optional). The label for the tree item. Default is value. When populating a cftree with data from a cfquery, display names are specified in a comma-separated list: display = "dept_name,emp_name."

PARENT (optional). Value for tree item parent.

IMG (optional). Image name or filename for the tree item. When populating a cftree with data from a cfquery, images or filenames for each level of the tree are specified in a comma-separated list. The default image name is "Folder."

A number of images are supplied and can be specified using only the image name (no file extension):

- cd
- computer
- document
- element
- folder
- floppy
- fixed
- remote

Use commas to separate image names corresponding to tree level—for example: img = "folder,document" img = ",document." To specify your own custom image, specify the path and file extension: img = "../images/page1.gif."

IMGOPEN (optional). Icon displayed with open tree item. You can specify the icon filename using a relative path. As with img, you can use an image supplied with ColdFusion.

HREF (optional). URL to associate with the tree item or a query column for a tree that is populated from a query. If href is a query column, then the href value is the value populated by the query. If href is not recognized as a query column, it is assumed that the href text is an actual HTML href. When populating a cftree with data from a cfquery, HREFs can be specified in a comma-separated list: href = "http://dept_server,http://emp_server."

TARGET (optional). Target attribute for href URL. When populating a cftree with data from a cfquery, targets are specified in a comma-separated list: target = "FRAME_BODY,_blank."

QUERY (optional). Query name used to generate data for the treeitem.

queryAsRoot (optional). Yes or No. Defines specified query as the root level. This option prevents having to create an additional parent cftreeitem.

EXPAND (optional). Yes or No. Yes expands tree to show tree item children. No keeps tree item collapsed. Default is Yes.

Usage

Note

Cftreeitem incorporates a Java applet, so a browser must be Java-enabled for cftree to work properly.

CFTRY / CFCATCH

Used with one or more cfcatch tags, the cftry tag allows developers to catch and process exceptions in ColdFusion pages. Exceptions include any event that disrupts the normal flow of instructions in a ColdFusion page, such as failed database operations, missing include files, and developer-specified events. cftry/cfcatch are exception handling tags.

Syntax

```
<cftry>
  ... Add code here
<cfcatch type = "exceptiontype">
  ... Add exception processing code here
</cfcatch>
  ... Additional cfcatch blocks go here
</cftry>
```

See Also

cferror, cfrethrow, cfthrow

Attributes

TYPE (optional). Specifies the type of exception to be handled by the cfcatch block. The following lists basic exception types you can use:

- Application
- Database
- Template
- Security
- Object
- missingInclude
- Expression
- Lock
- Custom_type
- Any (default)

For a list of advanced exception types, see "Advanced Exception types."

Usage

You must code at least one cfcatch tag within a cftry block. Code cfcatch tags at the end of the cftry block. ColdFusion tests cfcatch tags in the order in which they appear on the page.

If you specify the type to be Any, do so in the last cfcatch tag in the block so that all of the other tests are executed first.

Note

Specifying the type as Any causes the ColdFusion Application Server to catch exceptions from any CFML tag, data source, or external object, which your application may not be prepared to handle.

Applications can optionally use the cfthrow tag to raise custom exceptions. Such exceptions are caught with any of the following type specifications:

- type = “custom_type”
- type = “Application”
- type = “Any”

The custom_type type designates the name of a user-defined type specified with a cfthrow tag. cfcatch has a catch handler that can catch a custom type by pattern, providing the custom type is defined as a series of strings concatenated together by periods, as in “MyApp.BusinessRuleException. InvalidAccount.” cfcatch searches for a custom type match starting with the most specific and ending with the least specific. For example, you could define a type as follows:

```
<cfthrow type = "MyApp.BusinessRuleException.InvalidAccount">
```

cfcatch first searches for the entire type string defined in the cfthrow tag, as follows:

```
<cfcatch type = "MyApp.BusinessRuleException.InvalidAccount">
```

Then it searches for the next most specific:

```
<cfcatch type = "MyApp.BusinessRuleException">
```

Finally, it searches for the least specific:

```
<cfcatch type = "MyApp">
```

The order in which you code cfcatch tags designed to catch a custom exception type within an application does not matter. A cfcatch tag searches for the custom exception types from most specific to least specific.

If you specify the type to be "Application," the cfcatch tag catches only those custom exceptions that have been specified as having the Application type in the cfthrow tag that defines them.

The tags that throw an exception of type = "template" are cfinclude, cfmodule, and cferror.

An exception raised within a cfcatch block cannot be handled by the cftry block that immediately encloses the cfcatch tag. However, you can rethrow the currently active exception by using the cfrethrow tag.

You can use the cfcatch variable to access exception information:

- **Type**—Exception type, as specified in cfcatch.
- **Message**—The exception's diagnostic message, if one was provided. If no diagnostic message is available, this is an empty string.
- **Detail**—A detailed message from the CFML interpreter. This message, which contains HTML formatting, can help determine which tag threw the exception.
- **TagContext**—The tag stack: the name and position of each tag in the tag stack, and the full path names of the files that contain the tags in the tag stack. See the note that follows this list for more information.
- **NativeErrorCode**—type = "database" only. The native error code associated with this exception. Database drivers typically provide error codes to assist diagnosis of failing database operations. If no error code was provided, the value of NativeErrorCode is −1.
- **SQLSTATE**—type = "database" only. The SQLState associated with this exception. Database drivers typically provide error codes to assist diagnosis of failing database operations. If no SQLState value was provided, the value of SQLSTATE is −1.
- **ErrNumber**—type = "expression" only. Internal expression error number.
- **MissingFileName**—type = "missingInclude" only. Name of the file that could not be included.
- **LockName**—type = "lock" only. The name of the affected lock (set to anonymous if the lock was unnamed).
- **LockOperation**—type = "lock" only. The operation that failed (set to Timeout, Create Mutex, or Unknown).
- **ErrorCode**—type = "custom" only. A string error code.

- **ExtendedInfo**—type = "application" and custom only. A custom error message.

Advanced Exception Types

In addition to the basic exception types you can specify with the cfcatch type attribute, the following are advanced exception types you can specify in the type attribute.

COM.Allaire.ColdFusion.CFEXECUTE.OutputError
COM.Allaire.ColdFusion.CFEXECUTE.Timeout
COM.Allaire.ColdFusion.FileException
COM.Allaire.ColdFusion.HTTPAccepted
COM.Allaire.ColdFusion.HTTPAuthFailure
COM.Allaire.ColdFusion.HTTPBadGateway
COM.Allaire.ColdFusion.HTTPBadRequest
COM.Allaire.ColdFusion.HTTPCFHTTPRequestEntityTooLarge
COM.Allaire.ColdFusion.HTTPCGIValueNotPassed
COM.Allaire.ColdFusion.HTTPConflict
COM.Allaire.ColdFusion.HTTPContentLengthRequired
COM.Allaire.ColdFusion.HTTPContinue
COM.Allaire.ColdFusion.HTTPCookieValueNotPassed
COM.Allaire.ColdFusion.HTTPCreated
COM.Allaire.ColdFusion.HTTPFailure
COM.Allaire.ColdFusion.HTTPFileInvalidPath
COM.Allaire.ColdFusion.HTTPFileNotFound
COM.Allaire.ColdFusion.HTTPFileNotPassed
COM.Allaire.ColdFusion.HTTPFileNotRenderable
COM.Allaire.ColdFusion.HTTPForbidden
COM.Allaire.ColdFusion.HTTPGatewayTimeout
COM.Allaire.ColdFusion.HTTPGone
COM.Allaire.ColdFusion.HTTPMethodNotAllowed
COM.Allaire.ColdFusion.HTTPMovedPermanently
COM.Allaire.ColdFusion.HTTPMovedTemporarily

COM.Allaire.ColdFusion.HTTPMultipleChoices
COM.Allaire.ColdFusion.HTTPNoContent
COM.Allaire.ColdFusion.HTTPNonAuthoritativeInfo
COM.Allaire.ColdFusion.HTTPNotAcceptable
COM.Allaire.ColdFusion.HTTPNotFound
COM.Allaire.ColdFusion.HTTPNotImplemented
COM.Allaire.ColdFusion.HTTPNotModified
COM.Allaire.ColdFusion.HTTPPartialContent
COM.Allaire.ColdFusion.HTTPPaymentRequired
COM.Allaire.ColdFusion.HTTPPreconditionFailed
COM.Allaire.ColdFusion.HTTPProxyAuthenticationRequired
COM.Allaire.ColdFusion.HTTPRequestURITooLarge
COM.Allaire.ColdFusion.HTTPResetContent
COM.Allaire.ColdFusion.HTTPSeeOther
COM.Allaire.ColdFusion.HTTPServerError
COM.Allaire.ColdFusion.HTTPServiceUnavailable
COM.Allaire.ColdFusion.HTTPSwitchingProtocols
COM.Allaire.ColdFusion.HTTPUnsupportedMediaType
COM.Allaire.ColdFusion.HTTPUrlValueNotPassed
COM.Allaire.ColdFusion.HTTPUseProxy
COM.Allaire.ColdFusion.HTTPVersionNotSupported
COM.Allaire.ColdFusion.POPAuthFailure
COM.Allaire.ColdFusion.POPConnectionFailure
COM.Allaire.ColdFusion.POPDeleteError
COM.Allaire.ColdFusion.Request.Timeout
COM.Allaire.ColdFusion.SERVLETJRunError
COM.Allaire.ColdFusion.HTTPConnectionTimeout

Note

In order to see the tag stack displayed by TagContext, use the ColdFusion Administrator to enable the CFML stack trace. Under Debugging in the ColdFusion Administrator, choose the checkbox next to "Enable CFML stack trace."

CFUPDATE

The <cfupdate> tag updates existing records in data sources. <cfupdate> is a database manipulation tag.

Syntax

```
<cfupdate dataSource = "ds_name"
  dbType = "type"
  dbServer = "dbms"
  dbName = "database name"
  connectString = "connection string"
  tableName = "table_name"
  tableOwner = "name"
  tableQualifier = "qualifier"
  username = "username"
  password = "password"
  provider = "COMProvider"
  providerDSN = "datasource"
  formFields = "field_names">
```

See Also

cfinsert, cfprocparam, cfprocresult, cfquery, cfqueryparam, cfstoredproc, cftransaction

Attributes

dataSource (required). Name of the data source that contains your table. To connect to an ODBC data source that is not defined in the ColdFusion Administrator, specify __dynamic__. You must precede and follow the word dynamic with two underscore characters. When you use this attribute value, you must also specify all the ODBC connection information in a connectstring attribute.

dbType (optional). The database driver type:

- ODBC (default)—ODBC driver.
- Oracle73—Oracle 7.3 native database driver. Using this option, the ColdFusion Server computer must have Oracle 7.3.4.0.0 (or greater) client software installed.
- Oracle80—Oracle 8.0 native database driver. Using this option, the ColdFusion Server computer must have Oracle 8.0 (or greater) client software installed.

- Sybase11—Sybase System 11 native database driver. Using this option, the ColdFusion Server computer must have Sybase 11.1.1 (or greater) client software installed. Sybase patch ebf 7729 is recommended.
- OLEDB—OLE DB provider. If specified, this database provider overrides the driver type specified in the ColdFusion Administrator.
- DB2—DB2 5.2 native database driver.
- Informix73—Informix73 native database driver.

dbServer (optional). For native database drivers and the SQLOLEDB provider, specifies the name of the database server machine. If specified, dbServer overrides the server specified in the data source.

dbName (optional). The database name (Sybase System 11 driver and SQLOLEDB provider only). If specified, dbName overrides the default database specified in the data source.

connectString (optional). The contents of a connection string to send to the ODBC server. If you are connecting to a data source defined in the ColdFusion Administrator, you can use this attribute to specify additional connection details or to override connection information specified in the Administrator. If you are dynamically connecting to a datasource by specifying datasource = "__dynamic__," the connection string must specify all required ODBC connection attributes.

TableName (required). Name of the table you want to update. Note the following:

- ORACLE drivers—This specification must be in uppercase.
- Sybase driver—This specification is case sensitive and must be in the same case as that used when the table was created.

tableOwner (optional). For data sources that support table ownership (for example, SQL Server, Oracle, and Sybase SQL Anywhere), use this field to specify the owner of the table.

tableQualifier (optional). For data sources that support table qualifiers, use this field to specify the qualifier for the table. The purpose of table qualifiers varies across drivers. For SQL Server and Oracle, the qualifier refers to the name of the database that contains the table. For the Intersolv dBase driver, the qualifier refers to the directory where the DBF files are located.

USERNAME (optional). If specified, username overrides the username value specified in the ODBC setup.

PASSWORD (optional). If specified, password overrides the password value specified in the ODBC setup.

PROVIDER (optional). COM provider (OLE-DB only).

providerDSN (optional). Data source name for the COM provider (OLE-DB only).

formFields (optional). A comma-separated list of form fields to update. If this attribute is not specified, all fields in the form are included in the operation.

CFWDDX

The <cfwddx> tag serializes and deserializes CFML data structures to the XML-based WDDX format. You can also use it to generate JavaScript statements instantiating JavaScript objects equivalent to the contents of a WDDX packet or some CFML data structures. <cfwddx> is an extensibility tag.

Syntax

```
<cfwddx action = "action"
  input = "inputdata"
  output = "resultvariablename"
  topLevelVariable = "toplevelvariablenameforjavascript"
  useTimeZoneInfo = "Yes" or "No">
```

See Also

cfcollection, cfexecute, cfgraph, cfindex, cfobject, cfreport, cfsearch, cfservlet, cfservletparam, cfdump

Attributes

ACTION. Specifies the action taken by the cfwddx tag. Use one of the following:

- CFML2WDDX—Serialize CFML to WDDX format
- WDDX2CFML—Deserialize WDDX to CFML
- CFML2JS—Serialize CFML to JavaScript format
- WDDX2JS—Deserialize WDDX to JavaScript

INPUT (required). The value to be processed.

OUTPUT. The name of the variable to hold the output of the operation. This attribute is required for action = "WDDX2CFML." For all other actions, if this attribute is not provided, the result of the WDDX processing is outputted in the HTML stream.

topLevelVariable. Required when action = "WDDX2JS" or action = "CFML2JS." The name of the top-level JavaScript object created by the deserialization process. The object created by this process is an instance of the WddxRecordset object, explained in WddxRecordset Object. This attribute applies only when the action is WDDX2JS or CFML2JS.

useTimeZoneInfo (optional). Indicates whether to output time-zone information when serializing CFML to WDDX. If time-zone information is taken into account, the hour-minute offset, as represented in the ISO8601 format, is calculated in the date-time output. If time-zone information is not taken into account, the local time is output. The default is Yes.

Usage

Use this tag to serialize and deserialize packets of data used to communicate with the browser.

For complete information on WDDX, see the "Programming with XML" chapter in *Developing ColdFusion Applications.*

Appendix B
ColdFusion Function Reference

ColdFusion ships with nearly 200 functions you can use to perform complex data operations. This reference is extracted from the Macromedia documentation. You can find examples of how to use each function in the online documentation or in the books that ship with the boxed ColdFusion.

New Functions for ColdFusion 5

GetHTTPRequestData
User-Defined Functions

User-Defined Functions

You can now use CFScript to define custom functions for frequently used algorithms or procedures. This lets you write code once and use it many times in your pages. Custom functions are generally faster than equivalent custom tags and provide the convenience of return values. You can call custom functions anywhere that you can use a ColdFusion expression, such as in tag attributes, between # signs in output, and in CFScript code. You can pass a function name as an argument to another function. The isCustomFunction function has been added for ColdFusion 5.

You can define a custom function within a CFScript tag in any template. The definition must be visible when you call the custom function. The definition is visible if:

> The definition is in the same template as the call, even if it is after the call. (However, it is generally good practice to place the definition before the call.)

or

> The definition is in a template with cfinclude before the call.

Using CFScript, you define a function in a manner similar to defining JavaScript functions. You do not have to define a return type for your custom function, and it can be recursive (the body of a function can call the function).

To define a function, use the following syntax:

```
function functionName( [paramName1[, paramname2...]] ) {
CFScript Statements }
```

In addition to the current list of CFScript statements, two new statements can be used within the body of a function definition.

> `Var variableName = InitialValue`—Declares a variable local to the function.
>
> `Return expression`—Returns the specified value to the processing page and terminates processing in the function.

A new regular built-in CFML function has been added to determine if a name is a custom function. It can be used like any other CFML function:

> `isCustomFunction(name)`—Verifies that a function is a user-defined function. It is not necessary to call isdefined() before using isCustomFunction().

User-defined functions can be called with a variable number of arguments. The function must be called with at least as many arguments as there are named parameters. These arguments and additional arguments are accessible within the function through the Arguments variable. Here's an example that computes the sum of two or more arguments. The example contains two named parameters and can take an unlimited number of additional optional arguments.

```
function Sum2(a,b)
{
        var sum = a + b;
        var arg_count = ArrayLen(Arguments);
        var opt_arg = 3;
        for( ; opt_arg LTE arg_count; opt_arg = opt_arg + 1 )
        {
                sum = sum + Arguments[opt_arg];
        }
        return sum;
}

Sum2( 1 ); // error, not enough arguments
Sum2( 1,  3 ); // returns 4
Sum2( 1, 2, 3 ); // returns 6
```

The Arguments variable is an array of values. Arguments[1] is the first argument passed and Arguments[n] is the *n*th argument passed. You can determine how many arguments are passed by using ArrayLen(Arguments). The Arguments array parallels the named parameters. That is, if the function contains three named parameters, elements one through three of the Arguments array correspond to those parameters. However, within the function, all references to a particular argument should consistently use either the parameter name or the Arguments array. In the example, all references to the first argument would use either "a" or "Arguments[1]," but not both in different places.

Array Functions

ArrayAppend	ArrayAvg	ArrayClear	ArrayDeleteAt
ArrayInsertAt	ArrayIsEmpty	ArrayLen	ArrayMax
ArrayMin	ArrayNew	ArrayPrepend	ArrayResize
ArraySet	ArraySort	ArraySum	ArraySwap
ArrayToList	IsArray	ListtoArray	

Date and Time

CreateDate	CreateDateTime	CreateODBCDate
CreateODBCDateTime	CreateODBCTime	CreateTime
CreateTimeSpan	DateCompare	DateConvert

DateDiff	DateFormat	DatePart
Day	DayOfWeek	DayOfWeekAsString
DayOfYear	DaysInMonth	DaysInYear
FirstDayOfMonth	GetTimeZoneInfo	Hour
IsDate	IsLeapYear	IsNumericDate
Minute	Month	MonthAsString
Now	ParseDateTime	Quarter
Second	Week	XMLFormat
Year		

Decision

IsArray	IsAuthenticated	IsAuthorized	IsBinary
IsDate	IsDefined	IsDebugMode	IsLeapYear
IsNumeric	IsNumericDate	IsProtected	IsStruct
LSIsCurrency	LSIsDate	LSIsNumeric	ParameterExists

Display and Formatting

DateFormat	DecimalFormat	DollarFront
FormatBaseN	HTMLCodeFormat	HTMLEditFormat
LSCurrencyFormat	LSDateFormat	LSEuroCurrencyFormat
LSNumberFormat	LSTimeFormat	NumberFormat
ParagraphFormat	TimeFormat	YesNoFormat

Dynamic Evaluation

DE	Evaluate	IIf	SetVariable

International

DateConvert	GetLocale	GetTimeZoneInfo
LSCurrencyFormat	LSDateFormat	LSIsCurrency
LSIsDate	LSIsNumeric	LSNumberFormat

LSParseCurrency LSParseDateTime LSParseEuroCurrencyFormat
LSParseNumber LSTimeFormat SetLocale

List

ArrayToList ListAppend ListChangeDelims
ListContains ListContainsNoCase ListDeleteAt
ListFind ListFindNoCase ListFirst
ListGetAt ListInsertAt ListLast
ListLen ListPrepend ListQualify
ListRest ListSetAt ListSort
ListToArray ListValueCount ListValueCountNoCase

Mathematical

Abs Acos Asin Atn
BitAnd BitMaskClear BitMaskRead BitMaskSet
BitNot BitOr BitSHLN BitSHRN
BitXor Ceiling Cos DecrementValue
Exp Fix IncremenetValue InputBaseN
Int Log Log10 Max
Min Pi Ran Randomize
RandRange Round Sgn Sin
Sqr Tan

Query Functions

IsQuery QueryAddColumn QueryAddRow QueryNew
QuerySetCell QuotedValueList ValueList

String

Asc Chr Cjustify
Compare CompareNoCase DayOfWeekAsString
Find FindNoCase FindOneOf

FormatBaseN	GetToken	Insert
JSStringFormat	Left	Len
Ljustify	ListValueContent	ListValueCountNoCase
LSParseCurrency	LSParseDateTime	LSParseEuroCurrency
LSParseNumber	Ltrim	Mid
MonthAsString	ParseDateTime	REFind
REFindNoCase	RemoveChars	RepeatString
Replace	ReplaceList	ReplaceNoCase
REReplace	REReplaceNoCase	Reverse
Right	Rjustify	Rtrim
SpanExcluding	SpanIncluding	ToBase64
Ucase	Val	

Structure

IsStruct	StructClear	StructCopy	StructCount
StructDelete	StructFind	StructInsert	StructIsEmpty
StructKeyArray	StructKeyExists	StructKeyList	StructNew
StructSort	StructUpdate		

System

DirectoryExists	ExpandPath	FileExists
GetCurrentTemplatePath	GetDirectoryFromPath	GetFileFromPath
GetHTTPRequestData	GetMetricData	GetTempFile
GetTemplatePath	SetProfileString	

Other

CreateObject	CreateUUID	Decrypt
DeleteClientVariable	Encrypt	GetBaseTagData
GetBaseTagList	GetBaseTemplatePath	GetClientVariablesList
GetTickCount	Hash	PreserveSingleQuotes
QuotedValueList	StripCR	URLEncodedFormat
ValueList	WriteOutput	

Alphabetical List of ColdFusion Functions

Abs

Returns the absolute value of a number. The absolute value of a number is the number without its sign. See also Sgn.

Syntax

Abs(*number*)

number: Any number.

ACos

Returns the arccosine of a number in radians. The arccosine is the angle whose cosine is number. See also Cos, Sin, ASin, Tan, and Pi.

Syntax

ACos(*number*)

number: Cosine of the angle that is to be calculated. This value must be between −1 and 1, inclusive.

Usage

The range of the result is 0 to π. To convert degrees to radians, multiply degrees by 180. To convert radians to degrees, multiply radians by 180/π.

ArrayAppend

Appends an array index to the end of the specified array. Returns a Boolean TRUE on successful completion. See also ArrayPrepend.

Syntax

ArrayAppend(*array, value*)

array: Name of the array to which you want to append an index.

value: The value you want to place into the specified array in the last index position.

ArrayAvg

Returns the average of the values in the specified array.

Syntax

ArrayAvg(*array*)

array: Name of the array containing values you want to average.

ArrayClear

Deletes all data in the specified array. Returns a Boolean TRUE on successful completion. See also ArrayDeleteAt.

Syntax

ArrayClear(*array*)

array: Name of the array in which you want to delete data.

ArrayDeleteAt

Deletes data from the specified array at the specified index position. Note that when an array index is deleted, index positions in the array are recalculated. For example, in an array containing the months of the year, deleting index position [5] removes the entry for May. If you then want to delete the entry for November, you delete index position [10], not [11], since the index positions were recalculated after index position [5] was removed. Returns a Boolean TRUE on successful completion. See also ArrayInsertAt.

Syntax

ArrayDeleteAt(*array, position*)

array: Name of the array in which you want to delete index data specified in position.

position: Array position containing the data you want to delete.

ArrayInsertAt

Inserts data in the specified array at the specified index position. All array elements with indexes greater than the new position are shifted right by one. The length of the array increases by one index. Returns a Boolean TRUE on successful completion. See also ArrayDeleteAt.

Syntax

ArrayInsertAt(*array, position, value*)

array: Name of the array in which you want to insert data.

position: The index position in the specified array where you want to insert the data specified in value.

value: The value of the data you want to insert into the array.

ArrayIsEmpty

Determines whether the specified array is empty of data. Returns a Boolean TRUE if specified array is empty, FALSE if not empty. See also ArrayLen.

Syntax

ArrayIsEmpty(*array*)

array: Name of the array you want to check for data.

ArrayLen

Returns the length of the specified array. See also ArrayIsEmpty.

Syntax

ArrayLen(*array*)

array: Name of the array whose length you want to return.

ArrayMax

Returns the largest numeric value in the specified array.

Syntax

ArrayMax(*array*)

> *array:* Name of the array from which you want to return the largest numeric value.

ArrayMin

Returns the smallest numeric value in the specified array.

Syntax

ArrayMin(*array*)

> *array:* Name of the array from which you want to return the smallest numeric value.

ArrayNew

Creates an array of between one and three dimensions. Array elements are indexed with square brackets: [ ]. Note that ColdFusion arrays expand dynamically as data is added.

Syntax

ArrayNew(*dimension*)

> *dimension:* An integer value between 1 and 3.

ArrayPrepend

Adds an array element to the beginning of the specified array. Returns a Boolean TRUE on successful completion. See also ArrayAppend.

Syntax

ArrayPrepend(*array, value*)

array: Name of the array to which you want to prepend data.

value: The value you want to add to the beginning of the specified array.

ArrayResize

Resets an array to a specified minimum number of elements. ArrayResize can provide some performance gains if used to size an array to its expected maximum. Use ArrayResize immediately after creating an array with ArrayNew for arrays greater than 500 elements. Note that ColdFusion arrays expand dynamically as data is added. Returns a Boolean TRUE on successful completion.

Syntax

ArrayResize(*array, minimum_size*)

array: Name of the array you want to resize.

minimum_size: Minimum size of the specified array.

ArraySet

In a one-dimensional array, sets the elements in a specified range to the specified value. Useful in initializing an array after a call to ArrayNew. Returns a Boolean TRUE on successful completion. See also ArrayNew.

Syntax

ArraySet(*array, start_pos, end_pos, value*)

array: Name of the array you want to change.

start_pos: Starting position in the specified array.

end_pos: Ending position in the specified array. If this value exceeds the array length, elements are accordingly added to the array.

value: The value you want to add to the range of elements in the specified array.

ArraySort

Returns the specified array with elements numerically or alphanumerically sorted.

Syntax

ArraySort(*array, sort_type* [, *sort_order*])

array: Name of the array you want to sort.
sort_type: The type of sort to execute. Sort type can be:

- numeric—Sorts numerically
- text—Sorts text alphabetically, uppercase before lowercase
- textnocase—Sorts text alphabetically; case is ignored

sort_order: The sort order you want to enforce:

- asc (default)—Ascending sort order
- desc—Descending sort order

ArraySum

Returns the sum of values in the specified array.

Syntax

ArraySum(*array*)

array: Name of the array containing values you want to add together.

ArraySwap

Swaps array values for the specified array at the specified positions. ArraySwap can be used with greater efficiency than multiple CFSETs. Returns a Boolean TRUE on successful completion.

Syntax

ArraySwap(*array, position1, position2*)

array: Name of the array whose elements you want to swap.
position1: Position of the first element you want to swap.
position2: Position of the second element you want to swap.

ArrayToList

Converts the specified one-dimensional array to a list, delimited with the character you specify.

Syntax

ArrayToList(*array* [, *delimiter*])

array: Name of the array containing elements you want to use to build a list.

delimiter: Specify the character(s) you want to use to delimit elements in the list. Default is comma (,).

Asc

Returns the ASCII value (character code) of the first character of a string. Returns 0 if string is empty. See also Chr.

Syntax

Asc(*string*)

string: Any string.

ASin

Returns the arcsine of a number in radians. The arcsine is the angle whose sine is *number*. See also Sin, Cos, Pi, and Tan.

Syntax

ASin(*number*)

number: Sine of the angle that is to be calculated. This value must be between 1 and −1.

Usage

The range of the result is $-\pi/2$ to $\pi/2$ radians. To convert degrees to radians, multiply degrees by $\pi/180$. To convert radians to degrees, multiply radians by $180/\pi$.

Atn

Returns the arctangent of a number. The arctangent is the angle whose tangent is *number.* See also Tan, Sin, Cos, and Pi.

Syntax

Atn(*number*)

number: Tangent of the angle you want.

Usage

The range of the result is $-\pi/2$ to $\pi/2$ radians. To convert degrees to radians, multiply degrees by $\pi/180$. To convert radians to degrees, multiply radians by $180/\pi$.

AuthenticatedContext

Returns the name of the security context. See also IsAuthenticated, AuthenticatedUser, IsAuthorized, and CFAuthenticate.

Syntax

AuthenticatedContext()

AuthenticatedUser

Returns the name of the authenticated user. See also IsAuthenticated, AuthenticatedContext, and CFAUTHENTICATE.

Syntax

AuthenticatedUser()

BitAnd

Returns the bitwise AND of two long integers. See also BitNot, BitOr, and BitXor.

Syntax

BitAnd(*number1, number2*)

number1, number2: Any long integers.

Usage

Bit functions operate on 32-bit integers.

BitMaskClear

Returns number bitwise cleared with length bits beginning from start. See also BitMaskRead and BitMaskSet.

Syntax

BitMaskClear(*number, start, length*)

number: Long integer to be masked.
start: Integer specifying the starting bit for masking.
length: Integer specifying the length of mask.

Usage

Parameters *start* and *length* must be in the range from 0 to 31. Bit functions operate on 32-bit integers.

BitMaskRead

Returns the integer created from length bits of number beginning from start. See also BitMaskClear and BitMaskSet.

Syntax

BitMaskRead(*number, start, length*)

number: Long integer to be masked.
start: Integer specifying the starting bit for reading.
length: Integer specifying the length of mask.

Usage

Parameters *start* and *length* must be in the range from 0 to 31. Bit functions operate on 32-bit integers.

BitMaskSet

Returns number bitwise masked with length bits of mask beginning from start. See also BitMaskClear and BitMaskRead.

Syntax

BitMaskSet(*number, mask, start, length*)

number: Long integer to be masked.
mask: Long integer specifying the mask.
start: Integer specifying the starting bit in *number* for masking.
length: Integer specifying the length of mask.

Usage

Parameters *start* and *length* must be in the range from 0 to 31. Bit functions operate on 32-bit integers.

BitNot

Returns the bitwise NOT of a long integer. See also BitAnd, BitOr, and BitXor.

Syntax

BitNot(*number*)

number: Any long integer.

Usage

Bit functions operate on 32-bit integers.

BitOr

Returns the bitwise OR of two long integers. See also BitAnd, BitNot, and BitXor.

Syntax

BitOr(*number1, number2*)

number1, number2: Any long integers.

Usage

Bit functions operate on 32-bit integers.

BitSHLN

Returns number bitwise shifted without rotation to the left by count bits. See also BitSHRN.

Syntax

BitSHLN(*number, count*)

number: Long integer to be shifted to the left.

count: Integer specifying number of bits the number should be shifted.

Usage

Parameter count must be in the range from 0 to 31. Bit functions operate on 32-bit integers.

BitSHRN

Returns number bitwise shifted without rotation to the right by count bits. See also BitSHLN.

Syntax

BitSHRN(*number, count*)

number: Long integer to be shifted to the right.

count: Integer specifying number of bits the number should be shifted.

Usage

Parameter count must be in the range from 0 to 31. Bit functions operate on 32-bit integers.

BitXoR

Returns bitwise XOR of two long integers. See also BitAnd, BitNot, and BitOr.

Syntax

BitXor(*number1, number2*)

number1, number2: Any long integers.

Usage

Bit functions operate on 32-bit integers.

Ceiling

Returns the closest integer greater than a given number. See also Int, Fix, and Round.

Syntax

Ceiling(*number*)

number: Any real number.

Chr

Returns a character of a given ASCII value (character code). See also Asc.

Syntax

Chr(*number*)

number: Any ASCII value (a number in the range 0 to 255 inclusive).

Usage

Numbers from 0 to 31 are the standard, nonprintable ASCII codes. For example, Chr(10) returns a linefeed character and Chr(13) returns a carriage-return character. Therefore, the two-character string Chr(13) & Chr(10) is the newline string.

CJustify

Centers a string in the specified field length. See also LJustify and RJustify.

Syntax

CJustify(*string, length*)

string: Any string to be centered.

length: Length of field.

Compare

Performs a case-sensitive comparison of two strings. Returns a negative number if string1 is less than string2; 0 if string1 is equal to string2; or a positive number if string1 is greater than string2. See also CompareNoCase and Find.

Syntax

Compare(*string1, string2*)

string1, string2: Strings to be compared.

Usage

The comparison is performed on the ASCII values (character codes) of corresponding characters in string1 and string2. If many strings are sorted in increasing order based on the Compare function, they appear listed in dictionary order.

CompareNoCase

Performs a case-insensitive comparison of two strings. Returns a negative number if string1 is less than string2; 0 if string1 is equal to string2; or a positive number if string1 is greater than string2. See also Compare and FindNoCase.

Syntax

CompareNoCase(*string1, string2*)

string1, string2: Strings to be compared.

Cos

Returns the cosine of a given angle in radians. See also Sin, Tan, and Pi.

Syntax

Cos(*number*)

number: Angle in radians for which you want the cosine.

Usage

The range of the result is -1 to 1. To convert degrees to radians, multiply degrees by $\pi/180$. To convert radians to degrees, multiply radians by $180/\pi$.

CreateDate

Returns a valid date/time object. See also CreateDateTime and CreateODBCDate.

Syntax

CreateDate(*year, month, day*)

year: Number representing the year in the range 100–9999. Years from 0 to 29 are interpreted as 21st-century values. Years from 30 to 99 are interpreted as 20th-century values.

month: Number representing the month of the year, ranging from 1 (January) to 12 (December).

day: Number representing the day of the month, ranging from 1 to 31.

Usage

CreateDate is a subset of CreateDateTime. Time in the returned object is set to 00:00:00.

CreateDateTime

Returns a valid date/time object. See also CreateDate, CreateTime, CreateODBCDateTime, and Now.

Syntax

CreateDateTime(*year, month, day, hour, minute, second*)

year: Number representing the year in the range 100–9999.

month: Number representing the month of the year, ranging from 1 (January) to 12 (December).

day: Number representing the day of the month, ranging from 1 to 31.

hour: Number representing the hour, ranging from 0 to 23.

minute: Number representing the minute, ranging from 0 to 59.

second: Number representing the second, ranging from 0 to 59.

Usage

Years from 0 to 29 are interpreted as 21st-century values. Years from 30 to 99 are interpreted as 20th-century values.

CreateObject

Allows you to create COM, CORBA, and JAVA objects. *Note:* ColdFusion administrators can disable the CFOBJECT tag in the ColdFusion

Administrator Basic Security page, which also disables this function. Additionally note: On UNIX, COM objects are not currently supported by CreateObject.

CreateObject Topics

- COM
- CORBA
- JAVA

Object Types

Depending on the value of the type parameter, there are several additional parameters you can use. This table shows which parameters you can use with each object type.

Parameters Used with Object Types

Type	*Parameters*
COM	TYPE CLASS CONTEXT SERVER
CORBA	TYPE CONTEXT CLASS LOCALE
JAVA	TYPE CLASS

Sections that follow describe these values and parameters in greater detail.

CreateODBCDate

Returns a date in ODBC date format. See also CreateDate and CreateODBCDateTime.

Syntax

CreateODBCDate(*date*)

date: Date/time object in the period from A.D. 100 to A.D. 9999. Years from 0 to 29 are interpreted as 21st-century values. Years from 30 to 99 are interpreted as 20th-century values.

CreateODBCDateTime

Returns a date/time object in ODBC timestamp format. See also CreateDateTime, CreateODBCDate, CreateODBCTime, and Now.

Syntax

CreateODBCDateTime(*date*)

date: Date/time object in the period from A.D. 100 to A.D. 9999. Years from 0 to 29 are interpreted as 21st-century values. Years 30 to 99 are interpreted as 20th-century values.

Usage

When passing a date/time value as a string, make sure it is enclosed in quotes. Otherwise, it is interpreted as a number representation of a date/time object, returning undesired results.

CreateODBCTime

Returns a time object in ODBC time format. See also CreateODBCDateTime and CreateTime.

Syntax

CreateODBCTime(*date*)

date: Date/time object in the period from A.D. 100 to A.D. 9999.

Usage

When passing a date/time value as a string, make sure it is enclosed in quotes. Otherwise, it is interpreted as a number representation of a date/time object, returning undesired results.

CreateTime

Returns a valid time variable in ColdFusion. See also CreateODBCTime and CreateDateTime.

Syntax

CreateTime(*hour, minute, second*)

hour: Number representing the hour, ranging from 0 to 23.

minute: Number representing the minute, ranging from 0 to 59.

second: Number representing the second, ranging from 0 to 59.

Usage

CreateTime is a subset of CreateDateTime.

Time variables are special cases of date/time variables. The date portion of a time variable is set to December 30, 1899.

CreateTimeSpan

Creates a date/time object for adding and subtracting other date/time objects. See also CreateDateTime, DateAdd, and DateConvert.

Syntax

CreateTimeSpan(*days, hours, minutes, seconds*)

days: Number representing the number of days.

hours: Number representing the number of hours.

minutes: Number representing the number of minutes.

seconds: Number representing the number of seconds.

Usage

The CreateTimeSpan function creates a special date/time object that should be used only to add and subtract from other date/time objects or with the CFQUERY CACHEDWITHIN attribute.

CreateUID

Returns a Universally Unique Identifier (UUID) formatted as "XXXXXXXX-XXXX-XXXX-XXXXXXXXXXXXXXXX" where "X" stands for a hexadecimal digit (0–9 or A–F).

Syntax

CreateUUID()

Usage

Each UUID returned by the CreateUUID function is a 35-character-string representation of a unique 128-bit integer. Use the CreateUUID function when you need a unique string that you will use as a persistent identifier in a distributed environment. To a very high degree of certainty, this function returns a unique value; no other invocation on the same or any other system should return the same value.

UUIDs are used by distributed computing frameworks, such as DCE/RPC, COM+, and CORBA. With ColdFusion, you can use UUIDs as primary table keys for applications where data is stored on a number of shared databases. In such cases, using numeric keys may cause primary key constraint violations during table merges. By using UUIDs, you can eliminate these violations because each UUID is unique.

DateAdd

Returns a date to which a specified time interval has been added. See also DateConvert, DatePart, and CreateTimeSpan.

Syntax

DateAdd(*datepart, number, date*)

datepart: One of the following strings:

- yyyy—Year
- q—Quarter
- m—Month
- y—Day of year
- d—Day
- w—Weekday
- ww—Week
- h—Hour
- n—Minute
- s—Second

number: Number of units of *datepart* to add to *date* (positive to get dates in the future or negative to get dates in the past).

date: Date/time object in the period from A.D. 100 to A.D. 9999. Years from 0 to 29 are interpreted as 21st-century values. Years from 30 to 99 are interpreted as 20th-century values.

Usage

The *datepart* specifiers "y," "d," and "w" perform the same function—add a certain number of days to a given date. When passing a date/time value as a string, make sure it is enclosed in quotes. Otherwise, it is interpreted as a number representation of a date/time object, returning undesired results.

DateCompare

Performs a full date/time comparison of two dates. Returns -1 if date1 is less than date2; returns 0 if date1 is equal to date2; returns 1 if date1 is greater than date2. See the description of *datepart* for information on specifying the precision of the comparison. See also CreateDateTime and DatePart.

Syntax

DateCompare(*date1, date2* [, *datepart*])

date1: Date/time object in the period from A.D. 100 to A.D. 9999.

date2: Date/time object in the period from A.D. 100 to A.D. 9999.

datepart: Optional. The precision of the comparison. This parameter can have any of the following values:

- s—precise to the second.
- n—precise to the minute.
- h—precise to the hour.
- d—precise to the day.
- m—precise to the month.
- yyyy—precise to the year.

By default, precision is to the second.

Usage

When passing a date/time value as a string, make sure it is enclosed in quotes. Otherwise, it is interpreted as a number representation of a date/time object, returning undesired results. Years from 0 to 29 are interpreted as 21st-century values. Years from 30 to 99 are interpreted as 20th-century values.

DateConvert

Converts local time to Universal Coordinated Time (UTC) or UTC to local time based on the specified parameters. This function uses the daylight savings settings in the executing machine to compute daylight savings time, if required. See also GetTimeZoneInfo, CreateDateTime, and DatePart.

Syntax

DateConvert(*conversion-type, date*)

> *conversion-type:* There are two conversion types: “local2Utc” and “utc2Local.” The former converts local time to UTC time. The later converts UTC time to local time.
>
> *date:* Any ColdFusion date and time string. In order to create a ColdFusion date and time, use CreateDateTime.

Usage

When passing a date/time value as a string, make sure it is enclosed in quotes. Otherwise, it is interpreted as a number representation of a date/time object, returning undesired results.

DatedIff

Returns the number of intervals in whole units of type Datepart by which Date1 is less than Date2. See also DateAdd, DatePart, and CreateTimeSpan.

Syntax

DateDiff(*datepart, date1, date2*)

datepart: One of the following strings:

- yyyy—Year
- q—Quarter
- m—Month
- y—Day of year
- d—Day
- w—Weekday
- ww—Week
- h—Hour
- n—Minute
- s—Second

date1: Date/time object in the period from A.D. 100 to A.D. 9999.

date2: Date/time object in the period from A.D. 100 to A.D. 9999.

Usage

If you want to know the number of days between date1 and date2, you can use either Day of Year ("y") or Day ("d"). When datepart is Weekday ("w"), DateDiff returns the number of weeks between the two dates. If date1 falls on a Monday, DateDiff counts the number of Mondays until date2. It counts date2 but not date1. If interval is Week ("ww"), however, the DateDiff function returns the number of calendar weeks between the two dates. It counts the number of Sundays between date1 and date2. DateDiff counts date2 if it falls on a Sunday; but it doesn't count date1, even if it does fall on a Sunday. If date1 refers to a later point in time than date2, the DateDiff function returns a negative number. When passing date/time value as a string, make sure it is enclosed in quotes. Otherwise, it is interpreted as a number representation of a date/time object, returning undesired results. Years from 0 to 29 are interpreted as 21st-century values. Years from 30 to 99 are interpreted as 20th-century values.

DateFormat

Returns a formatted date/time value. If no mask is specified, DateFormat function returns date value using the dd-mmm-yy format. See also Now, CreateDate, and ParseDateTime.

Syntax

DateFormat(*date* [, *mask*])

date: Date/time object in the period from A.D. 1601 to A.D. 9999.
mask: Set of characters that are used to show how ColdFusion should display the date:

- d—Day of the month as digits with no leading zero for single-digit days.
- dd—Day of the month as digits with a leading zero for single-digit days.
- ddd—Day of the week as a three-letter abbreviation.
- dddd—Day of the week as its full name.
- m—Month as digits with no leading zero for single-digit months.
- mm—Month as digits with a leading zero for single-digit months.
- mmm—Month as a three-letter abbreviation.
- mmmm—Month as its full name.
- y—Year as last two digits with no leading zero for years less than 10.
- yy—Year as last two digits with a leading zero for years less than 10.
- yyyy—Year represented by four digits.
- gg—Period/era string. Currently ignored, but reserved for future use.

Usage

When passing a date/time value as a string, make sure it is enclosed in quotes. Otherwise, it is interpreted as a number representation of a date/time object, returning undesired results.

Note: On UNIX, there is a switch that provides fast date-time parsing. If you have enabled this switch, you must refer to dates in expressions in the following order: month, day, and year. For example:

```
<CFIF "11/23/1998" GT "11/15/1998">
```

If this switch is set, the default date format returned by the DateFormat() function cannot be parsed in an expression. However, if you specify a mask, indicating the correct order, such as, mm/dd/yyyy, the date returned by this function can be parsed.

The Fast Date/Time Parsing switch is set on the ColdFusion Administrator Server Settings page. Please refer to *Administering ColdFusion Server* for more information about ColdFusion settings.

DatePart

Returns the specified part of a date as an integer. See also DateAdd and DateConvert.

Syntax

DatePart(*datepart, date*)

datepart: One of the following strings:

- yyyy—Year
- q—Quarter
- m—Month
- y—Day of year
- d—Day
- w—Weekday
- ww—Week
- h—Hour
- n—Minute
- s—Second

date: Any date.

Usage

Years from 0 to 29 are interpreted as 21st-century values. Years from 30 to 99 are interpreted as 20th-century values. When passing a date/time value as a string, make sure it is enclosed in quotes. Otherwise, it is interpreted as a number representation of a date/time object, returning undesired results.

Day

Returns the ordinal for the day of the month, ranging from 1 to 31. See also DayOfWeek, DayOfWeekAsString, DayOfYear, DaysInMonth, DaysInYear, and FirstDayOfMonth.

Syntax

Day(*date*)

date: Any date.

Usage

Years from 0 to 29 are interpreted as 21st-century values. Years from 30 to 99 are interpreted as 20th-century values. When passing a date/time value as a string, make sure it is enclosed in quotes. Otherwise, it is interpreted as a number representation of a date/time object, returning undesired results.

DayOfWeek

Returns the ordinal for the day of the week. The day is given as an integer ranging from 1 (Sunday) to 7 (Saturday). See also Day, DayOfWeekAsString, DayOfYear, DaysInMonth, DaysInYear, and FirstDayOfMonth.

Syntax

DayOfWeek(*date*)

date: Any date.

Usage

Years from 0 to 29 are interpreted as 21st-century values. Years from 30 to 99 are interpreted as 20th-century values. When passing a date/time value as a string, make sure it is enclosed in quotes. Otherwise, it is interpreted as a number representation of a date/time object, returning undesired results.

DayOfWeekAsString

Returns the day of the week corresponding to day_of_week, an integer ranging from 1 (Sunday) to 7 (Saturday). See also Day, DayOfWeek, DayOfYear, DaysInMonth, DaysInYear, and FirstDayOfMonth.

Syntax

DayOfWeekAsString(*day_of_week*)

> *day_of_week:* Integer representing the day of the week, where 1 is Sunday, 2 is Monday, and so on.

Usage

Years from 0 to 29 are interpreted as 21st-century values. Years from 30 to 99 are interpreted as 20th-century values.

DayOfYear

Returns the ordinal for the day of the year. See also Day, DayOfWeek, DayOfWeekAsString, DaysInMonth, DaysInYear, and FirstDayOfMonth.

Syntax

DayOfYear(*date*)

> *date:* Any date.

Usage

DayofYear is aware of leap years. Years from 0 to 29 are interpreted as 21st-century values. Years from 30 to 99 are interpreted as 20th-century values. When passing a date/time value as a string, make sure it is enclosed in quotes. Otherwise, it is interpreted as a number representation of a date/time object, returning undesired results.

DaysInMonth

Returns the number of days in the specified month (Date). See also Day, DayOfWeek, DayOfWeekAsString, DayOfYear, DaysInYear, and FirstDayOfMonth.

Syntax

DaysInMonth(*date*)

date: Any date.

Usage

Years from 0 to 29 are interpreted as 21st-century values. Years from 30 to 99 are interpreted as 20th-century values. When passing a date/time value as a string, make sure it is enclosed in quotes. Otherwise, it is interpreted as a number representation of a date/time object, returning undesired results.

DaysInYear

Returns the number of days in a year. See also Day, DayOfWeek, DayOfWeekAsString, DayOfYear, DaysInMonth, DaysInYear, FirstDayOfMonth, and IsLeapYear.

Syntax

DaysInYear(*date*)

date: Any date.

Usage

DaysInYear is aware of leap years. Years from 0 to 29 are interpreted as 21st-century values. Years from 30 to 99 are interpreted as 20th-century values. When passing a date/time value as a string, make sure it is enclosed in quotes. Otherwise, it is interpreted as a number representation of a date/time object, returning undesired results.

DE

Returns its argument with double quotes wrapped around it and all double quotes inside it escaped. The DE (Delay Evaluation) function prevents the evaluation of a string as an expression when it is passed as an argument to IIf or Evaluate. See also Evaluate and IIf.

Syntax

DE(*string*)

string: String to be evaluated with delay.

DecimalFormat

Returns number as a string formatted with two decimal places and thousands separator. See also DollarFormat and NumberFormat.

Syntax

DecimalFormat(*number*)

number: Number being formatted.

DecrementValue

Returns integer part of number decremented by one. See also IncrementValue.

Syntax

DecrementValue(*number*)

number: Number being decremented.

Decrypt

Decrypts an encrypted string. See also Encrypt.

Syntax

Decrypt(*encrypted_string, key*)

encrypted_string: String to be decrypted.

key: String specifying the key used to encrypt encrypted_string.

DeleteClientVariable

Deletes the client variable specified by name. Returns a Boolean TRUE when variable is successfully deleted, even if variable did not previously exist. To test for the existence of a variable, use IsDefined. See also GetClientVariablesList.

Syntax

DeleteClientVariable(*"name"*)

name: Name of a client variable to be deleted, surrounded by double quotes.

Usage

If the client variable specified by name does not exist, an error is returned.

DirectoryExists

Returns YES if the directory specified in the argument does exist; otherwise, it returns NO. See also FileExists.

Syntax

DirectoryExists(*absolute_path*)

absolute_path: Any absolute path.

DollarFormat

Returns number as a string formatted with two decimal places, thousands separator, dollar sign. Parentheses are used if number is negative. See also DecimalFormat and NumberFormat.

Syntax

DollarFormat(*number*)

number: Number being formatted.

Encrypt

Encrypts a string. See also Decrypt.

Syntax

Encrypt(*string, key*)

string: String to be encrypted.

key: String specifying the key used to encrypt string.

Evaluate

The function evaluates all of its arguments, left to right, and returns the result of evaluating the last argument. See also DE and IIf.

Syntax

Evaluate(*string_expression1* [, *string_expression2* [, ...]])

string_expression1, string_expression2: Valid expressions to be evaluated.

Usage

String expressions can be arbitrarily complex. Note, however, that they are somewhat more complicated to write because they are inside a string. In particular, if the string expression is double-quoted, double quotes inside the expression must be escaped.

Exp

Returns *e* raised to the power of number. The constant *e* equals 2.71828182845904, the base of the natural logarithm. See also Log and Log10.

Syntax

Exp(*number*)

number: Exponent applied to the base *e*.

Usage

To calculate powers of other bases, use ^ (the exponentiation operator). Exp is the inverse of Log, the natural logarithm of number.

ExpandPath

Returns a path equivalent to the relative_path appended to the base template path. Note the following:

- ExpandPath creates a platform-appropriate path. You can use either a slash (/) or a backslash (\) in the specified relative path.
- The return value contains a trailing slash (or backslash) if the specified relative path contains a trailing slash (or backslash).

See also FileExists, GetCurrentTemplatePath, and GetFileFromPath.

Syntax

ExpandPath(*relative_path*)

relative_path: Any relative path. ExpandPath converts relative directory references (.\ and ..\)to an absolute path. The function throws an error if this argument or the resulting absolute path is invalid.

FileExists

Returns YES if the file specified in the argument does exist; otherwise, it returns NO. See also DirectoryExists, ExpandPath, and GetTemplatePath.

Syntax

FileExists(*absolute_path*)

absolute_path: Any absolute path.

Find

Returns the first index of an occurrence of a substring in a string from a specified starting position. Returns 0 if substring is not in string. The search is case sensitive. See also FindNoCase, Compare, FindOneOf, REFind, and Replace.

Syntax

Find(*substring, string* [, *start*])

substring: String being sought.

string: String being searched.

start: Starting position for the search.

FindNoCase

Returns the first index of an occurrence of a substring in a string from a specified starting position. Returns 0 if substring is not in string. The search is case insensitive. See also Find, CompareNoCase, FindOneOf, REFind, and Replace functions.

Syntax

FindNoCase(*substring, string* [, *start*])

substring: String being sought.

string: String being searched.

start: Starting position for the search.

FindOneOf

Returns the first index of the occurrence of any character from set in string. Returns 0 if no characters are found. The search is case sensitive. See also Find, Compare, and REFind functions.

Syntax

FindOneOf(*set, string* [, *start*])

set: String containing one or more characters being sought.

string: String being searched.

start: Starting position for the search.

FirstDayOfMonth

Returns the ordinal (the day's number in the year) for the first day of the specified month. See also Day, DayOfWeek, DayOfWeekAsString, DayOfYear, DaysInMonth, and DaysInYear.

Syntax

FirstDayOfMonth(*date*)

date: Any date.

Usage

Years from 0 to 29 are interpreted as 21st-century values. Years from 30 to 99 are interpreted as 20th-century values. When passing a date/time value as a string, make sure it is enclosed in quotes. Otherwise, it is interpreted as a number representation of a date/time object, returning undesired results.

Fix

Returns the closest integer less than number if number is greater than or equal to 0. Returns the closest integer greater than number if number is less than 0. See also Ceiling, Int, and Round.

Syntax

Fix(*number*)

number: Any number.

FormatBaseN

Converts a number to a string in the base specified by radix. See also InputBaseN.

Syntax

FormatBaseN(*number, radix*)

number: Number to be converted.

radix: Base of the result.

GetBaseTagData

Returns an object that contains data (variables, scopes, etc.) from a specified ancestor tag. By default the closest ancestor is returned. If there is no ancestor by the specified name, or if the ancestor does not expose any data (for example, CFIF), an exception will be thrown. See also GetBaseTagList.

Syntax

GetBaseTagData(*tagname* [, *instancenumber*])

tagname: Required. Specifies the ancestor tag name for which the function returns data.

instancenumber: Optional. Specifies the number of ancestor levels to jump before returning data. The default is 1.

GetBaseTagList

Returns a comma-delimited list of uppercase ancestor tag names. The first element of the list is the parent tag. If you call this function for a top-level tag, it returns an empty string. See also GetBaseTagData.

Syntax

GetBaseTagList()

GetBaseTemplatePath

Returns the fully specified path of the base template. See also GetCurrentTemplatePath, FileExists, and ExpandPath.

Syntax

GetBaseTemplatePath()

GetClientVariablesList

Returns a comma-delimited list of nonreadonly client variables available to a template. See also DeleteClientVariable.

Syntax

GetClientVariablesList()

GetCurrentTemplatePath

Returns the fully specified path of the template containing the call to this function. See also GetBaseTemplatePath, FileExists and ExpandPath.

Syntax

GetCurrentTemplatePath()

Usage

This function differs from GetBaseTemplatePath in that it will return the template path of an included template if the call is made from a template included with a CFINCLUDE tag, whereas GetBaseTemplatePath returns the template path of the top-level template even when the call to GetBaseTemplatePath is actually made from an included template.

GetDirectoryFromPath

Extracts the directory (with a \ (backslash)) from a fully specified path. See also ExpandPath and GetFileFromPath.

Syntax

GetDirectoryFromPath(*path*)

path: Fully specified path (drive, directory, filename, and extension).

GetFileFromPath

Extracts the filename from a fully specified path. See also ExpandPath and GetCurrentTemplatePath.

Syntax

GetFileFromPath(*path*)

> *path:* Fully qualified path (drive, directory, filename, and extension).

GetFunctionList

Returns a structure of functions that are available in ColdFusion.

Syntax

GetFunctionList()

GetLocale

Returns the locale for the current request. Locales are determined by the native operating system. A locale is an encapsulation of the set of attributes that govern the display and formatting of international date, time, number, and currency values. See also SetLocale.

Syntax

GetLocale()

Locale Support

ColdFusion can be expected to support the following locales with a default Windows NT installation.

Locales Supported by ColdFusion:

Dutch (Belgian)	French (Canadian)	Norwegian (Bokmal)
Dutch (Standard)	French (Standard)	Norwegian (Nynorsk)
English (Australian)	French (Swiss)	Portuguese (Brazilian)
English (Canadian)	German (Austrian)	Portuguese (Standard)
English (New Zealand)	German (Standard)	Spanish (Mexican)
English (UK)	German (Swiss)	Spanish (Modern)
English (US)	Italian (Standard)	Spanish (Standard)
French (Belgian)	Italian (Swiss)	Swedish

Note: The variable Server.ColdFusion.SupportedLocales is initialized at startup with a comma-delimited list of the locales that ColdFusion and the operating system support. GetLocale( ) will return an entry from that list. SetLocale will fail if called with a locale name not on that list.

GetMetricData

On Windows NT, GetMetricData returns all the internal data that is otherwise displayed in the Windows NT PerfMonitor. On UNIX, GetMetricData returns all of the internal data found by using CFStat. For it to work on NT you need to have turned on the PerfMonitor feature from the ColdFusion Administrator. See the Usage section for details of the structure that this function returns.

Syntax

GetMetricData(*monitor_name*)

monitor_name: The name of the performance monitor. On Windows NT, the performance monitor is PerfMonitor. On UNIX, it is CFStat.

Usage

On Windows NT, the function returns a ColdFusion structure with the following data fields:

- InstanceName
- PageHits

- ReqQueued
- DBHits
- ReqRunning
- ReqTimedOut
- BytesIn
- BytesOut
- AvgQueueTime
- AvgReqTime
- AvgDBTime
- CachePops

GetProfileString

Returns the value of an entry in an initialization file or an empty string if the value does not exist. An initialization file assigns values to configuration variables, also known as entries, that need to be set when the system boots, the operating system comes up, or an application starts. An initialization file is distinguished from other files by its .ini suffix, for example, boot.ini, Win32.ini, and setup.ini. See also SetProfileString.

Syntax

GetProfileString(*iniPath, section, entry*)

iniPath: Fully qualified path (drive, directory, filename, and extension) of the initialization file, for example, C:\boot.ini.

section: The section of the initialization file from which you would like to extract information.

entry: The name of the value that you would like to see.

GetTempDirectory

Returns the full path name of a directory, including the trailing slash. The directory that is returned depends on the account under which ColdFusion is running as well as a variety of other factors. Before using this function in an application, test to see the directory it returns under your account. See also GetTempFile.

Syntax

GetTempDirectory()

GetTempFile

Creates and returns the name of a temporary file in a directory whose name starts with (at most) the first three characters of prefix. See also GetTempDirectory.

Syntax

GetTempFile(*dir, prefix*)

dir: Directory name.

prefix: Prefix of a temporary file to be created in the directory specified by dir.

GetTemplatePath

Returns the fully specified path of the base template. Note that, for backward compatibility, GetTemplatePath is still supported. However, GetBaseTemplatePath supersedes this function and should be used in place of it in all code written after the release of ColdFusion 4.0. See also GetBaseTemplatePath, FileExists and ExpandPath.

Syntax

GetTemplatePath()

GetTickCount

Returns a millisecond clock counter that can be used for timing sections of CFML code or any other aspects of page processing.

Syntax

GetTickCount()

Usage

The absolute value of the counter has no meaning. Generates useful timing values by taking differences between the results of GetTickCount() at specified points during page processing.

GetTimeZoneInfo

Returns a structure containing time zone information for the machine on which this function is executed. The structure contains four elements with the following keys.

utcTotalOffset—Total offset of the local time in minutes from UTC (Universal Coordinated Time). A plus sign (+) indicates that a time zone is west of UTC, such as all of the time zones in North and South America. A minus sign (−) indicates that a time zone is east of UTC, such as the time zones in Germany.

utcHourOffset—Offset in hours of local time from UTC.

utcMinuteOffset—Offset in minutes after the hours offset is taken into account. For North America this will always be zero. However, for some countries that do not land exactly on the hour offset, the number will be between 0 and 60. For example, standard time in Adelaide, Australia, has an offset of 9 hours and 30 minutes from UTC.

isDSTOn—True if Daylight Savings Time (DST) is on in the host machine; False if DST is off.

See also DateConvert, CreateDateTime and DatePart.

Syntax

GetTimeZoneInfo()

GetToken

Returns the specified token in a string. Default delimiters are spaces, tabs, and newline characters. If index is greater than the number of tokens in string, GetToken returns an empty string. See also Left, Right, Mid, SpanExcluding, and SpanIncluding.

Syntax

GetToken(*string, index* [, *delimiters*])

string: Any string.

index: Any integer > 0 that indicates position of a token.

delimiters: String containing sets of delimiters.

Hour

Returns the ordinal value for the hour, in the range 0–23.

Syntax

Hour(*date*)

date: Date value to retrieve the hour part from.

Usage

Years from 0 to 29 are interpreted as 21st-century values. Years from 30 to 99 are interpreted as 20th-century values. When passing a date/time value as a string, make sure it is enclosed in quotes. Otherwise, it is interpreted as a number representation of a date/time object, returning undesired results.

HTMLCodeFormat

Returns HTML escaped string enclosed in <PRE> and </PRE> tags. All carriage returns are removed from string, and all special characters (> < " &) are escaped. See also HTMLEditFormat.

Syntax

HTMLCodeFormat(*string* [, *version*])

string: String being HTML escaped and preformatted.

version: The specific HTML version to use in replacing special characters with their entity references. Valid entries are:

- −1—The latest implementation of HTML
- 2.0—For HTML 2.0 (Default)
- 3.2—For HTML 3.2

HTMLEditFormat

Returns HTML escaped string. All carriage returns are removed from string, and all special characters (> < " &) are escaped. See also HTMLCodeFormat.

Syntax

HTMLEditFormat(*string* [, *version*])

string: String being HTML escaped.

version: The specific HTML version to use in replacing special characters with their entity references. Valid entries are:

- −1—The latest implementation of HTML
- 2.0—For HTML 2.0 (Default)
- 3.2—For HTML 3.2

Usage

By escaping all special characters, this function increases the length of the specified string. This can cause unpredictable results when performing certain string functions (Left, Right, and Mid, for example) against the expanded string.

IIF

The function evaluates its condition as a Boolean. If the result is TRUE, it returns the value of Evaluate(string_expression1); otherwise, it returns the value of Evaluate(string_expression2). Prior to using IIf, please read the Usage section and Note carefully. The IIf function is primarily intended for the conditional processing of dynamic expressions. For general conditional processing, see CFIF CFELSEIF CFELSE. For error handling, see CFTRY CFCATCH. See also DE and Evaluate.

Syntax

IIf(*condition*, *string_expression1*, *string_expression2*)

condition: Any expression that can be evaluated as a Boolean.

string_expression1: Valid string expression to be evaluated and returned if condition is TRUE.

string_expression2: Valid string expression to be evaluated and returned if condition is FALSE.

Usage

The IIf function is a shortcut for the following construct:

```
<CFIF condition>
  <CFSET result=Evaluate(string_expression1)>
<CFELSE>
  <CFSET result=Evaluate(string_expression2)><CFIF>
```

returning result.

The expressions *string_expression1* and *string_expression2* must be string expressions, so that they do not get evaluated immediately as the arguments of IIf. For example:

```
IIf(y is 0, DE("Error"), x/y)
```

will generate error if $y = 0$, because the third argument is the value of $x/0$ (not a valid expression).

Remember that ColdFusion evaluates *string_expression1* and *string_expression2*. To return the string itself instead of evaluating the expression, use the DE (delay evaluation) function.

Note: If you use pound signs (#) in either *string_expression1* or *string_expression2*, ColdFusion evaluates the part of the expression that is in pound signs first. By misusing pound signs, you can skew the results of the IIf function. In particular, if you use pound signs around the whole expression in *string_expression1*, it can cause the function to fail with the error 'Error Resolving Parameter' if there is an undefined variable in *string_expression1*.

IncrementValue

Returns integer part of number incremented by one. See also DecrementValue.

Syntax

IncrementValue(*number*)

number: Number being incremented.

InputBaseN

Returns the number obtained by converting string using the base specified by radix, an integer ranging from 2 to 36. See also FormatBaseN.

Syntax

InputBaseN(*string, radix*)

string: Any string representing number in base specified by *radix.*

radix: Base of number represented by string ranging from 2 to 36.

Insert

Inserts a substring in a string after a specified character position. Prepends the substring if position is equal to 0. See also RemoveChars and Len.

Syntax

Insert(*substring, string, position*)

substring: String to be inserted.

string: String to be inserted into.

position: Integer that indicates the character position in the string where the substring will be inserted.

Int

Returns the closest integer smaller than a number. See also Ceiling, Fix, and Round.

Syntax

Int(*number*)

number: Real number you want to round down to an integer.

Min

Returns the minimum, or smaller, value of two numbers.

Syntax

Min(*number1, number2*)

number1, number2: Any number.

See also Max.

IsArray

Returns TRUE if value is an array. See also Array Functions.

Syntax

IsArray(*value* [, *number*])

value: Variable name or array name.

number: Tests if the array has exactly the specified dimension.

IsAuthenticated

Returns TRUE if the user has been authenticated for any ColdFusion security context. If you specify the name of the security context, IsAuthenticated returns TRUE if the user has been authenticated for the specified ColdFusion security context. See also CFAUTHENTICATE, AuthenticatedContext, AuthenticatedUser, and IsAuthorized.

Syntax

IsAuthenticated([*security-context-name*])

security-context-name: The security context name.

IsAuthorized

Returns TRUE if the user is authorized to perform the specified action on the specified ColdFusion resource. See also IsAuthenticated.

Syntax

IsAuthorized(*resourcetype, resourcename* [, *action*])

resourcetype: String specifying the type of resource:

- Application
- CFML
- File
- DataSource
- Component
- Collection
- CustomTag
- UserObject

resourcename: String specifying the name of the resource. The value specified varies depending on the resource type:

Resourcetype specification	Resourcename specification
APPLICATION	Application name
CFML	CFML tag name
FILE	File name
DATASOURCE	Data source name
COMPONENT	Component name
COLLECTION	Verity collection name
CUSTOMTAG	Custom tag name
USEROBJECT	Object name

Resourcename is the actual resource that is protected, not to be confused with the rule name, which you specify in the ColdFusion Administrator.

action: String specifying the action for which authorization is requested. Do not specify this parameter for COMPONENT and CUSTOMTAG. For all other resource types, this parameter is required.

Resourcetype specification	Possible actions
APPLICATION	ALL USECLIENTVARIABLES
CFML	Valid actions for the tag specified by resourcename

Resourcetype specification	Possible actions
FILE	READ WRITE
DATASOURCE	ALL CONNECT SELECT INSERT UPDATE DELETE SP (stored procedure)
COMPONENT	No actions for this resource type
COLLECTION	DELETE OPTIMIZE PURGE SEARCH UPDATE
CUSTOMTAG	No actions for this resource type
USEROBJECT	Action specified via the ColdFusion Administrator

Usage

If you specify THROWONFAILURE=Yes in the CFAUTHENTICATE tag, you can enclose IsAuthorized in a CFTRY/CFCATCH block to handle possible exceptions programmatically.

IsBinary

Returns TRUE if value is binary; otherwise, the function returns FALSE. See also ToBinary, ToBase64, IsNumeric, and YesNoFormat.

Syntax

IsBinary(*value*)

value: Any value.

IsBoolean

Returns TRUE if value can be converted to a Boolean; otherwise, FALSE. See also IsNumeric and YesNoFormat.

Syntax

IsBoolean(*value*)

value: Any number or string.

IsDate

Returns TRUE if *string* can be converted to a date/time value; otherwise, FALSE. Note that ColdFusion converts the Boolean return value to its string equivalent, "Yes" and "No." See also ParseDateTime, CreateDateTime, and IsNumericDate.

Syntax

IsDate(*string*)

string: Any string value.

Usage

Years from 0 to 29 are interpreted as 21st-century values. Years from 30 to 99 are interpreted as 20th-century values.

IsDebugMode

Returns TRUE if debugging mode was set via the ColdFusion Administrator and FALSE if debugging mode is disabled.

Syntax

IsDebugMode()

IsDefined

Evaluates a string value to determine if the variable named in the string value exists. IsDefined returns TRUE if the specified variable is found, FALSE if not found. IsDefined provides an alternative to the ParameterExists function, eliminating the need for cumbersome expressions used to test for the existence of a variable:

```
Evaluate("ParameterExists(#var_name#)")
```

See also Evaluate.

Syntax

IsDefined(*"variable_name"*)

variable_name: A string value, the name of the variable you want to test for. This value must always be enclosed in quotation marks.

IsLeapYear

Returns TRUE if the year is a leap year; otherwise, FALSE. See also DaysInYear.

Syntax

IsLeapYear(*year*)

year: Number representing the year.

IsNumeric

Returns TRUE if string can be converted to a number; otherwise, FALSE. See also IsBinary.

Syntax

IsNumeric(*string*)

string: Any string value.

IsNumericDate

Evaluates "real value" of date/time object. Returns TRUE if the number represents "real value" of the date/time object; otherwise, FALSE. See also IsDate and ParseDateTime.

Syntax

IsNumericDate(*number*)

number: Real number.

IsProtected

Returns TRUE if the resource is protected in the security context of the authenticated user. See also IsAuthorized.

Syntax

IsProtected(*resourcetype, resourcename* [, *action*])

resourcetype: String specifying the type of resource:

- Application
- CFML
- File
- DataSource
- Component
- CustomTag
- UserObject

resourcename: String specifying the name of the resource. Resourcename is the actual resource that is protected, not to be confused with the rule name, which you specify in the ColdFusion Administrator. The value specified varies depending on the resource type:

Resourcetype specification	Resourcename specification
APPLICATION	Application name
CFML	CFML tag name
FILE	File name
DATASOURCE	Data source name
COMPONENT	Component name
COLLECTION	Verity collection name
CUSTOMTAG	Custom tag name
USEROBJECT	Object name

action: String specifying the action for which authorization is requested. Do not specify this parameter for COMPONENT and CUSTOMTAG. For all other resource types, this parameter is required.

Resourcetype specification	Possible actions
APPLICATION	ALL USECLIENTVARIABLES
CFML	Valid actions for the tag specified by resourcename

Resourcetype specification	Possible actions
FILE	READ WRITE
DATASOURCE	ALL CONNECT SELECT INSERT UPDATE DELETE SP (stored procedure)
COMPONENT	No actions for this resource type
COLLECTION	DELETE OPTIMIZE PURGE SEARCH UPDATE
CUSTOMTAG	No actions for this resource type
USEROBJECT	Action specified via the ColdFusion Administrator

Usage

The IsProtected function returns true only if the resource is protected by a rule in the security context or sandbox within which a request is being processed. An application may need to determine if a resource is protected and if the current user is authorized to use the resource. If a resource is not protected, then the IsAuthorized function returns true. In order to determine if a resource is explicitly protected with a rule, you must use the IsProtected function.

IsQuery

Returns TRUE if value is a query. See also QueryAddRow.

Syntax

IsQuery(*value*)

value: Query variable.

IsSimpleValue

Returns TRUE if value is a string, number, Boolean, or date/time value.

Syntax

IsSimpleValue(*value*)

value: Variable or expression.

IsStruct

Returns TRUE if variable is a structure. See also Structure Functions.

Syntax

IsStruct(*variable*)

variable: Variable name.

IsWDDX

Returns TRUE if the value is a well-formed WDDX packet and FALSE if not.

Syntax

IsWDDX(*value*)

value: Any WDDX packet.

Usage

Processes the WDDX packet specified using a validating XML parser which uses the WDDX DTD. If the parser processes without errors, TRUE is returned.

JSStringFormat

Returns a string that is safe to use with JavaScript.

Syntax

JSStringFormat(*string*)

string: Any string.

Usage

JSStringFormat escapes special JavaScript characters, such as the single quote ('), double quotes ("), and newline character so that you can put arbitrary strings safely into JavaScript.

LCase

Returns string converted to lowercase. See also UCase.

Syntax

LCase(string)

string: String being converted to lowercase.

Left

Returns the count of characters from the beginning of a string argument. See also Right, Mid, and Len.

Syntax

Left(*string, count*)

string: String from which the leftmost characters are retrieved.

count: Positive integer indicating how many characters to return.

Len

Returns the length of a string or a binary object. See also ToBinary, Left, Right, and Mid.

Syntax

Len(*string or binary object*)

string: Any string or binary object.

ListAppend

Returns list with value appended behind its last element. See also ListPrepend, ListInsertAt, and ListSetAt.

Syntax

ListAppend(*list, value* [, *delimiters*])

list: Any list.

value: Number or list being appended.

delimiters: Set of delimiters used in list.

Usage

When appending an element into a list, ColdFusion needs to insert a delimiter. If *delimiters* contains more than one delimiter, ColdFusion defaults to the first delimiter in the string, or , (comma) if *delimiters* was omitted. If you intend to use list functions on strings that are delimited by the conjunction ", " (comma-space), as is common in HTTP header strings such as the COOKIE header, we recommend that you specify delimiters to include both comma and space, because ColdFusion Server does not skip whitespace. For example,

ListAppend(*List, "MyCookie ", "," & CHR(32)*)

ListChangeDelims

Returns list with all delimiter characters changed to new_delimiter string. See also ListFirst and ListQualify.

Syntax

ListChangeDelims(*list, new_delimiter* [, *delimiters*])

list: List of delimiters being changed.

new_delimiter: String being used as a new delimiter.

delimiters: Set of delimiters used in list.

ListContains

Returns the index of the first item that contains the specified substring. The search is case sensitive. If the substring is not found in any of the list items, it returns zero (0). See also ListContainsNoCase and ListFind.

Syntax

ListContains(*list, substring* [, *delimiters*])

list: List being searched.

substring: String being sought in elements of list.

delimiters: Set of delimiters used in list.

ListContainsNoCase

Returns the index of the first element of a list that contains the specified substring within elements. The search is case insensitive. If no element is found, returns 0. See also ListContains and ListFindNoCase.

Syntax

ListContainsNoCase(*list, substring* [, *delimiters*])

list: List being searched.

substring: String being sought in elements of list.

delimiters: Set of delimiters used in list.

ListDeleteAt

Returns list with element deleted at the specified position. See also ListGetAt, ListSetAt, and ListLen.

Syntax

ListDeleteAt(*list, position* [, *delimiters*])

list: Any list.

position: Positive integer indicating the position of the element being deleted. The starting position in a list is denoted by the number 1, not 0.

delimiters: Set of delimiters used in list.

ListFind

Returns the index of the first occurrence of a value within a list. Returns 0 if no value is found. The search is case sensitive. See also ListContains and ListFindNoCase.

Syntax

ListFind(*list, value* [, *delimiters*])

list: List being searched.

value: Number or string that is to be found in the items of the list.

delimiters: Set of delimiters used in the list.

ListFindNoCase

Returns the index of the first occurrence of a value within a list. Returns 0 if no value was found. The search is case insensitive. See also ListContains and ListFind.

Syntax

ListFindNoCase(*list, value* [, *delimiters*])

list: List being searched.

value: Number or string being sought among elements of list.

delimiters: Set of delimiters used in list.

ListFirst

Returns the first element of the list. See also ListGetAt, ListLast, and ListQualify.

Syntax

ListFirst(*list* [, *delimiters*])

list: List whose first element is being retrieved.

delimiters: Set of delimiters used in the list.

ListGetAt

Returns the element at a given position. See also ListFirst, ListLast, ListQualify, and ListSetAt.

Syntax

ListGetAt(*list, position* [, *delimiters*])

list: List whose element is being retrieved.

position: Positive integer indicating the position of the element being retrieved.

delimiters: Set of delimiters used in list.

Usage

The first position in a list is denoted by the number 1, not 0.

ListInsertAt

Returns list with value inserted at the specified position. See also ListDeleteAt, ListAppend, ListPrepend, and ListSetAt.

Syntax

ListInsertAt(*list, position, value* [, *delimiters*])

list: Any list.

position: Position where the value is being inserted. The first position in a list is denoted by the number 1, not 0.

value: Number or list being inserted.

delimiters: Set of delimiters used in list.

Usage

When inserting elements into a list, ColdFusion needs to insert a delimiter. If *delimiters* contain more than one delimiter, ColdFusion defaults to the first delimiter in the string, or "," (comma) if delimiters was omitted. If you intend to use list functions on strings that are delimited by the conjunction ", " (comma-space), as is common in HTTP header strings such as the COOKIE header, we recommend that you specify delimiters to include both comma and space, because ColdFusion Server does not skip whitespace.

LJustify

Returns left-justified string of the specified field length. See also CJustify and RJustify.

Syntax

LJustify(*string, length*)

string: String to be left-justified.

length: Length of field.

ListLast

Returns the last element of the list. See also ListGetAt and ListFirst.

Syntax

ListLast(*list* [, *delimiters*])

list: List whose last element is being retrieved.

delimiters: Set of delimiters used in list.

ListLen

Returns the number of elements in the list. See also ListAppend, ListDeleteAt, ListInsertAt, and ListPrepend.

Syntax

ListLen(*list* [, *delimiters*])

list: Any list.

delimiters: Set of delimiters used in list.

ListPrepend

Returns list with value inserted at the first position, shifting all other elements one to the right. See also ListAppend, ListInsertAt, and ListSetAt.

Syntax

ListPrepend(*list, value* [, *delimiters*])

list: Any list.
value: Number or list being prepended.
delimiters: Set of delimiters used in list.

Usage

When prepending an element to a list, ColdFusion needs to insert a delimiter. If delimiters contain more than one delimiter, ColdFusion defaults to the first delimiter in the string, or "," (comma) if delimiters was omitted. If you intend to use list functions on strings that are delimited by the conjunction ", " (comma-space), as is common in HTTP header strings such as the COOKIE header, we recommend that you specify delimiters to include both comma and space, because ColdFusion Server does not skip whitespace.

ListQualify

Returns a list with a qualifying character around each item in the list, such as double or single quotes. See the List Functions table.

Syntax

ListQualify(*list, qualifier* [, *delimiters*] [, *elements*])

list: Any list of items or a variable that names a list.

qualifier: The character that is to be placed at the beginning and end of each item in the list.

delimiters: Set of delimiters used in list.

elements: Either the keyword "ALL" or "CHAR." If you specify "ALL," the function qualifies all items in the list. If you specify "CHAR," the function qualifies only items comprised of alphabetic characters; it does not qualify numeric items.

Usage

The new list may not preserve all of the delimiters in the previous list.

ListRest

Returns list without its first element. Returns an empty list (empty string) if list has only one element. See also ListFirst, ListGetAt, and ListLast.

Syntax

ListRest(*list* [, *delimiters*])

list: List whose elements are being retrieved.

delimiters: Set of delimiters used in list.

ListSetAt

Returns list with value assigned to its element at specified position. See also ListDeleteAt, ListGetAt, and ListInsertAt.

Syntax

ListSetAt(*list, position, value* [, *delimiters*])

list: Any list.

position: Any position. The first position in a list is denoted by the number 1, not 0.

value: Any value.

delimiters: Set of delimiters.

Usage

When assigning an element to a list, ColdFusion needs to insert a delimiter. If delimiters contain more than one delimiter, ColdFusion defaults to the first delimiter in the string, or "," (comma) if delimiters was omitted. If you intend to use list functions on strings that are delimited by the conjunction ", " (comma-space), as is common in HTTP header strings such as the COOKIE header, we recommend that you specify delimiters to include both comma and space, because ColdFusion Server does not skip whitespace.

ListSort

Sorts and delimits the items in a list according to the specified sort type and sort order.

Syntax

ListSort(*list, sort_type* [, *sort_order*] [, *delimiter*])

list: List to be sorted. The items in the list must be separated by commas or otherwise delimited.

sort_type: The type of sort to be executed. You can specify any of the following sort types:

- Numeric—sorts numbers.
- Text—sorts text alphabetically.
- Textnocase—sorts text alphabetically. The case is ignored.

sort_order: The order to be followed. You can specify any of the following:

- Asc (default)—Ascending sort order.
- Desc—Descending sort order.

delimiter: Specify the character(s) used to delimit elements in the list. Default is comma (,).

ListToArray

Converts the specified list into an array. See also ArrayToList.

Syntax

ListToArray (*list* [, *delimiter*])

list: Name of the list variable that contains the elements to be used to build an array. You can define a list variable with a CFSET statement. The items in the list must be separated by commas or otherwise delimited.

delimiter: Specify the character(s) used to delimit elements in the list. Default is comma (,).

ListValueCount

Returns the number of instances of a specified value in a list. The underlying search that finds the instances is case sensitive. See also ListValueCountNoCase.

Syntax

ListValueCount(*list, value* [, *delimiters*])

list: A list or the name of a list that is to be searched.

value: The string or number that the function is to find and count.

delimiter: Optional. Specify the character(s) used to delimit elements in the list. The default is a comma (,).

ListValueCountNoCase

Returns the number of instances of a specified value in a list. The underlying search that finds the instances is not case sensitive. See also ListValueCount.

Syntax

ListValueCountNoCase(*list, value* [, *delimiters*])

list: A list or the name of a list that is to be searched.

value: The string or number that the function is to find and count.

delimiter: Optional. Specify the character(s) used to delimit elements in the list. The default is a comma (,).

Log

Returns the natural logarithm of a number. Natural logarithms are based on the constant *e* (2.71828182845904). See also Exp and Log10.

Syntax

Log(*number*)

number: Positive real number for which you want the natural logarithm.

Log10

Returns the logarithm of number to base 10. See also Exp and Log.

Syntax

Log10(*number*)

number: Positive real number for which you want the logarithm.

LSCurrencyFormat

Returns a currency value using the locale convention. Default value is "local." See also LSEuroCurrencyFormat.

Syntax

LSCurrencyFormat(*number* [, *type*])

number: The currency value.

type: Currency type. Valid arguments are:

- none—(For example, 10.00)
- local—Default. (For example, $10.00)
- international—(For example, USD10.00)

Currency Output

The following list shows sample currency output for some of the locales supported by ColdFusion in each of the format types: local, international, and none.

Locale	**Format Type Output**
Dutch (Belgian)	Local: 100.000,00 BF International: BEF100.000,00 None: 100.000,00
Dutch (Standard)	Local: fl 100.000,00 International: NLG100.000,00 None: 100.000,00
English (Australian)	Local: $100,000.00 International: AUD100,000.00 None: 100,000.00
English (Canadian)	Local: $100,000.00 International: CAD100,000.00 None: 100,000.00
English (New Zealand)	Local: $100,000.00 International: NZD100,000.00 None: 100,000.00
English (UK)	Local: £100,000.00 International: GBP100,000.00 None: 100,000.00
English (US)	Local: $100,000.00 International: USD100,000.00 None: 100,000.00
French (Belgian)	Local: 100.000,00 FB International: BEF100.000,00 None: 100.000,00
French (Canadian)	Local: 100 000,00 $ International: CAD100 000,00 None: 100,000,00
French (Standard)	Local: 100 000,00 F International: FRF100 000,00 None: 100 000,00
French (Swiss)	Local: SFr. 100’000.00 International: CHF100’000.00 None: 100’000.00
German (Austrian)	Local: öS 100.000,00 International: ATS100.000,00 None: 100.000,00

Locale	Format Type Output
German (Standard)	Local: 100.000,00 DM International: DEM100.000,00 None: 100.000,00
German (Swiss)	Local: SFr. 100’000.00 International: CHF100’000.00 None: 100’000.00
Italian (Standard)	Local: L. 10.000.000 International: ITL10.000.000 None: 10.000.000
Italian (Swiss)	Local: SFr. 100’000.00 International: CHF100’000.00 None: 100’000.00
Norwegian (Bokmal)	Local: kr 100 000,00 International: NOK100 000,00 None: 100 000,00
Norwegian (Nynorsk)	Local: kr 100 000,00 International: NOK100 000,00 None: 100 000,00
Portuguese (Brazilian)	Local: R$100.000,00 International: BRC100.000,00 None: 100.000,00
Portuguese (Standard)	Local: R$100.000,00 International: BRC100.000,00 None: 100.000,00
Spanish (Mexican)	Local: $100,000.00 International: MXN100,000.00 None: 100,000.00
Spanish (Modern)	Local: 10.000.000 Pts International: ESP10.000.000 None: 10.000.000
Spanish (Standard)	Local: 10.000.000 Pts International: ESP10.000.000 None: 10.000.000
Swedish	Local: 100.000,00 kr International: SEK100.000,00 None: 100.000,00

LSDateFormat

Formats the date portion of a date/time value using the locale convention. Like DateFormat, LSDateFormat returns a formatted date/time value. If no mask is specified, LSDateFormat returns a date value using the locale-specific format.

Syntax

LSDateFormat(*date* [, *mask*])

date: Date/time object in the period from A.D. 100 to A.D. 9999.

mask: Set of characters that are used to show how ColdFusion should display the date:

- d—Day of the month as digits with no leading zero for single-digit days.
- dd—Day of the month as digits with a leading zero for single-digit days.
- ddd—Day of the week as a three-letter abbreviation.
- dddd—Day of the week as its full name.
- m—Month as digits with no leading zero for single-digit months.
- mm—Month as digits with a leading zero for single-digit months.
- mmm—Month as a three-letter abbreviation.
- mmmm—Month as its full name.
- y—Year as last two digits with no leading zero for years less than 10.
- yy—Year as last two digits with a leading zero for years less than 10.
- yyyy—Year represented by four digits.
- gg—Period/era string. Currently ignored, but reserved for future use

Usage

When passing date/time value as a string, make sure it is enclosed in quotes. Otherwise, it is interpreted as a number representation of a date/time object, returning undesired results.

LSEuroCurrencyFormat

Returns a currency value using the convention of the locale and the Euro as the currency symbol. Default value is "local." *Note:* The locale is set with the SetLocale function. See also LSParseEuroCurrency, LSCurrencyFormat, and SetLocale.

Syntax

LSEuroCurrencyFormat(*currency-number* [, *type*])

currency-number: The currency value.

type: Currency type. Valid arguments are:

- none—(For example, 10.00)
- local—Default. (For example, 10.00 ?)
- international—(For example, EUR10.00)

Usage

The LSEuroCurrencyFormat function can display the Euro symbol (€) only on Euro-enabled computers, such as Windows NT 4.0 SP4, that have Euro-enabled fonts installed.

This function is similar to LSCurrencyFormat, except that LSEuroCurrencyFormat displays the Euro currency symbol (€) or the international Euro sign (EUR) if you specify the type as local or international, respectively, and the Euro is the accepted currency of the locale.

The following list shows sample currency output for some of the locales supported by ColdFusion in each of the format types: local, international, and none.

Locale	**Format Type Output**
Dutch (Belgian)	Local: 100.000,00 € International: EUR100.000,00 None: 100.000,00
Dutch (Standard)	Local: € 100.000,00 International: EUR100.000,00 None: 100.000,00
English (Australian)	Local: €100,000.00 International: EUR100,000.00 None: 100,000.00
English (Canadian)	Local: €100,000.00 International: EUR100,000.00 None: 100,000.00
English (New Zealand)	Local: €100,000.00 International: EUR100,000.00 None: 100,000.00
English (UK)	Local: €100,000.00 International: EUR100,000.00 None: 100,000.00
English (US)	Local: €100,000.00 International: EUR100,000.00 None: 100,000.00
French (Belgian)	Local: 100.000,00 € International: EUR100.000,00 None: 100.000,00
French (Canadian)	Local: 100 000,00 € International: EUR100 000,00 None: 100 000,00
French (Standard)	Local: 100 000,00 € International: EUR100 000,00 None: 100 000,00

French (Swiss)	Local: € 100'000.00 International: EUR100'000.00 None: 100'000.00
German (Austrian)	Local: € 100.000,00 International: EUR100.000,00 None: 100.000,00
German (Standard)	Local: 100.000,00 € International: EUR100.000,00 None: 100.000,00
German (Swiss)	Local: € 100'000.00 International: EUR100'000.00 None: 100'000.00
Italian (Standard)	Local: € 10.000.000 International: EUR10.000.000 None: 10.000.000
Italian (Swiss)	Local: € 100'000.00 International: EUR100'000.00 None: 100'000.00
Norwegian (Bokmal)	Local: € 100 000,00 International: EUR100 000,00 None: 100 000,00
Norwegian (Nynorsk)	Local: € 100 000,00 International: EUR100 000,00 None: 100 000,00
Portuguese (Brazilian)	Local: €100.000,00 International: EUR100.000,00 None: 100.000,00
Portuguese (Standard)	Local: €100.000,00 International: EUR100.000,00 None: 100.000,00
Spanish (Mexican)	Local: €100,000.00 International: EUR100,000.00 None: 100,000.00
Spanish (Modern)	Local: 10.000.000 € International: EUR10.000.000 None: 10.000.000
Spanish (Standard)	Local: 10.000.000 € International: EUR10.000.000 None: 10.000.000
Swedish	Local: 100.000,00 € International: EUR100.000,00 None: 100.000,00

LSIsCurrency

Checks whether a string is a locale-specific currency string. Returns TRUE if string is a currency string, FALSE otherwise.

Syntax

LSIsCurrency(*string*)

string: The locale-specific currency string.

LSIsDate

Like the IsDate function, LSIsDate returns TRUE if string can be converted to a date/time value in the current locale, FALSE otherwise.

Syntax

LSIsDate(*string*)

string: Any string value.

Usage

Years less than 100 are interpreted as 20th-century values.

LSIsNumeric

Like the IsNumeric function, LSIsNumeric returns TRUE if string can be converted to a number in the current locale; otherwise, FALSE.

Syntax

LSIsNumeric(*string*)

string: Any string value.

LSNumberFormat

Formats a number using the locale convention. If mask is omitted, the number is formatted as an integer.

Syntax

LSNumberFormat(*number* [, *mask*])

number: The number you want to format.

mask: All LSNumberFormat mask characters apply except that ($) dollar, (,) comma, and (.) dot are mapped to their locale-specific counterparts.

LSNumberFormat Mask Characters:

Character	Meaning
_ (underscore)	Optional digit placeholder.
9	Optional digit placeholder. Same as _, but shows decimal places more clearly.
.	Specifies the location of a mandatory decimal point.
0	Located to the left or right of a mandatory decimal point, to force padding with zeros.
( )	Places parentheses around the mask if the number is less than 0.
+	Places + in front of positive numbers, – (minus sign) in front of negative numbers.
-	Place " " (space) in front of positive, – (minus sign) in front of negative numbers.
,	Separates thousands with commas.
L,C	Specifies left-justify or center-justify a number within the width of the mask column. L or C must appear as the first character of the mask. By default, numbers are right-justified.
$	Places a dollar sign in front of the formatted number. $ must appear as the first character of the mask.
^	Separates left from right formatting.

Note: If you do not specify a sign for the mask, positive and negative numbers will not align in columns. As a result, if you expect to display both positive and negative numbers in your application, use either the space or use - (hyphen) to force a space in front of positive numbers and a minus sign in front of negative numbers.

Usage

The position of codes in format masks determines where those codes will have effect. For example, if you place a dollar sign character at the far left of a format mask, ColdFusion displays a dollar sign at the very left edge of the formatted number. If you separate the dollar sign on the left edge of the format mask by at least one underscore, ColdFusion displays the dollar sign just to the left of the digits in the formatted number.

In all examples below, the numbers under the masks and the formatted output are used to clearly show the positions of characters.

Number	Mask	Result
4.37	$____.__	"$ 4.37"
4.37	_$___.__	" $4.37"
	12345678	12345678

This positioning idea can also be used to show where to place the – (minus sign) for negative numbers:

Number	Mask	Result
–4.37	–____.__	"– 4.37"
–4.37	_–___.__	" –4.37"
	12345678	12345678

There are four possible positions for any code character: far left, near left, near right, and far right. The left and right positions are determined by the side of the decimal point the code character is shown on. For formats that do not have a fixed number of decimal places, you can use a ^ (caret) to separate the left fields from the right.

Whether the code is placed in the far or near position is determined by the use of _ (underscore). Most code characters will have their effect determined by which of these of fields they are located in. The following example shows how to use the field to determine exactly where to place parentheses to display negative numbers:

Number	Mask	Result
3.21	C(_^_)	"(3.21)"
3.21	C_(^_)	" (3.21)"
3.21	C(_^)_	"(3.21) "
3.21	C_(^)_	" (3.21) "

LSParseCurrency

Converts a locale-specific currency string to a number. Attempts conversion through each of the three default currency formats (none, local, international). Returns the number matching the value of string. See also LSCurrencyFormat and LSParseEuroCurrency.

Syntax

LSParseCurrency(*string*)

string: The locale-specific string you want to convert to a number.

Currency Output

The following list shows sample currency output for some of the locales supported by ColdFusion in each of the format types: local, international, and none.

Locale	Format Type Output
Dutch (Belgian)	Local: 100.000,00 BFInternational: BEF100.000,00 None: 100.000,00
Dutch (Standard)	Local: fl 100.000,00 International: NLG100.000,00 None: 100.000,00
English (Australian)	Local: $100,000.00 International: AUD100,000.00 None: 100,000.00
English (Canadian)	Local: $100,000.00 International: CAD100,000.00 None: 100,000.00
English (New Zealand)	Local: $100,000.00 International: NZD100,000.00 None: 100,000.00
English (UK)	Local: £100,000.00 International: GBP100,000.00 None: 100,000.00
English (US)	Local: $100,000.00 International: USD100,000.00 None: 100,000.00
French (Belgian)	Local: 100.000,00 FB International: BEF100.000,00 None: 100.000,00
French (Canadian)	Local: 100 000,00 $ International: CAD100 000,00 None: 100 000,00
French (Standard)	Local: 100 000,00 F International: FRF100 000,00 None: 100 000,00
French (Swiss)	Local: SFr. 100'000.00 International: CHF100'000.00 None: 100'000.00
German (Austrian)	Local: öS 100.000,00 International: ATS100.000,00 None: 100.000,00
German (Standard)	Local: 100.000,00 DM International: DEM100.000,00 None: 100.000,00
German (Swiss)	Local: SFr. 100'000.00 International: CHF100'000.00 None: 100'000.00

Italian (Standard)	Local: L. 10.000.000 International: ITL10.000.000 None: 10.000.000
Italian (Swiss)	Local: SFr. 100'000.00 International: CHF100'000.00 None: 100'000.00
Norwegian (Bokmal)	Local: kr 100 000,00 International: NOK100 000,00 None: 100 000,00
Norwegian (Nynorsk)	Local: kr 100 000,00 International: NOK100 000,00 None: 100 000,00
Portuguese (Brazilian)	Local: R$100.000,00 International: BRC100.000,00 None: 100.000,00
Portuguese (Standard)	Local: R$100.000,00 International: BRC100.000,00 None: 100.000,00
Spanish (Mexican)	Local: $100,000.00 International: MXN100,000.00 None: 100,000.00
Spanish (Modern)	Local: 10.000.000 Pts International: ESP10.000.000 None: 10.000.000
Spanish (Standard)	Local: 10.000.000 Pts International: ESP10.000.000 None: 10.000.000
Swedish	Local: 100.000,00 kr International: SEK100.000,00 None: 100.000,00

LSParseDateTime

A locale-specific version of the ParseDateTime function, except that there is no option for POP date/time object parsing. Returns a date/time object. See also ParseDateTime and SetLocale.

Syntax

LSParseDateTime(*date-time-string*)

date-time-string: String being converted to date/time object. This string must be in a form that is readable in the current locale setting. By default the locale is set to English (US).

Usage

When passing a date/time value for the English (US) locale, the date-time string can be in any of the following forms:

Date-Time Composition	Example
dd mmmm yyyy	"25 January 1999"
hh:mm:ss	"8:30:00"
hh:mm:ss	"20:30:00"
mmmm dd, yyyy hh:mm:ss	"January 25, 1999 8:30:00"
hh:mm:ss mmm. dd, yyyy	"8:30:00 Jan. 25, 1999"
m/dd/yyyy hh:mm:ss	"1/25/1999 8:30:00"

Note that if you specify a year in the date, you should specify the full year.

If the date is formatted for a locale other than the English (US) locale, add or subtract the conversion time, depending on the locale. LSParseDateTime does not accept POP dates, nor does it have the capacity to convert dates to Greenwich Mean Time.

Years from 0 to 29 are interpreted as 21st-century values. Years from 30 to 99 are interpreted as 20th-century values.

LSParseEuroCurrency

Converts a locale-specific currency string that contains the Euro symbol (?) or sign (EUR) to a number. Attempts conversion through each of the three default currency formats (none, local, international). Returns the number matching the value of string. See also LSParseCurrency, LSEuroCurrencyFormat, and SetLocale.

Syntax

LSParseEuroCurrency(*currency-string*)

currency-string: The locale-specific string you want to convert to a number.

Usage

The LSParseEuroCurrency function can read the Euro symbol (€) only on Euro-enabled computers, such as Windows NT 4.0 SP4, that have Euro-enabled fonts installed.

This function is similar to LSParseCurrency, except that LSParseEuroCurrency parses only the Euro currency symbol (€) or the international Euro sign (EUR), not other currency symbols such as the dollar sign ($) or the pound sign (£).

LSParseNumber

Converts a locale-specific string to a number. Returns the number matching the value of string.

Syntax

LSParseNumber(*string*)

string: String being converted to a number.

LSTimeFormat

Returns a custom-formatted time value using the locale convention. See also LSParseDateTime.

Syntax

LSTimeFormat(*time* [, *mask*])

string: Any date/time value or string convertible to a time value.

mask: A set of masking characters determining the format:

- h—Hours with no leading zero for single-digit hours. (Uses a 12-hour clock.)
- hh—Hours with a leading zero for single-digit hours. (Uses a 12-hour clock.)
- H—Hours with no leading zero for single-digit hours. (Uses a 24-hour clock.)
- HH—Hours with a leading zero for single-digit hours. (Uses a 24-hour clock.)
- m—Minutes with no leading zero for single-digit minutes.
- mm—Minutes with a leading zero for single-digit minutes.
- s—Seconds with no leading zero for single-digit seconds.
- ss—Seconds with a leading zero for single-digit seconds.
- t—Single-character time marker string, such as A or P. Ignored by some locales.
- tt—Multiple-character time marker string, such as AM or PM

Usage

When passing date/time value as a string, make sure it is enclosed in quotes. Otherwise, it is interpreted as a number representation of a date/time object returning undesired results.

LTrim

Returns string with leading spaces removed. See also RTrim and ToBase64.

Syntax

LTrim(*string*)

string: String being left-trimmed.

Max

Returns the maximum, or higher, value of two numbers. See also Min.

Syntax

Max(*number1, number2*)

number1, number2: Any numbers.

Mid

Returns count characters from string beginning at start position. See also Left, Len, and Right.

Syntax

Mid(*string, start, count*)

string: Any string.

start: Starting position for count.

count: Number of characters being returned.

Minute

Returns the ordinal for the minute, ranging from 0 to 59. See also DatePart, Hour, and Second.

Syntax

Minute(*date*)

date: Any date.

Usage

Years from 0 to 29 are interpreted as 21st-century values. Years from 30 to 99 are interpreted as 20th-century values. When passing a date/time value as a string, make sure it is enclosed in quotes. Otherwise, it is interpreted as a number representation of a date/time object, returning undesired results.

Month

Returns the ordinal for the month, ranging from 1 (January) to 12 (December). See also DatePart, MonthAsString, and Quarter.

Syntax

Month(*date*)

date: Any date.

Usage

Years from 0 to 29 are interpreted as 21st-century values. Years from 30 to 99 are interpreted as 20th-century values. When passing a date/time value as a string, make sure it is enclosed in quotes. Otherwise, it is interpreted as a number representation of a date/time object, returning undesired results.

MonthAsString

Returns the name of the month corresponding to month_number. See also DatePart, Month, and Quarter.

Syntax

MonthAsString(*month_number*)

month_number: An integer ranging from 1 to 12.

Now

Returns the current date and time as a valid date time object. See also CreateDateTime and DatePart.

Syntax

Now()

NumberFormat

Creates a custom-formatted number value. If no mask is specified, returns the value as an integer with a thousands separator. See also DecimalFormat, DollarFormat, and IsNumeric.

Syntax

NumberFormat(*number* [, *mask*])

number: The number you want to format.

mask: Set of characters that are used to show how ColdFusion should display the number.

Mask characters:

Character	Meaning
_ (underscore)	Optional digit placeholder.
9	Optional digit placeholder. Same as _, but shows decimal places more clearly.
.	Specifies the location of a mandatory decimal point.
0	Located to the left or right of a mandatory decimal point, to force padding with zeros.
( )	Places parentheses around the mask if the number is less than 0.
+	Places + in front of positive numbers, – (minus sign) in front of negative numbers.

Character	Meaning
–	Place " " (space) in front of positive, – (minus sign) in front of negative numbers.
,	Separates thousands with commas.
L,C	Specifies left-justify or center-justify a number within the width of the mask column. L or C must appear as the first character of the mask. By default, numbers are right-justified.
$	Places a dollar sign in front of the formatted number. $ must appear as the first character of the mask.
^	Separates left from right formatting.

Note: If you do not specify a sign for the mask, positive and negative numbers will not align in columns. As a result, if you expect to display both positive and negative numbers in your application, either use the space or use – (minus sign) to force a space in front of positive numbers and a minus sign in front of negative numbers.

Usage

The position of codes in format masks determines where those codes will have effect. For example, if you place a dollar sign character at the far left of a format mask, ColdFusion displays a dollar sign at the very left edge of the formatted number. If you separate the dollar sign on the left edge of the format mask by at least one underscore, ColdFusion displays the dollar sign just to the left of the digits in the formatted number.

In all examples below, the numbers under the masks and the formatted output are used to clearly show the positions of characters.

Number	Mask	Result
4.37	$____.__	"$ 4.37"
4.37	–$___.__	" $4.37"
	12345678	12345678

This positioning idea can also be used to show where to place the – (minus sign) for negative numbers:

Number	Mask	Result
–4.37	–____.__	"– 4.37"
–4.37	_–___.__	" –4.37"
	12345678	12345678

There are four possible positions for any code character: far left, near left, near right, and far right. The left and right positions are determined by the side of the decimal point the code character is shown on. For formats that do not have a fixed number of decimal places, you can use a ^ (caret) to separate the left fields from the right.

Whether the code is placed in the far or near position is determined by the use of _ (underscore). Most code characters will have their effect determined by which of these of fields they are located in. The following example shows how to use the field to determine exactly where to place parentheses to display negative numbers:

Number	Mask	Result
3.21	C(__^__)	"(3.21)"
3.21	C__(^__)	" (3.21)"
3.21	C(__^)__	"(3.21) "
3.21	C__(^)__	" (3.21) "
	12345678	12345678

ParagraphFormat

Returns string with converted single newline characters (CR/LF sequences) into spaces and double newline characters into HTML paragraph markers (<P>). See also StripCR.

Syntax

ParagraphFormat(*string*)

string: String being converted to the HTML paragraph format.

Usage

ParagraphFormat is useful for displaying data entered into TEXTAREA fields.

ParameterExists

Returns TRUE if the specified parameter has been passed to the current template or has already been created during execution of the current template.

Otherwise returns NO. This function is provided for backward compatibility with previous versions of ColdFusion. You should use the function IsDefined instead. See also GetClientVariablesList and IsDefined.

Syntax

parameterExists(*parameter*)

parameter: Any syntactically valid parameter name.

ParseDateTime

Returns a date/time object from a string. See also LSParseDateTime, IsDate, and IsNumericDate.

Syntax

ParseDateTime(*date-time-string* [, *pop-conversion*])

date-time-string: String being converted to date/time object.

pop-conversion: POP or STANDARD. If you specify POP, the function takes the date/time string passed from a POP mail server and converts it to GMT (Greenwich Mean Time) for the English (US) locale. If you specify STANDARD or nothing, the function provides no conversion. See the Note for more information about parsing date-time strings that are not from the English (US) locale.

Usage

ParseDateTime is similar to CreateDateTime, except that it takes a string instead of specifically enumerated date/time values. Both ParseDateTime and CreateDateTime are provided primarily to increase the readability of code in compound expressions. Years from 0 to 29 are interpreted as 21st-century values. Years from 30 to 99 are interpreted as 20th-century values. When passing a date/time value as a string, make sure it is enclosed in quotes. Otherwise, it is interpreted as a number representation of a date/time object, returning undesired results.

Note: If the date is formatted for a locale other than the English (US) locale, you need to use the LSParseDateTime() function, then add or subtract the conversion time, depending on the locale. LSParseDateTime does not accept POP dates, nor does it have the capacity to convert dates to Greenwich Mean Time.

Pi

Returns the number 3.14159265358979, the mathematical constant, accurate to 15 digits. See also ASin, Cos, Sin, and Tan.

Syntax

Pi()

PreserveSingleQuotes

Prevents ColdFusion from automatically "escaping" single quotes contained in variable.

Syntax

PreserveSingleQuotes(*variable*)

> *variable:* Variable containing the string for which single quotes are preserved.

Usage

PreserveSingleQuotes is useful in SQL statements.

Quarter

Returns the number of the quarter, an integer ranging from 1 to 4. See also DatePart and Month.

Syntax

Quarter(*date*)

> *date:* Any date.

Usage

Years from 0 to 29 are interpreted as 21st-century values. Years from 30 to 99 are interpreted as 20th-century values.

When passing a date/time value as a string, make sure it is enclosed in quotes. Otherwise, it is interpreted as a number representation of a date/time object, returning undesired results.

QueryAddColumn

Adds a new column to a specified query and populates the column's rows with the contents of a one-dimensional array. Returns the query object with the additional column. Padding is added, if necessary, on the query columns to ensure that all columns have the same number of rows. See also CFQUERY, QueryNew, QueryAddRow, and QuerySetCell.

Syntax

QueryAddColumn(*query, column-name, array-name*)

query: Name of a query that was created with QueryNew.

column-name: The name of the new column.

array-name: The name of the array whose elements are to populate the new column.

Usage

You can add columns to any type of query object, such as queries retrieved with CFQUERY or queries created with QueryNew. The only type of query that you cannot use QueryAddColumn on is a cached query.

This function is particularly useful if you are an Oracle developer and would like to generate a query object from the arrays of output parameters which Oracle stored procedures can generate. Padding is added, if necessary, on the query columns to ensure that all columns have the same number of rows.

QueryAddRow

Adds a specified number of empty rows to the specified query. Returns the total number of rows in the query that you are adding rows to. See also QueryNew, QueryAddColumn, and QuerySetCell.

Syntax

QueryAddRow(*query* [, *number*])

query: Name of the query already executed.

number: Number of rows to add to the query. Default is 1.

QueryNew

Returns an empty query with a set of columns or an empty query with no columns. See Usage for more information. See also QueryAddColumn, QueryAddRow, and QuerySetCell.

Syntax

QueryNew(*columnlist*)

columnlist: Comma-separated list of columns you want to add to the new query or an empty string.

Usage

If you specify an empty string, you can add a new column to the query and populate its rows with the contents of a one-dimensional array using QueryAddColumn.

QuerySetCell

Sets the cell in a specified column to a specified value. If no row number is specified, the cell on the last row will be set. Returns TRUE. See also QueryAddColumn and QueryAddRow.

Syntax

QuerySetCell(*query, column_name, value* [, *row_number*])

query: Name of the query already executed.

column_name: Name of the column in the query.

value: Value to set in the specified cell.

row_number: Number of the row. Defaults to last row.

QuotedValueList

Returns a comma-separated list of the values of each record returned from a previously executed query. Each value in the list is enclosed in single quotes. See also ValueList.

Syntax

QuotedValueList(*query.column* [, *delimiter*])

query.column: Name of an already executed query and column. Separate query name and column name with a period (.).

delimiter: A string delimiter to separate column data.

Rand

Returns a random decimal number in the range 0 to 1. See also Randomize and RandRange.

Syntax

Rand()

Usage

To ensure even greater randomness, call Randomize before calling Rand.

Randomize

Seeds the random number generator in ColdFusion with the integer part of a number. By seeding the random number generator with a variable value, you help to ensure that the Rand function generates highly random numbers. See also Rand and RandRange.

Syntax

Randomize(*number*)

number: Any number.

Usage

Call this function before calling Rand. Although this function returns a decimal number in the range 0 to 1, it is not a random number and you should not use it.

RandRange

Returns a random integer between two specified numbers. Note that requests for random integers greater than 100,000,000 will result in nonrandom behavior. This restriction prevents overflow during internal computations. See also Rand and Randomize.

Syntax

RandRange(*number1, number2*)

number1, number2: Integer numbers less than 100,000,000.

ReFind

Returns the position of the first occurrence of a regular expression in a string, starting from the specified position. Returns 0 if no occurrences are found. This search is case sensitive. Returns the position and length of the first occurrence of a regular expression in a string if the returnsubexpressions parameter is set to True. See the description of the returnsubexpressions parameter and the "Usage" section for details. See also Find, REFindNoCase, and REReplace.

Syntax

REFind(*reg_expression, string* [, *start*] [, *returnsubexpressions*])

reg_expression: Regular expression used for search. This regular expression can include POSIX-specified character classes (for example, [[:alpha:]], [[:digit:]], [[:upper:]], and [[:lower:]]).

string: String being searched.

start: Optional. Starting position for the search. Default is 1.

returnsubexpressions: Optional. A Boolean value indicating whether a substring is returned. If you set this parameter to

TRUE, the function returns a CFML structure composed of two arrays containing the position and length of the first substring that matches the criteria of the search. You can retrieve the position and length of the matching subexpression by using the keys "pos" and "len." If there are no occurrences of the regular expression, the "pos" and the "len" arrays each contain one element that has a value of zero. If you set this parameter to FALSE, a scalar value is returned indicating the position of the first occurrence of a regular expression. The default value of this parameter is FALSE.

Usage

In order to find multiple instances of a substring, you must call REFind more than once, each time with a different starting position. To determine the next starting position for the function, use the returnsubexpressions parameter and add the value returned in the position key to the value in the length key.

If you do not use parentheses in the regular expression, the returnsubexpressions parameter returns single element arrays that denote the position and length of the first match found in the string.

If you do use parentheses to denote subexpressions within the regular expression, the returnsubexpressions parameter returns the position and length of the first match of the regular expression in the first element of the respective arrays; the position and length of the first instance of each subexpression within the regular expression are returned in subsequent elements of the arrays.

ReFindNoCase

Returns the position of the first occurrence of a regular expression in a string, starting from the specified position if the returnsubexpressions parameter is not set to True. Returns 0 if no occurrences are found.The search is case insensitive. Returns the position and length of the first occurrence of a regular expression in a string if the returnsubexpressions parameter is set to True. See the description of the returnsubexpressions parameter and the "Usage" section for details. See also Find, FindNoCase, REReplace, and REReplaceNoCase.

Syntax

REFindNoCase(*reg_expression, string* [, *start*] [, *returnsubexpressions*]) *reg_expression:* Regular expression used for search. This regular expression can include POSIX-specified character classes (for example, [[:alpha:]], [[:digit:]], [[:upper:]], and [[:lower:]]).

string: String being searched.

start: Optional. Starting position for the search. Default is 1.

returnsubexpressions: Optional. A Boolean value indicating whether a substring is returned. If you set this parameter to TRUE, the function returns a CFML structure composed of two single-element arrays containing the position and length of the first substring that matches the criteria of the search. You can retrieve the position and length of the matching subexpression by using the keys "pos" and "len." If there are no occurrences of the regular expression, the "pos" and the "len" arrays each contain one element that has a value of zero. If you set this parameter to FALSE, a scalar value is returned indicating the position of the first occurrence of a regular expression. The default value of this parameter is FALSE.

Usage

In order to find multiple instances of a substring, you must call REFind more than once, each time with a different starting position. To determine the next starting position for the function, use the returnsubexpressions parameter and add the value returned in the position key to the value in the length key.

If you do not use parentheses in the regular expression, the returnsubexpressions parameter returns single element arrays that denote the position and length of the first match found in the string.

If you do use parentheses to denote subexpressions within the regular expression, the returnsubexpressions parameter returns the position and length of the first match of the regular expression in the first element of the respective arrays; the position and length of the first instance of each subexpression within the regular expression are returned in subsequent elements of the arrays.

RemoveChars

Returns string with count characters removed from the specified starting position. Returns 0 if no characters are found. See also Insert and Len.

Syntax

RemoveChars(*string, start, count*)

string: Any string.
start: Starting position for the search.
count: Number of characters being removed.

RepeatString

Returns a string created from a string's being repeated a specified number of times. See also CJustify, LJustify, and RJustify.

Syntax

RepeatString(*string, count*)

string: String being repeated.

count: Number of repeats.

Replace

Returns string with occurrences of substring1 being replaced with substring2 in the specified scope. See also Find, ReplaceNoCase, ReplaceList, and REReplace.

Syntax

Replace(*string, substring1, substring2* [, *scope*])

string: Any string.
substring1: String to be replaced.
substring2: String that should replace occurrences of substring1.
scope: Defines how to complete the replace operation:

- ONE—Replace only the first occurrence (default).
- ALL—Replace all occurrences.

ReplaceList

Returns string with all occurrences of the elements from the specified comma-delimited list being replaced with their corresponding elements from another comma-delimited list. The search is case sensitive. See also Find, Replace, and REReplace.

Syntax

ReplaceList(*string, list1, list2*)

string: Any string.

list1: Comma-delimited list of substrings to be replaced.

list2: Comma-delimited list of replace substrings.

Usage

Note that the list of substrings to be replaced is processed one after another. In this way you may experience recursive replacement if one of your list1 elements is contained in list2 elements.

ReplaceNoCase

Returns string with occurrences of substring1 being replaced regardless of case matching with substring2 in the specified scope. See also Find, Replace, ReplaceList, and REReplace.

Syntax

ReplaceNoCase(*string, substring1, substring2* [, *scope*])

string: Any string.

substring1: String to be replaced.

substring2: String that should replace occurrences of substring1.

scope: Defines how to complete the replace operation:

- ONE—Replace only the first occurrence (default).
- ALL—Replace all occurrences.

ReReplace

Returns string with a regular expression being replaced with substring in the specified scope. This is a case-sensitive search. See also REFind, Replace, ReplaceList, and REReplaceNoCase.

Syntax

REReplace(*string, reg_expression, substring* [, *scope*])

string: Any string.

reg_expression: Regular expression to be replaced. This regular expression can include POSIX-specified character classes (for example, [:alpha:], [:digit:], [:upper:], and [:lower:]).

substring: String replacing reg_expression.

scope: Defines how to complete the replace operation:

- ONE—Replace only the first occurrence (default).
- ALL—Replace all occurrences.

ReReplaceNoCase

Returns string with a regular expression being replaced with substring in the specified scope. The search is case insensitive. See also REFind, REFindNoCase, Replace, and ReplaceList.

Syntax

REReplaceNoCase(*string, reg_expression, substring* [, *scope*])

string: Any string.

reg_expression: Regular expression to be replaced. This regular expression can include POSIX-specified character classes (for example, [:alpha:], [:digit:], [:upper:], and [:lower:]).

substring: String replacing *reg_expression*.

scope: Defines how to complete the replace operation:

- ONE—Replace only the first occurrence (default).
- ALL—Replace all occurrences.

Reverse

Returns string with reversed order of characters. See also Left, Mid, and Right.

Syntax

Reverse(*string*)

string: String being reversed.

Right

Returns the rightmost count characters of a string. See also Left, Len, and Mid.

Syntax

Right(*string, count*)

string: String from which the rightmost characters are retrieved.

count: Integer indicating how many characters to return.

RJustify

Returns right-justified string in the specified field length. See also CJustify and LJustify.

Syntax

RJustify(*string, length*)

string: String to be right-justified.

length: Length of field.

Round

Rounds a number to the closest integer. See also Ceiling, Fix, and Int.

Syntax

Round(*number*)

number: Number being rounded.

RTrim

Returns string with removed trailing spaces. See also LTrim and Trim.

Syntax

RTrim(*string*)

string: String being right-trimmed.

Second

For a date/time value, returns the ordinal for the second, an integer from 0 to 59. See also DatePart, Hour, and Minute.

Syntax

Second(*date*)

date: Any date.

Usage

When passing a date/time value as a string, make sure it is enclosed in quotes. Otherwise, it is interpreted as a number representation of a date/time object, returning undesired results.

SetLocale

Sets the locale to the specified new locale for the current session. *Note:* SetLocale returns the old locale in case it needs to be restored. See also GetLocale.

Syntax

SetLocale(*new_locale*)

new_locale: The name of the locale you want to set.

ColdFusion can be expected to support the following locales in a default Windows NT installation:

Dutch (Belgian)	French (Canadian)	Norwegian (Bokmal)
Dutch (Standard)	French (Standard)	Norwegian (Nynorsk)
English (Australian)	French (Swiss)	Portuguese (Brazilian)
English (Canadian)	German (Austrian)	Portuguese (Standard)
English (New Zealand)	German (Standard)	Spanish (Mexican)
English (UK)	German (Swiss)	Spanish (Modern)
English (US)	Italian (Standard)	Spanish (Standard)
French (Belgian)	Italian (Swiss)	Swedish

Note that the variable Server.ColdFusion.SupportedLocales is initialized at startup with a comma-delimited list of the locales that ColdFusion and the operating system support. GetLocale( ) will return an entry from that list. SetLocale will fail if called with a locale name not on that list.

SetProfileString

Sets the value of a profile entry in an initialization file. This function returns an empty string if the operation succeeds or an error message if it fails. See also GetProfileString.

Syntax

SetProfileString(*iniPath, section, entry, value*)

iniPath: Fully qualified path (drive, directory, filename, and extension) of the initialization file.

section: The section of the initialization file in which the entry is to be set.

entry: The name of the entry that is to be set.

value: The value to which to set the entry.

SetVariable

This function sets the variable specified by name to value and returns the new value of the variable. See also DeleteClientVariable and GetClientVariablesList.

Syntax

SetVariable(*name, value*)

name: Valid variable name.

value: String or number assigned to the variable.

Usage

When setting client variables, it is required that the client variable exists prior to using this function and that the ClientManagement attribute of CFAPPLICATION tag has been set to "Yes" for this template.

Sgn

Determines the sign of a number. Returns 1 if number is positive; 0 if number is 0; and −1 if number is negative. See also Abs.

Syntax

Sgn(*number*)

number: Any number.

Sin

Returns the sine of the given angle. See also ASin, Atn, Cos, Pi, and Tan.

Syntax

Sin(*number*)

number: Angle in radians for which you want the sine. If the angle is in degrees, multiply it by π()/180 to convert it to radians.

SpanExcluding

Returns all characters from string from its beginning until it reaches a character from the set of characters. The search is case sensitive. See also GetToken and SpanIncluding.

Syntax

SpanExcluding(*string, set*)

string: Any string.

set: String containing one or more characters being sought.

SpanIncluding

Returns all characters from string from its beginning until it reaches a character that is not included in the specified set of characters. The search is case sensitive. See also GetToken and SpanExcluding.

Syntax

SpanIncluding(*string, set*)

string: Any string.

set: String containing one or more characters being sought.

Sqr

Returns a positive square root. See also Abs.

Syntax

Sqr(*number*)

number: Number for which you want the square root.

Usage

Number must be greater than or equal to 0.

StripCr

Returns string with all carriage return characters removed. See also ParagraphFormat.

Syntax

StripCR(*string*)

string: String being formatted.

Usage

Function StripCR is useful for preformatted HTML display of data (PRE) entered into TEXTAREA fields.

StructClear

Removes all data from the specified structure. Always returns Yes. See also StructDelete, StructFind, StructInsert, StructIsEmpty, StructKeyArray, StructCount, StructKeyArray, and StructUpdate.

Syntax

StructClear(*structure*)

structure: Structure to be cleared.

StructCopy

Returns a new structure with all the keys and values of the specified structure. See also StructClear, StructDelete, StructFind, StructInsert, StructIsEmpty, StructKeyArray, StructKeyArray, and StructUpdate.

Syntax

StructCopy(*structure*)

structure: Structure to be copied.

Usage

This function throws an exception if structure does not exist.

StructCount

Returns the number of keys in the specified structure. See also StructClear, StructDelete, StructFind, StructInsert, StructIsEmpty, StructKeyArray, StructKeyArray, and StructUpdate.

Syntax

StructCount(*structure*)

structure: Structure to be accessed.

Usage

This function throws an exception if structure does not exist.

StructDelete

Removes the specified item from the specified structure. See also StructClear, StructFind, StructInsert, StructIsEmpty, StructKeyArray, StructCount, StructKeyArray, and StructUpdate.

Syntax

StructDelete(*structure, key* [, *indicatenotexisting*])

structure: Structure containing the item to be removed.

key: Item to be removed.

indicatenotexisting: Indicates whether the function returns FALSE if key does not exist. The default is FALSE, which means that the function returns Yes regardless of whether key exists. If you specify TRUE for this parameter, the function returns Yes if key exists and No if it does not.

StructFind

Returns the value associated with the specified key in the specified structure. See also StructClear, StructDelete, StructInsert, StructIsEmpty, StructKeyArray, StructCount, StructKeyArray, and StructUpdate.

Syntax

StructFind(*structure, key*)

structure: Structure containing the value to be returned.

key: Key whose value is returned.

Usage

This function throws an exception if structure does not exist.

StructInsert

Inserts the specified key-value pair into the specified structure. Returns Yes if the insert was successful and No if an error occurs. See also StructClear, StructDelete, StructFind, StructIsEmpty, StructKeyArray, StructCount, StructKeyArray, and StructUpdate.

Syntax

StructInsert(*structure, key, value* [, *allowoverwrite*])

structure: Structure to contain the new key-value pair.

key: Key that contains the inserted value.

value: Value to be added.

allowoverwrite: Optionally indicates whether to allow overwriting an existing key. The default is FALSE.

Usage

This function throws an exception if structure does not exist or if key exists and *allowoverwrite* is set to FALSE.

StructIsEmpty

Indicates whether the specified structure contains data. Returns TRUE if structure is empty and FALSE if it contains data. See also StructClear, StructDelete, StructFind, StructInsert, StructKeyArray, StructCount, StructKeyArray, and StructUpdate.

Syntax

StructIsEmpty(*structure*)

structure: Structure to be tested.

Usage

This function throws an exception if structure does not exist.

StructKeyArray

Returns an array of the keys in the specified ColdFusion structure. See also StructClear, StructDelete, StructFind, StructInsert, StructIsEmpty, StructKeyList, StructKeyExists, StructCount, and StructUpdate.

Syntax

StructKeyArray(*structure*)

structure: Structure from which the list of keys is to be extracted.

Usage

The array of keys returned by StructKeyArray is not in any particular order. In order to sort keys alphabetically or numerically, use ArraySort. Note that this function throws an exception if structure does not exist.

StructKeyExists

Returns TRUE if the specified key is in the specified structure and FALSE if it is not. See also StructClear, StructDelete, StructFind, StructInsert, StructIsEmpty, StructCount, StructKeyArray, and StructUpdate.

Syntax

StructKeyExists(*structure, key*)

structure: Structure to be tested.

key: Key to be tested.

Usage

This function throws an exception if structure does not exist.

StructKeyList

Returns the list of keys that are in the specified ColdFusion structure. See also StructKeyArray, StructClear, StructDelete, StructFind, StructInsert, StructIsEmpty, StructCount, and StructUpdate.

Syntax

StructKeyList(*structure,* [*delimiter*])

structure: Structure from which the list of keys are to be extracted.

delimiter: Optional. The value of this parameter indicates the character that will separate the keys in the list. By default, a comma (,) is used.

Usage

The list of keys returned by StructKeyList is not in any particular order. In order to sort keys alphabetically or numerically, use ListSort. Note that this function throws an exception if structure does not exist.

StructNew

Returns a new structure. See also StructClear, StructDelete, StructFind, StructInsert, StructIsEmpty, StructKeyArray, StructCount, and StructUpdate.

Syntax

StructNew()

StructSort

StructSort returns an array of structures containing top-level key names (strings) sorted according to the value of the specified sub-element. The value of the keys may be simple values or complex elements.

Syntax

StructSort(*Base* [*sortType, SortOrder, PathtoSubElement*])

base: A structure with one field (an associative array).

sorttype: may be "numeric," "text," or "textnocase." Default is "text."

sortorder: may be "ASC" (default) or "DESC."

pathtosubelement: specifies the path to apply to each of the top-level keys in order to reach the element whose value you wish to sort by. If unspecified, it defaults to nothing, meaning that the top-level entries will be sorted based on their own values.

Usage

The pathtosubelement string does not support array notation so only sub-structures of structures are supported.

StructUpdate

Updates the specified key with the specified value. Returns Yes if the function is successful and throws an exception if an error occurs. See also StructClear, StructDelete, StructFind, StructInsert, StructIsEmpty, StructKeyArray, StructCount, and StructKeyArray.

Syntax

StructUpdate(*structure, key, value*)

structure: Structure to be updated.
key: Key whose value is updated.
value: New value.

Usage

This function throws an exception if structure does not exist.

Tan

Returns the tangent of a given angle. See also Atn, ASin, Cos, Sin, and Pi.

Syntax

Tan(*number*)

number: Angle in radians for which you want the tangent. If the angle is in degrees, multiply it by $\pi()/180$ to convert it to radians.

TimeFormat

Returns a custom-formatted time value. If no mask is specified, the TimeFormat function returns time value using the hh:mm tt format. See also CreateTime, Now, and ParseDateTime.

Syntax

TimeFormat(*time* [, *mask*])

time: Any date/time value or string convertible to a time value.

mask: A set of masking characters determining the format:

- h—Hours with no leading zero for single-digit hours (uses a 12-hour clock)
- hh—Hours with a leading zero for single-digit hours (uses a 12-hour clock)
- H—Hours with no leading zero for single-digit hours (uses a 24-hour clock)
- HH—Hours with a leading zero for single-digit hours (uses a 24-hour clock)

- m—Minutes with no leading zero for single-digit minutes
- mm—Minutes with a leading zero for single-digit minutes
- s—Seconds with no leading zero for single-digit seconds
- ss—Seconds with a leading zero for single-digit seconds
- t—Single-character time marker string, such as A or P
- tt—Multiple-character time marker string, such as AM or PM

Usage

When passing a date/time value as a string, make sure it is enclosed in quotes. Otherwise, it is interpreted as a number representation of a date/time object, returning undesired results.

ToBase64

Returns the Base 64 representation of the string or binary object. Base64 is a format that uses printable characters, allowing binary data to be sent in forms and email and stored in a database or file. See also CFFILE for information about loading and reading binary data, CFWDDX for information about serializing and deserializing binary data, and IsBinary and ToBinary for checking for binary data and converting a Base 64 object to binary form.

Syntax

ToBase64(*string or binary_object*)

> *string or binary_object:* String or binary object that is to be converted to Base 64.

Usage

Base 64 provides 6-bit encoding of 8-bit ASCII characters. Because high ASCII values and binary objects are not safe for transport over Internet protocols such as HTTP and SMTP, ColdFusion offers Base 64 as a means to safely send ASCII and binary data over these protocols. In addition, Base 64 allows you to store binary objects in a database if you convert the data into Base 64 first.

ToBinary

Returns the binary representation of Base64 encoded data. See CFFILE for information about loading and reading binary data, CFWDDX for information about serializing and deserializing binary data, and IsBinary and ToBase64 for checking for binary data and converting it into printable form. See also Len for determining the length of a binary object.

Syntax

ToBinary(*string_in_Base64 or binary_value*)

string_in_Base64 or binary_value: String in Base 64 that is to be converted to binary or binary value that is to be tested to ensure that it is an acceptable binary value.

Usage

Base 64 provides 6-bit encoding of 8-bit ASCII characters. If you receive data in Base 64, you can re-create the actual binary object that it represents, such as a .gif , .jpeg, or executable file, by using the ToBinary function.

ToString

Attempts to convert a value of any type, including a binary value, into a string.

Syntax

ToString(*any_value*)

any_value: The value that is to be converted into a string.

Usage

If ToString cannot convert the value into a string, it throws an exception. All simple values can be converted into a string, even binary values that do not contain byte zero can be converted.

Trim

Returns string with both leading and trailing spaces removed. See also LTrim and RTrim.

Syntax

Trim(*string*)

string: String being trimmed.

UCase

Returns string converted to uppercase. See also LCase.

Syntax

UCase(*string*)

string: String being converted to uppercase.

URLDecode

Decodes a URL-encoded string. See also URLEncodedFormat.

Syntax

URLDecode(*urlEncodedString*)

urlEncodedString: A string that has been URL-encoded.

Usage

URL encoding refers to a data format where all high ASCII and nonalphanumeric characters are encoded using a percent sign followed by the two-character hexadecimal representation of the character code. For example, a character with code 129 will be encoded as %81. In addition, spaces can be encoded using the plus sign (+). Query strings in HTTP are always URL-encoded. URL-encoded strings can be created using the URLEncodedFormat function.

URLEncodedFormat

Returns a URL-encoded string. Spaces are replaced with +, and all nonalphanumeric characters with equivalent hexadecimal escape sequences. This function enables you to pass arbitrary strings within a URL, because ColdFusion automatically decodes all URL parameters that are passed to the template. See also URLDecode.

Syntax

URLEncodedFormat(*string*)

string: String being URL encoded.

Usage

URL encoding refers to a data format where all high ASCII and nonalphanumeric characters are encoded using a percent sign followed by the two-character hexadecimal representation of the character code. For example, a character with code 129 will be encoded as %81. In addition, spaces can be encoded using the plus sign (+). Query strings in HTTP are always URL-encoded. URL-encoded strings can be created using the URLEncodedFormat function.

Val

Returns a number that the beginning of a string can be converted to. Returns 0 if conversion is not possible. See also IsNumeric.

Syntax

Val(*string*)

string: Any string.

ValueList

Returns a comma-separated list of the values of each record returned from a previously executed query. See also QuotedValueList.

Syntax

ValueList(*query.column* [, *delimiter*])

query.column: Name of an already executed query and column. Separate query name and column name with a period (.).

delimiter: A string delimiter to separate column data.

Week

Returns the ordinal for the week number in a year, an integer ranging from 1 to 53. See also DatePart.

Syntax

Week(*date*)

date: Any date/time value or string convertible to date.

Usage

Years from 0 to 29 are interpreted as 21st-century values. Years from 30 to 99 are interpreted as 20th-century values. When passing date as a string, make sure it is enclosed in quotes. Otherwise, it is interpreted as a number representation of a date, returning undesired results.

WriteOutput

Appends text to the page output stream. Although you can call this function anywhere within a page, it is most useful inside a CFSCRIPT block. *Note:* When within the CFQUERY and CFMAIL tags, the WriteOutput function does not output to the current page, but instead writes to the current SQL statement or mail text. Do not use WriteOutput within CFQUERY and CFMAIL. This function writes to the page output stream regardless of conditions established by the CFSETTING tag.

Syntax

WriteOutput(*string*)

string: Text to be appended to the page output stream.

XMLFormat

Returns a string that is safe to use with XML.

Syntax

XMLFormat(*string*)

string: Any string.

Usage

XMLFormat escapes special XML characters so that you can put arbitrary strings safely into XML. The characters that are escaped by XMLFormat include the following:

greater than sign (>)
less than sign (<)
single quotation mark (')
double quotation mark (")
ampersand (&)

Year

Returns the year corresponding to date. See also DatePart and IsLeapYear.

Syntax

Year(*date*)

date: Any date/time value or string convertible to date.

Usage

Years from 0 to 29 are interpreted as 21st-century values. Years from 30 to 99 are interpreted as 20th-century values. When passing a date as a string, make sure it is enclosed in quotes. Otherwise, it is interpreted as a number representation of a date, returning undesired results.

YesNoFormat

Returns Boolean data as YES or NO. See also IsBinary and IsNumeric.

Syntax

YesNoFormat(*value*)

value: Any number or Boolean value.

Usage

The YesNoFormat function returns all nonzero values as YES and zero values as NO.

Appendix C

Common Errors and What to Do About Them

As you develop and debug your applications, you will undoubtedly come across many error messages. Often these error messages look frighteningly severe, when really it's just a matter of a simple typo somewhere in your code. Therefore, I have included this appendix as an aid in speeding up the debugging stage in your development. Here you can look up errors that you are likely to receive from your Web Server and from ColdFusion and see what is likely to be causing them. Then you can quickly get back to the fun stuff.

"Web Server Errors" is probably a misnomer; we might more correctly talk of HTTP errors, since the error codes and what they mean are platform neutral. That is, whatever action you take that causes an error will return the same error whether you're running Apache or IIS or what have you. I describe them this way to distinguish where in the process your page is triggering an error.

While there are a few bugs, here and there, and networks can occasionally act out due to their complexity, errors are almost always due to incorrectly written code. ColdFusion is a very stable, reliable platform. It doesn't act unpredictably. In my years of writing ColdFusion, I've encountered errors that couldn't ultimately be traced back to my own code *twice.* That's pretty good.

You're going to get errors. One comma out of place can crash your entire application. So, as passionately as you may shake your fist at your monitor, invoking all the dark arts as you swear your code is perfect, you might still take a moment and check over this list. *Just in case* ColdFusion is right . . . .

Web Server Errors

Some errors occur in the prepreprocessing stage in ColdFusion Application Server. Others are the result of badly formed requests, or web server errors. If you know what the errors mean, then you can more quickly infer the location of the code that's causing the error. You may even find that it is not your code at all that's causing the error, but rather something happening in the web server.

Status Codes

Every time you make an HTTP request, your web server returns back what are called *status codes.* A status code is a message indicating the success or failure of a web server's attempt to fulfill a request. Some status codes can indicate other things, too, such as the action taken.

There are actually five main levels of status codes, most of which the end user never sees. These are outlined in Table C.1.

Table C.1 Status Code Levels

Status Code Level	*Meaning*
100	Informational
200	Successful
300	Redirection
400	Client Errors
500	Internal Server Errors

Table C.1 indicates that any message you receive in the 400–499 range will be the result of a client error. Probably the status code you're most familiar with is the infamous "404 File Not Found" message. You see this message when the server is unable to fulfill your request because the resource (Web page) specified in your URL does not exist. This is an example of a client error, because the client (you and your little browser) asked for something impossible. You may also have seen Error 401, which indicates that you don't have the appropriate user credentials for accessing a resource, or Error 403 (Forbidden), which indicates a permission restriction on the files requested.

If you work on the web with any modicum of coherence, the status code you most frequently receive is 200. The contents of the 200 status code message are: "OK." This means that you asked for a particular page, and the server returned it to you successfully. You do not see this message, but it is in the response header. And, as you may quickly imagine, it is the stuff log files are made of. Let's take a look at the status code messages you're most likely to encounter and what they mean.

Table C.2 shows common client error messages (those in the 400 range) and what they are trying to tell you. If the client is sending data, an acknowledgement of a 4xx status code will suffice to close the connection.

Table C.2 Common Client Errors, What They Mean, and How to Fix Them

Error	*Meaning*
403	**Forbidden** Also "Permission Denied." This means that the server knows what you want it to do, but it doesn't want to do it. ColdFusion pages must reside in a directory with Execute permission. This error is most common on Microsoft's IIS; Netscape and O'Reilly Website automatically allow for APIs. To fix this on IIS, right-click on the site in question and choose Properties. Make sure that the "Execute" checkbox is selected.
404	**Resource Not Found** The server does not have the resource you asked it for. Check the name of your file, make sure you typed it correctly or that your hyperlink has it correctly spelled. Check the directory path specified and make sure that the file you're requesting is really in that directory. If it is, check your code for correct relative paths. Should ../../SomeFile.cfm really be ../SomeFile.cfm?
405	**Method Not Allowed** This error means that the method specified in the request header is not allowed for this server. In nearly every case the translation is this: you wrote <form method="POST" action= "SomeFile">. That is, you are POSTing form data and accidentally dropped the ".cfm" from the file name specified in the Action attribute of the form tag.
408	**Request Timeout.** The resource specified is available, but for some reason the process is taking longer than the specified timeout limit for the web server. Administrators specify a timeout limit in order to prevent orphaned threads from gradually using up all of a server's memory and processing cycles trying to fulfill a request. It is possible that you see this status code returned when you write a bad loop, write bad conditional logic, have a temporarily slow connection or slow server (perhaps because it has a great number of requests at once), or try to return 100,000 rows from your database at once.

Table C.3 shows common server errors (those in the 500 range). These are much less common but are scary, so they merit mention.

Table C.3 Common Server-Side Errors, What They Mean, and How to Fix Them

Error	*Meaning*
500	**Internal Server Error** The server encountered an unexpected condition which it could not resolve. This error can mean a great number of things. If you are running ColdFusion in a distributed environment and this error is recurring, make sure that the cfremote.ini file has the correct path to the web root.
503	**Service Unavailable** This error indicates that the web server is down temporarily or is unable to fulfill requests. This is sometimes due to overload. If you encounter this error often, try adding RAM to your web server.

You can also consult the Macromedia Knowledge Base if you encounter an error. It has a wealth of information regarding known bugs and even common user errors. Often the brief articles include how to fix things too.

ColdFusion Errors

They usually start with "An Error Occurred While Processing Your Request."

Error Resolving Parameter

This means that ColdFusion cannot determine the value of a variable. This could be for a number of reasons. Let's examine them.

Consider the following code. What's wrong with it?

```
<cfif MyVar is "ten">
    <cfoutput>#MyVar#</cfoutput>
</cfif>
```

The answer is that nothing is wrong with it per se, which is why it's a slightly difficult error to find. If you run the above code in your browser, you will see the error message shown in Figure C.1.

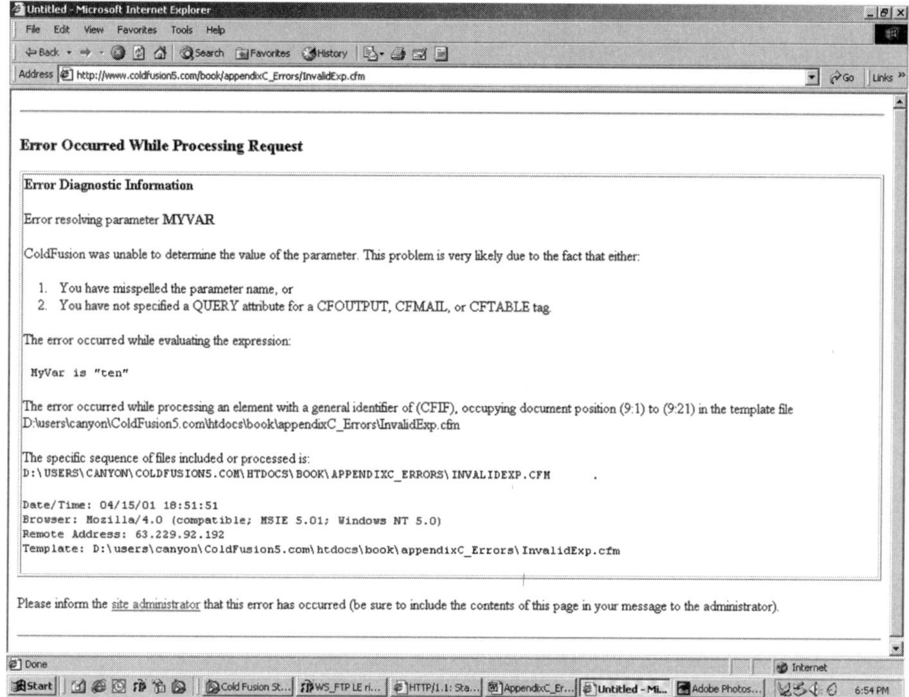

Figure C.1 You receive this error when you do not declare variables before referencing them.

The reason you get an error is that you have not declared the variable "MyVar" and have not set it to a value. It is therefore impossible for ColdFusion to evaluate the truthfulness of the <CFIF> statement (is it "ten" or "not ten"?)

Were we to declare our variable, we could alleviate this error. Try running this instead:

```
<cfset MyVar = "ten">

<cfif MyVar is "ten">
    <cfoutput>#MyVar#</cfoutput>
</cfif>
```

The addition of the variable declaration is emphasized above. This time we don't get an error.

Scope (Again)

Perhaps the above examples seem obvious. However, imagine you're working in a template of hundreds of lines of code, especially when using

<CFINCLUDE>, passing variables from page to page, resetting the scope for a variable (say, from URL to VARIABLES). Or say you're in a development stage and you're changing things around a lot. This sort of thing can be difficult to spot. Which brings us back to the question of scope.

Sometimes developers get this error *even when they have* declared their variables. How does that happen?

Scoping

When a variable without a scope prefix is referenced, ColdFusion searches the list of scopes in a consistent, nonarbitrary order to find its value. Table C.4 shows the order in which it searches.

Table C.4 ColdFusion Variable Scope, in Order

Search Order	*Variable Prefix*
1	Query Result variable (MYQUERYNAME.MyColumnName)
2	Local Variable (VARIABLES.MyVariable)
3	CGI Variable (CGI.MyVariable)
4	FILE Variable (File.MyVariable)
5	URL Variable (URL.MyVariable)
6	FORM Variable (FORM.MyFormFieldName)
7	COOKIE Variable (COOKIE.MyVariable)
8	CLIENT Variables (CLIENT.MyVariable)

There are several things to note in Table C.4, some of which may seem counterintuitive—for instance, the fact that ColdFusion looks for a variable in the query scope before looking in the local scope. And it is easy for developers to forget that a CGI or FILE variable will be found before a URL or FORM variable, since they work far more frequently with the latter two.

The way to avoid a lot of hassle here is to always prefix your variables with their proper scope. Instead of referring to #FirstName#, refer to getEmployeeNames.FirstName. Your code will run faster, because ColdFusion won't have to go hunting for the scope of your variable; you will cut down significantly on ill-spent debugging time; and your code will be more readable and easier for the developers of posterity to understand.

<NOTE>

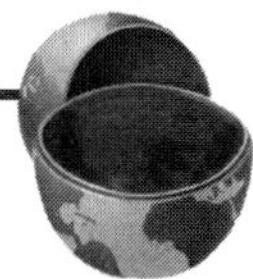

Remember that the scope prefix denotes only the scope of a variable; the scope itself determines where it is available, where its values are held, and how long its values will be available.

There are compelling reasons for always scoping variables: it improves performance, enhances readability, and prepares you with specificity if you modify your code. Some persons may argue that there are situations in which you do not want to prefix your variables. For instance, you may want the flexibility of having an action page accept a variable from two different scopes if you don't know how the user will pass them. My only answer to this is a question: why don't you know how the user will pass them?

The other significant thing to note about Table C.4 is this: when ColdFusion finds a variable in any given scope, *it stops looking*—just as when it satisfies a clause in a <CFIF> statement, it stops looking to satisfy further statements. It's not going to resolve a conflict; it will just execute at its first opportunity. That has important implications for the debugging process. It's time for a few short quizzes.

Without cheating, what will be the output of the following code and why?

Listing C.1 Can You Guess the Output of the Following Code?

```
<cfset Variables.FirstName = "Some Other Name">
<!----The query returns the result "James"--->
<cfquery datasource="AgentsDB" name="getUser">
    SELECT FirstName
    FROM Users
    WHERE UserID = 007
</cfquery>

<!---Reference the variable without its prefix--->
<cfoutput>
    #FirstName#
</cfoutput>
```

We might be tempted to say that the code will output "James," since the query is run *after* the locally set variable. However, the variable wasn't scoped, so ColdFusion went looking in predefined order for a FirstName variable. Therefore, the output of the above code is "Some Other Name."

The above code is perfectly legitimate, however, and both values can be accurately referenced by prefixing their scope:

```
<CFOUTPUT>#variables.FirstName#
              #getuser.FirstName#</CFOUTPUT>
```

or, like this:

```
<CFOUTPUT QUERY="getUser">
  #variables.FirstName# #getuser.FirstName#
</CFOUTPUT>
```

This does bring up the important issue of variable overwriting.

Without careful attention to your scope prefixes, you can overwrite your variables unintentionally. This can make it difficult to find the cause of an error in your code.

It is common practice to write variables declared in one scope into another scope that is more workable for the task at hand. For instance, in an earlier chapter I discussed the benefits of writing application and session variables into the request scope. Since structure values can be accessed very quickly by ColdFusion, it is not uncommon for developers to write FORM or URL variables into a structure. It such instances, you may find it difficult to trace the origin of your "parameter not defined" error.

Consider the following code. In what scope does the "MyName" variable reside by the time it is output?

Listing C.2 Make Sure You Know the Scope of Your Variables

```
<!---Set the name of this page so we can use it as its own
action page---->

<cfset thisPage = GetFileFromPath(CGI.SCRIPT_NAME)>

<!---Output "MyName" if it exists in any scope--->
<cfif isDefined("MyName")>
    Your name is <cfoutput>#MyName#</cfoutput>.
</cfif>

<cfoutput>
    <form action = "#thisPage#?MyName=Eben" name="MyForm"
          method="post">

</cfoutput>

<!---This form passes "Alison" as the value of "MyName", but
    the URL passes "Eben" as the value. What will our non-
    prefixed variable output? --->
```

```
        <input type="text" size="25" name="MyName"
value="Alison">
        <input type="submit" name="submit">
    </form>
```

Which scope will win in the race to become "MyName"? If you're not sure, consult Table C.4.

This example illustrates how you can easily overwrite your variables if you are not careful to prefix them. If we change our output statement to read #FORM.MyName#, then we can control the result more predictably. If it is imperative to have a variable with the same name available to us from different scopes, we can simply execute some conditional logic to determine its value.

A lot of things can go wrong in an enterprise-level application. Being explicit about the things you can control helps to eliminate unexpected results.

<NOTE>

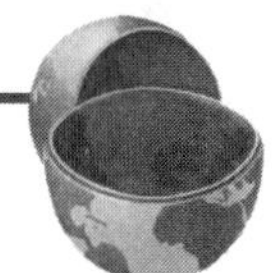

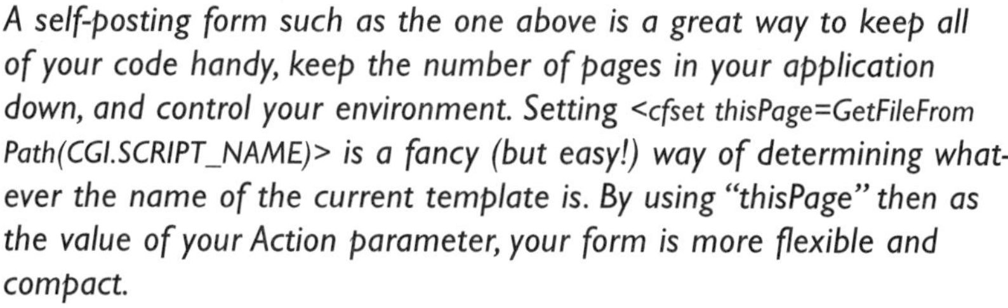

A self-posting form such as the one above is a great way to keep all of your code handy, keep the number of pages in your application down, and control your environment. Setting <cfset thisPage=GetFileFromPath(CGI.SCRIPT_NAME)> is a fancy (but easy!) way of determining whatever the name of the current template is. By using "thisPage" then as the value of your Action parameter, your form is more flexible and compact.

This discussion is especially important when you work with CLIENT and COOKIE variables for two reasons. The first is that they are set once, usually on a global page such as application.cfm, or after a login. That makes them a little trickier to keep track of. The second reason is that they reside on the client machine or on the server, and can persist for long periods of time. They also can be deleted or disabled. This makes their value somewhat more difficult to predict.

Let's extend the above example a little further. Having had the author beat you over the head with this variable prefixing business, you churlishly prefix all of your variables. However, business is booming, and your application expands somewhat. Now you need to test for the value of two variables. This brings up the related issue of conditional statements with regard to variables.

The Weakness of OR

It is a very common problem in ColdFusion applications for errors to stem from faulty logic. The following code will run fine, because FORM.FirstName is defined when the submit button is clicked:

Listing C.3 OR Is a Weak Logical Operator

```
<cfset thisPage = #GetFileFromPath(CGI.SCRIPT_NAME)#>

<cfif isDefined("FORM.FirstName") OR isDefined("FORM.Age")>
    Your name is <cfoutput>#FORM.FirstName#.</cfoutput><br>

</cfif>

<cfoutput>
    <form action = "#thisPage#" name="MyForm" method="post">
</cfoutput>
First Name: <input type="text" size="25"
name="FirstName"><br>
Age: <input type="text" size="25" name="MyAge"><br>
<input type="submit" name="submit">
```

Let's say that we want to collect the name and age of a user by modifying the above code. We'll just pop in an INSERT statement, as below, and go off to lunch.

Listing C.4 The Form with an SQL INSERT Statement

```
<cfset thisPage = #GetFileFromPath(CGI.SCRIPT_NAME)#>
<cfif isDefined("FORM.FirstName") OR isDefined("FORM.Age")>
    Your name is <cfoutput>#FORM.FirstName#.</cfoutput><br>

    <cfquery name="putUser" datasource="cf5DB">
        INSERT INTO Users (FirstName, Age )
        VALUES ('#FORM.FirstName#', #FORM.Age )
    </cfquery>
</cfif>

<cfoutput>
    <form action = "#thisPage#" name="MyForm" method="post">
</cfoutput>
First Name: <input type="text" size="25"
name="FirstName"><br>
Age: <input type="text" size="25" name="MyAge"><br>
          <input type="submit" name="submit">
    </form>
```

Returning from lunch, we are dismayed to see our co-workers shaking their heads sadly at us as we stroll into the office. What could be wrong? We *know*

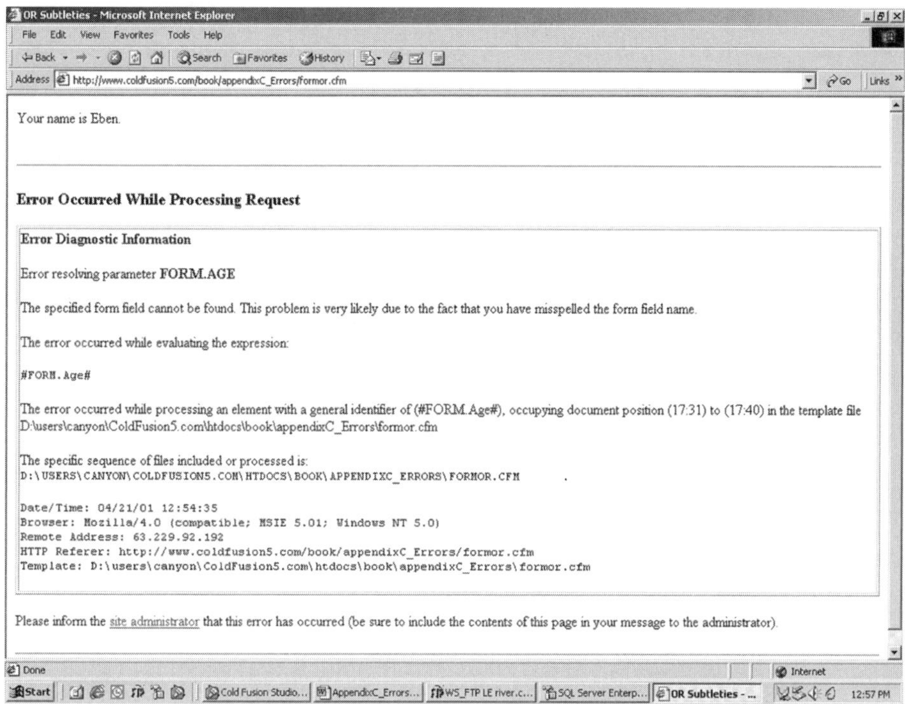

Figure C.2 The weakness of OR.

that the code we just wrote is okay, because all we did was add an insert statement using the variables already present. Right?

Wrong. We look at our monitor and see the ColdFusion error shown in Figure C.2.

The INSERT statement fails because it doesn't have the variable FORM.Age (because we called the form field "MyAge" instead of "Age"). So why didn't the page fail before, since we didn't touch that part of the code? As we learned earlier, the Boolean OR is the weakest conditional operator there is. You can string 50 false statements together, and if only one is true, the whole thing passes the test. In this code, ColdFusion checked for the existence of the "FirstName" field, and, finding it, never bothered to check for the existence of the "Age" field.

The lesson here is somewhat akin to the one about naming your database columns the same as the form controls that will supply their values: be certain that you are testing for variables in the exact same way that ColdFusion will. The consequence of not doing so is that your application will behave unpredictably. Since it may work the first 100 times you run it, be very diligent about following the rules of sound conditional logic.

Short-Circuit AND

As you may remember from the chapter on conditional logic, ColdFusion processes the Boolean AND operator in a *short-circuit evaluation.* Short-circuit evaluation means that any statement joined by the AND operator that contains even one false condition will cause the entire statement to return false. Since *both* conditions must be satisfied in two expressions joined by AND, then if the first condition is false, there's no point in evaluating the second condition, and it will not be evaluated at all by ColdFusion. Remembering this point can save you headaches in debugging your applications. It also means it's a good idea to put expressions that are most likely to fail first.

The Powerful NOT

In logic, negation is the most powerful operand. Conjuncting expressions with OR allows any one of a given list to be true, and the entire statement will return true. NOT, on the other hand, is powerful because it does not need to check for truth value very extensively—one mismatch and the entire list returns false. We can create some very unpredictable results with nested conditional statements using multiple logical operators. If you are experiencing problems with negation in complex logical statements, there are a couple of things you can do:

- See if you can break your code up into smaller logical units that will return the desired result. These may be easier to write, read, and debug.
- Insure that the variables or conditions you are testing against are persisting through the statement.
- Check the relationships between AND, OR, and NOT operators. As with queries, you can sometimes go a long way by writing out what you're trying to accomplish in plain language before you write the ColdFusion statement.

If it seems that logical errors are frequent in your applications, I strongly urge you to reread the chapter on conditional logic, and even to pick up a good logic book or two.

<NOTE>

Check out the modestly titled The Laws of Thought *by self-taught mathematician George Boole. His work forms a good deal of the basis for modern mathematical logic models. Boolean logic is also commonly employed in search engines on the web.*

Invalid Expression Format

With <CFOUTPUT>

A programmer often hears about this error when turning over code to the designer who will make it all presentable to the world. The error looks something like Figure C.3.

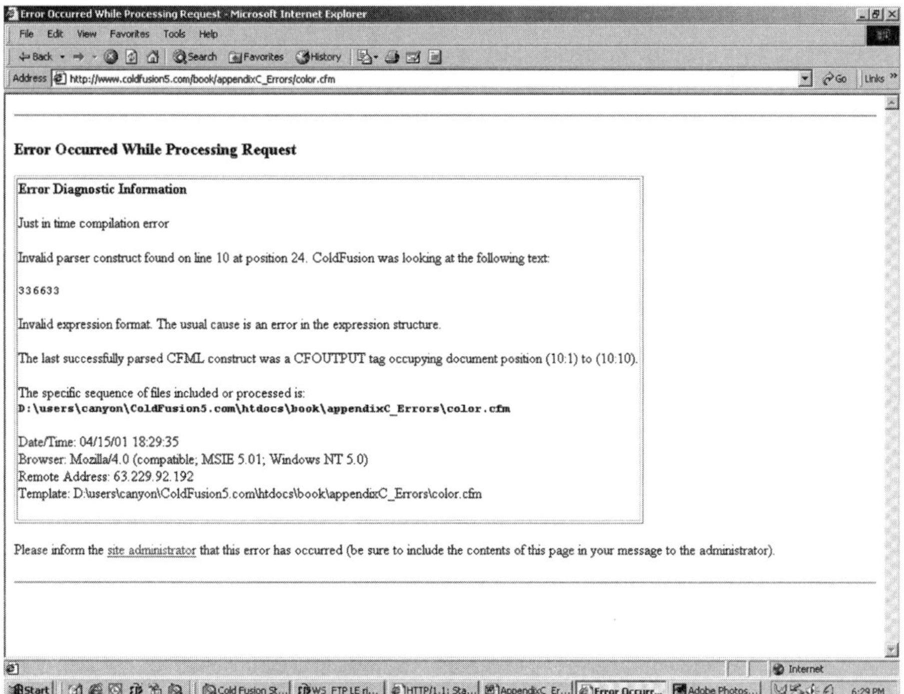

Figure C.3 You must escape pound signs within <CFOUTPUT>.

ColdFusion error screens are very helpful. This one does not tell you what code is problematic, though—it shows you the code *near* the problematic code. Here is the code that produced the error:

```
<cfset MyDate = DateFormat(Now())>
<cfoutput><font color=#336699>#MyDate#</font></cfoutput>
```

In this case, 336699 is not really a problem at all. It is the # sign that causes the problem, since it is inside a <CFOUTPUT> block. ColdFusion thinks that you want it to evaluate 336699 as an expression, and it can't. You must escape the pound sign, so that it doesn't try to evaluate something that is not an expression. The fix to the above code then is like this:

```
<cfoutput><font color=##336699>#MyDate#</font></cfoutput>
```

We are referencing the hexadecimal value for a lovely shade of blue within a pair of <CFOUTPUT> tags. A common scenario is for you, the programmer, to leave out font references altogether while you develop in order to facilitate code readability. Then you turn over your code to a designer, who adds font tags and images and makes things pretty. If you work this way, make sure to tell the designer to "Escape" the pound signs. Remember that escaping in ColdFusion means that you write the suspect character twice in a row, and ColdFusion knows to ignore them.

Another solution to the above situation is to put the <CFOUTPUT> statement on the inside of the <FONT> tag, like this:

```
<font color=#336699><cfoutput>#MyDate#</cfoutput></font>
```

But this is not always the most efficient solution. Use whichever is most appropriate for your entire template.

General Things to Check For

Sometimes it's hard to determine the root of the error you're getting. Perhaps it's one of those times (and you'll have them) when you find yourself writing frantically to a ColdFusion list, offering your kingdom for the answer to your "unfixable" error that is impossible to find. You can usually determine that you are in this desperate state; just look for "this doesn't make any sense . . ." or the more common "I KNOW I'M PERFECT BUT . . ." in the subject line of your email.

Typos

Look over your code for seemingly innocuous typos. One mistyped character can mean the difference between life and death.

I'll try to make this fun by replicating the games on the backs of cereal boxes. Which I only know about because of my daughter. Not because I like Cap'n Crunch or anything.

The code below will crash under certain circumstances and not others. It's not a trick question (that is, you have all of the information you need—the answer doesn't rely on what data types the columns in the database are, etc.). The error is just a typo. Can you find it?

```
<cfquery name="PutNewUser"
datasource="#Request.App.datasource#">
INSERT into USERS
(FirstName, LastName, Username, Password, Address1,
 Address2,      City, State, ZipCode,
    Country, PhoneNumber, PhoneNumber2,
    Newsletter, NewsletterType, Greeting, WebPageName,
    CompanyName, CompanyType, IsAdvertiser)
   VALUES
   (
   '#FORM.FirstName#',
   '#FORM.LastName#',
   '#FORM.Username#',
   '#FORM.Password#',
   '#FORM.Address1#',
   <cfif Trim(FORM.Address2) is not "">
         '#FORM.Address2#',
   <cfelse>NULL</cfif>
   '#FORM.City#',
   '#FORM.State#',
   #FORM.ZipCode#,
   '#FORM.Country#',
   '#FORM.PhoneNumber#',
   <cfif Trim(FORM.PhoneNumber2) is not "">
         '#FORM.PhoneNumber2#',
         <cfelse>NULL,</cfif>
   '#FORM.Newsletter#',
   '#FORM.NewsletterType#',
   '#FORM.Greeting#',
   '#FORM.WebPageName#',
   '#FORM.CompanyName#',
   '#FORM.CompanyType#', 1
   );
         </cfquery>
```

The above problematic code is a perfect example of the need for testing and testing your applications before you send them into the world. When using FORM variables, especially rather long forms such as this one, you must remember to fill out the form in the different ways that the user can.

The purpose of the above code is to collect information from a user via a plain HTML form and insert it into a database.

It appears clear from the above code that the application allows for two fields to be left blank by the user: Address2 and PhoneNumber2. This is a good idea, since many people do not require a second line for a suite or apartment address, and many people do not have a second relevant phone.

Which brings us to the answer.

The code tests for the existence of values for these variables in two CFIF statements. If a value is passed in the FORM.Address2 field, the code will insert that value. If the field is an empty string, the code inserts a NULL value into the Address2 column in the database. Same for the PhoneNumber2 form field.

Remember that ColdFusion compiles its SQL statement in preprocessing based on the ColdFusion code, and then it opens the database connection and passes the statement to the database.

Let's pretend to be ColdFusion for a moment. We get passed the form with all of the fields filled out. We read the template with the above code on it, process the conditional logic, and build the SQL statement just as it is written above, resolving the conditions into values. Since every field in the form was filled out, lines 14–18 now read as follows:

```
Some code ...
'555 Some Street',
'Apt. 12',
'New York City',
... Some more code ...
```

Each value is separated by commas to correspond with the columns specified in the column list at the beginning of the SQL statement. The same holds true for the PhoneNumber2 set of conditional statements. The SQL statement then gets passed to the database and completes as expected. We could test this page for a long time and never find the error.

The problem comes in line 17. What happens if a value for Address2 is not supplied? ColdFusion runs the code inside the CFELSE clause, which should insert a NULL value into the database. However, here is the SQL statement that ColdFusion will build:

```
Some code ...
'555 Some Street',
<NULL>
'New York City',
... Some more code ...
```

Can you see the problem yet? We forgot to put an extra comma in our CFELSE clause. This would be easy to do, since we already wrote one to separate the Address2 column from the City column for the code inside the CFIF clause on line 15. The above code, with the NULL value for Address2, will cause the statement to crash. The code for line 17 should read as follows:

```
<cfelse>NULL,</cfif>
```

<NOTE>

As you continue to develop, you can identify patterns regarding when you forget letters. You will also begin to identify words that cause you to mistype. For instance, I often write "datsource" for "datasource" (in which case ColdFusion tells me that "there is no attribute 'datsource' for CFQUERY").

Tips and Tricks for Debugging Your Applications

Here are a few general tips that you can use to speed up the process of bringing your application from the development server into production.

Use the Debugger

In ColdFusion Administrator, click Debug Options. This will show you a list of checkboxes to display information about processing your ColdFusion templates, including comma-delimited list of all FormFields submitted, the SQL Statement built by ColdFusion, processing time, and much more. This is an invaluable tool to use during the development process.

Make sure to limit the IP address that the debugging information is sent to. Since you cannot specify individual applications for which to output these variables, they will be output at the bottom of every single .cfm template that ColdFusion processes (including the ColdFusion Administrator itself). What you can control is the IP address that receives the debugging output. You specify the IP addresses to receive the debugging information by clicking the Debugging IPs link in the Server menu of ColdFusion 5. You can add several, as shown in Figure C.4.

<NOTE>

If you are behind a firewall on your LAN, you cannot type in the IP address of your own machine. You won't receive an error message of any kind, but

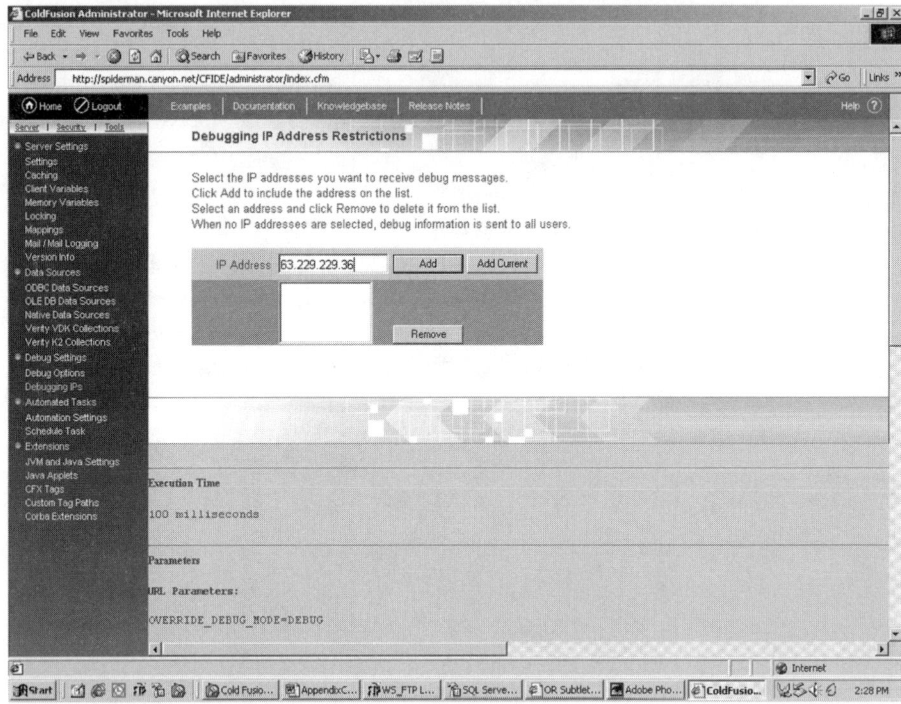

Figure C.4 Adding an IP address in ColdFusion Administrator to receive debugging output.

you won't see the debugging output either. If you are behind a firewall, you must specify the IP address of your firewall to see the debug output. This also means that everyone on your LAN will see the debug output too.

<CFOUTPUT> a Dummy Variable for Granular Control

Sometimes ColdFusion outputs errors that are not particularly specific. In order to determine exactly where ColdFusion stops processing (and therefore exactly where your code is breaking down), try the following:

At the very top of your page, create a simple variable like this: <CFSET Status="Everything is Cool">. Then write <CFOUTPUT>#Variables. Status# </CFOUTPUT>. If you see the output "Everything is cool", then the page is good to the point where the variable is visible. Keep moving the "output" and "abort" statement down through the page until the errant line of code is isolated.

You might be wondering when this is useful, since the error messages thrown by ColdFusion are so fantastically detailed. It actually is helpful not when ColdFusion is throwing an error, but when everything seems fine to ColdFusion, and the output is not what you intended.

For instance, I have found this technique useful if some conditional logic is used to create a display layer item, such as a table or a row. It also is useful in maintaining cross-browser compatibility, since different browsers display things more or less strictly. In working with very complex HTML tables, consider this trick.

You can also do this with ColdFusion 5's new <cfdump> tag.

<CFDUMP>

This tag was written for Macromedia Spectra as <cfa_dump> and has been generously supplied with ColdFusion 5 for the first time. You use <cfdump> during debugging to output a variable in a formatted table.

The <cfdump> tag allows you to output the name of a variable (which seems silly, since you have to specify it in the *var* attribute) or to output the current value of a variable. Consider the following situation:

```
<cfscript>
  idx = 21;
  idx = idx * 3.4;
  idx = idx / 0.9765;
</cfscript>
Dump: <cfdump var=#idx#>
```

Calling this page in a browser produces the following output for this simple variable:

```
Dump: 73.1182795699
```

The result in a browser is not particularly impressive for this simple variable—might as well use <cfoutput>, right? But your debugging is made a little more delightful by using the <cfdump> tag for more complex data types. That's where the real advantage comes in: your variable can be a simple variable, a query, a structure, an array, or a WDDX packet. It also makes a pretty blue table.

<CFDUMP> takes only one attribute, *var*, which is the name of the variable you want displayed. Just so you know what's going on under the hood,

the tag automatically generates the following JavaScript to create a display environment:

```
<script language="JavaScript">
  function cfadumpswitch(source) {
        target = source.parentElement.cells[1].style;
        if (target.display == 'none') {
              source.style.fontStyle = 'normal';
              source.style.backgroundColor = 'aaaaee';
              target.display = '';
        } else {
              source.style.fontStyle = 'italic';
              source.style.backgroundColor = 'silver';
              target.display = 'none';
        }
  }
  </script>
```

You cannot reference a complex datatype with <cfoutput> and expect to get anywhere. <cfdump> saves us the effort of looping over a structure (or whatever) and running the risk of introducing more problems. With <cfdump> it is simple! Check this out:

```
<cfset stThing = StructNew()>
<cfset stThing.Name = "Eben">
<cfset stThing.Phone = "555-1212">
<cfset stThing.Mood = "Happy">
<br>Dump: <cfdump var = #stThing#>
```

Load this page in a browser and voila, there you have your variable and all its values (Figure C.5).

Watch Out for Disparate Browser Behavior

If your application will have a wide audience, generally I recommend developing on Netscape 4.7. It is finicky and widely used. Forty percent of the 19 MB of code that is Microsoft Internet Explorer 5 is dedicated to handling poorly written code. Run the following code in IE 5:

```
<cfset thisPage = GetFileFromPath(CGI.SCRIPT_NAME)>
<cfif isDefined("URL.MyName")>
    Your name is <cfoutput>#URL.MyName#.</cfoutput><br>
</cfif>
<cfoutput>
<a href="#thisPage#?MyName=Eben Hewitt">Click Me</a> to post
the URL variable "Eben Hewitt".
</cfoutput>
```

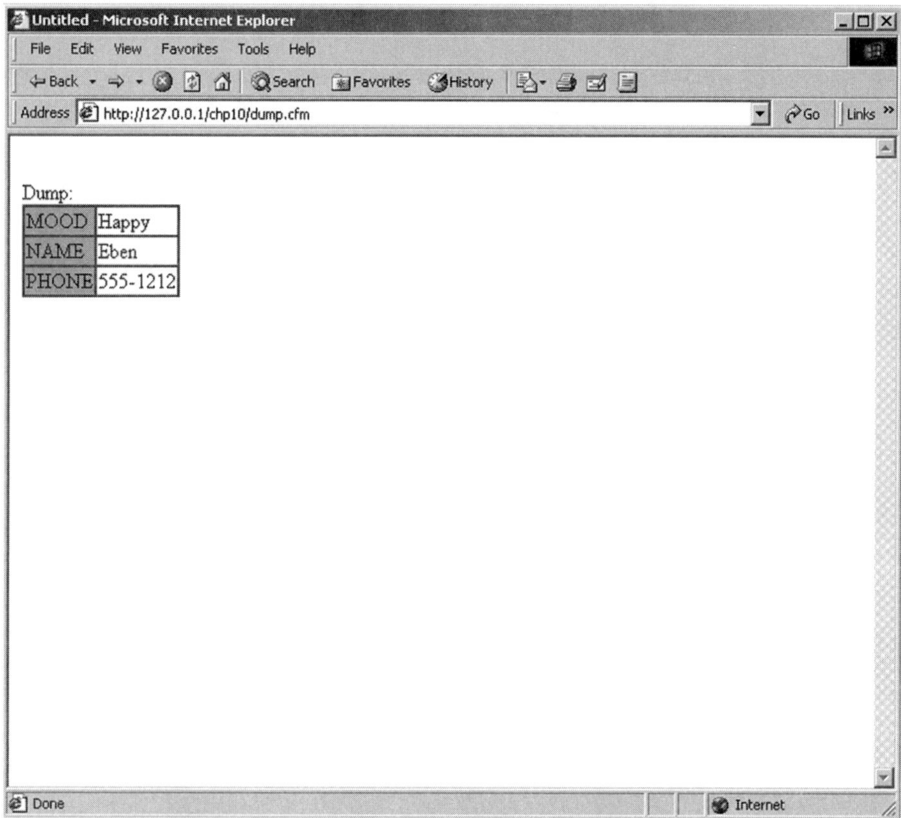

Figure C.5 Result of <cfdump>ing a ColdFusion structure.

The consideration here is that the value of the MyName variable contains a space. The two browsers have somewhat differing ideologies: When IE 5 encounters bad code, it tries to make up for it and display something. When Netscape encounters bad code, it is much less forgiving. The above code therefore works fine in IE 5. The browser just replaces the space in the passed URL variable with the URL encoded sign for a space ("%20"). When you run the same code in Netscape 4.7, you get a 400 error (Figure C.6).

The way to fix this is by setting a variable and putting the function URLEncodedFormat to work as follows:

```
<cfset MyName = "Eben Hewitt">

<cfoutput>
<a href="#thisPage#?MyName=#URLEncodedFormat(MyName)#">Click
Me</a>
</cfoutput>
```

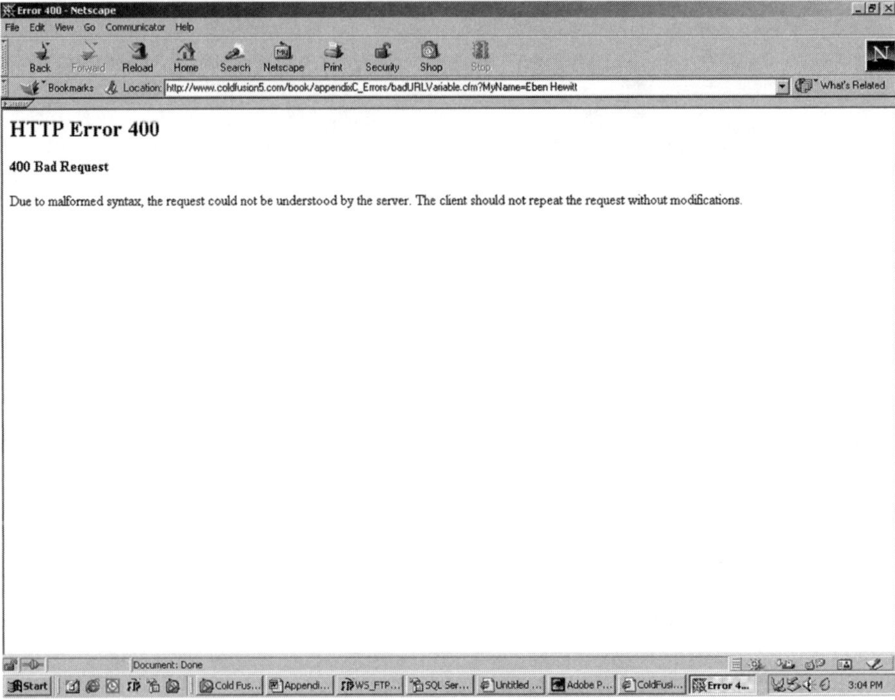

Figure C.6 Result of using spaces in a web address in Netscape 4.7.

SQL Errors

As a CF developer, it is critical that you understand the difference between the errors that ColdFusion returns to you and those that your database spits back.

Many errors that you will likely see in your ColdFusion work are database errors. Often they are not really errors at all, but indicate a lack of standardization between the application and the database.

The errors below are returned by Microsoft SQL Server, but are similar in report and behavior for other RDBMSs.

String Data Right Truncation

This error means literally that the data length allowed for the column is shorter than the data you're trying to stuff into it. SQL Server would have to truncate (cut off) the data passed to it in order to complete the INSERT or UPDATE statement. Look at this code quickly:

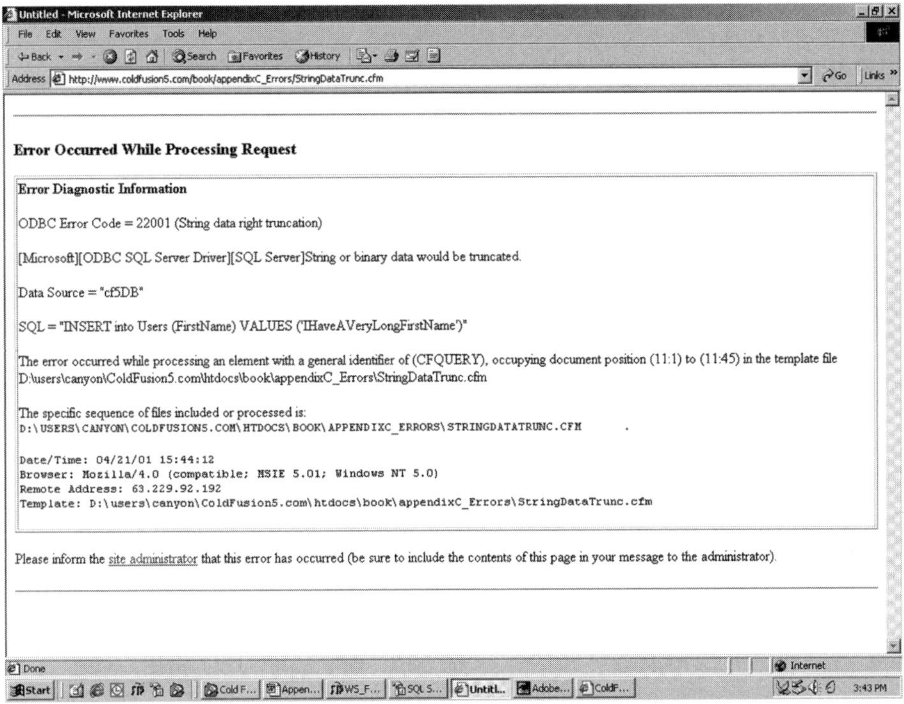

Figure C.7 String data right truncation errors mean you have allowed users to type more info into a form than the column will accept.

```
<!---The FirstName column is datatype VarChar. It is capable
of holding up to 8 characters.--->
<cfquery datasource = "cf5DB" name="putUser">
    INSERT into Users
    (FirstName)
    VALUES ('IHaveAVeryLongFirstName')
</cfquery>
```

Since the string we are trying to insert is longer than 8 characters, we get the error shown in Figure C.7.

To correct this problem we can do a couple of things. If your data is being submitted via a form, then you should make sure that the `size` attribute of your input tag is the same length as your database column (which you should do anyway). That's probably the smartest way, and the one with the least overhead. When a user tries to exceed the length allowed in the size attribute of the input field, her keys just stop working and she cannot type any further.

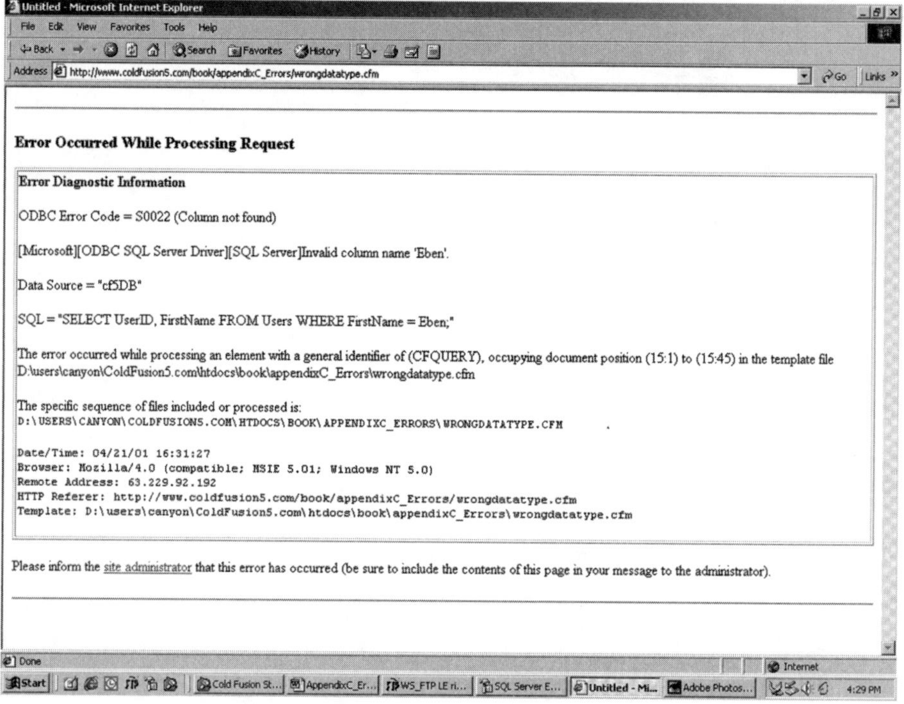

Figure C.8 Wrong data type error.

Bad Column Name

I include this error because it is one of the most misleading ones SQL Server returns. You've got a SELECT statement that retrieves the UserID and FirstName columns. It looks like this:

```
<!---UserID is the primary key, so it is an int datatype.
    The FirstName column is datatype VarChar.--->

<cfquery datasource = "cf5DB" name="putUser">
    SELECT UserID, FirstName
    FROM Users
    WHERE FirstName = #FORM.FirstName#;
</cfquery>
```

When we run this code, we see the error shown in Figure C.8.

What's the problem? We can see from the error message that SQL Server thinks we are passing it a column name instead of a value ("Eben") to find in the column "FirstName." The simple reason is that you must remember to put quotes around strings and you must not use quote marks of any kind on numeric or integer values. Were we to modify the code like this: WHERE FirstName = '#FORM.FirstName#,' it would run just fine.

<NOTE>

We would also get this error if we used double quote marks around our string, like this:

WHERE FirstName = "#FORM.FirstName#." Always use single quotes for strings and no quote marks for integers and numeric values.

Syntax Error or Access Violation

You receive this error when you have written an improper SQL statement. Check to make sure that your code complies with this list:

- Make sure that everything is spelled right. No, I mean really make sure. Half of the time that's your problem.
- Commas need to separate column names. Did you forget one?
- You must *not* have a comma after the last item in your list of columns or values. Improper syntax would be like this: SELECT UserID, FirstName, FROM Users.
- You can optionally end your SQL statement with a semicolon. This is a good idea if you are running two separate but related SQL statements inside the same <CFQUERY>
- Make sure you have declared everything correctly. In complex SQL statements, such as JOINs, it can be easy to incorrectly assign columns. Look briefly at the code below:

```
SELECT UserID, PL.PrivilegeLevel
FROM Users U
INNER JOIN PrivilegeLevel PL
    ON U.UserID = PL.UserID
WHERE FirstName = '#FORM.FirstName#'
```

When it runs this code, SQL will throw an error "Ambiguous column name." It doesn't know what you're referring to in your SELECT statement—the UserID in the Users table, or the UserID in the PrivilegeLevel table. In this case, it's a matter of scoping (or, more properly, aliasing) the columns with the tables, like this:

```
SELECT U.UserID, PL.PrivilegeLevel
FROM Users U
INNER JOIN PrivilegeLevel PL
    ON U.UserID = PL.UserID
WHERE FirstName = '#FORM.FirstName#'
```

To avoid syntax errors by making my statements more readable, I usually separate SQL keywords with a carriage return, like this:

```
SELECT UserID
FROM Users
WHERE FirstName = 'Zoe'
    AND MiddleInitial = 'A'
```

SQL is totally uninterested in my line returns. It works pretty well.

Reserved Words

Make sure that you do not use reserved words in naming your variables, your columns, or your tables. While the list of reserved words for various database systems would be very long indeed, you can check the complete list of reserved words for your RDBMS (they differ slightly from product to product).

Here is a list of words it is tempting to use for variables and columns. You must resist the temptation. They are all reserved, and you will catch an error if you refer to them at all outside their intended contexts.

ACTION	ACTIVE	AFTER	ALL
AVG	AUTHORIZATION	BACKUP	CACHE
CASE	CAST	CHAR	CHARACTER
CHECK	COMPUTED	CONNECTION	CURRENT
DATABASE	DATE	DATETIME	DAY
DEBUG	DEFAULT	DELETE	DISK
DISTINCT	DO	DOMAIN	DUMMY
EXEC	FILE	FOREIGN	FREETEXT
GENERATOR	IDENTITY	INPUT	INSERT
INT	INTERSECT	JOIN	KEY
LANGUAGE	LOGFILE	MANUAL	MATCH
MESSAGE	NEXT	NULL	OPEN
OPTION	OUTPUT	OVERFLOW	PAGE

PAGES	PASSWORD	PERMANENT	PRIVILEGES
PROCEDURE	PROTECTED	REFERENCES	RELATIVE
REPLICATION	SECOND	SELECT	SEQUENCE
SET	SIZE	SPACE	STABILITY
SQL	SQLCODE	SQLERROR	STATISTICS
SUSPEND	TABLE	TAPE	TIMESTAMP
TRANSACTION	TRANSLATE	TRUE	UNION
UNIQUE	USAGE	USE	USER
VALUE	VALUES	VARIABLE	VIEW
VOLUME	WAIT	WHEN	WHERE
WHILE	WORK	WRITE	YEAR
ZONE			

Notice that many of the reserved words above have special meaning for SQL Server, but multiple meanings in the English language in general. It is also tempting to use some of these reserved words, because they just describe exactly what you need. Watch out for the following situations:

- A common need in an application is to record the date of a transaction. Do not name your column "Date." Changing it to TransactionDate works, though.
- You might have a product line of shirts in your e-commerce site. Do not call your table or column "Size"; find a variation.
- Perhaps you have a site about families. Do not have a column called "Relative."
- Perhaps you have a website about labor issues for IT professionals. Do not call your column "Union."

You get the idea.

Cookies and <CFLOCATION>

One cannot set a cookie and then use <CFLOCATION> on the same page. You will not get an error, but your cookie will not be set. While this is not really an error, it is unexpected behavior that can have new developers really using a lot of indelicate language. And you will get an error later when trying to read the cookie. This can be very confusing, because all of your code will be correctly written (at least, each individual section of code will be correct in itself). Here is the reason for the behavior.

Think back to what we learned earlier in the section on HTTP and consider this example: You have a page called "Login.cfm," which takes the username and password from a user. It passes these variables to "LoginProcess.cfm," which checks against the database for a match. You then run some conditional logic that determines the behavior of the rest of the page. If there is a match for that username and password, set a cookie so we can remember them, and then use <CFLOCATION> to send them to "Welcome.cfm." That last part looks like this:

```
<!---They passed, so set the cookie and go to the welcome
page---->
<CFCOOKIE name=MyCookie' value="SomeValue" expires="never">
<CFLOCATION URL="Welcome.cfm">
```

This seems reasonable enough. However, the <CFLOCATION> tag does not send any data to the client. It simply redirects to the specified URL. Therefore, the cookie is never set, because the HTTP response header was never sent back to the client.

There are a couple of ways of dealing with this. One is to drop the <cflocation> and force the client to click into the Welcome.cfm page. This is not very elegant, but it works.

Another common way is to use JavaScript to perform the relocation. That would look like this:

```
<SCRIPT Language='JavaScript1.2'>
    location.href = 'Welcome.cfm'
</SCRIPT>
```

You could also use ColdFusion's <CFHEADER> tag to post data to the response header, like this:

```
<CFHEADER name='refresh' value='0'; URL='Welcome.cfm'>
```

The purpose of the CFHEADER tag is to set key-value pairs in the response header. So you can use its "Pragma" and "Expires" values (for instance) to make sure that the page you're viewing is not a cached copy.

Don't Put the String "Application.cfm" in a Template Name

ColdFusion does not allow two things regarding the Application.cfm file. First, you cannot access it directly (that is, you cannot type Application.cfm into the address bar in your browser and expect to see anything but an error).

Second, you can't put the string "application.cfm" anywhere in the name of a template. Because ColdFusion uses the CONTAINS statement to catch the first error, it will also throw this exception for MyNewApplication.cfm, even if its content is wholly innocuous. However, MyNewApplications.cfm (with an "s" before the ".cfm"), would be acceptable.

I hope that this appendix has offered you some greater understanding of common errors you might come across in developing your applications. You can use it as a reference as you work, and hopefully save yourself a lot of time.

Appendix D

Getting a ColdFusion Job

There are many resources for ColdFusion developers looking for work. This appendix will outline some of those available to you no matter where you are or what your current skill level is.

I include this appendix for a number of reasons. I wish I'd had it when I was first learning ColdFusion. It would have saved me a lot of time that I could have spent learning more useful stuff. I also love what I do so much that I want everyone to be as happy as I am. I imagine that you're not reading this book just for academic purposes; you're probably looking for a job or think that you will be in a few months.

The landscape for programmers has changed quite a bit in recent years, and it is not unusual for a programmer to work freelance—doing three-month stints here and there. Maybe the dot-com you worked for closed recently, or your family is looking to relocate. Perhaps you have outgrown your current position and are looking to increase your salary. Or maybe you are just starting out in web programming and are starting to think about giving up bartending for real this time. If you're a student nearing graduation, this is a perfect reference for you too.

Let's take a look at some skills you may be expected to know beyond ColdFusion itself.

Server Platforms

You may have to know server administration or architecture in order to be competitive. While it would be a rare or a rather small company that would have programmers performing administration of boxes, this knowledge is often desired by employers in order to assure compliance with their current systems, and it creates the most flexibility.

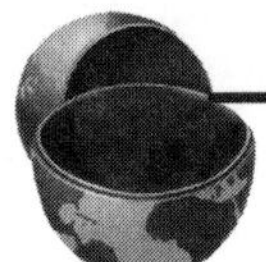

<TIP>

Currently, the overwhelming number of ColdFusion licenses purchased (83%) are for the Windows NT/2000 platform, with a meager 3% purchased for use on Linux platforms. The other 14% is divided between HP-UX and Sun Solaris servers. This may help you anticipate what platform employers are going to ask you to know.

Don't be fooled by this number, though. ColdFusion 4.5 for Linux was available only in beta version for a long time and would run only on RedHat 6.0 or better. With the release of ColdFusion 5.0, support has been expanded to include not only RedHat but also SuSE and Cobalt.

Database Software

While I use Microsoft SQL Server for the examples in this book, Oracle is of course a very popular RDBMS for organizations running ColdFusion. These are both rich and complex database management systems, and any knowledge of them that you can bring to the table will no doubt be helpful.

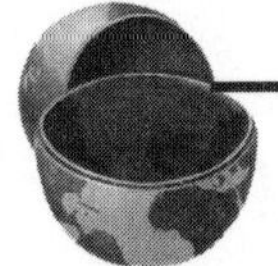

<TIP>

You can download a free 120-day evaluation version of Microsoft SQL Server 2000 at http://www.microsoft.com/downloads/search.asp?. You can download a free 30-day trial of Oracle 8i and 9i from http://otn.oracle.com/software/content.html. Both downloads are around 600 MB.

Of course you are not limited to these database servers. ColdFusion 5.0 ships with new support for a greater range of database software. The Merant 3.7 drivers make it easier to work with Informix 9, DB2, and others. If these are the database systems you already use, you're in luck! Check out the database chapters (9 and 10) for more information.

<NOTE>

Different relational database software products work differently with the SQL 92 standard language. There are a number of good books dedicated to these topics.

SQL statements written with the SQL92 standard will port to any RDBMS that is compliant with the standard without modification.

T-SQL (for Microsoft SQL Server) and PL/SQL (for Oracle) are really both dialects of the SQL language that have their own "extensions" or contributions to the language that will work only on their particular platform. In general, code written for Oracle can be ported for use on Microsoft SQL Server with some modification. Oracle 8i includes a utility for porting Microsoft SQL databases into Oracle. The same holds true for Microsoft Access 2000 and SQL Server, which has an "Upsizing Wizard" to bring Access databases into SQLServer. For instance, the datatype "Currency" in Access doesn't exist in SQL Server, where it's "money"; "memo" in Access corresponds with "text" in SQL Server, and so on.

Because Microsoft purchased the Sybase server to become its SQL Server product, the two systems were the same through SQL Server version 4.5. They still have many very similar features for the same reason.

Other Languages

Many development houses work with what their clients give them. The sites that clients bring to you can be written in any language. It is therefore helpful to know other web programming languages, as you will frequently see jobs that ask for not only ColdFusion, but also PHP, CGI, or ASP. Of course it never hurts to know XML, JavaScript, DHTML, or CSS.

CGI programs are often written in Perl, which you can download from www.perl.org or www.activestate.com.

PHP is available as a free download for Windows and Linux at www.php.net, where you can also find tutorials and other information.

ASP comes with Windows NT and 2000 servers. You can run ASP off a Linux box if you get a plug-in from ChiliSoft. This costs around $500.

There are a number of good books on all of these subjects. Make sure to check out the series devoted to XML published by Prentice Hall.

The Job Sites

The websites listed below have the purpose of hooking up employers with employees. Some specialize in ColdFusion jobs exclusively; others have a broader focus, such as IT jobs in general. They are listed here in no particular order.

JustColdFusionJobs.com ColdFusion jobs listed by state and city. This site features a number of jobs at Macromedia that they don't list on their website. Any given search is not likely to turn up more than 2 or 3 jobs. Employers sometimes list the position location as "anywhere" in order to turn up in a number of different result sets.

CFAdvisor.com This site is a free service to both employers and job seekers. It has a number of jobs listed, but some of them may be several months old.

FindADeveloper.com This site lists over 1,000 different employers for all areas of work related to web development.

HouseofFusion.com This site hosts a number of highly trafficked lists devoted to ColdFusion, many of which are hosted by Michael Dinowitz. CF-Talk sends out hundreds of emails a day from its members. It is a natural place for someone looking for a job to go—ask other developers, see if they need anyone to round out a project team. Sometimes companies hire interns as well.

Forums.Allaire.com The Allaire website is host to a classifieds section where you can post your skill set, and employers can post reference to a job they need a developer to do for them. As of this writing, the Macromedia site and the Allaire site have not yet merged completely, and so it is unclear where (if anywhere) you will be able to find this on the new website.

us.tekbay.com This site has a detailed set of searching tools that allow you to specify not only the location of your job, but also your skills. ColdFusion is on the list perhaps because the site itself is written in ColdFusion. They seem to have about 30 jobs throughout the United States for CF developers at any given time.

WebProgrammingJobs.com This site has an occasional ColdFusion job crop up, though it is really more devoted to C++ and like that.

Dice.com Typing in the key word "ColdFusion" often returns over a hundred jobs throughout the country. Many of the places that list with dice.com and monster.com are not the companies that you would work directly for—often they are employment agencies who act as representatives for you and the employer.

Monster.com This is much like Dice.com, and the two sites have been around for years. This is a very popular and trusted site, and a search for ColdFusion will often turn up well over a hundred jobs throughout the country.

TechieGold.com This site is also written in ColdFusion and lets you enter salary, skill, and location criteria. The great thing is that you don't have to sign up or become a member (though you will need to create an account to apply for a job online).

Other Good Ideas

Beyond cruising the websites above for job openings, you have a number of other options. You might make a very beautiful sign that reads "Will program for food" and hang around 47th and Lexington. However, other ways of going about it are equally efficient:

- Check out **Elance.com.** This website lets freelancers bid on projects that individuals and companies offer. A project is posted and described, and programmers may bid on the project, post their resumes, and make an argument for why they should get to do the project. Projects range from small e-commerce sites to WAP enabling a static site and more.
- Look for ISPs that host ColdFusion. They may need an administrator for their CF box, or they might be looking to bring some development in house. Look up the list of companies that host ColdFusion sites later in the appendices to get started.
- Go to different websites that have an office in the city you're interested in. Look for the ".cfm" extension on pages as you browse their website. Then look at the jobs section of their website.

- Check out the local universities. Even if you "know" that they run a certain platform, one job of a university is to teach students. They are also rather large organizations. That means that they often will run a number of different platforms throughout different departments and branches of a campus. One local university I know uses PHP and CGI on their public site running off UNIX servers. But their internal accounting system runs off a Windows platform with ColdFusion. So they need ColdFusion developers, even though you might not know it by looking quickly at their website.
- Read *ColdFusion Developer's Journal.* This is a good idea anyway, because it's a good magazine featuring articles by some of the leading developers in the industry. Many contributors are employees of Macromedia who create the products they're discussing, and companies looking for ColdFusion developers know to advertise there. If you are specifically looking for a job, however, you probably want to subscribe to the journal, since newsstands tend to leave it on the shelf two or three months. You want to make sure you have it as soon as it's released.
- Look at the websites of companies that you know develop ColdFusion. Look at Cybertrails.com Creative Services department in Phoenix, NoWalls.com in Salt Lake City, or a company like AbleCommerce.com in Washington state. Figleaf Software has offices in Atlanta and Washington, D.C. These companies have substantial product lines that are built on ColdFusion and Spectra technology, so they're likely to need developers at some point.
- Check out Macromedia itself. Allaire was based in Boston, but now that it has merged with Macromedia, the larger company also has offices in Dallas, Minneapolis, and San Francisco. Check out their website for job openings. Remember that ColdFusion Administrator is just a big ColdFusion application itself, as is Spectra, which means they need ColdFusion developers to write them.
- Get on a list. By joining CF-Talk (which produces hundreds of emails a day), or HouseOfFusion.com, or the CFDJ list, you can learn a lot from experts in the field. By joining the community like this, you may find it easier to get in touch with people who know of ColdFusion jobs.

- Take a class. Macromedia offers a variety of classes in ColdFusion, Spectra, HTML, and Java. These classes usually last two to four days and cost $1,200 to $3,000. This is a good way to get hands-on experience and meet people in the industry.
- Join a user group. The list of ColdFusion user groups is extensive. Often membership is sponsored, so it's free to members. This is a great way to connect with people working in ColdFusion development. The Macromedia website lists the current user groups by state. If there is not one in your area, contact Macromedia and they will help you get one going.

As you search for a job, remember that if you have used the expiring trial version of ColdFusion to develop up to this point, you can still use ColdFusion Express to continue your work. ColdFusion Express will not expire but has somewhat limited functionality (a number of tags are not supported).

Good luck!

Appendix E

Getting Certified in ColdFusion

There are programs and courses all over the world for developers who want to get certified in their specialty. Microsoft has dozens of opportunities for becoming certified. Oracle has a rather extensive and complex set of tracks for getting certified with their products. Luckily for us, Macromedia does too.

This book contains all of the information that you are likely to need to pass the certification.

This appendix answers some common questions about certification, offers you some tips about the test and the testing environment, and suggests some resources to help you study and learn more about ColdFusion certification. As a bonus, I've included a short sample test to help you prepare.

Common Certification Questions and Answers

There are a number of questions that developers frequently ask regarding the test. Here are some answers.

<NOTE>

If you are already a Macromedia ColdFusion 4.5 Certified Developer, you do NOT have to get recertified for 5.0—you're in! It's still a good idea to get familiar with the differences in versions, as there are many.

Why Get Certified?

These technical certifications have become huge enterprises for a number of reasons. For one, corporations have realized that the tests themselves, exam preparation software, courses, certification programs for the *instructors* for those courses, books, videos, websites, and other endless materials are very lucrative product lines in themselves. They also serve a number of actual purposes:

1. Perhaps the best reason is that they give you a good excuse to study. They help you focus your energy and your thinking as you program.
2. You'll become a better programmer because you have formalized your knowledge to a certain degree.
3. Because the test covers everything, you've got to get out of your rut a bit. That is, if all you love to do is write <CFINSERT> statements all over the place, signing up for the exam will make you brush up on your SQL.
4. You can distinguish yourself from your competition on the job market.
5. Get a raise.
6. Get listed on the Macromedia website as a ColdFusion Certified Developer.
7. Enjoy the logos and free gifts they send you when you pass.

<DISCLAIMER>

At the time of writing, the ColdFusion tests are undergoing some changes as Macromedia prepares the test for ColdFusion 5.0. Therefore, things may be a little different when you sign up for the test. Just check back with the resources I refer to here as you near test time to make sure that things are what you expect.

What Should I Expect?

It is useful for a developer to study for the test enough to pass it. It will make you a better programmer, and you really have to know your stuff. So I recommend having certification as something to aim for. However, you must make sure that your expectations are in alignment with reality to pass the test.

Am I Ready to Take the Test Now?

Dear Abby says, "If you have to ask, you aren't ready." Dear Abby was not talking about ColdFusion, but the general principle applies. Macromedia recommends that you have at least one year of developing ColdFusion applications under your belt before you try to take the test. They also recommend two years of high-level programming experience, and experience with Enterprise databases.

Academic knowledge is not a substitute for hands-on experience. While all of the material that you need in order to pass is in this book, do not drop it right now and run to the door expecting to pass.

How Do I Sign Up to Take the Test?

The test is currently offered through vue.com. To find the testing facility nearest you, visit their website or call 877-460-8679 (inside North America) or 952-995-8833 (outside North America).

VUE (Virtual University Enterprises) has more than 2,000 testing locations worldwide. Often these are in university testing centers or businesses.

How Much Does It Cost?

The test currently costs $150 U.S. The test fee is different in other countries. You can pay by credit card at vue.com.

What Do I Bring with Me?

You must present two forms of ID. One should have your picture on it (try your driver's license or passport). The other should have at least a signature. Make sure that you have your "candidate ID number" too. This is assigned to you by VUE when you sign up for the test.

How Long Does the Test Take?

You are allowed 60 minutes to complete the exam. I was nervous when I learned this, since you have to answer 61 questions. But in general the questions are brief, and the time allotment is more than generous. I finished my test in 24 minutes.

You need to allow more time than one hour, however, for the whole experience. Because there is a bit of other business for you to take care of, such as questionnaires and paperwork, you should set aside an hour and a half at least.

What Happens When I Get There?

Arrive early so you can scope the place out. No food or drinks will be allowed in the testing center. Once you sign in, you will be taken to a computer that is waiting for you with your test loaded onto it.

You will receive two blank pieces of scratch paper to use as you take the test. They will be taken back from you once you've finished the test.

Taking the Test

What Will I Be Tested On?

The following topics are the subject of the exam:

1. ColdFusion functionality
2. CFML language, general use, and syntax
3. HTML, HTTP and client (browser) behavior
4. Database concepts
5. SQL statements

The test does not divide its questions equally among these areas. The percentages below reflect the distribution of subject matter on which you will be tested.

1. 10% web fundamentals
2. 50% application development
3. 15–20% database concepts
4. 15–17% state management
5. 5% troubleshooting

What Is the Test Application Like?

Hopefully all of this will be explained to you by the person administering your test. Sometimes they skip it, in which case it is helpful to know.

You can mark questions for review. Which means that if you don't know the answer and you are concerned for time and feel you need to move on, you can return to the questions you marked and answer them later. This is a nice feature.

The test is multiple choice. Many questions have more than one correct answer, and you will be asked to indicate each correct answer. There is no partial credit; if you choose one correct and one incorrect answer on a question requiring two answers, you receive no credit whatsoever for that question.

Once you have completed the test, you will be presented with a screen showing each question number and how you answered it. You can go back and change your answer (provided that there is time remaining), or click a button to signify that you are satisfied with all of your answers.

What Score Do I Need to Pass?

The test is pass/fail, so you need to score 60% or better. Since the test is 61 questions, you need to get at least 37 of them right.

When Do I Get My Results?

Since the test is computerized, you get your results immediately. They will print you out a certificate that says that you took the test, whether or not you passed, and what your score is. This is presumably meant for your employer to verify that you were indeed taking the test, and not out playing pool with your buddies.

Note that if you fail, you must wait at least 30 days to take the test the second time. You may retake the test only twice within the same year.

What If I Need to Cancel?

You can cancel or reschedule your test up to 24 hours before your scheduled time. This is the only way to get a refund. If you cancel, you will be given a credit that you can use to schedule another time to take the exam.

What About the Fun Stuff?

If you pass, you will receive the ColdFusion Certified Professional Kit from Macromedia. It will contain a certificate suitable for framing, a disk with the Certified Professional Logo that you can use on your business cards, and other goodies like a welcome letter. You also get a gift. Allow two to three weeks for the kit to get to you, but you'll likely get it in a few days.

It will take several weeks for your name to show up on the Macromedia site. Once you're listed, it shows your name, the state you took the test in, and the date you passed.

How Do I Study for the Test?

I'm not going to insult you with advice about getting a good night's sleep and all that. There are a number of things you can do that will make you more comfortable; you know what those are. Here are some ideas to help you study:

Write Out Everything

It is not enough to read over material. Write it! Write out the tags, especially the ones that you're not familiar with. You have to write this stuff, upload it, and check it in your browser. If your job is not one where you get to sit around writing ColdFusion all day, or if there are a number of things in the language that you have not used much in your development, then this is imperative. Not familiar with structures? Sit at your desk and make a structure and populate it, manipulate the variables, and then clear it. Haven't had a chance to use WDDX? Now's the time. See if you can rewrite some code using <CFSCRIPT> (it will likely perform faster for you anyway!).

Go through the entire language—tags and functions—and write it out and make sure you've written it correctly. You'll find that this pays off in the long run, too—there is likely a world of functionality in there that you haven't explored yet.

Websites

A number of websites and tools have information on ColdFusion certification. Try these:

1. BrainBench.com. BrainBench charges for their tests (something like $20 each). They are not affiliated with any other company and are not trying to prepare you for the Macromedia exam per se. BrainBench offers a certification in its own right. You take the test with limited time (3 minutes

per question), and you receive a printed certificate ($7.95) if you pass. You take the test over the website.

2. CFCertification.com. This site allows you to take sample tests, and it's free. For $25 you can buy their study guide.
3. CentraSoft.com. CentraSoft makes a tool called CF_Buster which you can download for free from their website. The demo version doesn't expire and contains 61 questions for you to test yourself with from the comfort of your desktop. The commercial version has 500 questions.
4. ECertifications.com. They offer sample tests in ColdFusion and dozens of other IT topics. The site itself is handsomely written in ColdFusion!

Review Material

Read over sections in this book and any other ColdFusion books you may have, brushing up on topics that you don't feel comfortable with.

Allaire Alive

Allaire has offered short Flash clips viewable over their website which detail how different aspects of ColdFusion work, best practices, and other training topics. Many of these are led by Jeremy Allaire (creator of ColdFusion) and other top ColdFusion engineers. Whether or not these will make it to the Macromedia site we have yet to see. Currently they are located at http://www.Allaire.com/allairealive.

Courses

You can sign up for the Fast Track to ColdFusion course or the Advanced Course in ColdFusion offered by Macromedia-certified instructors. These courses last 2–3 days and are rather expensive ($1,200–$3,000). They are offered throughout the year, usually in the larger cities in any given state. Check the Macromedia website for more information.

Do-It-Yourself

Use the exercises and questions in this book to create flash cards. Get together with a friend and quiz each other. Read the tag and function references from start to finish.

Sample Test

The sample test below will give you an idea of the kinds of things you'll be asked on the test, how the questions might look, and the skill level you'll need to pass. If you don't get more than 90%, study a little more, code a little more, and then come back and quiz yourself again. These questions may be harder or easier than real test questions. Good luck!

1. **What is the output of the following code?**

```
<cfset one = "Hello">
<cfset two = "World">
<cfloop from="1" to="2" index="i">
<cfoutput>"#one#" & "#two#"</cfoutput>
</cfloop>
```

   a. The code will throw a ColdFusion error
   b. Hello & World Hello & World
   c. Hello Hello World World
   d. Hello World Hello World

2. **What languages can you use to write custom tags? (Choose three)**
   a. JavaScript
   b. Java
   c. C ++
   d. ColdFusion
   e. Visual Basic
   f. SQL

3. **Why will this code break?**

```
<cfquery datasource="cf5DB" name="myquery">
    INSERT INTO Users (FirstName, LastName)
    SET VALUES  = 'Eben', 'Hewitt'
</cfquery>
```

   a. The "SET" keyword is not used in INSERT statements.
   b. It is incorrect to use single quote marks around string values.

c. Parentheses are not used in INSERT statements.
d. "Database," not "Datasource," is the correct attribute to use in a <CFQUERY> tag.

4. What will be the result of the following code?

```
<cfcookie name="password" value="password" secure="No">
<cfset LoggedIn = "True">
<cflocation url="SomePage.html">
```

a. The cookie will be set on the client and the user will be redirected to "SomePage.html." SomePage.html will be aware of the value of the variable "LoggedIn."
b. The cookie will be set on the client and then ColdFusion will throw an error: it is illegal to specify anything other than .cfm files when using <CFLOCATION>.
c. The user will be redirected to "SomePage.html." The cookie will not be set. "SomePage.html" will have no awareness of the value of the "LoggedIn" variable.
d. The cookie will be set. The user will not be redirected. ColdFusion will throw an error: the correct attribute for the <CFLOCATION> tag is "template," not "url."

5. True or false: The default method of a <FORM> tag is "POST."

a. True
b. False

6. Which of the following are legal to use within a <CFIF> tag when comparing two expressions? (Choose two)

a. GTE
b. IS GREATER THAN
c. NEQ
d. =

7. Which of the following HTML tags were deprecated in HTML 4.0? (Choose two)

a. <DIV>
b. <HR>
c. <FONT>
d. <CENTER>

8. **ColdFusion creates certain variable scopes as structures. Choose *three* of them from the following list:**
   a. SESSION
   b. VARIABLES
   c. URL
   d. CLIENT
   e. CGI
   f. COOKIE

9. **True or False: OnRequestEnd.cfm will not be executed without a corresponding application.cfm file available to the current application.**
   a. True
   b. False

10. **What will be the output of the following code?**

```
<cfset FirstName = "Alison">
<cfset LastName = "Brown">
<cfswitch expression="#FirstName#">
    <cfcase value="Eben">
          Your first name is Eben.
    </cfcase>
    <cfcase value="Alison">
          Your first name is Alison.
                <cfswitch expression="LastName">
                      <cfcase value="Brown">
                            Your last name is Brown.
                      </cfcase>
                </cfswitch>
    </cfcase>
</cfswitch>
```

   a. Nothing. ColdFusion will throw an error.
   b. Your first name is Eben.
   c. Your first name is Alison. Your last name is Brown.
   d. Your first name is Alison.

11. **Why will the following code fail?**

```
<CFSCRIPT>
idx = 0;
if (isDefined("FORM.fieldnames"))
 {do while (idx LT ListLen(form.fieldnames))
  {
  idx = idx + 1;
```

```
  WriteOutput("<input type='hidden'
name='#ListGetAt(form.fieldnames, idx)#'

    value='#Evaluate("#ListGetAt(form.fieldnames,
idx)#")#'>");
  }
 }
</CFSCRIPT>
```

a. You cannot use ListGetAt for FORM variables. They are not returned as a list.
b. The "WriteOutput" statement is incorrectly constructed.
c. You cannot use tags inside a <CFSCRIPT> block.
d. There is no such thing as a "do while" loop. It should be a "for" loop.

12. Assuming today is March 27, 2002, what is the output of the following code?

```
<cfapplication name="TestApp">
<cfset application.ThisDate = "#Now()#">
<cfset strKeyArr = StructKeyArray(application)>

<cfloop from="1" to="#ArrayLen(strKeyArr)#" index="idx">
  <cfoutput>Key #idx# is #strKeyArr[idx]#,</cfoutput>
</cfloop>
```

a. Key 1 is APPLICATIONNAME, Key 2 is THISDATE,
b. Name = TestApp, ThisDate=02-Mar-27 00:00:00:00
c. Nothing. ColdFusion will throw an error.
d. Key APPLICATION is TestApp, Key THISDATE is 02-Mar-27 00:00:00:00

13. The following page is named "test.cfm." What would be output to the browser were the page accessed in the following manner: `'test.cfm?Render=Welcome&Style=Cool'`?

```
<cfscript>
    strMain = StructNew();
    if (IsDefined("URL.Render"))
          strMain.Render = URL.Render;
    else if (IsDefined("Form.Render"))
          strMain.Render = Form.Render;
    else
          strMain.Render = "Default";
</cfscript>
<cfoutput>#strMain.Render# #strMain.Style#</cfoutput>
```

a. Welcome Cool
b. The browser would output “Default” and ignore the Style=Cool query string.
c. The browser would output “Welcome” and *then* throw an error: “Style” is not a valid key in the strMain structure.
d. ColdFusion would throw an error: you cannot create a structure within a <CFSCRIPT> block.

14. Which function is used to retrieve information (such as variables and scopes) about an ancestor tag?

a. GetBaseTagData()
b. GetBaseTagInfo()
c. GetAncestorData()
d. GetCaller()

15. Which function returns the closest integer greater than a given number?

a. NextInt
b. Ceiling
c. Round
d. IntUp

16. The “Sales” table has 7,000 records for different products. The “NumberSold” column can be empty if a particular product has not yet been sold. What is the result of the following SQL?

```
<cfquery name="PutSales" datasource="SalesDB">
    UPDATE Sales
    SET NumberSold = NumberSold + 1
    WHERE 0 = 0
          <cfif NumberSold IS NOT NULL>AND 0 < 1</cfif>
</cfquery>
```

a. One record will be updated if there is no value yet in the NumberSold column.
b. All 7,000 records in the table will be updated.
c. Only products which have been sold at least once already will be updated.
d. ColdFusion will throw an error: the <CFIF> statement is improperly used, since ColdFusion cannot know the value of NumberSold in this context alone.
e. SQL will throw an error: it is illegal to add a number to a text string.

17. Surrounding your code with <CFLOCK> tags is crucial for which of the following situations? (choose one)

a. When reading or writing APPLICATION or SESSION variables.
b. When querying a database with a SELECT statement.
c. When looping over a result set, list, structure, or array.
d. When your code contains very complex or nested conditional logic.

18. How far up a directory tree will ColdFusion search for an Application.cfm file?

a. Within the current directory only.
b. A maximum of 4 directories.
c. It first looks in the current directory, then in the C:\Cfusion\Applications\ directory.
d. Until it reaches the web root of the current application.
e. Until it reaches the root of the web server.
f. All the way up the directory tree until it reaches the root of the hard drive.

19. What is the best choice for stopping the processing of a custom tag and returning to the caller page?

a. <CFABORT>
b. <CFEXIT>
c. <CFBREAK>
d. <CFRETURN>

20. What is the purpose of the <CFASSOCIATE> tag?

a. Associate a given authentication security context with a particular user.
b. Pass data from the parent custom tag into a child custom tag.
c. Pass data from the child custom tag back to the parent custom tag.
d. Link a custom tag to a particular application.

21. What is the output of the following code?

```
<CFHTTP URL="http://www.conditionallogic.com"
    METHOD="get"
    RESOLVEURL="true">
</CFHTTP>
<CFOUTPUT>#cfhttp.FileContent#</CFOUTPUT>
```

a. The code returns a data object containing variables.
b. The HTML code for the specified web page will be displayed.
c. The code will fail: cfhttp.FileContent is not a valid variable name.
d. The agent will retrieve the web page at the specified URL, and it will be displayed on the page.

22. You may use a trigger in conjunction with which of the following SQL keywords?

a. SELECT
b. UPDATE
c. INSERT
d. CONTROL
e. DELETE

23. How does CFPOP identify mail message numbers?

a. It doesn't.
b. As a parameter within CFID and CFTOKEN.
c. Relative to the position of emails in your message queue on the mail server. The ID numbers change when one is deleted.
d. With a unique identifier recorded in C:\Cfusion\Bin\Mail.

24. Which of the following file extensions may be indexed with <CFINDEX> in a Verity 2K collection? (Choose all that apply.)

a. .ppt
b. .doc
c. .pdf
d. .jpg
e. .htm
f. .cfm
g. .pl

25. Choose the true statements regarding the <CFTRANSACTION> tag.

a. It is used to support the COMMIT and ROLLBACK operations of your relational database.
b. You may nest <CFTRANSACTION> tags.

c. <CFTRANSACTION> is deprecated in ColdFusion 5.0. Where possible, you should use <CFLOCK> instead.
d. You may use a trailing slash (XML syntax) for writing a stand-alone <CFTRANSACTION/> tag.

26. Other than ColdFusion, which languages support WDDX?

a. C++
b. Perl
c. JavaScript
d. PHP
e. Java

27. Choose the true statements regarding WDDX:

a. OpenWDDX.org allows you to download a free SDK for working with WDDX.
b. WDDX is a proprietary language that ColdFusion employs to run probes.
c. JS2WDDX is a valid attribute of the WDDX tag.
d. WDDX is an acronym for "Web Distributed Data eXchange."

28. (Choose 1 answer) The <CFGRAPH> tag . . .

a. Integrates with Macromedia Generator to create dynamic reporting graphs.
b. Accepts "Pie," "Gannt," "Radius," and "Line" as possible values of the "TYPE" attribute.
c. Requires use of the child tags, <CFGRAPHPARAM> and <CFGRAPHITEM>.
d. Imports the Macr.CFGRAPH.Java.Class file to display dynamic graphs as Java applets.

29. What is the output of running this user-defined function and accompanying code?

```
<CFSCRIPT>
   function MoodRing(string)
        {
        return Replace(string, ":(", ":)", "ALL");
        }
</CFSCRIPT>
<CFSET MyVar = ":(">
<CFOUTPUT>#MoodRing(MyVar)#</CFOUTPUT>
```

a. Nothing. ColdFusion throws an error because of incorrect syntax.
b. :(
c. ALL
d. :)

30. Name the platforms that are supported by ColdFusion 5. (Choose all that apply.)

a. HP-UX
b. Sun Solaris
c. Linux RedHat 5.2 or better
d. Cobalt, RedHat 6 or better, and suSE
e. Windows 2000
f. Windows NT 4.0, service pack 4 or better

That is the end of the test. Please refer to the next page for the answers. If you score below a 27, mark the sections that you found difficult and study them before taking the actual test.

Sample Test Answers

Here are the answers to the sample test questions.

1. b
2. b, c, d
3. a
4. c
5. b
6. a, c
7. b, d
8. a, c, f
9. a
10. d
11. d
12. a
13. c
14. a
15. b
16. b
17. a
18. f
19. b
20. c
21. d
22. b, c, e
23. c
24. a, b, c, e, f
25. a, b, d
26. b, c, d
27. a, d
28. a
29. d
30. a, b, d, e

Appendix F

Best Practices

This chapter is a list of best practices for working with ColdFusion, divided into the following useful categories: Files, Speed & Performance, Database Issues, Security Issues, and General Issues. That means that these are guidelines for you to follow as you develop. While your code can certainly work if you don't do these, it might not perform as quickly, and it might be harder to follow. I urge you to come up with your own best practices as you work and pass them on to others for consideration.

Files

Give Your Files Meaningful Names

Prefix complex types like structure, arrays, and queries so that you can recognize them instantly as such. For instance, use "arr" for arrays, "str" for structures, "q" for queries. It's easy to understand "arrImageTypes," its relationships, and what kind of information you can expect from it. It's easier to understand "qGetAllUsers" than "gtusr." Be merciful to posterity.

It's also a good idea to give your templates lowercase names if you have to port to a UNIX platform after working with Windows. This one is hard to keep in mind, since ColdFusion is not case sensitive.

Comment Your Code

At the top of every template, include the following information as comments:

1. Template name
2. Author's name
3. Date created
4. Date last modified
5. Use (what pages call the template, the chain of events that the user might set in motion to call this particular page)
6. Purpose (what does this template do?)

Here is an example:

```
<!-----
    Template: act_AdAffiliateInsert.cfm

    Author: Eben Hewitt, eben@conditionallogic.com

    Purpose: Inserts a new Ad Affiliate profile into
                the Users table.

    Use: called from Step 2 of act_AdAffiliateSignUp.cfm

    Date Created: 2/16/01

    Date Last Modified: Tuesday, February 20, 2001 3:28:14 PM
----->
```

You know exactly what will be impacted if you change something, and you can easily debug this and its constellation templates. I urge you to follow this practice.

Always Use Application.cfm and OnRequestEnd.cfm

Even if you do not have a use for these files, ColdFusion will go hunting for them on every request. Your page processing time will speed up just by including empty files with these names in your site folder.

<NOTE>

Let us now be disabused of a commonly held yet fallacious belief: The truth is this: ColdFusion will search all the way up to the root of your server for an application.cfm file. That is, it only stops when it gets to C:\. Don't make it do all of this work, and don't let your applications be potentially exposed to a wandering application.cfm somewhere up the tree.

Set Defaults Only Once

This rule is stated as a corollary of the above, since it involves application.cfm. Many developers like to set applicationwide variables, such as a title or a datasource in application.cfm. But they don't check to see if their variables are defined, so they end up running the same code over and over. Use a check to see if a variable has been set. If it has, then move on. This will be slightly faster, and it is better programming form. Like this:

```
<cfif NOT isDefined("application.Datasource")>
  <cfset application.Datasource = "MyDatabase">
</cfif>
```

Use Relative Paths

Put your work into folders that make sense. This makes it easier to work with included files. If you use Flash with ColdFusion, you can create Flash menus that call the GetURL action and still work in every subdirectory.

Segment Your Code

Use indenting in your code so that you can easily read things that are embedded within each other. Let's say your table nested five tables deep isn't showing up in Netscape 4.7. It's happier to have to sort through this:

```
<table width="150" border="0" cellspacing="0">
    <tr>
       <td bgcolor="#311466">
            <!--- search box --->
            <p align="center">Search</p>
       </td>
    </tr>
</table>
```

than this:

```
<table width="150" border="0" cellspacing="0"><tr>
<td bgcolor="#311466"> <--- search box --->
<p align="center">Search</p></td></tr></table>
```

Use spacing in your templates so that you can follow them easily. ColdFusion won't mind. ColdFusion Studio, DreamWeaver, and other such programs can handle this for you so you don't sit there cobbling tabs and spaces together.

Speed and Performance

The following miscellaneous factors can speed your performance and encourage durability and scalability in your applications.

Rewrite Your Page If It Is Slower than 2000 Milliseconds

Two thousand milliseconds (two seconds) is the limit. If you use debugging output (as you should, see below), then you will be able to gauge how long it takes CFAS to process your request. I did not write "page," because you may have many levels of included files, queries, and so on that all have to run to make up a single request. If any request takes longer than 2000 milliseconds, it's a candidate for rewriting. We can generally exclude from this rule operations that you know will take a long time and rely on external factors, such as a <CFHTTP> call.

Use <cfswitch> Instead of <cfif>

This rule makes sense only on two occasions (though these are frequently confronted):

1. When you have a specific expression you can evaluate against.
2. When you have a set of more than three <cfelseif> clauses.

Your code will perform faster.

Use <cfscript> Instead of Three or More <cfset>s

When you use cfscript, the entire block gets sent to the engine at once. So ColdFusion has to make only one read. When you send three or more <cfset> statements, ColdFusion gets to interpret them once each, or three times. Therefore, the former is faster and cleaner.

Eschew IIF

The "immediate if" function (IIF) will process nearly two times slower than a cfif/cfelse block that accomplishes the same thing. Moreover, it is harder to read.

Database Issues

Let the Database Do the Work

If you are going to perform some aggregate function on data that resides in your database, do it there. That's what it is made to do. Your code will run faster. You can do *formatting* of data in your code, however, so you have more control.

For instance, SQL includes a number of aggregate and scalar functions that are also available in ColdFusion.

Functions that are replicated include most mathematical functions, date and time functions, trim string functions, and more. Remember that if you employ conditional logic or other ColdFusion code inside your SQL statement, ColdFusion will create the statement first and *then* send the SQL statement off to the database. You do not incur a longer database connection time by writing complex CF code in your <CFQUERY>s.

Use the Maxrows Attribute of the <cfquery> Tag

If you know how many rows you're supposed to get (say you're checking for the existence of a matching username and password that should be unique, and therefore have only one row return), set the maxrows attribute to "1," and give your database a break.

Don't Let Query-of-Queries Capability Make You Lazy

You might find it tempting with the query-of-queries capability new in ColdFusion to think about loading your entire 3,000-row product table into web server memory and start querying that for your e-commerce application. Depending on your site, this may not be careful designing or prudent use of resources. Determine what you need, and use only that. Determine your trade-offs and act according to greatest benefit (do some tests).

There are major benefits to the new query-of-queries capability; among these are the ability to perform cross-datasource joins, cross-datasource unions, and in-memory denormalization. And of course it is faster to retrieve memory-resident values. All of these can really bring together enterprise business applications; that doesn't make query-of-queries a license to slouch.

Security Issues

Do Not Use Hidden Fields to Pass Sensitive Information

You might be thinking, duh—because someone can do a view source in the browser and read the information. I'm not talking about people reading information you do not want them to read (that should be obvious). I am talking about allowing them to *modify* your data.

Let's say that you have a shopping cart that passes information about the products your user is purchasing, including the prices, passing in hidden form fields. If I view the source of this page and save it as an .htm file to my desktop, I can then edit the file. Once I have changed the prices to whatever I want, I can then pass the form to an absolute URL (instead of the relative URL specified in the form action attribute), and I can continue to check out normally.

This is not specifically a ColdFusion issue, since you might use hidden form fields in this way on an ASP, CGI site or any other kind of site. I'm not saying don't use hidden fields. I'm saying be careful what you pass in them.

Use Code for Security Contexts

It's a better idea to write your authentication frameworks into your code. If you overuse the CF Administrator's security contexts, you can get into porting hassles if you ever want to move your application. Avoid proliferating <cfauthenticate> tags.

Use <cflock> around <cfhttp> Calls

The <cfhttp> tag is used in a single thread by ColdFusion. Locking these calls will help cut down on p-code errors.

General Issues

Use Conditional Logic Logically

This may sound redundant, but it isn't. Conditional logic is a lot more than a couple of if/else statements. You must distill in your applications the *sine qua non* of each block and write your logic from that. You shouldn't have to check for more than two circumstances or current states at any given time, and you can often get away with one. The way you do this is by contextualizing your code. Nest your logic in a thoughtful, mathematical manner, and your pages will fly. They will also be simple to read and debug.

ColdFusion's short circuit logic aims to speed things up. You can do your part.

Copy Session and Application Variables into the Request Scope

I have Raymond Camden, Spectra Compliance Manager, to thank for telling me about this one. It is imperative that you write <cflock>s around references to session and application variables. So, instead of having to make sure that you've locked everything in all of the many places where you might refer to variables in both of these scopes, copy them to the REQUEST scope. In application.cfm, write this:

```
<CFLOCK TYPE="ReadOnly" SCOPE="Application" TIMEOUT=30>
  <CFSET Request.App = Duplicate(APPLICATION)>
</CFLOCK>


<CFLOCK TYPE="ReadOnly" SCOPE="Session" TIMEOUT=30>
    <CFSET Request.Ses = Duplicate(SESSION)>
</CFLOCK>
```

What you're doing is copying the structure that holds all of the application variables into the request scope, and then the same for session variables. Because you do it in application.cfm, you can reference these variables without having to lock them. But they act exactly the same way (as long as you *copy any changes back again* into the application and session scopes at the end of the page). Say you have a database that you set in application.cfm to be your global datasource, like this:

```
<cflock type="EXCLUSIVE" timeout="30" throwontimeout="Yes">
    <cfset Application.Datasource = "MyDatabase">
</cflock>
```

Then, when I later try to refer to it, I've got to lock that, too:

```
<cflock type="READONLY" timeout="10" throwontimeout="Yes">
          <cfquery name="getUsers"
          datasource="#Application.Datasource#">
</cflock>
```

This can get silly after a while.

Using the above trick, you can just refer to your variables like this instead:

```
<cfquery name="getUsers"
      datasource="#Request.App.Datasource#">
```

Note that you can also use the function StructCopy(APPLICATION) to accomplish the same thing if you prefer. And remember that you have to copy any potentially changed variables into their proper scope, once you've had your way with them in your page. So in OnRequestEnd.cfm. I usually do this:

```
<cflock name="RequestToApp" timeout="20"
         throwontimeout="Yes" type="READONLY">
    <cfset Application = StructCopy(Request.App)>
</cflock>
```

This will make your code shorter, cleaner, easier to read, and less error-prone. It will also make it easier to incorporate custom tags later.

Use Debugging Settings

There's not a reason in the world not to have the debugging options turned on throughout your development. They will cut down on your goofy time significantly.

First, in the Administrator, go to Debugging IPs in the Server menu (it's the default). Add your IP address to the form and hit Add Current.

Then return to the Server menu, choose Debugging Options, and check the boxes that you want to output. Note that if you choose *Show Detailed Processing Time Breakdown,* then you will have to restart your server.

Not only does the debugging output give you a good sense of what is running on each page and what variables are available, it can help you improve your design. For instance, if you see that a number of pages have a FORM variable present that you need only once or twice, then get rid of it, and reference it only where you need it.

Also, you will see all of the 45 CGI variables that are available to you. Some of these are new with ColdFusion 5.0, and they might give you ideas about what you can do in your ColdFusion pages that you hadn't thought of before.

For example, there's probably a good implementation of an intranet that can use the brand spanking new CGI.AUTH_USER variable, since it works in conjunction with NT challenge-response authentication.

I hope that these best practices make working with ColdFusion yield better results for you. If you come up with a best practice of your own, spread the word!

Appendix G

Wireless ColdFusion with WAP and WML

This appendix introduces you to the Wireless Application Protocol and the Wireless Markup Language. We will cover how you can use WML with ColdFusion to create dynamic websites for web-enabled cell phones and PDAs. Don't panic at the thought of having to learn another language. It's not all that hard to get started, and you'll be up and running in no time. We'll just examine the basic structure of the WML, and then you can apply much of what you've learned about ColdFusion here.

After this introduction on how to use ColdFusion with WAP and WML, you'll have a complete, working, data-driven wireless address book.

Wireless Application Protocol

WAP is a protocol, like HTTP, used to transfer information between a number of different kinds of wireless devices. These include web-enabled cellular phones, personal digital assistants, palmtops, so-called "smart-devices," and mini-computers. We have already started to see wireless appliances in cars.

As of this writing, WAP is still in iteration 1.2, though WAP 2.0 should be approved soon.

What It Is

The Wireless Application Protocol is a set of global, open standards that define the communications of wireless networks. Based on existing protocols, such as HTTP, WAP has been optimized for the wireless transfer of information.

WAP standards have been published by the WAP Forum since June of 1997. The Forum consists of more than five hundred members, including Ericsson, Motorola, Nokia, Microsoft, Hewlett-Packard, and IBM.

WAP is intended for quick, mobile use. This has a number of implications for us as we attempt to serve Internet sites across it:

1. You get only around 9600 bps.
2. It is not particularly reliable. From behind very much concrete your signal can get distorted or lost completely.
3. It is high-latency (your requests can commonly take a number of seconds).

For these reasons, WAP requires a number of complementary functions that often aren't necessary in HTTP. For instance, it can keep track of session state, even if your connection gets lost.

How It Works

The WAP Browser

First, you have to get a WAP browser. Just as you need an HTTP-enabled browsing program like Netscape or Internet Explorer to view pages on the web, so too you need a WAP-enabled browser for viewing on the wireless web.

A number of browsers are available, and unfortunately, they interpret Wireless Markup (the language that wireless pages are written in) very differently. Table G.1 shows many of the commonly available WAP browsers.

Table G.1 WAP Browsers

Browser	*Description*	*Where to Get It*
WinWAP3	Runs on Windows so you can view WAP content as you would in your regular browser. Looks like an HTTP browser, so it is familiar.	A 30-day trial is available from http://www.slobtrot.com. You can purchase the full version for $35.

Browser	*Description*	*Where to Get It*
Mobile Browser	This free browser toolkit is a popular development tool. It emulates the size and shape of the phone, making it easy to see what your code will look like in the real world. Skin-able!	http://www.openwave.com
Motorola	Gives you a good replication of how your code will run for this particular market segment.	http://www.Motorola.com
Ericsson	This toolkit includes a few different browsers.	http://www.Ericsson.com
Palm	WAPMan is the browser used for the Palm OS.	http://www.palmos.com/dev/tech/tools/emulator/

Note that this is a rather new technology, and therefore the browsers available for it are changing quickly.

Using a WAP browser, you can access pages written in WML, the Wireless Markup Language, which we will address in a moment. The WAP user makes a page request, the server housing the documents (which is often a standard HTTP server) communicates with what is known as the WAP gateway.

The WAP Gateway

The WAP Gateway has one purpose: to convert the housing server's required HTTP into WAP, so it can send a legible transfer back to the client browser. The gateway itself is really a set of software programs that make this conversion. Since this can be rather expensive and complex, the most common way of connecting to one of these gateways is to subscribe to the service of a gateway provider.

Wireless Markup Language

If you are familiar with XML, WML should be no problem. It is not an extensive language by any means, and you can learn enough in this appendix to get you started.

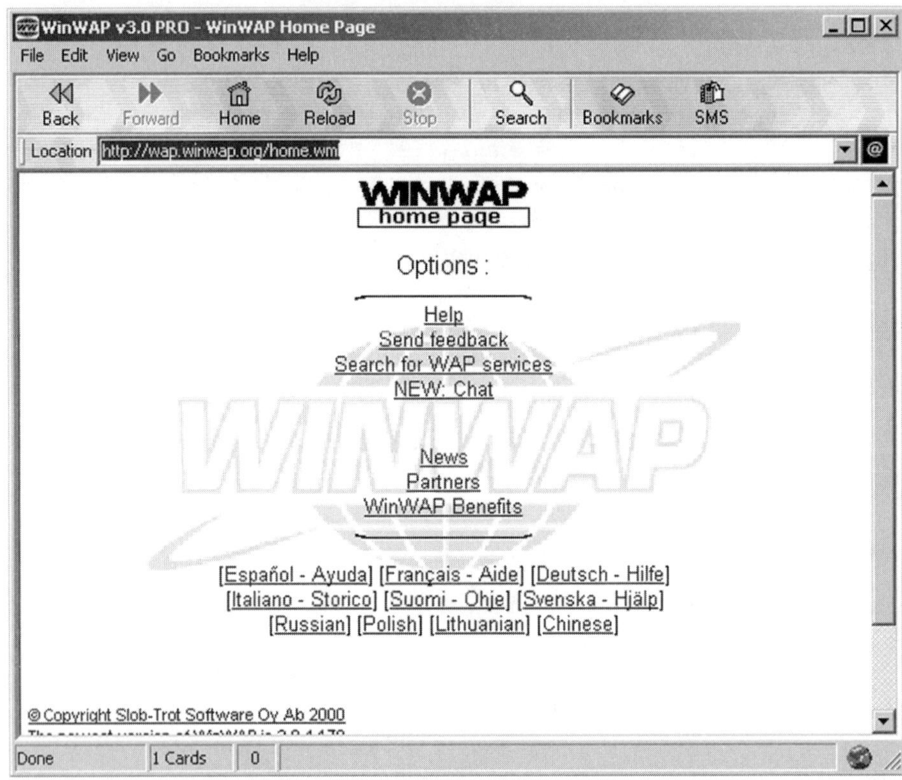

Figure G.1 A WAP Browser that runs on Windows.

What You Need

A WAP Browser or Phone Emulator

You should download any or all of the emulators mentioned in Table G.1. They're generally free (though some are free for only 30 days). You want more than one, because with wireless you've got compatibility issues to face. It's difficult to know what phones your users will have, so go ahead and test your work on a few different browsers. (See Figure G.1.)

I suggest that at least you use the Openwave UP.SDK (it used to be Phone.com).

WAP Content Type Support

In order to write your WML pages, you need nothing other than a plain text editor. If you are using ColdFusion Studio, you will be pleased to note that it has support for WML.

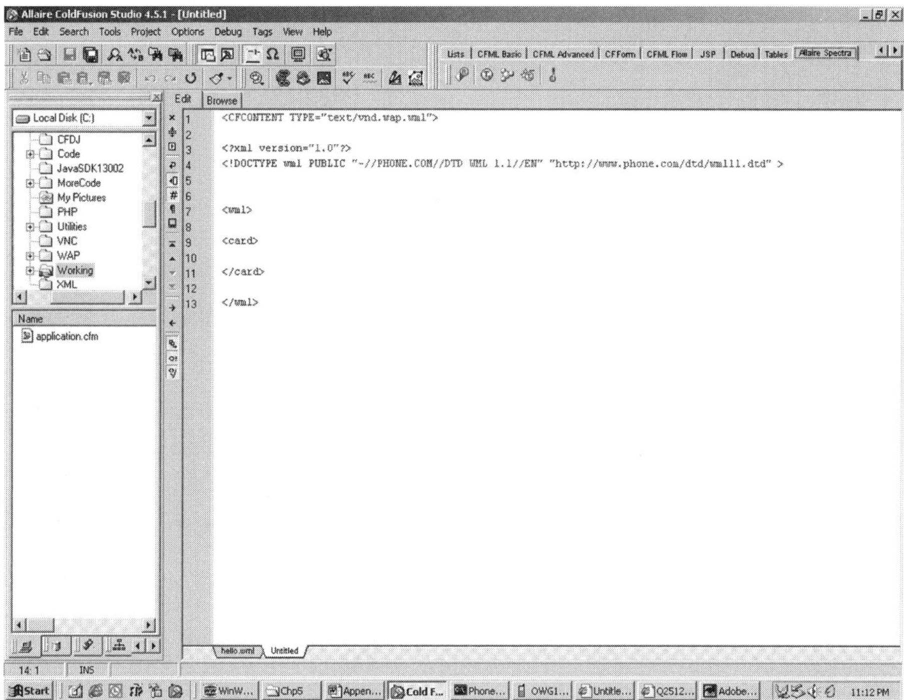

Figure G.2 Default WML document in ColdFusion Studio.

Click File > New. Choose the WML tab. Then choose "Dynamic (Using CF)." ColdFusion Studio will open a default document that looks something like Figure G.2.

All of the Phone.com business referred to in the default Studio document is okay. Phone became Openwave in late 2000, so it will be compatible with the documents you write.

What you will certainly need to do, however, is tell your web server that you are planning to accept WML. The output is XML compliant. It's a process no different than telling your web server to understand CFML and use cfserver.exe to process the requests (which outputs HTML-compliant text). Here, you're telling your web server to use the remote WAP gateway to process it. Also, with ColdFusion, Install Shield does that for you. With wireless (for now, anyway), you get to do it yourself.

<NOTE>

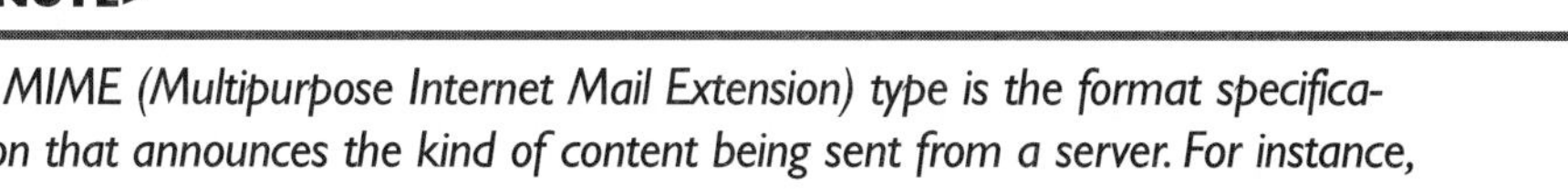

A MIME (Multipurpose Internet Mail Extension) type is the format specification that announces the kind of content being sent from a server. For instance,

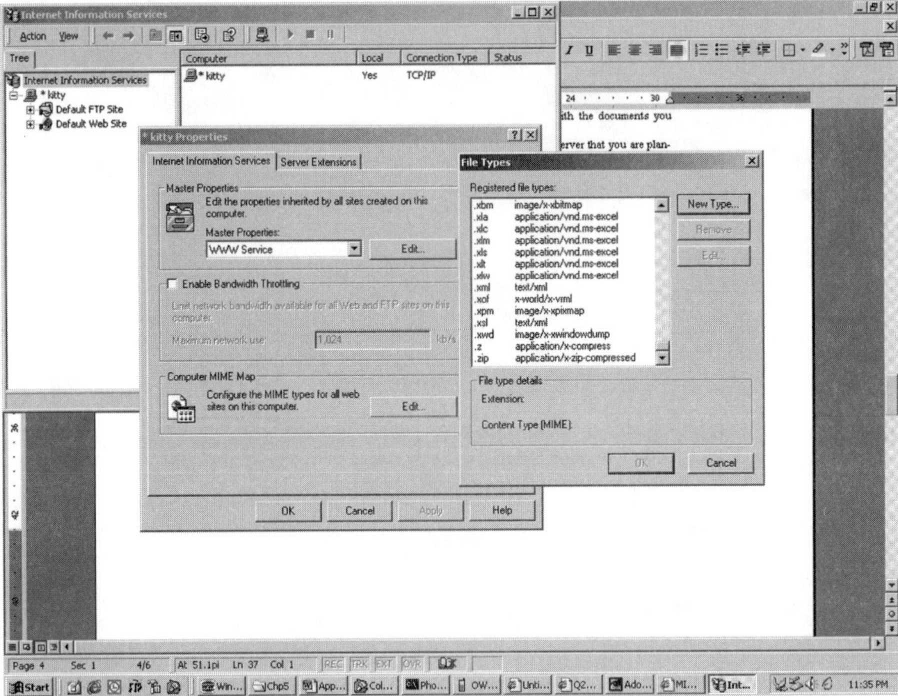

Figure G.3 Editing the MIME map in Internet Information Services.

the MIME type of HTML is text/HTML. The MIME type of a .gif image is image/gif. While these are predefined, you can also create your own.

So here is how you do that in Microsoft Internet Information Services:

1. Open IIS. You do this by going to Start > Programs > Administrative Tools > Internet Services Manager.
2. Right click on your machine name to bring up a menu. Select Properties.
3. Near the bottom you will see Computer MIME Map (Figure G.3). Click on Edit.
4. You will see a list of all currently available MIME types. Click New Type.
5. In the first (top) field, type: wml
6. In the second (bottom) field, type: text/vnd.wap.wml
7. Click `OK` three times. You're good to go.

WML—It's XML!

The Wireless Markup Language is an application of XML, the eXtensible Markup Language. By *application* in this context, I don't mean like a ColdFusion application, I mean that it is an instantiation of the abstract. This is what XML is itself—an application of SGML (Standard Generalized Markup).

SGML was created in 1986 by the International Organization for Standards (ISO—no, that's not a typo, it's French). Its purpose is to define a set of rules for "marking up" documents—that is, defining their structure and internal relations. So HTML is an instantiation of how to mark up HyperText documents.

XML is more flexible and less complex than SGML and has therefore been adopted as the abstract layer on which to base subsequent markup languages. (Also, you can send XML documents over http, which you can't do with SGML). XML is really a meta-language that defines how one can define tags, and the structural relationships between them. So we now have MathML, for instance, which is a way for mathematicians to exchange documents and have confidence that they will always be readable with each other. SMIL (pronounced "smile") is the Synchronized Multimedia Language, which is used to present video, audio, and graphic-rich presentations to users, especially those with disabilities.

New specifications crop up all the time. An exciting one is VoiceXML. The only VoiceXML browser as of this writing can be downloaded for free from IBM at http://alphaworks.ibm.com, and it is currently available for Windows only. The idea with VoiceXML is that you can access these documents via your regular telephone.

<NOTE>

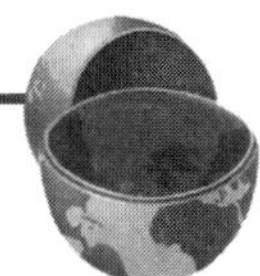

You can read a good deal about these specifications, and the entire proposals themselves, at http://www.w3c.org, home of the World Wide Web Consortium.

WML is the XML-based language for writing wireless sites, optimized to travel over the WAP. The point is that if you know much about XML, you're a long way toward knowing WML.

<NOTE>

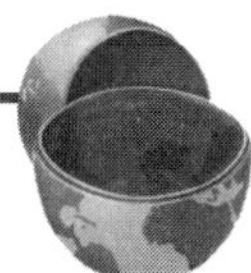

Another language commonly used to create wireless web pages is HDML. Since our larger purpose is to get you up and running with ColdFusion, we won't discuss it here.

Syntax

WML documents have the following structure:

1. An XML prolog
2. The <wml> tag.
3. A deck of more *cards* containing wml tags and your site content.

Here's what each is:

The XML Prolog

The first lines of the prolog tell the browser what document type to expect, and where on the Internet it can find the Document Type Definition that will help it interpret the markup. The standard prolog looks like this:

```
<?xml version="1.0"?>
<!DOCTYPE wml PUBLIC "-//WAPFORUM//DTD WML 1.2//EN"
    "http://www.wapform.org/DTD/wml12.xml">
```

The WML standard is currently in version 1.2. Check www.wapforum.org for updates.

The <wml> Tag

This is like the <HTML> tag in HTML; it tells the browser what kind of content to expect to have to interpret.

A Deck of Cards

In HTML, we view one Web page at a time. When we are interested in something, we click on it and initiate a new request. Because of the limited bandwidth that small wireless devices have to work with, and the limited display space on the phone, doing things this way would take a very long time for a basic set of transactions. Therefore, a call to a wireless page will return a *deck*. Each deck will contain a set of one or more (usually not more than eight) cards.

A card is a page to present to the user, generally encapsulating one small paragraph of text or a menu, for instance. Cards are batched in decks of related information and linked internally so that you needn't make a separate round trip each time you want to go to the next page. You can just call the next card in the deck that has already downloaded to the user's device.

Here are some important things to remember about writing WML:

1. All tag names are case sensitive.
2. You must enter all tag names in lowercase.

Write Your First Wireless Web Page

Open ColdFusion Studio or your text editor to a blank page. Type the following code:

```
<?xml version="1.0"?>
<!DOCTYPE wml PUBLIC "-//WAPFORUM//DTD WML 1.2//EN"
    "http://www.wapforum.org/DTD/wml12.dtd">

<wml>
    <card id="intro" title="I am like the HTML title tag">
          <p>Goodbye Cruel World!</p>
    </card>
    </wml>
```

<NOTE>

You must have no whitespace whatsoever between the XML prolog and the beginning of the document.

Open your WML browser and type the location of your document in the address bar. If you are using the Openwave SDK, your display should look like Figure G.4.

Here is a breakdown of your first WML page:

First, you declare the XML version. You then declare the document type as "wml" and tell the browser where it can find the definition for this document type, so it knows how to understand the markup.

Next, you announce the beginning of your deck with the <wml> tag. You define an individual card as an organized unit of information. The <p> and </p> tags, which are required, work much as they do in HTML. Then you type the text you want to display to your users, and close out your tags. Voila.

<NOTE>

You must use end tags in WML. There are certain tags that do not sensibly have end tags (such as the <hr> tag in HTML, or the <input> tag in WML. These are known as empty tags, *and you need to specify them using a trailing slash, like this: <input name="/login/"/>.*

The "title" attribute of the <card> tag does not show up in the Openwave emulator. I included it specifically to demonstrate this point. You need to check your WML in multiple devices or emulators.

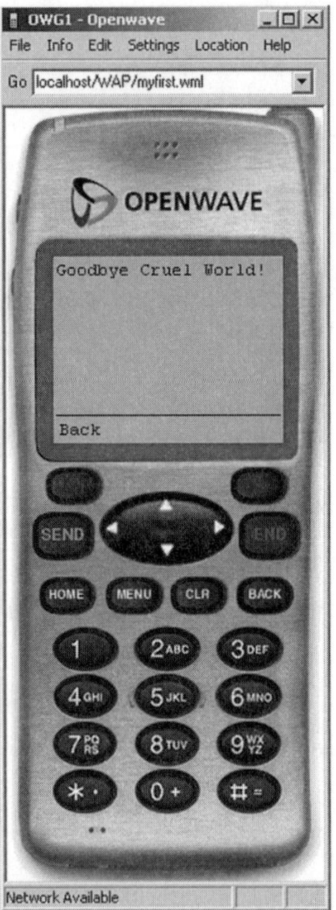

Figure G.4 Viewing a WML document in the Openwave emulator. Image of UP.SDK courtesy Openwave Systems Inc.

If You Got an Error

The most common error for beginning developers is the *406: No Acceptable Objects Found.* What it means is that you have inadvertently used the Accept-Language header and have not specified an Accept header other than text/plain and text/html. Since your WML pages have the .wml extension, the server determines that your type is octect/stream and returns an error.

To fix it, make sure that you have registered the wireless MIME type with your server. I have demonstrated above how to do this in IIS 5.0.

Also, you've probably noticed, when you launch your Openwave emulator, that you see two windows actually opened: the phone emulator window and a DOS window. The DOS window is a very helpful companion that displays a good deal of information about the request that was sent. Figure G.5 shows its output.

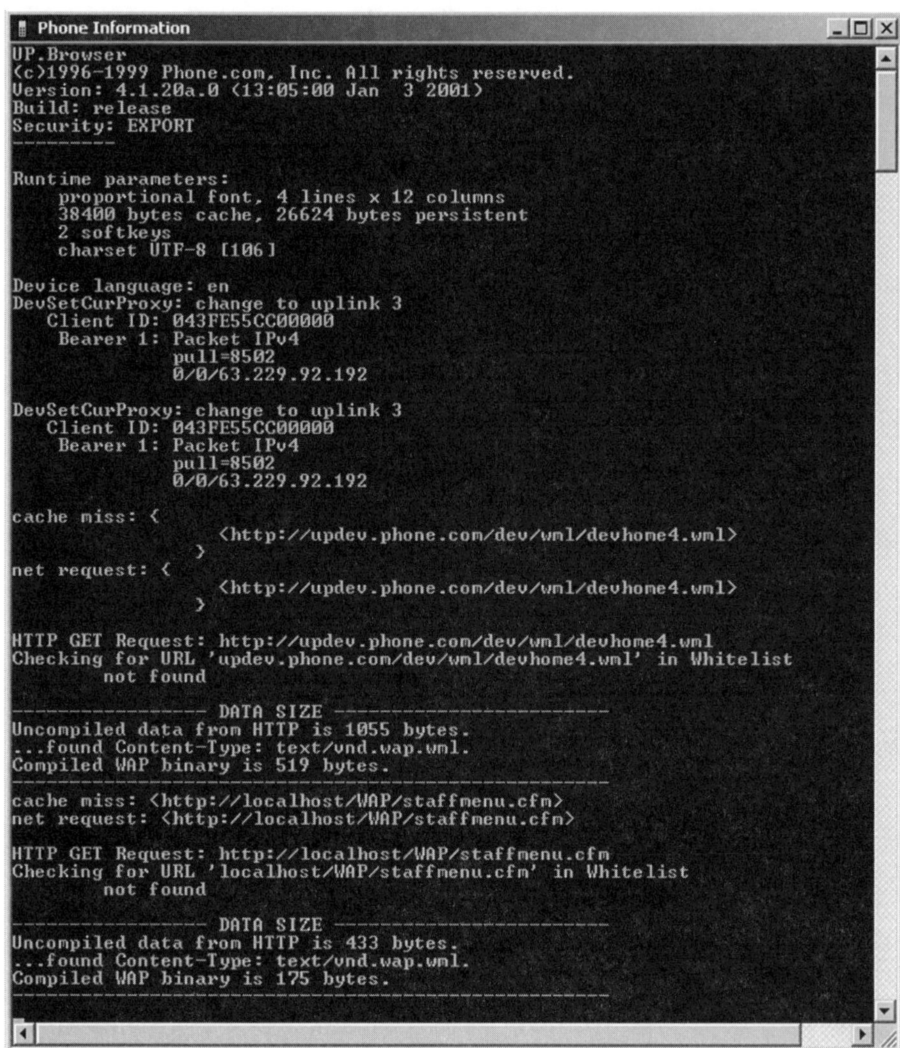

Figure G.5 Meta information about your WML page processing.

This can be a great tool when working with WML, much like the debugging output in ColdFusion Server.

Dynamic Wireless Websites

In order to present dynamic data with ColdFusion for a WAP device, we use the <CFCONTENT> tag. You may recall that the purpose of the <CFCONTENT>

tag is to change the page output to the designated MIME type. We can write whatever we want in ColdFusion, set the content type to WML in the first line of the page, and call that .cfm page from our web phone. It's really that easy. Here's how it looks:

```
<CFCONTENT type="text/vnd.wap.wml">
```

Let's use <cfcontent> to display at data-driven page in the Openwave browser. Our page will retrieve the first four records from the Users table. Type the following into Studio:

```
<cfcontent type="text/vnd.wap.wml"><?xml version="1.0"?>
<!DOCTYPE wml PUBLIC "-//WAPFORUM//DTD WML 1.2//EN"
    "http://www.wapforum.org/DTD/wml12.dtd">
<wml>

  <!----Retrieve the employees--->
       <cfquery name="getemployees" datasource="cf5db"
           maxrows="4">
           select firstname, lastname
           from users
       </cfquery>

  <!----Display them in a menu--->
   <card id="Menu">
   <p>
    <select name="menu" multiple="false">
        <cfoutput query="getemployees" >
            <option>#getemployees.lastname#,
                     #getemployees.firstname#</option>
         </cfoutput>
     </select>
    </p>
   </card>
</wml>
```

There are a number of things to notice about the listing.

The code uses the <CFCONTENT> tag to tell the browser to compile the wml. You make the declaration, run a simple query, and display the data as a <select> menu. If you are using the Openwave emulator, your output will look like Figure G.6.

If you are using WinWap 3.0, your page will look somewhat different. This browser outputs WML much like its HTML counterparts. The same page in WinWap 3.0 looks like Figure G.7.

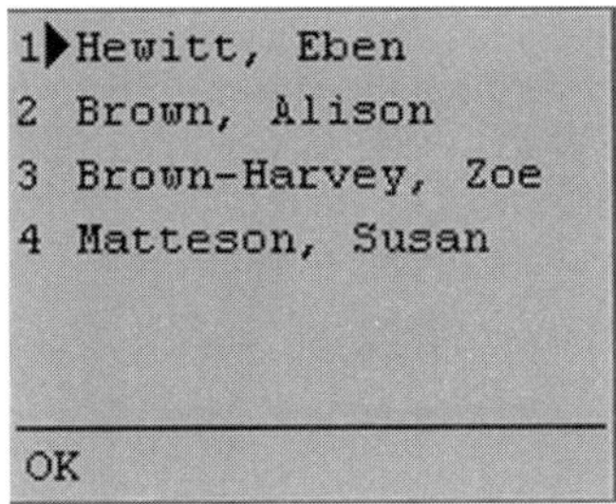

Figure G.6 Display of staff contact info.

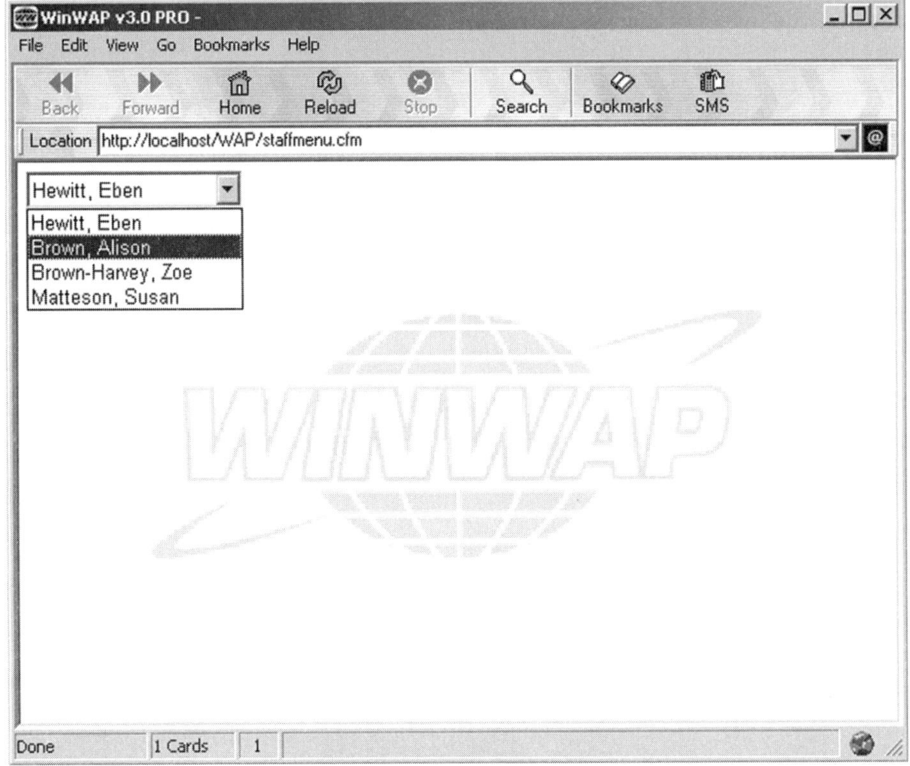

Figure G.7 The same card viewed in the WinWAP browser.

Navigating Between Cards

This would be a more user-friendly page if we had an introductory welcome screen, and then we could enter the menu. The best way to do this would be to send both the introductory card and the menu card in the same deck.

<NOTE>

This appendix is not intended to teach you all of WML or its counterpart scripting language, WMLScript. The idea is to learn just enough so that you can integrate ColdFusion with WML to make dynamic sites. If you are interested further, there are many good books on the topic.

The <go> Task

In WML, a *task* is an element that dictates an action to be performed. Perhaps the most common one is the <go> task, which performs the action of moving to a new card. Similarly, the <prev> task is used to return to the previous card.

So, in order to navigate between two cards in the same deck, we would use the <go> tag, and it works much the way you might use a local anchor in HTML. We are moving between local cards; that is, the initial request will have downloaded a number of cards so that the user does not have to make a round trip back to the server to see the next "page." Let's expand our little application to include two cards and the ability to jump between them.

We'll have an introductory card which we can click on to view the menu of employees:

```
<cfcontent type="text/vnd.wap.wml"><?xml version="1.0"?>
<!DOCTYPE wml PUBLIC "-//WAPFORUM//DTD WML 1.2//EN"
    "http://www.wapforum.org/DTD/wml12.dtd">
<wml>
<card id="welcome">
<do type="accept" label="go">
    <go href="#emplist"/>
</do>
<p align="center">Welcome to<br/>Core ColdFusion 5</p>
</card>

<cfquery name="menuitems" datasource="cf5db">
    select firstname, lastname
    from users
</cfquery>

<card id="emplist">
<do type="accept" label="go">
    <go href="#welcome"/>
</do>
<p>
```

```
<select name="menuchoice" multiple="false">
<cfoutput query="menuitems">
    <option>#firstname#</option>
</cfoutput>
</select>
 </p>
</card>
</wml>
```

There is a lot to notice here. First of all, we have the empty element <br/> tag. Since there is no closing tag for a <br>, we must signify this in order to comply with XML. We also notice that our query does not have to be inside the bounds of a card.

You can see that we have taken the "id" attribute of the card tag to specify a name for each card—in this case, "welcome" and "emplist." We can jump between cards in the same deck by using the go task like this: <go href= "#emplist"/>. So right away we notice that this is an empty element tag; that is, we must use the trailing slash. We notice, too, that it is similar to using an anchor in HTML to go to a specified place within the same document, without having to make a separate request. That work is done on the browser.

This would be a nicer introductory screen if it had an image. So let's include a little graphical logo at the top.

Incorporating Images

Using the <img> tag is almost as easy in WML as it is in HTML. The hard part is remembering that an empty tag in XML (and hence WML) requires a trailing slash. So the <img> tag looks like this:

```
<img src="CoreCF5.bmp" alt="Core CF 5" align="bottom"/>
```

One thing to note is that in WML, the "Alt" attribute of the <img> tag is required.

There are actually a number of other considerations for using images in WAP sites. To begin with, you may use only a one-bit bitmap black-and-white image. In some cases you will need to use a .wmbp (wireless bitmap) image. You will need to convert any image you want to use with a Photoshop plug-in called UnWired2B (available at http://www.rcp.co.uk/distributed/downloads) or an online converter tool (such as http://webcab.de.woe.htm). You need to keep your images under 128 pixels in both dimensions.

Now our first card now looks like this:

```
<card id="Welcome">
    <do type="accept" label="go">
```

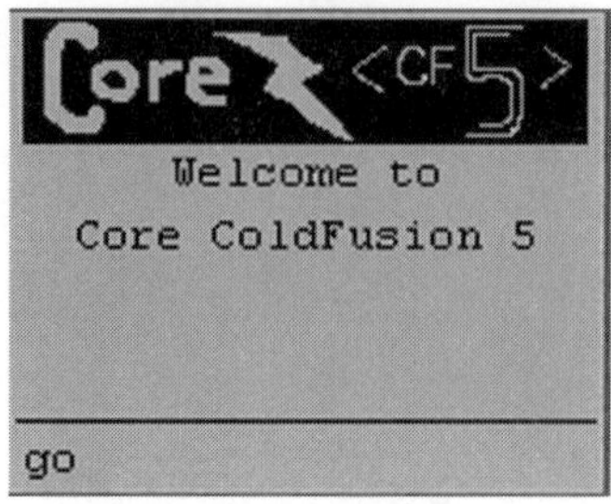

Figure G.8 Added bonus—my beautiful 1-bit artwork!

```
            <go href="#emplist"/>
    </do>
    <p align="center">
<img alt="Core CF 5 home" src="corecf5.bmp"
align="top"/>
    </p>
    <p align="center">Welcome to<br/>Core ColdFusion 5</p>
</card>
```

So as an added bonus to this chapter, you get to view my terrific one-bit image artwork. We will include the Core CF 5 logo on the welcome page, which now looks like Figure G.8.

Now that we've got our welcome screen, and are moving between cards, we need to make each select option a link so that we can drill down to more information about each employee.

Right now, if you were to click on an item, you would be returned to the default card ("Welcome"). In order to make each item in the list able to display specific information, we need to incorporate the <onpick> event.

OnPick Events

An event is something that can happen to an element of a WML page. In order to control events sensibly, you must bind an event to a task. Colloquially, we might say, "when such and such happens, do this." Here is how to specify each employee name in our select list as a separate URL that we can click on to see detailed information:

```
<option>
    <onevent type="onpick">
            <go href="empdetail.cfm?firstname=#firstname#"/>
    </onevent>
#firstname#
</option>
```

The translation of this code is: "When we pick a name from the list, go to the specified URL and pass it a parameter from the query." This works for just a few unique names. If we had two people named Zoe, however, two records would get returned on our action page. This is an undesirable result. So we can pass two parameters in the URL, separated with an ampersand. This is just like in ColdFusion, however, you must write the ASCII equivalent of the character when working with WML. So our two-parameter select option code would look like this:

```
<option>
    <onevent type="onpick">
          <go
href="empdetail.cfm?firstname=#firstname#&amp;lastname=#last
name#"/>
    </onevent>
#firstname#
</option>
```

The Result: An Address Book Application

This is the final code listing for the first page, which we will call "Welcome.cfm":

Listing G.1 Welcome.cfm

```
<cfcontent type="text/vnd.wap.wml"><?xml version="1.0"?>

<!DOCTYPE wml PUBLIC "-//WAPFORUM//DTD WML 1.2//EN"
    "http://www.wapforum.org/DTD/wml12.dtd">
<wml>
<card id="Welcome">
    <do type="accept" label="go">
          <go href="#emplist"/>
    </do>
    <p align="center">
    <img alt="Core CF 5 home" src="corecf5.bmp"
          align="top"/>
    Welcome to<br/>
    Core ColdFusion 5<br/>
    Address Book
    </p>
</card>

<cfquery name="menuitems" datasource="cf5db">
    select firstname, lastname
    from users
```

```
</cfquery>

<card id="emplist">
<p>
Choose an employee<br/>
to view contact info
<select name="menuchoice" multiple="false">
<cfoutput query="menuitems">
<option>
    <onevent type="onpick">
          <go
href="empdetail.cfm?firstname=#firstname#&amp;lastname=#last-
name#"/>
    </onevent>
#lastname#, #firstname#
</option>
</cfoutput>
</select>
 </p>
</card>
</wml>
```

And then our action page, which retrieves the specific employee chosen, is called "empdetail.cfm." It will look like this:

Listing G.2 EmpDetail.cfm

```
<cfcontent type="text/vnd.wap.wml"><?xml version="1.0"?>
<!DOCTYPE wml PUBLIC "-//WAPFORUM//DTD WML 1.1//EN"
    "http://www.wapforum.org/DTD/wml_1.1.xml">
<wml>
<card id="oneemp">

<p align="center"<Contact info for<br/>

<cfoutput>#firstname# #lastname#</cfoutput><br/>
    <cfquery name="getthisemp" datasource="cf5db">
         select phone, address, city, state
         from users
         where firstname = "#firstname#"
         and lastname = "#lastname#"
    </cfquery>

</p>

<p align="left">
    <cfoutput query="getthisemp">
         #phone#<br/>
```

```
            #address#<br/>
            #city#, #state#
        </cfoutput>
</p>

</card>
</wml>
```

So our final series of screens looks like this:

1. Welcome screen (Figure G.9).
2. Click anywhere and go to the next card, which is a list of employees (Figure G.10).
3. The record is retrieved and your drill-down data displayed (Figure G.11).

You can expand and improve on this by creating an intermediary screen which allows you to select only employees from a certain department. This way you won't bog down your device with a great number of records. Otherwise, you've got a pretty useful application.

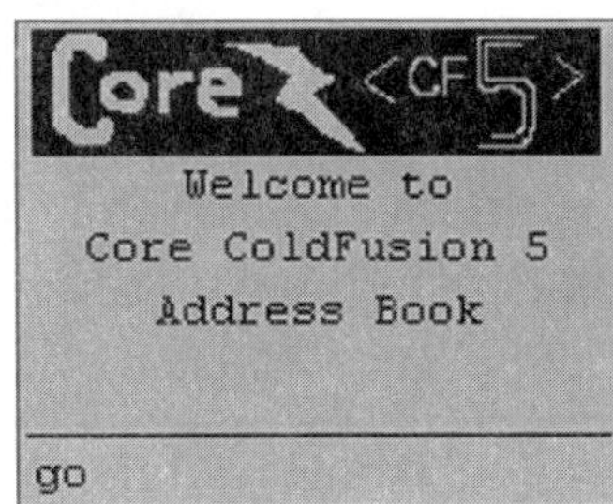

Figure G.9 Our address book welcome screen.

Choose an employee
to view contact info
1 Hewitt, Eben
2 Brown, Alison
3 Brown-Harvey, Zoe
4 Matteson, Susan
OK

Figure G.10 List of employees in address book.

Contact info for
Alison Brown
(520) 834-7565
606 Birch St.
Flagstaff, AZ
Back

Figure G.11 The drill-down record.

Wireless Style Guide

Below are some rules for you to follow as you create wireless sites. This is similar to Appendix F, "Best Practices," but the idea is extended for WML and WAP.

1. **Keep your deck below 600 bytes.** Expect a 2000-byte deck to take 10 seconds to transfer back to the client. You better be sending some smokin' content for that kind of wait! In general, your audience will have high latency, single-tasking devices. Use your knowledge of organizing web sites around navigation, anticipating logical user interaction processes. But apply the rule somewhat differently, keeping deck size in mind.
2. **Constrain your input fields with valid characters.** In order to cut down on user frustration, programmatically allow a maximum input size (credit cards would be 16 characters and no more), and constrain the user to valid data types (a credit card field should accept only numbers as valid input). This is happy for your users as much as it is for you—that latency overhead is a drag if you accidentally submit bogus input.
3. **Limit soft keys labels to 5 characters or fewer.** Some browsers cannot display more than this.
4. **Limit any text above form fields to 2 lines.** Otherwise, your text or image or important message can be truncated by some browsers.
5. **Use caching effectively.** You can alienate or otherwise irritate users if you force them to wait long periods of time downloading your up-to-the-second report. Don't set a deck to expire before it really must. Remember, unlike most Internet connections, which let you slouch around the web

> endlessly for no extra money, cell-phone users are paying big bucks every second they're online. If you make them wait, you're costing them money.

I suppose that if you were to glance at the above style guide and ask me to summarize it in 5 words or less, I might be able to distill this: *keep it short and sweet.*

A Word about Making Wireless Sites

Just remember that graphics are hardly the point for many of today's wireless web users. I'll probably eat these words in short order, but it is important for now to keep it simple and information-rich. It is no coincidence that the first and most prominent sites on the wireless internet were search engines and financial sites. Keep this in mind as you work.

An important consideration is to know what to do with the existing sites you have in HTML. My advice would be not to try to port these sites directly. They should be rewritten for WAP. This might sound like a drag, but it is the responsible thing to do, and it will keep your visitors happy. Filling out a form typing on a keyboard is very different from trying to input letters from a number pad on a phone. Don't force users to type in unnecessary information.

As wireless technology advances, we are witnessing even more exciting trends. For instance, now we're able to view Macromedia Flash movies on wireless devices. Check back frequently with http://www.wapforum.org and http://www.w3c.org for updates.

At this point, we're going to stop talking about WML. From here on out, making more advanced wireless applications becomes a WAP issue, and not a ColdFusion issue. There are many good WML books on the market. Many websites such as http://www.Openwave.com allow you to join as a developer and take advantage of the latest emulator or specification downloads. Have fun!

Appendix H

ColdFusion Resources, User Groups, and Hosts

A great number of resources are available to you on line as you use ColdFusion. This appendix is divided into three sections: General Resources, User Groups, and Hosting Companies. In the Resources section, you'll find a hard-won list of sites that have ColdFusion as their focus. These sites might teach you about how to use ColdFusion with COM, or have a set of tutorials. The important thing to note is that there is a strong, vibrant, supportive ColdFusion community. You are not alone!

Resources

In this section you're getting more than an annotated collection of bookmarks—it's like having your own ColdFusion Knowledge Base so you can join the community, get involved, get your questions answered, and continue your work fruitfully. You don't have to reinvent the wheel by discovering them all yourself. These are not in any particular order, so you can decide which ones you can best use.

Websites

http://www.corecoldFusion.com This book's companion website.

http://cfnews.weblogger.com A different tip every day.

http://www.cfcustomtags.com A great resource for custom tags and CF info.

http://www.teratech.com Michael Smith has a lot of free, useful resources here—including a ColdFusion tag wall poster and "cold cuts" (code snippets).

http://www.defusion.com Articles, resources, discussion.

http://www.vboston.com/DepressedPress/Content/ColdFusion/ Take the ColdFusion challenge, get custom tags and code snippets.

http://www.webmonkey.com A couple of articles related to specific CF development topics.

http://www.cfhub.com Lots of general info.

http://www.cfmcentral.com/gallery/ A good resource for custom tags, chat, jobs, and all things CF.

http://www.simplythebest.net/info/coldfusion.html A good list of ColdFusion-related web sites and a brief explanation of CF.

http://d.sefcik.cc/pgsql-coldfusion.html Tells you how to make postgresql work with CF on Solaris.

http://www.thescripts.com/serversidescripting/coldfusion Info for beginners.

http://www.cfmasters.com CF dev E-zine outlines how CF performs vs. ASP.

http://www.cfcode.com Forums by Robert Long.

http://www.coldfusiontraining.com Seminars you can take to boost your skills.

http://msdn.microsoft.com/library/periodic/period00/ColdFusion.htm High level overview of using SQL server with ColdFusion.

http://www.cfxtras.com Buy and sell custom tags, mailing list, training classes for those in Charlotte, NC.

http://community.borland.com/article/0,1410,23205,00.html How to use CFX tags to make ColdFusion talk to Interbase.

http://www.computerhelpbooks.com/c/Coldfusion/Coldfusion_Books.htm.

http://www.webtechcorp.com/coldfusion-training-course/coldfusion-training-course-301.htm ColdFusion training course in the UK.

http://www.webtricks.com/SourceCode/default.cfm Source code to a number of ColdFusion applications, like a Calendar, a Bingo game, a poll, and more.

http://www.cfmcentral.com Macromedia news, custom tags, jobs.

www.codebits.com Programming advice on a number of languages including ColdFusion.

http://www.members.dca.net/rbilson/cold_fusion.htm Rob Brooks-Bilson's collection of custom tags.

http://www.geocities.com/siliconvalley/campus/7521/coldfusionhelp.htm A few custom tags available for download.

http://www.forta.com The ColdFusion Product evangelist's website, dedicated to ColdFusion and books he's written—great!

http://www.cfadvisor.com/api-shl/engine.cfm Thorough.

http://www.developer.irt.org/script/fusion.htm Brief list of easy questions and answers.

http://forums.cfm-resources.com Forums.

http://www.cfsearch.com General enthusiasm.

http://www.builder.com/Programming/ColdFusion General tips, brief.

http://www.cfxtras.com CFX tags.

http://forums.allaire.com/coldfusion/ The forums are a great place to post questions about CF coding. Hundreds of developers here to help you out.

http://www.Allaire.com/allairealive A gallery of terrific 10-minute instructional videos on CF-related subjects.

http://devex.Allaire.com A repository for developers to share reusable components they create.

http://www.sys-con.com/coldfusion Home of the popular Sys-Con Media Cold Fusion Developer's Journal publication. They've got a great list you can join.

http://www.fusebox.org A popular methodology for writing ColdFusion that modularizes code for reuse.

http://www.figleaf.com/figleafhome/cfug/figpubs.htm A terrific resource of ColdFusion presentations.

http://www.defusion.com An online webzine devoted to all things ColdFusion.

http://www.HouseofFusion.com Home of Michael Dinowitz's cf-talk lists.

http://www.amkor.com/proving_grounds/ CF custom tags for download.

http://www.cfobjects.com Smart Objects—An initiative to apply object-orientation to CF.

http://www.ashleyking.com Ashely King's site.

http://www.deathclock.com/morpheus/cf.cfm Raymond Camden's site.

http://rtb.home.texas.net/cf/ A ColdFusion enthusiast.

http://www.four-runner.com Web development resources, including info on hosting and employment.

http://www.intrafoundation.com/freeware.html A lot of CFX tags for those interested in ColdFusion and C++.

http://www.experts-exchange.com/jsp/qList.jsp?ta=coldfusion A forum for questions and answers.

http://www.halhelms.com Hal Helms is a renowned teacher of ColdFusion and Team Allaire member.

http://groups.yahoo.com/group/cf-talk/ A mailing list dealing with CF language.

http://www.CFHub.com A resource for ColdFusion developers. Articles, tips, and code samples along with custom tags, CF hosting info, and an online directory.

http://www.cfvault.com Serious repository of custom tags and info.

http://www.intent.net/cfusion/module.htm Applications for sale.

http://packetderm.cotse.com/mailing-lists/ntbugtraq/2000/Jun/0020.html Information on Denial of Service attacks and ColdFusion server.

http://developer.irt.org/script/fusion.htm A list of FAQ (and answers).

http://www.cfcomet.com How to use COM with ColdFusion, some great articles and downloads.

http://www.flashcfm.com How to use Flash with ColdFusion. Downloads and tips.

http://www.forumspot.org Here is the place to download ColdFusion Forums (the first two versions anyway) for free.

http://www.zyxxy.com/cf_bit/ Some useful custom tags like <cf_julian> and <cf_incrementalpha>. Most are available for purchase.

http://www.spottedantelope.com/tools/cold_fusion/ A development company which makes their custom tags available for purchase. Check out <cf_Stalker>.

http://www.systemanage.com Charles Arehart, noted CF developer, can be found here. Useful articles on wireless in particular.

http://www.fusebox.org/fuseml/intro.htm One way to use UML with ColdFusion. Neat.

http://www.ektron.com Makers of the online WYSIWYG HTML editor used in Spectra.

http://www.ablecommerce.com Makers of online stores and auction software, totally written in ColdFusion.

Publications

ColdFusion Developers Journal (www.sys-con.com/coldfusion).

ColdFusion Advisor (www.cfadvisor.com).

Defusion (www.defusion.com).

User Groups

ColdFusion User Groups (CFUGs) have been thriving for years in the United States and around the world. There are user groups in nearly every state and in many areas abroad, including Germany, Pakistan, Hong Kong, Korea, France, Malaysia, South Africa, Barbados, Ireland, and many more. As of this writing, the number of user groups is over 150.

ColdFusion user groups often meet once a month to exchange information about ColdFusion, listen to guest speakers give presentations on new ColdFusion developments, try out their code, and like that. They're free to members if they can get a company to sponsor their events, which is often the case. User groups are an excellent way of learning fast, meeting people in your industry, and having fun. Just visit the Macromedia site to find out where the group meets in your city.

Starting a User Group

If there isn't one already in your city, you can start your own. Write to usergroups@macromedia.com requesting to start one up. You'll need a few things to get going, and Macromedia will ask you about them on your application.

- You'll need a Board of Directors. Sometimes people start them by themselves, but since it's a bit of work getting one together, it's a good idea to share the load.
- You must have a mission statement.
- Get a website (or at least a domain for now), usually with a .org extension, since user groups are not for profit. You'll use this as your chief mode of announcing meetings and special events.

Once Macromedia has approved your new group, they really go a long way toward helping you get off the ground and making sure it's a success. They offer you marketing tools, advice, and assistance, send out emails announcing your first meeting, and more.

You can find a complete list of all of the user groups on the web at the following address: http://devex.allaire.com/developer/usergroups/findusergroup.cfm.

List of User Groups

Just in case the online list is no longer there when you read this, here is a list of user groups in the United States. If they don't have a site up yet, I've included the email address of the group organizer so you can contact them about joining.

Alabama (Birmingham) www.birminghamcoldfusion.com

Alabama (Huntsville) www.nacfug.org

Arizona (Phoenix) www.azcfug.org

Arizona (Tucson) www.tucsoncfug.org

California (Bay Area) www.bacfug.org

California (Southern California) www.sccfug.org
California (Southern California-Los Angeles) www.sccfug.org
California (Southern California-Orange County) www.sccfug.org
California (Sacramento) www.jelproductions.com
California (San Diego) www.sdcfug.org
Connecticut (Hartford) graves@rapidcf.com
Connecticut (New Haven) www.cfug.cshore.com
Connecticut (Stamford-Westchester) bah@abodofoto.com
Illinois (Chicago) www.chicfug.org
Illinois (East Central) http://205.198.253.95/
Illinois (Quad Cities) http://www.qc-cfug.org/
Illinois (Springfield) ashbagd@mail.ioc.state.il.us
Colorado (Colorado Springs) astarkey@mentiscorp.com
Colorado (Denver) www.nccfug.com
Colorado (Rocky Mountain) www.mtncfug.com
Florida (Gainesville) no site yet
Florida (Jacksonville) www.missionboard.com/jaxcfug
Florida (Naples) no site yet
Florida (Orlando) www.cf.itcenter.org
Florida (Pensacola) no site yet
Florida (South Florida) www.cfug-sfl.org
Florida (Tallahassee) no site yet
Florida (Tampa Bay) www.cfug.stampedenetwork.com
Georgia (Atlanta) www.acfug.org
Georgia (Atlanta) www.Figleaf.com
Idaho (Boise) www.cfidaho.org
Indiana (Central Indiana) www.hoosierfusion.com
Indiana (Northern Indiana) www.nicfug.org
Iowa (Cedar Valley) www.chandlerresearch.com/crweb/community/cvcfug/adbout.html
Kentucky (Louisville-Lexington) www.loulexcfug.com
Maryland (Baltimore) www.Figleaf.com
Maryland www.cfug-md.org

Maryland (Southern Maryland) www.smdcfug.org
Massachusettes (Boston) www.cfugboston.org
Michigan (Detroit) http://www.detroitcfug.com/
Michigan (Mid-Michigan) http://www.fusemonkey.com/
Minnesota (Twin Cities) www.colderfusion.com
Missouri (Kansas City) www.kcfusion.org
Missouri (Southern Missouri) jeremiah.andrick@noble.net
Missouri (St. Louis Metro Area) www.psiwebstudio.com/cfug/
Montana (Helena) tmarino@falcon.com
Nebraska (Omaha) Mkruger@CFWebtools.com
Nevada (Las Vegas) pegarm@lvcm.com
New Hampshire (Concord) www.nhcfug.org
New Jersey (Central) HNguyen7@prius.jnj.com
New Jersey (Northern) www.njcfug.org
New Jersey (Southern) m-stewart@home.com
New Mexico (Albuquerque) www.nmcfug.org
New York (Albany) www.anycfug.org
New York (Long Island) www.licfug.org
New York (New York City) www.nycfug.org
New York (Rochester) www.roch-cfug.org
North Carolina (Charlotte) www.charlotte-cfug.org
North Carolina (Greenville) no site yet
North Carolina (Raliegh) www.ccfug.org
North Dakota romm@magician.com
Ohio (Mid-Ohio Valley) hannum@ohio.edu
Ohio (Cleveland) www.cfugonline.org
Ohio (Columbus) www.oacfug.org
Oklahoma (Oklahoma City) Glen-Collymore@ouhsc.edu
Oklahoma (Tulsa) www.tulsacfug.org
Oregon (Portland) www.pdxcfug.org
Oregon (Roseburg) sbland@douglasesd.k12.or.us
Pennsylvania (Harrisburg) jimr321@cs.com
Pennsylvania (Lehigh Valley) www.lvcfug.org

Pennsylvania (Philadelphia) www.pacfug.org
Pennsylvania (Pittsburgh) www.pghcfug.org
Pennsylvania (State College) www.cfug-sc.org
Rhode Island (Providence) www.teamcfm.com/ricfug
South Carolina (Greenville) http://www.epilogsys.com/ucpcug/public/focusgps/cfug.cfm
Tennessee (Knoxville) doug@colknox.com
Tennessee (Memphis) mkubicki@univ-solutions.com
Tennessee (Nashville) www.ncfug.org
Texas (Austin) www.cftexas.outer.net
Texas (Dallas-Fort Worth) www.dfwcfug.org
Texas (San Antonio) www.sacfug.org
Utah (Utah State College) jnelson@nstep.net
Utah (Salt Lake City) www.slcfug.org
Utah (Provo) http://exciteworks/uvcfug
Vermont (Montpelier) www.mtbytes.com/cfug/
Virginia (Hampton Roads) www.hrcfug.org
Virginia (Northern Virginia) www.Figleaf.com
Virginia (Richmond) http://richmond-cfug.btgi.net/
Washington DC www.Figleaf.com
Washington (Seattle) www.cfseattle.org
Washington (Walla-Walla) sarahlewis@alhena-design.com
Wisconsin (Milwaukee) www.metomilwaukee.com/usr/cfug
Wyoming (Jackson) www.4pines.com/projects/cfug/

Companies That Host ColdFusion Sites

Perhaps you want to develop ColdFusion, but you don't have the resources to host your own server. That's okay! There are hundreds of hosting companies out there who can host your ColdFusion site for you. Some are dedicated to ColdFusion and Spectra; others are general hosting companies who provide ColdFusion services.

There are nearly 50,000 ColdFusion servers installed, but not all of them are hosting companies. Many are universities, research labs, and private corporations. And remember that there are a number of important questions that your hosting provider should be able to answer. Hopefully this section will help you sort through the hype and get a host who is right for you. A number of the sites in my list are online resources that will direct you to dozens of actual hosting companies.

List of ColdFusion Hosting Companies

This is certainly not a complete list, as there are hundreds of hosts in the United States alone. In order to find a good host, I suggest you look at the Hosting partners list on the Macromedia Site. Macromedia Hosting Partners are companies that have had an application approved by Macromedia, listing how many people they have dedicated to maintaining their ColdFusion services, what their backup plans are, what the connection speed is, and like that. So a lot of companies don't quite make it. You can be pretty sure that if your host is a Macromedia hosting partner, they're reliable.

If there is something special that the companies below support, I note it parenthetically.

1stChoiceSite.com

ABICommerce.net (AbleCommerce hosting)

CFXHosting.com

ColdWorks.com

CrystalTech.com (9 GB traffic!)

Cybertrails.com (Oracle, SQL Server, Macromedia partner)

Datapipe.com/coldfusionhosting.htm

Dellhost.com

HostMySite.com

ICN.net (as low as $15 per month for CF)

Interland.com

Intermedia.net (CyberCash, WebTrends, Exchange)

Media3.net (since 1995)

Minerva.net

Pegasus Web (NT and Unix)

PowerSurge.net

PurpleHosting.com (does Spectra too!)

Skynetweb.com
Tristarweb.com
Virtualscape.com
WhekWeb.com
WeAreCFHosting.com
WebHosting.com

Questions to Ask a ColdFusion Hosting Company

Trusting your work to an outside hosting vendor is a little scary. You can reduce the anxiety by knowing the answers to all of the following questions. Even if you think that you won't be using a real-time credit card processor, it might be a good idea to find out which ones your potential host supports, just in case your work expands in that direction one day.

It's a big drag to switch hosts if you discover that you aren't pleased. I've worked with a client who had to move her company's website from one host to another. She wanted to handle the move herself, and with the database, custom tags, CFX tags, paths, hard-coded local references, supporting Word and .pdf documents, it took her more than four months to get the site moved and running normally again. It's not nothing to do it. And, of course, companies that you move your site away from aren't necessarily very interested in helping you leave them. So once you are ready to put up a site, or to move your existing site to a new server, I urge you to take the following things into account first. You also might get a sense, when asking these questions, how helpful the hosting company is likely to be if you have a serious problem later on.

Have You Disabled Any ColdFusion Tag?

There are a number of ColdFusion 5 tags that you can turn off in the administrator for security reasons. These tags are very powerful, and are used to manipulate files and directories, and even your system registry. For instance, the <CFFILE> tag can be used to delete files from the server. Some companies who provide a shared environment turn these tags off in order to prevent having to think about certain security issues. Do you use any of the following tags in your applications, or think you will in the future?

- CFCONTENT
- CFDIRECTORY

- CFFILE
- CFOBJECT
- CFREGISTRY
- CFADMINSECURITY
- CFEXECUTE
- CFFTP
- CFLOG
- CFMAIL
- DBTYPE=DYNAMIC
- CONNECTSTRING

<CFFILE> is a very popular and useful tag. If you ISP or host doesn't support it, you could be quite limited.

You can view these tags (and turn them off) in ColdFusion 5 Administrator by going to Security > Tag Restrictions.

What Databases Do You Support?

Ask—even if you're not planning on using a big RDBMS for your sites. If they don't support Oracle or SQL Server, they probably don't have very much money—which would make me wonder about their connections and support options too.

Are You a Macromedia Hosting Partner?

You might want to go with one of the Macromedia Hosting Partners. As mentioned above, they've got to pass a test by Macromedia, so you know they've had to meet rigorous demands about backups, support, and connection speed. Also, they are *required* as partners to run the latest version of ColdFusion. There's a lot of stuff you can do in version 5 that you can't do in 4.5. And there are a lot of hosts out there running version 4.0 (which was released more than two years ago). If they make it their business to run the latest version, they're serious about ColdFusion (not just about hosting). You can find a list of ColdFusion hosting partners at http://www.allaire.com/Partners/Search.

How Many Datasources Do I Get?

Ask how many datasources you get with each hosting package. Often you are limited to one or two, and usually you have to pay a lot extra to get more than that. This might not be a concern for you if you're just planning on doing development or practice work. However, even then, you might be interested in testing out ColdFusion 5's sexy new querying capabilities, which allow you to join results from multiple datasources. This is also a classic place for hidden costs to creep in.

How Can I Interact with My Database?

If you have a database whose structure might change with some frequency, be very careful about getting the answer you want to this question. Often hosting companies require you to email their support staff, and then they make the changes to the database that you request when they get around to it. This can mean *days.* I have also noticed, even at some of the big hosting companies, that often they don't have dedicated database server admins. If you start to color outside the lines a bit, they might not know what you're talking about (for instance, I've sent hosting companies a database backup that I was told wasn't a database, and therefore they couldn't do anything with it).

So ask what the process for changing your database is. It is rare to find a host that will allow you to log in to the common SQL server and start executing DTS packages. Your login may not be allowed stored procedure privileges. That might be okay with you, and it might not.

If you need really heavy and frequent database access and modification, you might be forced to consider going with a dedicated server. This can run hundreds (or thousands) of dollars a month. And you'll need your own software licenses for everything. So then you're really in a different conversation.

Comparison Shopping

You can also shop around at websites that compare different hosting companies. Many of these will tell you what kind of services a particular hosting company offers in addition to ColdFusion, and they may have rankings based on criteria you want to know about. You might start with these:

www.HostCompare.com

www.HostIndex.com

www.HostSearch.com

www.WebHosters.com

There are hundreds of good hosts across the country. I hope that this appendix helps you find what you need for ColdFusion hosting.

Appendix I

SQL Function Reference

The following section provides a reference for generally useful SQL functions. Look over it in order to familiarize yourself with the rich options you have when working with data in ColdFusion. You may save yourself a good deal of trouble if you know what functions you already have to work with. Note that a number of functions are the same in ColdFusion as they are in SQL, and so it won't be quite as daunting to learn them.

This is not a complete reference; it is meant to be useful as you develop ColdFusion applications. Variables are specified in *italics*.

String Functions

String functions perform operations on string values (Table I.1). They return usually string, but occasionally numeric, values. Any character expression is abbreviated here as *char*.

Table I.1 SQL String Functions

Function	*Operation*	*Example and Result*
ASCII	Returns ASCII code of leftmost character in *char*	select ASCII(1) 49
CHAR	Converts an integer ASCII code to a character	select char(126) ~
CHARINDEX	Returns position of the first *char*	select charindex('b', 'eben')
	in the second *char*	2
LEFT	Returns leftmost *integer_*	select left ('ColdFusion', 3)
	expression characters in *char*	Col
LEN	Returns number of characters in a given character *string*	select len('ColdFusion') 10
LTRIM	Trims leading whitespace of *char*	select ltrim('ColdFusion') ColdFusion
REPLACE	Finds all instances of the second *char* in the first *char* and replaces them with the third *char*	Select REPLACE ('ColdFusion','o', '5') C5ldFusi5n
REVERSE	Returns the reverse of *char*	Select REVERSE ('ColdFusion') noisuFdloC
RIGHT	Returns rightmost *integer* characters in *char*	Select RIGHT ('ColdFusion', 4)sion
RTRIM	Strips whitespace off the end of *char*	select RTRIM ('ColdFusion') ColdFusion
SOUNDEX	Returns four-character SOUNDEX code for *char*	Select SOUNDEX ('ColdFusion') C431
SPACE	Returns *integer* number of spaces	Select space(5)
STR	Returns character data converted from numeric data. Takes this syntax: STR(*float_expression*[, *length*[, *decimal*]])	SELECT STR(123.45, 5, 1) 123.5
SUBSTRING	Returns length number of characters according to this syntax:	SELECT substring('Eben Hewitt', 6, 1)

Function	*Operation*	*Example and Result*
	SUBSTRING(*expression, start, length*)	H
UPPER	Returns *char* in uppercase	select UPPER('coldfusion') COLDFUSION

SQL Mathematical Functions

To save space, and because many of the SQL mathematical functions are duplicated in ColdFusion functions, I will abbreviate the mathematical functions somewhat here. In Table I.2, the "example and Result" cell shows an example of an acceptable use of the function, and the line beneath shows the result of executing the function with that sample data. In order to use the examples as given from within ColdFusion, you should alias the function result so you can reference the alias from <CFOUTPUT>.

Table I.2 SQL Mathematical Functions

Function	*Operation*	*Example and Result*
ABS	Returns absolute value of *numeric _expression*	*SELECT abs((42 + 20) - 170.33)*108.33
ACOS	Returns arccosine of *float_ expression* between 1 and -1	SELECT acos(-1) 3.1415926535897931
ASIN	Returns arcsine of *float_expression*	SELECT asin(1) 1.5707963267948966
ATAN	Returns arctangent of *float_ expression*	SELECT atan(45) 1.5485777614681775
ATN2	Returns angle, in radians, whose tangent is between the two *float_expression* values.	SELECT atn2(60, 45) 0.92729521800161219
CEILING	Returns the smallest integer greater than or equal to *numeric_ expression*	SELECT ceiling(4.35) 5

Table I.2 Continued

Function	*Operation*	*Example and Result*
COS	Returns the trigonometric cosine of *float_expression*	SELECT cos(45.983) -0.41678583316938139
COT	Returns the trigonometric cotangent of *float_expression*	SELECT cot(180) 0.74699881441404437
DEGREES	Given an angle in radians, returns the angle in degrees of *numeric_expression*	SELECT degrees(17) 974
EXP	Returns exponent value of *float_expression*	SELECT exp(3.14) 23.103866858722185
FLOOR	Returns largest integer less than or equal to *numeric_ expression*	SELECT floor(33.567) 33
LOG	Returns natural logarithm of float_expression	SELECT log(15) 2.7080502011022101
LOG10	Returns base-10 logarithm of float_expression	SELECT log10(15) 1.1760912590556813
PI	Returns the constant *pi* to 16 places	SELECT pi() 3.1415926535897931
POWER	Returns the value of *x* raised to *y*	SELECT power(10,3) 1000
RADIANS	Returns angle in radians, given an angle *numeric_expression* in degrees	SELECT radians(90) 1
RAND	Returns a random float between 0 and 1	SELECT Rand() 0.94359739042414437
ROUND	Returns *numeric_expression*, rounded to *length*	SELECT Round (2.1546687, 5) 2.1546700
SIGN	Returns +1 if *numeric_expression* is positive, -1 if it is negative	SELECT sign(-23) -1
SIN	Returns the trigonometric sine of the given angle *float_expression* in radians	SELECT sin(90) 0.89399666360055785
SQUARE	Returns square of *float_expression*	SELECT Square(5) 25.0

Function	*Operation*	*Example and Result*
SQRT	Returns square root of *float_expression*	SELECT sqrt(25) 5.0
TAN	Returns tangent of *float_expression*	SELECT tan(45) 1.6197751905438615

SQL Aggregate Functions

Aggregate functions are occasionally referred to *as set functions.* They allow you to make a summary of columnar data. While there are more aggregate functions than the ones listed below, these are ANSI-92 standard and should therefore apply across RDBMSs.

Avg

Returns the average (mean) of all the values, or only the DISTINCT values, in the expression. Example:

```
        SELECT "AveragePrice" = AVG(ProductPrice)
        FROM Products
```

Count

Returns the total number of non-null values in the expression. Example:

```
<cfquery name="CountProductRows" datasource="ProductsDB">
        SELECT COUNT(ProductName) as num
        FROM Products
</cfquery>
<cfoutput query="CountProductRows">#num#</cfoutput>
```

Count (*)

Using the wildcard in place of an expression with COUNT returns the number of rows, including null-value rows. You may not use COUNT(*) with DISTINCT. For an example of COUNT, see above.

This is probably most useful when you are building an application and need to know the number of rows in your table.

Max

Returns the maximum value in the expression. Example:

```
<cfquery name="Item" datasource="ProductsDB">
        SELECT Max(Price) as num
        FROM Item
</cfquery>
<cfoutput query="Item"<#num#</cfoutput>
```

Min

Returns the minimum value in the expression. Example:

```
<cfquery name="Item" datasource="ProductsDB">
        SELECT Min(Price) as num
        FROM Item
</cfquery>

<cfoutput query="Item">#num#</cfoutput>
```

Sum

Returns the sum of all values, or only DISTINCT values, in the expression. NULL values are ignored. SUM may be used only for columns of numeric data types. Example:

```
<cfquery name="Item" datasource="ProductsDB">
        SELECT Sum(Price) as num
        FROM Item
</cfquery>
<cfoutput query="Item">#num#</cfoutput>
```

SQL Date/Time Functions

I have found that a number of developers have questions about the date/time functions. It can be confusing to remember what your result will be when you run certain date/time functions against your database. I have therefore gone into more detail and used examples below and displayed the system output.

Of course, you use any and all of these within a <CFQUERY> tag from within a ColdFusion template.

Dateadd

Example:

```
SELECT DATEADD(Year, -10, getdate()) AS [DateAdd]
```

Outputs:

```
          DateAdd
---------------------------
      1991-05-28 17:36:06.553

(1 row(s) affected)
```

The above example demonstrates two concepts at once: the DATEADD function, and the fact that you can *subtract* a date using date add. You simply add a negative number.

Datediff

Returns the number of *dateparts* between two specified dates. DATEDIFF is structured as follows:

DATEDIFF(*datepart, startdate, enddate*)

Example:

DATEDIFF(Week, "27 Mar 1999", getdate()) AS [DateDiff]

Outputs:

```
DateDiff
-----------
114
(1 row(s) affected)
```

—which is to say that the difference in weeks from March 27, 1999, until today's date (May 28, 2001) is 114.

Datename

Returns the name of the specified *datepart* in the *date* as a character string. Here is its structure:

DATENAME(*datepart, date*)

Example:

SELECT DATENAME(month, getdate()) AS [DateName]

Will output:

```
DateName
------------------------------
May
(1 row(s) affected)
```

"May" is output because the SQL Server Function "getdate()" is invoked, as in other examples, to retrieve the current system date.

Datepart

Returns the specified *datepart* in the *date* as an integer. Here is the structure:

DATEPART(*datepart, date*)

Example:

SELECT DATEPART(quarter, getdate()) AS [DatePart]

The example above outputs the following, since May, which is the current system month at time of writing, is in the second quarter:

```
DatePart
-----------
2
(1 row(s) affected)
```

Day

Returns the *day* specified in *date* as an integer value.
Example:

SELECT DAY("26 Mar 99") AS [Day]

Will output:

```
Day
-----------
26
(1 row(s) affected)
```

Since the first number in the date string represents the day, this is correct.

Getdate

Returns the current system date and time. Takes no parameters.

SELECT getdate() AS Now

will output something like the following (depending on what the current date and time is):

```
Now
---------------------------
2001-09-28 18:54:47.173
(1 row(s) affected)
```

Month

Returns the month specified in *date* as an integer:

SELECT MONTH(getdate()) AS thisMonth

Returns:

```
thisMonth
-----------
5
(1 row(s) affected)
```

Year

Returns year specified in *date* as an integer:

SELECT YEAR(getdate()) AS thisYear

Returns:

```
thisYear
-----------
2001
(1 row(s) affected)
```

<NOTE>

getdate() and many more of these are not valid functions in Microsoft Access or other desktop relational database systems. Check your database documentation for more information on functions in your system.

Index

Note: Page references in **bold type** refer to tables and figures.

A

B

C

E

F

N

O

P

Q

R

S

T

U

V

W

X

Y

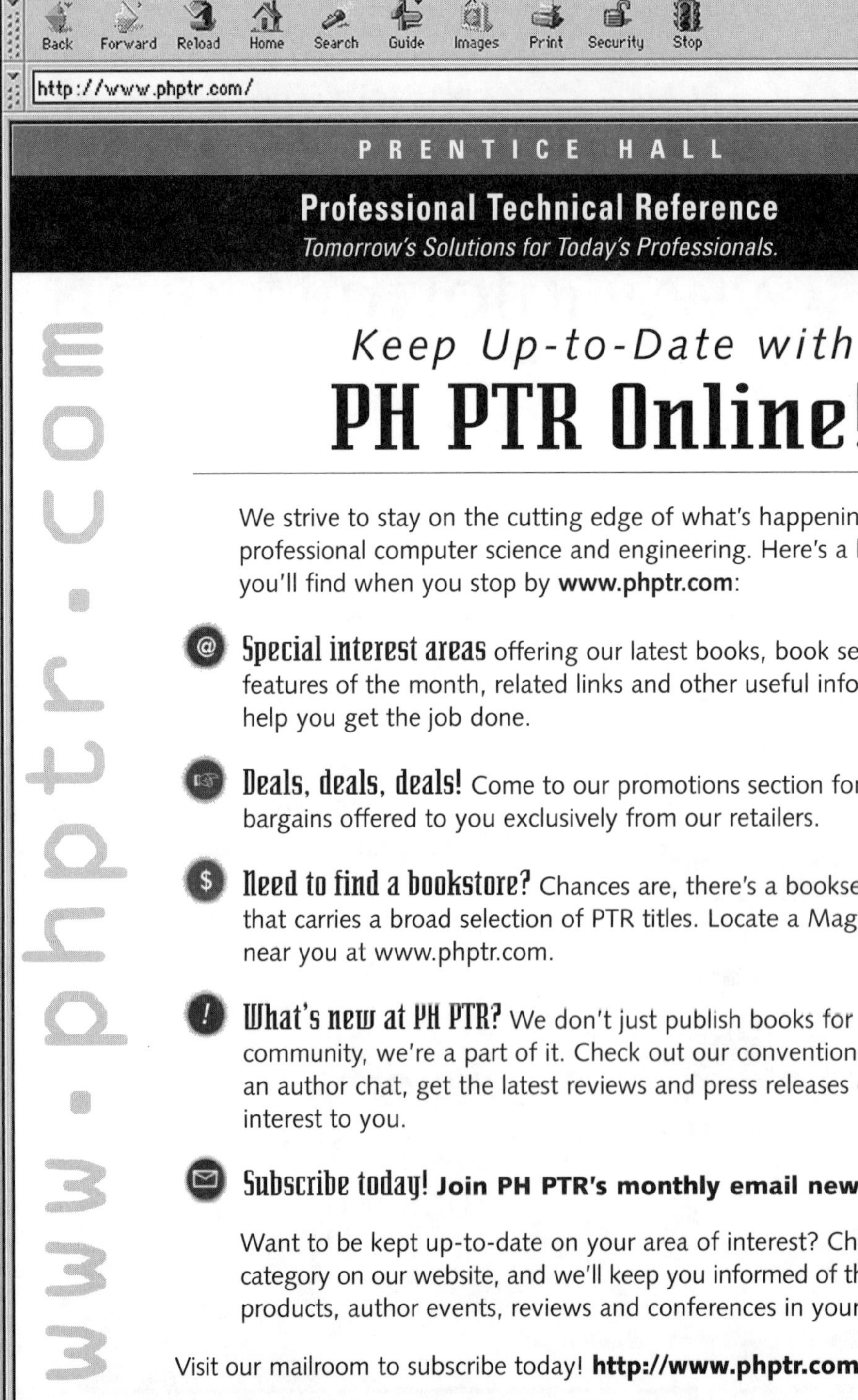
Prentice Hall: Professional Technical Reference
Back Forward Reload Home Search Guide Images Print Security Stop
PH PTR
http://www.phptr.com/
PRENTICE HALL
Professional Technical Reference
Tomorrow's Solutions for Today's Professionals.
www.phptr.com
Keep Up-to-Date with
PH PTR Online!
We strive to stay on the cutting edge of what's happening in professional computer science and engineering. Here's a bit of what you'll find when you stop by www.phptr.com:
Special interest areas offering our latest books, book series, software, features of the month, related links and other useful information to help you get the job done.
Deals, deals, deals! Come to our promotions section for the latest bargains offered to you exclusively from our retailers.
Need to find a bookstore? Chances are, there's a bookseller near you that carries a broad selection of PTR titles. Locate a Magnet bookstore near you at www.phptr.com.
What's new at PH PTR? We don't just publish books for the professional community, we're a part of it. Check out our convention schedule, join an author chat, get the latest reviews and press releases on topics of interest to you.
Subscribe today! Join PH PTR's monthly email newsletter!
Want to be kept up-to-date on your area of interest? Choose a targeted category on our website, and we'll keep you informed of the latest PH PTR products, author events, reviews and conferences in your interest area.
Visit our mailroom to subscribe today! http://www.phptr.com/mail_lists

LICENSE AGREEMENT AND LIMITED WARRANTY

READ THE FOLLOWING TERMS AND CONDITIONS CAREFULLY BEFORE OPENING THIS DISK PACKAGE. THIS LEGAL DOCUMENT IS AN AGREEMENT BETWEEN YOU AND PRENTICE-HALL, INC. (THE "COMPANY"). BY OPENING THIS SEALED DISK PACKAGE, YOU ARE AGREEING TO BE BOUND BY THESE TERMS AND CONDITIONS. IF YOU DO NOT AGREE WITH THESE TERMS AND CONDITIONS, DO NOT OPEN THE DISK PACKAGE. PROMPTLY RETURN THE UNOPENED DISK PACKAGE AND ALL ACCOMPANYING ITEMS TO THE PLACE YOU OBTAINED THEM FOR A FULL REFUND OF ANY SUMS YOU HAVE PAID.

1. **GRANT OF LICENSE:** In consideration of your payment of the license fee, which is part of the price you paid for this product, and your agreement to abide by the terms and conditions of this Agreement, the Company grants to you a nonexclusive right to use and display the copy of the enclosed software program (hereinafter the "SOFTWARE") on a single computer (i.e., with a single CPU) at a single location so long as you comply with the terms of this Agreement. The Company reserves all rights not expressly granted to you under this Agreement.
2. **OWNERSHIP OF SOFTWARE:** You own only the magnetic or physical media (the enclosed disks) on which the SOFTWARE is recorded or fixed, but the Company retains all the rights, title, and ownership to the SOFTWARE recorded on the original disk copy(ies) and all subsequent copies of the SOFTWARE, regardless of the form or media on which the original or other copies may exist. This license is not a sale of the original SOFTWARE or any copy to you.
3. **COPY RESTRICTIONS:** This SOFTWARE and the accompanying printed materials and user manual (the "Documentation") are the subject of copyright. You may not copy the Documentation or the SOFTWARE, except that you may make a single copy of the SOFTWARE for backup or archival purposes only. You may be held legally responsible for any copying or copyright infringement which is caused or encouraged by your failure to abide by the terms of this restriction.
4. **USE RESTRICTIONS:** You may not network the SOFTWARE or otherwise use it on more than one computer or computer terminal at the same time. You may physically transfer the SOFTWARE from one computer to another provided that the SOFTWARE is used on only one computer at a time. You may not distribute copies of the SOFTWARE or Documentation to others. You may not reverse engineer, disassemble, decompile, modify, adapt, translate, or create derivative works based on the SOFTWARE or the Documentation without the prior written consent of the Company.
5. **TRANSFER RESTRICTIONS:** The enclosed SOFTWARE is licensed only to you and may not be transferred to any one else without the prior written consent of the Company. Any unauthorized transfer of the SOFTWARE shall result in the immediate termination of this Agreement.
6. **TERMINATION:** This license is effective until terminated. This license will terminate automatically without notice from the Company and become null and void if you fail to comply with any provisions or limitations of this license. Upon termination, you shall destroy the Documentation and all copies of the SOFTWARE. All provisions of this Agreement as to warranties, limitation of liability, remedies or damages, and our ownership rights shall survive termination.
7. **MISCELLANEOUS:** This Agreement shall be construed in accordance with the laws of the United States of America and the State of New York and shall benefit the Company, its affiliates, and assignees.
8. **LIMITED WARRANTY AND DISCLAIMER OF WARRANTY:** The Company warrants that the SOFTWARE, when properly used in accordance with the Documentation, will operate in substantial conformity with the description of the SOFTWARE set forth in the Documentation. The Company does not warrant that the SOFTWARE will meet your requirements or that the operation of the SOFTWARE will be uninterrupted or error-free. The Company warrants that the media on which the SOFTWARE is delivered shall be free from defects in materials and workmanship under normal use for a period of thirty (30) days from the date of your purchase. Your only remedy and the Company's only obligation under these limited warranties is, at the Company's option, return of the warranted item for a refund of any amounts paid by you or replacement of the item. Any replacement of SOFTWARE or media under the warranties shall not extend the original warranty period. The limited warranty set forth above shall not apply to any SOFTWARE which the Company determines in good faith has been subject to misuse, neglect, improper installation, repair, alteration, or damage by you. EXCEPT FOR THE EXPRESSED WARRANTIES SET FORTH ABOVE, THE COMPANY DISCLAIMS ALL WARRANTIES, EXPRESS OR IMPLIED, INCLUDING WITHOUT LIMITATION, THE IMPLIED WARRANTIES OF MERCHANTABILITY AND FITNESS FOR A PARTICULAR PURPOSE. EXCEPT FOR THE EXPRESS WARRANTY SET FORTH ABOVE, THE COMPANY DOES NOT WARRANT, GUARANTEE, OR MAKE ANY REPRESENTATION REGARDING THE USE OR THE RESULTS OF THE USE OF THE SOFTWARE IN TERMS OF ITS CORRECTNESS, ACCURACY, RELIABILITY, CURRENTNESS, OR OTHERWISE.

IN NO EVENT, SHALL THE COMPANY OR ITS EMPLOYEES, AGENTS, SUPPLIERS, OR CONTRACTORS BE LIABLE FOR ANY INCIDENTAL, INDIRECT, SPECIAL, OR CONSEQUENTIAL DAMAGES ARISING OUT OF OR IN CONNECTION WITH THE LICENSE GRANTED UNDER THIS AGREEMENT, OR FOR LOSS OF USE, LOSS OF DATA, LOSS OF INCOME OR PROFIT, OR OTHER LOSSES, SUSTAINED AS A RESULT OF INJURY TO ANY PERSON, OR LOSS OF OR DAMAGE TO PROPERTY, OR CLAIMS OF THIRD PARTIES, EVEN IF THE COMPANY OR AN AUTHORIZED REPRESENTATIVE OF THE COMPANY HAS BEEN ADVISED OF THE POSSIBILITY OF SUCH DAMAGES. IN NO EVENT SHALL LIABILITY OF THE COMPANY FOR DAMAGES WITH RESPECT TO THE SOFTWARE EXCEED THE AMOUNTS ACTUALLY PAID BY YOU, IF ANY, FOR THE SOFTWARE.

SOME JURISDICTIONS DO NOT ALLOW THE LIMITATION OF IMPLIED WARRANTIES OR LIABILITY FOR INCIDENTAL, INDIRECT, SPECIAL, OR CONSEQUENTIAL DAMAGES, SO THE ABOVE LIMITATIONS MAY NOT ALWAYS APPLY. THE WARRANTIES IN THIS AGREEMENT GIVE YOU SPECIFIC LEGAL RIGHTS AND YOU MAY ALSO HAVE OTHER RIGHTS WHICH VARY IN ACCORDANCE WITH LOCAL LAW.

ACKNOWLEDGMENT

YOU ACKNOWLEDGE THAT YOU HAVE READ THIS AGREEMENT, UNDERSTAND IT, AND AGREE TO BE BOUND BY ITS TERMS AND CONDITIONS. YOU ALSO AGREE THAT THIS AGREEMENT IS THE COMPLETE AND EXCLUSIVE STATEMENT OF THE AGREEMENT BETWEEN YOU AND THE COMPANY AND SUPERSEDES ALL PROPOSALS OR PRIOR AGREEMENTS, ORAL, OR WRITTEN, AND ANY OTHER COMMUNICATIONS BETWEEN YOU AND THE COMPANY OR ANY REPRESENTATIVE OF THE COMPANY RELATING TO THE SUBJECT MATTER OF THIS AGREEMENT.

Should you have any questions concerning this Agreement or if you wish to contact the Company for any reason, please contact in writing at the address below.

Robin Short
Prentice Hall PTR
One Lake Street, Upper Saddle River, New Jersey 07458

About the CD-ROM

Contents

Thirty-day evaluation copies of all these Macromedia tools: ColdFusion 5.0 Enterprise Application Server for Windows, Linux, and Solaris; ColdFusion Studio 4.5—the complete IDE for creating and deploying ColdFusion applications; HomeSite 4.5—the award-winning HTML editor; Macromedia Spectra 1.5 Application Framework—written in ColdFusion with approximately 450 custom tags, Spectra enables e-commerce, personalization, and content management for the entire spectrum of a website's users; JRun Java Server 3.0.1 for Linux and Windows—the complete Java and JSP server, including Allaire's JSP tags; Free Macrodmedia Flash Toolkit for ColdFusion—comes with Flash tools that can enhance your sites' user interface and functionality, including a calendar, a calculator, and more.

All of the book's source code. Note that source code on the CD-ROM may not match exactly with the code found in the book. In the folder called "Store," you will find the complete code for the e-commerce site. In the folder called "WAP_AddressBook," you will find the complete code base for creating the WAP address book. You can view this in a WAP browser on a Web-enabled cell phone or a Web phone emulator. Locations for downloading such browsers can be found in Appendix G.

An unrestricted copy of ColdFusion Express for ColdFusion 4.5. With ColdFusion Express, you are limited to just the fundamental tags and server interaction, but your license is free and won't expire. Can be used for development in cost-aware environments.

System Requirements

Windows 95 or later

Soundcard and speakers

16MB RAM

4× CD-ROM drive

800 × 600 resolution set to 256 colors

Microsoft Internet Explorer 4 or Netscape 3.04 or later

Please see Chapter 4, "Installing ColdFusion Server," for complete system requirements for ColdFusion Server products.

Technical Support

If you are having problems with the evaluation software, please contact Macromedia at http://www.macromedia.com/support/ or http://www.allaire.com/support/index.cfm.

Prentice Hall does not offer technical support for this software. However, if there is a problem with the media, you may obtain a replacement copy by e-mailing your problem to disc_exchange@prenhall.com.